Ira Gershwin
John Wayne
Lucille Ball
Fred Astaire
Orson Welles
Dolores Del Rio

THE RKO
STORY

RKO RADIO PICTURES, INC.
DAILY TALENT REQUISITION

RKO RADIO PICTURES, INC.
CALL SHEET

DATE FRI. 11/1/40

DIRECTOR Sam Wood   TITLE KITTY FOYLE

PRODUCTION No. 285

NAME	TIME
MADE UP READY TO WORK	
Ginger Rogers	9:00 AM
James Craig	"
Polly Bailey	"
Extras as req.	9:30 AM
Patricia Conway	2:30 PM

STANDINS:
| Dorothy Fenter | 8:30 AM |
| Jack Irwin | " |

STAFF AND CREW READY AT PATHE   9:00 AM

THE RKO STORY

Richard B. Jewell with Vernon Harbin

ARLINGTON HOUSE

Published in Great Britain 1982 by
Octopus Books Limited
59 Grosvenor Street,
London W1

First published in the United States by
Arlington House, A Division of Crown
Publishers, Inc. Inquiries should be
addressed to Crown Publishers Inc.,
One Park Avenue, New York 10016.

© 1982 Octopus Books Limited

Library of Congress
Catalog Card Number 81-22100
ISBN 0-517-546566

10 9 8 7 6 5 4 3 2 1
First edition

Produced by Mandarin Publishers Limited
22a Westlands Road, Quarry Bay,
Hong Kong

Printed in Hong Kong

Text by Richard B. Jewell
Consultant Editor: Vernon Harbin

The publishers would like to thank
John Douglas Eames for originating
the concept for this series of studio
histories.

Contents

For Lynne and Louise, who endured this enterprise with remarkable forbearance

Acknowledgements

The RKO Story was written in a small office on Vermont Avenue in Los Angeles, adjacent to a warehouse of marvellous studio records which made the project feasible in the first place. For providing office space and access to films and documents, I am indebted to RKO General Incorporated and, most especially, to the company's West Coast manager, John Munro-Hall, whose courtesy, generosity and encouragement were unflagging throughout. Karen Murphy and Jack Curtis of RKO–Los Angeles and Martha Abrams and Ruth Zitter of RKO–New York also gave freely of their time and expertise as the project took shape.

My research on the history of RKO began when I was a doctoral student at the University of Southern California. It is a pleasure to acknowledge the efforts of Irwin Blacker, Arthur Knight, John Russell Taylor, David Malone and Art Murphy, who read an earlier version of the book and provided guidance, advice and many perceptive insights.

Pandro S. Berman and Bert Granet shared their knowledge and experience of RKO in personal conversations, and Mr Berman was kind enough to lend some of his personal stills.

Terry Roach, Sam Gill, Bob Cushman and the staff of the Academy of Motion Picture Arts and Sciences Library were always efficient and patient, despite the heavy demands made upon them. I would also like to extend my sincere thanks to the following who, in addition to the Academy, helped with the research and/or the gathering of photographic stills:

Robert Knutson and Janet Lorenz (University of Southern California), Audree Malkin (University of California at Los Angeles), Saul Jaffe and Betty Jones (Vitaprint, New York), Holly Yasui (University of Wisconsin), Mary Corliss (The Museum of Modern Art, New York), Tom Bodley (Samuel Goldwyn Productions), Bob Colman (Hollywood Poster Exchange) Mike Hawks (Eddie Brandt's Saturday Matinee), Ron Haver (Los Angeles County Museum of Art) and Marc Wanamaker. I want also to single out Joanne Yeck, my chief research assistant, whose cooperation and enthusiasm never wavered throughout the long and sometimes exasperating gestation period.

I should like to thank Allen Eyles for reading the manuscript, and for offering constructive suggestions and thoughtful criticism. I am also grateful to the general editor, Robyn Karney, whose tireless attention contributed greatly to making it a better book.

Finally, I am most deeply indebted to my partner and consultant editor, Vernon Harbin. Mr Harbin went to work for RKO in 1931, rising from a job in the fan mail department to an important executive position, and weathering all the changes in management that took place at this volatile studio through the years. Even after the company ceased production, he continued on, running the West Coast offices of RKO General until mid-1976. Vernon collaborated on the gathering of stills, helped create the text with his memories, insights and thorough understanding of the company's evolution, and made corrections of my sometimes fanciful, often thoroughly misguided, interpretations of events and relationships without ever once raising his voice. He is a true gentleman, and without his contributions, *The RKO Story* would be a lesser work indeed.

Richard B. Jewell
Los Angeles, 1982.

Preface

The two previous volumes in this series – *The MGM Story* by John Douglas Eames and *The Warner Bros. Story* by Clive Hirschhorn – provided a basic structure for the writing of *The RKO Story*. Nonetheless, a number of choices had to be made as the project evolved, and the following remarks are intended to help the reader understand those choices.

First, it was decided to describe every feature film that the studio produced and/or released in the United States. The only exceptions to this rule come near the end of RKO's history when it turned over distribution of its own product, plus some independently-made films, to other companies, including Universal-International and Warner Bros. Since these films were all originally intended to be handled by RKO's film exchanges, they are included in the book.

RKO set up distribution offices in London in 1930, releasing some independently-produced films in Britain that it did not market in America. The corporation also made some features in Britain that, likewise, never found their way across the Atlantic. These films are not included in the main body of the text, but are listed in a special appendix entitled 'RKO British Production and Distribution'.

In terms of format, RKO's films have been grouped according to the year of general release in the US. On some occasions, the studio would open a picture in Los Angeles just before the end of a year to qualify it for Academy Award considerations. In instances where this manouevre was successful and the film actually earned at least one Oscar nomination, the picture is listed in the year before its general release in order to conform with the Academy's catalogue of honours. Other productions (such as **The Best Years Of Our Lives** and **Mourning Becomes Electra**) had special 'road-show' engagements before wide release. These are incorporated under the year of their 'road-show' presentations.

One often finds bewildering discrepancies among the various sources that list picture credits. In the early years of RKO, there are sometimes even differences between the final main title credits and those enumerated in the advertising materials for a given picture. Consequently, Vernon Harbin and I decided that the final authority for credit information in the individual picture write-ups would be the final main title of the picture itself. On occasion there are errors in these main titles; in such cases, every effort has been made to provide the correct information. Where there is no producer, or other seemingly obvious credit, it is because there is no record of such a credit.

Sprinkled throughout the text are various financial figures. The yearly profit-and-loss statements are extracted, by and large, from the corporation's annual stockholder reports. Data on production costs, gross film rentals and profits (or losses) on individual films come from company records and relate to the initial release throughout America and the rest of the world. Some pictures (**King Kong**, for example) were successful in their first runs and then earned even more in subsequent reissues. Others (like **Citizen Kane**) were considered financial failures at the end of their original release, but eventually entered the black due to re-releases. However, the first release was of paramount importance to the studio and to the creative people involved, so only these financial figures have been enumerated.

One of the most exasperating problems we encountered concerns the names of various individuals. Actors and behind-the-camera personnel often changed their names completely (Michael St Angel became Steven Flagg, then reverted back to Michael St Angel), altered the spelling (Theodore Von Eltz became Theodor Von Eltz) or played even more bizarre games (writer Robert D. Andrews later became Robert Hardy Andrews). Once again, the final title has been used as ultimate authority, though some attempt has been made to smooth out the many inconsistencies.

In the early days when William LeBaron was head of production, he was automatically overall producer on most films even if the work was designated to an associate producer or supervisor. Thus, to avoid meaningless repetition (WLB) signifies a LeBaron production.

Throughout its history, RKO generally took a back seat to such competitors as MGM, Paramount and Warner Bros. in the area of contract performers. Consequently, it was often forced to borrow leading actors from these and other companies. An effort has been extended to point out these borrowings as they relate to specific movies. Remakes, both of a studio's own films and of other companies' pictures, were also a fact of Hollywood life and are mentioned in individual picture discussions.

RKO maintained an active short unit, grinding out hundreds of two-reel comedies, sports films, documentary studies and so forth to supplement its feature productions. This book does not deal with short subjects, except insofar as their Academy Award performance is concerned.

For reasons too lengthy to enumerate, it has not been possible to view every one of the pictures described herein. Whenever a film was unavailable for screening, I consulted a number of critical reviews and then reflected the consensus of opinion in the evaluative remarks on the picture in question. The main sources utilized for this purpose were *The New York Times, The Los Angeles Times, Variety, The Hollywood Reporter, The Motion Picture Herald, The Monthly Film Bulletin, Film Daily* and *Harrison's Reports*.

Two reference guides were especially helpful in the preparation of *The RKO Story*. Denis Gifford's *British Film Catalogue (1895–1970)*, published by David and Charles, was the principal source used to generate the 'RKO British Production and Distribution' section, and Robert Osborne's *50 Golden Years Of Oscar*, published by ESE California in association with the Academy of Motion Picture Arts and Sciences, provided information about the performance of RKO films in the Academy Awards over the years.

Introduction

Legend has it that Radio-Keith-Orpheum was born in a Manhattan oyster bar in October 1928, during a conversation between two famous American business tycoons – Joseph P. Kennedy and David Sarnoff – but it is necessary to flash back almost a decade to discover the roots of the organization.

Robertson-Cole, a British import/export concern whose primary business was Rohmer automobiles, had also profitably exported film for various Hollywood independents. By 1919, Rufus S. Cole and H. F. Robertson decided to involve themselves more directly with the motion picture industry. They allied themselves with Exhibitors Mutual Distributing Corporation (an outgrowth of the venerable Mutual Film Corp.), then formed their own distribution company and, finally, decided to build their own studio and make their own pictures. In 1921 they looked about for an appropriate site and fixed upon Colegrove: 13.5 acres of property owned by the Hollywood Cemetery Association and bounded on two sides by Gower Street and Melrose Avenue. Soon seven buildings, including three production stages, were going up but, impatient to get started, the new movie men started rolling the cameras before the studio was even finished.

The first picture actually produced by Robertson-Cole was **The Wonder Man**, starring the famous French boxer Georges Carpentier and directed by John G. Adolfi. This was filmed at Solax Studios in Fort Lee, New Jersey. In Hollywood **Kismet**, featuring Otis Skinner, became the initial on-the-lot production; exterior scenes were shot as the studio took shape, while interior work was completed at Haworth Studios. **The Mistress Of Shenstone**, a Pauline Frederick vehicle directed by Henry King, followed closely behind and was hailed as the first 'official' studio production.

Robertson-Cole's next-door neighbour at this time was the United Studios, a rental facility where First National and other companies made their pictures. Paramount bought this property in 1926, and Paramount Pictures and RKO functioned side-by-side for many years, separated only by a fence.

In 1922, Robertson-Cole was reorganized and its name changed to Film Booking Offices of America, Inc., commonly referred to as FBO. Though the company was still owned principally by Britishers, an American group headed by P. A. Powers, Joseph I. Schnitzer and Harry M. Berman (whose son Pandro would become RKO's most prolific and successful producer) bought into the organization and took active roles in its operation. Action films, westerns and homespun dramas were filmed on the lot, but FBO functioned primarily as a distribution organization during this period. P. A. Powers was essentially in charge and even changed the name to The Powers Studios for a short time. He lined up deals with Hunt Stromberg, Gene Stratton-Porter, Ethel Clayton, and British, French and Italian companies for the release of their films. The biggest stars to appear in FBO pictures were Anna Q. Nilsson, Warner Baxter, Ralph Lewis, Irene Rich and sagebrush heroes Fred Thomson and Harry Carey.

Powers departed from FBO in October 1923, and Major H. C. S. Thomson, who represented the British banking interests, arrived from India to succeed him. Thomson hired B. P. Fineman as studio production chief, a job he held from 1924 until January 1926, during which time his wife Evelyn Brent emerged as one of FBO's biggest stars, along with

several more cowboys including Bob Custer, Yakima Canutt and Tom Tyler, as well as 'Strongheart' the dog. FBO's films were unpretentious and made both quickly and cheaply. Compared to Metro–Goldwyn–Mayer, Paramount and Fox, the studio was strictly a minor league outfit distributing filler product for the neighbourhood trade.

This state of affairs was expected to change when Joseph P. Kennedy, using the Boston banking house of Hayden, Stone and Co. as an intermediary, bought FBO from the British interests in February 1926. Kennedy soon installed Edwin King as his production head, but there was no appreciable change in the company thrust. Even after William LeBaron, former head of production at Paramount's eastern studios, took charge of filmmaking in 1927, FBO continued to churn out a mediocre stream of melodramas, indifferent comedies, and a proliferation of low budget westerns. New western series were launched starring Bob Steele, 'little buckeroo' Buzz Barton, the canine 'Ranger' and Tom Mix, whose days of high-riding were drawing to a close. Joe E. Brown, actor-director Ralph Ince, Bessie Love and Douglas Fairbanks Jr appeared in occasional FBO specials. Few of the films from the Kennedy–LeBaron company had budgets that exceeded $75,000.

Meanwhile, a few blocks away on Sunset Boulevard, the Warner brothers detonated the greatest single explosion in motion picture history: 'talkies'. The Warners' commitment to sound in *Don Juan* and then, more significantly, *The Jazz Singer* (1927) elevated them from an outfit of FBO dimensions to one of the top movie companies in the world. Hollywood scrambled on to the bandwagon of sound and, as we shall see, gave birth to a new child of the revolution with RKO.

Referred to derisively as the 'squawkies', and pronounced a 'fad', a 'novelty', and a 'public curiosity' that would disappear in a matter of months, talking pictures defied all the industry's sceptics. Warner Bros.' first 'all-talker', *The Lights Of New York*, blasted off to unprecedented box-office heights in 1928, prompting a wild burst of technical energy that swept through Hollywood companies and theatres throughout the world. Every important organization began installing sound equipment in its studios and movie houses, building new

'talkie' stages and sound-proofing existing ones, and combing the dramatic woods for players with pleasing voices and that crucial ability to seem natural while directing their speeches to microphones hidden in flower pots and other ingenious locations.

The public's omnivorous appetite for sound entertainment invoked a business boom for those companies that could deliver the goods. Warner Bros.' profits leaped from $2 million in 1928 to $17 million in 1929, and Paramount, Fox and MGM also published cheerful balance sheets that year. Another enterprise was reaping enormous profits as well. This was A. T. & T., whose Western Electric subsidiary had cornered the entire market on the production and installation of sound equipment.

Enter David Sarnoff, president of Radio Corporation of America (RCA). Sarnoff was aware of the enormous potential revenue to be earned from sound movie paraphernalia, and commissioned his engineers to design the necessary machinery. They obliged with a sound-on-film (optical sound) system which RCA promptly trademarked 'Photophone'. But Photophone had a large stumbling block in its path to success – the important motion picture companies had already signed exclusive agreements with Western Electric for the use of their system, so Sarnoff began casting about for some other foothold within the Hollywood enclave. He found it in FBO.

In January 1928, Joseph Kennedy announced that RCA had acquired a 'substantial interest' in FBO. The original statement also mentioned prominently that FBO films would utilize the Photophone reproduction and synchronization method and that RCA's new invention would be 'available to the entire motion picture industry'. Thus, RCA planned to use FBO as a showcase for Photophone and, possibly, as a base from which to attack the near-monopoly of Western Electric.

The sound revolution crushed many small film companies and producers who were unable to meet the financial demands of sound conversion. It also provoked titanic power struggles among the larger studios, each of which was jockeying for top position in the Hollywood hierarchy. Theatres were one measure of supremacy, and companies built and bought them with wild abandon, almost like properties in a Monopoly

game. The late Twenties were also marked by 'merger fever'; rumours flew constantly about the amalgamation of different companies into 'super-studios' that could dominate the filmmaking world: Fox plus MGM, Paramount plus Warner Bros., Warner Bros. plus First National (one merger that did eventually materialize).

Though FBO now had the economic muscle of RCA backing it up, the studio remained vulnerable in this highly charged atmosphere. The obvious problem was its lack of theatres. Sarnoff and Kennedy discovered the solution in an affiliation between FBO and the Keith-Albee-Orpheum circuit of vaudeville houses. Although many of the 700 K-A-O Theatres in the US and Canada could not be converted into showplaces for sound films, the agreement gave FBO a guaranteed outlet for its pictures and provided a nucleus from which a theatre empire could be constructed.

In October 1928, the famous oyster bar meeting took place, and one of the largest business compacts in the history of the American film industry was effected. RCA, through an equitable exchange of stock, gained control of both Keith-Albee-Orpheum and FBO, resulting in the birth of a giant $300 million corporation.

The merger was confirmed on October 23, 1928, and the venture was officially named the Radio-Keith-Orpheum Corporation, with David Sarnoff as chairman of its board of directors. Executive positions were filled in the final month of the year. Hiram Brown, whose business experience included the public utilities field and the leather trade, but nothing remotely related to show business, became president of the corporation. Sarnoff rationalized his selection of Brown by arguing that since RKO had no exact parallel in the amusement field, it needed a man with strong administrative skills to co-ordinate the enterprise. Sarnoff expected that Brown, who was supposed to be an 'organizational genius', would rapidly pick up the special requirements and nuances of motion picture commerce.

The film production arm also received a new president: Joseph I. Schnitzer. Unlike Brown, Schnitzer was well-acquainted with the movie business. He had been an FBO executive since 1922 and was its ranking vice-president when the merger was announced. To make room for Schnitzer, Joseph Kennedy voluntarily resigned from the organization. Never a factor in the new company, Kennedy moved on to make an outsized reputation in banking, diplomatic and – especially through his famous sons, John, Robert and Edward – political circles. Lee Marcus assumed the vice-presidency of the production company, and B. B. Kahane became its secretary–treasurer, with William LeBaron continuing as production chief.

Early in 1929, industry trade journals began to carry a series of hyperbolic advertisements heralding the new film company. The first of these featured a bare-chested god-like figure, towering over a modern metropolis. It proclaimed: A TITAN IS BORN ... ECLIPSING IN ITS STAGGERING MAGNITUDE AND FAR-REACHING INTERESTS ANY ENTERPRISE IN THE HISTORY OF SHOW BUSINESS. The superlatives continued: ONE MAMMOTH UNIT OF SHOWMANSHIP ... FULFILLMENT OF DARING DREAMS ... COLOSSUS OF MODERN ART AND SCIENCE. One of David Sarnoff's fondest wishes was to forge an alliance between radio (RCA controlled the NBC network) and the movies, and so RKO productions were trade-named 'Radio Pictures'. To reinforce the concept, RKO adopted, as its now famous logograph, a giant radio tower perched atop the world, beeping out its signal of 'A Radio Picture'.

The purpose of the ballyhoo was to dissolve any connection between the new, dynamic RKO and its puny forbear, FBO. Sarnoff was committed to making RKO an industry leader, not a shoddy operation cranking out quickie westerns and insipid melos for undiscriminating filmgoers. To demonstrate

William LeBaron, RKO's first production chief, who was succeeded by David O. Selznick in 1931.

his determination, he authorized Schnitzer to purchase the screen rights to Florenz Ziegfeld's musical extravaganza **Rio Rita** for $85,000. A few months later, another musical, **Hit The Deck**, was cornered for more than $100,000. Both received substantial advertising copy as the first of many special events which could be expected from the new 'Titan' of the studios.

RKO continued to grow throughout 1929. The Corporation bought the Proctor theatre chain in New York and New Jersey, and six Pantages houses on the West Coast. At 780 Gower Street (RKO's official Hollywood address), $500,000 was spent on talking picture construction. In addition, the 'RKO ranch' became a reality when the studio purchased 500 acres in the San Fernando Valley near Encino for the construction of large standing sets, and for filming exterior scenes in westerns and other action pictures.

In October 1929, RKO celebrated its first birthday. This event, however, was somewhat eclipsed by the stock market crash – eclipsed for everybody but David Sarnoff, who remained barely dismayed by the turn of events. The future of talking pictures looked bright, **Rio Rita** was a hit, and his new creation promised to show a tidy profit in its first short production year. Sarnoff and his associates entertained grandiose dreams for the future: they envisaged RKO as a giant entertainment conglomerate that would someday combine films, vaudeville shows, radio broadcasts, and television (then in the experimental stage) into a symbiotic package.

But David Sarnoff's grand design was never realized. Throughout the 27 years of activity that followed, RKO existed in a perpetual state of transition: from one regime to another, from one set of production policies to the next, from one group of filmmakers to an altogether different group. Being a less stable studio than its famous competitors, the company never 'settled down', never discovered its real identity. It failed to develop a singular guiding philosophy or continuity of management for any extended period. As a result, RKO's films tended to reflect the personality of the individual in charge of the studio at any given time – and since this time was always short, a dizzying number of diverse individuals became involved in RKO's creative affairs over the years, and the pictures never evolved an overall style unique to the studio.

Executive producer Merian C. Cooper, a leading studio figure in the early 30s and co-director/producer of **King Kong**.

This uncomfortable state of affairs, marked by continual financial fragility as well as creative turmoil, nonetheless had much to do with the creation of the exceptional and idiosyncratic pictures that have become RKO's hallmark. While other companies with steadier managements and well-defined production philosophies concentrated on a limited array of films, RKO created classics of nearly every type: the musical (**Swing Time**), the western (**Cimarron**), comedy (**Bringing Up Baby**), the horror film (**King Kong**), the woman's film (**Kitty Foyle**), the suspense thriller (**Notorious**), the adventure film (**Gunga Din**), the *film noir* (**Out Of The Past**), the socially conscious film (**Crossfire**) – plus the most extraordinary and influential picture of the entire Hollywood studio era: **Citizen Kane**.

Dorothy Arzner, one of Hollywood's very few women directors, on the set of **Christopher Strong** (1933).

Executive producer William LeBaron led the parade of studio decision-makers. He gave RKO its first giant hit (**Rio Rita**) and its only *bona fide* Best Picture Oscar-winner (**Cimarron**), but little else. LeBaron came from the theatrical world and had considerable silent film experience, but he was slow to adapt to the demands of the new sound medium. Few of his productions pleased the critics, the public, or David Sarnoff who replaced him with a new executive producer.

The hand-picked successor was David O. Selznick, an arrogant young genius who began, almost immediately, to upgrade the company's artistic reputation. In a year and a half under Selznick, RKO produced **Symphony Of Six Million**, **What Price Hollywood?**, **A Bill Of Divorcement**, **Topaze**, **King Kong** and other auspicious films, as well as signing future luminaries Katharine Hepburn and Fred Astaire. Unhappily, David Selznick found himself at loggerheads with corporate president Merlin Aylesworth over a sacred Hollywood concern: final creative authority. He left RKO in early 1933 – a major loss from which the studio would never entirely recover.

Illustrious Hollywood composer Max Steiner, RKO's first resident musical director.

Merian C. Cooper, a Selznick protégé, accepted Aylesworth's offer to replace his mentor. An explorer and documentary film-maker before he came to Hollywood, Cooper favoured adventure films packed with action and romance, but ill-health prevented him from fully implementing his production philosophy. Indeed, the films that stand out from the Cooper period (**Little Women**, **Morning Glory**, **Flying Down To Rio**) are worlds apart from **King Kong**, the masterpiece he co-produced and co-directed under Selznick.

Director George Cukor with Katharine Hepburn on location for **Little Women** (1933).

Youthful producer Pandro S. Berman was called on to fill the gap during two periods of Cooper's absence through illness and then became official production chief when Cooper gave up the job. Always a shrewd judge of talent, Berman noted the chemistry between Fred Astaire and Ginger Rogers in **Flying Down To Rio** and decided to star them in **The Gay Divorcee**. Thus began the legendary Astaire–Rogers partnership, and a series of popular and critically esteemed musicals that almost single-handedly kept RKO afloat during the middle years of the Depression. Though Berman superintended other fine pictures, including **Of Human Bondage** which made Bette Davis a star, he was never comfortable with the job of executive producer, preferring to concentrate on individual films. In mid-1934, he returned to the producer ranks and surrendered overall production responsibility to studio president B. B. Kahane.

Kahane maintained a policy of benevolent neglect, leaving the creative teams to get on with the job once he had approved a project. His approach paid dividends in 1935 when the studio released such memorable movies as **The Informer, Roberta, Becky Sharp, Alice Adams** and **Top Hat**.

Despite these successes, Kahane was relieved of his duties when a corporate shake-up placed Leo Spitz in charge of the organization. President Spitz appointed Sam Briskin, a Columbia Pictures veteran, as his studio chief. Briskin's two years at the helm represented a backward step for RKO's artistic reputation. Though the company released more films than ever before, most were second-rate comedies and melodramas. Nearly all the best pictures made during Briskin's tenure, including **Follow The Fleet, Winterset, Swing Time** and **Stage Door**, were personally produced by Pandro Berman.

above: George Schaefer (left), president of RKO Radio Pictures, with executive producer Pandro S. Berman. *right:* Leslie Howard and Bette Davis with director John Cromwell (with moustache) on the set of **Of Human Bondage** (1934).

what Schaefer wanted, for he felt fully capable of making all the important company decisions, including the creative ones.

Schaefer was determined to turn RKO into a 'prestige' studio, emphasizing quality productions based on respected literary and theatrical properties. He also hoped to take a leadership position in Hollywood by hiring promising talents and giving them an opportunity to fashion aesthetically ambitious films. This policy enticed an intractable and brilliantly gifted young man named Orson Welles, and his Mercury Theatre group, to RKO. A stormy association followed, yielding **Citizen Kane** before it terminated, but most of Schaefer's ideas misfired disastrously. Though other triumphs were recorded (**My Favorite Wife, All That Money Can Buy, Suspicion, The Magnificent Ambersons**), Schaefer's films nearly bankrupted the company before he resigned in 1942.

Art directors Van Nest Polglase (right) and Perry Ferguson working on the designs for **Gunga Din** (1939).

When Briskin went back to Columbia in late 1937, Leo Spitz implored Berman to take over production again. He reluctantly agreed, but his first year yielded no pictures of special distinction. This initial disappointment was dispelled by **Gunga Din, Love Affair, Bachelor Mother, The Hunchback Of Notre Dame** and other fine movies, all released in the extraordinary Hollywood year of 1939. This, however, was Pan Berman's final year with RKO. Discontented with the policies of new corporate president George Schaefer, Berman accepted a position with MGM, leaving Schaefer in full command of RKO. This was precisely

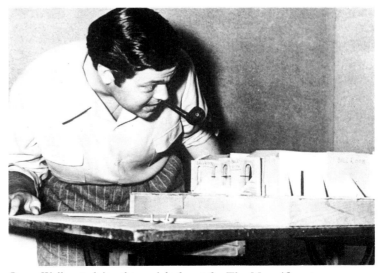

Orson Welles studying the model of a set for **The Magnificent Ambersons** (1942).

Summoned to perform emergency surgery on RKO's weakened corporate body, new production head Charles Koerner vowed to turn out 'audience' pictures, rather than wooing the intelligentsia. By offering the by then war-weary public a cinematic smorgasbord that included horror films, detective yarns, war pictures, comedies, topical potboilers and an occasional musical, Koerner made the company prosperous again within a miraculously short span of time. And once RKO was on firm financial ground, he gave the green light to projects of limited box-office potential such as **Days Of Glory** and **None But The Lonely Heart**. Koerner's lasting fame, though, is based largely on a group of horror films with such lurid titles as **Cat People, I Walked With A Zombie** and **The Leopard Man**. Made on meagre budgets by producer Val Lewton, they introduced new psychological subtleties into a rigidly formularized genre, and secured Lewton a place as an innovator.

Charles Koerner died of leukemia in 1946, forcing corporate president N. Peter Rathvon to take over production

Producer Dore Schary with Dorothy McGuire on the set of **Till The End Of Time** (1946).

for one very good year. During that year RKO released **Till The End Of Time, Notorious, The Best Years Of Our Lives, It's A Wonderful Life** and **The Farmer's Daughter**. Rathvon's own role in the making of these films was minimal; most were either independently produced, or co-productions between RKO and other organizations. Rathvon, who thankfully had no illusions about his own creative abilities, hired writer-producer Dore Schary as head of production in 1947.

Producer-director Leo McCarey (left), Ingrid Bergman, Bing Crosby and Charles Koerner on the set of **The Bells Of St Mary's** (1945).

below: Alfred Hitchcock directing **Notorious** (1946) on location.

One of the rare pictures of Howard Hughes, this one taken around 1946 shortly before he took over RKO.

Schary regarded film as a medium of constructive social commentary, and his commitment to serious issues was manifested in such 'problem' pictures as **Crossfire, They Live By Night** and **The Boy With Green Hair**. But Schary's tastes were catholic, and he also sponsored an assortment of other engrossing films such as **Out Of The Past, I Remember Mama** and **The Set-Up**.

In 1948, the most dramatic change to date was visited upon RKO – a change which brought lasting damage to the company, and sowed the seeds of its final destruction. The famed multi-millionaire tycoon and movie producer Howard Hughes bought control of the studio. Ruthless, despotic and unstable, Hughes' lack of orthodoxy completely changed the character of the company. Lawsuits abounded, and talent left in droves to escape the curtailment of artistic freedom by RKO's McCarthyist new owner boss. Under Hughes, the studio's output of feature films was cut drastically, and only a handful achieved any artistic credibility. A list of productions that included such astounding disasters as **The Conqueror,**

Cameraman Harry Stradling (left) and director Otto Preminger, both borrowed from other studios for **Angel Face** (1953).

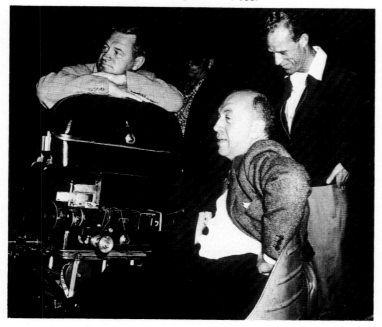

Son Of Sinbad and the long-delayed **Jet Pilot**, made RKO the laughing stock of Hollywood. The few decent films to emerge under the RKO logo during the first half of the 1950s were almost all independently produced (**The Thing, Rashomon, Face to Face,** etc.).

Hughes sold RKO to General Teleradio Inc. in 1955. Its president, T. F. O'Neil, was mainly interested in RKO's backlog of completed pictures which he intended to release to television, but he vowed to keep making movies and hired William Dozier as his production topper. As ill luck would have it, Dozier's films were no better than those of Hughes. Its reputation in ruins and its finances depleted, RKO ceased making films in 1957.

The supreme irony of RKO's existence is that the studio earned a position of lasting importance in cinema history largely *because* of its extraordinarily unstable history. Since it was the weakling of Hollywood's 'majors', RKO welcomed a diverse group of individualistic creators and provided them, at least until the Hughes era, with an extraordinary degree of freedom to express their artistic idiosyncracies.

Janet Leigh and director Josef von Sternberg on the set of the Hughes flop **Jet Pilot** (1957).

A number of important figures built their careers at 780 Gower Street: Irene Dunne, George Cukor, Katharine Hepburn, Fred Astaire, Ginger Rogers, Max Steiner, Garson Kanin, Dalton Trumbo, Orson Welles, George Stevens, Edward Dmytryk, Robert Wise, Robert Ryan, Robert Mitchum, Lucille Ball and many others. Some might never have been given a chance by the stronger companies, while others almost certainly would have found advancement more difficult.

David Sarnoff must have felt considerable exasperation through the years as he watched his step-child lurch along from one crisis to another, yet, undeniably, RKO *did* manage to carve out a special place in Hollywood, for it never became predictable and it never became a factory. Its unique volatility generated a corporate psycho-drama that reflects, to an uncanny extent, the rise and fall of the studio system itself. And it also generated more than 1000 pictures – some forgettable, some too awful to contemplate, and a handful of the best movies ever made. All are here, along with the cast of characters who helped make the RKO story one of the most stupendous roller coaster rides in the history of show business.

1929

To demonstrate its commitment to sound, RKO decided to release only 'all talking' pictures in 1929, its first year. The production year was therefore an abbreviated one, with only 12 pictures going out under the 'Beeping Tower' logo. The last of the FBO's, with stars such as Tom Rix, Bob Steele, Olive Borden, Buzz Barton and Ranger, were issued at regular intervals during the first seven months. Some of these were partial 'talkies', while others were old-fashioned silents.

The 1930s was RKO's greatest decade, a decade that gave birth to **King Kong, Little Women, The Informer, Bringing Up Baby, Gunga Din** and many other fondly remembered titles – not to mention the Astaire–Rogers musicals. These years also represent perhaps the wildest corporate adventure in the annals of any show business organization: instability became the RKO watchword, with management leaders coming and going in dizzying shifts and the possibility of financial collapse never far from 780 Gower St. It was a wild and woolly epoch, packed full of the triumphs and tragedies that make behind-the-scenes history sometimes more dramatic than Hollywood's calculated screen fictions.

The Hiram Brown–Joseph I. Schnitzer regime sowed the seeds of trouble that would bear fruit for years to come. Flushed with the success of **Rio Rita** and several of its other early productions, the corporation continued to expand, annexing more and more theatres and contracting to manage two colossal entertainment palaces being constructed in Manhattan's Radio City. The executives also agreed to move their eastern headquarters to Rockefeller Center when that complex of skyscrapers was completed. In January 1931, RKO purchased the historic Pathé organization, including its studio, its newsreel, its distribution network and its contract performers. It seemed good business to operate this new acquisition as a separate entity, so RKO Pathé was christened with Lee Marcus as president and Charles R. Rogers as production chief.

RKO's saga is glutted with sad examples of bad timing, and this period had more than its share. While the corporation forged boldly ahead, the business climate in the United States grew steadily worse. Movies, which had seemed 'depression-proof' for a time, began to receive a chilly reception from a public preoccupied with the realities of life. To combat the wave of audience apathy, admission prices were slashed and double features became commonplace, yet nothing made a major impact. RKO found itself in an especially vulnerable position. Still an industry infant, it lacked the creative talent to compete with the contract artists of MGM, Paramount, Warner Bros., etc. Not that all those studios were prospering either – by 1933, nearly every Hollywood company except MGM was flirting with bankruptcy.

Hoping to upgrade the mediocre level of RKO films, David Sarnoff hired David O. Selznick to take charge of studio production in the fall of 1931. Selznick met the challenge by immediately cancelling a mindless farrago then being shot called *ChiChi And Her Papas*, cleaning out the dead wood from the former regime, and instituting a search for the kind of talent the publicity staff could boast about. Former production topper William LeBaron remained under contract, drawing a huge salary and doing very little to earn it. Selznick eventually persuaded Ben Schulberg of Paramount to take LeBaron off RKO's hands. Mr LeBaron would have much better luck there, producing the Mae West hits and eventually becoming Paramount studio head.

A period of rigid economizing coincided with Selznick's entry into RKO affairs. This led to the elimination of RKO Pathé as a separate studio making theatrical feature

Roberta (1935)

1939

films. Selznick was placed in charge of all production, forcing Charles R. Rogers out of the organization. A group headed by Rogers later wrested control of Universal from Carl Laemmle, and Rogers ran production at that studio from 1936 to 1938.

Early in 1932, Merlin 'Deac' Aylesworth replaced Hiram Brown as RKO corporate president. Aylesworth was a lawyer and the president of the RCA-controlled National Broadcasting System. He soon became the loudest and most tenacious exponent of radio–film cooperation, a fact that did not endear him to many Hollywood leaders who viewed the airwaves as filmdom's chief competitive enemy. The incredible aspect of Aylesworth's appointment was that he planned to devote only half his time to his new job. He would retain the presidency of NBC, spending mornings on RKO business, and dedicating his afternoons to the broadcasting concern. Aylesworth was supposed to have boundless energy, but anyone could see that this was an ill-considered, foolhardy arrangement.

The organization spent much of 1932 cutting costs, including expenditure on theatres which had become a steady drain on corporate finances. The end of the year, however, brought the completion of Radio City and the necessity of adding two elephantine houses to RKO's already strained exhibition operations. Radio City Music Hall, a 6200-seat palace intended for the presentation of stage shows and vaudeville entertainments, and the RKO Roxy, a 3700-seat auditorium for movies and live performances, were part of a stupendous Rockefeller dream that lost massive amounts of money from the first days their doors were opened. After 16 days, and losses that totalled $180,000, the Music Hall switched to motion picture programmes which helped the balance sheet but made the RKO Roxy an obvious redundancy. Back in the 'Titan' days when the initial commitment was made, the concept of these remarkable edifices as the RKO flagship theatres must have been thoroughly intoxicating; now the brutal realities of the Depression had turned them into a liability which Radio-Keith-Orpheum could ill afford.

The outlook was brighter at the studio, where David Selznick was making impressive strides. He eliminated many minor talents drawing major salaries, while promoting a few old-line individuals (such as Pandro Berman) who showed exceptional promise. His eye for talent brought Merian C. Cooper, George Cukor, Katharine Hepburn, Fred Astaire and other blue-chip prospects into the fold, and thanks to his careful and inventive management, RKO movies began to make an impression.

Despite nurturing such triumphs as **What Price Hollywood?**, **A Bill Of Divorcement** and **King Kong**, David O. Selznick left RKO in early 1933. The corporation suffered crushing losses of more than $10 million in 1932, which provoked Merlin Aylesworth to assume final authority regarding the approval of all scripts and budgets. Selznick regarded this interference in his operations as intolerable and quit. And who could blame him? The notion of Aylesworth – an organization man with no Hollywood experience – making all-important creative decisions was ludicrous, and when the studio lost Selznick, it lost the foremost production genius ever to enter its employ. The record of his films throughout the remainder of the decade – including *Dinner At Eight*, *David Copperfield*, *A Star Is Born*, *The Prisoner Of Zenda*, *Intermezzo* and *Gone With The Wind* – is a testament to his unrivalled abilities.

Merian C. Cooper, the adventurous producer and co-director of **King Kong**, took over Selznick's job. Cooper had a big challenge ahead of him for, at that very moment, RKO was collapsing into equity receivership. Early in 1933, a US District Court in New York appointed

Love Affair (1939)

left: Bebe Daniels and John Boles in **Rio Rita** (1929)

the Irving Trust Company as Receiver of Radio-Keith-Orpheum. This meant that the corporation was essentially bankrupt. The function of Irving Trust, a powerful New York financial concern, was not to run RKO, but to participate in the formulation of economizing and reorganizational plans which would protect stockholder interests and, it was hoped, prop the enterprise back on its feet. RKO's embarrassment was shared by its next-door neighbour, Paramount, which went into receivership at almost exactly the same time. Paramount, however, was able to solve its fiscal problems in a relatively short time, while RKO's languishment in '77B' (as receivership later came to be known in reference to the appropriate section of the Bankruptcy Act of 1934) would last into the next decade.

Merian C. Cooper approached his work with gusto, turning out films that were made quickly, cheaply and, by and large, competently. In September of 1933, he suffered a mild heart attack and took a few months off to recover. Pandro S. Berman, Cooper's principal assistant at the time, was asked to oversee all studio production until his boss' return. Cooper did return in mid-December – for two months. Once again his health began to fail and he embarked on another extended vacation, throwing the studio into general turmoil. Employees wondered whether Mr Cooper would ever run the lot again, and it was a well-known fact that Berman preferred producing individual films to superintending a full slate of pictures. The rumours were laid to rest in May 1934 when Merian C. Cooper resigned his executive position with RKO.

Emerging from the chaos of the Cooper period was a break-through that would boost RKO's artistic reputation and financial performance throughout the rest of the thirties. The huge success of Warner Bros.' innovative *Forty-Second Street* brought back the musical, which had been out of favour with audiences since 1930. RKO's **Melody Cruise**, a minor 1933 effort, was a success and persuaded the studio brass to make a somewhat more elaborate song-and-dance vehicle called **Flying Down To Rio**, in which a pair of dancers in supporting roles danced nimbly away with the picture. Their names were Fred Astaire and Ginger Rogers. Ginger had played a small role in *Forty-Second Street* before signing with RKO in 1933 – an arrangement that brought her mostly 'B' film roles until **Rio** came along. Fred was originally antagonistic to the notion of being teamed with a 'movie queen', but Pandro S. Berman talked him into it. The pair were to make eight more RKO films together, and became the biggest box-office attraction in company history.

The most profitable Astaire–Rogers film was **Top Hat**, released in 1935. This very special year also included RKO's most honoured film, **The Informer**, another giant Astaire–Rogers–Irene Dunne hit, **Roberta**, and the first feature made in three-strip Technicolor, **Becky Sharp**. J. R. McDonough, president of the production company, was now in charge of the studio, and B. B. Kahane was now head of production. The job had been dumped on Kahane following a disagreement between McDonough and Pandro Berman which resulted in Berman's return to the producer ranks.

The next executive shake-up occurred in late 1935 when Floyd Odlum purchased half of RCA's controlling interest in RKO. Odlum was a major American financier, director of the Foreign Power Company, United Fruit Company and the Italian Superpower Corporation. He was no stranger to movie enterprise either; his Atlas Corporation held considerable investments in Paramount, Warner Bros. and Loew's (MGM), and he intended to make sure RKO was run in a no-nonsense, businesslike fashion. His handpicked executives were Leo Spitz, a Chicago attorney who had once defended Al Capone, and Samuel Briskin, a Columbia Pictures veteran. Spitz became corporate president, replacing Merlin Aylesworth who was made chairman of the board, while Briskin took over the production reins from Kahane.

Thanks to an upsurge in the American economy, RKO showed respectable profits in 1936 and 1937. But, in fact, the Spitz–Briskin alliance was not constructive. Most of the films

centre: Margot Graham and Victor McLaglen in **The Informer** (1935)
right: David Manners and Katharine Hepburn in
A Bill Of Divorcement (1932)

produced were negligible, the studio failed to build any major new personalities and Katharine Hepburn's status was severely damaged. Sam Briskin's only noteworthy accomplishment was the signing of Walt Disney to a distribution deal. The first Disney–RKO feature release, **Snow White And The Seven Dwarfs**, became one of the blockbuster hits of the decade.

The Hepburn situation was particularly exasperating. Having skyrocketed to success in such early films as **A Bill Of Divorcement**, **Morning Glory** and **Little Women**, the sublime actress foundered helplessly as a series of bad pictures undermined her credibility with film patrons. (**Spitfire**, **Sylvia Scarlett** and **A Woman Rebels** were especially damaging.) In 1938, a group of independent theatre owners placed her at the top of their 'box-office poison' list, and even her superlative performance in **Bringing Up Baby** did not find favour with the public. When Hepburn refused to appear in **Mother Carey's Chickens**, RKO executives were happy to release her from her contract. The plucky Miss Hepburn was no dead duck, however, as her subsequent career was to prove.

There was ample cause for rejoicing when Pandro S. Berman, a proven talent, replaced Sam Briskin as head of production in 1938. Berman understood the studio's special problems better than anyone, having served it since its inception. His first full year as executive producer contained some disappointments (such as **Room Service**), but he had an excellent slate of pictures in preparation when George J. Schaefer replaced Leo Spitz as president of Radio-Keith-Orpheum in late 1938.

Schaefer, who had spent more than a quarter of a century in the motion picture industry and was vice-president and general manager of United Artists at the time, was brought to RKO by the Rockefellers. Owners of considerable RKO stock and in league with David Sarnoff (still a behind-the-scenes power), the Rockefellers were displeased with the policies of Floyd Odlum's executives and felt the corporation needed firm, active leadership. Schaefer approached his task with fervour, demanding final

say on everything, including studio decisions. This policy, plus the president's wholesale recruitment of independent production units, so infuriated Pandro Berman that he quit RKO in 1939. His departing legacy was the best group of pictures in company history, including **Gunga Din**, **Love Affair**, **Bachelor Mother** and **The Hunchback Of Notre Dame**.

If Pandro Berman's leave-taking put the full-stop to an era for RKO, **The Story Of Vernon And Irene Castle** added the exclamation mark. **Vernon And Irene Castle** was the ninth and last of the Astaire–Rogers pictures. With their films no longer sure box-office winners and the two stars chafing to pursue solo careers, RKO acquiesced in the termination. The most famous, profitable and artistically ambitious series in RKO annals had played itself out.

During George Schaefer's first full year as president, RKO underwent a radical metamorphosis. After years of producing nearly all of its own product, the studio became involved with a number of independents who would be responsible for a significant percentage of future releases. Turning away from a long period of economic restraint, the studio began competing for the most prestigious literary properties, signing up freelance stars (Carole Lombard, Cary Grant, Charles Laughton and others) and luring bold but untested new talents like Orson Welles. Schaefer obviously intended to turn RKO into a 'quality' studio, one known for ambitious, masterful productions rather than the 'B'-level melodramas, erratic comedies and escapist musicals which had characterized its past.

As 1939 came to a close, the corporation was almost free of receivership, but the outbreak of World War II and the progress of a US government suit concerning such trade practices as block booking and blind bidding caused an aura of insecurity to settle over all of Hollywood. One point was certain – RKO had definitely found a strong president, determined to lead his company to a position of industry pre-eminence. David Sarnoff's original grandiose vision for RKO was alive and well, and resting firmly in the hands of one man: George J. Schaefer.

★★★★★★★★★★★★★★★★★

1929

★★★★★★★★★★★★★★★★★

In 1929, the studio amassed a substantial contingent of talent to spearhead its quest for greatness. The first actors placed on the payroll were Bebe Daniels, Betty Compson, Richard Dix, Sally Blane and Rudy Vallee. Luther Reed, Malcolm St Clair and Wesley Ruggles were the top directors. James Ashmore Creelman, Jane Murfin, Wallace Smith and J. Walter Ruben became contract writers and studio head William LeBaron, a writer by trade, agreed to take an active hand in story matters, as well as production. Victor Baravalle was appointed as the studio's musical director, and the Oscar Levant–Sidney Clare partnership was employed to write songs. Max Ree took charge of a conglomerate department that included art direction, set and costume design, and props.

The company used 'It's RKO – Let's Go' as an advertising slogan and, following the general trend of the time, made sure that practically every picture contained some kind of musical component.

Three films brought in a lion's share of the profits: **Street Girl, The Vagabond Lover** and the studio's first immense hit, **Rio Rita**. Net corporate profit for this initial auspicious year amounted to $1,669,564.

Syncopation, the first 'Radio' picture, was, in fact, sandwiched in between two FBO programmers, and was also the initial 'all talking' film utilizing the RCA Photophone system. Although bandleader Fred Waring and His Pennsylvanians received star billing, they were seen only twice in the picture, whose story focused on Barbara Bennett (left) and Bobby Watson (right) as a dance team whose marriage is threatened by villainous millionaire Ian Hunter (centre). Some additional diversion was supplied by Morton Downey, Verree Teasdale, Osgood Perkins, Dorothy Lee and McKenzie Ward, all as members of the jazz nightclub scene. Bert Glennon directed (dialogue direction by Bertram Harrison and James Seymour), from Frances Agnew's adaptation of a Gene Markey novel (Markey provided the dialogue) and, despite mediocre acting, cliché-ridden speeches and less-than-perfect synchronization, the film – supervised by Robert Kane and shot in New York – played two weeks at the New York Hippodrome and broke all house records. The public was obviously enchanted by this freshest of screen entertainments: the musical. Songs: 'Jericho' Leo Robin, Richard Myers; 'Mine Alone' Herman Ruby, Myers; 'I'll Always Be In Love With You' Bud Green, Sammy Stept.

The first 'official' RKO production, **Street Girl**, was a typical concoction of the early sound era in which Betty Compson (centre) starred as a violinist, and the manager of a quartet of jazz musicians who call themselves 'The Four Seasons'. She and band member John Harron (at piano) fall in love, but complications arise when Ivan Lebedeff, a prince from the girl's Balkan homeland, pays court to her. Everything, however, works out in the end, with piano-pounding boy and violin-plucking girl joined blissfully together. Though only average fare, the William LeBaron production (associate producer Louis Sarecky) attracted over $1.1 million in box-office rentals on an initial investment of $211,000. RKO was at last well and truly (and profitably) launched. Directed by Wesley Ruggles from a Jane Murfin screenplay (based on a story by W. Carey Wonderly), the cast included Jack Oakie (left, borrowed from Paramount), Ned Sparks (right), Guy Buccola (centre right), Joseph Cawthorn, Doris Eaton and Gus Arnheim and His Ambassadors. The picture inspired two RKO remakes: *That Girl From Paris* (1937) starring Lily Pons and *Four Jacks And A Jill* (1942) with Anne Shirley. Songs: 'My Dream Memory', 'Lovable And Sweet', 'Broken Up Tune' Oscar Levant, Sidney Clare.

The real-life Moore brothers – Tom, Matt (centre) ▷ and Owen (left) – with a wealth of silent film credits between them, had never worked together in a picture. Producer William LeBaron remedied this situation by teaming them in **Side Street** (GB: **The Three Brothers**), the story of three O'Farrells, one a policeman, the second an ambulance surgeon and the third a racketeer. Unknown to the underworld brother, his men lay a trap for the cop. The gangster learns the truth, rushes to the rendezvous and is mowed down by his cohorts, dying in the arms of his two brothers. Though the Irish brogues often got a little too thick (as did the plot contrivances), the Moores – under Malcolm St Clair's direction – performed well in a film that managed, at times, to be genuinely gripping in spite of its elements of implausible melodrama. George O'Hara and Jane Murfin wrote the screenplay from a story by St Clair adapted by John Russell. Also in it: Frank Sheridan (right), Emma Dunn, Kathryn Perry (Mrs Owen Moore in real life), Charles Byer, Arthur Housman, Walter McNamara and Mildred Harris (a silent film star and ex-wife of Charles Chaplin).

The science of eugenics seemed a ripe subject for burlesque, but **The Very Idea** completely failed to do it justice. Allen Kearns (left) and Doris Eaton (centre) played a married couple frustrated by their failure to have a baby. Eaton's brother, (Frank Craven, right) happens to be the author of a book on such matters and selects a perfect couple (Hugh Trevor and Sally Blane) who are hired to produce a superior offspring for the childless young marrieds. When baby arrives, the proud parents naturally don't want to give it up, leading to a considerable quantity of lame farce until the inevitable news is announced: Kearns and Eaton are at last going to have a child of their own. Made cheaply, the film was a botch in all respects and something of an omen of many future unsuccessful RKO stabs at mirth. Producer William LeBaron was responsible for the screenplay (from his play of the same title), and the sorry enterprise clearly called into question his ability to run the studio. Actor Craven shared the directing credit with Richard Rosson, Myles Connolly was the associate producer, and Olive Tell and Theodore von Eltz ◁ were also cast.

△

'The ruthless sea rogue and the titian-haired dancing girl in a throbbing tropic love duel', boomed the publicity for **The Delightful Rogue**, whose story and screenplay (by Wallace Smith) offered sporadic bursts of electricity, but hardly made the screen throb. A decidedly greasy Rod La Rocque (left) played the rogue, a pirate in fact, who sails to Tapit and encounters American dancer Rita LaRoy (right), the object of Charles Byer's jealous affections. Byer soon finds himself in the rogue's clutches and, in order to win her beau's release, LaRoy must spend the night in La Rocque's cabin. Nothing occurs but chatter; nevertheless, Byer is reduced to a green-eyed frenzy, prompting the disgusted dancer to set sail with the gentlemanly rogue. The principals gave their all to this call of the wild and steamy, but to little avail. William LeBaron again produced, with Henry Hobart as his associate, A. Leslie Pearce was the director and Lynn Shores the pictorial director. Bert Moorehouse, Ed Brady, Harry Semels and Samuel Blum were among the supporting players. One song, 'Gay Love' by Oscar Levant and Sidney Clare, was featured.

The one undoubted 'Titan' released in 1929 was **Rio Rita**, a lavish musical western brought to the screen following a 62-week run on Broadway. Though it may seem an exotic piece of screen antiquity by today's standards, the picture was one of the prime entertainments of its era, and earned $2.4 million in box-office rentals. Bebe Daniels (left), in her first talking picture, and John Boles (right), a Universal contract star borrowed for the occasion, topped the cast. Boles played a Texas ranger on the trail of the notorious bandit, El Kinkajou. He meets Rita (Daniels), they fall in love, but immediately drift apart because her brother is one of the ranger's suspects. It seems for a time that Rita will marry the villain Ravenoff, but he is soon revealed to be the Kinkajou and the final ceremony unites her with the ranger. Interwoven with the romance and intrigue, in alternating scenes, was a comic subplot which had Chick Bean (Bert Wheeler) trying to arrange a divorce through an unscrupulous lawyer named Lovett (Robert Woolsey). Director Luther Reed simply froze the stage show on celluloid, paying minimal attention to cinematic quality. Nevertheless, the sheer spectacle of **Rio Rita** redeemed its stodginess – especially Max Ree's art direction and costuming. The river barge finale, shot in two-strip Technicolor, remains a feast for the eyes. Pearl Eaton staged the dances. Producer William LeBaron's decision to spare no expense paid handsome dividends and looked forward to later musical triumphs for the studio. Director Reed, who also adapted the Guy Bolton–Fred Thompson stage book, cast Georges Renevant (the heavy), Dorothy Lee, Don Alvarado and Helen Kaiser in supporting roles. One song, 'You're Always In My Arms', was specially written for the film. Other songs included: 'Rio Rita', 'Following The Sun Around', 'If You're In Love You'll Waltz', 'The Ranger's Song' Harry Tierney, Joseph McCarthy. MGM later bought the property and made its own version in 1942, starring Kathryn Grayson, John Carroll and Abbott and Costello.

Olive Borden starred in director William J. Cowen's undernourished melodrama **Half Marriage**. The silly screenplay (by Jane Murfin, working from George Kibbe Turner's original), had Miss Borden (left) playing Judy Paige, a society girl who, much to the disappointment of her parents, elopes with a young architect called Dick (Morgan Farley, right). What her folks don't know is that Judy and Dick are already secretly married anyway, and it takes a rival suitor (Anderson Lawler) to jump to his death from Judy's apartment before all is revealed and resolved. Future gossip columnist Hedda Hopper played Olive's mamma, and other featured players for associate producer Henry Hobart included Ann Greenway, Sally Blane and Richard Tucker. Two songs, 'After The Clouds Roll By' and 'You're Marvelous', by Sidney Clare and Oscar Levant, and a few vaudeville-style gags from Ken Murray, briefly enlivened the proceedings. (WLB).

△
A familiar trip to the battleground of boxing, **Night Parade** (GB: **Sporting Life**) presented Hugh Trevor (right) as a middleweight champion seduced into throwing the big fight by Aileen Pringle (centre). The machinations of Pringle and racketeer Robert Ellis (left) are revealed at the crucial moment and, spurred on by a good woman (Dorothy Gulliver) and a wise father (Lloyd Ingraham), Trevor gets up off the canvas and wins. The mouldy tale, based on a play by Hyatt Daab, Edward Paramore Jr and George Abbott, was not helped by James Gruen and George O'Hara's punch-drunk screenplay, Malcolm St Clair's sluggish direction, or the notably dismal performances of Ingraham, Pringle and Ellis. Also cast: Ann Pennington, Lee Shumway, Heinie Conklin and Charles Sullivan. Louis Sarecky was the associate producer. (WLB).

△
Jazz Heaven was a whimsical and appealing Tin Pan Alley tale that concerned a songwriter (John Mack Brown, right, on loan from MGM) and his girl (Sally O'Neil, left) who are battling to complete the tune that will make them rich and happy. In the end, of course, they succeed – with the help of a pair of music publishers named Kemple and Klucke, played by Joseph Cawthorn and Albert Conti who, between them, stole the show. Clyde Cook, Blanche Frederici and Henry Armetta were also featured for associate producer Myles Connolly. J. Walter Ruben and Cyrus Wood provided the screenplay (story by Pauline Forney and Dudley Murphy), and the zippy direction was by Melville Brown. The lovers' song, 'Someone', was actually composed by Oscar Levant and Sidney Clare. (WLB).

△
RKO viewed as much as possible in musical terms during its initial year, and **Tanned Legs**, directed by Marshall Neilan, was no exception. Oscar Levant and Sidney Clare again provided the songs which, on this occasion, were rather awkwardly injected into a comedy-drama about hi-jinx in a seaside resort. June Clyde (right) starred as a leggy young lady determined to straighten out her wayward family. Mom (Nella Walker) and Dad (Albert Gran) are dallying with partners much younger than they, and sister Sally Blane is treading on thin ice with a dissolute young bounder played by Edmund Burns. Though she almost forfeits her reputation and her true love Arthur Lake (left) in the process, the resilient heroine manages to bring her errant relations to their senses. William LeBaron, however, should have had more sense than to sponsor this less-than-scintillating exercise. Tom Geraghty wrote the screenplay, providing supporting parts for Dorothy Revier, Ann Pennington, Allen Kearns and Lincoln Stedman. Louis Sarecky was the associate producer. Songs included: 'With You, With Me', 'You're Responsible'.

△
Crooner Rudy Vallee top-lined **The Vagabond Lover**, one of the studio's solid box-office successes. The James Ashmore Creelman story and screenplay had Vallee as Rudy Bronson, a hick from Waterville who completes a correspondence course with America's 'Saxophone King' and then heads for Long Island to meet the great man. Rebuffed by his idol, Rudy poses as the King, enjoys a limited success, is exposed as an imposter, but finally wins praise and a job offer from the jaundiced mail-order monarch himself. Along the way, Rudy (left) also captures the heart of comely Sally Blane (right). Marie Dressler (centre) was by far the best thing in the picture, playing Blane's dowager aunt who tramples on the smug, pseudo-intellectual members of Long Island society – especially one Mrs Todhunter (Nella Walker). Vallee was as stiff as a frozen mackerel throughout, and the rest of the acting faltered considerably, but audiences, who flocked to see Rudy perform with his Connecticut Yankees band, didn't seem to mind. Marshall Neilan directed for associate producer Louis Sarecky, and their cast also included Charles Sellon, Norman Peck, Danny O'Shea, Eddie Nugent and – as the Saxophone King – Malcolm Waite. Songs included: 'A Little Kiss · Each Morning', 'Heigh-Ho Everybody' Harry Woods; 'If You Were The Only Girl' Clifford Grey, Nat D. Ayer; 'I'll Be Reminded Of You' Ed Heyman, Ken Smith; 'I Love You, Believe Me, I Love You' Rubey Cowan, Phil Bartholomae, Phil Boutelje. (WLB).

A sour note was sounded by **Dance Hall**, RKO's final release of the decade. Vina Delmar's story required shipping clerk Arthur Lake (right) to attempt to dance his way into Olive Borden's heart, but he is thwarted by dashing aviator Ralph Emerson who swoops in and plucks the delectable prize away. Not for long, however, since time proves the flyer unworthy, and, by the final fade, Borden (left) and Lake are cemented together, dancing partners for life. The film collapsed in the critical areas of acting (Arthur Lake was the weakest of the weak), dialogue (the screenplay by Jane Murfin and J. Walter Ruben contained a steady stream of 'Goshes', 'Gees' and other incisive expressions) and direction (Melville Brown, bumbling along in the alien world of sound pictures), which didn't leave much to be said for it. Yet, somehow, it managed to be mildly diverting from time to time. Associate Henry Hobart supervised the production, and the supporting cast included Joseph Cawthorn, Margaret Seddon, Lee Moran, Helen Kaiser, Tom O'Brien
◁ and George Irving. (WLB).

1930

★ ★ ★ ★ ★ ★ ★ ★ ★ ★ ★ ★ ★ ★ ★

★ ★ ★ ★ ★ ★ ★ ★ ★ ★ ★ ★ ★ ★ ★

In February 1930, Radio-Keith-Orpheum stock was considered a Wall Street best buy. One broker conjectured that the company's theatres would entertain 500 million customers during the year and the stock could possibly show earnings of $10 per share. Buoyed by such optimistic forecasts, the organization continued to expand. More theatres joined the RKO chain, making a grand total of 175 film palaces by the end of the year. It was reported that the company had spent $33 million in net acquisition of capital assets during 1929 and 1930.

The studio signed director Herbert Brenon, who had made such silent successes as *Peter Pan*, *Beau Geste* and *The Great Gatsby*, director-actor Lowell Sherman and performers Joel McCrea, Irene Dunne, Evelyn Brent, Mary Astor and blackface radio stars Amos 'n' Andy. Bert Wheeler and Robert Woolsey inaugurated their own series of lunatic comedies.

By the end of 1930, RKO's fortunes had done a complete turnabout. Its pictures had shown no discernible improvement, and the worsening Depression transformed many of its profitable theatres into money-sapping edifices. Embarrassingly, vaudeville programs, which were still prevalent in most of the houses, appeared to be sustaining the company.

A worried Joseph Schnitzer began to assert himself. He started reading plays and scripts and promised to take an active hand in production. Rumours that the president of Radio Pictures would replace William LeBaron as head of production were echoing through the Hollywood hills by December.

The studio released 29 films in 1930. They were a desultory collection, and no big hits were produced. **Check And Double Check** and **Hook, Line and Sinker** earned the largest profits.

Despite the downturn in business at year's end, RKO reported net profits of $3,385,628 for 1930.

Second Wife, featuring Conrad Nagel and Lila Lee, offered a rather drab domestic plot, redeemed by quality writing and finely honed performances. In it, Lee (left) marries widower Nagel (right) despite suitor Hugh Huntley's poisonous prophecy that she cannot fill the gap left by Nagel's first wife. When her husband deserts her to attend to his seven-year-old son who is ill in Switzerland, the now pregnant Lee decides she can never live with him again, and prepares to run away with Huntley – until he refuses to accept her baby. Considerably chastened, she is reconciled with Nagel and her stepson. The efforts of writers Hugh Herbert and Bert Glennon (basing their script on Fulton Oursler's play *All The King's Men*), director Russell Mack and the actors, including Freddie Burke Frederick (as the seven-year-old), and Mary Carr, the kindly housekeeper, made this a cultivated tearjerker. Myles Connolly was the associate producer. (WLB). RKO remade the film in 1936 with Gertrude Michael, Walter Abel and Erik Rhodes.

Seven Keys To Baldpate already boasted an illustrious history when RKO brought it to the screen as the first Richard Dix showpiece. Based on Earl Derr Biggers' novel, the tale had been produced in 1917 with George M. Cohan (who had also written a successful stage version) and then again in 1925 with Douglas MacLean. The studio would re-tool it twice more: in 1935 with Gene Raymond and in 1947 with Phillip Terry. The story – an equal mixture of mystery, melodrama and farce – revolved around William Magee (Dix, right), a successful author whose forthcoming marriage is threatened because he hasn't completed an overdue manuscript. The writer repairs to the Baldpate Inn for some peace and quiet, promising to complete the book within 24 hours, but the Inn becomes a beehive of frantic activity when $200,000 is stolen. Finally the sheriff arrives, locks up everyone but the writer, and the multiple mysteries are solved. All except one, that is. The final twist was that all the on-screen activity was actually the substance of Magee's novel, which he finishes just in time. Too convoluted and too cute for mystery purists, the film was nonetheless a lively diversion, with Dix passing the test set by his first RKO role. Director Reginald Barker and dialogue director Russell Mack kept Jane Murfin's screenplay zipping along, with help from Miriam Seegar (left), Margaret Livingston, Lucien Littlefield, Joseph Allen, DeWitt Jennings, Nella Walker, Alan Roscoe, Crauford Kent and Harvey Clark. Louis J. Sarecky was the associate producer. (WLB).

Seeking out an exotic location, RKO dropped anchor in Fiji for **Girl Of The Port**, and came up with another hackneyed melodrama. This time it was about an English lord (Reginald Sharland) who flees to the island paradise to overcome his desperate fear of fire – a condition induced by his war time experiences. Sharland (right) is on the road to alcoholic amnesia when he meets showgirl Sally O'Neil (left), who helps him deal with his phobia. Jealous heavy Mitchell Lewis forces Sharland to participate in a native fire-walking ritual, but the hero conquers his fear, walking right through the flames and into the arms of his beloved showgirl. Beulah Marie Dix adapted John Russell's story, Bert Glennon directed (dialogue director Frank Reicher), and the cast also included Crauford Kent, Arthur Clayton, Duke Kahanamoku, Gerald Barry, Renee Macready and John Webb Dillon. Bertram Millhauser was associate producer. (WLB).

The studio's second major musical, **Hit The Deck**, made money, but it never approached the previous year's *Rio Rita* in popularity. Based on the Vincent Youmans musical play (book by Herbert Fields) of the same title, which was in turn based on Hubert Osborne's 1922 theatrical comedy *Shore Leave*, the film starred Jack Oakie (centre) as aptly named sailor Bilge Smith and Polly Walker as Looloo, owner of a seaside coffee shop who falls for him. Luther Reed adapted the property for the screen, and directed it with the same approach he had brought to *Rio Rita*, with approximately the same inert results. In addition to the obvious drawbacks of a photographed stage play, the picture was little more than an awkward excuse to mainline as many musical numbers (Pearl Eaton staged the dances) as possible in a short period of time. Walker performed capably as the girl whose sudden wealth sabotages her dreams of romance, but Oakie (borrowed from Paramount) was not versatile enough to meet the demands of his role, and comedy turns by Harry Sweet, Franker Woods and Roger Gray brought only sporadic chuckles. Partial Technicolor did add some visual richness. William LeBaron

personally supervised with a cast that also featured Marguerite Padula, June Clyde, Ethel Clayton, Wallace MacDonald and Del Henderson. RKO sold it to MGM who remade it in 1955 with Jane Powell, Tony Martin and Debbie Reynolds. Songs included: 'Keeping Myself For You' Sidney Clare, Vincent Youmans; 'Sometimes I'm Happy', 'Hallelujah' Leo Robin, Clifford Grey, Youmans; 'Sez You – Sez Me' Harry Tierney.

The vocal talent of Bebe Daniels (left) was about all that **Love Comes Along** offered in the way of entertainment. Rummaging about for a star vehicle for Miss Daniels, William LeBaron happened upon Edward Knoblock's play *Conchita*, turned over the adaptation to Wallace Smith and instructed Oscar Levant and Sidney Clare to prepare some appropriate tunes. Under Rupert Julian's torpid direction, the resultant melodrama sputtered and wheezed its way on to the screen, finally conking out completely. All about an actress stranded on the mythical island of Caparoja, it surveyed her warbling in a local tavern, her stormy love affair with a devil-may-care sailor and the difficulties hatched by her relationship with the island potentate. LeBaron would have been better off if he had tossed out the plot and just photographed his star singing for 80 minutes. Other cast members included Lloyd Hughes (right), badly miscast as the romantic sailor, Montagu Love (the insidious potentate), Ned Sparks, Lionel Belmore, Alma Tell and Evelyn Selbie. Henry Hobart was the associate producer. Songs included: 'Night Winds', 'Until Love Comes Along'.

While most of RKO's films were currently light, frivolous and insubstantial, **The Case of Sergeant Grischa** went to the opposite extreme. William LeBaron believed the Arnold Zweig novel to be 'one of the greatest war books' and insisted that the film version be just as uncompromising and harrowing as its source. The famous silent film director Herbert Brenon, together with scenarist Elizabeth Meehan, was charged with the screen translation, and LeBaron fully expected the finished picture to be sufficiently important and controversial to draw a respectable audience. Instead, it was so tedious, so lacking in credibility, and so devoid of dramatic intensity, that it flopped totally. Chester Morris (left) played Grischa, a simple-minded Russian soldier who escapes from a German prisoner-of-war camp. He hides out with a girl named Babka (Betty Compson, right) for a time, but finally his longing for his homeland overcomes him. Wearing the identity tag of a dead Russian spy, the sergeant is soon recaptured by the Rhinelanders and sentenced to death. Their ruthlessness and disdain for justice is driven home when proof of Grischa's innocence is brushed aside and he is executed. What LeBaron felt would be 'the most discussed film that was ever produced', was one of the most quickly forgotten. Also cast: Jean Hersholt, Alec B. Francis, Gustav von Seyffertitz, Paul McAllister, Leyland Hodgson, Bernard Siegel and Frank McCormack.

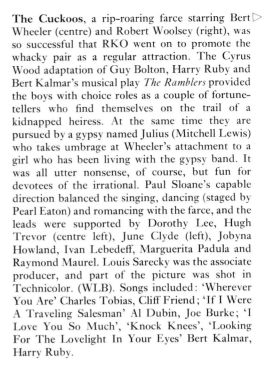

Rod La Rocque (right) played a cavalier Mexican bad guy with a sentimental streak in **Beau Bandit**. The trivial story, by Wallace Smith, opened with La Rocque and his deaf-mute accomplice (Mitchell Lewis) about to rob a bank, despite hot pursuit from 'Bob-Cat' Manners (Walter Long) and his posse. The singing of Doris Kenyon distracts the outlaw, and soon he is masterminding a scheme to free her from the clutches of skinflint banker Charles B. Middleton (left) and get her married to her real love George Duryea (later to be known as Tom Keene, star of a low-budget Western series). Any similarities to *The Story Of Robin Hood* were, in this second-rater, purely coincidental. Lambert Hillyer directed; Henry Hobart was associate producer. Also cast: James Donlan, Charles Brinley, Barney Furey and Bill Patton. (WLB).

Former FBO star Evelyn Brent (left) returned to her old studio for **Framed**, a routine potboiler directed by George Archainbaud. Paul Schofield's script (dialogue Wallace Smith) had Brent as a nightclub hostess whose one objective in life is to avenge the death of her father, killed during a holdup by police inspector William Holden (no relation to the star of *Sunset Boulevard* and *Bridge On The River Kwai*). Her intentions become confused when the inspector's son (Regis Toomey, right) falls in love with her. Soon her passion for the son overcomes her hatred of the father, and it all ends happily when she foils a plan by bootlegger Ralf Harolde to bump off both of them. Henry Hobart was the associate producer, and Maurice Black, Robert Emmett O'Connor and Eddie Kane were in it too. (WLB).

Romance in high society was the subject of **Lovin' The Ladies**, a minor Richard Dix starrer. Dix, an electrician, becomes the guinea pig in Allen Kearns' experiment to prove that any two people can be made to fall in love. Passing Dix (right) off as a proper gentleman, Kearns introduces him to sophisticate Renee Macready, but the plan goes haywire when Kearns' fiancée Lois Wilson (left) falls for the dashing commoner. At the fade, Dix ashamedly confesses the subterfuge, but Wilson marries him anyway. Producer William LeBaron's play *I Love You* provided the basic plot which J. Walter Ruben adapted. Melville Brown's direction kept the convoluted story intelligible, and Edward Cronjager, Dix's favourite cameraman, supplied the vivid photography. The supporting players included Rita LaRoy, Virginia Sale, Selmer Jackson, Anthony Bushell and Henry Armetta. Louis Sarecky was the associate producer.

In **Alias French Gertie** (GB: **Love Finds A Way**), Bebe Daniels and Ben Lyon (who were shortly to marry in real-life), portrayed a pair of engaging safecrackers who meet when both fasten upon the same diamond cache at the same moment. The rest of the picture documented the pair's seesaw relationship as Lyon (right) constantly slipped back to his old habits, despite Bebe's (left) attempts to convince him to go straight and settle down with her. Wallace Smith's screen adaptation from Bayard Veiller's play *The Chatterbox*, also gave featured roles to Robert Emmett O'Connor, Daisy Belmore, John Ince, Betty Pierce, Maude Turner Gordon, Nella Walker and Charles Giblyn. George Archainbaud was the director, Henry Hobart the associate producer. The picture was a remake of FBO's *Smooth As Satin* (1925) which starred Evelyn Brent. (WLB).

The Cuckoos, a rip-roaring farce starring Bert Wheeler (centre) and Robert Woolsey (right), was so successful that RKO went on to promote the whacky pair as a regular attraction. The Cyrus Wood adaptation of Guy Bolton, Harry Ruby and Bert Kalmar's musical play *The Ramblers* provided the boys with choice roles as a couple of fortune-tellers who find themselves on the trail of a kidnapped heiress. At the same time they are pursued by a gypsy named Julius (Mitchell Lewis) who takes umbrage at Wheeler's attachment to a girl who has been living with the gypsy band. It was all utter nonsense, of course, but fun for devotees of the irrational. Paul Sloane's capable direction balanced the singing, dancing (staged by Pearl Eaton) and romancing with the farce, and the leads were supported by Dorothy Lee, Hugh Trevor (centre left), June Clyde (left), Jobyna Howland, Ivan Lebedeff, Marguerita Padula and Raymond Maurel. Louis Sarecky was the associate producer, and part of the picture was shot in Technicolor. (WLB). Songs included: 'Wherever You Are' Charles Tobias, Cliff Friend; 'If I Were A Traveling Salesman' Al Dubin, Joe Burke; 'I Love You So Much', 'Knock Knees', 'Looking For The Lovelight In Your Eyes' Bert Kalmar, Harry Ruby.

Based on S. N. Behrman's play *The Second Man*, **He Knew Women** took a sardonic view of romance and of the upper crust. Lowell Sherman (left) made his RKO debut as a lazy writer who becomes captivated by the ample fortune of widow Alice Joyce (right), which attracts him even more than the romantic allegiance of lovely Frances Dade. She almost ruins his chances with the widow by announcing that he has compromised her, whereupon young chemist David Manners who is in love with Frances takes a potshot at Sherman. The shot is poorly aimed but impresses Dade nonetheless; she changes her attitude completely toward this formerly despised suitor. Money (and love) triumph as Sherman and Joyce, Manners and Dade are united in the end. Hugh Herbert directed (receiving pictorial assistance from Lynn Shores). Herbert also collaborated on the screenplay with William Jutte, managing to make it witty and engaging, although it remained very slight and a little static. Myles Connolly was the associate producer. (WLB).

◁ **The Runaway Bride** quickly found a place to hide – in storage vaults rather than movie theatres. Donald Crisp directed Jane Murfin's screenplay (based on a play by Lolita Ann Westman and H. H. Van Loan) which told the ludicrous story of a pair of innocent lovebirds, Mary Astor (right) and Lloyd Hughes (left), who somehow get involved with a jewel heist, a cutpurse chamber maid, a fake hospital run by gangsters and various other incredulities. If everyone's Atlantic City honeymoon were like this one, Niagara Falls would have to hire Barnum and Bailey to compete. Also wading through the nonsense were Paul Hurst, David Newell, Natalie Moorhead, Edgar Norton and Francis McDonald for associate producer William Sistrom (who would supervise some of the studio's 'Saint' pictures in later years.) (WLB).

A boatload of characters and a labyrinthine plotline kept **Midnight Mystery** director George B. Seitz on his toes. Betty Compson (right), Lowell Sherman, Rita LaRoy, Ivan Lebedeff, Raymond Hatton, Marcelle Corday and June Clyde were among the combustible personalities being ferried by Hugh Trevor (left) to his island castle off the coast of Maine. Storms, both natural and emotional, soon erupt, culminating in Sherman's murder of Lebedeff. Compson who, in addition to being Trevor's fiancée, happens to be a mystery story writer, totes up the clues and then tricks Sherman into confessing his crime. Beulah Marie Dix's adaptation of Howard Irving Young's play *Hawk Island* was hardly Hitchcock, but managed to tickle the fancy of sleuth addicts. Bertram ◁ Millhauser was the associate producer. (WLB).

Jack Mulhall played **The Fall Guy** (GB: **Trust Your Wife**), a young drug clerk who loses his job and is soon mixed up with the underworld, as personified by one 'Nifty' Herman (Thomas E. Jackson). A cache of illegal drugs is found in Mulhall's possession by government agent Pat O'Malley, but all ends happily when the hero dupes 'Nifty' into spilling the beans. Besides personal exoneration, Mulhall is rewarded with a job as O'Malley's assistant. Mae Clarke (right), who was immortalized in *The Public Enemy* when James Cagney pushed a grapefruit in her face, topped the supporting cast, which included Ned Sparks (left), Wynne Gibson, Tom Kennedy and Alan Roscoe. All their performances were adequate, but director Leslie Pearce's stagebound direction robbed the comedy-drama of any true vitality. Tim Whelan wrote the adaptation of George Abbott and James Gleason's Broadway hit, and the associate producer was William Sistrom. (WLB).
▽

Inside The Lines was cloak-and-dagger hokum, indifferently acted by Betty Compson (left) and Ralph Forbes. The Earl Derr Biggers novel (adapted by Ewart Adamson with dialogue by John Farrow) concerned attempts to destroy the British fleet during World War I. Ralph and Betty are in love, but each thinks the other is spying for the Germans. Thankfully, both turn out to be British agents and, together, they prevent the treacherous Hindu Amahdi (Mischa Auer, right) from blowing up England's chances to whip the Kaiser. Roy Pomeroy supplied the perfunctory direction, and doubled as associate producer. His cast also featured Montague Love, Ivan Simpson, Reginald Sharland, Betty Carter, Evan Thomas and William von Brincken. (WLB).
▽

Mistaken identity was the key ingredient in ▷ **Shooting Straight**, a vehicle for Richard Dix (right) in which he played 'Lucky' Larry Sheldon, a gambler on the run because he thinks (mistakenly) that he has committed a murder. When the train on which he is making his getaway meets an accident, 'Lucky' recuperates in the home of minister James Neill, who believes him to be a travelling evangelist. Dix grows attached to both his new identity and to the minister's daughter (Mary Lawlor, centre), but the day of reckoning inevitably arrives. However, instead of the prison sentence which he expects, 'Lucky' finds that another man has confessed to the murder, whereupon he decides to continue his personal regeneration with the approval of his understanding sweetheart. J. Walter Ruben patched together the contrived screenplay from Wallace Smith's adaptation of a Barney Sarecky story; Mathew Betz (left), George Cooper, William Janney and Robert Emmett O'Connor were also cast, and George Archainbaud directed for associate producer Louis Sarecky. (WLB).

A revamped remake of a Famous Players silent production, **Conspiracy** focused on the determination of Bessie Love (right, borrowed from MGM) and her brother Bert Moorehouse to wreck a drug ring responsible for their father's death. With assistance from young reporter Hugh Trevor and mystery writer Ned Sparks, they succeed in trapping all the villains. The Christy Cabanne-directed film did not, however, manage to trap many customers. Total film rentals added up to a paltry $138,000. Beulah Marie Dix adapted the Robert Baker – John Emerson play, providing supporting roles for Ivan Lebedeff, Rita LaRoy, Gertrude Howard, Otto Matiesen (left), Walter Long and Donald Mackenzie. Associate producer: Bertram Millhauser. (WLB).
▽

Bebe Daniels (right) undertook a straight dramatic ▷ role in **Lawful Larceny**. The Jane Murfin scenario, based on Samuel Shipman's play, required her to insinuate herself into the confidence of Olive Tell, a siren who has vamped Miss Daniels' simpleton husband (Kenneth Thomson) out of a considerable fortune. Adopting Olive's methods, Bebe retrieves the money and out-manoeuvres crooked smoothie Lowell Sherman (left) in the process. Sherman's presence alone, plus his fast-paced direction, made this one of the year's better melos. Purnell Pratt, Maude Turner Gordon, Helene Millard, Bert Roach and Louis Payne played secondary roles, and Olive Tell's real-life husband, Henry Hobart, was the associate producer. **Lawful Larceny** was a remake of a 1925 Paramount film which starred Hope Hampton and Conrad Nagel. (WLB).

'Youth Whoops It Up In The Rumble Seat!' read one publicity catch-line for **She's My Weakness**. It turned out to be a bumpy ride for all concerned, especially leading players Sue Carol, a Fox contract actress borrowed for the part, and Arthur Lake. Director Melville Brown not only failed to coax performances of any conviction from his stars, but his frozen camera style brought the narrative to a monotonous standstill. The Howard Lindsay–Bertrand Robinson play, *Tommy*, on which the film was based, was pretty dull to begin with, and J. Walter Ruben's script added very little pizzazz to the story of Lake's (right) difficulties in marrying his sweetheart Carol (left). But the problems, which involved the crucial sale of a piece of land, and the machinations of a scheming uncle who interferes with both real estate and romance, all came right in the end. Boy got girl, but most members of the viewing public surely didn't care. Also cast: William Collier Sr, Lucien Littlefield, Helen Ware, Alan Bunce, Emily Fitzroy and Walter B. Gilbert. Henry Hobart was associate producer. (WLB).

Dixiana, another William LeBaron production, was surely RKO's largest disappointment of the year. A glamour-filled musical in the *Rio Rita* mould, it reunited director-adaptor Luther Reed with Bebe Daniels, Wheeler and Woolsey, Dorothy Lee and other participants in RKO's first big smash, but in place of John Boles, Everett Marshall was the romantic lead. Although Marshall was as stiff as a board throughout, he was only one of many minus factors contributing to the failure of the movie. An overabundance of musicals had glutted the market, making the overfed patrons far more discriminating. And, since neither the songs, the dances, the direction, the costumes or even the Technicolor sequences in **Dixiana** offered anything fresh or above the ordinary, it wound up a $300,000 loser. Set against a Mardi Gras background, the Anne Caldwell original concerned the class conflicts which impede a love match between Daniels, a circus performer, and Marshall, who hails from the southern aristocracy. Further disrupting matters is Ralf Harolde (centre), a big-time gambler who wants Daniels (right) and intends to ruin her man. The heroine eventually takes control of her own destiny, exposing the evil intentions of the gambler and breaking down the barriers between Marshall (left) and herself. Bert Wheeler and Robert Woolsey added some humorous window dressing as members of the circus troupe, and Joseph Cawthorn, Jobyna Howland and Bill Robinson were also featured. Victor Baravalle was the musical director, Pearl Eaton again staged the dances, and Max Steiner, whose film music career would blossom at RKO in the years to come, earned his first orchestration credit. Songs included: 'Dixiana' Benny Davis; 'Here's To The Old Days', 'My One Ambition Is You', 'A Lady Loved A Soldier', 'Guiding Star' Anne Caldwell, Harry Tierney.

John Galsworthy's grim novel about blighted fortune, **Escape**, was chosen as the material for RKO's first venture into foreign production. Co-produced with Basil Dean in England, and released as an Associated Radio Picture, the movie top-starred the charismatic British stage actor Gerald du Maurier (right, father of Daphne) as Matt Denant, a World War I hero sentenced to five years hard labour for the accidental killing of a repugnant detective. Driven to the edge of insanity, Denant makes his escape and, with the aid of several women, dodges the authorities for a considerable period of time. Finally cornered in the vestry of a country church, the fugitive gives himself up to save the parson the necessity of further shielding him. Basil Dean adapted and directed, and his leading man was ably supported by a cast that included Jean Cadell (left), Mabel Poulton, Marie Ney, Edna Best, Ann Casson, Madeleine Carroll, Ian Hunter and Edward Addison. John E. Burch was sent from Hollywood as assistant director, and Jack Kitchen to edit, but the venture – advertised as 'adult entertainment' – failed to rouse any enthusiasm in the US. Joseph L. Mankiewicz directed a 1948 remake for 20th Century-Fox, in Britain.

Irene Dunne (right) made her screen debut in **Leathernecking** (GB: **Present Arms**), an unpretentious but silly adaptation (by Jane Murfin) of a Herbert Fields–Richard Rodgers–Lorenz Hart stage musical, denuded of its original Rodgers and Hart songs. Eddie Foy Jr played a buck private who, in order to sweep society girl Dunne off her feet, conceives ingenious schemes like impersonating a captain and arranging for a fake shipwreck. Each brainstorm boomerangs, and yet he still ends up on a desert island with his beloved. Miss Dunne is not impressed, but following relentless Hollywood logic, they end up together anyway. And, for good measure, he gets promoted to captain. Audiences, unaroused by this cornucopia of foolishness, gave it the thumbs down. Edward Cline directed, and Ken Murray, Louise Fazenda, Lilyan Tashman, Ned Sparks, Benny Rubin, Rita LaRoy, Fred Santley, William von Brincken (left) and Claude King (centre) were also implicated in the picture's downfall, as were dance director Pearl Eaton and associate producer Louis Sarecky. Even 20 minutes of colour footage didn't help. Songs included: 'All My Life' Benny Davis, Harry Akst; 'Evening Star', 'Careless Kisses', 'Mighty Nice And So Particular' Oscar Levant, Sidney Clare. (WLB).

The most interesting thing about **Danger Lights** was its use of a 'wide stereoscopic' film process invented by George K. Spoor and P. J. Berrggren. The new breakthrough did provide a greater illusion of depth and added punch to the action sequences, but its many drawbacks – chief of which was the prohibitive cost of the 63.5 mm film and cameras – forced RKO to scrap the experiment after this one. Special equipment was also needed to project the film, a financial burden which few theatre owners were interested in shouldering as the Depression worsened. **Danger Lights** provided an old-fashioned love triangle set against a railroading backdrop. The male leads, Louis Wolheim and Robert Armstrong, were gentlemanly to a fault, with Wolheim saving

Armstrong's life in spite of the latter having snaked his girl (Jean Arthur, illustrated centre with Wolheim) away from him. When Wolheim later suffers a critical brain injury, Armstrong (centre left) reciprocates by rushing his pal to Chicago for treatment from an eminent specialist. Director George B. Seitz added his own emphasis to James Ashmore Creelman's already over-emphatic scenario, and Hugh Herbert, Frank Sheridan, Robert Edeson, Alan Roscoe, William P. Burt and James Farley contributed proficient supporting performances. Myles Connolly supervised and received associate producer credit and Hugh Herbert was dialogue director. Master cinematographer Karl Struss took charge of the specialized photography. (WLB).

Half Shot At Sunrise offered the intermittently amusing escapades of two American doughboys AWOL in Paris with the military police in hot pursuit. James Ashmore Creelman's story, with dialogue by Anne Caldwell and Ralph Spence, was obviously tailored to the talents of Bert Wheeler (left) and Robert Woolsey (centre). Though this was only their second starring effort, the Wheeler–Woolsey formula was already clearly established, with the comedians' strength lying, not in their singing and dancing, but in their delivery of flippant dialogue passages, often laced with juicy *double entendres*. Wheeler, as here, acted the role of naïve straight man who sets up the worldly, acidulous Woolsey for premium one-liners, and a romantic interest for Wheeler was another obligatory element. Dorothy Lee (right), playing the vivacious Annette in this one, currently held a monopoly on the team's sweetie market (she had filled the role in each of their four films). Paul Sloane directed and Henry Hobart was associate producer. Also cast: George MacFarlane, Edna May Oliver, Leni Stengel, Hugh Trevor, Roberta Robinson, John Rutherford, and the dancing group known as The Tiller Sunshine Girls. Max Steiner received his first credit as musical director. Song: 'Nothing But Love' Anne Caldwell, Harry Tierney. (WLB).

The Pay-Off (GB: **The Losing Game**), a banal and incredible story adapted by Jane Murfin from a play by Samuel Shipman and John B. Hymer. All about a world-weary gang leader who falls for an ingenue and chooses to go to the electric chair to safeguard her and her fiancé from prosecution, it starred Lowell Sherman (right), who also directed. The depiction of a crucial hold-up in a jewellery store was one of the most bungled pieces of movie-making in the annals of cinema, and demonstrates Sherman's technical clumsiness. Yet, as an actor, he generally transcended the parts he was given, and his screen presence in this one was the element that made it possible to endure the film. Yet another William LeBaron–Henry Hobart production, the cast featured Marian Nixon (left) as the ingenue and William Janney as her boyfriend, with Hugh Trevor, George F. Marion, Helene Millard, Walter McGrail, Robert McWade and Alan Roscoe in support. Lynn Shores again assisted Sherman as pictorial director. RKO re-cycled the story in 1938, calling it *Law Of The Underworld* with Chester Morris and Anne Shirley.

Joel McCrea (right) starred in his first he-man role for the studio in **The Silver Horde**, which dealt with a battle for control of the Yukon salmon fisheries. Evelyn Brent (left) played a notorious dancehall tart, and Jean Arthur was the girl whom the hero really loves, though she thinks Brent has enticed him away from her. Gavin Gordon featured as the villain determined to brook no business competition from McCrea and Louis Wolheim, but they master him in the end. Rex Beach's red-blooded story (adapted by Wallace Smith) contained frequent brawls but little else to attract one's attention. George Archainbaud's unenthusiastic direction smothered the material and also his supporting players (Raymond Hatton, Blanche Sweet, Purnell Pratt, William B. Davidson and Ivan Linow). William Sistrom was associate producer. (WLB).

Establishing a policy of raiding the air-waves that would continue for years, the studio signed well-known radio comedians Amos (Freeman Gosden, right) 'n' Andy (Charles Correll, left) and starred them in a specially contrived vehicle called **Check And Double Check**. As cab drivers hired to transport Duke Ellington and his Cotton Club Orchestra to a high society ball, the duo become involved with Sue Carol and Charles Morton, whose desire to marry is jeopardized by Morton's inability to locate a deed to some family property. After a considerable amount of slapstick, as well as ethnic repartee, the stars end up in a haunted house where they discover the crucial document. The combined efforts of director Melville Brown, writers Bert Kalmar and Harry Ruby (adaptation and continuity by J. Walter Ruben), the principal actors, and the second-string performers, added up to little more than standard, middle-grade entertainment, yet the movie became so successful that Amos 'n' Andy were rated RKO's top stars by the end of the year. In studying the pattern of gross receipts, however, the company discovered that the picture had zero 'hold-over' value. Apparently audiences turned out to see the black-face duo out of pure curiosity but, having viewed them once on celluloid, seemed to have no more interest in the radio personalities. They were 'freaks of the screen, good for one film only'. Completing one of the fastest revolutions of the wheel of fortune in show business history, the two new stars were unceremoniously dumped, and never made another feature for RKO. Bertram Millhauser was the associate producer, and the cast also included Irene Rich, Ralf Harolde, Edward Martindel, Russ Powell and Rita LaRoy. Songs included: 'Three Little Words', 'Ring Dem Bells' Kalmar, Ruby; 'Old Man Blues' Irving Mills, Duke Ellington. (WLB).

Written by Tim Whelan and Ralph Spence and directed by Edward Cline, **Hook, Line And Sinker** was one of the best and most successful of the Bert Wheeler (left) and Robert Woolsey (right) pictures. Dorothy Lee (centre), provided the feminine interest for the fifth time in a row and was the key to the daffy plot. Portraying the heiress to a dilapidated resort hotel which the two clowns agree to help her restore and manage, she falls for Wheeler, defying her mother's wish that she marry two-faced Ralf Harolde. Luckily, mother (Jobyna Howland) is landed by Woolsey, who immediately gives his okay to the nuptials of his pal and his new step-daughter. This all takes place at the fade-out, after two rival bands of gangsters have transformed the hotel into something that closely resembles Swiss cheese. Hugh Herbert as a seedy house detective, and Natalie Moorhead as a phony duchess in league with the crooks, provided capital support in a film that contained more than the standard number of funny lines and situations. George F. Marion Sr. Stanley Fields and William B. Davidson were also in it for associate producer Myles Connolly (WLB).

1931

★★★★★★★★★★★★★★★★★

1931

★★★★★★★★★★★★★★★★★

On 29 January, 1931, RKO assimilated the Pathé Exchange – its Culver City studio and its contract stars, who included Constance Bennett, Ann Harding, Helen Twelvetrees and Bill Boyd. The idea was to operate RKO Pathé as an autonomous unit within the corporate structure. Lee Marcus was made president, Charles R. Rogers was signed to head production and Courtland Smith to superintend the newsreel arm.

By mid-year, the icy grip of the Depression began to close on RKO and its new acquisition. The organization started losing hundreds of thousands of dollars each week, and a decision was made to merge the separate distribution organizations of RKO and RKO Pathé. This was the first step in a process that would lead to the complete disappearance of RKO Pathé as a producer of theatrical feature films.

David O. Selznick joined RKO as head of production in November. By that time the company was, incredibly, close to total collapse. Its stock had plummetted from a high of 50 to a low of 1⅞ and a recapitalization plan had to be prepared to keep the corporation afloat.

In addition to the Pathé actors, RKO acquired the services of Dolores Del Rio. She would partially fill the gap left by Bebe Daniels, who departed for Warner Bros., though Del Rio would not actually be seen in a Radio picture until 1932. The financial crisis also resulted in a year-end 'fat-trimming' that would cost the jobs of associate producer Myles Connolly, directors Harry Hoyt and Paul L. Stein and writers Tim Whelan and Anthony Coldeway. One who weathered the tornado was future leader Pandro S. Berman, who was promoted to the rank of associate producer.

Fifty films were released, 33 by RKO Radio and 17 by RKO Pathé. Few made money in another deflating year, though **Cracked Nuts**, **The Common Law** and **The Public Defender** did post small profits.

The corporation's net loss for 1931 was $5,660,770.

Lowell Sherman injected some refinement into **The Royal Bed** (GB: **The Queen's Husband**), a suggestively titled burlesque that was neither lusty nor particularly humorous. Robert E. Sherwood's play (adaptation by J. Walter Ruben) cast Sherman (right) as the lethargic and henpecked king of a mythical island in the North Sea. The plot begins to simmer after his termagant queen (Nance O'Neil) leaves on a trip to America; the country is soon beset by revolution and daughter Mary Astor (centre) reveals that she is in love with a commoner (Anthony Bushell, left) and not the crown prince (Hugh Trevor) who her mother has decided she must marry. The king, however, uncharacteristically asserts himself, quells the revolutionaries and officiates at the secret marriage of the princess to her bourgeois lover. Sherman directed the film, also casting Robert Warwick, Alan Roscoe, Gilbert Emery, J. Carrol Naish and Frederick Burt. Henry Hobart was production supervisor. (WLB).

First released in 1930 by Pathé, **Sin Takes A Holiday** was acquired by RKO as part of its takeover package and distributed by RKO Pathé early in 1931. It was a representative domestic drama with Constance Bennett (right) caught between Kenneth MacKenna (left), who has married her as a matter of convenience, and Basil Rathbone, a cultivated European who introduces her to the charms and allures of a Parisian lifestyle. It is, however, MacKenna who Bennett really loves and, although Rita LaRoy tries to throw Cupid for a loop, love prevails when MacKenna confesses that Bennett is unquestionably the woman for him. Paul L. Stein directed the racy screenplay by Horace Jackson, based on a Robert Milton–Dorothy Cairns story. E. B. Derr was the producer, and his cast also included Louis John Bartels, John Roche, ZaSu Pitts, Kendall Lee, Fred Walton, Murrell Finley and Helen Johnson.

Helen Twelvetrees (right) had one of her better roles as **Millie** in the Charles R. Rogers production based on Donald Henderson Clarke's novel (screenplay by Charles Kenyon). After her first innocent love affair goes sour, Millie throws herself recklessly into the feverish romantic merry-go-round of the big city. One day she is shocked to discover that her own daughter has fallen under the spell of a former admirer, and she guns him down to protect the girl's honour. Rhetorical fireworks burst forth in the inevitable courtroom climax, and soap-opera addicts had a ball. John Francis Dillon directed, with a solid supporting cast that included Lilyan Tashman, Robert Ames (left), Joan Blondell, John Halliday, James Hall, Anita Louise, Edmund Breese, Frank McHugh and Franklin Parker. Note: Charles Rogers produced the film independently; it was acquired by RKO when Rogers agreed to become the production chief of RKO Pathé, but was released as a Radio picture.

Another Pathé film acquired by RKO, **The** ▷
Painted Desert would have been thoroughly
forgettable but for Edward Snyder's superior
photography of the California desert, and the
appearance of Clark Gable (right) in a minor role.
Bill Boyd (centre, long before his Hopalong
Cassidy days) was the star, complemented by old-
timer William Farnum and heart-throb Helen
Twelvetrees. Tungsten mining provided the narrative framework in which standard sagebrush
conflicts were elaborated – without much enthusiasm by any of the participants. Howard
Higgin directed from a story and screenplay by
Tom Buckingham and himself. E. B. Derr produced the film and J. Farrell MacDonald, Charles
Sellon, Will Walling, Guy Edward Hearn and
Wade Boteler were in it too. Though this version
enjoyed medium-magnitude stars and a respectable budget, RKO later realized that the story was
'B' level through and through and remade it in
1938 as part of the George O'Brien series of
programmer Westerns. (RKO Pathé.)

Director Herbert Brenon, who was having con- ▷
siderable difficulty adapting to the new 'talkie'
medium, tried to cash in on one of his silent
successes with **Beau Ideal**. Brenon had directed
Percival C. Wren's *Beau Geste* (1927) for Paramount, but this further excursion with the
Foreign Legion contained none of the intoxicating
frissons of the earlier picture. The novel by Wren,
as transformed for the screen by Elizabeth Meehan
and Paul Schofield, concerned the quest of Otis
Madison (Lester Vail, left, borrowed from MGM)
to locate his boyhood friend John Geste (Ralph
Forbes, right) in the wilds of Arabia. He finally
discovers him confined in a hell-hole prison
for disgraced Legionnaires. After considerable
derring-do involving a treacherous Emir (George
Rigas) and an aptly named 'Angel of Death' (Leni

Stengel), the men set out for England where the
beautiful Loretta Young (on loan from First
National) awaits them. Marred by rotten dialogue and overwrought acting (especially Hale
Hamilton's performance as Major LeBaudy),
Beau Ideal lost $330,000 and earned consider-
ation as the most wretched picture turned out by
the studio in what was, generally, to be a very poor
year. Also cast: Irene Rich, Frank McCormack,
Otto Matiesen, Don Alvarado, Bernard Siegel,
Myrtle Stedman, Joseph DeStefani, John St Polis
and Paul McAllister. William LeBaron produced.

Cimarron, written by Howard Estabrook from
the best-selling novel by Edna Ferber, was conceived as an epic project and its final cost
($1,433,000) far surpassed any previous RKO
budget. Ambition was rewarded when the 131-
minute film won the 'Best Picture' Oscar, picked
up two other Academy Awards (for Estabrook's
script and Max Ree's art direction), and received
many additional accolades (sadly, it would be the
only RKO picture – with the exception of Sam
Goldwyn's *The Best Years Of Our Lives*, which the
studio distributed in 1946 – to win the top industry
honour). Set in Oklahoma during the great land
rush of 1889, and spanning its development to
1929, **Cimarron** top-starred Richard Dix (illustrated centre) as Yancey Cravat. Cravat, an
American knight errant who champions the cause
of the downtrodden (Indians included) through his
actions and through the influential newspaper he
publishes, is also a restless wanderer. He periodi-
cally leaves for years at a time, while his patient
wife Sabra (Irene Dunne) carries on his newspaper
and his fight for justice. Much of the film rested on
Miss Dunne's able shoulders, and audiences were
encouraged to suffer with her during her extended
periods of abandonment, and to marvel at her
spirit and fortitude. Obviously Edna Ferber,
producer William LeBaron, and director Wesley
Ruggles believed that the combination of Yancey's
passion and Sabra's indomitability made America
great. The large cast included Edna May Oliver,
Estelle Taylor, Nance O'Neil, William Collier Jr,
Rosco Ates, George E. Stone, Stanley Fields and
Robert McWade. Despite all the publicity and
kudos, the depressed business climate of the day
wrecked the film's box-office performance, and
Cimarron recorded a $565,000 loss. A major
reissue in 1935 helped redress the balance. MGM
later bought the property and remade it for release
in 1960 with Glenn Ford and Maria Schell.

Despite its sensationalistic title and advertising campaign ('Every Inch A Man – Bought Body And Soul By His Wife'), **Kept Husbands** was a lukewarm melo directed by Lloyd Bacon. Joel McCrea (right) played a proud steelworker who wins the hand of a millionaire's daughter (Dorothy Mackaill, centre) but soon loses his self-respect. Following a period of domestic strife, they solve their problems when the frivolous wife agrees to live within the limitations of her husband's earned income. Associate producer Louis Sarecky penned the original story which Forrest Halsey and Alfred Jackson adapted colourlessly. Also cast: Ned Sparks, Robert McWade, Florence Roberts and a trio of silent film luminaries: Mary Carr, Clara Kimball Young and Bryant Washburn (left). William LeBaron produced.

After *Kept Husbands*, **Lonely Wives** had their turn. The story required Edward Everett Horton (left) to tackle two roles: a business-like attorney and a vaudeville impersonator named 'The Great Zero'. The lawyer, whose pretty wife (Esther Ralston) has been away for some time, hires 'Zero' to deceive his mother-in-law so that he can spend an evening fooling around with Laura LaPlante. The wife naturally chooses to return on that very night, provoking the usual farcical complications which soon come to a boil. Walter De Leon wrote the screenplay from a European stage success, and added a fair amount of literate banter, but Russell Mack's direction added nothing. Patsy Ruth Miller (right), Maude Eburne, Spencer Charters, Maurice Black and Georgette Rhodes were other members of producer E. B. Derr's cast. (A Pathé production, acquired by RKO in the takeover).

Pity the poor viewers who had to suffer through **The Lady Refuses**, an unsavoury melodrama directed with contemptuous indifference by George Archainbaud. Betty Compson (left) was top-cast as a lady destined to become a street-walker until a titled gentleman (Gilbert Emery) hires her to rescue his son from the clutches of a designing woman. She accomplishes her mission and ends up with the young man's father as her prize. Wallace Smith's screenplay, based on a Robert Milton–Guy Bolton story, made for a gruelling 72 minutes, with the going especially painful whenever tongue-tied John Darrow (right), as the son, was on screen. Other members of the cast included Margaret Livingston, Ivan Lebedeff, Edgar Norton and Daphne Pollard. Bertram Millhauser was associate producer. (WLB).

Mary Astor (right) scored a hit in **Behind Office Doors**, directed by Melville Brown, Astor played private secretary Mary Linden who, out of devotion to paper company executive Robert Ames, masterminds his career. His blindness to her love and talents, however, leads the heroine into the arms of Ricardo Cortez (left), but Ames soon pushes the panic button for his indispensible assistant and sweetens the offer with a marriage proposal. Featherweight stuff, but audiences embraced it nonetheless. Carey Wilson authored the screenplay (from Alan Brener Schultz's novel), with parts in it for Catherine Dale Owen, Kitty Kelly, Edna Murphy, Charles Sellon, George MacFarlane and William Morris. Associate producer: Henry Hobart. (WLB).

Beyond Victory was a muddled anti-war polemic full of pacifist lectures but not much trenchant drama. The events that led four troopers to enlist are detailed (in flashback), with the overall point being that they were fools to leave their families and sweethearts behind and get involved in the killing game. When production ended, the picture was such a mess that episodes with Helen Twelvetrees and June Collyer had to be cut out completely, and Edward H. Griffith was assigned to shoot extensive retakes. His dedicated attempts at alchemy could not, however, change dross into gold. E. B. Derr was the producer, John Robertson received the directing credit, and Horace Jackson and James Gleason wrote the story and screenplay. Bill Boyd, playing another stout-hearted hero, top-lined a cast that included scenarist Gleason (left), ZaSu Pitts (right), Fred Scott, Lew Cody, Marion Shilling, Lissi Arna, Theodore von Eltz, Mary Carr, Russell Gleason (son of James), Frank Reicher and Wade Boteler. (RKO Pathé).

The 'W' Plan, a well-staged espionage drama, took Brian Aherne (centre) behind German lines to sabotage the enemy's grandiose scheme to blow up towns and villages occupied by the British. The German mining operation is in the form of a W – thus the rather unengaging title. Aherne acted with proper restraint, and dedication to the cause, and Madeleine Carroll lent attractive support as his sweetheart from pre-war days. Victor Saville adapted the novel by Graham Seton (additional dialogue by Miles Malleson and Frank Launder) and also directed; the supporting cast included Gibb McLaughlin, Gordon Harker, Cameron Carr, C. M. Hallard, Milton Rosmer, Mary Jerrold and George Merritt. The film was a British International production distributed by RKO in America. Though it was not very successful in the States, **The 'W' Plan** contained more excitement than most of the studio's homegrown product.

What does it take to make a philandering bachelor settle down? The answer, according to **Bachelor Apartment**, was Irene Dunne (centre). Lowell Sherman (right) played the smooth seducer with wit and magnetism, who alternately flirts with Dunne's sister (Claudia Dell), and fights off the unwelcome attentions of former silent star Mae Murray. Sherman also directed, meeting the demands of the John Howard Lawson story (screenplay by J. Walter Ruben) – he drew a charming performance from Dunne and made the final product a sophisticated comedy of relative distinction under associate producer Henry Hobart. The featured players also included Norman Kerry, Kitty Kelly, Ivan Lebedeff, Noel Francis, Purnell Pratt (left) and Charles Coleman.

Rugged actor Louis Wolheim took his first shot at directing with **The Sin Ship**. Wolheim (right, on loan from the Caddo company) also played the captain of a two-masted schooner filled with men lusting for delectable Mary Astor (left). The hard-bitten captain is the chief lothario, but Astor fends everyone off until, in the end, she accepts Wolheim. Also aboard: minister-cum-crook Ian Keith, conscienceless seaman Alan Roscoe and ambitious mate Hugh Herbert. Detective Russell Powell pops up to dispatch Keith when they finally reach port. Myles Connolly was the supervisor, and actor Herbert wrote the screenplay from Keene Thompson and Agnes Brand Leahy's story. Lynn Shores was pictorial director. (WLB). Note: This was Wolheim's last picture; he died in February, 1931, before its release.

Bert Wheeler and Robert Woolsey (centre) went on another rampage in **Cracked Nuts**. The screenplay by Al Boasberg (dialogue by Boasberg and Ralph Spence) took aim at the political arena and most of its satiric projectiles were on target. Woolsey was Zander Ulysses Parkhurst – Zup for short – who wins the kingship of El Dorania in a crap game. General Bogardus (Stanley Fields, borrowed from Paramount) envisions King Zup six feet under and hatches various schemes to make his dream come true. Meanwhile, Wheeler is fighting his own battle with Edna May Oliver over Dorothy Lee. Edna May, who eventually becomes King Zup's secretary of war, has no use for the ne'er-do-well Wheeler and does not want him sniffing around her niece. Edward Cline directed this unbridled lunacy with breathless but coherent abandon, and his supporting cast included Leni Stengel, Boris Karloff and Frank Thornton. Douglas MacLean, a star comedian during the silent era, functioned as associate producer, and also contributed to the script. (WLB).

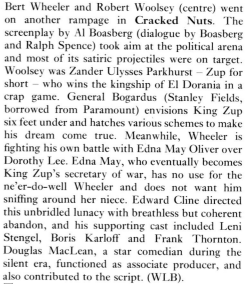

A. A. Milne, best known as the creator of Christopher Robin and Winnie the Pooh, provided the thriller material for **The Perfect Alibi** (GB: **Birds Of Prey**). Milne's play *The Fourth Wall*, which had run for two seasons on Broadway, concerned a murder so carefully planned that the murderers (there are two of them) feel they are undetectable. Following a suspense formula that would become the nearly exclusive property of Alfred Hitchcock in later years, the identity of the villains is revealed to the audience but not to the other characters in the story. Producer-director Basil Dean also adapted Milne's play to the screen with results that were mostly uneven. Above-average acting by C. Aubrey Smith, Robert Loraine (right) and Warwick Ward helped to salvage the enterprise which did offer a fair number of gripping moments, and Dorothy Boyd (left), Frank Lawton and Ellis Jeffreys were also in it. The picture was made in England by Associated Radio Pictures.

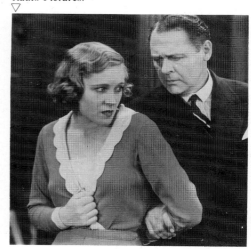

Sweepstakes, one of the year's most ludicrous comedy efforts, featured Eddie Quillan (left) as a jockey whose horse, Six-Shooter, rockets to victory whenever he chants 'whoop-te-do'. Lew Lipton delivered the story and screenplay (dialogue Ralph F. Murphy), which also spotlighted James Gleason as the rider's loyal pal, Marian Nixon (centre) as his love object and Lew Cody (right) as the heavy determined to reign over the sport of kings. Albert Rogell directed with a shaky hand for producer Charles R. Rogers (his first RKO Pathé credit) and associate producer Harry Joe Brown, and supporting players included Paul Hurst, Frederick Burton, Billy Sullivan, Lillian Leighton and King Baggott, a well-respected silent director now embarking on a thespian career. Song: 'How About Me Calling You My Sweetheart' Ted Snyder, Mort Harris.

Wishing to keep peace in the family, William LeBaron provided Bert Wheeler (right) a chance to make good *sans* Robert Woolsey in **Too Many Cooks**. The outcome proved to be just as tedious as Woolsey's *Everything's Rosie*. Frank Craven's dippy play (screenplay by Jane Murfin) revolved around the antics of 13 members of the Cook family, all of whom take an active interest in the courting affairs of Wheeler and the ubiquitous Dorothy Lee (centre). In keeping with the adage from which the title derives, the lovers' brew is spoiled; so was humour, romance and any other diverting ingredient. William Seiter, who would be given superior RKO material in the future, directed, with a supporting group that included Rosco Ates (left), Robert McWade, Sharon Lynn, Hallam Cooley, Florence Roberts, Clifford Dempsey and Ruth Weston. Douglas MacLean was the associate producer.

Following his success in *Skippy*, Jackie Cooper (left) was imported from Hal Roach Studios to play **Young Donovan's Kid** (GB: **Donovan's Kid**). The treacly story of a six-year-old orphan adopted by a violent gunman, it traced the gunman's reformation under the influence of the dirty-faced youngster and a virtuous lady. Richard Dix (right) played the tough guy and Marion Shilling the girl in J. Walter Ruben's adaptation of a novel by Rex Beach. Director Fred Niblo endeavoured to inject as much emotion as possible into the tale, but his hypodermic failed him and the end product was just ho-hum amusement. Louis Sarecky was the associate producer. Also cast: Frank Sheridan, Boris Karloff, Fred Kelsey, Wilfred Lucas, Florence Roberts, Stanley Fields and Dick Alexander. **Young Donovan's Kid** was a remake of Paramount's 1923 production *Big Brother*, which had featured Tom Moore. (WLB).

Melodrama and comedy intermingled in **White Shoulders**, another far-fetched potboiler derived from another Rex Beach novel. In it, Mary Astor (left) is near starvation when Jack Holt (right, on loan from Columbia), a multi-millionaire, sweeps into her life and marries her. Though obviously in love with Holt, Astor impulsively runs away with Ricardo Cortez, who is more entranced with the heroine's jewellery than anything else. Further snags involve Mary's former husband, from whom she has never been legally divorced. Director Melville Brown and screenwriter J. Walter Ruben (additional dialogue Jane Murfin) extricated their star from this artificial briar patch by having the first husband murdered and Cortez jailed as the killer, thereby freeing the sorrowful Miss Astor to return to the affluent Holt. Kitty Kelly, Sidney Toler, Robert Keith and Nicholas Soussanin also had significant roles for associate producer Henry Hobart. The picture was a remake of *Recoil* (Rex Beach's original title), made in 1924 by J. Parker Read for Goldwyn-Cosmopolitan release. (WLB).

With Constance Bennett, Helen Twelvetrees and Ann Harding among its stars, it is understandable that RKO Pathé would specialize in 'woman's pictures' – of which **Born To Love** was an above-average example. The setting was wartime London where Constance Bennett (right), an American hospital worker, falls head-over-heels in love with aviator Joel McCrea. He leaves her with child and is subsequently shot down behind German lines. Assuming her hero to be dead, Bennett provides her child with a new father (Paul Cavanagh, left), but McCrea returns, and Bennett is separated from her offspring. She and the audience suffer at the unnatural condition and, although she and McCrea are finally reunited, the baby dies, making for a firm three-handkerchief ending. Paul L. Stein directed from Ernest Pascal's story and screenplay, with a cast that included Anthony Bushell, Louise Closser Hale, Frederick Kerr, Mary Forbes, Elizabeth Forrester, Claude King, Edmond Breon and Reginald Sharland.

Gregory LaCava came on board for **Laugh And Get Rich**, a homespun comedy about life in a boarding house run by Edna May Oliver (left). Though the film was agreeable in an unprepossessing sort of way, director-writer LaCava would make a number of better RKO pictures. Oliver contributed her usual superior work as domestic top-sergeant, but Hugh Herbert was the cast standout, playing her indolent but good-hearted husband. Herbert's get-rich schemes were the main subject of conflict until one of his long-forgotten inventions finally pays off, but there was also a romantic sub-plot involving Herbert and Oliver's daughter, Dorothy Lee (right). LaCava wrote the screenplay and Ralph Spence added some dialogue; their efforts were based on a story by Douglas MacLean who doubled as the associate producer. Russell Gleason, John Harron, Charles Sellon, George Davis, Robert Emmett Keane, Maude Fealy, Louise MacIntosh and Lita Chevret led the supporting cast. (WLB).

If it is true that 'by thine works ye shall be known', it was unfortunate that RKO's reputation was coming increasingly to rest on such folderol as **Three Who Loved**. Betty Compson (left) was the main character, a Swedish lass who comes to America to wed sweetheart Conrad Nagel (borrowed from MGM). The film shaped up as old-fashioned triangle stuff with Robert Ames (right) doing his best to steal Compson away from his pal Nagel. Screenwriter Beulah Marie Dix (adapting a story by Martin Flavin) evidently decided this plot was going nowhere, so she shifted her approach to a drama of conscience. Ames is sent to prison for a crime committed by Nagel. Nagel and Compson are living comfortably with their young son when the convict breaks out five years later. Just as Ames is about to complicate matters, the police shoot him, but the guilt-ravaged Nagel confesses his crime anyway. The brave Swedish mother tells him she'll be waiting when he's served his time. George Archainbaud directed, maintaining a remarkably straight face under the circumstances. Robert Emmett O'Connor, Bodil Rosing, Dickie Moore and Fred Santley also appeared for associate producer Bertram Millhauser. (WLB).

Transgression, based on a novel by Kate Jordan, centred on Kay Francis (left, borrowed from Paramount) who leaves her husband (Paul Cavanagh, borrowed from Fox) to run off with Spaniard Ricardo Cortez (right). After despatching a letter to Cavanagh explaining why she has left him, Francis learns that her lover is having an affair with a peasant girl. The girl's father shoots Cortez, and Francis, sadder but wiser, rushes home to intercept the letter. A blackmail element heightens the suspense, but all is well in the end, with Francis realizing her husband's true worth. Herbert Brenon's direction was more fluid than in his previous attempts at talkies, and he did a satisfactory job of transferring Elizabeth Meehan's scenario (additional dialogue by Benn W. Levy) to the screen. William LeBaron personally produced, with decorative performances supplied by Nance O'Neil, Doris Lloyd, John St Polis, Ruth Weston, Adrienne d'Ambricourt and Wilfred Noy. Paramount had filmed the story in 1924, calling it *The Next Corner* and employing Cortez for the same Latin lover role he played in this version.

Scriptwriter J. Walter Ruben was given a chance to direct with **The Public Defender**, and cranked out a competent melo in which he utilized Richard Dix (left) to good effect. George Goodchild's novel *The Splendid Crime*, adapted by Bernard Schubert, was topical fare about a bank failure, the three crooks (Purnell Pratt, Frank Sheridan and Carl Gerard) who are responsible and the daring young broker (Dix) who ferrets out the full story for the ruined depositors. Ruben's work was confident, and he got the most from a large cast that included Alan Roscoe, Boris Karloff (right), Paul Hurst, Nella Walker, Ruth Weston, Edmund Breese, Robert Emmett O'Connor, Phillip Smalley and, as the love interest, Shirley Grey (on loan from Samuel Goldwyn). Louis Sarecky was the associate producer. (WLB).

Based on a novel by Robert W. Chambers, **The Common Law** furnished Constance Bennett (left) with an attractive role, and became one of the few hit films of a very lean year. Bennett played a forward-thinking young woman who has already been sharing an apartment with Lew Cody in Paris when she agrees to pose for struggling artist Joel McCrea (right). They soon fall in love, and the rest of the story is comprised of stormy breakups and reconciliations, attempts by Cody to sabotage the affair and the shocked exhortations of McCrea's Tarrytown, New York family when they discover what has been happening to him in decadent Europe. Director Paul L. Stein and screenwriter John Farrow (dialogue by Horace Jackson) kept a firm grip on the heady material, making it both lively and literate. Charles R. Rogers produced, Harry Joe Brown was his associate, and Robert Williams, Hedda Hopper and Walter Walker were noteworthy in supporting roles. Marion Shilling, Paul Ellis and Yola D'Avril were also cast. The film was a remake of 1916 and 1923 silent versions, both released by the Selznick organization. (RKO Pathé).

Among producer Charles R. Rogers' attempts to ▷
lure the lady customers to the box-office was **A Woman Of Experience**, a trifling melodrama that cast Helen Twelvetrees (centre) as a spy who samples the intoxicating champagne of European love. Smitten by young naval officer William Bakewell, Twelvetrees must nevertheless carry out her mission and become the 'companion' of German agent Lew Cody. She is wounded in action and learns she has but six months to live. The gallant Bakewell marries her anyway, despite the objections of his mother who knows more about the heroine's checkered past than her son does. 'Her charms were arms against the enemy' read one promotional teaser, and director Harry Joe Brown did his best to play up the lurid angles of John Farrow's play *The Registered Woman*, which Farrow also scripted (with additional dialogue by Ralph F. Murphy). H. B. Warner (left), ZaSu Pitts, C. Henry Gordon (right), Nance O'Neil, George Fawcett, Franklin Pangborn and Edward Earle were others in the cast. (RKO Pathé).

In his quest for an RKO answer to Garbo and Dietrich, William LeBaron found Lili Damita (then under contract to Samuel Goldwyn) and starred her in **The Woman Between** (GB: **Madame Julie**). However, despite lavish production values and Victor Schertzinger's adroit direction, the enterprise failed – due largely to the inability of adaptor Howard Estabrook to invent a high-powered climax to the *risqué* story. The plot had a beautiful French modiste (Damita, right) marrying widower O. P. Heggie, much to the displeasure of his son (Lester Vail, borrowed from MGM) and daughter (Miriam Seegar, left). The bored young wife and the angry young son are soon drawn together, with Damita eventually agreeing to run away with Vail. The final confrontation between husband and wife is a complete fizzle: Damita decides to stay with Heggie for reasons which were entirely obscure, and the picture faded out, leaving Vail – and the audience – more than a little mystified and frustrated. Anita Louise, Ruth Weston, Lincoln Stedman, Blanche Frederici, William Morris and Halliwell Hobbes were also featured. Estabrook based his scenario on a play by Irving Kaye Davis, and director Schertzinger composed the song 'Close To Me' used in the picture.
▽

Life on the road for the itinerant drummer was the subject of **Traveling Husbands**, a limp diversion directed by Paul Sloane. Frank Albertson (centre left, borrowed from Fox), Carl Miller, Hugh Herbert and Spencer Charters portrayed the salesmen, with not a Willy Loman among them. But then this watery blend of melodrama, comedy and moral inspiration was hardly Arthur Miller territory. Evelyn Brent (left) topped the female performers in Humphrey Pearson's story and screenplay, which also gave roles to Constance Cummings (centre right), Dorothy Peterson, Gwen Lee, Frank McHugh, Stanley Fields (right), Rita LaRoy, Lucille Williams and Purnell Pratt. The associate producer was Myles Connolly. Song: 'There's A Sob In My Heart' Max Steiner, Humphrey Pearson. (WLB).
▽

Robert Woolsey's attempt to solo without Bert Wheeler produced the immediate nosedive and subsequent crackup of **Everything's Rosie**. Though Woolsey (left) was certainly the funnier of the two comedians, he needed his partner as a foil and he also needed good material in order to flourish. Al Boasberg's story, scripted by Tim Whelan with dialogue by Boasberg and Ralph Spence, abandoned the humorist to his own devices, and there are only so many *shticks* one can build around a cigar. Woolsey played a medicine show fakir teamed with 'Rosie' (Anita Louise, right) whom he adopted when she was only three. She is now blossoming into womanhood, and working the carnivals with Woolsey. Her step-dad is eventually brought face-to-face with the parents of her proper young man (John Darrow), with predictable *faux pas* and complications following, before the equally predictable happy ending. The studio's blunder in providing Woolsey with his own starring vehicle was, happily, never to be repeated. Clyde Bruckman provided the unenthusiastic direction and Louis Sarecky was the associate producer. Also cast: Florence Roberts, Clifford Dempsey, Lita Chevret, Alfred James and
◁ Frank Beal. (WLB).

The deceptive nature of appearances was the focus of **High Stakes**, a pleasant farce starring Lowell Sherman (right) and Mae Murray (left). The film's major dupe is Edward Martindel, who believes that his brother (Sherman) is a worthless drunk and that his starry-eyed new wife (Murray) worships him. In reality, she and her cohort, Leyland Hodgson, worship money, and are in league to chisel as much as possible from Martindel. It is Sherman, of course, who steps in, reveals the truth, and rids his sibling of the two schemers. Working from a Willard Mack play and a J. Walter Ruben screenplay, Sherman also directed in spirited style. Henry Hobart was the associate producer. Also cast: Karen Morley, Ethel Levey, Alan Roscoe, Maude Turner Gordon, Charles Coleman and Phillip Smalley. (WLB).
▽

Technicolor was called on to pep up **The Runaround** (GB: **Waiting For The Bride**), but its hues could not compensate for a lack of dramatic and comedic values and the film lost $160,000. All about a dancing girl who has none of the instincts of her gold-digging friends, it starred Mary Brian (left, on loan from Paramount). At one point Miss Brian even turns down a $1000 bracelet because it includes the generous donor's apartment key as a bonus gift. Her good behaviour is, of course, rewarded when she is united in matrimony with playboy Geoffrey Kerr (centre). The hamfisted farcical services of Joseph Cawthorn, Marie Prevost (right) and Johnny Hines were provided, under the stuttering direction of William James Craft (dialogue direction Allen Fagan). Alfred Jackson and Barney Sarecky adapted Sandah Owen's original for associate producer Louis Sarecky. Why this minor fluff of a film was made in colour remains anybody's guess.
▷

Director Fred Niblo squeezed a good deal of ▷ honest suspense from **The Big Gamble**, a remake of the 1926 film *Red Dice*, which had featured Rod La Rocque. Bill Boyd (centre left) assumed the La Rocque role, playing a gambler who wants to pay off his considerable debts before bidding adieu to the cruel, cruel world. Gangster Warner Oland works out the solution, planning to collect a $100,000 insurance policy when Boyd dies, but Dorothy Sebastian rekindles Boyd's interest in living, and together they triumph over the nefarious heavy. Though the Octavus Roy Cohen tale (screenplay by Walter DeLeon and F. McGrew Willis) raced along under Niblo's taut direction, it did pause on occasion for comic interludes with James Gleason and ZaSu Pitts, which were welcome breaks in the mounting tension. Charles R. Rogers produced with Harry Joe Brown as his associate. Also cast: June MacCloy, William Collier Jr, Ralph Ince, Geneva Mitchell and Jack Richardson (centre), (RKO Pathé).

△ The haste with which RKO was disgorging Wheeler and Woolsey vehicles began to show in **Caught Plastered**. It had the usual cardboard villains, romantic subplot and passages of vaudeville patter, but the fusion of elements (story by Douglas MacLean, adaptation and dialogue by Ralph Spence) was lacklustre throughout. Renovating a drug store instead of a hotel on this occasion, Bert Wheeler (centre) and Robert Woolsey (right) run headlong into Jason Robards Sr, a sneaky real estate man who wants to foreclose on the property, and its owner, kindly old Lucy Beaumont. Dorothy Lee (left) is caught in the middle between the two opposing forces, inclining, as usual, towards Mr Wheeler. William Seiter directed, and author MacLean was associate producer. Charles B. Middleton, DeWitt Jennings, Josephine Whittell and James Farley completed the cast. Song: 'I'm That Way About You' Victor Schertzinger. (WLB).

Finally adopting a production policy that indicated some common sense, RKO Pathé launched a series of cheap and very rapidly made westerns starring Tom Keene (formerly known as George Duryea). Written and directed by Robert. F. Hill, the first offering was **Sundown Trail** in which Keene (left) was the manager of a ranch inherited by Marion Shilling (centre). A city slicker, she has no interest in either her foreman or the Wild West, but this attitude changes completely during the picture's 51-minute duration. Standard genre ingredients included a clutch of desperados, and Keene's outlaw pal who decides to go straight. Other players: Nick Stuart (right), Hooper Atchley, Stanley Blystone, Alma Chester, William Welsh, Murdock MacQuarrie and Louise Beavers. The production was supervised by Fred Allen and featured one song, 'I Built A Gal' by Arthur Lange and writer-director Hill.

Rebound, originally a Broadway hit by Donald Ogden Stewart, seemed promising material for a romantic screen comedy, but it was spoiled by some tedious philosophizing on the merits of love. Edward H. Griffith directed with firmness and grace, and his actors generally seemed in tune with their roles, but the script (adapted by Horace Jackson) wrecked its chances of success with movie audiences. All about Bill Truesdale (Robert Ames, centre right), who marries Sara (Ina Claire, centre left, borrowed from Samuel Goldwyn and given top billing) after his true love Evie (Myrna Loy, right) ties the knot with Lyman Patterson (Hale Hamilton), the story allowed for the reintroduction of Evie into Bill's affections and the subsequent deterioration of his marriage. He comes to his senses in time to save his wife from the designs of suitor Johnnie Coles (Robert Williams, left), and banishes the flighty Evie from his life forever. As might be expected in a Stewart composition, there were many witty lines, but the serious passages

threw the whole venture off balance and it lost $215,000. Hedda Hopper, Walter Walker, Louise Closser Hale and Leigh Allen were also cast. Harry Joe Brown was associate producer. (RKO Pathé).

The Gay Diplomat, a routine cloak-and-dagger fable, is chiefly memorable as Pandro S. Berman's initial production. Berman was William LeBaron's assistant when Henry Hobart, the supervisor assigned to the film, walked off. LeBaron gave Berman the job, and thereby launched the career of the man who became RKO's bread-and-butter producer throughout the better part of the decade. Ivan Lebedeff (left) portrayed a dashing Russian

officer dispatched to Bucharest to neutralize a woman spy responsible for leaks in the Russian communication system. Genevieve Tobin (right, borrowed from Universal) was the first suspect, but since Lebedeff falls in love with her, audiences knew she must be innocent. And indeed she was – Betty Compson (her star status had deteriorated somewhat by now) turned out to be the Rumanian Mata Hari. Richard Boleslavsky directed from a Benn W. Levy story, which Doris Anderson adapted (additional dialogue by Alfred Jackson). Also in the cast: Ilka Chase, Purnell Pratt, Colin Campbell, Arthur Edmund Carew, Edward Martindel, John St Polis, George Irving and Rita LaRoy.

There was a great deal of artifice in **Devotion**, a Cinderella-type tale directed by Robert Milton, whose chief assets were its principals, Ann Harding (left) and Leslie Howard (right). Pamela Wynne's novel *A Little Flat In The Temple*, on which Horace Jackson and Graham John based their screenplay, called for Miss Harding to fall in love with attorney Howard at first sight and then to adopt the guise of a middle-aged governess in order to be close to him. A strong bond soon develops between the governess and Howard's young son (Douglas Scott), but the interference of Robert Williams, an accused murderer defended by Howard, and Olive Tell, the hero's as-yet-undivorced wife, churns the waters mightily. The mess is cleaned up in the end, with barrister and governess joining together in accordance with the immutable laws of such romantic fantasy. All in all, it was an appealing treat for dreamers and idealists. Harry Joe Brown was the associate producer, utilizing O. P. Heggie, Louise Closser Hale, Dudley Digges, Alison Skipworth, Doris Lloyd, Ruth Weston and Joan Carr in lesser roles. Leslie Howard appeared by courtesy of MGM. (RKO Pathé).

Only a nimble director like Gregory LaCava could keep track of a feast for gossips like **Smart Woman** and, fortunately, William LeBaron chose him for the task. Myron C. Fagan's play *Nancy's Private Affair*, as scripted by Salisbury Field, contained more back-and-forth action than a tennis tournament. Mary Astor (right) played the central character, who returns from a trip abroad to find that her husband Robert Ames (left) has been appropriated by shallow blonde Noel Francis. Using wealthy Englishman John Halliday to make Ames jealous, she succeeds in separating the lovebirds, but then decides that her husband is damaged goods and that she prefers the Britisher anyway. But on the way to Reno with Halliday, where she intends to get a quickie divorce, Astor exercises her woman's prerogative one last time and resolves to stay married to her thoroughly repentant husband! Anyone who entered this loopy comedy in the middle surely left with a migraine headache. Edward Everett Horton topped the supporting players, who also included Ruth Weston, Gladys Gale, Alfred Cross and Lillian Harmer. Bertram Millhauser earned the associate producer credit.

Bad Company was poorly received in its own day, but the film's stature has grown over the years; it is now considered one of the most intriguing gangster films of the early thirties. Anticipating *The Godfather* in its emphasis on family relationships and the psychological implications of criminality, the film was directed by Tay Garnett and starred Helen Twelvetrees (left) and Ricardo Cortez. Cortez swaggered through the role of Goldie Gorio, a psychotic mobster who refuses to relax his grip on Steven Carlyle (John Garrick), a young lawyer who wants out of the rackets. Carlyle eventually marries Helen King (Twelvetrees); it is she who must bear the tragic weight of the circumstances when she learns that both her husband and her brother (Frank Conroy, right) are engulfed in the rackets. And it is she who ultimately throws caution aside and kills Gorio in an attempt to salvage her family before all hope has vanished. Cortez and Twelvetrees both chewed up the scenery as the melodrama unfolded – a fact that contemporary reviewers carped about at length. However, most of the critics overlooked the clever contribution of Garnett, who directed with an instinctive feel for the elements of the newly-developing genre while, at the same time, embellishing those elements with clever symbolism, doses of black humour and special expressionistic touches. The screenplay by Thomas Buckingham and the director, suggested by Jack Lait's novel *Put On The Spot*, also highlighted Paul Hurst, Frank McHugh, Kenneth Thomson, Arthur Stone, Emma Dunn, Harry Carey and Edgar Kennedy. Harry Joe Brown was the associate producer. (RKO Pathé).

A movie combining the talents of Erich von Stroheim (left), Lili Damita (right), Adolphe Menjou and Laurence Olivier could not be all bad, but **Friends And Lovers** came close to it. Von Stroheim played Victor Sangrito who is shot to death while whipping his wife (Damita). This clears the decks for the development of a turgid love triangle involving Menjou and Olivier as two British military men contending for the widow's affections. Wallace Smith's adaptation of Maurice DeKobra's novel, *The Sphinx Has Spoken*, contained a good deal of squabbling but little true drama. Victor Schertzinger directed the soggy William LeBaron production with a cast that included Hugh Herbert, Frederick Kerr, Blanche Frederici, Vadim Uraneff and Jean Del Val. Director Schertzinger and Max Steiner collaborated on the musical score of this film, which contrived to lose $260,000.

With MGM's Marie Dressler emerging as a giant star, RKO hoped to build the inimitable Edna May Oliver (left) into a rival attraction. Juliet Wilbur Tompkins' story **Fanny Foley Herself** (GB: **Top Of The Bill**) was not, however, a good choice for the unveiling of a new RKO leading lady. This sometimes sentimental, sometimes farcical drama about a vaudeville performer (Oliver) and her two daughters, Helen Chandler (centre left), and Rochelle Hudson (right), self-destructed thanks to enervated direction and absurd plot contrivances. At one point Miss Oliver, who believes daughter Hudson has been compromised, boards a plane, flies through rain and fog, makes a parachute jump and then battles through muck and mud to reach her daughter, only to learn that she is as happy as a bee with new husband John Darrow. Edna May maintained her composure throughout, though she must have been grimacing underneath. Director Melville Brown again proved himself an anachronism in the world of sound film sophistication, and screenwriter Carey Wilson (additional dialogue Bernard Schubert) shouldered part of the blame for the debacle. Also in it: Hobart Bosworth (centre right), Florence Roberts, Robert Emmett O'Connor and Harry Stubbs. The film was shot in Technicolor, with John E. Burch as production supervisor. (WLB).

Future RKO queen Ginger Rogers (right) received third billing in **The Tip-Off** (GB: **Looking For Trouble**). A clever gangster spoof written for the screen by Earl Baldwin from a story by George Kibbe Turner, it featured a Candide-like Eddie Quillan who blunders into the middle of a mob feud, making just the right move whenever he seems about to be annihilated. Befriending him – and making off with the picture in the process – is thick-skulled, anti-grammatical fighter Robert Armstrong (left), whose sweetheart Baby Face (Rogers) keeps him on a leash thanks to her superior vocabulary. Albert Rogell's effervescent direction (dialogue direction Ralph F. Murphy) was just right for the story, which also included parts for Joan Peers, Ralf Harolde, Mike Donlin, Ernie Adams, Charles Sellon and Cupid Ainsworth. The associate producer was Harry Joe Brown. (RKO Pathé).

Freighters Of Destiny was the pretentious title of a Tom Keene western that only cost a total of $39,000 to make. The title refers to the venerable wagons that ferried settlers to the uncivilized West, with Keene (right) and his father in charge of a wagon train which is continually harassed by a violent band of outlaw plug-uglies who shoot up the wagons and steal them whenever they can. It turns out that a local banker, who wants to acquire the 'freighter' franchise for himself, is behind the attacks. Barbara Kent (left) took care of the feminine requirements, and Billy Franey managed to add a few moments of comedy. Adele Buffington's screenplay and Fred Allen's direction were routine, but Ted McCord's cinematography deserved special praise. Also cast: Mitchell Harris, Frederick Burton, Frank Rice, William Welsh, Fred Burns and Charles Whittaker. (RKO Pathé).

Plenty sentimental and making no apologies for it, **Consolation Marriage** (GB: **Married In Haste**) provided Irene Dunne (left) with her first solo starring opportunity. Dunne and Pat O'Brien (borrowed from Howard Hughes' Caddo Company) played two jilted lonely-hearts who, believing they have lost everything that is romantic and lovely in life, make a match of convenience: a consolation marriage. It is filled with the charm and attraction of small things such as dogs, babies, picnics and mutual good humour. But what becomes their deep love for one another is unrealized until both of their former sweethearts again become available. Jarring reunions with the respective 'dream' lovers bring the couple back together for a fade-out clinch that spells future bliss. Paul Sloane directed this fanciful soufflé with a suitably light touch, and Humphrey Pearson fashioned the engaging screenplay from Bill Cunningham's story. Lester Vail and Myrna Loy featured as the original love objects, with Matt Moore, John Halliday and baby Pauline Stevens (right) also appearing. Max Steiner and associate producer Myles Connolly wrote the theme music, entitled 'Devotion'.

Homespun radio philosopher Seth Parker (Phillips Lord, left) came to Hollywood for **Way Back Home** (GB: **Old Greatheart**), and the result was a sweet and appealing little picture with a few laughs and a few tugs at the heartstrings. Jane Murfin wrote the script to order, working in the characters from the radio show (Ma Parker played by Effie L. Palmer, Lizzie by Mrs Phillips Lord and Cephus by Bennett Kilpack), plenty of Down East atmosphere (barn dances, taffy-pulling, singing bees), and a few melodramatic twists to jazz up the proceedings. RKO also imported Frank Albertson from Fox and Bette Davis (right) from Universal (not yet a star, her services were acquired for the sum of $300 per week for three weeks) to play a pair of young lovers who, aided by Parker, eventually conquer the forces bent on keeping them apart. Pandro S. Berman supervised for producer William LeBaron and director William Seiter, and the cast also featured Frankie Darro, Dorothy Peterson, Stanley Fields, Oscar Apfel and Raymond Hunter.

A bland remake of a 1919 Paramount release which had starred Robert Warwick and Wanda Hawley, **Secret Service** told the story of a Union officer (Richard Dix, right) who falls in love with a Confederate general's daughter (Shirley Grey, left, again borrowed from Samuel Goldwyn). Dix and his brother (William Post Jr) are dispatched behind enemy lines to locate defensive weaknesses so that the Yankee forces can break through and bring the war to a speedy termination. After a series of less-than-thrilling adventures, Dix is imprisoned by the Rebels; he goes to the guard house sustained by the knowledge that his beloved will be waiting when the fighting ends. J. Walter Ruben directed from Bernard Schubert's screenplay (based on William Gillette's stage original), and the associate producer was Louis Sarecky. Nance O'Neil, Harold Kinney, Gavin Gordon, Florence Lake, Frederick Burton, Clarence Muse and Eugene Jackson rounded out the cast. (WLB).

◁Director Wesley Ruggles and writer Howard Estabrook joined forces for **Are These Our Children?** and the result was in many ways superior to the sprawling *Cimarron* which they also worked on together. Ruggles' story, as scripted by Estabrook, focused on Eddie (Eric Linden, left), a decent lad who is unwittingly drawn into a devil's cauldron of liquor, fast women and crime. A drunken binge results in Eddie's accidental shooting of an aged delicatessen owner. Even his own trial does not impress itself on the foolish, naive youth until he hears the death sentence pronounced. Tough-minded throughout, the film contained no last minute contrivances for a happy ending: at the finish, Eddie is on his way to prison where he will be executed. Casting mostly unknown and largely juvenile actors, including Ben Alexander, Mary Kornman, Billy Butts, Rochelle Hudson (centre), William Orlamond, Arline Judge, Roberta Gale, Bobby Quirk and Beryl Mercer (right), Ruggles netted an ensemble of solid performances for associate producer Louis Sarecky. **Are These Our Children?** achieved a strong sense of verisimilitude, and meaningful comment on contemporary life that was unusual to RKO's pictures. (WLB).

Men who go down to the sea in ships were nowhere to be found in **Suicide Fleet**. This consistently artificial thriller had something to do with a clash between German U-boats and an American 'mystery' vessel, but it was all just an excuse to knot together Bill Boyd (centre right), Robert Armstrong (left) and James Gleason (centre left) – three Coney Island characters in love with the same girl (Ginger Rogers, right). The jocular elements worked pretty well, but the naval manoeuvres were pure hooey, and funnier (unintentionally) than the scenes designed to evoke laughter. Lew Lipton penned the screenplay (dialogue by F. McGrew Willis), from a story by Commander Herbert A. Jones. Albert Rogell directed, and Harry Joe Brown was the associate producer. In support: Frank Reicher, Ben Alexander, Henry Victor, Hans Joby, and Harry Bannister, who was under contract to RKO Pathé at the 'request' of Ann Harding, his then wife. (RKO Pathé).

Sneaking in with very little fanfare at year's end was **The Big Shot** (GB: **The Optimist**), a dopey comedy about a young hotel clerk who is conned into purchasing some worthless swamp land. But the land, as was the way with such diversions, turns out to include a valuable sulphur spring. Director Ralph F. Murphy cast Eddie Quillan (left) as the guileless real estate speculator, Maureen O'Sullivan (centre, borrowed from Fox) as the heroine who rushes to tell Quillan about his good fortune before he is duped again, and Arthur Stone as a grumpy Civil War veteran who takes a shine to the lad. The acting contingent, which also included Mary Nolan, Rosco Ates, Belle Bennett, Louis John Bartels, Otis Harlan and William Eugene (right), did their best, but the insipid story by George Dromgold and Hal Conklin (screenplay by Earl Baldwin and Joseph Fields) defeated every effort. Harry Joe Brown was the associate producer for Charles R. Rogers. (RKO Pathé).

★★★★★★★★★★★★★★★★★★

1932

★★★★★★★★★★★★★★★★★★

One of the corporation's worst years from a loss stand-point, 1932 was, ironically, the best year for talent acquisition that the studio would ever enjoy. David O. Selznick's seasoned eye fastened on George Cukor, Merian C. Cooper, Katharine Hepburn and Fred Astaire, all of whom signed RKO contracts. In addition, Selznick recruited Kenneth Macgowan as story editor (he would soon become a producer) and, despite an order to dump all members of the LeBaron coterie, retained Pandro S. Berman as his personal assistant. Berman quickly proved his value and returned to the producing ranks.

RKO Pathé was phased out completely as a separate production wing of the corporation. Its Culver City Studio (the venerable Thomas H. Ince plant from the silent era) became mainly a rental lot. Both Charles R. Rogers, the chief of RKO Pathé production, and William LeBaron moved on to other companies, leaving David O. Selznick in complete charge of studio film-making.

The inevitable shake-up in the upper echelons occurred early in the year when Joseph I. Schnitzer resigned as president of the production company, and Merlin Aylesworth replaced Hiram Brown as chief executive of the parent corporation. B. B. Kahane, the secretary-treasurer, was promoted to Schnitzer's old job, Ned E. Depinet became vice-president of distribution and Harold B. Franklin took over the theatre division. Lee Marcus, formerly president of RKO Pathé, was given a vague position as 'liaison officer' between the studio and home office.

But the best news was that RKO began to make a better class of product. Selznick's impact on the quality of Radio Pictures was dramatic, despite penny-pinching economic strictures forced on him by the Depression atmosphere.

Losses for the year totalled more than $10 million, but it was hardly a profitable year for anyone in Hollywood. Paramount's deficit in the same period amounted to $21 million, and Warner Bros. reported losses of $14 million.

Of the 47 films released, the year's best money-makers were **Bring 'Em Back Alive**, **A Bill of Divorcement** and **The Phantom Of Crestwood**.

The studio ushered in the new year with a Wheeler ▷ and Woolsey starrer called **Peach O'Reno**. Tim Whelan's story (adaptation and dialogue by Whelan, Ralph Spence and Eddie Welch) once again cast Robert Woolsey (left) in the role of a shyster lawyer, with Bert Wheeler (right) as his partner. They run a 'quickie' divorce racket in Nevada which metamorphoses into a gambling casino in the evenings. To avoid a strong-arm gambler (Mitchell Harris) who is intent on plugging the man who arranged his wife's divorce, Wheeler cavorts in drag through much of the picture. The touch was hardly original but, thanks to William Seiter's frolicsome direction, it did generate a certain amount of humour. William LeBaron was the producer, and John E. Burch supervised. Dorothy Lee, Zelma O'Neal, Joseph Cawthorn, Sam Hardy, Arthur Hoyt and Cora Witherspoon provided the major support. Song: 'From Niagara Falls To Reno' Richard A. Whiting, Harry Akst, Grant Clarke.

Men Of Chance was another day at the races, but it failed to spell thoroughbred entertainment. The picture's primary virtues were its racing footage, and some behind-the-grandstands insights into gambling manipulations keenly observed by director George Archainbaud. The Louis Weitzenkorn story (adaptation and dialogue by Louis Stevens) was another matter entirely; Mary Astor (right) is dispatched to pull a Circe-routine on Diamond Johnny (Ricardo Cortez) so she can poison his horse before the big race. Never trust a woman – she ends up marrying him, the horse wins from the off, and the vicious opposition forces are ruined in the process. Most of the script's wretched dialogue was forced on the two stars, but supporting characters John Halliday (left), Ralph Ince, Kitty Kelly, James Donlan and George Davis had to cope with their share of bad lines as well. Pandro S. Berman was the associate producer. (WLB). ▽

Only hard-core western addicts found anything to savour in **Partners**, one of the more anaemic of the Tom Keene oaters. The story and dialogue (by Donald W. Lee) cast suspicion on the hero for the murder of old peddler Billy Franey. Breaking away when the sheriff comes to arrest him, Keene (centre right) and his wonder horse Flash follow the clues to bad guy Lee Shumway and justice is done. Keene then rounds up the girl (Nancy Drexel, right) and the peddler's grandson (Bobby Nelson, centre left), and all three become 'pards' for life. Fred Allen directed with a supporting cast that included Otis Harlan, Victor Potel (left), Carlton King, Ben Corbett, and the world's champion roper, Fred Burns. (RKO Pathé). ▽

Panama Flo was such a rampant disaster that ▷ only one question seems relevant: how did this picture ever come to be made? Producer Charles R. Rogers and his associate Harry Joe Brown must have noticed the narrative weaknesses that ran through Garrett Fort's script, but they never bothered to rectify them. The most damaging of the incoherencies was the sudden transformation of Charles Bickford (left), the obvious heavy for much of the story, into the romantic hero, and the concomitant flip-flop of Robert Armstrong from apparent champion to deceitful murderer. Perhaps the filmmakers (including director Ralph Murphy) expected the steamy jungle atmosphere and heroine Helen Twelvetrees' (right) unbridled histrionics to defuse the audience's critical sensibilities; instead viewers were confounded and angered by the degree of pictorial ineptitude which they witnessed in this absurd story of a honky-tonk girl stranded in Panama, who ends up as housekeeper to a man who will otherwise send her to jail for fleecing his pocketbook. Other unfortunate cast members: Marjorie Peterson, Maude Eburne, Paul Hurst, Reina Velez and Hans Joby. Arthur Miller (not to be confused with the illustrious playwright) contributed the one element of interest – the photography. RKO remade the picture in 1939 with Lucille Ball, calling it *Panama Lady*. (RKO Pathé).

Edna May Oliver was at her peak in **Ladies Of The Jury**, a comedy about the trial of a young actress (Jill Esmond) accused of shooting her elderly husband. As a society matron chosen for jury duty, Oliver (right) savaged the courtroom in her own unique style. Interrogating witnesses whenever she felt like it and addressing the incensed judge (Robert McWade, left) with total informality, she managed to set precedents that pushed legal decorum back a thousand years. Ably assisted by Lowell Sherman's direction, Marion Dix's jocular adaptation of a play by John Frederick Ballard, and capital supporting performances from Rosco Ates, Ken Murray, Kitty Kelly and Cora Witherspoon, Edna May proved she was fully capable of carrying the kind of picture tailored to her talents. William LeBaron produced what was one of the better comedy efforts of his term at RKO. Douglas MacLean was his associate producer, and Salisbury Field and Eddie Welch both contributed dialogue. Also cast: Charles Dow Clark, Helene Millard, Kate Price, Lita Chevret, Florence Lake, Guinn Williams and Leyland Hodgson. Helen Broderick and Victor Moore starred in a 1937 remake called *We're On The Jury*.

Dolores Del Rio received full star treatment in her first RKO picture, the appropriately titled **Girl Of The Rio** (GB: **The Dove**). Unfortunately, a plethora of close-ups of the gorgeous actress could not counterbalance Herbert Brenon's sluggish direction or Elizabeth Meehan's half-hearted script, and the film bombed badly. The plot concerned the efforts of cabaret dancer Del Rio (right) to fend off the advances of sneering Mexican *caballero* Leo Carrillo (left) and secure the release of her *novio* (Norman Foster, centre), whom Carrillo has had removed to a foreign prison. The Willard Mack play, based on a magazine story by Gerald Beaumont and mounted by David Belasco on Broadway, had been a pleasing amalgam of comedy, suspense and romance, but this celluloid version (associate producer Louis Sarecky) had only meagre amounts of each. Also cast: Stanley Fields, Frank Campeau, Lucile Gleason and Ralph Ince. A remake of a 1928 Norma Talmadge silent picture released by United Artists, it would be brought back to life in 1939 as *The Girl And The Gambler*, starring Steffi Duna, Tim Holt, and Leo Carrillo again portraying the stereotyped *caballero*. Song: 'Querida' Victor Schertzinger. (WLB).

Another faraway location was on view in **Prestige**, but the results were not many notches above *Panama Flo*. This time it was a penal colony in Indochina to which Ann Harding (left) journeys in search of her fiancé. He is commandant of the French facility, a man fighting a losing battle with alcohol because of the rigours of jungle life. Melvyn Douglas (borrowed from Samuel Goldwyn) played the part, with Adolphe Menjou (right) in attendance as his chief nemesis. Tay Garnett's direction succeeded in conveying the monotony, stifling heat and other discomforts of the setting, but, unfortunately, the story by Harry Hervey (adaptation by Garnett and Rollo Lloyd and screenplay by Francis Edwards Faragoh) had similar characteristics. It went nowhere, and wasted Miss Harding's beauty and obvious talent. Ian MacLaren, Guy Bates Post, Carmelita Geraghty, Creighton Hale and Clarence Muse also appeared, plus co-adaptor Rollo Lloyd who was also dialogue director. Harry Joe Brown was the associate producer. Song: 'I Don't Know What You Do To Me' Harold Lewis, Bernie Grossman. (RKO Pathé).

◁ The studio tried to resuscitate the career of silent star Pola Negri (illustrated) by top-casting her in **A Woman Commands**, her first talking picture. Given solid support by Roland Young as the Serbian king who decrees she must marry him, and Basil Rathbone, portraying an army captain nearly ruined by her and for whom she sacrifices her life, the star's acting was respectable, and the picture as such proved to be palatable melodrama. Paul L. Stein, who had handled one of the raven-haired actress' first films in Berlin, directed her, and brought a semblance of style to Horace Jackson's somewhat turgid screenplay (based on a story by Thilde Forster). Art director Carroll Clark and wardrobe designer Gwen Wakeling furnished sumptuous sets and costumes, but it was all for naught. La Negri's 'piquant' (the studio's euphemism for thick and guttural) accent was a liability impossible to overcome. The film lost $265,000, and the star made no more pictures for the company. Charles R. Rogers produced, Harry Joe Brown was the associate and the supporting cast included H. B. Warner, Anthony Bushell, Reginald Owen, May Boley, Frank Reicher, George Baxter and David Newell. Originally intended as an RKO Pathé release, the film was eventually distributed as a Radio picture. Song: 'Promise You'll Remember Me For I'll Remember You' Nacio Herb Brown, Gordon Clifford.

△

Constance Bennett's talents were displayed to good advantage in **Lady With A Past** (GB: **Reputation**), a cosmopolitan comedy well-handled by director Edward H. Griffith. The point of the title is that Miss Bennett (left) has no romantic past to boast about; indeed, she is a bashful, intelligent young lady and not happy about that at all. Off to Europe she goes to develop her personality and, she hopes, her love life. At first she is forced to hire an 'admirer' to take her dancing and to the cafés, but before long she becomes a *succès de scandale* whose name appears in the Paris papers regularly. The studio borrowed Ben Lyon (right) from Warner Bros. to impersonate the paid escort and David Manners from First National to handle the role of a young bachelor stunned by Bennett's transformation. Both did excellent jobs, topping a gifted supporting troupe that numbered Don Alvarado, Albert Conti, Merna Kennedy, Astrid Allwyn, Donald Dillaway, Blanche Frederici, John Roche and Nella Walker among its members. Horace Jackson wrote the well-spiced screenplay from a novel by Harriet Henry, and Harry Joe Brown was associate producer. (RKO Pathé).

△

The first RKO picture to carry David O. Selznick's 'executive producer' credit was **The Lost Squadron**, an aerial thriller directed by George Archainbaud. Although hardly a masterwork, the film did have a certain originality, and was very well made. Both of these attributes – with extra emphasis on originality – would become characteristics of the Selznick product. The story centred on three members of a World War I flying squadron who take jobs as movie stunt flyers after the war ends. They find work with a maniacal director (Erich von Stroheim, centre, type cast) who eventually murders one of them for reasons of jealousy. The two remaining pals then take their revenge. The acting of principals Richard Dix (right), Robert Armstrong and Joel McCrea tended to be a bit wobbly, but the aviation sequences were anything but. They would still be labelled spectacular by today's standards. Wallace Smith fashioned the screenplay from a story by Dick Grace (additional dialogue Herman J. Mankiewicz and Robert S. Presnell), and an interesting cast also featured Mary Astor (left), Dorothy Jordan, Hugh Herbert, Ralph Ince, Marjorie Peterson, Ralph Lewis and William Davidson. **The Lost Squadron** indicated that Selznick would, indeed, raise the level of RKO production.

Cheers for **Carnival Boat**, a vigorous action story set in and among the lumber camps. Given only 61 minutes to play with, scenarist James Seymour, adapting a story by Marion Jackson and Don Ryan, managed to work in a runaway train, a ride on a cable car, a monumental brawl between hero Bill Boyd (left) and Fred Kohler, and a climactic log jam which Boyd breaks up in Paul Bunyon fashion. The title refers to a show boat that transports Ginger Rogers (right) into the lumberjacks' lives, causing some disagreement between Boyd and his father Hobart Bosworth over the young man's future plans. Director Albert Rogell laced the action and romance with fair comedy relief, chiefly provided by Edgar Kennedy and Harry Sweet. All in all, it was a bustling, amiable little picture of which Charles R. Rogers and associate producer Harry Joe Brown did not need to feel ashamed. The players also included Marie Prevost, Charles Sellon, Eddie Chandler and Walter Percival. (RKO Pathé).

▽

Tom Keene westerns were strictly low-brow fodder, but their miniscule budgets made them the only consistently profitable pictures coming out of the studio during this era. **The Saddle Buster**, for example, cost $38,000 and earned a profit of $25,000. The original story by Cherry Wilson was mildly novel in that it included no good guy–bad guy conflict at its core. Instead, the rodeo saga concerned a cowpoke (Keene, centre) who loses his nerve after 'Black Peril', a man-trampling bronco nearly crushes him to death. Following a period of brooding over his cowardly impulses, Keene returns to the arena, rides 'Black Peril' to a standstill, and wins enough money to pay for the hospitalization of another rider who has tangled with the vicious horse. He also earns the love of Helen Foster (left) as an extra reward. Fred Allen directed, Oliver Drake wrote the screenplay and Marie Quillan (right), Robert Frazer, Richard Carlyle, Fred Burns, Charles Quigley and Harry Bowen also appeared. (RKO Pathé).

▽

△

Bert Wheeler (right) and Robert Woolsey superimposed their own brand of madness on the wild, wild west in **Girl Crazy**. Arriving in Custerville, Arizona, in a wrecked taxicab drawn by a tired and disgusted team of horses, the two city-slickers soon find themselves at odds with Stanley Fields (left), who specializes in annihilating the local sheriffs. This comes as a result of Eddie Quillan's decision to turn his father's cattle ranch into a whoopee resort with a jazz orchestra, show girls and a gambling concession, and his call for assistance to his two pals from back home. Wheeler eventually becomes sheriff (in a rigged election), but this time Fields is frustated in his attempts to add another tin star to his morbid collection. Based on a stage success by John McGowan and Guy Bolton, with music by George and Ira Gershwin, this William Seiter-directed romp was expensive by 1932 standards, and failed to earn any profits. Still, it represented better-than-average Wheeler and Woolsey entertainment. William LeBaron produced (his last picture for RKO), employing several writers to draft the finished script: Herman J. Mankiewicz (adaptation), Eddie Welch and Walter DeLeon (dialogue), Tim Whelan (screenplay). The feminine acting contingent featured Mitzi Green, Dorothy Lee, Kitty Kelly and Arline Judge, and Brooks Benedict, Lita Chevret and Chris-Pin Martin were also cast. RKO later sold its rights to MGM, which produced a remake in 1943 starring Mickey Rooney and Judy Garland. Songs included: 'I Got Rhythm', 'Embraceable You', 'Bidin' My Time', 'Sam And Delilah' George and Ira Gershwin.

Young Bride featured Helen Twelvetrees (illustrated) and Eric Linden in a nondescript story about a starry-eyed young girl who marries the man of her dreams and then finds that he is a loud-mouthed, insensitive braggart. The two stars, capably directed by William Seiter, maintained admirable restraint throughout, despite the Hugh Stanislaus Stange stage material (adapted by Garrett Fort with additional dialogue by Ralph Murphy and Jane Murfin) which continually veered in the direction of bathos. Harry Joe Brown was the associate producer, and the cast also included Arline Judge, Cliff Edwards, Rosco Ates, Blanche Frederici, Polly Walters and Edmund Breese. (RKO Pathé).

The Office Girl (GB: **Sunshine Susie**) was a British remake of a successful German musical comedy entitled *Die Privatsekretaerin*. Renate Mueller (right) reprised her starring role as a young stenographer who goes to Vienna, finds work in a bank and becomes involved with the managing director, whom she mistakes for a low-salaried clerk. Around this core were wound several comic scenes and a number of songs sung by Miss Mueller. Victor Saville adapted Franz Schulz's story, and directed from a scenario by Robert Stevenson. The major supporting players were Owen Nares (left, as the managing director), Jack Hulbert and Morris Harvey. The film was a Gainsborough Pictures production, acquired for US distribution by RKO. Songs: 'Today I Feel So Happy', 'Just Because I Lost My Heart To You', 'I'll Get There In The End', 'I Have My Aunt Eliza' Paul Abraham, Desmond Carter.

Symphony Of Six Million (GB: **Melody Of Life**), a Fannie Hurst weepie directed by Gregory LaCava, was a film of 'firsts': it was Pandro Berman's first associate producer assignment under Selznick; it was the first film for Russian-born actor Gregory Ratoff, who played the father of physician Ricardo Cortez; it was the first time an elaborate surgical procedure was filmed; and it was embellished by one of Max Steiner's first complete musical scores. The narrative, as scripted by Bernard Schubert and J. Walter Ruben (additional dialogue James Seymour), concerned a doctor who sacrifices his ideals for money and social position and then bungles an operation on his own father. In an ending designed to puncture the resistance of even the most cynical, Cortez rescues his situation by performing miraculous surgery on his true love, Irene Dunne (illustrated, with Cortez). The overwhelming strings of Max Steiner's score swamped the drama on occasion and Cortez's limited acting abilities were evident throughout, yet the movie was still a genuine victory in its overall impact. Humorous scenes featuring Ratoff were especially well-drawn and adroitly depicted. Anna Appel, Noel Madison, Lita Chevret, John St Polis, Julie Haydon, Helen Freeman, Josephine Whittell, Oscar Apfel and Eddie Phillips were others in the cast.

J. Walter Ruben's inspired screenplay and skilful direction made **The Roadhouse Murder** one of the studio's most diverting thrillers. Eric Linden (right) played Chick Brian, a cub reporter who pretends to be a murderer and dispatches articles to his newspaper supposedly written by the culprit. Soon a web of circumstantial evidence closes around his breach of journalistic ethics, and he finds himself convicted of the killings. Dorothy Jordan (left, borrowed from MGM) was also featured, with Purnell Pratt, Rosco Ates, David Landau, Bruce Cabot, Phyllis Clare, Gustav von Seyffertitz, Roscoe Karns and William Morris in other notable roles for associate producer Willis Goldbeck. Gene Fowler contributed additional dialogue to Ruben's script, which was based on a novel by Maurice Level.

David Selznick brought John Barrymore (right) to RKO for **State's Attorney** (GB: **Cardigan's Last Case**), the far-fetched tale of a brilliant criminal lawyer with underworld connections. Director George Archainbaud gave Barrymore free reign to emote, and the histrionically-inclined actor took full advantage. His performance was so overwrought in several scenes that it wrecked the necessary balance between star and co-workers. The Louis Stevens story and Gene Fowler-Rowland Brown screenplay gave key roles to Helen Twelvetrees (left) as the wayward but wistful girl whose love leads Barrymore to bare his soul, and William (Stage) Boyd (borrowed from Paramount and not to be confused with the RKO Pathé star) as the gangster chief destroyed by his former lawyer in the courtroom finale. Associate producer James Kelvin McGuinness' supporting players including Jill Esmond, Mary Duncan, C. Henry Gordon, Oscar Apfel, Ralph Ince, Albert Conti, Frederick Burton and Paul Hurst. Lee Tracy and Margot Grahame were featured in an RKO remake, *Criminal Lawyer*, released in 1937.

Elements of the old haunted-house chiller showed up in **Ghost Valley**, another Tom Keene western directed by Fred Allen for associate producer Harry Joe Brown. In it, Merna Kennedy inherits some property in a ghost-town, including an overlooked gold mine. The usual shudder routines were employed by Mitchell Harris (right) to scare the heroine into selling, but Keene (left), also part heir to the property, foils the bad guy's designs. Adele Buffington wrote the mediocre screenplay, and Billy Franey, Harry Bowen, Kate Campbell and Ted Adams also appeared. (RKO Pathé).

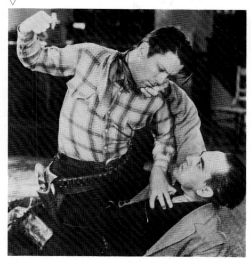

Though its title suggested a Tom Keene horse-opera, **Westward Passage** took place far from the open range. There was more than a slight whiff of Noel Coward in the air, as Ann Harding (right) and Laurence Olivier (left) portrayed a pair of love birds who can't refrain from bickering. After they marry, frustrated writer Olivier decides that the friction is hurting his career; this leads to divorce, Miss Harding's rebound marriage to Irving Pichel and a reconciliation and subsequent elopement between the made-only-for-each-other battlers. Margaret Ayer Barnes wrote the novel which Bradley King adapted, with dialogue by Humphrey Pearson. Robert Milton directed smartly, drawing fine performances from the principals, as well as supporting actors ZaSu Pitts, Juliette Compton, Irene Purcell, Don Alvarado, Florence Lake, Edgar Kennedy and child player Bonita Granville. Associate producer Harry Joe Brown's film was light and appealing, but the patrons didn't agree, and it lost $250,000. (RKO Pathé).

Ricardo Cortez delivered one of his finest performances in **Is My Face Red?**, an adaptation of a Ben Markson–Allen Rivkin play, written for the screen by Markson and Casey Robinson. Cortez was William Poster, a scandal-mongering journalist unfettered by considerations of propriety or good taste. Droll, shrewd and hopelessly vain, Cortez (right) managed to create a scathing portrayal without making his character too repellent for audiences to swallow. Naturally Cortez/Poster gets his come-uppance, but old flame Helen Twelvetrees (left) is there to console him after the fall. Adding to the excitement were Jill Esmond, Robert Armstrong, Arline Judge, ZaSu Pitts, Clarence Muse and Sidney Toler. Director William Seiter made the most of his script and cast, and Harry Joe Brown was the associate producer.

What Price Hollywood? was a special picture that reflected David Selznick's romantic view of his chosen profession, and provided George Cukor with his first important directorial success with a movie that was to become the prototype of the *A Star Is Born* pictures. The story by Adela Rogers St John and screenplay by Jane Murfin and Ben Markson (Gene Fowler and Rowland Brown also received a vague writing credit) traced the rise of a Brown Derby waitress from obscurity to movie stardom. The central role went to Constance Bennett (left), who, in the superb first half, made her transformation entirely credible. Lowell Sherman, too, turned in a bravura performance as a dipsomaniac director who helps her along her way, and Gregory Ratoff was excellent as the Selznick-inspired movie mogul; while the glimpses of behind-the-scenes film-making remain among the best ever committed to celluloid. The picture starts to go wrong when a love interest for Bennett (Neil Hamilton as a millionaire polo player) enters the proceedings. Hamilton's performance was woefully deficient and, even worse, his presence forced Sherman (right) into the background. Five years later when Selznick returned to the material for the first *A Star Is Born*, he and his writers ironed out the kinks by combining the Sherman and Hamilton characters into one man. And thus, one of the most durable plots in Hollywood history came into being. Cukor would make another version himself, starring Judy Garland and James Mason, more than 20 years later for Warner Brothers. **What Price Hollywood?** also featured Brooks Benedict and Louise Beavers in its cast, for associate producer Pandro S. Berman. (RKO Pathé).

Booted and spurred and ready for action, Tom Keene (left) found himself at odds with bosomy Marie Wells in **Beyond The Rockies**. And that was the one twist in Oliver Drake's screenplay, based on a story by John P. McCarthy. Instead of the usual bearded macho villain, Miss Wells is the outlaw boss of a ranch which is also an outpost for rustlers. Aided by pals Julien Rivero and Ernie Adams (right), the hero puts chivalry aside and concentrates on his task of bringing justice to the uncivilized territory. Director Fred Allen churned out another moderate cowpoke success, using Rochelle Hudson, Hank Bell, William Welsh, Tom London and Ted Adams in supporting parts. Harry Joe Brown was the associate producer. (RKO Pathé).

Survival was the big issue in **Roar Of The Dragon** – both the survival of Richard Dix (right) and his compatriots who must hold off a guerilla horde in war-weakened Manchuria, and the survival of the production at the pay-box window. Though Dix and certain members of his party lasted through the demolition, audiences took no pleasure in the Wesley Ruggles-directed effort and it soon withered away, unloved and unmourned. One of the damaging weaknesses was Danish actress Gwili Andre (centre), another Garbo impersonator who was supposedly a woman of mystery. She took her part very literally, always appearing to be in a state of puzzlement. Edward Everett Horton and ZaSu Pitts (left) battled valiantly to inject some comedy relief between the bursts of machine gun fire, but they had very thin material with which to work. Arline Judge, Dudley Digges, C. Henry Gordon, William Orlamond, Arthur Stone, Toshi Mori, Will Stanton and Jimmy Wang also portrayed characters in the Howard Estabrook screenplay (based on George) Kibbe Turner's *A Passage To Hong Kong* and a story by Merian C. Cooper and Jane Bigelow). William LeBaron was to be credited as producer, but this fell away as part of his contract settlement.

Miracles do happen in Hollywood, despite what the sceptics say. Dorothy Wilson (right), an RKO secretary, was chosen to play the lead in **The Age Of Consent**, turned in a pleasing performance, and earned herself a studio contract. Director Gregory LaCava teamed Miss Wilson with Richard Cromwell (on loan from Columbia) in this interesting (and inexpensive) study of college life. Instead of the usual survey of sophomoric girl-chasing and fraternity partying, Martin Flavin's drama explored the problems and confusions of students in search of themselves. The two leading actors played a pair of star-crossed under-graduates, each of whom gets involved in a near disastrous romantic incident due to a misunderstanding about the relative values of education and marriage. LaCava's deft touch enriched the screenplay by Sarah Y. Mason and Francis Cockrell. Also cast for associate producer Pandro S. Berman: Arline Judge, Eric Linden (left), John Halliday, Aileen Pringle, Reginald Barlow and, in an unbilled bit, Betty Grable. H. N. Swanson, former editor of *College Humor* magazine, was the technical advisor. He would soon become an RKO story editor and associate producer, then later one of Hollywood's most prominent literary agents.

Richard Walton Tully's play **Bird Of Paradise** was one of the most heavily doomed undertakings in RKO history. David Selznick inherited the property from the LeBaron organization and decided to make it one of the big films of the year. King Vidor was borrowed from MGM to direct, and Joel McCrea (centre right) and Dolores Del Rio (centre left) were cast in the starring roles. Upon the crew's arrival in Hawaii for extensive location shooting, a 'kono wind' commenced, bringing overcast skies and nearly continuous rainfall. At one point, Vidor had to employ natives to nail palm fronds back on trees denuded by the winds. After 24 working days – of which only one had been clear – the weary film troop limped back to Hollywood, where other problems plagued them until shooting was completed. In spite of everything, **Bird Of Paradise** turned out tolerably well. Highlighted by the sparkling photography of Clyde DeVinna, Edward Cronjager and Lucien Andriot, the picture succeeded in capturing the exotic ambience of Polynesia. The biggest drawback was the story: a succession of RKO writers (Wells Root, Wanda Tuchock and Leonard Praskins received screen credit) were unable to elevate Tully's original above the heavy-breathing melodramatic level. An overwrought hodge-podge of action sequences and native superstitions, and an object lesson in the perils of miscegenation, the plot never coalesced into articulate drama. Culture-crossed lovers Del Rio and McCrea did all right in the sensual love scenes, but their acting created several unintentionally funny moments elsewhere, such as the segments in which McCrae instructs the island princess in the English language. Max Steiner composed the eloquent score. Also cast: John Halliday, Richard 'Skeets' Gallagher, Bert Roach, Creighton Chaney (Lon's son, known later in his career as Lon, Jr), Wade Boteler, Arnold Gray, Reginald Simpson and Napoleon Pukui. RKO sold its story rights to Twentieth Century-Fox who remade it in 1951, with Louis Jourdan, Debra Paget and Jeff Chandler in the starring roles.

Great white hunter Frank Buck gave the company ▷ one of its most profitable films of 1932 with **Bring 'Em Back Alive**. Produced by the Van Beuren Corporation, which also made short films and cartoons for RKO release, this documentary was photographed on location in the Malayan jungle and featured clashes between a tiger and a black leopard, a crocodile and a python, and a titanic struggle between a tiger and a python. Humorous sequences, including the frustrated attempts of natives to transport a captured baby elephant (illustrated), were intercut to lighten the proceedings. Buck's famous book of the same title provided the inspiration for the picture, and he doubled as both star and narrator, with Edward Anthony (the book's co-author) also appearing. Clyde E. Elliott was the director, and Gene Rodemich composed a musical score. RKO's advertising staff smelled strong exploitation possibilities and responded with a bang-up campaign which drew a gratifying response from the public, assuring that further jungle adventures of Mr Buck would be preserved on celluloid.

Oscar winner Norman Taurog directed Bert Wheeler (left) and Robert Woolsey (centre) in **Hold 'Em Jail**. Another unbridled burlesque, this one was set in a prison run by a man who adores football. Slapstick veteran Edgar Kennedy (right) played the warden, and five different writers (story by Tim Whelan and Lew Lipton; screenplay by Walter DeLeon, S. J. Perelman and Eddie Welch) made him happy by including an absurd pigskin contest between two rival penitentiaries as the set piece of the film. Edna May Oliver (centre right) also contributed, though only in a minor role, but Wheeler–Woolsey stalwart Dorothy Lee was missing this time. Betty Grable (centre left) replaced her, playing the warden's daughter. Taurog moved things along in rapid-fire fashion, and the film boasted first class production values. Still, the formula elements in the duo's pictures were becoming tediously predictable and this one ended up a $55,000 loser. Also cast: Robert Armstrong, Rosco Ates, Warren Hymer, Paul Hurst, G. Pat Collins, Stanley Blystone, Jed Prouty and Spencer Charters. Harry Joe Brown was the associate producer.

The choicest oddity on the 1932 programme was **The Most Dangerous Game** (GB: **The Hounds Of Zaroff**). A pet project of associate producer Merian C. Cooper, the film related the story of a mad Russian count (Leslie Banks) who, having grown bored with hunting animals, stalks humans on his private island. Into his clutches fall Fay Wray (left), Robert Armstrong and Joel McCrea (right). The directorial team of Ernest B. Schoedsack and actor Irving Pichel handled James Ashmore Creelman's adaptation of a story by Richard Connell, turning it into a modest success. The plot has been re-cycled many times, including for RKO's *A Game Of Death* (1945) and the United Artists release *Run For The Sun* (1956), as well as for innumerable radio and television versions. With respect to the studio's history, this first production seems the most important, since it can be viewed as a sort of warm-up exercise for *King Kong*. Several of the same sets were used in both films, and Cooper, Schoedsack, Wray, Armstrong, and Max Steiner who composed the stirring score, segued directly into the tale of the mighty ape. Noble Johnson, Steve Clemento and Dutch Hendrian were also in it.
▽

The Tiffany Thayer novel which provided the basis for **Thirteen Women** had exciting possibilities, but they were negated by Bartlett Cormack and Samuel Ornitz's lacklustre screenplay and George Archainbaud's like-minded direction. Irene Dunne (left) and Ricardo Cortez topped the cast, though neither was given much to do. The picture actually belonged to Myrna Loy (right), as a half-caste who sets out to destroy 12 women who snubbed her during her college days. She's pretty successful, too, though her homicidal activities soon become routine and monotonous. Besides Dunne and Loy, the other ladies involved were Jill Esmond, Mary Duncan, Kay Johnson, Florence Eldridge, Julie Haydon, Harriet Hagman, Elsie Prescott, and Peg Entwistle, who committed suicide by jumping off the famous Hollywood sign after the completion of the picture (a comment on its quality perhaps?). C. Henry Gordon, Edward Pawley, Blanche Frederici and Wally Albright ◁ were other members of the cast.

Hell's Highway demonstrated David Selznick's interest in fresh, controversial subject matter. An indictment of the chain-gang system, the film was released shortly before Warner Bros.' *I Am A Fugitive From A Chain Gang*. It did not have the innate dramatic strength of the more famous Warner picture, but it still succeeded in depicting the brutalizing conditions endured by penal work crews. The screenplay by Samuel Ornitz, Robert Tasker and director Rowland Brown presented Richard Dix (illustrated) as a tough con, suffering the tortures of merciless overseers, bad food and unsanitary conditions. The arrival of his younger brother (Tom Brown) with a new batch of prisoners complicates his plans to break out. When the opportunity for freedom finally comes, Dix's concern for his injured sibling seals his doom. Rochelle Hudson, C. Henry Gordon, Oscar Apfel, Stanley Fields, John Arledge, Warner Richmond, Charles Middleton, Fuzzy Knight and Clarence Muse lent support to the two principals. A bit heavy on the sermonizing and melodrama, **Hell's Highway** was, nevertheless, a film that took risks and deserved plaudits for doing so.
▽

'Danger's my meat, chief,' Tom Keene (left) informs his Texas ranger superior in **Come On Danger!**, and off we go on a wild west frolic containing plenty of bare-knuckled action and guns a-blazin'. It seems that a woman (Julie Haydon, right) is the source of trouble, but in truth Robert Ellis has started rumours about Haydon to deflect suspicion from himself and his band of marauders. Keene gets revenge on Ellis, who had killed his ranger brother, and takes a shine to the unjustly accused young lady as well. Robert Hill directed from a screenplay by David Lewis and Lester Ilfeld (story by Bennett Cohen). Rosco Ates, William Scott, Frank Lackteen, Wade Boteler, Roy Stewart and Harry Tenbrook completed the cast. This was the first Keene vehicle released as a Radio picture. RKO remade it ten years later with Tim Holt.
▽

△

Corporate president Merlin Aylesworth and his staff were constantly on the lookout for ways to combine radio and film into a mutually beneficial package. They hit upon an interesting scheme for the joint exploitation of a mystery tale entitled **The Phantom Of Crestwood**. The studio produced Bartlett Cormack and J. Walter Ruben's story for release in October. Beginning in August and continuing for six weeks, the NBC radio network presented a dramatization of **The Phantom**. The climactic episode was not broadcast, however; instead, listeners were encouraged to submit their own endings with prizes parcelled out for the best dramatic solutions. The gimmick may have helped, for the film, a convoluted brain twister with no real freshness to it, made $100,000 in profits. Karen Morley (left, borrowed from MGM) played the pivotal role of a kiss-and-tell specialist who blackmails five men for half a million dollars. She is murdered before she can collect, prompting co-star Ricardo Cortez (right) to subject all the potential killers to the third degree. Ruben directed from Cormack's screenplay, using

Anita Louise, Pauline Frederick, H. B. Warner, Mary Duncan, Sam Hardy and Tom Douglas in other featured roles. Also cast: Richard 'Skeets' Gallagher, Ivan Simpson, Aileen Pringle, George E. Stone and Robert McWade. Merian C. Cooper was the associate producer.

Marian Marsh (right), Reginald Denny (centre right), Richard Bennett, Norman Foster (centre left), Irving Pichel, Nydia Westman, Thomas E. Jackson and Larry Steers (left) suffered a multitude of indignities at the hands of writer William A. Drake in **Strange Justice**. Victor Schertzinger's murky direction implied sincere contempt for this tale of a wrongfully convicted young chauffeur who is about to be electrocuted when the man he supposedly murdered drops by Sing Sing to clear up the misunderstanding. J. G. Bachmann produced for King Motion Pictures, an independent outfit which had made a deal to release its films through RKO. The King productions had only two ways to go after this witless drivel – up, or under. ▷

△

Clemence Dane's play **A Bill Of Divorcement** is memorable for Katharine Hepburn's screen debut, as well as for other reasons. Top-starred John Barrymore (centre) played a man who has been confined in a mental institution for 25 years, but who escapes on the day his wife (Billie Burke) divorces him. Barrymore's performance for director George Cukor was restrained and poignant – solid evidence of how superb the 'great profile' could be when handled properly and given a challenging role. But the real story centred on Hepburn (right) as Barrymore's daughter. With her realization that there is mental disease in her family, and that the only possible path for her is to give up her lover (David Manners) and remain childless, the film turned into an emotional tragedy that was made wrenchingly believable by this daring and unique screen personality. There had been serious doubts among the RKO brass about Miss Hepburn's abilities before the film was made. She erased them completely with her performance, though it is doubtful that even David Selznick dreamed he had launched the career of one of the greatest actresses in cinema history. Others cast were Paul Cavanagh, Henry Stephenson (left), Gayle Evers and Elizabeth Patterson, and the adaptation was by Howard Estabrook and Henry Wagstaff Gribble. **A Bill of Divorcement** was a remake of a British picture released in America in 1922 by Associated Exhibitors; RKO mounted it again in 1940, starring Adolphe Menjou and Maureen O'Hara.

The Theft Of The Mona Lisa was a maddening example of high-class cinematic achievement which fell flat on its face in American theatres. Made in Germany by director Geza von Bolvary from Walter Reisch's marvellous script, it told the story of a poor Italian glazier who falls in love with a Parisian hotel maid. The maid happens to resemble da Vinci's famous 'Mona Lisa', so the young man steals the painting to impress her. She is more impressed by lucre and runs away with a rich man. The heartbroken lad is soon imprisoned, becoming a national hero when he informs the court that he stole the painting to restore it to his Italian homeland. Willy Forst (illustrated) played the earnest glazier and Trude von Molo the frivolous maid. Their work displayed real artistry, as did all other aspects of the production, but domestic viewers found it slow and boring and avoided it like the plague. Gustav Grundgens, Fritz Odemar, Max Gulstarff, Rosa Valetti and Paul Kemp were also in the cast. RKO picked up the American rights from Superfilm, a German production outfit.

Little Orphan Annie, based on Harold Gray's famous comic strip and starring Mitzi Green (left) as the loquacious heroine, was a hit for the studio. Wanda Tuchock and Tom McNamara's screenplay gave Annie ample opportunities to do good (her apparent *raison d'être*) and to utter her favourite exclamation, 'leaping lizards'. Edgar Kennedy (right) as Daddy Warbucks, and Buster Phelps, playing a wide-eyed child who is the object of some of Annie's beneficence, gave fine accounts of themselves, and the other supporting players, including May Robson, Matt Moore, Kate Lawson and Sidney Bracy were all above average. John Robertson directed and Max Steiner arranged the music.

The Sport Parade brought together a clutch of appealing characters but, unfortunately, the movie didn't add up to much. The star was Joel McCrea (left), playing a sports writer who somehow manages to win a wrestling championship. Buzzing about McCrea were crooked wrestling promoter Walter Catlett; tipsy photographer Richard 'Skeets' Gallagher; rival William Gargan, vying with McCrea for the affections of Marian Marsh; and, stealing everyone's thunder, Robert Benchley as a droll, mistake-prone radio announcer. Though the film did survey numerous sporting events, its story (screenplay by Corey Ford and Francis Cockrell, based on original material by Jerry Horwin) had very little to do with the real world. Dudley Murphy's direction was altogether amateurish, but the picture was worth seeing for Benchley's bibulous performance. Clarence H. Wilson and Ivan Linow (right) were also in it.

Former RKO president Joseph I. Schnitzer set up Jefferson Pictures Corporation to produce independent films after he resigned from the studio. It was to be a short-lived endeavour, and Men Are Such Fools demonstrated why. With Leo Carrillo and Vivienne Osborne (right) topping the cast, the film was silent film fodder through and through, maladroitly directed by William Nigh. Carrillo and wife Osborne arrive in America hoping to make good in the world of music. She is soon dallying with Earle Foxe (left), and her husband is soon in jail for Foxe's murder. Behind bars he composes a stirring march, with the aid of fellow prisoners who all seem to have vocal or instrumental abilities. The criminals responsible for the antiquated plotline were Thomas Lloyd Lennon (story) and Viola Brothers Shore (adaptation and dialogue). Also cast: Una Merkel, Joseph Cawthorn, Tom Moore, J. Farrell MacDonald, Paul Hurst, Albert Conti, Lester Lee and Eddie Nugent. RKO distributed for Jefferson Pictures.

Although executive producer David Selznick discouraged the comparison because its cost was some $800,000 less than *Cimarron*, The Conquerors was cast in the same epic mould as RKO's Oscar-winner. Richard Dix (left) and Ann Harding (right) were teamed for this special, and William A. Wellman was borrowed from Warner Bros. to direct Robert Lord's screenplay, based on a story by Howard Estabrook. The film encompassed life in the United States from 1870 to the early 1930s, focusing on one American family (headed by Dix and Harding) whose three generations triumph over a variety of hardships, and lay the foundations of a great Midwestern banking institution in the process. Thematically, the script hammered home the idea that after each of its periods of economic crisis, America has not only recovered but forged ahead to greater prosperity. It was obviously designed to provide inspiration for cheerless Depression audiences. Selznick predicted it would be 'one of the biggest pictures ever made', but it failed to make an impression at the box office, and it completed its run as a $230,000 debit in studio account books. The sluggish, episodic structure was one problem, Richard Dix's overblown performance another, and the heavy propaganda of the final speech a third. Sadly, bravura montage transitions by Slavko Vorkapich went largely unappreciated, as did the quality supporting work of Edna May Oliver and Guy Kibbee, and Max Steiner's outstanding score. Also: Julie Haydon, Donald Cook, Walter Walker, Wally Albright, Marilyn Knowlden, Harry Holman, Jason Robards.

Tom Keene (right) was earning $3,347 per picture at this juncture (compared to Ann Harding's $93,913 salary for *The Conquerors*), so who could blame him if he seemed a bit lackadaisical at times. **Renegades Of The West** was one of those times, with the top cowboy somnambulating his way through Frank Richardson Pierce's story (screenplay Albert Shelby LeVino) about a man who goes to jail to get the goods on cattle thieves who have done away with his father. A baby appeared for the hero's adoption, adding some sweetening for saccharine tastes, and Betty Furness (left) furnished feminine decoration, but it was still one of Keene's most slack-jawed oaters. Casey Robinson directed, B. F. Zeidman was the associate producer, and Rosco Ates, James Mason (not to be confused with the later star), Carl Miller, Max Wagner, Rockcliffe Fellowes, Roland Southern and Jules Cowles were also involved. The film was a remake of FBO's *The Miracle Baby*, which starred Harry Carey in 1923.

▽

△

Rockabye was an out-and-out disaster that damaged David Selznick's credibility precisely when the renewal of his RKO contract was under consideration. The studio bought the rights to Lucia Bronder's teary paean to mother love from Gloria Swanson, then rushed it into production because of certain commitments to exhibitors and to Constance Bennett (right), its star. George Fitzmaurice, who had directed several Greta Garbo films, as well as Rudolph Valentino's triumphant *Son Of The Sheik*, was borrowed from MGM, and Selznick negotiated a deal with Paramount to use Phillips Holmes as the leading man. The finished film was so wretched that George Cukor was summoned to direct two weeks of retakes, with Joel McCrea taking over Holmes' role. The salvage job was eventually deemed worthy of release, though it was still one of the year's most abysmal efforts. Bennett was criminally miscast as an actress who forsakes her lover rather than disrupt the twin spiritual harmonies of family and motherhood. The only hearts broken by this weeper belonged to RKO executives. Final credits for directing and writing went to Cukor and Jane Murfin respectively. Paul Lukas (left), Jobyna Howland, Walter Pidgeon, Clara Blandick, Walter Catlett and June Filmer (centre) also appeared. **Rockabye** was the final feature to go out as an RKO Pathé release. Songs: 'Till The Real Thing Comes Along' Edward Eliscu, Harry Akst; 'Sleep, My Sweet' Jeanne Borlini, Nacio Herb Brown. ▷

△
Secrets Of The French Police contained six murders and one suicide, a Svengali-like plotter, a fetching damsel hypnotized to act the role of a lost Russian princess, underground passages, night burial and an astonishing number of other thriller ingredients – all delivered up in 55 minutes of screen time. Director Edward Sutherland did a fair job of making the muddled script (by Samuel Ornitz and Robert Tasker, based on a series of magazine articles by H. Ashton-Wolfe) coherent. Gregory Ratoff (left) played an evil hypnotist with appropriate menace, and Murray Kinnell handled the role of a French sleuth competently. Gwili Andre (right) as the phony princess was vacant throughout, though she was only supposed to be hypnotized part of the time. Others wrapped up in this malevolent spider web of intrigue: Frank Morgan, John Warburton, Rochelle Hudson, Christian Rub, Arnold Korff, Kendall Lee, Lucien Prival and Guido Trento.

Former FBO silent director Ralph Ince steered **Men Of America (GB: The Great Decision)** and also played the principal heavy. Neither his directorial experience nor his acting abilities were displayed to good advantage, as the film proved to be a mediocre western which dissuaded the studio from building an action series around Bill Boyd. Boyd (right) played the newest inhabitant of Paradise Valley who becomes the first suspect when a rash of robberies and murders afflicts the community. Teaming with Charles 'Chic' Sale (left), an old Indian fighter and manager of the local general store, Boyd wages war against the real culprits, a crew of escaped convicts from Leavenworth prison. The moral of the story was that the he-man western climate was 'mighty rough' on urban rats. It was also rough on action buffs who had to sit through long stretches of 'Chic' Sale's homilies and cornpone humour before the guns began to blaze. Samuel Ornitz and Jack Jungmeyer wrote the poorly constructed screenplay from a story by Humphrey Pearson and Henry McCarty. Pandro S. Berman was the associate producer, and the cast also included Dorothy Wilson (probably wishing she were back in the studio secretarial pool), Henry Armetta, Alphonz Ethier, Theresa Maxwell Conover, Eugene Strong, Fatty Layman, Fred Lindstrand and Frank Mills.

Gregory LaCava directed RKO's funniest film of ▷ the year, **The Half-Naked Truth**. A breathless romp at the expense of the publicity racket, the plot followed the career of Lee Tracy (centre right) from carnival shill to top New York advertising man and back again. Lupe Velez (left) as the object of his gimmicks and his affections, and frog-voiced Eugene Pallette (centre left) as Tracy's assistant Achilles, both added considerably to the merriment. The screenplay was by LaCava and Corey Ford, based on Ben Markson and H. N. Swanson's story which was, in turn, suggested by David Freedman's story, *Phantom Fame*. It contained one classic farcical sequence in which Tracy blackmails theatrical impresario Frank Morgan – a compromising snapshot of Morgan and Velez is the instrument and takes on a life of its own, cropping up in larger and ever more detailed versions whenever he turns around. Eventually reducing Morgan to blubbering gelatin, Tracy's ploy succeeds and so did the film – boisterously. Associate producer Pandro S. Berman's cast also included Shirley Chambers, Franklin Pangborn, Robert McKenzie (right) and Mary Mason.

mortified by some of his activities. A matter of special concern to her is the behaviour of her husband's convivial butler (Gargan) who cannot seem to grasp his proper station in life. Tom, in turn, finds his wife's friends to be droning bores. The Horace Jackson screenplay followed the protagonist's disentanglement from the marriage, and his retreat to the arms of his real love. Edward H. Griffith's tasteful direction found favour with critics who bestowed near unanimous plaudits on the film. It did excellent business during the Roxy engagement, but Depression audiences, as a whole, were not enthusiastic about the less-than-earth-shaking problems of the privileged class and the film eventually lost $110,000. Also cast: Neil Hamilton, Henry Stephenson, Leni Stengel and Donald Dillaway. David Selznick personally produced, George Folsey photographed, and Van Nest Polglase received credit for the lavish art direction. Warner Bros. later bought the rights to the play and remade it as *One More Tomorrow* in 1946, starring Dennis Morgan, Ann Sheridan and Alexis Smith.

The Animal Kingdom (GB: **The Woman In His House**), based on a Broadway play by Philip Barry, was considered special enough to be the premiere attraction at the RKO Roxy in Radio City. Leslie Howard (right), William Gargan and Ilka Chase, who had captivated audiences in the stage version, repeated their performances, and Myrna Loy (centre, borrowed from MGM) and Ann Harding (left) were added to the cast. Howard played Tom Collier, an amiable man who takes a proper wife (Loy) and soon discovers he has made a mistake. Unlike the agreeable artist (Harding) he had formerly loved, Tom's wife is positively

Edna May Oliver (right) teamed up with James Gleason (left) to solve two murders, two love affairs and other matters of crime and romance in **Penguin Pool Murder** (GB: **The Penguin Pool Mystery**). Miss Oliver portrayed angular school-marm Hildegarde Withers, who dresses like Queen Mary and carries a silver-handled umbrella, rain or shine. On an outing to the Battery Park Aquarium, she happens upon the body of Gerald Parker (Guy Usher) floating in the penguin's tank. Wise-cracking, know-it-all inspector Oscar Piper (Gleason) is called in and finds no scarcity of suspects, including the aquarium director

(Clarence H. Wilson) who had threatened Parker for selling him out in the stock market, Parker's beautiful and unfaithful wife (Mae Clarke) and one of her lovers (Donald Cook). The mystery culminates in a courtroom scene wherein Miss Withers springs a trap on the real murderer: the widow's lawyer and present lover (Robert Armstrong). The combination of Oliver and Gleason, plus the merriment and mystery as directed by George Archainbaud and scripted by Willis Goldbeck (from a novel by Stuart Palmer and story by Lowell Brentano), added up to one killing entertainment. It also led RKO to launch a new series around the Withers and Piper characters. Kenneth Macgowan earned his first associate producer credit, and the remainder of the cast included Edgar Kennedy, James Donlan and Gustav von Seyffertitz.

∇

★★★★★★★★★★★★★★★★★
1933
★★★★★★★★★★★★★★★★★

In February, David O. Selznick, having reached an impasse with corporate president Merlin Aylesworth over the question of final production authority, quit RKO for MGM. Merian C. Cooper, Selznick's former assistant, replaced him as production chief.

Just before Cooper assumed his position, RKO collapsed into equity receivership. Studio president B. B. Kahane continued to trim production-related costs, letting go of such highly paid individuals as production manager Sam Jaffe, writer Howard Estabrook and montage specialist Slavko Vorkapich. In six months, he reduced the writers' payroll by 50 per cent.

The studio also lost director George Cukor, who accompanied Selznick to MGM, and Constance Bennett, whose star-status went into eclipse. She left the studio before the end of the year. Two important additions, however, were director John Ford, signed originally to make one picture and then persuaded by Kahane to make three more, and J. R. McDonough, an executive vice-president of RCA who joined RKO as general manager of the corporation. Considered to be David Sarnoff's right-hand man, McDonough's initial tasks were to take some of the pressure off over-burdened Merlin Aylesworth and to help with the court-ordered reorganization of RKO.

In September, the studio was jolted by the news that Merian C. Cooper had suffered a heart attack. Principal assistant Pandro S. Berman took over production while Cooper recuperated. He returned to his job in mid-December.

Corporate losses for the year totalled $4,384,064 – less than half the deficit of the previous year. The two blockbuster hits were **King Kong** and **Little Women**, with **Morning Glory, One Man's Journey, Flying Down To Rio** and **Melody Cruise** also performing well. Westerns were phased out, but musicals made a dramatic comeback. During 1933, 49 pictures were released, of which 41 came from the studio, and 8 were independent productions.

Irene Dunne (centre) and Charles Bickford (left) were ill-used in **No Other Woman**, an arch and banal melodrama directed by J. Walter Ruben. Bickford played a happy-go-lucky steel worker whose ambitious wife (Dunne) finds a way to make him a millionaire. Emotionally unprepared to deal with his good fortune, he soon falls under the spell of temptress Gwili Andre, leading to a sensational divorce trial and his eventual humiliation and imprisonment. Wanda Tuchock and Bernard Schubert wrote the strained scenario from a story by Owen Francis, and Eugene Walter's play *Just A Woman*. Also cast: Eric Linden (right), Christian Rub, Leila Bennett, J. Carrol Naish, Buster Miles and Hilda Vaughn. All in all, it was one of the most feeble films made during David O. Selznick's tenure. The picture was a partial remake of *Just A Woman*, based on Walter's play, and released by First National in 1925 with Claire Windsor and Conway Tearle.

Lili Damita laboured valiantly to salvage **Goldie Gets Along** and almost managed it, despite the cliché-laden script by William A. Drake (from a book by Hawthorne Hurst), and Malcolm St Clair's dreary direction. Miss Damita (left) made a charming Goldie LaFarge who abandons her New Jersey home and her sweetheart (Charles Morton) to seek the spotlights of Hollywood. On her way west she gets mixed up in a beauty contest racket engineered by Sam Hardy. Wriggling away from Hardy, she proceeds to the movie capital where (would you believe it), her old beau is now a leading man in films. Soon she is his equal, but when Morton informs her that he is quitting and going back to New Jersey, she hesitates and then, her voice cracking with emotion, begs him to take her along. Poor Goldie is fed up with the world of glamour, while audiences were just fed up – period – with her brainless story. Other sacrificial victims: Nat Pendleton (right), Lita Chevret, Arthur Hoyt, Henry Fink, Bradley Page and Lee Moran. J. G. Bachmann produced for King Motion Pictures, with RKO functioning as distributor.

Bronco-buster Tom Keene (left) was mistaken for notorious killer 'Denver Ed' in **The Cheyenne Kid**. It took plenty of shooting, a flurry of fisticuffs, and even a well-aimed vial of acid to straighten out the misunderstanding, but all ended well, with Tom in the embrace of heroine Mary Mason (right). Robert Hill directed this undistinctive chapter in the Keene series, from a story by W. C. Tuttle and screenplay by Jack Curtis. Also cast: Rosco Ates, Otto Hoffman, Al Bridge, Alan Roscoe and Anderson Lawler. The tale had been filmed under the title *Man In The Rough* with Bob Steele for FBO in 1928 and would sally forth again as *The Fargo Kid* in 1940, starring Tim Holt.

W. W. Jacobs' celebrated story, and a stage version of it by Louis N. Parker, provided the inspiration for **The Monkey's Paw**. C. Aubrey Smith (left) played Sergeant Major Morris, who carries the accursed amulet from India to England, where Ivan Simpson (centre left) and Louise Carter (right) take advantage of its three wishes to their everlasting sorrow. Director Wesley Ruggles made the horror palpable, the climactic scene in which the couple's dead son returns from the grave being particularly effective. Graham John wrote the screenplay, including an 'it was all a dream' tag calculated to make audiences feel a bit better about the disturbing events. That was a mistake, for it short-circuited the frightening impact of all that had come before. Pandro S. Berman was the associate producer; the secondary players included Bramwell Fletcher (centre right, the son), Betty Lawford, Winter Hall, Herbert Bunston, Nena Quartaro, LeRoy Mason, J. M. Kerrigan and Nigel De Brulier. Though a competent effort, the picture did not attract much business and was Wesley Ruggles' last directorial job for RKO.

It took two directors – Harlan Thompson and Slavko Vorkapich – to handle **The Past Of Mary Holmes**, but neither was able to keep principal actors Helen MacKellar (right) and Eric Linden under control. Each tried to out-do the other, yielding 70 minutes of frantic scene chewing. Rex Beach's novel, as adapted by Marion Dix and Edward Doherty for associate producer Bartlett Cormack, concerned a former opera star (MacKellar) who loses her voice, takes to the gin bottle, and plunges herself and her son (Linden), whom she blames for her impairment, into a gutter existence. To get revenge and her name in the papers, she concocts a story about Linden killing a man-about-town. The court trial displayed some of the most dreadful acting ever captured on celluloid, before the mother's mandatory change of heart, and subsequent capture of the real killer led to a happy ending. Jean Arthur (left) and Richard 'Skeets' Gallagher were also featured, and Ivan Simpson (centre), Clay Clement, J. Carrol Naish, Rosco Ates, Rochelle Hudson, John Sheehan, Franklin Parker, Edward Nugent and Jane Darwell completed the cast. The film was a remake of *The Goose Woman* (Beach's original title), a 1925 Universal production which starred Louise Dresser, Jack Pickford and Constance Bennett.

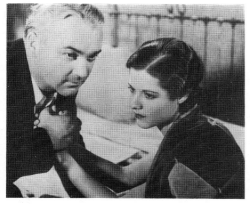

Once again digging around in its own backyard for inspiration, RKO came up with **Lucky Devils**, a romance about Hollywood's death-defying stunt men. The formula plot centred on reckless veteran Bill Boyd (left) who begins to lose his nerve after falling in love. This was, of course, just a pretext to show off a plethora of hair-raising stunts: autos crashing into plate glass windows, a fight on a burning roof, a death ride through tumultuous rapids, etc. Director Ralph Ince did a passable job of orchestrating the components in Agnes Christine Johnston and Ben Markson's screenplay, based on a story by Casey Robinson and real-life stunt man Bob Rose. Bill Boyd was assisted by lovely Dorothy Wilson (right) as his pregnant wife, William Gargan as his virile, good-humoured pal, and an able support group that included stunt man Rose, Rosco Ates, William Bakewell, Julie Haydon, Bruce Cabot, Rochelle Hudson, Creighton Chaney, Phyllis Fraser, Betty Furness and Ward Bond. Merian C. Cooper, who had a taste for vigorous, action-oriented pictures, was associate producer.

Jack Oakie (left) navigated his way through **Sailor Be Good**, a so-so comedy directed by James Cruze. Having grown attached to the Navy uniform in *The Fleet's In* and RKO's *Hit The Deck*, Oakie gave a roaring impersonation of Jonesy, a gob boxing champion who spars for the affections of Vivienne Osborne (right). As 'Red', the dance-hall hostess with a sailor in every port, Miss Osborne was the most interesting character, but scenarists Viola Brothers Shore and Ethel Doherty didn't provide her with much to do. Instead, they concentrated on Jonesy, marrying him off to society debutante Gertrude Michael and then arranging his release from the social register for a return to the ring – and 'Red'. The rest of the cast, including George E. Stone, Lincoln Stedman, Max Hoffman Jr, Huntley Gordon, Gertrude Sutton and Charles Coleman was mainly required to stand around and appear interested in the goings-on. Ralph Spence and Viola Brothers Shore wrote the wise-cracking dialogue, and Joseph I. Schnitzer and Samuel Zierler produced for Jefferson Pictures Corporation.

One of David O. Selznick's last RKO triumphs ▷ was **Topaze**, an adaptation of Marcel Pagnol's play about a mousy French schoolteacher who learns the wicked ways of the business world and then turns them to his advantage. Selznick was apprehensive about the play's satirical thrust (notorious box-office cyanide) but felt it would have a chance in the market place if John Barrymore played the lead role. Barrymore (illustrated) agreed, and Harry D'Arrast was hired to direct. With the assistance of screenwriter Ben Hecht (working from Benn W. Levy's adaptation of the drama) and a superb cast (especially Myrna Loy, Reginald Mason, Jackie Searl, Jobyna Howland and Albert Conti), they turned out a delightfully parodic tale that still seems fresh and bracing today. One of the plot elements in **Topaze** made Myrna Loy (on loan from MGM) the mistress of Reginald Mason. This relationship was shown quite openly for what it was, and even discussed at several moments. When, however, RKO decided to re-release the film in 1936, it was rejected by industry censor Joseph Breen because of the existence of this promiscuous relationship without 'compensating moral values'. Thus, a picture considered eminently suitable for public viewing in 1933 and named one of the best American films of the year by the National Board of Review, was later banned from domestic theatres, thanks to the infamous Production Code. And if movies of the late 1930s and 1940s seem bland compared to pre-1934 offerings, this story suggests why. The French produced three screen versions of the play, released in 1932, 1936 and 1952.

There was a great deal of plot in **The Great Jasper**, but the main emphasis was on character. Richard Dix (right) played the eponymous hero, an irresponsible and irresistible charmer who gets in enough hot water to last three lifetimes. The H. W. Hanemann–Robert Tasker screenplay, based on Fulton Oursler's novel, followed Jasper Horn from woman to woman and from job to job, until he finds his niche as a rich and famous fortune teller in Atlantic City. The day of reckoning finally arrives when his bastard son (by the wife of a former employer), practising the same heartless wiles as his father, ruins the happiness of Jasper's legitimate son. Ably directed by J. Walter Ruben, Richard Dix did his best to impersonate a man who, according to studio publicity, 'kept too many home fires burning', but he didn't radiate the charisma necessary to be a fully acceptable Don Juan. Still, the film was adequate entertainment, and boasted strong secondary performances from Edna May Oliver (left), Florence Eldridge (as Jasper's prudish wife) and Bruce Cabot. Wera Engles, Walter Walker, David Durand, Betty Furness and James Bush were also cast. Kenneth Macgowan was the associate producer.

'He's not just a movie actor, he's a real guy,' says Edgar Kennedy of Tom Keene (left) in **Scarlet River**, a tiny gem of a picture about a western movie company running out of wide open spaces in which to operate. Kennedy played the frustrated director of the film-within-a-film, starring (who else?) Tom Keene. Eventually the crew ends up at Scarlet River Ranch, which evil foreman Creighton Chaney (Lon Jr) is trying to wrest from Dorothy Wilson (right). Keene steps out from in front of the cameras, proving Kennedy's statement on target by saving the girl and subduing the villain. Otto Brower directed from a slightly self-conscious but amiable screenplay by Harold Shumate. The players included Betty Furness, Rosco Ates, Billy Butts, Hooper Atchley, Jack Raymond, James Mason and Yakima Canutt, with cameos by Joel McCrea, Myrna Loy and Bruce Cabot (glimpsed in the studio commissary). David Lewis was the associate producer.

W. Somerset Maugham provided the brittle, sarcastic material for **Our Betters**, a Constance Bennett vehicle about social pretensions and Anglo-American relationships. Director George Cukor was on the job from day one of shooting which guaranteed that the outcome would be altogether superior to the wretched *Rockabye* the previous year. Bennett (foreground) portrayed an American hardware heiress who marries titled gentleman Alan Mowbray. Discovering that he is only interested in her money and has no intention of giving up his mistress (a brief appearance by Finis Barton) Bennett takes her revenge on the entire London social milieu. Jane Murfin and Harry Wagstaff Gribble wrote the articulate adaptation for producer David O. Selznick, and Charles Rosher was responsible for the hard-edged photography. Violet Kemble-Cooper, Phoebe Foster, Charles Starrett, Grant Mitchell, Anita Louise (standing), Gilbert Roland, Minor Watson and Hugh Sinclair played other significant roles. ▽

Junior Durkin (left) played a 17-year-old amateur sleuth in **Man Hunt**, a J. G. Bachmann production that was amateurish through and through. Sam Mintz and Leonard Praskins authored the script, following the correspondence-school detective through a night replete with murder, the discovery of a fortune in stolen diamonds, and a confrontation with the bald-headed killer. Charlotte Henry (right) appeared as the girl in distress. Irving Cummings was the director, and allowed precocious Mr Durkin to run wild, thus assuring that his film would be acceptable to Saturday matinee crowds but not to anyone else. Dorothy Reid (actually billed as Mrs Wallace Reid), Arthur Vinton, Edward Le Saint, Richard Carle and Carl Gross Jr were also in it. **Man Hunt** was made independently by King Motion Pictures and released by RKO. ▽

Christopher Strong provided Katharine Hepburn (illustrated) with her first starring role as Lady Cynthia Darrington, a record-breaking aviatrix who falls passionately in love with Sir Christopher Strong (Colin Clive). Their affair culminates in pregnancy, but Sir Christopher cannot bring himself to desert his kindly wife (Billie Burke). Facing an impossible situation, Lady Cynthia commits suicide by deliberately crashing her airplane. Hepburn's performance and the taut direction of Dorothy Arzner added new dimensions to the soap opera genre; and the script (by Zoe Akins, from the novel by Gilbert Frankau) created a screen persona for Miss Hepburn that she would build upon for the rest of her career — independent, intelligent, courageous but, at the same time, vulnerable and sadly wistful due to her separation from orthodox life styles. The only significant flaw was the casting of Colin Clive as her lover; he appeared so stiff and ineffectual throughout that one had trouble believing the heroine would have anything to do with him, much less sacrifice her life on his account. The cast also included Helen Chandler, Ralph Forbes, Irene Browne, Jack LaRue and Desmond Roberts; David Selznick personally produced, employing Pandro S. Berman as his associate.

From primordial jungle to last stand atop the Empire State Building came **King Kong**, the simian superstar of one of the most original motion pictures ever made. Known at various times in its production history as *The Beast*, *The Eighth Wonder* and *Kong* before the final title was determined, the picture began principal photography in August 1932 but was not released until March 1933, the Depression's darkest hour. This was, in truth, Merian C. Cooper's film. He conceived the idea, and co-directed and co-produced (with Ernest B. Schoedsack). Cooper's own love of adventure and his Barnum-like abilities were captured in the character of Carl Denham, the entrepreneur who leads the expedition to Kong's island. Robert Armstrong played the part – by far the best role and performance of his career. David O. Selznick had little to do with the picture, but when he and B. B. Kahane saw how it was developing, they squeezed other budgets to provide extra funds for its completion. The final cost was $300,000 over the original budget. Technically, **King Kong** was a stupendous feat of special effects wizardry. Chief technician Willis O'Brien's staff, including E. B. Gibson, Marcel Delgado, Fred Reese, Orville Goldner, Carroll Sheppird, Mario Larrinaga and Byron L. Crabbe, breathed life into the 50-foot ape and the other prehistoric monsters that roam through his island. Their work set a standard of excellence against which all future 'trick' pictures would be measured. On the narrative level, James Ashmore Creelman and Ruth Rose completed the screenplay from Cooper and Edgar Wallace's original story. Among the script's inspired action elements were battles between Kong and various gigantic beasts, his rampage through the streets of New York and his final, futile attempts to swat the killer airplanes that riddle his body with machine gun bullets. The story also provided a classic role for Fay Wray, as the beauty whose charms emasculate the beast. Her immortal screams, mixed with the ape's thunderous growls (sound effects by Murray Spivack) nearly blew the tops off theatres in 1933. Also cast: Bruce Cabot (as the rather ineffectual love interest), Frank Reicher (as the ship's captain), Sam Hardy, Noble Johnson, James Flavin, Steve Clemento and Victor Wong. One must not forget Max Steiner's musical score – it remains one of the most dynamic compositions in the history of film music. Before its release, MGM offered to buy **King Kong** for $400,000 more than its negative cost ($672,000). RKO wisely refused to sell, and the film earned $1,761,000 in film rentals, despite the Depression. Periodic re-issues also proved very successful. Dino De Laurentiis acquired the rights and produced a much publicized, stratospherically-budgeted, up-dated, and very poor version in 1976, with Jeff Bridges and Jessica Lange, released by Paramount.

Lionel Barrymore (right, borrowed from MGM) was the chief inducement to see **Sweepings**, a lumbering family drama directed by first-time RKO helmsman John Cromwell. Building from the ashes of the Chicago fire, Barrymore founds one of the city's great department stores. He dreams that his children will take over and continue to expand his empire, but each of them disappoints him in turn. In the end, the work is entrusted to an associate (Gregory Ratoff, left) who had been with the founder from the start. Lester Cohen's adaptation of his own novel was stuffy and lugubrious, and although Barrymore delivered an affecting performance, the rest of the cast (including Eric Linden, William Gargan, Gloria Stuart, Alan Dinehart, Helen Mack, Lucien Littlefield, George Meeker and Esther Muir) hardly distinguished themselves. David O. Selznick received his last executive producer credit, and Pandro S. Berman was the associate. RKO remade the picture in 1939 under the title *Three Sons*, with Edward Ellis in the Barrymore role, and William Gargan cast again, but playing the part taken by Alan Dinehart in this version.

India Speaks was a laughable attempt to blend a staged drama about a white man who violates the sanctity of a Hindu temple, with documentary travelogue footage of the country. The advertising promised all sorts of titillations ('an amazing adventure in a fabulous land where a thousand golden temples hide a million sins'), but the Walter Futter production delivered, instead, a number of repellent views of native culture, including loathsome beggars, starving children and religious fanatics who have spikes driven through their faces. Richard Halliburton (left), an author and adventurer, played the main part in the staged story and also spoke the narration. There *were* some interesting moments, including insights into Buddhism and shots of the garden spots of Kashmir, but viewers who came expecting something exotic and spicy no doubt left in an understandable state of rage. Since there was no directorial credit, one assumes that either Futter or Halliburton was in charge. Norman Houston wrote the dialogue, and Peverell Marley, Robert Connell and H. T. Cowling photographed. RKO distributed for the Futter Corporation.

The bad guys in **Son Of The Border** were a mob preying on stage coaches bringing gold into the new territory. Tom Keene (left), in charge of the law and order contingent, mistakenly kills his friend Creighton Chaney (right), who is mixed up with the outlaws, and then adopts the dead man's kid brother (David Durand). Except for some well-staged action scenes, there was not much meat here for carnivorous western zealots. Lloyd Nosler directed Wellyn Totman's story and screenplay, which gave roles to Julie Haydon, Edgar Kennedy, Al Bridge, Charles King and Claudia Coleman. Nicholas Musuraca shot the picture for associate producer David Lewis.

In the wake of a dispute related to their new contract, and one outing for Columbia called *So This Is Africa*, Bert Wheeler and Robert Woolsey returned to their home base to begin a new series, of which **Diplomaniacs** was the first instalment. The comic components remained the same as before in this zany story of Willy Nilly (Wheeler, right) and Hercules Glub (Woolsey, left) who are sent to a Geneva peace conference as representatives of the Adoop Indians. There was one difference, though – that of cost. The film came in at $242,000 as compared to $408,000 for *Hold 'Em Jail* and $532,000 for *Girl Crazy*. It was easier to turn a profit at the lower figure, and **Diplomaniacs** clicked to the tune of $65,000. Joseph L. Mankiewicz and Henry Myers wrote the screenplay from a story by Mankiewicz, providing roles for Marjorie White, Louis Calhern, Phyllis Barry, Hugh Herbert, Edgar Kennedy and Richard Carle. William Seiter directed, Merian C. Cooper received his first credit as executive producer and Sam Jaffe was the associate producer. Song: 'Sing To Me' Harry Akst, Edward Eliscu.

Irene Dunne gained stature with **The Silver Cord**, a Sidney Howard play smoothly directed by John Cromwell. This tale of suffocating mother love involved two battles – the first between Dunne (left) and Laura Hope Crews over Crews' elder son Joel McCrea (right), and the second between Crews and Frances Dee (borrowed from Paramount) who loves the other son, Eric Linden. The film was packed with long rhetorical speeches and included some unintentionally humorous moments, such as the mother imploring her sons to come back for their overcoats as they rush off to rescue Dee, who has attempted suicide. **The Silver Cord** did, however, provide Miss Dunne with an opportunity to deliver a firm, powerful performance, thus raising her standing in the constantly shifting polls of Hollywood popularity. Son-devouring Crews also fared well in Jane Murfin's screenplay. Helen Cromwell, Gustav von Seyffertitz, Reginald Pasch and Perry Ivins were also cast; Pandro S. Berman produced and Charles Rosher supervised the photography.

One wonders what David Sarnoff and NBC-RKO president Merlin Aylesworth thought of **Professional Sweetheart** (GB: **Imaginary Sweetheart**), an audacious satire on radio programming. William Seiter directed Ginger Rogers (right) as Glory Eden, Purity Girl of the Ippsie-Wippsie radio hour sponsored by a man named Ipswitch (Gregory Ratoff), fondly known as the wash cloth king. A much ballyhooed romance develops between Glory and Jim Davey (Norman Foster, left, borrowed from Fox), a Kentucky hayseed, and their subsequent wedding is broadcast live. Nutty complications follow when Glory falls in love with rustic living. It requires a merger of Ipswitch's concern with his hated rival, the Kelsey Dishrag Company, to get Glory back on the air for the Ippsie-Kelsey Clothie programme. The madcap screenplay by Maurine Watkins gave roles to ZaSu Pitts, Frank McHugh, Allen Jenkins, Franklin Pangborn, Edgar Kennedy (as Kelsey), Lucien Littlefield, Frank Darien and Sterling Holloway. H. N. Swanson was associate producer. Song: 'My Imaginary Sweetheart' Harry Akst, Edward Eliscu.

A punctual murderer kept his engagements in ▷ **Tomorrow At Seven**, a rather anaemic mystery starring Chester Morris (right) and Vivienne Osborne. The biggest enigma of all was why the victims make themselves available at the appointed hour, since the specialist in homicide (who uses an ace of spades as his calling card) always informs them in advance of their forthcoming demise. Anyway, a pair of bumbling detectives, played by Allen Jenkins (left) and Frank McHugh (centre), get after Mr Ace, making it *de rigueur* that thriller novelist Morris, who is collecting material for a book on the Ace (when he isn't romancing Miss Osborne, the daughter of one of the victims) will solve the puzzle. Ralph Spence's screenplay was not without wit or invention, but Ray Enright's flat direction allowed much of the excitement to evaporate. Henry Stephenson, Grant Mitchell, Oscar Apfel, Cornelius Keefe, Edward Le Saint, Charles B. Middleton, Virginia Howell and Gus Robinson constituted the supporting cast. Joseph I. Schnitzer and Samuel Zierler produced this Jefferson Pictures Corporation potboiler.

A 16-room hospital, complete in every detail from ether and iodoform to operating tables and wards, was constructed for **Emergency Call**. The sets by Van Nest Polglase and Al Herman actually contained a good deal more interest than Houston Branch and Joseph L. Mankiewicz's screenplay (based on a story by John B. Clymer and James Ewens) which was clotted with clichés from beginning to end. Bill Boyd (right) portrayed a promising surgeon who discovers that his hospital is controlled by ambulance-chasing racketeers preying on the halt, sick and injured. When defective anaesthetic causes his pal William Gargan to die on the operating table, Boyd mounts a crusade and disinfects the place of all appropriate vermin. Edward Cahn directed as if he wanted desperately to be done with it – and who could blame him? Wynne Gibson (left), Betty Furness, Reginald Mason, Edwin Maxwell, George E. Stone, Merna Kennedy, Oscar Apfel, Ruth Fallows and Jane Darwell led the supporting cast and Alberta Vaughn, an FBO star of the 1920s, played a bit part. The associate producer was Sam Jaffe.

Ferret-like George E. Stone's big ideas got the best of him in **The Big Brain** (GB: **Enemies Of Society**), a Sy Bartlett story and script (continuity by Warren Duff) which did not, unfortunately, yield a big picture. Stone rises from New York barbershop bootblack to successful promoter of worthless stocks. It appears he might even get away with his swindling, having arranged for simpleton Phillips Holmes (right) to take the rap, until a lady smokes him out. The lady is Fay Wray (left), and she has precisely the same effect on the Machiavellian brain as she did on the beast in *King Kong*. Her charms cause Stone to let down his guard long enough for the authorities to put the clamps on him. George Archainbaud's unenthusiastic direction was matched by the acting of the principals and the supporting cast, which included Minna Gombell, Lilian Bond, Berton Churchill, Reginald Mason, Sam Hardy, Edgar Norton, Charles McNaughton and Lucien Littlefield. Reginald Owen was the one exception, giving a lively performance as one of Stone's associates. Samuel Bischoff produced the Admiral Productions film, RKO distributed.
▽

Melody Cruise rekindled the studio's interest in musicals and also launched a blossoming RKO talent: director Mark Sandrich. After writing and directing shorts (including the Academy Award-winning *So This Is Harris*) and assisting Norman Taurog on *Hold 'Em Jail*, Sandrich was promoted to features by Merian C. Cooper, at the insistence of Lou Brock, head of the short subject department, who was associate producer on **Melody Cruise**, his first RKO feature. Typical of first-time directors, Sandrich indulged in a wide variety of camera pyrotechnics including trick wipes, split screens and superimpositions, but he did not allow these gimmicks to interfere with the story, or disturb the musical sequences of his picture. The story (screenplay by Sandrich and Ben Holmes) was set on board a steamship bound for California from New York. Millionaire Phil Harris (right), and Charles Ruggles (left, borrowed from Paramount), whose job is to keep Harris out of the matrimonial clutches of a bevy of designing females (one of them Betty Grable), are among the passengers. The film quickly assumed the trappings of classic farce with Ruggles, especially, emerging as a polished and witty practitioner of the form. Will Jason and Val Burton wrote the musical numbers, which were fairly forgettable, but Sandrich infused the action with such energy and *joie de vivre* (and a ballet staged by Dave Gould) that the movie became one of the company's major hits of the year. Helen Mack, Greta Nissen, Chick Chandler, June Brewster (centre), Shirley Chambers, Florence Roberts and Marjorie Gateson were also featured. Songs included: 'Isn't This A Night For Love', 'This Is The Hour', 'I Met Her At A Party', 'He's Not The Marrying Kind'.

There was a modest amount of pleasure to be derived from **Flying Devils** (GB: **The Flying Circus**), a foray into the blue yonder which starred Arline Judge (left), Bruce Cabot (right), Eric Linden (centre left) and Ralph Bellamy (centre right). A carnival air circus provided the setting for triangle theatrics, with Linden falling for Judge, who is married to Bellamy, and the latter seeking revenge. The ultimate confrontation takes place in mid-air, where Linden's noble brother (Cabot) sabotages Bellamy's plans and dies for his trouble. Bellamy also conveniently crashes, freeing Miss Judge to make a proper attachment to Mr Linden. Critics blasted the film for its tired plot and inferior dialogue (screenplay by Louis Stevens and Byron Morgan from a story by Stevens), as well as the consistently deficient performances of the top-liners. Nevertheless, director Russell Birdwell, best known as one of the demon press agents of the era, was able to pump enough zip into the proceedings to please the public; it became a bantam box-office hit. Cliff Edwards, June Brewster, Frank LaRue and Mary Carr led the support, and David Lewis was the associate producer. ▷

Screenwriter Harold Shumate and director Otto Brower made the one unforgivable 'B' western mistake in **Cross-Fire**: they allowed the over-elaborate plot to get in the way of the action. The result was a dull Tom Keene horse opera, occasionally enlivened by rib-tickling bits of business from old pro Edgar Kennedy. Keene (left) was somewhat in the background in this one, the story of five grizzled westerners who became outlaws when one of them is unjustly accused of murder. The old-timers were played by Lafe McKee, Charles K. French, Nick Cogley, Jules Cowles and Thomas Brower, with Betty Furness (right), Edward Phillips, Stanley Blystone, Murdock MacQuarrie and Kid Wagner also participating. David Lewis was the associate producer, and Tom MacNamara wrote additional dialogue for this final chapter in the Tom Keene series. The film should not be confused with RKO's famous study of anti-semitism, released in 1947 as *Crossfire*.

Constance Bennett (left) was badly miscast in **Bed Of Roses**. She played a callous reform school 'graduate' who is determined to have her 'bed of roses' no matter what the cost. As is usual with such plots, she eventually sees the error of her ways, but too late, alas, for audiences, who lost sympathy with so crude and despicable a character as she was made to seem. Joel McCrea (right), as the captain of a Mississippi River cotton barge, and John Halliday, as a prominent New Orleans publisher, competed for the low-bred lady's affections, and Pert Kelton turned in a respectable Mae West impersonation as Constance's accomplice. Wanda Tuchock wrote the contrived screenplay; Gregory LaCava directed, and teamed with Eugene Thackrey to write the dialogue. Samuel Hinds, Franklin Pangborn, Tom Francis, Robert Emmett O'Connor, Eileen Percy and Jane Darwell also appeared for producer Pandro S. Berman. Miss Bennett's star status was now in jeopardy, thanks to pictures like this one and *Rockabye*.

Double Harness was one of the year's liveliest comedies, thanks to the charm and finesse of Ann Harding (left), and the suavity and polish of William Powell. Edward Poor Montgomery's play, as adapted by Jane Murfin, addressed itself to the old problem of the women who tricks her man into marriage, then sets about earning his love honestly. Powell (right), always at ease in a playboy role, and his ash-blonde leading lady, matched each other step-for-step under John Cromwell's exemplary direction. Also cast: Lucile Browne, Henry Stephenson, Lilian Bond, George Meeker, Reginald Owen, Kay Hammond, Leigh Allen, Hugh Huntley and Wallis Clark. Kenneth Macgowan was the associate producer.

Headline Shooter (GB: **Evidence In Camera**) was a cheaply made but efficient grafting of a fictional tale onto footage of actual fires, earthquakes, floods, and other natural disasters. Wallace West's story was written for the screen by Agnes Christine Johnston and Allen Rivkin with additional dialogue by Arthur Kober. The screenplay glorified reckless newsreel photographer William Gargan (left), who is married to his work but in love with fellow journalist Frances Dee (right). She yearns for romance, and a more stable life, and inclines towards gentlemanly Ralph Bellamy for a time. But a final confrontation with gangsters, which threatens the lives of all three principals, convinces the heroine that the 'shooter' is the only man who can make her happy. As he had in *The Sport Parade*, Robert Benchley added a few inspired moments of hilarity as a radio announcer, while Jack LaRue, Gregory Ratoff, Wallace Ford, Betty Furness, Hobart Cavanaugh, June Brewster, Franklin Pangborn and Dorothy Burgess did well in support. David Lewis was the associate producer and Otto Brower directed. ▽

The search for a dead gangster's hidden fortune prompted the action in **Before Dawn**, directed by Irving Pichel. This inexpensive spine-tingler included a haunted house, a clairvoyant, a mysterious death mask and a superfluity of murders and 'accidental' deaths. Stuart Erwin (left, borrowed from MGM) enjoyed success as a detective who hits upon the idea of employing clairvoyant Dorothy Wilson (right) to help in the solving of crime. The psychic lady soon discerns the evil designs of crazed medico Warner Oland. Pichel drove the story along at lightening speed, and provided an hour's worth of pleasure for chiller fans. Dudley Digges, Gertrude W. Hoffmann, Oscar Apfel, Jane Darwell and Frank Reicher were also in the cast. Edgar Wallace, whose fertile pen had produced more than 200 novels, 1000 short stories and 20 plays, wrote the original story in Hollywood shortly before his death in 1932, and Garrett Fort wrote the screenplay. The associate producer was Shirley Burden.

A potboiler that never even simmered, **No Marriage Ties** featured an energetic but self-defeating performance by Richard Dix. Cast as a heavy-drinking roué, Dix (right) becomes the nation's greatest advertising man by means of fraud and deception. His life is shattered by the threatened exposure of his unethical business methods and the suicide of a former fiancée but, after hitting the skids, he is rescued from speakeasy limbo by Elizabeth Allan (left, borrowed from MGM). The exertions of five writers (Arch Gaffney and Charles W. Curran who wrote the play, Sam Mintz who adapted it and H. W. Hanemann and Arthur Ceasar who penned the dialogue) failed to rescue the story from run-of-the-mill tedium, and J. Walter Ruben directed without distinction. Associate producer William Goetz's cast also featured Doris Kenyon, Alan Dinehart, David Landau, Hobart Cavanaugh, Hilda Vaughn and Charles Wilson.

◁ Writer Ruth Rose and her husband, director Ernest B. Schoedsack, who collaborated on *King Kong* and its sequel, also contributed **Blind Adventure** to the studio program. This mystery drama set in London's West End was a strange, muddled fiction about thugs and thieves who live in close proximity to highly respectable Britishers. An American, played by Robert Armstrong (right), stumbles upon the den of criminals and, assisted by charming burglar Roland Young and plucky heroine Helen Mack (left), noses around until the many bewilderments are cleared up. The creators tried unsuccessfully to achieve a jocular tone but the end product was laboured and disappointing. Ralph Bellamy, John Miljan, Laura Hope Crews, Henry Stephenson, Phyllis Barry, John Warburton, Marjorie Gateson, Beryl Mercer, Tyrell Davis, Forrester Harvey, George K. Arthur and Ivan Simpson were also in it for associate producer David Lewis.

Katharine Hepburn collected her first Academy Award for **Morning Glory**. Cast to type as a garrulous New Englander who arrives in New York with one burning ambition – to be an actress – she delivered an effervescent performance under the careful direction of Lowell Sherman. The story (based on a play by Zoe Akins, adapted by Howard J. Green) was all about how, after a series of disappointments, Eva Lovelace (Hepburn) gets her big chance when blonde star Mary Duncan attempts to strong-arm producer Adolphe Menjou for more money just before the curtain rises on her new play. The producer fires his star, Eva takes her place and triumphs. A love triangle involving Hepburn (right) with Menjou (left) and writer Douglas Fairbanks Jr was grafted uncomfortably onto the main plot, and Sherman failed to disguise the stage origins of the story. Still, Hepburn was sufficiently bewitching to banish one's reservations. Life imitated art for RKO, which now had a rapidly ascending star of its own in Miss Hepburn. Also cast: C. Aubrey Smith, Don Alvarado, Richard Carle, Tyler Brooke, Fredric Santley and Geneva Mitchell. Pandro S. Berman produced. In 1957, the studio remade the film as *Stage Struck*, with Susan Strasberg, Henry Fonda and Christopher Plummer.

After scoring in *Professional Sweetheart*, Ginger ▷ Rogers (centre) and Norman Foster (left, on loan from Fox) were again teamed to pleasing effect in **Rafter Romance**. Novelist John Wells' cute story had Foster and Rogers, each hard-pressed to make ends meet, entering into an arrangement with landlord George Sidney (right) to occupy the same Greenwich Village apartment. She has access during the evening, when he is at work, and he takes over while she sells ice boxes during the day. The two 'roommates' have never met, but nonetheless form definite opinions about one another. He believes her to be a fussy, fidgety old spinster, while she visualizes him as a crabby, belligerent upstart. When they do meet — away from the apartment — they naturally fall in love, all the while complaining of their distaste for their respective lodgers. In due course the truth is revealed and, under William Seiter's lively direction, a superior RKO comedy was delivered. Robert Benchley, Laura Hope Crews, Guinn Williams and Sidney Miller were also cast. H. W. Hanemann and Sam Mintz wrote the screenplay (adaptation by Glenn Tryon) for associate producer Kenneth Macgowan. RKO remade it as *Living On Love* in 1937, with James Dunn and Whitney Bourne.

A healer of hearts as well as bodies was physician Eli Watt (Lionel Barrymore, left) in **One Man's Journey**. Returning to the rural community where he was reared, the doctor irons out difficulties in the path of true love for Dorothy Jordan and James Bush and repeats the service for Joel McCrea (right) and Frances Dee. He also attends to all the ailments of the townspeople, often receiving vegetables as recompense for his services. An uplifting testimonial to the human capacity for self-sacrifice and nobility, the Katharine Haviland-Taylor story, written for the screen by Lester Cohen and Samuel Ornitz, impressed critics and filmgoers alike. The impeccable direction was the work of John Robertson, Pandro S. Berman produced, and the cast also included May Robson, David Landau, Buster Phelps, June Filmer, Oscar Apfel, Samuel Hinds and Hale Hamilton. Both Barrymore and Robson were borrowed from MGM. The 1938 remake, entitled *A Man To Remember* with Edward Ellis and Anne Shirley, proved even more popular than this original version. ▽

Something resembling Noah's flood struck the world in **Deluge**, toppling skyscrapers and generally causing devastation. Most of the action took place somewhere about 40 miles from 'where New York City was'. Here a battle develops between hero Sidney Blackmer (left) and villain Fred Kohler over Peggy Shannon (right), presumed to be the only woman still alive in that part of the world. Most of the special effects were crudely executed, but they were certainly superior to the fatuous plot, frenzied acting and mundane dialogue of this early forerunner of the 'disaster' movie. Felix E. Feist directed from a screenplay by John Goodrich and Warren B. Duff, based on S. Fowler Wright's novel. Admiral Productions made the low-grade drivel, employing Samuel Bischoff as associate producer and Lois Wilson, Matt Moore, Ralf Harolde, Samuel Hinds and Edward Van Sloan in secondary roles. ▷

◁ **Midshipman Jack** was the inconsequential story of a shiftless lad who finally comes of age, thanks to the military discipline at the US Naval Academy. Bruce Cabot (left) played the title role, learning lessons in pride and loyalty which he then passes along to the eager freshmen who are his responsibility. He even gets to marry the Commander's daughter (Betty Furness) in the end. Christy Cabanne directed from a screenplay by Frank Wead and F. McGrew Willis for associate producer Glendon Allvine. Arthur Lake (right) and his sister Florence added humorous diversion, and Frank Albertson (centre), John Darrow, Purnell Pratt and Margaret Seddon were also in it. RKO re-cycled the story as *Annapolis Salute* in 1937, starring James Ellison and Marsha Hunt.

There was nothing good to be said about **Flaming** ▷ **Gold**, a convoluted melo starring Bill Boyd (right) and Pat O'Brien (left). A pair of wildcatters punching holes in the Mexican desert, they are soon attacked by the giant World Wide Oil Company which is determined to put them out of business. Just why World Wide would care about these small fry is never made clear, and neither is a subsequent brouhaha that develops between the two pals after Boyd marries Mae Clarke (on loan from MGM). A new gusher came in at the end, soiling the faces of the principals but reaping no box-office by-product for the studio. Ralph Ince's sluggish direction elicited run-of-the-mill performances from Boyd and Clarke, with Pat O'Brien contributing the few good moments. Malcolm Stuart Boylan and John Goodrich wrote the screenplay from a story by Houston Branch. Robert McWade, Helen Ware and Rollo Lloyd were also cast for associate producer Sam Jaffe.

The seen-it-all-before plot of **Chance At Heaven** was so slight and whimsical, that its familiarity did not even breed contempt. In it, dumb little rich girl Marian Nixon motors into the life of poor boy Joel McCrea (right) in her 12-cylinder roadster, upsetting the future plans of his worthy girl friend Ginger Rogers (left). The marriage of McCrea and Nixon is a predictable bust, but good sport Ginger hangs around to pick up the pieces. At least she understands how to bake a pie, which is more than her wealthy rival can handle. Vina Delmar wrote the story, which Julian Josephson and Sarah Y. Mason adapted. William Seiter's direction un-earthed more comedy in the tale than was actually there, and he drew some side-splitting moments from his leading lady. Also cast: Andy Devine, Lucien Littlefield, Virginia Hammond, George Meeker and Ann Shoemaker. The associate producer was H. N. Swanson.

Constant shifts from comedy to drama and back again kept audiences at **Aggie Appleby, Maker of Men** (GB: **Cupid In The Rough**) speculating about what manner of picture they had paid to see. Even after it was over, viewers still weren't sure, because director Mark Sandrich and screenwriters Humphrey Pearson and Edward Kaufman (original play by Joseph O. Kesselring) hadn't given them enough clues. As the title intimated, it was all about Aggie (Wynne Gibson, centre) who makes over Charles Farrell (left) from a softie to a tough mug, and William Gargan (right) from a hard-boiled type to a near pansy. Farrell and Gibson played everything straight and sincere, while Gargan and ZaSu Pitts dived for the funny bone at every opportunity. Nonetheless, the mish-mash featured good dialogue and catchy performances and was not altogether destroyed by its schizophrenia. Betty Furness, Blanche Frederici and Jane Darwell had secondary roles in the Pandro S. Berman production.

Irene Dunne (left), Walter Huston (right), Bruce Cabot, Edna May Oliver, Conrad Nagel, Sam Hardy and Mitchell Lewis brought Sinclair Lewis' characters to life in **Ann Vickers**. Jane Murfin's screenplay watered down the novel's content considerably, but with its distinguished cast and John Cromwell's polished direction, it still made for an appealing film. Miss Dunne played the eponymous heroine whose damaging relationship with an army officer turns her against men. Years later, as head of a model detention home for women, she meets a judge (Huston, borrowed from MGM) who changes her attitude to the opposite sex. Endless impediments stand in their way, not least of which has Huston jailed for eight years on a trumped-up bribery charge, but finally, they are happily united. The story's episodic structure contained a number of dramatic punctuations, each illuminated satisfactorily by a cast that also included Murray Kinnell, Helen Eby-Rock, Gertrude Michael, J. Carrol Naish, Sarah Padden and Reginald Barlow. Pandro S. Berman produced; Van Nest Polglase and Charles Kirk were responsible for the immaculate art direction.

Ace Of Aces was the story of a sensitive artist (Richard Dix, right) who goes reluctantly to war and is transformed by its ugly realities into a blood-thirsty aerial killer. The hero's obsession with glory destroys his relationship with society debutante Elizabeth Allan (left, borrowed from MGM), who had insisted on his participation in the hostilities in the first place. Eventually Dix is killed, and Allan is left alone to ponder the realization that her true love actually ceased to exist when he fired his first shot. J. Walter Ruben's direction did nothing to enliven John Monk Saunders' stale plot and leaden characterizations (screenplay by Saunders and H. W. Hanemann). Ralph Bellamy, Theodore Newton, Nella Walker, Anderson Lawler, Frank Conroy, Joe Sauers (later Sawyer), Arthur Jarrett, William Cagney (James' brother), Grady Sutton, Betty Furness and Edward Gargan went along for the ride. Stock footage from the Howard Hughes epic *Hell's Angels* was used in some of the flying sequences. Sam Jaffe was the associate producer.

Goodbye Love attempted to be nothing more than a frivolous confection and failed to achieve even that, sinking under the ponderous direction of H. Bruce Humberstone. A satirical broadside at the alimony racket, the story wasted the talents of farceur Charles Ruggles (right), who played a butler pretending, for part of the picture, to be an English lord and big game hunter, and Verree Teasdale (left), a slinky blonde gold-digger. Supporting players Sidney Blackmer, Mayo Methot, Phyllis Barry, Ray Walker, John Kelly, Grace Hale and Luis Alberni also went for nothing. Hampton Del Ruth wrote the threadbare story, with continuity and dialogue by Del Ruth and George Rosener and additional dialogue by John Howard Lawson. Joseph I. Schnitzer and Samuel Zierler co-produced for Jefferson Pictures Corporation. The film was Jefferson's goodbye picture; the independent ceased operations after its completion.

Constance Bennett's swan song for RKO was ▷ **After Tonight** (GB: **Sealed Lips**), an impoverished spy yarn written by Jane Murfin, Albert Shelby LeVino and Worthington Miner from a story by Murfin. The film showed a $100,000 loss, thus convincing studio executives that the actress' box-office charisma had vanished. In fact, Bennett (left) was more than adequate as a beautiful and accomplished Russian spy operating in Austria during World War I; the film's other wretched components were what doomed it to failure. Romantic conflict turned on the far-fetched device of the spy falling in love with Austrian counter-intelligence officer Gilbert Roland (right), whose job is to trap all foreign agents. Roland's wooden acting detracted from the love story, and George Archainbaud's perfunctory direction defused its potential tension and suspense. It was just an all-round botch, for which the star took a large and undeserved portion of the blame. H. N. Swanson was the associate producer, and the cast also included Edward Ellis, Sam Godfrey, Lucien Prival, Mischa Auer, Ben Hendricks Jr, Leonid Snegoff and Evelyn Carter Carrington. Song: 'Buy A Kiss' Val Burton, Will Jason.

Alfred Santell directed **The Right To Romance**, a monotonous melodrama about the effects of repressing one's amorous impulses. Ann Harding (left) played Dr Margaret Simmons, a plastic surgeon with offices in New York, who has allowed her professional dedication to bury her natural inclinations for romance and fun. On vacation in California, she runs into aviator Robert Young (right, on loan from MGM) who awakens her to life's blissful possibilities. They marry, but everything goes wrong – including the movie. Conflict emerges between sober woman and carefree man, but there was little humour or genuine pathos to imbue their disintegrating alliance with interest. Sidney Buchman and Henry McCarty wrote the screenplay from a story by associate producer Myles Connolly, giving additional roles to Nils Asther, Sari Maritza, Irving Pichel, Helen Freeman, Alden Chase, Delmar Watson, Louise Carter, Bramwell Fletcher, Patricia O'Brien, ◁ Howard Hickman and Thelma Hardwick.

Little Women was a smash hit, and one of the most important pictures ever produced by the studio. It revitalized interest in the 'classics' and in costume pictures, driving most of the Hollywood companies into a mad scramble to acquire similar material. Production chief David O. Selznick decided to film Louisa May Alcott's episodic novel about the highs and lows of a New England family during the Civil War era, but he departed for MGM before it went into production. His successor Merian C. Cooper kept the project alive, assigned Kenneth Macgowan to produce, and squeezed extra funding to upgrade the cast. Returning from MGM to direct was George Cukor. He handled the Academy Award-winning adaptation by Sarah Y. Mason and Victor Heerman with such finesse that it firmly established his reputation as a major cinematic talent. Katharine Hepburn (back centre) topped the cast, playing tomboyish Jo, and received first class support from Joan Bennett (centre), Frances Dee (right) and Jean Parker (left) as her sisters Amy, Meg and Beth respectively. Paul Lukas, Douglass Montgomery, Edna May Oliver, Spring Byington, Henry Stephenson, John Davis Lodge, Samuel Hinds, Mabel Colcord and Marion Ballou also appeared in this nostalgic triumph, photographed in the style of finely-etched ferrotypes by master cinematographer Henry Gerrard. For once, RKO's timing was impeccable. Depression audiences were ripe for the film's evocation of life in a simpler, more innocent and auspicious world. In addition, the movie business had come under fire in 1932 and 1933 for presenting an abundance of violent and sexually titillating material. **Little Women** was just the kind of film the bluenoses felt should be produced. They proclaimed it, sent their children to see it, and made it part of school curricula. RKO was the ultimate beneficiary, amassing profits of $800,000 on this irresistibly entertaining picture. The Alcott story had first been filmed by Paramount in 1919; it was remade by MGM in 1949 with June Allyson and Elizabeth Taylor in the cast.

Screenwriter Dwight Taylor spruced up John Van Druten's play, *Behold We Live*, and gave it a happy ending, but **If I Were Free** (GB: **Behold We Live**) was still only humdrum entertainment. Irene Dunne (centre) starred as the proprietor of a London antique shop who falls in love with bibulous lawyer Clive Brook (right) after she has already suffered a calamitous marriage to Nils Asther. Miss Dunne's taste in men leaves a good deal to be desired, especially since Brook's wife (Lorraine MacLean) won't even consider giving him a divorce. But Hollywood conventions lead to a change of attitude on the wife's part, and everything ends pleasantly. Elliott Nugent directed for associate producer Kenneth Macgowan. The best thing about the film was its acting, including the supporting work of Henry Stephenson, Vivian Tobin, Laura Hope Crews, Tempe Pigott and Mario Dominici (left).

▽

Astonishingly, executive producer Merian C. Cooper managed to complete a sequel to *King Kong* in the same year the original was released. **The Son Of Kong** brought back Robert Armstrong as Carl Denham, Frank Reicher as the ship's captain and Victor Wong as the Chinese cook. The Ruth Rose screenplay was devised for a small budget and its cheapness proved its undoing. The first three-quarters of the film was tepid melodrama set in an exotic port to which Armstrong as Carl Denham, Frank Reicher as the escape a horde of New Yorkers determined to sue them for unleashing Kong's rampage. A series of unlikely events leads them back to the great ape's island, where the special effects magicians finally get a chance to show off. Their work is simply not up to par, however. The various monsters, as well as the final devastating earthquake, cannot be compared to the brilliant sleight-of-hand performed in the original. Since Willis O'Brien and most of his technical crew also laboured on *King Kong*, the paltry budget and the rush to complete the film, must have compromised their artistry. As for the titular hero, Kong's offspring turns out to be a cuddly teddy bear of a beast scarcely 30 feet tall. Armstrong helps the simian escape from a quicksand bog; thereafter, the albino gorilla hangs around, saving Armstrong and ingenue Helen Mack (both illustrated with Son of Kong) from a number of horrible deaths, and mugging for the camera whenever possible. Obviously sonny didn't inherit much of papa's primordial energy, and neither did his picture. Also cast: John Marston, Lee Kohlmar and Ed Brady. Ernest B. Schoedsack directed and Archie Marshek was the associate producer.

▽

△

Flying Down To Rio was a watershed film in RKO history. It introduced one of the most famous teams in the chronicle of Hollywood musical filmmaking – Fred Astaire and Ginger Rogers (both illustrated) – and it inaugurated a series of pictures that would make the studio a leader in the production of musicals throughout the rest of the decade. Dolores Del Rio and Gene Raymond were top-billed, but Rogers and Astaire, playing members of Raymond's itinerant band, and billed fourth and fifth respectively, stole the film from its stars. This is not to denigrate the work of the latter pair: Raymond, as a flying song writer, and Del Rio, as a gorgeous Brazilian engaged to Raul Roulien, delivered engaging performances that paid off nicely within the confines of the fanciful narrative. But Astaire was a natural-born star and Rogers complemented him perfectly; when they danced the screen glowed white-hot, and who could compete with that? Associate producer Lou Brock's story, directed by Thornton Freeland, may not challenge the best Astaire–Rogers efforts, but it has a kind of outrageous exuberance that makes it endearing.

Among the memorable moments concocted by scenarists Cyril Hume, H. W. Hanemann and Erwin Gelsey (from a play by Anne Caldwell) are Raymond extemporizing a love ballad to Del Rio on the piano which he has installed in his private airplane; the famous aerial ballet climax (dance direction by Dave Gould) with scores of chorus girls, anchored to the wings of airplanes, dancing and doffing their clothes for all of Rio to see; and finally Raul Roulien's flamboyant exit from Del Rio's life, accomplished by leaping from a commercial airliner high in the clouds. Fortunately, he remembers his parachute. **Flying Down To Rio** was, and is, a lot of fun. And in the captivating 'Carioca' number (nominated for an Academy Award) a pair of performers emerged who would be RKO's class act for years to come: Fred and Ginger. Blanche Frederici, Walter Walker, Etta Moten, Roy D'Arcy, Maurice Black, Armand Kaliz, Paul Porcasi, Reginald Barlow and Eric Blore were also cast. The exceptional musical score included: 'Music Makes Me', 'Orchids In The Moonlight', 'Flying Down To Rio' Vincent Youmans, Edward Eliscu, Gus Kahn.

★★★★★★★★★★★★★★★★

1934

★★★★★★★★★★★★★★★★

Early in the year, Merian C. Cooper's health again began to fail, and he resolved to take an extended vacation in Hawaii. Pandro S. Berman was once more persuaded to step in as production topper during his absence. When he returned in May, Cooper resigned his position, but agreed personally to produce two large-scale films for the company: **She** and **The Last Days of Pompeii**.

In the meanwhile, J. R. McDonough had been named president of RKO Radio Pictures and B. B. Kahane, who had formerly held that title, was made president of a subsidiary called RKO Studios. Ned Depinet was promoted to the presidency of the distribution arm.

Pandro S. Berman was supposed to continue as head of production, but a blow-up occurred in June which allowed Berman to return to his real love: the production of individual pictures. The conflict arose between Berman and J. R. McDonough over the always sensitive issue of final production authority. McDonough, who had been working for RKO less than a year and had no training or experience in the creative areas of film, began interfering in story selection, casting and other matters that Berman rightly considered his responsibility. The subsequent show-down left RKO without a production chief, so B. B. Kahane reluctantly agreed to fill the gap. He soon instituted a 'unit production' concept, which meant that each staff producer would be responsible for a set number of features with Kahane providing advice where needed. *Time* magazine referred to RKO as 'Hollywood's most mismanaged studio' during this period, but the system would have some very positive results.

Mark Sandrich and George Stevens emerged as directors of consequence, but their former boss in the short unit, Lou Brock, was fired after his disastrous mismanagement of **Down To Their Last Yacht**. Lee Marcus, whose company service dated back to RKO's beginnings, was placed in charge of the short films.

The studio released 44 films in 1934. The net loss for the year was $310,575, —a major improvement over previous years. Top money-makers were **The Gay Divorcee, Anne Of Green Gables** and **The Silver Streak**.

Left-wing writer John Howard Lawson was to become one of the most celebrated members of the 'Hollywood Ten' during the years of McCarthy witchhunting. One could certainly discern his anti-capitalism bias in **Success At Any Price**, an unoriginal story partially redeemed by the earnest acting of Douglas Fairbanks Jr (right). Fairbanks played Joe Martin, a man who spits on the laws and mores of his time, manipulates the world of big business to make more and more money and to gain more and more power, then falls victim to his own ruthless tactics. Lawson and co-scenarist Howard J. Green, adapting Lawson's play *Success Story*, appended an unconvincing happy ending, but they made sure that the story's implicit condemnation of cut-throat competition as an evil by-product of free enterprise economics came through in unadulterated fashion. Other members of associate producer H. N. Swanson's cast: Genevieve Tobin (left), Frank Morgan, Colleen Moore, Edward Everett Horton, Nydia Westman, Allen Vincent, Henry Kolker and Spencer Charters. J. Walter Ruben directed.

◁ Jean Parker (right, borrowed from MGM) and Tom Brown (centre) proved that love can triumph over anything in **Two Alone** – over anything, that is, but a dull and dreary scenario. Parker played an orphan and Brown a reform school runaway, both enslaved by psychotic dirty old man Arthur Byron (left). After the conventional melodramatics are played out, the girl's real father (Willard Robertson) reveals his identity and sees that the lovers are properly married. Elliott Nugent's flaccid direction perfectly matched the turgid Josephine Lovett–Joseph Moncure March screenplay, in the service of which ZaSu Pitts, Beulah Bondi, Nydia Westman, Charley Grapewin, Emerson Treacy and Paul Nicholson also laboured. Dan Totheroh's play, *Wild Birds*, was the source of this excruciating 80-minute picture, overseered by associate producer David Lewis.

Hips, Hips Hooray was unremarkable, mildly successful, Wheeler–Woolsey fare. Veteran funny men Harry Ruby and Bert Kalmar wrote the songs and (with Edward Kaufman's assistance) the screenplay for associate producer H. N. Swanson. The story introduced Bert Wheeler (right) and Robert Woolsey (left) as salesmen peddling a new brand of lipstick that comes in several flavours. When the cosmetics activity begins to bog down, the two clowns get themselves involved in a cross-country auto race, which enabled director Mark Sandrich to punch in plenty of Keystone Kop-style gags. Torch singer Ruth Etting (centre), Thelma Todd, Dorothy Lee, George Meeker, Phyllis Barry, James Burtis, Matt Briggs and Spencer Charters were all there too. Songs included: 'Keep Romance Alive', 'Keep On Doin' What You're Doin', 'Tired Of It All'.

In desperate need of a romantic leading man to match its numerous female starlets, RKO signed handsome Czechoslovakian stage actor Francis Lederer (left) and starred him in **Man Of Two Worlds**. Ainsworth Morgan's novel, as written for the screen by Morgan and Howard J. Green, constituted a strange choice with which to launch a future matinée idol. Lederer was cast as a Nanook-like Eskimo introduced into British culture by Henry Stephenson (right). After a wide-eyed tour of civilized living and a dramatic rebuff from Elissa Landi, whose attentions he mistakes for love, the Arctic native returns to his own people. There was some method in the studio's apparent madness: fearing Lederer's European accent might be a severe handicap, producer Pandro S. Berman and director J. Walter Ruben decided to provide him with a role that required only a smattering of English. The actor responded well, playing Aigo the Eskimo with an ingratiating blend of naïvete and bemusement. Audiences didn't buy it and the film lost $220,000. Also cast: J. Farrell MacDonald (centre), Steffi Duna, Sarah Padden, Walter Byron, Forrester Harvey, Ivan Simpson, Lumsden Hare, Christian Rub, Emil Chautard and Gertrude Wise.

Keep 'Em Rolling had precisely that effect on audiences cornered by its sentimental goo; most viewers were soon headed for the exits. Walter Huston (right, borrowed from MGM) was uncomfortably cast as a regular Army sergeant whose love for a horse named Rodney causes him to go AWOL and to face a possible court-martial. Rodney, it seems, had saved Huston's life during the big war, and had also performed the super-equine feat of dragging a cannon to an allied camp where the weapon was needed to repulse a German attack. A new breed of insensitive military officers are about to auction Rodney off when Huston lights out with the nag; all ends cheerily, of course, thanks to a special Presidential decree retiring Rodney with a full ration of oats and appointing Huston as his caretaker. Associate producer William Sistrom, director George Archainbaud and screenwriter Albert Shelby LeVino (story by Leonard Nason) should all have been put out to pasture for whipping up this mawkish brew. Frances Dee, Minna Gombell, Frank Conroy, G. Pat Collins, Robert Shayne (left), Ralph Remley and officers and enlisted men from Fort Myer, Virginia, where exterior scenes were shot, also took part. 'Caisson Song', composed by First Lieutenant E. L. Gruber, was featured.

The Meanest Gal In Town was a pitiful excuse for a comedy which featured ZaSu Pitts as the owner of a dry goods store. Russell Mack bore primary responsibility, having both written the screenplay (with Richard Schayer and H. W. Hanemann) and directed it. El Brendel (right), as a barber trying to scrape up enough money to marry Miss Pitts (left), Pert Kelton, as a stranded showgirl who upsets the Pitts–Brendel romance, 'Skeets' Gallagher, as a fast-talking salesman, and James Gleason, as the local wiseacre who ends up marrying Miss Kelton, all strained to make something of the amorphous plot. It was a hit-and-miss proposition from the first frame, with the misses coming out on top. Associate producer H. N. Swanson's supporting cast included Edward McWade, Arthur Hoyt, Morgan Wallace and Wallis Clark. Arthur Horman wrote the original story.

John Ford's first production for RKO, **The Lost Patrol**, was another reflection of executive producer Merian C. Cooper's preference for adventure stories set in faraway locales. The Dudley Nichols screenplay (adaptation by Garrett Fort) originated as a story by Philip MacDonald about a British patrol that loses its bearings in the Mesopotamian desert and is slowly picked apart by unseen Arab sharpshooters. Victor McLaglen (centre), Boris Karloff (left), Wallace Ford (right), Reginald Denny, J. M. Kerrigan, Billy Bevan, Alan Hale, Brandon Hurst, Douglas Walton, Sammy Stein, Howard Wilson and Paul Hanson comprised the all-male cast. Unlike most of Ford's work – and the escapist tendencies then predominant in Hollywood filmmaking – **The Lost Patrol** was absolutely unremitting in its sense of hopeless-

ness and futility. Even the solace of religion, so prominent in the director's canon, is missing here. Karloff, who mouths Biblical phrases throughout, finally loses his mind and, dressed as John the Baptist, marches out to meet the Arabs. They gun him down without a moment's hesitation. Despite its depressing tone, the picture proved to be a modest financial and critical success, perhaps because its unusual subject matter and approach made it stand out from the log jam of homogenized American pictures. Cliff Reid was the associate producer, and variations of the basic plot would later appear in *Bad Lands* (RKO, 1939), *Bataan* (MGM, 1943) and *Sahara* (Columbia, 1943). A silent version of the tale released by British International in 1929, had used Cyril McLaglen, brother of Victor, in the same starring role.

The tattered arm of coincidence showed up whenever **Long Lost Father** began to flounder. Screenwriter Dwight Taylor, working from a novel by G. B. Stern, arranged a reunion between John Barrymore (left), who had deserted his family many years before, and his daughter Helen Chandler (right). Both end up working for Alan Mowbray in his Happy Hour nightclub. Though Chandler detests her ne'er-do-well dad at first, she comes to love and admire him after he helps to free her of a robbery charge and points her in the direction of a proper mate. Ernest B. Schoedsack's pedestrian direction pointed to the fact that action-adventure was more his forte than comedy-drama. The secondary players: Donald Cook, E. E. Clive, Claude King, Reginald Sharland, Ferdinand Gottschalk, Natalie Moorhead, Doris Lloyd, Phyllis Barry, Tempe Pigott, Herbert Bunston, Charles Irwin and John Rogers. Kenneth Macgowan was the associate producer.

Frank Buck (illustrated) returned from the jungles of Ceylon, Malaya and Northern India with a sequel to *Bring 'Em Back Alive* entitled **Wild Cargo**. This time Buck concentrated on the ingenious methods employed to trap animals – including elephants, tigers, leopards and a giant tapir – rather than skirmishes between various beasts. One bit of excitement was a fight to the death between a panther and a python, won by the crafty serpent. Armand Denis directed, with Nicholas Cavaliere and Leroy G. Phelps supplying the excellent photography. Courtney Ryley Cooper wrote dialogue and narration, based on the book of the same title by Buck and Edward Anthony. The Van Beuren organization produced and, although the film did not cause as much stir as Mr Buck's initial compilation, it still earned a profit of $100,000 for its distributor, RKO.

The studio bought Lula Vollmer's play *Trigger* with Dorothy Jordan in mind, but Katharine Hepburn (illustrated) fell in love with the story and prevailed upon Pandro Berman to assign it to her. The final result, retitled **Spitfire**, proved to be one of the major miscalculations of the distinguished actress' career. Adapted by Miss Vollmer and Jane Murfin, and directed by John Cromwell, the picture was an asinine hodgepodge about poverty and backwoods religion, interwoven with a flaccid love triangle linking Hepburn to Robert Young (on loan from MGM) and Ralph Bellamy. She delivered one of her most frenetic performances as illiterate mountain girl Trigger Hicks, who mixes quaint oaths with hymn singing and flings rocks at the very people for whom she prays. Martha Sleeper, Louis Mason, Sara Haden, Virginia Howell, Sidney Toler, High Ghere, John Beck and Therese Wittler were also in it. A case of near-lethal miscasting, this Pandro S. Berman production kicked off a wave of public disenchantment with Katharine Hepburn that would eventually result in her being labelled 'box-office poison'.

This Man Is Mine starred Irene Dunne (left) in a flimsy love triangle with Ralph Bellamy (right) as the apex. In it, Dunne battled with an unscrupulous Constance Cummings (on loan from Darryl Zanuck's Twentieth Century organization) for Bellamy's affections and finally won, though the big question was why the two superior women expended so much energy on so sappy a hero in the first place. Director John Cromwell gave a great deal more than he got from Jane Murfin's adaptation of *Love Flies In The Window*, a play by Anne Morrison Chapin. So did art directors Van Nest Polglase and Carroll Clark, who designed the elegant sets, and David Abel, who photographed them with sparkling precision. Supporting players Kay Johnson and Sidney Blackmer feasted on the script's few witty lines, and Charles Starrett, Vivian Tobin, Louis Mason, Adda Gleason and Herbert Evans also appeared for producer Pandro S. Berman.

ZaSu Pitts (left), now being given an occasional lead, was surrounded by Pert Kelton (right), Nat Pendleton, Edward Everett Horton and Ned Sparks in **Sing And Like It**. This burlesque concerned a gangster (Pendleton) who sponsors the singing career of Miss Pitts. The mug exerts so much pressure that she becomes a success, even though her warbling is dissonance personified. The movie was essentially a one-joke affair, with the joke re-commencing each time the 'singer' opened her mouth. Marion Dix and Laird Doyle typed out the passable screenplay from a story by Aben Kandel. William A. Seiter directed, and the cast also included Richard Carle, John M. Qualen, Matt McHugh, Stanley Fields, Joseph Sauers, William M. Griffith, Grace Hayle, Roy D'Arcy and Florence Roberts, for associate producer Howard J. Green. Song: 'Your Mother' Dave Dreyer, Roy Turk.

An above-average programmer, **The Crime Doctor** offered a master-mind detective (Otto Kruger, illustrated) who plots the perfect crime. Believing his wife (Karen Morley, borrowed from MGM) to be unfaithful, Kruger kills a woman who has been blackmailing the suspected lover (Nils Asther) and cleverly pins the homicide on Asther. John Robertson directed Jane Murfin's adaptation of a story by Israel Zangwill with dexterity, eliciting respectable performances from Judith Wood, William Frawley, Donald Crisp, Frank Conroy, J. Farrell MacDonald, Fred Kelsey and G. Pat Collins, as well as the principal players. David Lewis was the associate producer. No doubt to pacify the Breen office, the filmmakers compromised their deft story by including an epilogue in which everything turns out to have been a fiction written by the criminologist for publication. Thus Hollywood sleight-of-hand transformed tragedy into comedy in the twinkling of an eye. The film was a remake of *The Perfect Crime*, a 1928 FBO partial-'talkie' that starred Clive Brook and Irene Rich.

Wanda Tuchock (a writer) and George Nicholls Jr (an editor) collaborated on the direction of **Finishing School**, and their inexperience showed in every frame of the picture. Frances Dee (right) is sent off to Crockett Hall, an institution for daughters of the socially élite, where she learns plenty about the extravagances, absurdities and hypocrisies of the educational establishment, and of the world at large. Her indoctrination is so disheartening that she is contemplating suicide when poor boy Bruce Cabot rattles up in his shabby Ford and takes her away from all the phonies. The performances were the only above-average ingredient in this threadbare picture, especially Billie Burke's portrayal of Dee's selfish mother, and Ginger Rogers' (left) of her worldly roommate. The Tuchock–Laird Doyle script, from a story by David Hempstead, also gave employment to John Halliday, Beulah Bondi, Sara Haden, Helen Freeman, Marjorie Lytell, Adalyn Doyle and Dawn O'Day (soon to be known as Anne Shirley). Kenneth Macgowan was the associate producer, and borrowed Billie Burke from Samuel Goldwyn.

Clive Brook (right) and the luminous Diana Wynyard (centre), the British stars of the Academy Award-winning *Cavalcade* (Fox, 1933) were re-united in **Where Sinners Meet** (GB: **The Dover Road**). The story had Brook as a man who has experienced two unhappy marriages, devoting himself to preventing others from making the same mistake. Corralling two eloping couples in his home, he so engineers things that each is given a foretaste of what their future married life will be. His ploy works so successfully that the men flee abruptly, leaving Brook with two women on his hands. Wynyard (borrowed from MGM) and Reginald Owen (left) made up one twosome and Billie Burke (borrowed from Samuel Goldwyn) and Alan Mowbray the other, in H. W. Hanemann's adaptation of *The Dover Road*, a play by A. A. Milne. J. Walter Ruben's careful direction brought out the personalities of the various characters, with the overall result being merry if insubstantial entertainment. Pandro S. Berman enjoyed his first executive producer credit, with David Lewis as his associate, and Gilbert Emery, Phyllis Barry, Walter Armitage, Katherine Williams, Robert Adair and Vernon Steele also in the cast. The film was a remake of *The Little Adventuress*, a 1927 DeMille-Producers Distributing Corporation film featuring Vera Reynolds and Victor Varconi.

It took more than an average suspension of disbelief to appreciate **Stingaree**. Still, if one let down one's guard and surrendered to the film's fantastic improbabilities, there was much romance and exhilaration to be found. It was all about an Australian opera singer who falls for an unconventional bandit called 'Stingaree'. The outlaw robs not for profit, nor even to aid the poor, but chiefly to satisfy his sense of the absurd. In his most flamboyant escapade, he steals the gold-braided uniform of the Governor General, attends the opera star's homecoming concert dressed as the high official, then kidnaps her and carries her off on a white horse *á là* Rudolph Valentino. The movie top-cast Richard Dix (right), in his best role in years as the bandit, and Irene Dunne (left) as the lady. The Becky Gardiner screenplay (adaptation by Lynn Riggs and Leonard Spigelgass from a series of stories by E. W. Hornung) also gave Miss Dunne a chance to showcase her vocal talents. William A. Wellman directed for associate producer David Lewis, and their cast included Mary Boland, Conway Tearle, Andy Devine, Henry Stephenson, Una O'Connor, George Barraud, Reginald Owen, 'Snub' Pollard, Billy Bevan and Robert Greig. The story had first been filmed as a 12-episode silent serial, produced by the Kalem Company and called *The Adventures Of Stingaree*. Songs included: 'Stingaree Ballad', 'Tonight Is Mine' Gus Kahn, W. Franke Harling; 'I Wish I Were A Fisherman', 'Once You're Mine' Edward Eliscu, Max Steiner.

Too many writers with too many different comedic notions turned **Strictly Dynamite** into a lame and frazzled satire on radio comedy shows. When the smoke cleared, about all one remembered was Jimmy Durante: his malapropisms and his famous profile. The 'Schnozzle' (left, borrowed from MGM), played a radio funny man who is running out of jokes, hires Norman Foster (on loan from Fox) to write some, and soon finds himself in the middle of a marital squabble involving Foster's wife (Marian Nixon) and Durante's temperamental broadcasting partner (Lupe Velez, right, borrowed from MGM). Robert T. Colwell and Robert A. Simon penned the original story, Maurine Watkins and Ralph Spence wrote the screenplay and Milton Raison and Jack Harvey added dialogue; the whole package was, to quote one of Jimmy Durante's famous remarks, a 're-voltin' development'. Elliott Nugent directed, H. N. Swanson was associate producer and William Gargan, The Mills Brothers, Eugene Pallette, Minna Gombell, Sterling Holloway, Leila Bennett, Franklin Pangborn, Berton Churchill, Irene Franklin and Jackie Searle were also featured. Songs included: 'Swing It Sister', 'Oh, Me! Oh, My! Oh, You!' Harold Adamson, Burton Lane; 'Money In My Clothes' Irving Kahal, Sammy Fain; 'I'm Putty In Your Hands' Durante, Adamson; 'Hot Patatta', Durante.

A musical exercise written on a blackboard, a high-heeled slipper stained with blood, a dead ant in the bottom of a highball glass and a partly empty bottle of whisky were the crucial clues in **Murder On The Blackboard**, volume two of the Hildegarde Withers–Oscar Piper mystery series. Miss Withers (Edna May Oliver, right) must endure the sneers of detective Piper (James Gleason), who finds her clue-mania absurd, before bagging the killer of her school's music teacher and, thereby, completing her lesson in detection for the red-faced cop. George Archainbaud's taut direction captured the spirit of Stuart Palmer's original story and Willis Goldbeck's screenplay, and associate producer Kenneth Macgowan made it look as if it cost much more than it actually did. Also cast: Bruce Cabot (centre), Gertrude Michael (left), Tully Marshall, Fredrik Vogeding, Edgar Kennedy, Regis Toomey, Jackie Searle, Barbara Fritchie, Gustav von Seyffertitz, Tom Herbert and Jed Prouty.

Nobility of majestic proportions was on display in **The Life Of Vergie Winters**, a competent tearjerker more than a little reminiscent of *Only Yesterday* and *Back Street* (Universal, 1932). Ann Harding (right) portrayed the spiritual paragon, a woman who loves John Boles (left, on loan from Fox) and welcomes his attentions 'without benefit of clergy'. She accepts her fate philosophically, sacrificing everything for her man, and enduring gossip, slander and malicious persecution for 22 years. She even gives up her daughter and watches the child being raised in the lap of luxury while she remains ostracized, and finally takes the blame for Boles' murder to protect his good name. Harding's saintly performance, under the sincere direction of Alfred Santell, kept the Jane Murfin screenplay (based on a novel by Louis Bromfield) from degenerating into pure treacle. Betty Furness played the love child of the Harding–Boles liaison (Bonita Granville played her briefly as a younger girl) and Helen Vinson Boles' cold, selfish wife. Also cast in the Pandro S. Berman production: Frank Albertson, Creighton Chaney, Sara Haden, Molly O'Day, Ben Alexander, Donald Crisp, Maidel Turner, Cecil Cunningham and Wesley Barry. Together, cast and crew succeeded in making the film a burnt offering to the purity of love and sacrifice.

The madcap comedy of Bert Wheeler (left) and Robert Woolsey (right) seemed to work best when transported to some faraway time and place. In **Cockeyed Cavaliers**, the 16th century British setting and costumes added an extra dimension to the usual burlesque. This time Wheeler was a kleptomaniac, constantly getting himself and Woolsey into trouble. The pair are mistaken for the king's physicians and subsequently invade the estate of the Duke of Weskit (Robert Greig). The high point in Edward Kaufman and Ben Holmes' script (additional dialogue Grant Garrett and Ralph Spence) was a parody of the famous scene in MGM's *Queen Christina* in which Greta Garbo (who has been dressed as a boy) reveals her true identity to John Gilbert. Mark Sandrich's crackling direction realized the full potential of the comic elements, and Thelma Todd, Dorothy Lee, Noah Beery, Henry Sedley, Jack Norton, 'Snub' Pollard, Billy Gilbert and Franklin Pangborn also contributed. Associate producer: Lou Brock. Songs: 'Dilly Dally', 'I Went Hunting And The Big Bad Wolf Was Dead' Will Jason, Val Burton.

△

A favourite quest in Depression movies was for a prosperous son-in-law to extricate a formerly wealthy family from the doldrums. **We're Rich Again**, based on a play by Alden Nash, was a mediocre contribution to this theme. Reginald Denny played the vacillating matrimonial object and Joan Marsh the prospective bride, with Billie Burke (right, borrowed from Samuel Goldwyn) as her pampered mother, Grant Mitchell (centre) as her distraught ex-millionaire father, and Edna May Oliver (left) as her polo-playing grandmother. They were all in fine fettle, but Marian Nixon, playing a meddling character named Arabella, spoiled it. Arabella's incessant yammering was supposed to be funny, but it proved supremely irritating instead. Director William Seiter deserved much of the blame for allowing the actress to go overboard; both he and Nixon needed a lesson in comic deportment. Others in the Ray Harris screenplay were Larry 'Buster' Crabbe, Gloria Shea, Edgar Kennedy, Otto Yamaoka, Lenita Lane, Dick Elliott and Andreas De Segurola. Associate producer: Glendon Allvine. Song: 'Senorita' Albert Hay Malotte.

Bette Davis scorched the screen in **Of Human ▷ Bondage**, the most prestigious RKO picture of the year. John Cromwell who directed, also suggested the casting of Davis, thereby atoning for his recent *Spitfire* debacle. As its title implied, the W. Somerset Maugham novel, adapted by Lester Cohen, dealt with emotional enslavement. Leslie Howard (left), playing well-to-do but club-footed medical student Philip Carey, is obsessed with Mildred (Davis, right), a sluttish waitress who abuses him. The plot builds to a climax in which he finally summons the courage to tell Mildred that she disgusts him, whereupon she erupts in a venomous assault, revealing the depths of her ignominy and also laying bare the flaws in Carey's character. Afterwards, she lays waste his apartment, destroying his paintings and books, and burning the bonds that sustain him. In this one scene, it is possible to watch the baptism of a great actress and a major star. Unfortunately for RKO, Warner Bros., who had loaned them Miss Davis for the picture and still controlled her $750 per week contract, would reap the benefits of her future box-office pull. Though awe-struck critics lauded the movie in their reviews, audiences were not as enthusiastic and it wound up a $45,000 loser. Davis' portrayal was too uncompromisingly vicious for contemporary tastes, and film patrons never quite forgave Howard for taking her back as often as he did. Producer Pandro S. Berman also employed Frances Dee, Kay Johnson, Reginald Owen, Reginald Denny and Alan Hale in the cast. Warner Bros. later purchased the rights and re-made the story in 1946 with Paul Henreid and Eleanor Parker starring. A 1964 version, released by MGM, featured Laurence Harvey and Kim Novak.

△

Bachelor Bait would have been just one more thoroughly forgettable farce but for one notable fact: the RKO feature film debut of director George Stevens. Stevens had been working for associate producer Lou Brock on short subjects; now he acquitted himself sufficiently well to earn his chances at more challenging films. Edward and Victor Halperin's story, scripted by Glenn Tryon, was all about Romance Inc., a matrimonial agency run by Stuart Erwin (right, on loan from MGM). Erwin becomes so wrapped up in uniting others that he almost marries off the girl he loves (Rochelle Hudson, borrowed from Fox) to a millionaire. Sexy gold-digger Pert Kelton (left) steps in at just the right moment, giving Erwin a chance to rectify the mistake he is about to make. Stevens' efficient direction did not hint at his major triumphs to come, but he did get the maximum number of laughs from an altogether minimal script. 'Skeets' Gallagher, Berton Churchill, Grady Sutton and Clarence H. Wilson led the support.

△

Let's Try Again (GB: **Marriage Symphony**) was another lecture on the flawed wisdom of hasty divorce, which starred Clive Brook and Diana Wynyard (borrowed from MGM) as a married couple who are three anniversaries past the seven-year-itch. Temptation enters their respective lives in the guise of Helen Vinson and Theodore Newton, and Brook (right) and Wynyard (left) seriously contemplate divorce. However, by the final fade their relationship seems well on the

mend. Worthington Miner adapted Vincent Lawrence's play *Sour Grapes*, and also directed for associate producer Myles Connolly. Miner's approach to the material was overbearingly sober, and the upshot was flat, toothless entertainment that garnered only $183,000 in total film rentals. A comparable low-budget film should have brought in revenues of approximately $250,000 during this period. Also featured: Irene Hervey, Arthur Hoyt and Henry Kolker.

Richard Dix's fans (mostly female), who had come to expect a dashing recklessness in his characterizations, weren't disappointed by **His Greatest Gamble**. The surprising element was the plot, which had a battle going on between Dix (right) and his divorced wife over their lovely daughter. Sentenced to 15 years in jail for unintentionally killing a woman, the hero breaks out after learning that the mother's influence has made his daughter spineless, waning and neurotic. He rescues her, reinvigorating her spirit and health before turning her over to the man she loves and turning himself over to the prison authorities. Dorothy Wilson (centre, borrowed from Charles R. Rogers) played the grown-up daughter, Bruce Cabot her fiancé and Erin O'Brien-Moore (left) the vampirish mother. John Robertson directed a cast that also included Edith Fellows, Shirley Grey, Leonard

Carey and Eily Malyon. Sidney Buchman and Harry Hervey wrote the screenplay, based on a story by Salisbury Field. Myles Connolly was the associate producer of this unusual variation on a standard woman's film plot.

A suspense comedy with mystical overtones, **Their Big Moment** (GB: **Afterwards**) paired ZaSu Pitts (centre) and 'Slim' Summerville (left, borrowed from Universal) with indifferent results. The Marion Dix–Arthur Caesar screenplay (from a play by Walter Hackett) dealt with Miss Pitts' discovery of real psychic abilities in the middle of a phony séance. James Cruze (who had directed the first important epic western, *The Covered Wagon*) further weakened his now faltering reputation by overseeing this unfortunately muddled effort. It also featured Kay Johnson, William Gaxton (right), Bruce Cabot, Julie Haydon, Huntley Gordon and Tamara Geva. The associate producer was Cliff Reid.

Joan Lowell (front right), a female Frank Buck, but with a considerably more undisciplined imagination, starred in **Adventure Girl**, the 'fact and fiction' account of her trip to an unnamed Caribbean country. Setting out with her father and two sailors on a 48-foot schooner, the adventuress first encounters a hurricane, then discovers an ancient Spanish map hinting of buried treasure, and finally arrives in the kingdom of the Mayas where she is nearly burned at the stake by enraged natives. Footage of Joan's battles with an octopus, a shark and a boa constrictor were designed to add to the thrills, but only the most unsophisticated viewers bought it for anything more than the sheer baloney it was. And low-budget baloney at that. Herman Raymaker directed, Ferrin Frazier wrote the text, and Captain Wagner, Bill Sawyer and Otto Siegler also appeared. The Van Beuren organization produced the film, based on a book of the same title by Miss Lowell.

RKO bought Wilhelm Speyer's stage play **Hat, Coat And Glove** with John Barrymore in mind, but the famous actor's 'health' was not up to the task, and the studio was forced to look elsewhere for a leading man. Ricardo Cortez (right) was eventually borrowed from Warner Bros. to play the role of a lawyer who agrees to defend his wife's lover against a murder charge on the condition that she will not testify and will return to her husband after the trial. The three titular items of clothing become crucial pieces of evidence introduced into the lengthy and tedious courtroom proceedings. Barbara Robbins (centre) as the wife and John Beal (left) as her young lover topped director Worthington Miner's cast, which also included Dorothy Burgess, Paul Harvey, Sara Haden, Margaret Hamilton, David Durand, Murray Kinnell, Frederick Sullivan and Gale Evers. Francis Faragoh wrote the dull screenplay for associate producer Kenneth Macgowan. The studio remade the tale in 1944 with Tom Conway and Audrey Long, calling it *A Night Of Adventure*.

▽

The Fountain, a weighty film directed by John Cromwell, was guilty of the ultimate Hollywood sin: it was boring. Adapted by Jane Murfin (dialogue by Samuel Hoffenstein) from Charles Morgan's best-selling novel, it was a sad story of marital sacrifice and the cruel nature of war. Ann Harding (right) is married to Paul Lukas (borrowed from Universal), a German officer serving in World War I, when she meets and falls in love with British soldier Brian Aherne (left). Lukas returns, a one-armed victim of poison gas, and Harding bravely attempts to nurse him back to health. He soon discerns that his wife is caring for him out of duty and pity – not love – but there are no recriminations. He condones her new attachment before dying. Intelligent, tasteful and superbly phographed by Henry W. Gerrard, the film was undone by its laborious pacing, long-winded dialogue and undue restraint, which resulted in a box-office deficit of $150,000. Also cast: Jean Hersholt, Ralph Forbes, Violet Kemble-Cooper, Sara Haden, Ian Wolfe, Frank Reicher and Ferike Boros. Pandro S. Berman produced.

▽

It is sometimes said that a film is so bad that it's good, meaning that the sheer ineptitude of the undertaking may have a perverse entertainment value: **Down To Their Last Yacht** (GB: **Hawaiian Nights**) would very probably qualify for such a description by today's campy standards, but in its own time it came to be regarded as the worst film ever produced by RKO. The basic idea of millionaires forced to live on their yacht and work for a living had possibilities, but this plot soon disintegrated to be replaced by a South Sea island story full of nonsensical pandemonium. At the end, the yacht is blown to bits so rich and poor can live together and think about nothing but 'love'. The film had a number of amazing ingredients – loin-clothed natives behaving like gangsters, a blonde queen (Mary Boland, centre left) who enjoys feeding her guests to the sharks, and hula dancers who obviously learned to shimmy in a Broadway chorus line (dance director Dave Gould) – but there was little humour, less social comment and no intelligence to be found in the surreal production. The other bewildered performers who struggled against the tidal wave of inanity included Sidney Fox, Polly Moran (centre right), Sidney Blackmer (left), Ned Sparks, Sterling Holloway, Marjorie Gateson, Irene Franklin, Charles Coleman and Tom Kennedy (right). One would think they had all wandered onto the set one day and tried to make up a Polynesian musical as they went along, although the credits (director Paul Sloane; screenplay Marion Dix and Lynn Starling; story Herbert Fields and Lou Brock) belied this possibility. The film's biggest loser was Lou Brock. Much can be forgiven an indulgent producer if his efforts are successful. Brock was renowned around the RKO lot for his tendency to allow pictures to overrun their budget estimates and for his sanguine disregard for proper authorizations. Since both *Melody Cruise* and *Flying Down To Rio* had been hits, his carryings-on were tolerated until he completed this appallingly bad picture. In short order, Mr Brock was pounding the Hollywood pavements, looking for a new job. The (also wretched) songs included: 'South Sea Bolero' Max Steiner, Ann Ronell: 'Tiny Little Finger On Your Hand' Val Burton, Will Jason; 'Malakamokalu' Cliff Friend, Sidney Mitchell; 'Funny Little World', 'Beach Boy' Ann Ronell.

▽

△

Audiences were beginning to get wise to the predictable nature of RKO's female-oriented dramas. They turned up their handkerchiefs at **The Age Of Innocence**, another expedition into the familiar territory of *Back Street* (Universal, 1932) and *The Life Of Vergie Winters*. This time the love affair central to the plot is wrecked by the severe moral constraints of Victorian society. Irene Dunne (right) and John Boles (left, borrowed from Fox), the famous *Back Street* tandem, were the victims who are prevented from marrying because she is in the process of divorcing her husband. Boles weds Julie Haydon instead, but this hardly dampens his enthusiasm for Dunne. She finally terminates the relationship, sending Boles back to his wife, though the love between them will never be extinguished. Edith Wharton's novel which formed the basis for the film (along with a stage version by Margaret Ayer Barnes) had won the Pulitzer Prize in 1920, but by 1934 its social comment was completely passé. The upshot, directed by RKO first-timer Philip Moeller, was a ponderous business which, while not lacking in histrionics, was devoid of true emotion, and failed to be the romantic tragedy envisaged by producer Pandro S. Berman and his staff. Sarah Y. Mason and Victor Heerman's screenplay also gave roles to Lionel Atwill, Helen Westley, Laura Hope Crews, Herbert Yost, Theresa Maxwell Conover, Edith Van Cleve and Leonard Carey. In an unusual loan arrangement, cinematographer James Van Trees and his crew were brought over from the Twentieth Century lot and gave the film a splendid visual treatment.

According to RKO advertising **The Richest Girl In The World** was 'the season's most electrifying comedy drama, lavish with humour, romance and glamour'. For once, the claim was only slightly exaggerated. The splendid story and screenplay by Norman Krasna, who would soon become a premiere Hollywood writer, concerned a wealthy girl who switches places with her secretary to be sure men pursue her for reasons other than her fortune. Assured comedienne Miriam Hopkins (left, borrowed from Paramount) portrayed the heiress, with Fay Wray (on loan from Twentieth Century) as the real secretary and Joel McCrea (right) as the principal love interest. William A. Seiter's solid direction underscored the script's witty dialogue and moments of genuine hilarity, and he also coaxed wry performances from Henry Stephenson, Reginald Denny, Beryl Mercer, George Meeker, Wade Boteler, Herbert Bunston, Burr McIntosh and Edgar Norton. Pandro S. Berman personally produced, having purchased the screenplay with his own money during a period when Norman Krasna was blackballed by Louis B. Mayer of MGM.
▽

◁ **Dangerous Corner** took its title from a line in the script which compared the telling of truth to an automobile skidding round a dangerous corner. And that was the theme of J. B. Priestley's play: the devastating consequences of total candour. Virginia Bruce (centre left, borrowed from MGM), Conrad Nagel, Melvyn Douglas (right), Erin O'Brien-Moore (left), Betty Furness (centre right), Henry Wadsworth and Doris Lloyd are drawn into a series of damaging confessions, revealing their suppressed passions and guilty secrets, while attempting to determine the circumstances surrounding the suicide of Ian Keith and the theft of a large sum of money. A trick denouement turns back the clock, retrieving the world of half-truths and deceptions so that everything ends happily. It was a clever and different type of screen fiction, well-acted by the principals, but directed without much style by Phil Rosen. Anne Morrison Chapin and Madeleine Ruthven wrote the screenplay, and B. P. Fineman, who had been FBO studio head in the mid-1920s, brought the property to his old lot and served as the associate producer.

The Gay Divorcee (GB: **The Gay Divorce**) pointed towards RKO's major triumphs of the rest of the decade. Despite Fred Astaire's disinclination to be teamed with anyone, the picture cemented the Astaire–Rogers combination, and its plot contained the basic formula for most of their later efforts. Adapted by Dorothy Yost, Edward Kaufman and George Marion Jr from Dwight Taylor, Kenneth Webb and Samuel Hoffenstein's stage success, the story presented the conspiracy of attorney Edward Everett Horton and busybody aunt Alice Brady to secure a divorce for Rogers through the employment of a professional co-respondent – a man hired to give the impression that she is having a clandestine affair with him. Fred (left), playing an American dancer, is immediately infatuated with Ginger (centre), when they meet in the London docks. He pursues her for weeks without success, and is ultimately mistaken by her for the despised co-respondent; after considerable pandemonium, all misconceptions are clarified and the two lovers unite in the end. Interwoven with the mistaken identity plot were humorous subplots of a quasi-screwball comedy nature featuring Brady, Horton, Eric Blore and ◁ Erik Rhodes, the actual co-respondent (right). The silly subplots, along with the actors themselves, would also reappear in subsequent musicals. Finally, the fundamental Astaire–Rogers production team coalesced on **The Gay Divorcee**: producer Pandro S. Berman and director Mark Sandrich topped a group which also comprised art directors Van Nest Polglase and Carroll Clark, who took responsibility for the quintessential art deco design of the pictures, musical director Max Steiner and cameraman David Abel (Dance direction Dave Gould). Songs from the excellent score included: 'Night And Day' Cole Porter; 'Don't Let It Bother You', 'Let's K-nock K-nees' Mack Gordon, Harry Revel; 'A Needle In A Haystack', 'The Continental' Con Conrad, Herb Magidson.

△
Gridiron Flash (GB: **The Luck Of The Game**) was a cheap but satisfying 'B' picture, written and directed by Glenn Tryon (from a story by Nicholas Barrows and Earl Snell). Eddie Quillan (right) was the 'cherub', a tough guy recruited from a penitentiary team to upgrade the football fortunes of Bedford College. Quillan at first agrees to help the bedraggled Bedford squad in exchange for the opportunity to pull a few jobs on the side, but he is soon in love with the campus queen (Betty Furness, left, borrowed from MGM) and becomes infected with the school spirit. After several misunderstandings, he shows up and wins the big game in the final minute of play. Louis Sarecky, a name much in evidence during the LeBaron period, was the associate producer. Helping to make it funny and intermittently exciting were Grant Mitchell, Lucien Littlefield, Edgar Kennedy, Grady Sutton, Joseph Sauers (Sawyer), Allen Wood and Margaret Dumont.

Wednesday's Child was the pathetic story of a youth who is the victim of his parents' broken marriage. Adapted by Willis Goldbeck from a play by Leopold Atlas, it told how the boy (Frankie Thomas, right) is forced to testify during the divorce action, then finds himself in military school because neither father (Edward Arnold, left) nor mother (Karen Morley, borrowed from MGM) has room for him in their lives. At the end, however, the father has a change of heart, takes the boy out of school, and makes a home for the two of them. Despite this sentimentalized tag, this was one of RKO's most affecting dramas of the year, sensitively directed by John Robertson. Associate producer Kenneth Macgowan's cast also included Robert Shayne, Frank Conroy, Shirley Grey, Paul Stanton, David Durand, Richard Barbee, Mona Buns, Elsa Janssen, and the real-life father of Frankie Thomas, Tom Franklin, who would appear in many later RKO films under his real name, Frank M. Thomas. The studio remade the picture in 1946, calling it *Child Of Divorce* and substituting a girl (Sharyn Moffett) for the boy.

Though people didn't speak of 'mid-life crises' in 1934, Frank Morgan (centre, borrowed from MGM) had one in **By Your Leave**, a clichéd romantic boomerang tossed off by scriptwriter Allan Scott from a play by Gladys Hurlbut and Emma B. C. Wells. Morgan, having arrived at that time in life when men begin to shrink from the shadow of advancing age, decides to prop up his sinking ego by taking a vacation apart from his wife Genevieve Tobin (left, on loan from Warner Brothers). His lark turns into a miserable fiasco, but Miss Tobin meets Neil Hamilton in the meantime, and they are soon contemplating a romantic voyage on Hamilton's yacht. Morgan makes amends just in time, and his confession of love causes the wife to cancel her plans. He never discovers, however, that what was decidedly not sauce for the gander came dangerously near to being sauce for the goose. Pandro S. Berman produced, Lloyd Corrigan directed and Marian Nixon, Gene Lockhart, Margaret Hamilton (right), Betty Grable, Glenn Anders, Charles Ray and Lona Andre also participated.

A superior Wheeler–Woolsey farce, **Kentucky Kernels** (GB: **Triple Trouble**) chronicled the comedians' adoption of a precocious youth, played by 'Spanky' McFarland (the famous 'Our Gang' trouper), and their subsequent journey to the land of mint juleps to claim the boy's inheritance. There, 'Spanky' (centre, on loan from Hal Roach Studios) ignites a feud between families headed by Noah Beery and Lucille LaVerne, forcing Mr Wheeler (right) and Mr Woolsey (left) to strain their wits in order to keep their skins. George Stevens supplied the high-octane direction, working from a pacy screenplay by Bert Kalmar, Harry Ruby and Fred Guiol (story by Kalmar and Ruby). Mary Carlisle, Sleep 'n' Eat (later known as Willie Best), Margaret Dumont, Louis Mason, Paul Page, Frank McGlynn Jr, Richard Alexander and William Pawley had other roles, and H. N. Swanson was the associate producer. Kalmar and Ruby provided two songs, 'One Little Kiss' and 'Supper Song'.

Dashiell Hammett, author of *The Thin Man* and *The Maltese Falcon*, was responsible for **Woman In The Dark** which concerned itself with the question of whether or not a transgressor can ever live down his former mistakes. Ralph Bellamy (left), recently out of jail for manslaughter, wants simply to be left alone, but he is persecuted by sheriff Granville Bates and soon finds himself in the middle of an imbroglio involving Fay Wray (centre) and her former lover, bad guy Melvyn Douglas. Hammett's story (scripted by Sada Cowan with additional dialogue by Marcy Klauber and Charles Williams) came complete with mystery elements and a twist ending, but it was one of the author's lesser achievements, soon forgotten by all but a few thriller buffs. Phil Rosen directed a cast that also featured Rosco Ates (right), Reed Brown Jr, Ruth Gillette and Nell O'Day. Burt Kelly was the associate producer for Select Productions, an independent company.

Producer Kenneth Macgowan, director George Nicholls Jr and screenwriter Sam Mintz joined forces to create one of the most pleasing financial and critical successes of the year. In an attempt to emulate the appeal of *Little Women*, **Anne Of Green Gables** was given the same tone, the same homespun atmosphere, the same concern for character. The showmanship department pulled off a minor coup on the picture – Dawn O'Day, a largely unknown actress, won the role of Anne Shirley, the quixotic young heroine of the L. M. Montgomery novel on which the picture was based. Realizing the latent publicity value, the studio convinced Miss O'Day to change her professional name to: Anne Shirley (right). The actress would be known as Anne Shirley for the rest of her career, thus identifying herself forever with the character she played so warmly and beguilingly. The supporting cast featured Tom Brown (left) as the girl's sweetheart, O. P. Heggie and Helen Westley as her foster parents, Sara Haden as a gossipy, troublemaking neighbour and Murray Kinnell as the local school teacher. Gertrude Messinger, Charley Grapewin, Hilda Vaughn and June Preston also appeared. **Anne Of Green Gables** was a remake of a 1919 Realart picture, directed by William Desmond Taylor and starring Mary Miles Minter.

The award for the year's most outrageous plot fabrication belonged to **The Silver Streak**. Roger Whately's story, scripted by Whately, H. W. Hanemann and Jack O'Donnell, told of a breakneck 2000 mile train trip which must be made in 19 hours in order to deliver iron lungs to a Nevada town where an epidemic of infantile paralysis has broken out. Sally Blane (centre), Charles Starrett (right), Hardie Albright (left) and William Farnum topped director Thomas Atkins' cast, which also included Irving Pichel, Arthur Lake, Theodore von Eltz, Guinn Williams, Edgar Kennedy and Doris Dawson. The Burlington Zephyr also received a prominent credit for 'portraying' the Silver Streak. Glendon Allvine associate-produced the picture, which contained enough high-speed excitement to make audiences overlook the story's rampant implausibilities; it earned $107,000 in profits. Note: The Twentieth Century-Fox film of the same title, released in 1976, bore no relation to this one, other than that it concerned an express train.

In the dark recesses of the studio, **Lightning** ▷ **Strikes Twice** was wryly referred to as a 'commitment' special. All about hoydenish Steffi Duna contractual obligations to performers Thelma Todd (centre), Pert Kelton, 'Skeets' Gallagher (right) and Chick Chandler. Indeed, the story by Marion Dix and Ben Holmes, scripted by Joseph A. Fields and John Grey, smacked of absolute desperation. A black cat's midnight caterwauling upsets a butler's nerves, his bullets upset the police department, two cops disappear down a manhole and the butler flees into hiding. Thus began a mystery-comedy-melodrama that went precisely nowhere. Ben Holmes directed and Lee Marcus earned his first credit as associate producer. It was hardly an auspicious beginning for the man who would soon be superintending all of the company's

'B' releases. Other 'committed' cast members: Ben Lyon (left), Laura Hope Crews, Walter Catlett, Jonathan Hale, Margaret Armstrong, John Davidson, Fred Kelsey, Edgar Dearing and Roger Gray.

Some beautiful footage of New Guinea (photographed for a Merian C. Cooper picture that was never completed) was about all that **Red Morning** – a supposedly serious melodrama – offered in the way of audience diversion. The trite screenplay by John Twist and Wallace Fox, compounded by Fox's flaccid direction and the inept acting of the entire cast, made this seem like another 'commitment' special. All about hoydenish Steffi Duna (illustrated), who survives the scuttling of her father's ship by its mutinous crew, encounters with hostile natives, and other outlandish perils before she and her fiancé Regis Toomey finally set sail for a more placid destination, it contained more unintentional howlers than a year's supply of Mascot westerns. Also cast: Raymond Hatton, Mitchell Lewis, Charles Middleton, George Lewis, Francis McDonald, Arthur 'Pat' West, Brandon Hurst, Willie Fung, Olaf Hytten, Alphonz Ethier, Lionel Belmore and James Marcus. Cliff Reid was the associate producer.

RKO's Christmas gift to the masses was **The Little Minister**, based on the novel and play by Sir James Barrie. Katharine Hepburn was top-starred as Babbie, an enchanting gypsy girl whose love for the new cleric of a Scottish village results in near-tragedy. For the minister's dour, stiff-necked congregation resent his falling in love, especially with what they regard as a wanton. The church elders almost dismiss him, and he is accidentally stabbed (but survives the ordeal). Though she was once again playing a fiery outsider, this Hepburn creation (right) was much more attractive than the coarse and gullible Trigger Hicks of *Spitfire*. John Beal (left) was acceptable as the title character himself, whose rigidity and maternal fixation are gradually erased by his relationship with Babbie. Pandro S. Berman produced, sparing no expense in the recreation of the Scottish township. Indeed, the sets (art direction by Van Nest Polglase and Carroll Clark; interiors by Hobe Erwin) and costumes (by Walter Plunkett) lent the film a sense of total authenticity. Richard Wallace directed from a screenplay by Jane Murfin, Sarah Y. Mason and Victor Heerman (additional scenes by Mortimer Offner and Jack Wagner), with Miss Hepburn contributing suggestions for the ending, some of which were adopted. Alan Hale, Donald Crisp, Lumsden Hare, Andy Clyde, Beryl Mercer, Billy Watson, Dorothy Stickney, Mary Gordon and Frank Conroy rounded out the large cast. An engaging and high-class production in every way, **The Little Minister** was also RKO's most expensive film of the year ($648,000 negative cost) and the most expensive film in which Katharine Hepburn had ever appeared. It did respectable business everywhere it played, but nevertheless lost $9000. Both Paramount and Vitagraph had released versions of the same story in 1921, starring Betty Compson ◁ and Alice Calhoun respectively.

The Depression was beginning to ease throughout America and, feeling cautiously optimistic about the future, RKO's board of directors allocated $500,000 for studio expansion. The work, completed during the following year, added three sound stages, dressing rooms, scene docks, film vaults and a three-story office building.

During 1935, RKO acquired distribution rights to 'The March of Time' a dramatized news featurette produced by Henry R. Luce's *Time* magazine. These shorts would accompany the studio's feature releases for several years to come, with a new issue appearing on an average of once a month.

In October, Floyd Odlum and his Atlas Corporation acquired half of RCA's controlling interest in the corporation, with an option to buy the other half within two years. Odlum's entry into RKO affairs heralded an executive shakeup. Leo Spitz was made president of Radio-Keith-Orpheum, and Merlin Aylesworth was 'elevated' to the position of chairman of the board of directors. Towards the end of the year, Samuel Briskin took over from B. B. Kahane as vice-president in charge of studio production. Briskin came from Columbia, where he had been general manager of the Cohn studio for eight years.

Producers Merian C. Cooper and Kenneth Macgowan left RKO in 1935, Cooper to become executive vice-president of Pioneer Pictures, while Macgowan joined Darryl F. Zanuck's newly formed Twentieth Century-Fox organization. To replace these gentlemen, the studio promoted Edward Kaufman and Robert Sisk into the producer ranks. Kaufman had formerly been a staff writer and Sisk the company's head of publicity in New York. Among the year's talent acquisitions were composer Irving Berlin, who would work on the Astaire-Rogers series, and opera singer Lily Pons.

Though there were the usual disappointments, 1935 was a vintage year for RKO production. **Top Hat** was a giant hit, closely followed by **Roberta**, and **The Informer**, **Star Of Midnight**, **Alice Adams** and **In Person** also performed solidly at the box-office. A total of 43 films were released, four of them produced by independents.

The corporation's final financial statement showed profits of $684,733. It was the first year RKO had made money since 1930.

After ignoring the genre for more than a year, RKO opened the year with a western starring Richard Dix (right) and Martha Sleeper (borrowed from MGM). **West Of The Pecos** was based on one of Zane Grey's most durable novels, adapted to the screen by Milton Krims and John Twist. The elements were thoroughly familiar: a quick-draw hero suspected of cattle rustling, a girl masquerading as a boy to facilitate her passage through the rough country, a Comanche attack which generates plenty of high-pitched excitement, a tough and vicious villain bent on the destruction of the hero, etc. Director Phil Rosen took all the clichés and somehow managed to blend them into a fresh brew. He was assisted in his alchemy by the superior performances of the two stars and supporting performers Samuel Hinds, Fred Kohler and Maria Alba. Other members of associate producer Cliff Reid's cast: Sleep 'n' Eat (Willie Best), Louise Beavers, Pedro Regas, G. Pat Collins (left), Russell Simpson, Maurice Black, George Cooper and Irving Bacon. RKO remade the film in 1945 starring Robert Mitchum.

Grand Old Girl was intended as an assault on the emotions, but its stolid approach and well-worn contrivances left audiences stonily unmoved. Wanda Tuchock's story, adapted by Arthur T. Horman and scripted by Milton Krims and John Twist, was a hymn in praise of the American school teacher. May Robson (left, borrowed from MGM), a public servant for some 38 years, is given the boot for meddling in local politics and standing up to a petty gambler who preys on innocent children. After a series of lugubrious episodes, the President of the US (one of Miss Robson's former pupils, of course) steps in to deliver a speech extolling the patriotic virtues of school teaching, motherhood and so on. Robson, and co-stars Mary Carlisle (right, also borrowed from MGM) and Fred MacMurray (borrowed from Paramount) attempted to stand firm against this avalanche of contrived sentimentality, but they were soon buried under its rubble, along with director John Robertson and associate producer Cliff Reid. Other dazed cast members were Alan Hale, Etienne Girardot, William Burress, Hale Hamilton, Edward Van Sloan, Fred Kohler Jr, Onest Conley, Ben Alexander, George Offerman Jr, and Gavin Gordon as the President.

◁ For those filmgoers particularly interested in fashion, **Gigolette** (GB: **Night Club**) offered 16 changes of outfit for its star, Adrienne Ames (left). There was little else, however, to warrant the viewers' attention in this hackneyed tale of an impoverished society girl who goes to work in the Club Hee-Haw, a New York clip-joint of prohibition vintage owned by Ralph Bellamy. Miss Ames, of course, played the central character, eventually falling for Donald Cook (right) who gets the wrong impression about her relationship with Bellamy after she is promoted to the job of gigolette (an escort for lonely male guests) in Bellamy's swanky Casino de Monaco. Gordon Kahn's tissue-thin screenplay also contained parts for Robert Armstrong, Harold Waldridge, Robert T. Haines and Grace Hampton. Charles Lamont directed; Burt Kelly was the associate producer for Select Productions.

Star Of Midnight featured William Powell (right) as Clay Dalzell, a character seemingly plagiarized from Nick Charles whom Powell had impersonated so winningly in MGM's *The Thin Man* (1934). Dalzell is a debonair lawyer suspected of murder. He sets about solving the crime in order to establish his own innocence, but he is constantly thwarted by the police and by gangsters, each group shadowing the hero for their own reasons. Ginger Rogers (left) co-starred as Powell's romantic consort and, if she did not complement him as well as Myrna Loy had in the MGM picture, her work was nonetheless several notches above adequate. The Howard J. Green–Anthony Veiller–Edward Kaufman screenplay (from a novel by Arthur Somers Roche), abetted by Stephen Roberts' reliable direction, appealed to a wide audience, and earned profits of $265,000 for RKO. Supporting players: Paul Kelly, Gene Lockhart, Ralph Morgan, Leslie Fenton, J. Farrell MacDonald, Russell Hopton, Vivien Oakland and Robert Emmett O'Connor.

Anatole France's novel *The Crime Of Sylvestre Bonnard* came to the screen as **Chasing Yesterday**, a sweet but slow-gaited little picture without much dramatic horsepower (screenplay by Francis Edwards Faragoh). O. P. Heggie (centre) played French bibliophile Bonnard who has been searching for one book for 40 years. An old love letter leads him to the daughter (Anne Shirley, left) of a former flame; when the multiple complications are sorted out, he not only has his book but is also the guardian of the girl. Etienne Girardot turned in an effectively chilling performance as the villain of the piece, but Trent Durkin (also known as Junior Durkin, right), Miss Shirley's love interest, appeared rigid and uncomfortable in his scenes, of which there were mercifully few. Helen Westley, Elizabeth Patterson, John Qualen, Doris Lloyd and Hilda Vaughn were in it too, for director George Nicholls Jr and associate producer Cliff Reid.

Captain Hurricane purported to be a 'true picture' of life on Cape Cod where (according to studio publicity) 'the women, waiting the return of their husbands from the sea, sit in dignified aloofness watching the parade of summer visitors'. To avoid the sedentary vigil becoming a little tedious for the customers, the screenplay (by Josephine Lovett, based on Sara Ware Bassett's novel *The Taming Of Zenas Henry*) contained enough plot to service half a dozen movies. In the main, it was about old salt James Barton (left, making his film debut after a successful Broadway run as Jeeter Lester in *Tobacco Road*) who wants to retire and enjoy his bachelorhood, but is forced to return to the sea to earn enough money to prevent foreclosure on his home. He comes back to the Cape a hero, having saved the lives of the crew when the ship caught fire off the coast of Mexico. Helen Westley, Helen Mack (borrowed from Paramount), Gene Lockhart (right), Henry Travers, Douglas Walton, Otto Hoffman, Harry Stubbs, J. Farrell MacDonald, Forrester Harvey and Stanley Fields also appeared, cluttering up a film which was, at heart, a character study. The sluggish direction was by John Robertson, and Frank O'Heron (formerly the company's vice-president for business affairs) served as associate producer of this $126,000 box-office flounder. It ◁ was O'Heron's first and last production for RKO.

Up and coming Ginger Rogers starred – *sans* Fred Astaire – in **Romance In Manhattan**, but the picture really belonged to Francis Lederer (left). Given a more suitable role than his Eskimo persona of *Man Of Two Worlds*, Lederer portrayed a boisterously optimistic Czech immigrant who maintains his smile and positive outlook despite the many disappointments he finds in inhospitable New York. Chorus girl Rogers (right) befriends the helpless foreigner and, following standard Hollywood logic, comes to love him. Jane Murfin and Edward Kaufman's excellent screenplay, based on a story by Norman Krasna and Don Hartman, made for brisk, uplifting entertainment under the solid direction of Stephen Roberts. Also cast: Arthur Hohl, Jimmy Butler, J. Farrell MacDonald, Helen Ware, Eily Malyon, Lillian Harmer, Donald Meek, Sidney Toler, Oscar Apfel and Reginald Barlow. Pandro S. Berman produced.

John Cromwell's hitherto honourable record as a director was considerably blemished by **Village Tale**, a tawdry little melo set in a tawdry little Iowa town populated by cretins, gossips, bullies, and others of similarly unattractive ilk. Allan Scott's inept screenplay (from a novel by Phil Stong) focused on a feud between Randolph Scott (left, borrowed from Paramount) and Arthur Hohl (borrowed from Columbia) over Kay Johnson (right), Hohl's wife. Everyone concerned struggled to elevate this mindless farrago, but no amount of effort could rescue it from its lack of action, sympathy and credibility. Others caught floundering: Robert Barrat, Janet Beecher, Edward Ellis, Dorothy Burgess, Donald Meek, Andy Clyde, Guinn Williams, Ray Mayer, T. Roy Barnes and DeWitt Jennings.

Bowing to pressures from religious and civic ▷ groups, as well as Joseph Breen's censorship office, Hollywood studios no longer dared feature underworld leaders as glamorous heros, and thus **The People's Enemy** – a watchable melo – offered a thoroughly offensive gangster as its central figure. Preston Foster played Vince, a gangland millionaire who crowns his despicable acts by deserting his wife and child when they need him most. Naturally the rat pays in the end with a prison sentence while Melvyn Douglas (centre) becomes the beneficiary of the suffering wife (Lila Lee, left). Crane Wilbur directed from a story by Edward Dean Sullivan and screenplay by Sullivan and Gordon Kahn. The cast also included Shirley Grey, Rosco Ates, William Collier Jr, Sybil Elaine (right) and Herbert Rawlinson. Burt Kelly was the associate producer for Select Productions.

Pathos, drama, comedy, youthful romance and atmospheric beauty were all combined to little effect in **A Dog Of Flanders**, feebly directed by Edward Sloman. An idyllic tale, it contained a noble dog, an art contest and a juvenile love triangle uniting Frankie Thomas (left), Helen Parrish and Richard Quine, all of which was designed to draw cheers and tears from the audience but mainly appeared to induce sleep. Ainsworth Morgan wrote the screenplay from Dorothy Yost's adaptation of a novel by 'Ouida'. O. P. Heggie, DeWitt Jennings, Ann Shoemaker (right), Christian Rub, Frank Reicher, Nella Walker, Addison Richards, Joseph Swickard, Sarah Padden, Harry Beresford and 'Lightning' (centre) filled out the cast. The associate producer was William Sistrom. Metro had done an earlier version in 1924 with Jackie Coogan, and Twentieth Century-Fox released another in 1959, starring David Ladd. ▽

In striking contrast to *A Dog Of Flanders*, **Laddie** ▷ was a triumph of the sweet and sentimental, skilfully adapted from the Gene Stratton-Porter novel by Ray Harris and Dorothy Yost and splendidly directed by George Stevens. A visual poem to the honest virtues of rural Indiana living, the story as such concerned John Beal's (left) romantic pursuit of Gloria Stuart (borrowed from Universal) and the parental obstacles with which they must contend. Stealing the picture from the two top-liners was little sister Virginia Weidler (right), a disarming elf capable of evoking pathos or humour with equal dexterity. Willard Robertson and Dorothy Peterson were featured as Beal's parents, Donald Crisp as Stuart's stern father, and William Bakewell as her prodigal brother. Also cast: Gloria Shea, Charlotte Henry, Jimmy Butler, Grady Sutton, Greta Meyer and Mary Forbes. FBO had made a version of the story in 1926; RKO would film it again in 1940 with

Tim Holt and Joan Carroll. Producer Pandro S. Berman was so impressed by George Stevens' management of this version that he later assigned him *Alice Adams* as a reward.

△
Enchanted April proved to be a horrible box-office dud, and hastened Ann Harding's (right) demise as an RKO star. Director Harry Beaumont attempted to balance syrupy romantic sequences with wild and zany comedy episodes, but made a mess of it all. The plot had Harding and Katharine Alexander taking an April holiday at an old villa in San Salvatore, Italy, where they accept Jessie Ralph and Jane Baxter as paying guests. All four women are suffering from various romantic ailments, and want nothing more than to distance themselves from men for a while. Crowding in on them are a plethora of eccentric characters headed by Reginald Owen, whose self-imposed grandiloquence was the only genuinely funny element in the film. Harding's estranged husband (Frank Morgan, on loan from MGM) also shows up, whereupon they become awkwardly and unconvincingly reconciled. Samuel Hoffenstein and Ray Harris deserved censure for their confusing and misconceived screenplay (based on a novel by 'Elizabeth', and a play by Kane Campbell). Ralph Forbes (left), Charles Judels and Rafaela Ottiano completed the cast. The picture represented one of Kenneth Macgowan's most dismal failures as an RKO producer.

At a time when RKO had given up competing for ▷ the most expensive novels and dramatic properties, Pandro S. Berman insisted that the company spend whatever was necessary to acquire **Roberta**, a Broadway hit with a book by Otto Harbach and music by Jerome Kern. Producer Berman's determination paid wonderful dividends; the picture earned $770,000 in profits and boosted the careers of Fred Astaire, Ginger Rogers and Irene Dunne. Like *Flying Down To Rio*, **Roberta** seems clearly out of balance. Irene Dunne was the main star and her love affair with Randolph Scott (borrowed from Paramount) represented the central focus of the plot. Astaire and Rogers (illustrated centre) were brilliant when on screen, but simply weren't there enough. One especially longs for more Ginger Rogers in the picture. Her portrayal of the phony Polish Countess Scharwenka was a delight, signalling her development as an outstanding screen comedienne. This is not to imply that Miss Dunne was inadequate as Stephanie, the dress designer who happens also to be a real Russian princess. She performed and sang admirably, without much support from the wooden Mr Scott. Jane Murfin, Sam Mintz and Allan Scott's screenplay (additional dialogue Glenn Tryon), based on a novel by Alice Duer Miller as well as the Broadway play, bogged down into an interminable fashion show near the end. In the parade of models, one can spot Lucille Ball, making her first RKO appearance. A little over 20 years later, her company would purchase the entire studio for the production of television programmes. Also cast: Helen Westley, Claire Dodd, Victor Varconi, Luis Alberni, Ferdinand Munier, Torben Meyer, Adrian Rosley and Bodil Rosing. William Seiter provided the agreeable direction. RKO later sold the property to MGM, which released a remake entitled *Lovely To Look At* in 1952 featuring Kathryn Grayson, Red Skelton and Howard Keel. Songs included: 'Yesterdays', 'Let's Begin', 'Smoke Gets In Your Eyes' Otto Harbach, Jerome Kern; 'Lovely To Look At' Kern, Dorothy Fields, Jimmy McHugh; 'I'll Be Hard To Handle' Kern, Otto Harbach, Bernard Dougall; 'I Won't Dance' Oscar Hammerstein II, Dorothy Fields, Jimmy McHugh, Kern.

◁**Strangers All** offered a fairly unilluminating portrait of a mother, her three sons and one daughter, whose different attitudes and ambitions make them virtual strangers under the same roof. Charles Vidor directed this domestic brouhaha, coaxing passable performances from mother May Robson (centre); Preston Foster (right), the stable bread-winner of the family; William Bakewell (left) who imagines he is a great actor; James Bush, a birdbrained radical whose goal is to save the masses from the capitalists, and daughter Florine McKinney who, while away at college, gets married without consulting the family. Comedy tended to overpower drama, but neither strain was well articulated in Milton Krims' scenario, based on a play by Marie M. Bercovici. Samuel Hinds, Clifford Jones, Suzanne Kaaren, Leon Ames, Reginald Barlow and Paul Stanton were also cast. The associate producer was Cliff Reid who supervised the picture.

Nine people were caught in a tightening net of sinister circumstances in **Murder On A Honeymoon**. One of them happens to be Hildegarde Withers (Edna May Oliver, centre), the snoopy school teacher who never misses a clue, thus ensuring that the true killers will be unmasked in the end. The screenplay, by Seton I. Miller and Robert Benchley (based on a novel by Stuart Palmer), was one of the best in the 'Murder On' series, with plenty of barbed repartee between Withers and Inspector Oscar Piper, again portrayed by James Gleason (right). Director Lloyd Corrigan capitalized on the Catalina Island locations, contrasting their picturesque beauty with the spooky atmosphere and scientific sleuthing of the story. Lola Lane, George Meeker, Dorothy Libaire, Harry Ellerbee, Chick Chandler, Sleep 'n' Eat (Willie Best), Leo G. Carroll, DeWitt Jennings, Spencer Charters, Arthur Hoyt (left), Matt McHugh, Morgan Wallace and Brooks Benedict completed the cast, each of them making a valuable contribution to the Kenneth Macgowan ◁ production.

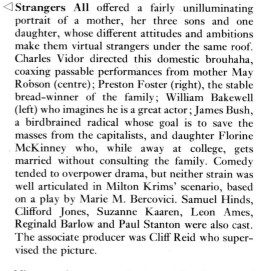

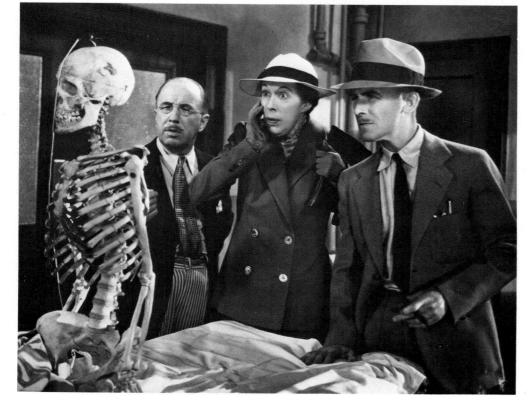

The year's elegant surprise package was a film ▷
version of Liam O'Flaherty's novel, **The
Informer**, about a dull-witted lout who sells out
his best friend for a twenty-pound note, and then
is over-whelmed by the consequences of his act.
With associate producer Cliff Reid supervising, it
was made inexpensively ($243,000 negative cost)
as the first picture of John Ford's new three-
picture RKO deal. The subject matter proved
ideal for Ford, a close student of Irish literature
and history, and his direction brought forth the
most prestigious film that RKO had ever produced. Dudley Nichols' screenplay about the
ravages of conscience, Ford's creation of the
constricted, fog-enshrouded ambience of Dublin
during the Black and Tan occupation and Victor
McLaglen's portrayal of gutter Judas, Gypo
Nolan, elicited hosannas of praise from critics
everywhere. The National Board of Review named
it best film of 1935 and it garnered Academy
Awards for Ford, Nichols, McLaglen (illustrated)
and Max Steiner (Musical Score). Other important
collaborators were Joseph August, who supervised
the atmospheric photography, George Hively,
whose bravura editing earned an Oscar nomination, and supporting players Heather Angel
(borrowed from Universal), Preston Foster,
Margot Grahame, Wallace Ford, Una O'Connor
(left), J. M. Kerrigan, Joseph Sauers (Sawyer),
Neil Fitzgerald, Donald Meek, D'Arcy Corrigan,
Leo McCabe, Gaylord Pendleton and Francis
Ford. The reputation of **The Informer** has
declined in recent years. Before his death, even
Ford dismissed it as not one of his favourites. Yet
one cannot deny the consummate skill with which
every detail was handled and the ultimate power of
the drama. It remains an affecting cinematic
accomplishment and, considering its tiny budget,
will always represent one of the miracle productions of the studio system. Few filmmakers have
ever done so much with so little. British
International released a silent version of the story
in 1929, and Paramount completed a loose remake
called *Uptight* in 1968, with a black cast directed
by Jules Dassin.

◁ A sorry botch of material calculated for its
emotional impact, **Break Of Hearts** did
Katharine Hepburn's career almost as much
damage as *Spitfire* had done. Charting the stormy
amorous relationship between a magnetic orchestra conductor (Charles Boyer, left) and a
budding composer (Hepburn, right), the picture
sank in a sea of threadbare clichés, frantic dialogue
and flaccid direction (by Philip Moeller). Other
casualties included John Beal, playing second-
fiddle to Boyer for Hepburn's affections, Inez
Courtney and Jean Howard as two of the
conductor's admirers, and Lee Kohlmar attempting to inject a few laughs into the dull plot as a
member of the orchestra. Ferdinand Gottschalk,
Sam Hardy, Helene Millard, Susan Fleming and
Anne Grey also appeared, but only Jean Hersholt,
playing Hepburn's music master, enjoyed a role
equal to his thespian abilities. Sarah Y. Mason,
Victor Heerman and Anthony Veiller collaborated
on the script (story by Lester Cohen), failing to
unearth anything resembling freshness in any of its
various developments. Robert de Grasse's glossy
camera work and Max Steiner's orchestration
could not redeem this hapless endeavour which
producer Pandro S. Berman evidently persuaded
Hepburn into against her wishes.

A title like **The Nitwits** could only mean that the
screen's nitwittiest actors, Bert Wheeler (right)
and Robert Woolsey, were running amok once
again. Having involved themselves in almost every

type of plot, it was inevitable that the duo would
eventually get mixed up in a murder mystery.
This one involved the 'Black Widow', a blackmailer terrorizing the city; Betty Grable (left)
played Wheeler's girl friend who becomes one of
the suspects until Dr Wheeler and Sherlock
Woolsey stumble upon the real culprit. Fred Guiol
and Al Boasberg put together the script from a
story by Stuart Palmer, and George Stevens
enriched it with sturdy direction. Fred Keating,
Evelyn Brent, Erik Rhodes, Hale Hamilton,
Charles Wilson, Arthur Aylesworth, Willie Best
and Lew Kelly also took part in the slapstick
events, of which Lee Marcus was the associate
producer. Songs included: 'Music In My Heart'
Dorothy Fields, Jimmy McHugh; 'You Opened
My Eyes' L. Wolfe Gilbert, Felix Bernard.
▽

A low-budget musical comedy designed to take advantage of the public's current enthusiasm for the genre, **Hooray For Love** stumbled along its well-worn path. The trivial music, sloppily integrated into Marc Lachmann's story (screenplay by Lawrence Hazard and Ray Harris) held minimal attraction for audiences growing accustomed to the excellence of the Astaire–Rogers pictures. The plot surveyed the misfortunes of Gene Raymond, a producer of musical entertainments, who ends up bankrupt and in jail. He ultimately wins Ann Sothern (borrowed from Columbia) and watches gleefully as his show becomes a smash, but the upbeat finale could not redeem all the mediocrity that had come before. Only Lionel Stander's performance as Chowsky, a Russian orchestra conductor, and the appearances of Bill Robinson (left), Jeni LeGon and 'Fats' Waller (right) added a few bursts of vitality. Walter Lang directed, Felix Young was the associate producer, Sammy Lee staged the musical numbers, and the cast also included Maria Gambarelli (of ballet fame), Thurston Hall, Pert Kelton, Georgia Caine, Etienne Girardot and Sam Hardy. Songs included: 'Hooray For Love', 'You're An Angel', 'I'm In Love All Over Again', 'I'm Living In A Great Big Way' Dorothy Fields, Jimmy McHugh.

Richard Dix (right) regained hero status in **The Arizonian**, a fast-paced, action-filled and enjoyable western directed by Charles Vidor. The story and screenplay by Dudley Nichols (who would later write the classic *Stagecoach*) provided Dix with the role of marshal Clay Tallant, Silver City's ambassador of law and order, circa 1880. Tallant is joined in his war against the evil Mannen gang by reformed outlaw Tex Randolph (Preston Foster). Together they protect the honest townsfolk, show proper respect for womanhood (especially Margot Grahame, who added the romantic spark) and vanquish the outlaws (led by Louis Calhern). James Bush, J. Farrell MacDonald, Ray Mayer, Willie Best, Joseph Sauers (Sawyer) and Francis Ford rounded out the cast for associate producer Cliff Reid. The story was remade in 1939 as *The Marshall Of Mesa City*, starring George O'Brien.

She, H. Rider Haggard's classic fantasy about eternal youth, was savoury material for producer Merian C. Cooper's exotic tastes. Cooper wanted Joel McCrea and Frances Dee for the important roles of Leo and Sally, two of the three adventurers (Nigel Bruce, right, as Holly was the other) who happen upon the kingdom of Kor, ruled by 'Hash-A-Mo-Tep' (She Who Must Be Obeyed). Neither McCrea nor Dee was available, forcing him to settle for Randolph Scott (standing centre, borrowed from Paramount) and Helen Mack. Helen Gahagan (left), a movie world unknown, was chosen to play the title character. In order to include some additional elements of excitement (such as a glacial avalanche), screenwriter Ruth Rose transplanted the story from Africa to the Arctic. As directed by Irving Pichel and architect Lansing C. Holden, the film contained a number of impressive components: fabulous sets, striking costumes and superb special effects. But its liabilities outweighed its virtues. The Rose screenplay (with additional dialogue by Dudley Nichols) was stilted and bathetic, and the acting of Scott and Mack proved especially limp, even by their own modest standards. Helen Gahagan performed with majesty and proper wistfulness – to no avail. The movie lost $180,000 and aborted Miss Gahagan's brief motion picture career. Years later she would gain eminence in another arena – politics – during a bitter race for the US Senate with Richard M. Nixon. Also cast: Gustav von Seyffertitz, Lumsden Hare, Samuel Hinds and Noble Johnson. Silent versions were released in 1919 and 1926, and Ursula Andress starred in a 1965 version, distributed by MGM in America. ▷

◁Hollywood's most eagerly awaited feature was **Becky Sharp**, the first full-length production in three-strip Technicolor. The film had been in the pipeline since 1933 when John Hay Whitney and his cousin, Cornelius Vanderbilt Whitney, formed Pioneer Pictures at the suggestion of their friend Merian C. Cooper. The Whitneys were not just interested in making motion pictures; as the company name suggested, they wished to blaze new trails in the entertainment industry. *La Cucaracha*, an award-winning short completed in the 'perfected' Technicolor process in 1934, encouraged them to charge ahead, and William Makepeace Thackeray's classic novel *Vanity Fair*, about a social-climbing adventuress and her escapades among a gallery of rich, titled, crafty and insensitive pre-Victorian characters, was chosen as the subject matter for this special production. Kenneth Macgowan supervised with the patience of Job, coping with an unceasing succession of problems. The biggest of these came a few weeks into production when director Lowell Sherman developed pneumonia and died; Rouben Mamoulian was hired, threw out his predecessor's footage and began anew. Star Miriam Hopkins also came down with pneumonia during the filming, but fortunately recovered. When the picture was finally released, it generated a near unanimous double-edged response from critics. The vivid and artistic use of colour received unqualified praise, whereas the dramatic elements were deemed woefully inadequate. Mamoulian and Robert Edmond Jones, the skilled art director, carefully worked out colour schemes to underscore the varying moods of the story. The Duchess' ball, for example, which takes place on the eve of the Battle of Waterloo, was an astonishing *tour de force* in illustrating how visual elements can reflect and symbolise dramatic themes. Unfortunately, less care was evident in the Francis Edwards Faragoh screenplay (based on Langdon Mitchell's play *Becky Sharp*, as well as the Thackeray original). It unfolded in deadly dull fashion, despite tolerable performances from Frances Dee, Nigel Bruce and Cedric Hardwicke. Though the Academy saw fit to bestow an Oscar nomination on Miss Hopkins (illustrated) for her portrayal of Becky, the frivolous anti-heroine who rises from the mud of a battlefield to the foot of a throne, she was badly miscast and contributed to the picture's indifferent box-office performance. Other members of the very large cast included: Billie Burke, Alison Skipworth, Alan Mowbray, G. P. Huntley Jr, William Stack, George Hassell, William Faversham, Charles Richman, Doris Lloyd, Colin Tapley and Olaf Hytten. Before the picture's release, some industry experts were predicting that colour would supplant black-and-white overnight, just as sound had quickly made silent films anachronistic. But **Becky Sharp** gave evidence that 'the play' was still 'the thing'; although other studios would use Technicolor for occasional productions throughout the rest of the decade, colour, alone, could not guarantee success. Earlier screen versions of *Vanity Fair* included a 1923 release, starring Mabel Ballin, and a 1932 picture, featuring Myrna Loy.

Old Man Rhythm, a college comedy with lots of music, rated a D-minus as entertainment. The idea was for wealthy George Barbier (borrowed from Paramount) to enrol in college to save his son (Charles 'Buddy' Rogers) from all those gold-digging coeds. A convention of writers (story by Lewis Gensler, Sig Herzig and Don Hartman; screenplay by Sig Herzig and Ernest Pagano; additional dialogue by H. W. Hanemann) managed to squeeze one or two laughs out of the excuse for a plot, which was sandwiched between the wall-to-wall musical numbers staged by Sam White and choreographed by Hermes Pan. Edward Ludwig directed this exercise in tedium for Zion Myers, a former assistant to Pandro Berman, who clearly fumbled his first chance as associate producer; his cast included Barbara Kent, Grace Bradley, Betty Grable, Eric Blore, Erik Rhodes, John Arledge, Johnny Mercer (left), Donald Meek and Evelyn Poe (right). Songs: 'I Never Saw A Better Night', 'Old Man Rhythm', 'Boys Will Be Boys', 'Comes The Revolution' 'When You Are In My Arms', 'There's Nothing Like a College Education' Johnny Mercer, Lewis Gensler.
▽

Producer Kenneth Macgowan and director John Cromwell made every effort to capture the spirit of Mazo de la Roche's novel **Jalna** and met the challenge with considerable success. Set in and around a vast farm estate in Canada, the picture focused on the Whiteoak family – their loves, quarrels, jealousies and problems resulting from ill-matched marriages. There was perhaps a bit too much plot here for a 75-minute film, but the actors, whose personalities meshed perfectly with the characters portrayed, filled it with fascinating moments. Ian Hunter (borrowed from Warner Brothers) and Kay Johnson topped the cast, which also included C. Aubrey Smith (centre left), Nigel Bruce, David Manners, Peggy Wood (right), Jessie Ralph (centre, seated), Molly Lamont, Theodore Newton, Halliwell Hobbes (centre right), George Offerman Jr, Clifford Severn (left) and Forrester Harvey. Anthony Veiller wrote the script, based on Garrett Fort and Larry Bachmann's adaptation of ◁ the novel.

A better-than-average programmer, **Hot Tip** linked the talents of James Gleason (right) and ZaSu Pitts, who were seemingly born to play opposite one another. The William Slavens McNutt story (screenplay by Hugh Cummings, Olive Cooper and Louis Stevens) presented Gleason as a horse racing sucker whose wife (Pitts) loathes and abominates gambling. Their daughter's sweetheart needs $200, prompting Gleason to return to the race track where he soon finds himself 'handicapped' in every sense of the word. Gleason and Ray McCarey co-directed, with William Sistrom as associate producer. Margaret Callahan, Russell Gleason, Ray Mayer, Willie Best, J. M. Kerrigan (left), Arthur Stone, Rollo Lloyd, Del Henderson, Donald Kerr and Kitty McHugh were also in it.

After the disastrous *Spitfire*, the respectable but financially disappointing *Little Minister* and the dismal *Break of Hearts*, Katharine Hepburn (right) desperately needed a strong vehicle to revitalize her fading fortunes. She got it in **Alice Adams**, the film that also earned first-line directorial status for George Stevens. Booth Tarkington's Alice, the lovely small town girl snubbed by society because of her father's lack of money and ambition, was a character well-suited to the actress' talents, and Hepburn played her with a poignant blend of self-deceptive idealism and agonized frustration. Stevens' comedy training was evident in the film's best scene where the Adams family invites Alice's beau, proper-born Fred MacMurray (2nd left, borrowed from Paramount), to a dinner that degenerates into one of the most hilarious and, at the same time, painfully lacerating fiascos in American cinema history. A counterfeit happy ending requiring MacMurray to confess his love suddenly and Hepburn to respond, 'Gee Whiz!', was the only false note in Pandro S. Berman's production. Dorothy Yost, Mortimer Offner and Jane Murfin adapted Tarkington's novel for the screen, with roles for Fred Stone, Evelyn Venable, Frank Albertson, Ann Shoemaker (left), Charley Grapewin, Grady Sutton, Hedda Hopper, Jonathan Hale and Hattie McDaniel (2nd right). The picture was a hit and returned Hepburn (temporarily) to the public's good graces. King Vidor had directed a 1923 version of the story, starring his wife Florence Vidor.
▽

The team of distinctive talents attached to the ▷
Astaire–Rogers movies scored a collective triumph
with **Top Hat**. Pandro S. Berman's production
featured a bravura score by Irving Berlin, supple
direction by Mark Sandrich, jocular supporting
performances by Edward Everett Horton (left),
Helen Broderick (2nd left), Eric Blore (left centre)
and Erik Rhodes (right), quintessential art deco
design by Van Nest Polglase and Carroll Clark,
and a plot that built on one incredibly elaborate
romantic misunderstanding – in short, the film
epitomized the Fred (centre right) and Ginger
(centre) formula. Astaire initially disliked the
Dwight Taylor–Allan Scott screenplay (story by
Taylor) intensely, feeling that it required him to
play 'an objectionable young man without charm
or sympathy or humour'. Some rewriting rectified
this problem, and he emerged as the thoroughly
witty and appealing Jerry Travers, who has to
chase Dale Tremont (Ginger) across Europe
before finally convincing her that he is *not* the
husband of Helen Broderick. Astaire–Rogers
films, however, are remembered principally for
their musical numbers, and this one had more than
its fair share of Berlin classics, all suitably and
engagingly choreographed by Astaire and Hermes
Pan. The picture opened at Radio City Music
Hall, easily smashing all previous attendance
records. Its subsequent world release was equally
spectacular, making it the most lucrative picture
produced by RKO during the decade ($3,202,000
in film rentals). **Top Hat** also secured a premium
position for Ginger Rogers and Fred Astaire; at
the end of 1935, the team ranked fourth among the
top star attractions in the movie business. Songs
included: 'No Strings', 'Isn't This A Lovely Day',
'Cheek To Cheek', 'The Piccolino', 'Top Hat,
White Tie And Tails'.

Kenneth Macgowan's final RKO production was
The Return Of Peter Grimm, for the title role
of which he borrowed Lionel Barrymore from
MGM. A remake of a 1926 Fox silent that featured
Alec B. Francis and Janet Gaynor, it told the story
of a man who came back from the dead to redeem
the mess he had made of life. The film's problem
was its tone: uncertain whether to play straight or
go for the laughs, director George Nicholls Jr
allowed the unfolding events to teeter clumsily
between comedy and drama. Mostly he opted for
the sober approach – a mistake, for the whiskered
David Belasco play (script by Francis Edwards
Faragoh) was ripe for burlesque. Barrymore (right)
responded to it with a steady but uninspired
performance; other cast members, notably Allen
Vincent as Barrymore's untoward nephew, Helen
Mack as his adopted daughter and James Bush as
Mack's true love, wobbled throughout. Edward
Ellis, Donald Meek, George Breakston (left),
Lucien Littlefield, Ethel Griffies, Ray Mayer and
Greta Meyer did their best under the circum-
stances. It all added up to a regrettable coda to
Macgowan's RKO career. His future productions
would come out under the Twentieth Century-
Fox banner.

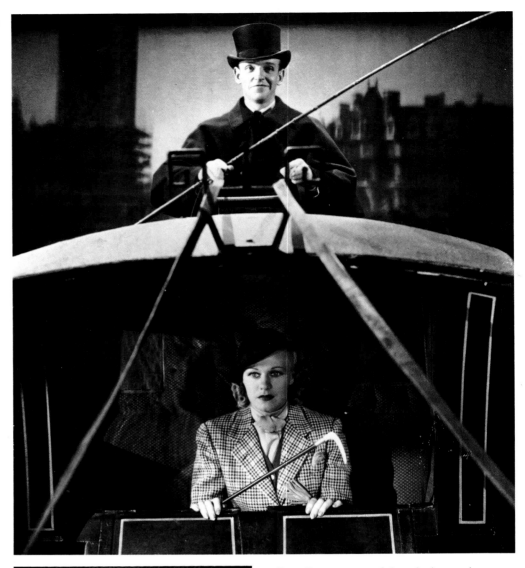

His Family Tree was ripe with old chestnuts.
James Barton (centre), the operator of a pub in
Ireland, journeys to Center City, USA to find out
why his son (William Harrigan, left) hasn't answered any of his letters. It seems the offspring is
trying to cover up his heritage in order to win a
mayoralty election, and has even changed his name
from Murphy to Murphree. Barton blabs the
truth, much to the chagrin of the son's social-
climbing wife (Marjorie Gateson), but saves the
day by bringing in the city's Irish votes in the nick
of time. The Joel Sayre–John Twist screenplay,
inspired by *Old Man Murphy*, a play by Patrick
Kearney and Henry Wagstaff Gribble, gave hypocrisy and snobbery the knockout but packed very
little box-office punch. Also cast: Margaret
Callahan, Addison Randall (right), Maureen
Delany, Clifford Jones, Ray Mayer, Herman Bing,
Pat Moriarty and Ferdinand Munier. The director
was Charles Vidor, with Cliff Reid as associate
producer. This was James Barton's second and last
RKO vehicle.

Rounding up most of the reigning cowboy stars,
including Hoot Gibson (centre), Bob Steele, Harry
Carey (right), Tom Tyler, and old-timers William
Desmond, Franklyn Farnum and William
Farnum, RKO rumbled back into frontier history
with **Powdersmoke Range**. The picture was
loaded with action in the finest tradition of William
Colt MacDonald's 'Three Mesquiteer' novels, one
of which provided the basis of the picture. Harry
Carey stood out as Tucson Smith, whose purchase
of a ranch throws him into conflict with local
mayor Sam Hardy, a greedy politico lining his
coffers through cattle rustling and gin making.
Hardy hires killer Tom Tyler to eliminate Carey,
but Tyler soon joins forces with the white hats
(including Guinn Williams, left) who sterilize
Hardy's den of thievery. Cliff Reid was the
associate producer, and Wallace Fox directed from
a screenplay by Adele Buffington. The supporting
cast included Boots Mallory, Ray Mayer, Adrian
Morris, Buzz Barton, Wally Wales, Art Mix,
Buffalo Bill Jr and Buddy Roosevelt.

In the mode of *Little Women*, *Anne of Green Gables* and *Laddie*, **Freckles** was another homespun fantasy aimed at the broadest cross section of potential filmgoers. Edward Killy and William Hamilton directed with warmth, realizing a good deal of sympathy and whimsical amusement from the Gene Stratton-Porter novel, scripted by Dorothy Yost. Tom Brown (left) portrayed the title character, an orphan who secures a watchman's job in an Indiana lumber camp around the turn of the century. The plot dealt with a burgeoning romance between Brown and Carol Stone (centre left) and the rescue of an impish youngster (Virginia Weidler, centre right, on loan from Paramount) from a group of bandits. Lumsden Hare, James Bush (right), Dorothy Peterson, Addison Richards, Richard Alexander, George Lloyd, Louis Natheaux and Wade Boteler were other members of producer Pandro S. Berman's cast. The story had been filmed twice before, by Paramount in 1917 and FBO in 1928; there would be another remake in 1960, released by Twentieth Century-Fox.

▽

Lurking beneath the 19th century Argentinian setting of **Hi, Gaucho!** was a trite western scripted by Adele Buffington from a story by director Thomas Atkins. Steffi Duna (right) and John Carroll (left, in his screen debut) played starry-eyed lovers whose cattle-ranching families are bitter rivals. After bandit raids, fist-fights, hard-riding chase scenes and other stereotyped oater conventions, the gaucho and his senorita are rounded up for an ardent finale. Walter Plunkett's costumes were the only authentic – and colourful – thing about the picture. Early RKO stalwarts Rod La Rocque and Montagu Love topped a supporting cast that also included Ann Codee, Tom Ricketts, Paul Porcasi and Enrique DeRosas. John E. Burch was the associate producer. Songs included: 'Song Of The Open Road', 'Bandit Song', 'Little White Rose' Albert Hay Malotte.

▽

Merian C. Cooper's production of **The Last Days Of Pompeii** was an improvement on *She*, but it cost substantially more to make, and lost $237,000 at the box-office. The screenplay by Ruth Rose (from a story by James Ashmore Creelman and Melville Baker; adaptation by Boris Ingster) bore no resemblance to Sir Edward Bulwer-Lytton's novel of the same name, other than the historical period and the climactic destruction of Pompeii with the eruption of Mount Vesuvius. Opting for a mixture of decadence and sanctification *à la* Cecil B. De Mille, the writers invented the tale of Marcus, a blacksmith who becomes obsessed with money and power after the death of his wife and son. On a trip to Judea, Marcus' adopted son is healed by Jesus, yet Marcus refuses to act when he sees the healer about to be crucified. The hero finally undergoes a spiritual awakening as the lava engulfs Pompeii, and sacrifices his own life so that his son and a slave girl may escape. Though Preston Foster (right) performed adequately in the lead role, acting honours definitely belonged to Basil Rathbone (left) as Pontius Pilate. His compelling portrait of a clever, haughty man, forever tortured by the memory of the innocent teacher whom he sentenced to death, ranks among the foremost interpretations of Pilate on film. Director Ernest B. Schoedsack managed the large cast (including Alan Hale, David Holt, John Wood, Dorothy Wilson,

Louis Calhern, Wyrley Birch, Gloria Shea, Frank Conroy, William V. Mong, Murray Kinnell and Henry Kolker) well, but allowed the drama to sag at crucial points. One of the chief disappointments was the relatively meagre level of the spectacle. The obligatory gladiatorial scenes were less than dynamic, and the special effects simulating the devastation of Pompeii did not measure up to the best work of chief technician Willis O'Brien and his staff of wizards. **The Last Days Of Pompeii** was a tolerable film that fell short of the great ambitions of its producer – and of RKO. Note: RKO re-released the picture on a double-bill with *She* in 1949. The two films did well enough to recoup their original losses.

With director George Stevens moving on to bigger things, Bert Wheeler (right) and Robert Woolsey (centre right) were left with writer Fred Guiol calling the shots on **The Rainmakers**. The film didn't even aspire to mediocrity, but the fault lay less with the director than with the material (story by Guiol and Albert Treynor; screenplay by Grant Garrett and Leslie Goodwins). The verbal aspect of the duo's comedy, always heavily dependent on sexual *double-entendres*, had been restricted almost out of existence by the ever-watchful Production Code office so, to compensate, the writers piled on more and more slapstick, making the film appealing to 'kiddies' but not to most adult audiences. Even the return of Dorothy Lee (centre left) had no appreciable impact on this tale of two 'scientists' who bring their rain-producing apparatus to a California bean-growing community. It was a topical subject blown to bits by a tornado of moth-eaten gags. Others in the picture were Berton Churchill, George Meeker, Frederic Roland (left) and Edgar Dearing. Lee Marcus was the associate producer. Song: 'Isn't Love The Grandest Thing?' Jack Scholl, Louis Alter.

▽

The Three Musketeers had originally been planned as a vehicle for Francis Lederer and director John Ford. When it finally reached the screen, however, it was directed by Rowland V. Lee and featured Walter Abel (right) as d'Artagnan and Paul Lukas (centre, borrowed from MGM), Moroni Olsen (2nd left) and Onslow Stevens (left) as the musketeer trio. Though all turned in acceptable performances, the screenplay by Lee and Dudley Nichols failed to tap the rich vein of romanticism and excitement in the Alexander Dumas original. Max Steiner's florid musical score helped somewhat, but the picture remains one of the more commonplace versions of a classic swashbuckling tale. Cliff Reid was the associate producer, and Margot Grahame, Heather Angel, Ian Keith, Rosamond Pinchot, John Qualen, Ralph Forbes, Nigel De Brulier, Murray Kinnell, Lumsden Hare and Miles Mander completed the cast. More famous treatments of the same novel include the 1921 United Artists release, starring Douglas Fairbanks, the 1948 MGM production, starring Gene Kelly, and the 1973 Twentieth Century-Fox release, starring Michael York and Raquel Welch.

Even Helen Broderick and Eric Blore, so efficient in the Astaire–Rogers pictures, were powerless to redeem a piece of moronic silliness known as **To Beat The Band**. This musical farce, directed by Ben Stoloff and featuring Matt Malneck and Johnny Mercer's music, must have been thrown together in a big hurry by writers George Marion Jr (story) and Rian James (screenplay). Its comedic moments failed to amuse, and its plot, concerning the quest of Hugh Herbert (left, borrowed from Warner Brothers) to marry a widow within three days and thereby inherit $59 million, bordered on the incomprehensible. Associate producer Zion Myers supervised his second musical flop in a row. Roger Pryor (right), Fred Keating, Phyllis Brooks (centre), Evelyn Poe, Johnny Mercer, Ray Mayer, Joy Hodges and the California Collegians were also in it, and the numbers were staged by Sam White. Songs included: 'If You Were Mine', 'Eeny Meeny Miney Mo', 'Santa Claus Came In The Spring', 'I Saw Her At Eight O'Clock', 'Meet Miss America'.

In Person, a pleasant vehicle for Ginger Rogers, utilized George Brent (imported from Warner Brothers) as her romantic foil. Rogers (centre) portrayed the vainglorious Carol Corliss, a film personality who adopts outlandish disguises to avoid her clamouring admirers. Brent (right) takes up with the star at an out-of-the-way mountain resort and, to her great surprise, is not at all impressed by her true identity. Screenwriter Allan Scott, using a story by Samuel Hopkins Adams as inspiration, chronicled Brent's taming of this Hollywood-era shrew. Director William Seiter made a competent job of transferring the script to screen, calling on Alan Mowbray (left), Grant Mitchell, Samuel S. Hinds, Joan Breslau, Louis Mason, Spencer Charters and Edgar Kennedy for support. Pandro S. Berman produced, Hermes Pan created a couple of sterling dance routines for Miss Rogers, and Oscar Levant and Dorothy Fields wrote the songs. These included: 'Don't Mention Love To Me', 'Got A New Lease On Life', 'Out Of Sight, Out Of Mind'.

Annie Oakley, a fictionalized biography of the famous female sharpshooter by Joseph A. Fields and Ewart Adamson, was adapted to the screen by Joel Sayre and John Twist, and made for sturdy entertainment. More a romantic melodrama than a western, the story centred on Annie (Barbara Stanwyck, left) and her passion for Toby Walker (Preston Foster, right), who claims to be the world's greatest marksman until she bests him. After the mandatory period of professional rivalry and romantic conflict, they are finally united by a marksman superior to both of them – Cupid. George Stevens directed his fourth satisfying film of 1935, and Melvyn Douglas, Moroni Olsen (as Buffalo Bill), Pert Kelton, Andy Clyde, Margaret Armstrong, Delmar Watson and Adeline Craig completed the cast for associate producer Cliff Reid. One note for the changing times department: a humorous subplot involved the attempts of Sitting Bull (Chief Thunderbird), travelling with the Wild West show, to cope with urban life. Today, the joshing treatment of his frustrations would be considered in very poor taste.

Associate producer William Sistrom dusted off ▷
Seven Keys To Baldpate and re-mounted it with
Gene Raymond (right) playing the role that had
launched Richard Dix's RKO career in 1930.
Raymond played the writer who repairs to the
Baldpate Inn for peace and quiet, planning to
finish a novel in 24 hours. Once there, the actor's
job called for little more than to register perpetual
amazement as all manner of motley characters
disturb his concentration. Among them: Eric
Blore as a detective, Murray Alper as a small-time
crook, Margaret Callahan (left) as the romantic
diversion, Moroni Olsen as the heavy with Ray
Mayer as his double-crossing assistant, and Henry
Travers as the hermit-ghost of the inn. Walter
Brennan also scored in a humorous bit at the
beginning of the film. Anthony Veiller and Wallace
Smith wrote the screenplay, based on a novel by
Earl Derr Biggers and a dramatization by George
M. Cohan. Others in the cast were Grant Mitchell,
Erin O'Brien-Moore, Erville Alderson, Harry
Beresford and Emma Dunn. They were directed
by the team of William Hamilton and Edward
Killy, who succeeded in freshening up the slightly
mouldy material. RKO would put it up on the
screen one more time, in 1947 with Phillip Terry.

Hollywood's reputation as a place where anything
can happen was put to the test in **Another Face**
(GB: **It Happened In Hollywood**). The story
(by Thomas Dugan and Ray Mayer) had gangster
Brian Donlevy (left) undergoing plastic surgery,
then bumping off the doctor and heading for
Hollywood to parade his new profile in front of the
cameras. The only hitch is that he overlooks nurse
Molly Lamont, who fingers him when he shows up
in the movies. Hairbrained publicity man Wallace
Ford decides to capture the crook while the
cameras are turning for the attendant exploitation
value, thereby throwing the whole studio into peril
when the set-up is muffed. It was all sheer hokum,
but audiences hungry for a peek at the world
behind the cameras made it a respectable hit. Cliff
Reid was the associate producer, Christy Cabanne
directed and Garrett Graham and John Twist
wrote the energetic screenplay. Also cast: Phyllis
Brooks (right), Erik Rhodes, Alan Hale, Addison
Randall, Paul Stanton, Charles Wilson, Hattie
McDaniel and Si Jenks.

The third chapter in Frank Buck's (illustrated)
jungle adventures had an exciting title – **Fang
And Claw** – but there wasn't much in it that
audiences had not seen in his two previous films.
Essentially a demonstration of various methods of
trapping, it showed the capture of a tiger, two huge
pythons, a baby hippopotamus, an alligator, a bird
of paradise and several other wild beasts, plus the
usual bunch of mischievous monkeys, and caged
birds chirping sweetly. The film was technically
superior to the earlier documentaries, thanks to the
fine photography of Harry E. Squire and Nicholas
Cavaliere, and to Buck's confident direction.
Winston Sharples composed the music for the Van
Beuren release. Audiences seemed to be tiring of
trips to the Asiatic bush; this venture earned
profits of only $46,000 for RKO.

Opera star Lily Pons (right) made her motion
picture debut in **I Dream Too Much** as a
provincial French girl who falls in love with an
American composer (Henry Fonda, left, borrowed
from Walter Wanger). Complications arise when
her singing career takes off while his operatic
composition falls flat; undaunted, she gets her man
by transforming his opera into a successful musical
comedy. Producer Pandro S. Berman, who hoped
to make Miss Pons an RKO star in the mould of
Columbia's Grace Moore, provided her with John
Cromwell as director, and a winning score by
Jerome Kern and Dorothy Fields, but the screenplay by Edmund North and James Gow (original
story by Elsie Finn and David G. Wittels)
sabotaged their efforts. A clumsy mélange of high
brow artistry (Miss Pons singing arias from various
operas, including 'Caro Nome' from *Rigoletto*) and
low-jinks comedy (Eric Blore cavorting with a
trained seal named Duchess), it was further
weakened by soggy dialogue. Though handtailored
to showcase the heroine's unquestionable vocal
gifts, the film, not surprisingly, flopped. Osgood
Perkins, Lucien Littlefield, Lucille Ball, Mischa
Auer, Paul Porcasi and Scott Beckett were others
in the cast. Songs included: 'I Dream Too Much',
'The Jockey On The Carousel', 'I'm The Echo', 'I
Got Love'.
▽

We're Only Human featured Preston Foster
(left) as a reckless, lone-wolf cop who thinks he can
lick all the crooks in the world singlehanded. James
Gleason, a more sober and calculating officer,
eventually convinces him that 'by the book' is the
better way. Nonetheless, Foster's original instincts
surface during the slam-bang finale in which he
wipes out an entire gang by himself. James Flood
matched the *macho* demands of Rian James'
screenplay (based on a story by Thomas Walsh)
with taut direction. Jane Wyatt (right, borrowed
from Universal) gave a good account of herself as a
news reporter who seems always to be in the wrong
place at the right time, and Arthur Hohl, John
Arledge, Jane Darwell, Moroni Olsen, Christian
Rub, Mischa Auer, Harold Huber and Rafaela
Ottiano were also cast. Former staff writer Edward
Kaufman functioned as associate producer.
▽

★★★★★★★★★★★★★★★★★★

1936

★★★★★★★★★★★★★★★★★★

The signing of a distribution deal with Walt Disney was a highlight in company affairs. Disney's foresight regarding television was a major factor in his decision to join RKO. Knowing of the studio's close ties with RCA, then a leading sponsor of video development, Disney cemented a deal with Sam Briskin after negotiations with his former distributor, United Artists, fell apart. Briskin had worked with Walt and Roy Disney around 1930 when the brothers were using Columbia as a releasing outlet.

Production chief Briskin also signed up a number of new RKO producers during the year. Edward Small, pioneer Jesse L. Lasky, and ace producer-director Howard Hawks all agreed to make films for the company. With Pandro Berman's unit the only dependable creative entity within the studio confines, these gentlemen were a much needed asset, and the studio was also fortunate in acquiring the services of George and Ira Gershwin to compose for the 'A' musical pictures. However, Max Steiner, the brilliant composer of scores for **King Kong**, **The Informer** and many other RKO titles, departed for Warner Bros. – a major loss to the studio; and Ann Harding, whose drawing power had faded substantially since the early part of the decade, was not rehired when her contract came to an end.

On the executive front, B. B. Kahane moved to Columbia in mid-year, taking approximately the same job vacated by Sam Briskin when he came to RKO. Kahane was an able executive who had contributed significantly to RKO's successes over the years, but new management had demoted him, and he felt it was time to get out. J. R. McDonough, likewise demoted by the Spitz–Briskin regime, stayed on in a lesser capacity. Finally, Sid Rogell, who would be an important studio functionary for years to come, arrived to take on the job of studio manager.

RKO released 39 films during the year. With certain exceptions, they were not an enduring group. **Follow The Fleet** and **Swing Time** were the top money hits, while **The Ex-Mrs. Bradford**, **The Bride Walks Out** and **Walking On Air** also performed well at the box-office.

Corporate profits amounted to $2,514,734. It was a good year for the entire industry with weekly theatre attendance increasing to 81 million patrons and industry grosses up $250,000,000 over the previous year.

Follow The Fleet departed from the usual Astaire–Rogers blueprint. Its screenplay by Dwight Taylor and Allan Scott (based on Hubert Osborne's play *Shore Leave*) did not depend on a mistaken identity component and it portrayed the two stars (illustrated), less-than-convincingly, as a sailor and a dance hall girl, both slightly impoverished and worried about money. The usual comedy contingent was also missing, its place taken by a romantic subplot involving Randolph Scott (borrowed from Paramount) and Harriet Hilliard (later Harriet Nelson). Still, the essence and style of the picture were in keeping with previous successes. The Navy uniform provided an attractive alternative to Fred Astaire's usual tuxedo, and he and Ginger quarrelled and made up and, above all, danced with their customary *joie de vivre* (numbers staged by Hermes Pan). Mark Sandrich's direction was solid; Irving Berlin's score, if not quite as bewitching as his tunes for *Top Hat*, contained the sublime 'Let's Face The Music And Dance' and had much to recommend it; and the production values ensured by Pandro S. Berman's supervision were munificent and dazzling. There were weaknesses: Randolph Scott, playing Astaire's sailor pal, was clearly out of his depth, and the missing comedy performers left a noticeable gap, making this the least funny of the Astaire–Rogers cycle. Nevertheless, the imperfections didn't bother lovers of these unique musicals, and, once again, RKO had a huge hit in its programme. Cast in supporting roles were Betty Grable, Astrid Allwyn, Harry Beresford, Russell Hicks, Brooks Benedict and Lucille Ball. Though RKO's *Hit The Deck* (1930) had been an earlier musical version of Osborne's *Shore Leave*, this film was based on the original play, not on the Jack Oakie picture. A silent *Shore Leave* had been made in 1925 by Inspiration and released by First National, starring Richard Barthelmess and Dorothy Mackaill. Songs included: 'We Saw The Sea', 'Let Yourself Go', 'I'm Putting All My Eggs In One Basket', 'I'd Rather Lead A Band', 'Get Thee Behind Me, Satan', 'But Where Are You?'
▽

One of the most bizarre films ever produced by a ▷ Hollywood studio, **Sylvia Scarlett** now enjoys a cult following among cinema buffs all over the world. In its day, however, it was considered by many to be the worst 'A' picture ever released by RKO. The pet project of Katharine Hepburn and director George Cukor, it opened divertingly with Hepburn (left), Brian Aherne (right) and Cary Grant attempting to become 'con artists' in Victorian England. This plot line soon dissolved, and the film meandered off in a variety of unexpected directions, all tied loosely together by the overall theme of illusion versus reality. As its thrust becomes more and more diffused, its characters become more and more unsympathetic and it finally concludes with a blurred, implausible resolution. One element that especially disturbed audiences was Hepburn's masquerading as a boy through much of the action, even though the reason for the disguise disappears near the beginning of the picture. Her wooing by both men and women was supposed to be funny, but didn't play that way. No picture ever did more damage to Miss Hepburn's public esteem than this one. Cary Grant (borrowed from Paramount) did score a minor victory. Playing disreputable cockney Jimmy Monkley, Grant was able to display a flair for comedy and an acting range not evident in his earlier films. Gladys Unger, John Collier and Mortimer Offner collaborated on the screenplay, basing it on Compton Mackenzie's novel. Edmund Gwenn, Natalie Paley, Dennie Moore and Lennox Pawle also appeared. Producer Pandro S. Berman was so horrified by the audience's violent antipathy when **Sylvia Scarlett** was first screened that he told Hepburn and Cukor he never wanted to see either of them again. He later calmed down, though the picture was a total flop ($363,000 loss).

With Pandro S. Berman supervising and Charles Vidor directing, **Muss 'Em Up** (GB: **The House Of Fate**) was a classy crime melodrama. A successful combination of laughter and thrills, it starred Preston Foster as witty, hard-boiled detective Tip O'Neil. Erwin Gelsey's script, based on a novel by James Edward Grant, uncorked the mystery with the killing of a millionaire's pet dog, then added kidnapping, ransom demands and homicide. Foster (centre right) played his role in the finest tradition of the Dashiell Hammett school of tough-guy theatrics; other standouts were millionaire Alan Mowbray (right), Ralph Morgan (as Mowbray's eccentric brother-in-law), and Guinn Williams (Foster's chauffeur and body-guard). Margaret Callahan (centre left), Maxie Rosenbloom, Molly Lamont, John Carroll, Florine McKinney, Robert Middlemass (left), Noel Madison, Maxine Jennings, Harold Huber, Clarence Muse, Paul Porcasi, Ward Bond and John Adair completed the cast. Well-paced and cleverly plotted, **Muss 'Em Up** easily overcame its miserable title. Note: The title did have a certain topicality. New York police commissioner Lewis J. Valentine had used a similar expression while instructing his men how to treat criminals during gangland roundups.

Somewhat reminiscent of *Morning Glory*, **Chatterbox** starred Anne Shirley (left) as a stage-struck Vermont girl who storms the bastions of show business in New York. Her Broadway debut in 'Virtue's Reward' is a total fiasco, but she finds happiness anyway – in the arms of Phillips Holmes. Shirley made the guileless neophyte appealing and director George Nicholls Jr surrounded her with a benign contingent of supporting players that included Edward Ellis, Erik Rhodes, Margaret Hamilton, Granville Bates, Lucille Ball (right), Allen Vincent, George Offerman Jr, Maxine Jennings, Richard Abbott, Wilfred Lucas and Margaret Armstrong. Holmes seemed ill-at-ease throughout. Sam Mintz wrote the delicate adaptation of David Carb's play for new associate producer Robert Sisk.

Director Stephen Roberts worked hard on **The Lady Consents**, but his assured and sensitive handling of the picture's unoriginal plot was unable to transform it into anything special. P. J. Wolfson's story (screenplay by Wolfson and Anthony Veiller) focused on Ann Harding (centre), as the wife of successful physician Herbert Marshall (left, borrowed from Paramount), who discovers that a younger and more vivacious girl (Margaret Lindsay, right, borrowed from Warner Bros.) is usurping her husband's affections. Harding steps gracefully aside, allowing Marshall to play out the romance and so discover the basic error of his judgment. While the performances of the two actresses were sound, this was not one of Herbert Marshall's most memorable pieces of work. He was overshadowed by his on-screen father, Edward Ellis, who wisely and sincerely labours to keep the marriage together. Walter Abel, Hobart Cavanaugh and Ilka Chase also appeared for associate producer Edward Kaufman. Note concerning the ever-watchful eye of the viewing public: RKO was inundated by letters from outraged members of various American and Canadian glass blowers' unions, protesting the inclusion of a scene in which beer was served in a tin can.

Two In The Dark, a confused mystery directed by Ben Stoloff from a novel by Gelett Burgess, presented Walter Abel (right) as an amnesiac worried by the possibility that he has participated in the murder of a theatrical producer. Unemployed actress Margot Grahame (left) comes to Abel's rescue by helping him to resurrect his past, even though she suspects he may indeed be a killer. It took intense powers of concentration to follow the film's convoluted plot, which made it a loser with whodunnit fans as well as average theatre patrons. Seton I. Miller wrote the screenplay, giving additional roles to Wallace Ford, Gail Patrick, Alan Hale, Leslie Fenton, Eric Blore, Erin O'Brien-Moore, Erik Rhodes, J. Carrol Naish and Addison Randall. Zion Myers was the associate producer. The studio reverted to the novel's original title, *Two O'Clock Courage*, when it remade the picture in 1945 with Tom Conway and Ann Rutherford.

Non-stop gags superbly realized by Leigh Jason's crackling direction made **Love On A Bet** one of the year's most sympathetic comedies. Gene Raymond (centre) wagers that he can depart from New York in his underwear and arrive in Los Angeles 10 days later with a good suit, $100 in cash and a sweetheart to boot. How he accomplishes his goals was the subject of P. J. Wolfson and Philip G. Epstein's script, based on a story by Kenneth Earl. Raymond was in top form as the transcontinental hitchhiker, and so were Helen Broderick (left), an acidulous motorist who gives him a lift, and Wendy Barrie (right, borrowed from Paramount), as Miss Broderick's niece who marries the hero in the end. William Collier Sr, Spencer Charters, Walter Johnson, Addison Randall, Eddie Gribbon and Morgan Wallace had supporting roles for associate producer Lee Marcus.

Richard Dix (right) struck gold, romance and an endless vein of clichés in **Yellow Dust**, a minor western directed by Wallace Fox. After four years of collegiate studies in mineralogy, Dix teams up with grizzled prospector Andy Clyde and, in short order, they find the mother lode. On the way to register their claim, they interrupt a stage coach holdup and save damsel Leila Hyams (left) from the outlaws. Events in the Cyril Hume–John Twist script (suggested by Dan Totheroh and George O'Neil's play) continue along this dusty, well-worn trail with Dix winning the girl and killing the claim-jumping crook (Onslow Stevens, complete with malevolent moustache) in a climactic gun-duel. Associate producer Cliff Reid's cast also included Moroni Olsen, Jessie Ralph, Victor Potel, Ethan Laidlaw and Ted Oliver. One of the few Hollywood staples being upgraded by the studio during this period was the western; **Yellow Dust**, however, made no contribution to the advances in quality.

Bert Wheeler (centre right) and Robert Woolsey (centre left) had enjoyed remarkable longevity by RKO standards, but they were nearing the end of their Radio Pictures career. **Silly Billies**, featuring the duo as a dentist and his assistant who invade Gold Rush territory, was compared unfavourably to a 'Popeye' cartoon by the *New York Times*. The problem had been intensifying for several years: a kind of comedic *rigor mortis* had set in, and neither the actors nor their writers or directors seemed able to shake it off. They continued to rely on the same tired plot formulas and the same hackneyed verbal repartee. Though they were made on small budgets, the Wheeler–Woolsey efforts now regularly lost money. It did not take an acute sense of hearing to detect the death knell that was beginning to toll. Fred Guiol directed **Silly Billies** from a story by Thomas Lennon and screenplay by Al Boasberg and Jack Townley. Dorothy Lee (centre), Harry Woods, Ethan Laidlaw, Chief Thunderbird, Delmar Watson and Richard Alexander were also members of associate producer Lee Marcus' cast, and the obligatory song was 'Tumble On Tumbleweed' by Dave Dreyer and Jack Scholl.

The Farmer In The Dell was supposed to showcase Fred Stone as a new Will Rogers. He did a fair job of the impersonation, though cagey Will would never have set foot in a story this weak. Stone (left) was Pa Boyer, patriarch of an Iowa farm family who are perfectly content with their lot until Ma (Esther Dale) insists they move to Hollywood. Her goal is to engineer a movie career for daughter Jean Parker (centre, borrowed from MGM), but, instead, it is Pa who becomes the character star. Undeterred, Ma 'goes Hollywood' in a big way, nearly wrecking her daughter's love life before Pa blows up and brings everyone back to earth. The script by Sam Mintz and John Grey, from a novel by Phil Stong, was of very little consequence, but then nothing in director Ben Holmes' film was either, with the exception of a witty and flamboyant performance by Moroni Olsen as the director who discovers Pa's hidden abilities. Robert Sisk was the associate producer. Also cast: Frank Albertson, Maxine Jennings, Ray Mayer, Lucille Ball, Rafael Corio, Frank Jenks, Spencer Charters, John Beck (right) and, in a bit part, Tony Martin.

The call of the wild echoed through **Two In Revolt**, an interesting novelty picture starring a dog and a horse. Lightning (right) and Warrior are born on the same day, become fast friends and then take off for the freedom of the wilderness. They are reunited when a wolfpack attacks a herd of wild horses led by Warrior, and Lightning helps drive the marauders off. They eventually return to their youthful trainer (John Arledge, left) who grooms Warrior for the big race. He wins, of course, with some extra encouragement from the strong-hearted German shepherd. The human performers, who included Louise Latimer (centre) as Arledge's sweetheart, Moroni Olsen as a racehorse breeder, and Emmett Vogan as a crooked gambler, were no match for the animals; every time they showed up in the Ferdinand Reyher–Frank Howard Clark–Jerry Hutchison screenplay (story by Earl Johnson and Thomas Storey), the picture's pace decelerated somewhat. Thankfully, the dog and horse were accorded enough of the 60-minute running time to make it exciting. Glenn Tryon deserved special credit for his exacting direction under challenging circumstances, and associate producer Robert Sisk also merited praise for giving this 'star-less' film first-cabin treatment. Other cast members: Harry Jans, Willie Best, Murray Alper, Ethan Laidlaw and Max Wagner.

Helen Broderick (right) replaced Edna May Oliver in **Murder On A Bridle Path**, yet another in the series of Hildegarde Withers–Oscar Piper mysteries. Since the screen persona of Miss Withers had been moulded by the inimitable Oliver, no one could ever be a fully acceptable substitute, but Broderick, who was a superb character actress, did pretty well. The circumstances in this case were set in motion by the death of flirtatious grass widow Sheila Terry, who is slain on the bridle path in New York's Central Park. Clandestine amours, back alimony, a wrecked bicycle and a forged jail release all serve to complicate the puzzle and test the deductive powers of Hildegarde and Inspector Piper (James Gleason, left). Four literary brains (Dorothy Yost, Thomas Lennon, Edmund North and James Gow) concocted the teasing screenplay from a novel by Stuart Palmer, offering secondary parts to Louise Latimer, Owen Davis Jr, John Arledge, John Carroll, Leslie Fenton, Christian Rub, Willie Best, John Miltern, Spencer Charters, James Donlan, Gustav von Seyffertitz, Frank Reicher and Harry Jans. Edward Killy and William Hamilton co-directed efficiently for associate producer William Sistrom.

Having given up on Ann Harding (right), RKO pushed her into **The Witness Chair**, a laboured whodunnit that was an embarrassment to all involved. The plot had something to do with Harding's 'righteous' murder of an embezzler (Douglass Dumbrille) who is about to elope with the innocent daughter (Frances Sage) of her beloved (Walter Abel). Miss Harding's actions backfire when Abel finds himself accused of the murder. A flashback structure was utilized, perhaps to add zest to the wafer-thin story, but it only succeeded in over-stretching the plot. Dumbrille made a convincing heavy, but the other characters – played by Moroni Olsen, Margaret Hamilton, Maxine Jennings, William Benedict, Paul Harvey (left), Murray Kinnell, Charles Arnt and Frank Jenks – were drab and dusty. George Nicholls Jr didn't waste much energy on the direction of Rian James and Gertrude Purcell's excruciating screenplay (story: Rita Weiman). The associate producer was Cliff Reid. Once a beautiful and magnetic star, Ann Harding left RKO in disgrace following **The Witness Chair**. A number of years would pass before she returned to work for the studio.

In **Special Investigator**, Richard Dix (right) played a brilliant criminal lawyer who chalks up a sensational track record – defending the worst members of the mob. When, however, his G-man brother is gunned down by the criminals, he reconsiders his deeds, joins the Department of Justice, and goes 'under cover' to exact appropriate revenge. Based on a story by Erle Stanley Gardner and forcefully directed by Louis King, the picture contained enough red-blooded melodrama to earn a profit of $91,000. Dix gave one of his most natural performances, and J. Carrol Naish was excellent as the brutal gang leader. Also cast: Margaret Callahan, Erik Rhodes (centre), Owen Davis Jr, Ray Mayer, Harry Jans, Joseph Sawyer, Sheila Terry (left), J. M. Kerrigan, Jed Prouty and Russell Hicks. Louis Stevens, Thomas Lennon and Ferdinand Reyher hammered out the script for associate producer Cliff Reid.

In a year littered with expensive failures, one unexpected success surprised even the studio executives. **The Ex-Mrs. Bradford** was another thinly disguised reworking of the 'Thin Man' formula with William Powell (right), on this occasion, playing a famous surgeon suspected of a series of murders by police inspector James Gleason. The doctor soon assumes the role of sleuth, solving the crimes and clearing his name. Jean Arthur (left) handled the role of Powell's wife with assurance, abetted by that superb refugee from the Astaire–Rogers series, Eric Blore, as the butler, and a supporting cast that included Robert Armstrong, Lila Lee, Grant Mitchell, Erin O'Brien-Moore, Ralph Morgan, Frank M. Thomas, Lucile Gleason, Frank Reicher, John Sheehan, Paul Fix, Charles Richman and Frankie Darro. The mystery was nimbly structured and the humour urbane and ingratiating, yet the film offered nothing new. Once again the audience encountered Powell, gracefully solving a dangerous puzzle and sparring wittily with Arthur (rather than Myrna Loy or Ginger Rogers). Nonetheless, movie consumers were evidently famished for this kind of entertainment, and **The Ex-Mrs. Bradford**, directed by Stephen Roberts from a screenplay by Anthony Veiller based on James Edward Grant's story, was the third most profitable film of the year for RKO. Edward Kaufman served as associate producer.

△

Dancing Pirate was the second and last Pioneer three-strip Technicolor feature to be distributed by RKO. Feeling they had erred in picking a 'high-brow' piece of material (*Becky Sharp*) for their first colour venture, the Pioneer executives (including Merian C. Cooper) moved in the opposite direction. They chose a trifling fantasy about a Boston dancing master shanghaied by a crew of picturesque (and harmless) pirates. The plot (story: Emma Lindsay-Squier; adaptation: Jack Wagner, Boris Ingster; screenplay: Ray Harris, Francis Edwards Faragoh) was just a flimsy excuse for a parade of exotic settings and costumes designed to exhaust the spectrum of colour possibilities. Starring Steffi Duna (left), directed by Lloyd Corrigan and designed by Robert Edmond Jones (all had worked on the initial Technicolor short, *La Cucaracha*), **Dancing Pirate** was pretty but disappointing. It lacked an interesting story; the comedy was ineffectual, and the score – by no less than Richard Rodgers and Lorenz Hart – a dud. This final Pioneer experiment quickly self-destructed at the pay-box window. Also featured, for producer John Speaks, were Charles Collins (right) and Frank Morgan, plus Luis Alberni, Victor Varconi, Jack LaRue, Alma Real, William V. Mong, Mitchell Lewis, Julian Rivero, John Eberts and the Dancing Cansinos (Rita Hayworth's family). Songs included: 'Are You In Love?', 'When You're Dancing The Waltz'.

△

Fred Stone was public bulwark number one in **Grand Jury**, the story of a law-abiding citizen outraged by legal practices that permit killers to go unpunished. Aided by reporter Owen Davis Jr (right), who happens to be in love with Stone's grand-daughter Louise Latimer (left), he mounts a crusade to round up a bunch of murdering racketeers. The crusade was a success, but the movie, alas, was not. Joseph A. Fields and Philip G. Epstein's screenplay brought nothing fresh to the story by James Edward Grant and Thomas Lennon, and neither did Albert S. Rogell's perfunctory direction. Among others wasted in the Lee Marcus production were Guinn Williams, Harry Beresford, Frank M. Thomas (centre), Harry Jans, Margaret Armstrong, Charles Wilson, Russell Hicks, Billy Gilbert, Robert E. Keane, William Davidson, G. Pat Collins, Billy Arnold, Thomas Jackson and Edward Gargan.

A minor masterpiece, but now largely forgotten ▷ even by dogged aficionados of the western, **The Last Outlaw** featured Harry Carey (left) as a famous bad man who gets out of jail after serving 25 years. He discovers things have deteriorated somewhat in his old hangout of Broken Knee, now called Center City. Progress has brought with it bad manners, noise pollution, incompetent politico sheriffs and, most ridiculous of all, dude cowboys who sing to spectators from the movie screen. Long before *Ride The High Country* (MGM, 1962) and *Lonely Are The Brave* (Universal International, 1962), **The Last Outlaw** chronicled the losing of the west, poking affectionate fun at the modern west while developing a story to demonstrate the superiority of certain simple, old-fashioned frontier virtues and abilities. Journeyman Christy Cabanne directed the John Twist–Jack Townley script (based on an original story by John Ford and E. Murray Campbell) for associate producer Robert Sisk. The cast included Hoot Gibson (right), Tom Tyler, Henry B. Walthall, Margaret Callahan, Ray Mayer, Harry Jans, Frank M. Thomas, Russell Hopton, Frank Jenks, Maxine Jennings and Fred Scott. Song: 'My Heart's On The Trail' Nathaniel Shilkret, Frank Luther.

An inferiority complex may sound more tragic than comic, but it was clearly a laughing matter in **Bunker Bean** (GB: **His Majesty, Bunker Bean**). The titular hero, a mousy office drudge, gains confidence from a crystal gazer who informs him that he is the reincarnation of both Napoleon and an Egyptian pharaoh. Convinced of his innate powers of conquest, he wins the love of the boss' daughter and soon becomes a big shot, much to the chagrin of her desk-pounding father. Owen Davis Jr (left) played the worm who turns, Louise Latimer (right) his romantic *vis-à-vis* and Robert McWade her dyspeptic father. William Hamilton and Edward Killy were the directors for associate producer William Sistrom. The screenplay, by Edmund North, James Gow and Dorothy Yost, realized most of the laughs inherent in Harry Leon Wilson's original novel and a play by Lee Wilson Dodd. Also in it: Jessie Ralph, Lucille Ball, Berton Churchill, Edward Nugent, Hedda Hopper, Ferdinand Gottschalk, Leonard Carey, Russell Hicks, Pierre Watkin, and Sybil Harris as the crystal gazer. Earlier versions of the tale were produced by Paramount in 1918 and Warner Bros. in 1925.

▽

Let's Sing Again was the first of a series of Bobby Breen musicals produced by Sol Lesser's Principal Productions for RKO release. Eight-year-old wonder boy Breen developed his talents on radio with Eddie Cantor and, thus, came to the movies a thoroughgoing entertainer. The plots tailored for him were mawkishly sentimental, requiring the tenor-cum-soprano to suffer bravely until the ineluctably uplifting denouement. Along the way, the narratives would creak and groan, yielding outlandish opportunities for Breen (centre) to demonstrate his vocal abilities. In this case, the precocious youngster runs away from an orphanage and joins a travelling show, where he is adopted by Henry Armetta (right), playing a stereotyped screen Italian. The climax comes in New York where Bobby is improbably reunited with his operatic father through the miracle of music. Kurt Neumann directed from a screenplay by Don Swift and Sam Jarrett. The supporting players included George Houston (left), Vivienne Osborne, Grant Withers, Inez Courtney, Richard Carle, Lucien Littlefield and Ann Doran. Songs included: 'Let's Sing Again' Jimmy McHugh, Gus Kahn; 'Lullaby' Hugo Riesenfeld, Selma Hautzik; 'Farmer In The Dell' Samuel Pokrass, Charles O. Locke, Richard E. Tyler.

Although Bret Harte's name was above the title, **M'Liss** bore only a casual resemblance to his novel about a rip-roaring mining camp on which the film was based. Screenwriter Dorothy Yost softened the book's tough core and transformed it into an idyllic romance involving naive mountain girl Anne Shirley (left) and earnest school master John Beal (right). Miss Shirley had an instinct for this type of homespun role, and her charming performance helped make **M'Liss** a pleasant lollipop of a movie. Also deserving of praise were George Nicholls Jr, who directed with an elfin touch, and character actors Guy Kibbee, Moroni Olsen, Douglass Dumbrille and Frank M. Thomas who handled their limited roles with professional finesse. Ray Mayer, Barbara Pepper, William Benedict, Arthur Hoyt, Margaret Armstrong, James Bush and Esther Howard were in it too, for associate producer Robert Sisk. Mary Pickford had starred in a 1918 version of the story, and Universal also filmed it, as *The Girl Who Ran Wild*, with Gladys Walton in 1922.

Edward Small, formerly production chief of Reliance Pictures, joined RKO as a producer and gave the company a breezy comedy hit – **The Bride Walks Out** – in his first effort. The P. J. Wolfson–Philip G. Epstein screenplay (based on a story by Howard Emmett Rogers) contained a routine plot, but offered high-quality dialogue and amiable comic characters. Leigh Jason directed at a rapid clip, managing to wheedle something constructive from practically every actor present. Barbara Stanwyck (right) was top-cast as a bride with caviar tastes forced to live on a hamburger diet by her doting but low-salaried husband (Gene Raymond). They eventually split up, bringing millionaire idler Robert Young (centre, borrowed from MGM) into Stanwyck's orbit before love ultimately triumphs over luxury. Young contributed one of his best performances, and Helen Broderick (left) and Ned Sparks were in top form as a couple always on the verge of marital warfare. Also cast: Anita Colby, Vivien Oakland, Willie Best, Robert Warwick, Billy Gilbert, Ward Bond, Edgar Dearing, Wade Boteler and Hattie McDaniel.

A remake of a 1930 Conrad Nagel–Lila Lee vehicle, **Second Wife** was unquestionably the worst RKO film of the year (*Sylvia Scarlett* notwithstanding). Audiences in theatres everywhere hooted its trite story, platitudinous dialogue and extended histrionics. Thomas Lennon's dehydrated script (based on a play by Fulton Oursler), aggravated by Edward Killy's meat-axe direction, left the actors between the proverbial rock and hard spot. Walter Abel (left) played the husband who is faced with a choice between journeying abroad to comfort his ill, 10-year-old son or remaining at home with his new wife, who is about to have their first child. An intelligent decision would have been for Abel to stay out of this picture in the first place. Gertrude Michael (right, borrowed from Paramount) appeared as the wife, Erik Rhodes as an admirer who tries to break up the marriage and Lee Van Atta as the boy struck down by typhoid. Producer Lee Marcus' supporting cast also included Emma Dunn, Brenda Fowler, Frank Reicher and George Breakston.

Ann Sothern (left) and Gene Raymond (right) had RKO executives **Walking On Air**, which was also the title of one of the studio's best 'B' musicals. Engagingly scripted by Bert Kalmar, Harry Ruby, Viola Brothers Shore and Rian James from a story by Francis M. Cockrell, the plot turned on Miss Sothern's hiring of Raymond to pose as an effete French count. His job is to insult and alienate her father (Henry Stephenson) and aunt (Jessie Ralph) to such an extent that they will be glad to let her marry recently-divorced (and heavily alimonied) Alan Curtis. Raymond eventually decides he wants the young lady for himself and mounts a radio campaign to win her. Director Joseph Santley maintained buoyancy throughout, whipping the romance, comedy, music and suspense into a delightful 68-minute package. Edward Kaufman produced, with George Meeker, Gordon Jones, Maxine Jennings, Anita Colby and Patricia Wilder in secondary roles. Songs included: 'Cabin On The Hilltop' Bert Kalmar, Harry Ruby; 'My Heart Wants To Dance', 'Let's Make A Wish' Kalmar, Ruby, Sid Silvers.

Mary Of Scotland was carefully calculated to undo the *Sylvia Scarlett* damage and bring Katharine Hepburn (right) back to public favour. Using Maxwell Anderson's drama as a basis, Academy Award winners Dudley Nichols and John Ford collaborated on a motion picture that fairly reeked of prestige. Producer Pandro S. Berman gave it V.I.P. treatment, employing a huge cast and making it the second most expensive production of the year (only *Swing Time* cost more). Though the final product received respectful praise from the critics, it flopped with the public, further diminishing Hepburn's industry reputation. The reasons for failure were obvious. This chronicle of the life-and-death struggle for supremacy between two iron-willed women – Mary Stuart, and Elizabeth I of England – was long, ponderous, episodic and ultimately passionless. In short, it was an utter bore. The excitement

that scenarist Nichols and director Ford had provided in *The Informer* was missing here; even Hepburn's acting seemed oddly guarded and bloodless. Only Fredric March's performance as the Earl of Bothwell, who made Mary forget her throne, had some fire to it, thus contributing to Ford's reputation as a male-oriented director incapable of guiding strong actresses. Also featured were Florence Eldridge (left) as Queen Elizabeth, Douglas Walton as Lord Darnley and Moroni Olsen as John Knox, and the rest of the cast included John Carradine, Robert Barrat, Gavin Muir, Ian Keith, William Stack, Ralph Forbes, Alan Mowbray, Frieda Inescort and Donald Crisp. The disappointing results of **Mary Of Scotland** placed RKO in a desperate position: something had to be done to resuscitate Katharine Hepburn's career before the negative tide became irreversible.

Now considered by many to be the best of the ▷ Astaire–Rogers musicals, **Swing Time** earned its reputation primarily through its sensational dance numbers – especially 'Bojangles of Harlem', in which Fred Astaire danced with a triplicate shadow in a bravura example of creative special effects, and 'Never Gonna Dance', perhaps the most dazzling wooing-and-surrender number in the entire cycle. After a momentary absence in *Follow The Fleet*, the humorous element reappeared with Helen Broderick and Eric Blore once again in attendance and Victor Moore joining the entourage as Pop, Astaire's sidekick. A delicious spoof occurred near the beginning when Astaire, pretending to be a clumsy bumpkin, takes a 'hoofing' lesson from Ginger at the Gordon Dancing Academy. She throws up her hands, sure she could never teach this clod anything and is promptly fired by her boss (Blore) for incompetence (that is, refusing to accept money from a sucker). Astaire then proceeds to prove that Ginger is the best teacher in the world by dancing a complicated routine that elicits one of Blore's incomparable stunned expressions of amazement. If *Swing Time* had a weakness, it was the story (screenplay by Howard Lindsay and Allan Scott, story by Erwin Gelsey). Though Astaire–Rogers plots had never been much more than cleverly orchestrated excuses for the musical set pieces, this one – about professional gambler 'Lucky' Garnett, whose big problem is to keep from earning $25,000 whereupon he will be forced to marry his home town sweetheart (Betty Furness) – was even sillier and flimsier than most. Pandro S. Berman again produced, utilizing Hermes Pan to stage the dance ensembles and George Stevens to direct. It was Stevens' only film with the Astaire–Rogers team and, generally, his direction hardly differed from that of Mark Sandrich. Georges Metaxa, John Harrington, Pierre Watkin, Abe Reynolds, Gerald Hamer, Edgar Dearing and Frank Jenks also took part. The superlative score was by Jerome Kern and Dorothy Fields. Songs included: 'Pick Yourself Up', 'Waltz In Swing Time', 'A Fine Romance', 'It's Not In The Cards', 'The Way You Look Tonight'.

What would happen if a conscientious member of a state prison parole board found that his own son was a notorious public enemy up for parole? **Don't Turn 'Em Loose** answered the question succinctly, if melodramatically. Lewis Stone (borrowed from MGM) played the father who succumbs to his weaker impulses, signs the parole order and then must shoot down son Bruce Cabot (right, also borrowed from MGM) to prevent him from causing further mayhem. As an indictment of flabby parole regulations, the picture was pretty addle-brained, but it did work on a more modest, potboiler level. Harry Segall and Ferdinand Reyher's screenplay, based on a story by Thomas Walsh, had tension and a few genuine shocks, to which Ben Stoloff's direction did full justice. Also cast: James Gleason, Louise Latimer, Betty Grable, Grace Bradley (left), Nella Walker, Frank M. Thomas, Harry Jans, John Arledge, Frank Jenks, Maxine Jennings, Gordon Jones and Addison Randall. The associate producer was Robert Sisk.

Wheeler (left) and Woolsey (right) crashed an archaeological expedition in **Mummy's Boys**. The notion of dispatching the venerable RKO jokesters to the land of the pharaohs held promise, but it was in no way fulfilled, thanks to a plethora of musty jokes, mummified slapstick and lacklustre performances. The infamous Egyptian curse certainly took its toll on this picture. Among those suffering from it were screenwriters Jack Townley, Philip Epstein and Charles Roberts (story: Townley and Lew Lipton), director Fred Guiol, associate producer Lee Marcus and second-string performers Barbara Pepper (centre), Frank M. Thomas, Willie Best, Francis McDonald, Frank Lackteen, Charles Coleman, Mitchell Lewis and Frederick Burton. The only standout was Moroni Olsen, giving a suitably shuddery impersonation of an insane villain. In retrospect, it seems that RKO should have left this one at rest in the tomb. ▽

Ann Sothern (left) and Gene Raymond (right), by now a fully fledged RKO team, scored another hit in **Smartest Girl In Town**. Infused with sharp dialogue and clever comic situations, the Viola Brothers Shore screenplay (based on a story by Muriel Scheck and H. S. Kraft) dealt with the hectic love affair between an agency model (Sothern) who poses for magazine advertisements and a millionaire (Raymond) whom she mistakes for a fellow model. Helen Broderick, Eric Blore and Erik Rhodes added to the fun, feasting on three juicy supporting roles, and Joseph Santley's direction never faltered, constantly injecting the flip plot with extra vitality. Producer Edward Kaufman's secondary players also included Harry Jans, Frank Jenks, Alan Curtis, Edward Price and Rolfe Sedan. Song: 'Will You?' Gene Raymond.

A muddled exposé of college football 'fixes', **The Big Game** may be best remembered as the first screenwriting task of a Brooklyn youth destined for success in the field of popular fiction: Irwin Shaw. The picture hardly suggested the potential of its writer; it tried, yet failed decisively, to meld a routine college romance with a boneheaded thriller about an attempt by gangsters to kidnap the star quarterback on the eve of the critical contest. James Gleason, Philip Huston, June Travis (borrowed from Warner Bros.), Bruce Cabot (centre right, borrowed from MGM), Andy Devine (centre left, borrowed from Universal), John Arledge and Guinn Williams were the featured performers in this Pandro S. Berman production, directed by George Nicholls Jr. Shaw's script, based on a novel by Francis Wallace, also contained roles for C. Henry Gordon, Frank M. Thomas, Barbara Pepper, Edward Nugent, Margaret Seddon, Billy Gilbert, John Harrington, Murray Kinnell and eight members of the most recent All-American football squad.

▽

Whatever **Daniel Boone** may have lacked, it wasn't plot. Screenwriter Daniel Jarrett, working from an original story by Edgecumb Pinchon, concentrated on the famous Boone-led pioneering journey from North Carolina to the wilds of Kentucky. However, he also added subplots about marauding Indians led by meany John Carradine (symbolically garbed in a skunkskin cap) and the treachery of aristocratic Virginia lawmakers who usurp the lands cleared by Boone and his fellow settlers. George O'Brien (left), though a bit overweight, made a worthy and stalwart Boone; he was aided by Heather Angel as the romantic lead and George Regas (right) as the faithful Indian sidekick who saves Boone when he is being burned at the stake. Except for the wildly gesticulating histrionics of Carradine, director David Howard underplayed everything, making the film a strangely muted example of the action adventure. It wasn't history, but it wasn't pure romantic fantasy, either. Others in the cast were Ralph Forbes, Clarence Muse, Dickie Jones, Huntley Gordon, Harry Cording, Aggie Herring. Crauford Kent and Keith Kenneth. George A. Hirliman was the producer for his own independent production company; RKO was the distributor.

▽

Another chapter in the studio's periodic love affair with aerial drama, **Without Orders** boiled down to a rivalry between fliers Robert Armstrong (right) and Vinton Haworth for the love of stewardess Sally Eilers (left). Miss Eilers' romantic choice is made for her when the cowardly Haworth bails out of his crippled airliner, forcing the stewardess to take the controls. Aided by radio instructions from Armstrong, she lands the ship and its passengers safely. Director Lew Landers, piloting his first of many RKO productions, kept the Peter B. Kyne story (screenplay: J. Robert Bren and Edmund L. Hartmann) airborne throughout its 64-minute running time. Helping to add to the sky-high excitement were Frances Sage, Charley Grapewin, Ward Bond, Frank M. Thomas, May Boley, Arthur Loft and Walter Miller. Cliff Reid served as associate producer. Note: Director Landers was previously known in Hollywood as Louis Friedlander.

▽

Wanted! Jane Turner was sturdy, reliable but uninspired melodrama, produced by Cliff Reid and directed by Edward Killy. All about mail theft and the postal authorities who combat it, the film featured Lee Tracy (right) and Gloria Stuart (left, borrowed from 20th Century-Fox) as the heroic combination. The writers (story idea suggested by Julius Klein, story by John Twist and Edmund L. Hartmann, screenplay by Twist) constructed their narrative around 'Jane Turner', a name used by the crooks for the general delivery pickup of their ill-gotten loot. A real (innocent) Jane Turner shows up, complicating the designs of both good guys and bad. Judith Blake played the actual Jane Turner, Barbara Pepper was the imposter and Paul Guilfoyle made a properly sinister heavy. Others in the cast were John McGuire, Frank M. Thomas, Patricia Wilder, Willard Robertson and Irene Franklin.

▽

◁ Producer Pandro S. Berman believed strongly that **A Woman Rebels** would return Katharine Hepburn to the front rank of Hollywood stardom. Hepburn found the material (based on a novel by British author Netta Syrett) 'mediocre' but agreed to undertake the film after a good deal of urging from Berman. The central character, Pamela Thistlewaite, seemed a perfect Hepburn heroine. A nonconformist in strict Victorian society, Pamela asserts herself on such subjects as a woman's right to work, to live alone, to read whatever she pleases and to choose her own husband. The film, however, proved to be more of a tearjerker than a treatise on the freedom of women. Miss Thistlewaite has an illegitimate child (by Van Heflin) and, after a considerable period of suffering, finally discovers happiness in the arms of a faithful suitor (Herbert Marshall). Mark Sandrich's direction lacked suitable grace and polish, making the Anthony Veiller–Ernest Vajda script seem remote and insubstantial, and without much relevance to a 1936 audience. The decision once again to cast Hepburn (illustrated) as a fiery eccentric, courageously standing her ground against the forces of social dehumanization and intellectual sterility, was also imprudent. Although she certainly played the role better than any other actress could, this was precisely the Hepburn persona that audiences now found tiresome. The public demonstrated its aversion to the character and the picture by carefully avoiding theatres that played it. Costing a modest amount for a Hepburn vehicle, the lamentable film lost $222,000 – even more than *Mary Of Scotland*. Rather like Helen Gahagan bathed in the flames in *She*, Miss Hepburn was withering away rapidly, much to the horror of the RKO brains trust who appeared powerless to do anything about her waning appeal and prestige. The cast also included Elizabeth Allan, Donald Crisp, Doris Dudley, David Manners, Lucile Watson, Eily Malyon, Margaret Seddon, Molly Lamont, Lionel Pape and Constance Lupino.

△

Make Way For A Lady was the last – and also the least – of three 'sweet and innocent' 1936 comedies starring Anne Shirley (left). The plot, fashioned by Gertrude Purcell from a novel entitled *Daddy And I* by Elizabeth Jordan, called for the ingenue to meddle innocently in the private affairs of her widowed father (Herbert Marshall, right). Misunderstanding his true needs and feelings, she almost succeeds in arranging a marriage between Marshall and a woman he detests (Margot Grahame). Despite passable direction by David Burton, the picture was both highly improbable and consistently bland, even by 'B'-unit standards. Gertrude Michael, Taylor Holmes, Clara Blandick, Frank Coghlan Jr, Maxine Jennings, Mary Jo Ellis, Murray Kinnell, Helen Parrish and Willie Best were also among those appearing for associate producer Zion Myers.

The fifth of the studio's Hildegarde Withers–Oscar Piper whodunnits, **The Plot Thickens** (GB: **The Swinging Pearl Mystery**) cast ZaSu Pitts (right) as the schoolmarm sleuth with James Gleason (left) back again as the hard-boiled inspector. The substitution of Miss Pitts for Edna May Oliver and Helen Broderick left the comedy intact, but detracted from the dynamics of the mystery plot. One had to strain awfully hard to buy fluttery ZaSu as a model of rational thinking. In any event, screenwriters Clarence Upson Young and Jack Townley (story by Stuart Palmer) made no allowance for the limitations of the new leading lady, teasing her with two seemingly unrelated murders which prove to be mere peccadilloes leading to the real issue: a cleverly engineered scheme by a band of international crooks to steal a treasure from an art museum. Thanks to the miscasting of Pitts, and Ben Holmes' sub-standard direction, this was the most anaemic chapter in an otherwise felicitous RKO series. Also cast: Owen Davis Jr, Louise Latimer, Arthur Aylesworth, Paul Fix, Richard Tucker, Barbara Barondess, James Donlan, Agnes Anderson and Oscar Apfel. William Sistrom was the associate producer.

The ingredients of **Night Waitress** were depressingly stale – a shadowy, waterfront setting, smugglers, double-crossers and other assorted cops and robbers. The constituent parts were combined without a trace of originality or imagination, making this Margot Grahame (right) vehicle one of the dullest offerings of the year. Joseph Henry Steele's debut as associate producer was thoroughly forgettable, thanks in part to Marcus Goodrich's cluttered screenplay (story by Golda Draper) and Lew Landers' take-it-or-leave-it direction. Miss Grahame seemed out of place as a low-life character working in a seaport cafe, but the *coup de grace* was delivered by her romantic counterpart Gordon Jones. He tried but completely failed to charm as a former rum runner. Vinton Haworth (centre), Marc Lawrence (left), Billy Gilbert, Donald Barry, Otto Yamaoka, Paul Stanton, Arthur Loft and Walter Miller also appeared. Russell Metty's sharply detailed black-and-white photography turned out to be the only superior aspect of this clumsy cheapie.

Chapter two of the Bobby Breen story found the youthful song belter deep in the land o' cotton. But not for long. Circumstances send him packing to New York where he is coldshouldered by his own grandmother (May Robson) and made miserable by a coterie of nasty cousins. With some assistance from butler Charles Butterworth, Breen (illustrated) ultimately melts grandma's heart and wins the favour of all the other New Yorkers who count. He even manages to import his old mammy (Louise Beavers), which makes the boy's new life in Yankeeland complete. The young star now enjoyed a following among sentimentalists and undiscriminating lovers of musicals, but he would never challenge the sovereignty of child superstar Shirley Temple, although his pictures made money for producer Sol Lesser and his Principal company, and for RKO. Earle Snell, Harry Chandlee and William Hurlbut developed the **Rainbow On The River** screenplay from a novel by Mrs C. V. Jamison. Director Kurt Neumann also cast Alan Mowbray, Benita Hume, Henry O'Neill, Marilyn Knowlden, Lillian Yarbo, Stymie Beard, Eddie 'Rochester' Anderson, Betty Blythe, Theresa Maxwell Conover, Clarence Wilson, Lew Kelly, Lillian Harmer and the Hall Johnson choir. Songs included: 'Rainbow On The River' Paul F. Webster, Louis Alter; 'Flower Song' Hugo Riesenfeld, Selma Hautzik; 'Old Folks At Home', 'De Camptown Races' Stephen Foster; 'Waitin' For The Sun' Karl Hajos.

RKO's final and most prestigious 1936 production was **Winterset**, Maxwell Anderson's thinly disguised examination of the Sacco and Vanzetti case. The biggest challenge lay with scenarist Anthony Veiller, whose job was to eliminate most of Anderson's blank verse and to substitute a happy ending for the original tragic denouément. He did such a skilful job, somehow keeping the profound rhythms of Anderson's work intact, that even the playwright was delighted by the transformation. The execution, 15 years previously, of a high-minded liberal for a crime he did not commit, furnished the motivation of Pandro S. Berman's production, which focused primarily on the efforts of the dead man's son (Burgess Meredith) to clear his father's name. These efforts also give rise to a strange, swift romance between Meredith and his co-star Margo that interferes with the youth's determined purpose. Alfred Santell's direction did very little to obscure the stage origins of the drama, but its impassioned outcry against injustice and mob hysteria came through clearly, and critics went overboard in their appreciation. Three members of the stage production – Meredith (left), Eduardo Ciannelli (right) and Margo (2nd left) – repeated their original roles, supported by John Carradine, Maurice Moscovitch (centre), Paul Guilfoyle, Edward Ellis (centre right), Stanley Ridges, Mischa Auer, Willard Robertson, Alec Craig (2nd right), Barbara Pepper, Murray Alper and Paul Fix. Studio executives had hoped that **Winterset** would gain the reputation and box-office success of *The Informer*, to which it was widely compared. It did not, losing some money and winning no major awards; still, the film was an artistically prominent piece of work and came to be regarded, quite rightly, with pride by the studio that made it.

RKO sailed blithely into the new year on the strength of its best financial showing since the early days of the company. In line with the consolidation of various subsidiaries (including RKO Studios Inc., the RKO Distributing Corporation and the RKO Pathé Studios Corporation) into RKO Radio Pictures, Inc., a new logo was introduced. Each new film would henceforward proclaim 'RKO Radio Pictures Presents' instead of 'Radio Pictures Presents'. Now known primarily as RKO rather than Radio, the studio would begin to assert its independence from broadcasting, and demonstrate its full commitment to film – a commitment that had often been questioned in the past.

Former NBC president Merlin Aylesworth resigned as chairman of the RKO board of directors, and, in October, it was announced that Samuel Briskin was leaving his position as production head. Though the studio had certainly made money during his tenure, Briskin had hired a number of unreliable second-rate producers, had demonstrated an inability to handle certain profligate filmmakers and had failed to develop a talent pool – especially in the acting area – of any consequence. In addition, the quality of RKO pictures had deteriorated steadily under his guidance, with the 1937 releases even more disappointing than those of 1936. Leo Spitz asked Pandro Berman to step once more into the breach and head studio production; Berman accepted the job with considerable reluctance.

RKO's talent acquisitions included Joe Penner and Parkyakarkas, a pair of radio comedians who would find movie customers harder to please, and Joan Fontaine (whose eventual success only came after she left RKO). The studio, together with the rest of Hollywood and Broadway, mourned the tragic loss of George Gershwin, who died after completing the score for **A Damsel In Distress**.

The fullest production year in company history, 1937 generated 56 films, but most were programmers, lacking in stars and solid production values. On the credit side, however, Walt Disney's first animated feature, **Snow White And The Seven Dwarfs**, opened in special engagements in December and rocketed to immediate success.

The corporation's net profit for 1937 was $1,821,165 – some $600,000 less than the figures posted for the year before. Top box-office grosses included **Snow White And The Seven Dwarfs** (most of its revenues were recorded in 1938), **Shall We Dance, Sea Devils, There Goes My Girl** and **That Girl From Paris**.

We Who Are About To Die was based on the ▷ true story of David Lamson who spent 13 months in San Quentin penitentiary before the Supreme Court reversed his murder conviction. Evidently writer John Twist felt Lamson's account needed to be juiced up, so he injected nearly every cliché imaginable into his screenplay: the devoted lover (Ann Dvorak, borrowed from Warner Bros.) working with a quick-witted sleuth (Preston Foster) to find proof of her man's innocence, explosions of cruelty and violence within the prison walls, a last-minute reprieve as the hero (John Beal, centre) is being led to his execution, etc. Christy Cabanne directed this strained melo for producer Edward Small. Ray Mayer, Gordon Jones, Frank Jenks, J. Carrol Naish, Russell Hopton, Frank M. Thomas, Paul Hurst, John Wray, Barnett Parker, Willie Fung, John Carroll, DeWitt Jennings and Howard Hickman (left) were also in it.

The frightful acting of Smith Ballew (right) brought **Racing Lady** to a screeching halt. A recent recruit to the screen from radio, Ballew's impersonation of a millionaire auto manufacturer pulled the rug from under the professional performances of Ann Dvorak (left, borrowed from Warner Bros.) playing an enthusiastic horsewoman, and Harry Carey as her father. The plot, based on two original stories (one by Damon Runyon, the other by J. Robert Bren and Norman Houston) and written for the screen by Dorothy Yost, Thomas Lennon and Cortland Fitzsimmons, concerned Ballew's purchase of a thoroughbred, and his employment of Miss Dvorak to train the horse. A romantic interest grows between them until the girl realizes that her boss has a distorted sense of sportsmanship and cares about the horse only for the publicity value it brings his business. As if Ballew's histrionics weren't damaging enough, Wallace Fox's predictable direction further weakened the picture. Berton Churchill, Frank M. Thomas, Ray Mayer, Willie Best, Hattie McDaniel, Harry Jans, Lew Payton, Harlan Tucker and Alex Hill were others in the cast. Song: 'Sweeter All The Time' Andy Iona Long, Lysle Tomerlin.
▽

A news photographer and a blue-blooded debutante, who want to marry, have to overcome the obstacles set in their path by the girl's patrician father. Their efforts to do so (successfully, of course), formed the comedic core of **They Wanted To Marry**. As scripted by Paul Yawitz and Ethel Borden (story by Larry Bachmann and Darwin L. Teilhet), it was an inoffensive, seen-it-all-before trifle. Betty Furness (right, borrowed from MGM) played the girl, Gordon Jones (left) her journalist sweetheart and Henry Kolker the disapproving dad, with E. E. Clive, Patsy Lee Parsons, Frank M. Thomas, Charles Wilson, William Benedict and Diana Gibson lending assistance. Lew Landers directed and Zion Myers produced.
▽

△

A passable remake of *Ladies On The Jury* (1932), **We're On The Jury** cemented the comedy team of Victor Moore (right) and Helen Broderick (left), who had been paired to good advantage in *Swing Time*. Producer Lee Marcus dusted off the old John Frederick Ballard play, turned the adaptation over to Franklin Coen and cornered Ben Holmes to direct. With Broderick giving her usual solid performance as haughty Mrs Dean who has no use for legal proprieties but sniffs out the real facts of the murder case, and Moore enjoying some antic moments as real estate salesman J. Clarence Beaver (known affectionately as Pudgy to Mrs Dean), the picture provided a congenial way of passing the time. Joseph Henry Steele was the associate producer. Also cast: Robert McWade (repeating his role as the judge), Philip Huston, Louise Latimer, Vinton Haworth, Maxine Jennings, Frank M. Thomas, Colleen Clare, Billy Gilbert, Charles Lane and Charles Middleton.

△

Former exhibitor David L. Loew's first independent production for RKO release was **When's Your Birthday?**, a comedy starring the man with the inimitable mouth, Joe E. Brown (illustrated). Introduced as a youngster pursuing a very unsuccessful boxing career to pay for his astrology studies, Brown eventually secures a job as a fortune teller in a carnival concession and thenceforward leads such a hectic life that his boxing activities seem mild by comparison. The romantic attentions of Marian Marsh and Suzanne Kaaren are a major source of complication, adding the eternal triangle to the signs of the zodiac which Brown seeks to understand. Harry Clork wrote the whimsical screenplay, working from a play by Fred Ballard which Harvey Gates, Malcolm Stuart Boylan and Samuel M. Pike had adapted. Harry Beaumont directed, drawing rollicking performances from a cast that included Fred Keating, Edgar Kennedy, Maude Eburne, Margaret Hamilton, Minor Watson, Frank Jenks, Don Rowan, Granville Bates, Charles Judels, a dog named Corky and former silent film performer Bull Montana. The picture's opening cartoon sequence (produced by Leon Schlesinger) was shot in Technicolor. Robert Harris served as associate producer for David L. Loew Productions.

That Girl From Paris was the biggest hit of Lily Pons' movie career. Pandro S. Berman utilized the talents of several writers (story by Jane Murfin suggested by a story by J. Carey Wonderly; adaptation by Joseph A. Fields; screenplay by P. J. Wolfson and Dorothy Yost), and they succeeded in brewing up a musical comedy-romance with above-average slapstick and farcical complications. Opera purists must have been outraged by this tale, which had the golden-voiced soprano attached to a swing band (though she did sing 'Una Voce Poco Fa' from Rossini's *The Barber Of Seville*); but it captured the fancy of less lofty viewers, and garnered $1,163,000 in film rentals. Leigh Jason brought some witty direction to the saga of French opera star Pons (right) who baulks at a marriage of convenience and follows handsome American band leader Gene Raymond to the US where she involves him and his band of three in her immigration difficulties. Jack Oakie (left), Mischa Auer and Frank Jenks comprised the band with Herman Bing, Lucille Ball, Patricia Wilder, Vinton Haworth, Gregory Gaye, Willard Robertson, Rafaela Ottiano and Ferdinand Gottschalk also contributing strong support work. A loose remake of *Street Girl* (1929), the story would be filmed again in 1942 as *Four Jacks And A Jill*. Songs included: 'Love And Learn', 'The Call To Arms', 'Seal It With A Kiss', 'Moon Face', 'My Nephew From Nice' Arthur Schwartz, Edward Heyman; 'Tarantella' Panofka.

▽

Robert Sisk's production of **Don't Tell The Wife** was a middling laugh-getter about a dim-witted innocent (Guy Kibbee, right) whose unintentional blunders result in foiling a band of stock manipulators. Though Christy Cabanne's direction was undistinguished and the Nat Perrin script (based on George Holland's play *Once Over Lightly*) depended on comic conceits of a very low order, the fusion of characters and performers was sufficiently amusing to keep audiences attentive. Una Merkel (left, borrowed from MGM) as the titular wife, Lynne Overman (centre, borrowed from Paramount) playing a former racketeer who can't resist the chance for one more big hit, and Guinn Williams as a thick-headed gang member, each enjoyed a few humorous moments. Also cast: Thurston Hall, Frank M. Thomas, William Demarest, Lucille Ball, Harry Tyler, George Irving, Bradley Page and Si Jenks.

▽

△

A straightforward action melodrama, and a good one at that, **Sea Devils** pitted Coast Guard tough guy Victor McLaglen (centre left) against Preston Foster (right), whose personality is too much like McLaglen's for his own good. Spiced with numerous fistfights and an exciting rescue at sea, the dramatic conflict turned on McLaglen's determination to marry off daughter Ida Lupino (centre right) to seaman Donald Woods (left). Lupino, however, falls in love with Foster, causing immediate friction between father and daughter and father and suitor. Frank Wead, John Twist and P. J. Wolfson's script was a model of neat construction, pacing and dialogue, and director Ben Stoloff translated it to the screen with appropriate panache. Edward Small, who seemed to have better luck with programmers and 'in-between' films than with 'A' pictures, produced. Also cast were Helen Flint, Gordon Jones, Pierre Watkin, Murray Alper, Billy Gilbert and Barbara Pepper. The outstanding photography of J. Roy Hunt and Joseph August, abetted by Vernon Walker's special effects, was another plus factor in this financially profitable and entertaining adventure film.

△

Christy Cabanne's direction and the performances of Lee Tracy (centre), Margot Grahame and Eduardo Ciannelli elevated **Criminal Lawyer** above its pulp-fiction origins, making the film one of the most carefully wrought and incisive RKO dramas of 1937. Tracy played a lawyer who climbs steadily (and sneakily) to the position of district attorney but, in fact, his legal standing is a cover for gangland activitives. He is being groomed for the governor's mansion when he has a change of heart, motivated by his sincere feelings for Miss Grahame. His subsequent confession before a grand jury ruins his career, but also sinks the story's chief rat (Ciannelli). Erik Rhodes added a few diverting comedy turns, while the rest of the cast, including Betty Lawford, Frank M. Thomas, Wilfred Lucas, William Stack, Lita Chevret (left), Aileen Pringle, Kenneth Thomson and Theodore von Eltz, also acquitted themselves nicely. G. V. Atwater and Thomas Lennon wrote the screenplay from Louis Stevens' original story. Cliff Reid produced this popular remake of *State's Attorney* (1932). Song: 'Tonight, Lover, Tonight' Jack Stern, Harry Tobias.

A routine and thoroughly predictable melo, **Park Avenue Logger** (GB: **Millionaire Playboy**) cast George O'Brien (right) as the scion of a wealthy New York family. O'Brien's father (Lloyd Ingraham) unaware that his son has become a wrestling champion known as the Masked Marvel, sends him to an Oregon lumber camp to 'become a man'. There, the hero knocks the daylights out of the lumberjacks, exposes the crooked operations of two scheming foremen and helps a gorgeous girl (Beatrice Roberts) to make a success of her crippled father's logging business. George A. Hirliman produced for his own independent company, and David Howard directed. Dan Jarrett and Ewing Scott provided the action-dominated screenplay from a *Saturday Evening Post* story by Bruce Hutchison. Also cast: Willard Robertson, Ward Bond (left), Bert Hanlon, Gertrude Short, George Rosener and Robert Emmett O'Connor. The associate producer was Leonard Goldstein.

In another vain attempt to propel Katharine Hepburn back to the top, Pandro S. Berman produced **Quality Street**, an adaptation of James M. Barrie's play, with a scenario by Mortimer Offner and Allan Scott and direction by George Stevens. Barrie, of course, had been the source of one of Hepburn's most charming roles in *The Little Minister*, and Stevens had handled an earlier 'comeback' picture, *Alice Adams*. This time the combination failed. The story concerned one Phoebe Throssel (Hepburn, right), a lady teetering on the brink of spinsterhood and casting about for a husband before all hope is gone. Miss Hepburn's performance seemed to reflect some of her growing personal frustration; it was overwrought almost to the point of hysteria, obliterating the sentimental and gently amusing intent of the material. The supporting cast included Franchot Tone (centre, borrowed from MGM), Eric Blore, Fay Bainter (left), Cora Witherspoon, Estelle Winwood, Florence Lake, William Bakewell and Joan Fontaine (her first appearance for RKO). Despite splendid photography by Robert deGrasse, painstaking art direction and set design by Hobe Erwin, and the quaint costumes of Walter Plunkett, RKO had another Hepburn bomb ($248,000 loss) on its hands, prompting serious discussions among the executives about the actress' overall worth to the company. **Quality Street** was a remake of a 1927 MGM silent which starred Marion Davies.

China Passage, a tepid programmer, was destined for the lower half on neighbourhood double bills. The weaknesses began with the story (by Taylor Caven) and screenplay (by Edmund L. Hartmann and J. Robert Bren), a tedious shipboard mystery which included multiple murders and the disappearance of the precious '500' diamond. Edward Killy's stagey direction and a cluster of undernourished performances sealed the picture's fate. Vinton Haworth (right) and Gordon Jones (left) playing two adventurers charged with guarding the diamond, Constance Worth as a government customs agent, and Leslie Fenton and Alec Craig as the gem thieves and killers, were the principal passengers on this ship of fools. Other members of producer Cliff Reid's cast: Dick Elliott, Frank M. Thomas, George Irving, Billy Gilbert, Joyce Compton, Philip Ahn, Lotus Long (centre) and Huntley Gordon.

The Soldier And The Lady (GB: **Michael Strogoff**) was an intriguing anomaly – a cooperative venture between a European producer and RKO's Hollywood production machinery. Frenchman Joseph Ermolieff came to Pandro S. Berman with French and German versions of Jules Verne's *Michael Strogoff* already on celluloid. Producer Berman, struck by the epic sweep of the drama and the spectacular battle footage, purchased the English language rights – a deal that also included access to the negative of the French version. Berman hired Anton Walbrook, who had starred in both European pictures, put Mortimer Offner, Anthony Veiller and Anne Morrison Chapin to work on the screenplay, and assigned George Nicholls Jr to direct. The completed picture cleverly intercut new footage with old, making for a homogeneous total package. Its plot followed Strogoff (Walbrook, centre), the Czar's personal courier, to Siberia in 1870. He carries with him the strategy that will defeat the rebellious Tartars. After an encounter with beautiful spy Margot Grahame (right), an emotional scene in which he is forced to deny his own mother (Fay Bainter) and a stomach-churning moment in which he is apparently blinded by one of villain Akim Tamiroff's men, Strogoff finally delivers the key message and Russia is saved. Comic relief by Eric Blore and Edward Brophy, playing two unlikely journalists covering the action, was pretty witless but, otherwise, the picture measured up to RKO's expectations. Also cast: Elizabeth Allan (left, borrowed from MGM), Paul Guilfoyle, William Stack, Paul Harvey and Michael Visaroff.

John Ford's three-picture commitment to RKO ▷ ended with **The Plough And The Stars**. This particular experience so soured his attitude to the studio that he never again worked as an RKO contract director (although he later made a deal to release his independently produced Argosy films through RKO in the 1940s). Problems arose after shooting was completed. With Ford vacationing on his yacht, Sam Briskin and others previewed the film and, feeling changes were necessary, assigned George Nicholls Jr to reshoot certain scenes. Ford was outraged when he learned the film had been tampered with, and ultimately demanded that his name be removed from the credits. He had no contractual right to do this, and RKO declined to accommodate him. In fact, the film's problems were larger in scope than the director cared to admit. Sean O'Casey's original play, set during the Irish rebellion of 1916, had been an ironic commentary on the tragic futility and foolhardiness of Irish national politics. It observed that the Irish with their natural love of fiery oratory and talent for bickering were often as impractical as they were foolishly brave. Dudley Nichols' adaptation altered the resonances of the original, concentrating instead on a classic struggle between love and duty as symbolized by the battle between a rebel officer (Preston Foster, right) and his wife (Barbara Stanwyck, left), who is determined to keep her man out of the fighting. Ford drew performances from his two stars which were no more than adequate, and much of the drama seemed strained and irresolute. Perhaps the most lasting contribution of **The Plough And The Stars** was the introduction of several performers from Dublin's Abbey Theatre, including Barry Fitzgerald, Eileen Crowe, Denis O'Dea, F. J. McCormick and Arthur Shields. Una O'Connor, Moroni Olsen, Bonita Granville, J. M. Kerrigan, Erin O'Brien-Moore and Cyril McLaglen also appeared for associate producers Cliff Reid and Robert Sisk. The disappointment caused by the failure of this film ended RKO's interest in 'prestige' pictures – at least for the remainder of Leo Spitz's presidency.

The Man Who Found Himself was the assembly-line tale of a doctor who renounces his Hippocratic oath, then re-embraces it at the climactic moment. At least the setting was different – physician John Beal (left) performs his crucial surgery while high in the clouds in a flying hospital – though the picture never got far off the ground. Newcomer Joan Fontaine (centre), featured as the nurse who coaxes Beal back to his proper calling, gave a fetching performance. Alice F. Curtis provided the story material, and four screenwriters (J. Robert Bren, Edmund L. Hartmann, G. V. Atwater and Thomas Lennon) were needed to record all the obligatory clichés. Cliff Reid produced, Lew Landers directed and the cast also included Philip Huston (right), Jane Walsh, George Irving, James Conlin, Frank M. Thomas and Diana Gibson.

A hectic romance between an heiress and a penniless young man, a missing stamp worth $10,000, a case of mistaken identity and a job that involves a mythical wife were a few of the too many plot elements in **Too Many Wives**. As scripted by Dorothy Yost, Lois Eby and John Grey from a story by Richard English, they added up to one more strained and tedious comedy which audiences avoided with alarming uniformity. Total film rentals for this William Sistrom-produced turkey came to $122,000. The unfortunate performers included Anne Shirley (centre) as the heiress, John Morley (left) as her romantic foil, Gene Lockhart (right) as her father, and Dudley Clements, Barbara Pepper, Frank Melton, Charles Coleman, Dot Farley, Jack Carson and George Irving. Ben Holmes directed with all the finesse of a blacksmith.

Preston Foster (centre) played picturesque gambler John Oakhurst in **The Outcasts Of Poker Flat**. The screenplay, as written by John Twist and Harry Segall for producer Robert Sisk, was actually an amalgamation of two Bret Harte stories, *The Luck Of Roaring Camp* and *The Outcasts Of Poker Flat*. Its saga of love, conflict and sacrifice occurred against a California gold rush backdrop and featured Jean Muir (borrowed from Warner Bros.) as Helen Colby, the school teacher who tries to reform gambler Oakhurst; Margaret Irving (left) as the Duchess, his green-eyed associate; Virginia Weidler (right, borrowed from Paramount) as 'Luck', the tiny mascot of the roughneck mining camp; and Van Heflin as Reverend Samuel Woods who, like Oakhurst, falls in love with Miss Muir. Bret Harte's strong suit as a writer was always his feeling and appreciation for his characters, but this Christy Cabanne-directed effort reduced Harte's people to one-dimensional and uninteresting creatures. Sadly, the film emerged as just another routine western. Frank M. Thomas, Si Jenks, Dick Elliott, Al St John, Bradley Page, Richard Lane, Monte Blue, Billy Gilbert and Dudley Clements contributed decorative performances. Harry Carey had starred in a 1919 Universal version of the tale, and it was filmed again by 20th Century-Fox in 1952 with Dale Robertson and Anne Baxter.

Anatole Litvak made his Hollywood directorial debut with **The Woman I Love** (GB: **The Woman Between**). Litvak had directed a celebrated French version of the story which was based on the novel *L'Equipage* by Joseph Kessel. RKO spared no expense in introducing the director to American motion pictures, borrowing Paul Muni (right) from Warner Bros. and Louis Hayward from Universal to play the principals in a love feud that erupts over Miriam Hopkins (left). Nevertheless, the emotional dramatics, played out against the wartime manoeuvres of a French flying squadron, never caught fire and the film swiftly expired at the box office (net loss to RKO: $266,000). Part of the problem was rooted in Ethel Borden's irresolute screenplay, but the uninspired performances of the three principals proved even more lethal and, for that, Mr Litvak deserved a significant portion of the blame. Colin Clive, Minor Watson, Elizabeth Risdon, Paul Guilfoyle, Wally Albright, Mady Christians, Alec Craig, Owen Davis Jr, Sterling Holloway, Vince Barnett, Adrian Morris, Donald Barry, Joe Twerp and William Stelling completed producer Albert Lewis' large cast. The only outstanding element in the film was Arthur Honegger and Maurice Thiriet's musical score which had also been used in Litvak's French picture.

Aside from Onslow Stevens' intermittently engaging portrayal of a superstitious racehorse owner, **You Can't Buy Luck** was an inept comedy-drama that earned a place beside RKO's other third-class programme pictures. Martin Mooney and Arthur T. Horman's screenplay (story by Mooney) cast Stevens (centre) as Joe Baldwin, a man who believes that the more he helps others financially, the more luck his horses will have on the track. A murder is introduced, and Baldwin is arrested and convicted – all to make the sanctimonious point that a man's charity should be based on a sincere desire to help others, not his own selfishness. Director Lew Landers did his best to pep up this pretentious and flimsy rubbish, but the basic material stifled his efforts. Also cast: Helen Mack (right), Vinton Haworth, Maxine Jennings, Paul Guilfoyle, Frank M. Thomas, Richard Lane, Murray Alper, Hedda Hopper, Dudley Clements, Barbara Pepper and Willie Best (left).

The only Astaire–Rogers musical of 1937 was ▷ **Shall We Dance**. It contained many wonderful features, including a dazzling score by George and Ira Gershwin (their first and last for Fred and Ginger), a witty roller skating sequence, and an imaginative ending that is arguably the best in the entire series. However, the Allan Scott–Ernest Pagano script (suggested by a story by Lee Loeb and Harold Buchman and adapted by P. J. Wolfson), about the high-velocity romance between a world-renowned ballet dancer (Astaire, left) and an equally well-known revue artiste (Rogers, right), seemed like a rehash of earlier efforts, full of multiple misunderstandings, and characters who had been glimpsed, perhaps, a time too often. Edward Everett Horton as Astaire's impresario and Eric Blore as a hotel official appeared to be sleepwalking through their roles after years of similar work. Dancing took a back seat to singing in this picture and, since the primary strength of the team's productions had always been the scintillating dance routines, this may have disappointed some members of the audience. The decreased number of dances (staged by Hermes Pan, ballet by Harry Losee), the familiarity of the plot recipe, and the slightly warmed-over characters all may have contributed to the indisputable shrinkage in the Astaire–Rogers audience. **Shall We Dance** returned a profit of $413,000, but this was well below the plus figures on previous pictures. Jerome Cowan, Ketti Gallian, William Brisbane, Harriet Hoctor and Ann Shoemaker also performed for producer Pandro S. Berman and director Mark Sandrich. Songs included: 'Let's Call The Whole Thing Off', 'Shall We Dance', 'I've Got Beginner's Luck', 'They All Laughed', 'They Can't Take That Away From Me'.

Behind The Headlines, a zesty 'B' melodrama, featured Lee Tracy (right) in the familiar guise of indefatigable newshawk, hustling, this time, for a radio station. Tracy's innate competitiveness places him in a difficult position with his lady love (Diana Gibson, left) who reports the local events for a rival newspaper and takes umbrage at his successful 'scooping'. In the end, the hero rescues his girl from a gang of thieves, thus salvaging their relationship. Richard Rosson's confident direction brought out the best in the leads, as well as in supporting troops Donald Meek, Paul Guilfoyle, Philip Huston, Frank M. Thomas, Tom Kennedy, Doodles Weaver, Ralph Robertson, Art Thalasso and Edith Craig. Edmund L. Hartmann and J. Robert Bren wrote the crafty screenplay (story by Thomas Ahearn) for producer Cliff Reid. Russell Metty's cinematography and Vernon L. Walker's special effects also helped to make **Behind The Headlines** a standout in a year of indifferent RKO programmers.

Another firm example of RKO's gift for manufacturing entertaining 'B' westerns, **Border Cafe** offered 65 breezy minutes of comedy, romance and action. Seemingly inspired by *The Last Outlaw*, the picture played up the clash between modern era gangsters (J. Carrol Naish played the chief villain) and men still in tune with the code of the old west. Once again, Harry Carey was the embodiment of dependable western virtues which, of course, triumph in the end, and John Beal (left) brought credibility to the role of a Boston ne'er-do-well who, under Carey's tutelage, rapidly transforms himself into a stalwart cowboy. The fiery Armida (right), as the entertainer in the establishment of the title, was an unlikely but effective romantic foil for Beal. George Irving, Leona Roberts, Marjorie Lord, Lee Patrick, Paul Fix, Max Wagner and Walter Miller were also in it. Producer Robert Sisk, director Lew Landers and writers Thomas Gill (story) and Lionel Houser (screenplay) all made valuable contributions to this satisfying genre picture.
▽

Mysterious aerial smugglers, a device for controlling airplanes in flight via a radio beam, a high-energy romance, and a rivalry between two small-town newspaper correspondents, were all woven into the Richard Flournoy–Richard Macaulay screenplay for **Riding On Air**. Joe E. Brown (centre) portrayed one of the correspondents, whose interest in the radio beam invention and whose determination to catch the smugglers, involve him in non-stop complications. With Guy Kibbee as an oily stock swindler and Florence Rice as the girl for whom Brown and his rival Vinton Haworth battle throughout, the picture offered plenty of thrills and laughs for Joe's fans and others as well. Edward Sedgwick's lively direction kept the independent feature on track for producer David L. Loew. Anthony Nace, Harlan Briggs (centre right), Andrew Tombes, Clem Bevans (centre left) and Harry C. Bradley (right) led the support. The original plot idea came from a series of *Saturday Evening Post* stories by Richard Macaulay.
▽

Another bird's-eye-view behind the scenes of a newspaper, **There Goes My Girl** detailed the dirty tricks perpetrated by managing editor Richard Lane to sabotage the marriage of his star reporter (Ann Sothern, left) to a rival newspaperman (Gene Raymond, right). The film, more than a bit reminiscent of Ben Hecht and Charles MacArthur's *The Front Page*, contained plenty of squabbling and much frenetic activity, but not much real humour. One scene was a gem of farce among the overall dross: a fake murder interrupts the marriage ceremony just as vows are being exchanged, and Sothern, true to the dedication of her calling, abandons her betrothed at the altar in pursuit of the story. Ben Holmes, working from George Beck's story and Harry Segall's screenplay, provided the erratic direction, for producer William Sistrom. Also cast: Gordon Jones, Frank Jenks, Bradley Page, Joan Woodbury, Marla Shelton, Alec Craig, Joseph Crehan, William Corson and Maxine Jennings.
▽

△
Broad-shouldered, square-jawed George O'Brien, after playing Daniel Boone and a larruping lumberjack in his last two films, returned to his familiar posture astride a horse in **Hollywood Cowboy**. Dan Jarrett and Ewing Scott's screenplay gave viewers two pictures for the price of one by casting O'Brien (left) in the role of a western star who goes to Wyoming for a picture and, upon its completion, becomes actively involved in a real range war. As directed by co-scenarist Scott, the story tilted in the direction of comedy, with Joe Caits (as O'Brien's writer pal) and Frank Milan (a wealthy dude rancher) earning a large percentage of the laughs. Also cast: Cecilia Parker, Maude Eburne (right), Charles Middleton, Lee Shumway, Walter De Palma, Al Hill, William Royle, Al Herman, Frank Hagney, Dan Wolheim and Slim Balch. Leonard Goldstein was the associate producer for George A. Hirliman Productions.

Another harmless and mildly humorous Guy Kibbee trifle, **The Big Shot** cast the rotund innocent as a small town veterinary surgeon who is contented with his lot even after a mysterious uncle leaves him a fortune. However, his ambitious and domineering wife (Cora Witherspoon, left) decides that the bequest must be used to launch their daughter (Dorothy Moore, right) upon a social career in the metropolis where the uncle lived. There, Kibbee (centre) discovers that he has also inherited the leadership of a notorious band of gangsters from the uncle. Edward Killy directed from a script by Arthur T. Horman and Bert Granet (story by Lawrence Pohle and Thomas Ahearn). Also cast: Gordon Jones, Russell Hicks, Frank M. Thomas, Dudley Clements, George Irving, Maxine Jennings, Barbara Pepper, Tom Kennedy, John Kelly, Eddie Gribbon, Al Hill and Donald Kirke. RKO secured the services of Mr Kibbee and Miss Witherspoon from MGM. Apart from its title, this picture had nothing in common with *The Big Shot* of 1931, or with a Warner Bros. film of the same title, with Humphrey Bogart, released in 1942.

New Faces of 1937 was originally intended as the first of a series of musical revues designed to introduce new RKO talent to the movie-going public. The plot, concocted by a cluster of writers (story George Bradshaw; adaptation Harold Kusell, Harry Clork, Howard J. Green; screenplay Nat Perrin, Philip G. Epstein, Irv S. Brecher; additional sketch David Freedman), concerned a crooked theatrical producer (Jerome Cowan) who deliberately mounts flop shows. Since the shows have numerous backers (the producer has sold more than 100 per cent of each), he pockets the surplus and then sets about producing another deliberate bomb. Mel Brooks tapped the same basic concept for his sublime first film *The Producers*, but the RKO team used it mainly as a clothes line on which to peg (clumsily) a multitude of gags, songs and dances. Broadcasting personalities Milton Berle, Joe Penner (right) and Parkyakarkas (left) topped a huge cast that also included Harriet Hilliard, William Brady, Thelma Leeds, Tommy Mack, Bert Gordon, Lorraine Krueger (centre), the Four Playboys, the Rio Brothers, the Loria Brothers, the Brian Sisters, the Three Chocolateers, Ann Miller and Dewey Robinson. Director Leigh Jason battled unsuccessfully to impose some order on the wildly divergent acts and slapstick events. Containing not a single memorable musical number or inspired comedy routine, this tedious mish-mash caused the studio embarrassment a-plenty. Theatre owners and audiences displayed such hostility towards the Edward Small production in general, and Penner and Parkyakarkas in particular, that RKO cancelled plans to make a 'New Faces of 1938'. Songs included: 'New Faces' Charles Henderson; 'The Widow In Lace' Walter Bullock, Harold Spina; 'When The Berry Blossoms Bloom' Joe Penner, Hal Raynor; 'Love Is Never Out Of Season', 'Penthouse On Third Avenue', 'It Goes To Your Feet', 'If I Didn't Have You' Lew Brown, Sammy Fain.

George O'Brien (right) abandoned the wide open spaces of the western range for the near-limitless vastness of the Pacific Ocean in **Windjammer**. Cast in the role of a deputy state's attorney who becomes involved with a gang of smugglers after he attempts to subpoena millionaire sportsman Brandon Evans aboard the latter's yacht, O'Brien is ultimately cast adrift in a flimsy boat with Evans, the millionaire's comely daughter (Constance Worth, left) and her weakling suitor (Gavin Gordon). As written for the screen by Dan Jarrett and James Gruen (from a story by Major Raoul Haig), the tale had fewer action sequences than other O'Brien pictures, though it did include a dilly of a fight between the hero and bad guy William Hall. Ewing Scott directed and associate producer David Howard supervised for George A. Hirliman Productions. Stanley Blystone, Lal Chand Mehra, Ben Hendricks, Lee Shumway, Frank Hagney and Sam Flint were also cast.

A lame send-up of domestic competitions, **Meet The Missus** presented Victor Moore (centre right) as the henpecked victim of wife Helen Broderick's (right) contest-mania. She's much too busy to attend to the normal round of household chores until she is picked as a finalist in the Happy Noodles Housewives' competition. Off she goes to Atlantic City with Moore, who has been taking care of the cooking, bed making, etc. and – you guessed it – wins the big prize (which is tendered mainly to get rid of her and her husband). Jack Townley, Bert Granet and Joel Sayre, working from a story by Jack Goodman and Albert Rice, blended the ingredients, which came out pretty stale despite the watchful eye of director Joseph Santley. Anne Shirley (left) was wasted as the daughter of the topsy-turvy couple, and Alan Bruce (centre left), as her boyfriend, endured the same fate. Edward H. Robins, William Brisbane, Frank M. Thomas, Ray Mayer, Ada Leonard, George Irving, Alec Craig, Willie Best, Virginia Sale and Jack Norton also appeared for producer Albert Lewis.

Super-Sleuth boasted one virtue that immediately made it superior to other programme releases: originality. The Gertrude Purcell–Ernest Pagano screenplay (based on a play by Harry Segall) proffered Jack Oakie (right) as a fat-headed movie detective who, believing he actually embodies the cool powers of reasoning which his celluloid alter-ego always displays, undertakes to solve a real mystery which is baffling the Los Angeles police. The narrative concept yielded much genuine humour, and even some suspense, when Oakie unwittingly enlists the aid of the very man he is trying to capture. Ben Stoloff's direction emphasized the gap between movie-inspired methods of crime detection and those that operate in the actual world; seldom before had Hollywood done justice to this rich vein of comic possibilities. Rendering able assistance was a cast that included Ann Sothern (centre), Eduardo Ciannelli, Alan Bruce, Edgar Kennedy (left), Joan Woodbury, Paul Guilfoyle, Bradley Page, Willie Best, William Corson, Alec Craig, Richard Lane, Paul Hurst, George Rosener, Fred Kelsey, Robert Emmett O'Connor, Phillip Morris and Dick Rush. Edward Small produced.

The plot of **Flight From Glory** centred on villain Onslow Stevens' recruitment of maverick pilots to fly run-down airplanes over the Andes Mountains. Stevens keeps his discredited flyers in constant debt, charging them for food, liquor and lodging until, one by one, they crack up in their worm-eaten crates. Introduced into this suicidal atmosphere is cowardly Van Heflin (centre) and his beautiful bride Whitney Bourne (left). Being the only attractive woman in the vicinity, Bourne brings more than a dollop of emotional combustion with her. At the finale, the wild-eyed Heflin takes Stevens for one last flight, clearing the decks for Bourne to exit with Chester Morris (right, borrowed from Columbia), the picture's real hero. Tautly directed by Lew Landers from David Silverstein and John Twist's no-nonsense screenplay (story by Robert D. Andrews), **Flight From Glory** was an unquestionable victory for producer Robert Sisk. Also cast: Richard Lane, Paul Guilfoyle, Solly Ward, Douglas Walton, Walter Miller, Rita LaRoy and Pasha Khan.

On Again – Off Again was mostly the latter – a wilted Bert Wheeler (centre right) and Robert Woolsey (left) effort about two quarrelling partners who run a pill factory. They decide to settle their differences in a wrestling match – winner to manage company for a year, loser to become winner's valet. Wheeler loses, and the picture then degenerated into colourless master–servant farce. Everyone involved appeared to be having some difficulty just going through the motions. Lee Marcus produced, and Edward Cline directed from a Nat Perrin–Benny Rubin script. Marjorie Lord (right), Patricia Wilder, Esther Muir (centre left), Paul Harvey, Russell Hicks, George Meeker, Maxine Jennings, Kitty McHugh, Hal K. Dawson, Alec Hartford and Pat Flaherty were also in it. The basic story material originated as *A Pair Of Sixes*, a play written by Edward H. Peple and filmed in 1918 by Essanay. A musical version entitled *Queen High* was produced on Broadway in 1926 and filmed by Paramount in 1930. Songs: 'One Happy Family', 'Thanks To You' Dave Dreyer, Herman Ruby.

Hideaway, directed by Richard Rosson, presented Fred Stone (left) as a worthless squatter who devotes his wits and energies to avoiding anything that resembles work. Stone's laziness seemed to penetrate every fibre of the picture, making it one of the year's dullest stabs at comedy. Even the inclusion of some sympathetic gangsters (led by J. Carrol Naish, centre) failed to lift the story out of the doldrums. The stock characters included Emma Dunn as Stone's shrewish, overworked wife, Marjorie Lord as his pretty daughter and Tommy Bond as a pint-sized hayseed whose slingshot strikes terror in the gangsters' hearts. J. Robert Bren and Edmund L. Hartmann's screenplay, based on a stage drama by Melvin Levy, also employed William Corson, Ray Mayer (right), Bradley Page, Paul Guilfoyle, Dudley Clements, Alec Craig, Lee Patrick, Charles Withers, Otto Hoffman and Bob McKenzie. The producer was Cliff Reid.

In a pretty dire programmer called **You Can't Beat Love**, Preston Foster (left) played a wealthy young attorney who never backs down from a dare and ends up running for mayor against the incumbent, who just happens to be his sweetheart's father. Foster eventually steps aside, but not before he exposes the mayor's grafting henchmen. This comedy-romance, scripted in run-of-the-mill fashion by David Silverstein and Maxwell Shane (story Olga Moore) also suffered from Christy Cabanne's lifeless direction and the lukewarm performances of Foster, Joan Fontaine (right) and Frank M. Thomas. Producer Robert Sisk also cast Herbert Mundin, William Brisbane, Alan Bruce, Paul Hurst, Bradley Page, Berton Churchill, Harold Huber, Paul Guilfoyle and Barbara Pepper.

Though it was by no means a bad film, **The Toast Of New York** was the year's biggest financial disaster. It starred Edward Arnold (borrowed from B. P. Schulberg Productions) as 'Jubilee Jim' Fisk, one of the tycoons who ruled Wall Street after the Civil War. A highly romanticized biography, the picture traced Fisk's meteoric rise to power, his open warfare with fellow magnates Daniel Drew (Donald Meek) and Cornelius Vanderbilt (Clarence Kolb), the rupture of his closest friendship (with Cary Grant) which occurs when he implements a maniacal scheme that threatens the fragile economic balance of the entire nation, and finally his assassination. Arnold (right) brought a refreshing vigour to his role, Jack Oakie added humour as one of his close associates, and Frances Farmer (centre, borrowed from Paramount) made a fitting object for Arnold's (and Grant's) affections. Only Cary Grant (left, also borrowed from Paramount) came off poorly in a part that was not well-drawn. Produced by Edward Small and directed by Rowland V. Lee from a script by Dudley Nichols, John Twist and Joel Sayre (based on a book by Bouck White and story by Matthew Josephson), the picture cost much too much ($1,072,000). Edward Arnold did not have sufficient box-office appeal to carry such a production, and the resulting studio loss was a blistering $530,000. Thelma Leeds, Billy Gilbert, Stanley Fields, George Irving, Frank M. Thomas, Russell Hicks, Oscar Apfel, Dudley Clements, Lionel Belmore, Robert McClung, Robert Dudley, Dewey Robinson, Gavin Gordon, Joyce Compton and Virginia Carroll rounded out the huge cast. Songs included: 'The First Time I Saw You', 'Ooh, La, La' Nathaniel Shilkret, Allie Wrubel; 'Temptation Waltz' Shilkret, L. Wolfe Gilbert.

The conventional wisdom that inexpensive service yarns yield good box-office returns again proved true with respect to **Annapolis Salute** (GB: **Salute To Romance**). Though it was just a feeble remake of *Midshipman Jack* (1933), the picture, directed by Christy Cabanne, grossed $272,000 in film rentals and earned a nice profit. Filmed by Russell Metty on location at the Naval Academy, the real backgrounds were at odds with the artificial story of midshipman James Ellison (right, borrowed from Harry Sherman) and his battles with father Harry Carey and rival Van Heflin (centre) over his courting of Academy belle Marsha Hunt (left, borrowed from Paramount). John Twist wrote the unconvincing screenplay from a story by director Cabanne, and Robert Sisk produced. Also cast: Ann Hovey, Arthur Lake, Dick Hogan, Marilyn Vernon and John Griggs.

Make A Wish was typical Bobby Breen material: a modern day fairy tale about the relationship between a youthful prodigy and a Broadway composer (Basil Rathbone, left), which is cemented at a Maine camp for boys. Complicating matters are the boy's mother (Marion Claire), her jealous fiancé (Ralph Forbes), and three comic book villains (Henry Armetta, Leon Errol and Donald Meek) whose goal is to steal Rathbone's latest operetta. Resourceful Master Breen (right) asserts himself, undoing all the adult damage and making sure the show goes on. Kurt Neumann directed the Gertrude Berg–Bernard Schubert–Earle Snell screenplay (story by Berg) with a commendably gentle touch. The cast also included Billy Lee, Herbert Rawlinson, Leonid Kinskey and Fred Scott. Associate producer Edward Gross supervised the film for Sol Lesser's Principal Productions. Songs: 'Make A Wish', 'Music In My Heart', 'Old Man Rip' Oscar Strauss, Louis Alter, Paul E. Webster.

Still hoping to make box-office magnets of Joe Penner and Parkyakarkas, the studio turned the two comedians loose in **The Life Of The Party**. The resultant picture was on a par with *New Faces of 1937*. Joseph Santley's story, as scripted by Bert Kalmar, Harry Ruby and Viola Brothers Shore, was a diffuse hodge-podge of songs, dances, slapstick gags and tender romance, embellished with glossy production values. Gene Raymond (centre), cast as a young man who will lose $3 million if he marries before he is 30 and Harriet Hilliard (centre left), who initially favours a career above marriage, handled the love plot and much of the singing. Ann Miller contributed some welcome crisp tap routines and Penner, Parkyakarkas, Victor Moore (centre right), Billy Gilbert and Helen Broderick provided the so-called comedy. Producer Edward Kaufman and director William Seiter also utilized Richard Lane (left standing), Franklin Pangborn, Margaret Dumont, Ann Shoemaker (right), Jane Rhodes, George Irving, Winifred Harris and Charles Judels in secondary roles. Songs included: 'Roses In December' Herb Magidson, George Jessel & Ben Oakland; 'So You Won't Sing', 'Life Of The Party', 'Yankee Doodle Band' Herb Magidson, Allie Wrubel.

Forty Naughty Girls sounded like a film designed for an Elk's Club smoking room but was, in fact, the final Hildegarde Withers–Oscar Piper whodunnit. The murder of a press agent in a theatre dressing room and the even more mysterious killing of the show's leading man, which takes place in full view of the audience, send Oscar (James Gleason, right) and Hildegarde (ZaSu Pitts, left) into action. While the inspector stubbornly follows the obvious clues to prop man Frank M. Thomas, Miss Withers ferrets out the evidence that proves Alan Edwards (centre) is the actual culprit. Produced by William Sistrom and directed by Edward Cline, the picture (screenplay by John Grey, story by Stuart Palmer) was only a pallid imitation of the earlier chapters in the series. Also featured in support: Marjorie Lord, George Shelley, Joan Woodbury, Tom Kennedy, Alden Chase, Edward Marr, Ada Leonard, Donald Kerr and Barbara Pepper.

△

Saturday's Heroes, RKO's contribution to the cinema's annual pigskin parade, combined the usual end runs, forward passes and last second touchdowns with an exposé of professionalism in college football. George Templeton's story centred on star quarter-back Van Heflin (left) who, after being burned by the system, works out a solution to its inherent hypocrisy. His ideas include frank acknowledgement by universities that their athletes are subsidized; the picture even offered an example of how the proposed solution might work.

To prevent it from becoming too much of a homily, screenwriters Paul Yawitz, Charles Kaufman and David Silverstein included a standard romantic subplot involving Heflin with Marian Marsh, plus some comedy relief from Frank Jenks and Al St John. Edward Killy directed with minimal enthusiasm for producer Robert Sisk. Also cast: Richard Lane, Alan Bruce (centre), Minor Watson, Willie Best, Walter Miller (right), Crawford Weaver, George Irving, Dick Hogan and Charles Trowbridge.

The superior acting abilities of Barbara Stanwyck (right) and Herbert Marshall (centre) failed to redeem a piece of arrant foolishness entitled **Breakfast For Two**. Marshall was badly miscast as a happy-go-lucky Broadway playboy who is leading a reckless existence until fiery-tempered Texas heiress Stanwyck comes into his life. How she breaks up his romance with gold-digging actress Glenda Farrell (borrowed from Warner Bros.), takes away his income and leads him to the altar as the final stage in the reformation process, were the main plot points in the ludicrous Charles Kaufman–Paul Yawitz–Viola Brothers Shore screenplay (story David Garth). Director Alfred Santell gave the film plenty of gloss, but was powerless to protect it from its wretched plot. Eric Blore (left), Etienne Girardot, Donald Meek, Frank M. Thomas and Pierre Watkin also appeared for producer Edward Kaufman.
▽

RKO's finest film of the year was **Stage Door** – a sterling comedy-drama about a group of young actresses waiting and hoping for their 'big break'. Producer Pandro S. Berman envisioned the Edna Ferber–George S. Kaufman hit play as a Katharine Hepburn–Ginger Rogers vehicle from the moment the studio purchased the rights. Gregory LaCava returned to RKO to direct and rewrote much of the story and dialogue (which had already been recast by screenwriters Morrie Ryskind and Anthony Veiller) so that the final picture was quite different from the Ferber–Kaufman original. The film had special significance for Katharine Hepburn. Needing a hit desperately, she was cast as a society girl who comes to New York determined to make it as an actress, eventually gets her chance, and triumphs. The role was quite similar to her Academy Award-winning characterization in *Morning Glory*. Adolphe Menjou (centre), another participant in the earlier film, was again enlisted to play a philandering producer. Ginger Rogers (left), portraying a witty, sarcastic broad who measures success in purely material terms, made an inspired foil for Miss Hepburn (foreground centre); their barbed exchanges rank among the best examples of pungent dialogue in 1930s American comedy. Backing them up in a most delightful boarding house were such performers as Lucille Ball, Andrea Leeds, Gail Patrick, Ann Miller and the marvellous Eve Arden (complete with omnipresent cat draped round her neck). Despite Pandro Berman's belief that the film would be a blockbuster and the four Oscar nominations that it received, **Stage Door** was something of a box-office disappointment, earning profits of only $81,000. Some 'experts' blamed Hepburn for the letdown – a ridiculous charge for she was totally ingratiating throughout. Constance Collier, Samuel S. Hinds, Franklin Pangborn, William Corson, Pierre Watkin, Grady Sutton, Frank Reicher, Jack Carson, Phyllis Kennedy, Margaret Early, Jean Rouverol, Elizabeth Dunne, Norma Drury, Jane Rhodes, Peggy O'Donnell and Harriet Brandon were other members of the cast. Song: 'Put Your Heart Into Your Feet And Dance' Hal Borne,
◁ Mort Greene.

Fred Astaire had been pressuring the RKO brass ▷ to do a picture without Ginger Rogers for years; **A Damsel In Distress** gave him his chance but didn't turn out quite as he had hoped. The picture did have its attractions: impeccable production design and art direction by Van Nest Polglase and Carroll Clark, a memorable score by George and Ira Gershwin, expert supporting performances from George Burns (front) and Gracie Allen (centre) and a droll screenplay by Ernest Pagano, S. K. Lauren and P. G. Wodehouse (from Wodehouse's original story). And Astaire (right) was, as ever, wit and debonair charm personified in the role of an American musical comedy composer storming the stuffy battlements of the British gentry to win his lady love. The big problem was new leading lady Joan Fontaine, who was still learning her craft as an actress and could not keep pace with the polished Mr Astaire. While Ginger Rogers' screen persona complemented Astaire's, Fontaine's detracted from his strengths. In their one 'dance' number, director George Stevens went to such lengths to camouflage Fontaine's lack of ability that the result almost bordered on the absurd. Lacking a romantic dancing partner, much of Astaire's 'hoofing' in the film was done with Burns and Allen whose dance timing proved as good as their comedy timing. The threesome's romp through a funhouse was especially inspired and earned an Oscar for dance director Hermes Pan. Still, nothing could compensate for the absence of a capable female lead; **Damsel**, a remake of a 1920 Pathé release, became Fred Astaire's first box-office loser. Pandro S. Berman produced with a cast that also included Reginald Gardiner, Ray Noble, Constance Collier, Montagu Love, Harry Watson and Jay Duggan. Songs included: 'Things Are Looking Up', 'Nice Work If You Can Get It', 'A Foggy Day In London Town', 'I Can't Be Bothered Now', 'Put Me To The Test', 'Stiff Upper Lip'.

Connoisseurs of slapstick got their money's worth in **Fit For A King**, a Joe E. Brown comedy scripted by Richard Flournoy and directed by Edward Sedgwick. The story, about a cub reporter assigned to cover an archduke who is being trailed by assassins, climaxed in a long chase sequence involving automobiles, motorcycles, bicycles and a haycart which Brown (left) rides until it falls to pieces. It was thoroughly mindless, of course, but audiences supported it anyway. Also cast: Harry Davenport as the archduke, Helen Mack (right) as an unlikely princess and Paul Kelly as a rival newspaperman constantly out-scooping the star, plus Halliwell Hobbes, John Qualen, Donald Briggs, Frank Reicher, Russell Hicks and Charles Trowbridge. RKO distributed for David L. Loew Productions.

Hollywood pioneer Jesse L. Lasky's first RKO production, **Music For Madame**, was wrecked by its inane Gertrude Purcell–Robert Harari screenplay (story by Harari). Nino Martini (right, of Metropolitan Opera fame) is on the road to Hollywood when jewel thieves trick him into singing at a wedding party, steal an expensive pearl necklace, and then threaten to kill the baritone if he ever sings again. Acute audience members realized, of course, that RKO was not going to pay Mr Martini's salary without giving him plenty of opportunities to use his golden voice, which was why they had to endure the tortured plot devices required to liberate him from his predicament. Any pretence that director John Blystone had of forging some sort of entertainment from the wretched story dissolved quickly, and so did the lines at the box office – the picture lost $375,000. Joan Fontaine (left), Alan Mowbray, Billy Gilbert, Alan Hale, Grant Mitchell, Erik Rhodes, Lee Patrick (centre), Frank Conroy, Bradley Page, Ada Leonard, Alan Bruce, Romo Vincent, Barbara Pepper, Edward H. Robins, George Shelley and Jack Carson lent their support to no avail. Songs included: 'Music For Madame' Herb Magidson, Allie Wrubel; 'King Of The Road' Nathaniel Shilkret, Eddie Cherkose; 'I Want The World To Know', 'Bambina' Rudolf Friml, Gus Kahn; 'Vesti La Guibba' (from Leoncavallo's *Pagliacci*). ▽

RKO's 1937 comedies were long on slapstick but short on originality, as **There Goes The Groom** amply demonstrated. Its familiar story focused on a wacky family, scrambling to cover up its financial problems and casting about to lure a wealthy son-in-law into the fold. Burgess Meredith (left) arrives fresh from a gold strike in Alaska and the chase is on. Meredith is originally ticketed for Louise Henry (his school sweetheart) but ends up with younger sister Ann Sothern (centre). Routinely directed by Joseph Santley from a screenplay by S. K. Lauren, Dorothy Yost and Harold Kusell (from an original story by David Garth), the film did occasionally tickle the funny bone, and also provided Meredith with an opportunity to demonstrate comic abilities that had not been hinted at in *Winterset*. Also cast: Mary Boland (right), Onslow Stevens, William Brisbane, Roger Imhof, Sumner Getchell, George Irving, Leona Roberts and Adrian Morris. The producer was Albert Lewis.

△
A cursory remake of *Rafter Romance*, **Living On Love** presented James Dunn (right) and Whitney Bourne (left) as occupants of the same apartment inhabited by Ginger Rogers and Norman Foster in 1933. Since he is only there by day, and she only at night, the two characters develop a strong antipathy to each other as room-mates while falling in love as strangers who meet away from the confines of their dingy home base. The basic premise, scripted by Franklin Coen from John Wells' novel, still had some comic stamina left in it, but much of the humour was smothered by Lew Landers' stodgy direction. Also cast: Joan Woodbury, Solly Ward, Tom Kennedy, Franklin Pangborn, Kenneth Terrell, James Fawcett and Chester Clute.

Shortly before signing an agreement with producer-director Herbert Wilcox to provide the studio with a quota of British-made pictures, RKO began distributing his **Victoria The Great**, an expensive and dignified biography of the British monarch which Wilcox had completed under his Imperator Film Productions banner. The film starred Wilcox's future wife Anna Neagle (right), who handled the title role with appropriately regal grace. Adopting a degree of poetic licence, the plot concentrated on both the early and late years of the queen's 60-year reign, emphasizing her relations with Prince Albert (Anton Walbrook, left), Prince Ernest (Walter Rilla), Lord Melbourne (H. B. Warner), Lord Palmerston (Felix Aylmer), the Duke of Wellington (James Dale), Gladstone (Arthur Young), Disraeli (Derrick de Marney), President Lincoln (Percy Parsons) and other famous figures of her eponymous age. Though not made with American audiences in mind, the film's respectful tone, coupled with its emphasis on Victoria's humanity, proved appealing to a broad spectrum of the public. Exactly 100 years after ascending the throne, Victoria Regina demonstrated she still had ample charisma. Based on distribution rights alone, RKO made a nifty profit on the picture. Miles Malleson and Charles de Grandcourt authored the screenplay which was shot at the London Film Studios, Denham, England. The final sequences were in Technicolor. Additional cast members: Mary Morris, Charles Carson, C. V. France, Gordon McLeod, Greta Wegener, Paul Leyssac and Hugh Miller.
▽

Fight For Your Lady presented Ida Lupino entertaining the patrons of a Budapest nightclub with a ventriloquist act. The real dummies, however, were all behind the cameras of this bumbling musical farce. A quintet of writers (story by Jean Negulesco and Isabel Leighton; screenplay by Ernest Pagano, Harry Segall and Harold Kusell) hatched the story of an American singer (John Boles, left) who, having been jilted by Margot Grahame, decides to pay court to Miss Lupino (right, borrowed from Paramount). This is tantamount to suicide, since she happens to be married to Europe's most formidable duelist (Erik Rhodes, centre) whose swordsmanship has already claimed 44 victims. Under Ben Stoloff's direction, nearly every gag fell flat, and a supporting cast populated by good character actors failed to provide even moderate diversion. Jack Oakie, Gordon Jones, Billy Gilbert, Paul Guilfoyle, George Renavent, Charles Judels, Maude Eburne, Charles Coleman, Leona Roberts and Forrester Harvey were among those present. Albert Lewis produced. Song: 'Blame It On The Danube' Harry Akst, Frank Loesser.

Hitting A New High represented a new low in Hollywood's treatment of opera stars. Since signing Lily Pons (centre), the studio chiefs had been desperately attempting to popularize her obviously sophisticated appeal. In this instance, she was forced to dress in a costume of feathers, twitter when she talked and answer to the name of 'Ooga-Hunga, the Bird Girl'. The screenplay by Gertrude Purcell and John Twist (story Robert Harari and Maxwell Shane) made this the idea of demon publicist Jack Oakie (right), who presents the aspiring singer to the show business world as a sweet-singing missing link from Africa. Raoul Walsh's direction, the musical numbers by Jimmy McHugh and Harold Adamson, and the comic interpolations of Eric Blore and Edward Everett Horton (left) could not redeem the cockeyed premise. The film lost a bundle and brought down the curtain on the RKO career of Miss Pons. It also hastened producer Jesse L. Lasky's exit from the studio. Others in the cast were John Howard (background, in yachting cap), Eduardo Ciannelli, Luis Alberni, Jack Arnold (formerly Vinton Haworth) and Leonard Carey. Songs included: 'Je Suis Titania' (from *Mignon*) Thomas; 'Nightingale Song' (from *Paristys*) Saint-Saens; 'I Hit A New High', 'This Never Happened Before', 'Let's Give Love Another Chance' McHugh, Adamson.

High Flyers was the Bert Wheeler–Robert Woolsey swan song. Written for the screen by Benny Rubin, Bert Granet and Byron Morgan (from a play by Victor Mapes), the picture contained an occasional funny line, and even a gag or two that had not been used before, but mostly it was *deja vu* and bad *deja vu* at that. Woolsey (left) and Wheeler played carnival con artists dispensing flying lessons to all the suckers in the vicinity. They soon find themselves involved with a group of jewellery smugglers in need of transportation. Spicy Lupe Velez (right) emerged triumphant from the overall tedium, tossing off imitations of Dolores Del Rio, Simone Simon and Shirley Temple and upstaging everyone around her. Lee Marcus produced, Edward Cline directed and Marjorie Lord, Margaret Dumont, Jack Carson, Paul Harvey, Charles Judels, Lucien Prival, Herbert Evans, Herbert Clifton and George Irving were also cast. Wheeler and Woolsey were unquestionably RKO's senior performers, having appeared in at least one film for the company in every year of its existence. But now they were finished – as a motion picture act, and as a second-rate comedy duo. Approximately one year after the release of **High Flyers**, Robert Woolsey died of a kidney ailment. Songs: 'I Always Get My Man', 'Keep Your Head Above Water', 'I'm A Gaucho' Dave Dreyer, Herman Ruby.

Although its subject was nitroglycerine, **Danger Patrol** was only moderately absorbing. The plot centred on Harry Carey (left), a veteran transporter of the volatile substance used to squelch oil field blazes, who forbids daughter Sally Eilers to marry John Beal (right) because Beal is also involved in the suicidal vocation. At the climax, Carey grasps the inevitability of their love, gives the youngsters his blessing and then takes over an especially dangerous mission from Beal. As scripted by Sy Bartlett from a story by Helen Vreeland and Hilda Vincent, the mission naturally led to the star's heroic demise. Lew Landers directed with the occasional exciting touch, but allowed Carey to dominate the action and overpower his co-stars Beal and Eilers. Above-average performances were given by featured players Frank M. Thomas, Crawford Weaver, Lee Patrick, Edward Gargan and Paul Guilfoyle, with Solly Ward, Ann Hovey, Richard Lane, Walter Miller, George Shelley, Vinton Haworth and Herman Brix (later known as Bruce Bennett) also cast. ▷

To prevent a raid on the city treasury, mayor Fred Stone (left) broke a few laws himself in **Quick Money**. Stone, a thorn in the side of confidence men Berton Churchill and Paul Guilfoyle, is slated for political oblivion via a recall election so he sabotages the balloting, using both legal and illegal methods to accomplish his purpose. Fortunately, he is able to unmask the crooks before the votes are counted. Arthur T. Horman's story (screenplay by Franklin Coen, Bert Granet and Horman) formed the basis of this unpretentious but lively dramatic comedy. Director Edward Killy cast Harlan Briggs as a foolish local banker, Dorothy Vaughan as the mayor's wife and Dorothy Moore as his daughter. Also in it: Gordon Jones, Sherwood Bailey, Frank M. Thomas, Jack Carson, Kathryn Sheldon, Dick Elliott, James Farley, William Franey, Fuzzy Knight and Hattie McDaniel (right).

Allan Scott's screenplay for **Wise Girl** required million dollar heiress Miriam Hopkins (left, borrowed from Samuel Goldwyn) to adopt the disguise of a pauper, invade the Greenwich Village artists' colony and attempt to gain custody of her divorced sister's two children from their intractable father (Ray Milland, right). Produced by Edward Kaufman and directed by Leigh Jason, the narrative contained an adequate amount of charm, wit and slapstick hokum to entertain the average movie patron. Ivan Lebedeff, much on view in RKO films of the LeBaron period, returned in a caricatured supporting part, with Walter Abel, Henry Stephenson, Alec Craig, Guinn Williams, Betty Philson, Marianna Strelby, Margaret Dumont, Jean DeBriac, Rafael Storm, Gregory Gaye, Richard Lane and Tom Kennedy completing the cast. Scott's screenplay was based on a story by himself and Charles Norman.

Walt Disney's historic **Snow White And The Seven Dwarfs** (illustrated) premiered at the Carthay Circle Theatre in Los Angeles on 21 December 1937. From there it swept through America – and the world – inspiring an avalanche of critical and customer approval wherever it played. The full-length animated feature, adapted from Grimm's Fairy Tales by Ted Sears, Otto Englander, Earl Hurd, Dorothy Ann Blank, Richard Creedon, Dick Rickard, Merrill de Maris and Webb Smith, had been a sizeable gamble on Disney's part, requiring three years, $1,500,000 in production expenses, 570 artists and 250,000 drawings to complete. But it paid dividends that were beyond even its creator's expectations. Besides attracting a record-breaking $8,500,000 in gross film rentals, the picture became a merchandizing bonanza, with Snow White dolls, toys, books, records and other novelties flooding the nation. Although RKO did not profit from the subsidiary marketing, it was more than happy to be the distributor of this Technicolor blockbuster. Using multiplane animation techniques that set a standard of excellence for the entire field, the Disney staff brought to life a host of memorable characters – Snow White, the wicked queen, the prince and, of course, the redoubtable dwarfs. They were the most recognizable folklore figures in the world for years after the film's release. Though it is impossible to enumerate all the important contributors to **Snow White**, here are a few major names: David Hand (supervising director); Perce Pearce, Larry Morey, William Cottrell, Wilfred Jackson and Ben Sharpsteen (sequence directors); Hamilton Luske, Vladimir Tytla, Fred Moore and Norman Ferguson (supervising animators). Walt Disney's formula for success, as evidenced by **Snow White**, was simple. He gave the public quality entertainment no matter what the cost. RKO's executives could have learned a

good deal from their new associate's show business philosophy. Songs included: 'Some Day My Prince Will Come', 'Snow White', 'Whistle While You Work', 'With A Smile And A Song', 'I'm Wishing' Frank Churchill, Larry Morey, Paul J. Smith.

The last of the RKO Gene Raymond–Ann Sothern pictures was also, predictably, the weakest of the lot. **She's Got Everything** recounted the efforts of Victor Moore and Helen Broderick (left) to promote a properly luxurious marriage for the recently impoverished Miss Sothern (right). Coffee magnate Raymond represents the ideal

catch and the predestined twosome eventually tie the knot, in spite of Moore's meddling which nearly spoils everything. More than plot weaknesses spoiled the picture, with the indifferent performances of the two stars and Joseph Santley's forced direction representing two painfully obvious problems. The trite screenplay by Harry Segall and Maxwell Shane also gave roles to Parkyakarkas, Billy Gilbert, William Brisbane, Herbert Clifton, Alan Bruce, Solly Ward, Alec Craig, Fred Santley, Richard Tucker, George Irving and Jack Carson. Albert Lewis was the producer. Song: 'It's Sleepy Time In Hawaii' Leon & Otis Rene.

★★★★★★★★★★★★★★★★★★

1938

★★★★★★★★★★★★★★★★★★

Katharine Hepburn's association with RKO ended in 1938. Early in the year the actress was allowed to make *Holiday* for Columbia; it was the first time the studio had ever permitted Miss Hepburn to work for another production company, and an indication that she was no longer considered to be of unique value. When she returned to RKO, the actress' prestige had fallen to an all-time low. Pressure from disgruntled exhibitors, plus the disheartening box-office performance of **Bringing Up Baby**, forced company executives to consider the possibility that she had exhausted her value as a screen personality. They assigned her a part in **Mother Carey's Chickens** which she refused to take, and this prompted the termination of her contract.

RKO also gave up on Joan Fontaine during the year. The company chiefs felt her potential was minimal, and dropped her from the studio roster along with producers Howard Hawks, Edward Kaufman, Jesse L. Lasky and Edward Small. Quite obviously Sam Briskin's talent roundup had been, by and large, a failure. Two inventive individuals did make breakthroughs on a small picture entitled **A Man To Remember**: director Garson Kanin and writer Dalton Trumbo.

Leaving 'A' production to Pandro Berman, corporate president Leo Spitz focused his attention on the 'B' unit, advocating the filming of crime subjects, 'exploitation' films and homespun, sentimental diversions. One of Spitz's continuing bequests to RKO was the popular 'Saint' series, which continued its run for some time after his departure from the company.

Floyd B. Odlum decided not to exercise his option on the large block of corporate stock still owned by RCA, thereby forfeiting the chance to take complete control of RKO operations. Odlum evidently had reservations about the movie company's future prospects. He deferred to the other behind-the-scenes power – David Sarnoff of RCA, and the Rockefellers, who also had substantial holdings in RKO – to determine future company policy. When Leo Spitz resigned the presidency and returned to his law practice late in the year, the Rockefellers (with Sarnoff's approval) made the decision to bring in George J. Schaefer, formerly of United Artists, to reshape the organization. He became the fourth corporate president in RKO's brief history.

RKO's profits fell to $173,578 in 1938. The business recession of the period had much to do with declining revenues, but this was also another disenchanting year for studio product. Top money earners among the 42 releases were **The Saint In New York, Sky Giant, A Man To Remember, Mother Carey's Chickens** and **Condemned Women**.

Double Danger cast Preston Foster (left) as an author of mystery stories, who also happens to be a gentleman jewel thief lusting after the Konjer diamonds. Played tongue-in-cheek by director Lew Landers, this lightweight mystery featured Whitney Bourne (centre left) who also has a yen for diamonds and develops one for Foster, Samuel S. Hinds and Donald Meek as a police commissioner and an eccentric jeweller pooling their resources to track down the thieves, Cecil Kellaway (right) as a phony valet and Paul Guilfoyle (centre right) as the principal heavy. At the finale, Foster gets the girl and reforms, vowing to write one last book entitled 'The End of the Gentleman'. And commissioner Hinds doesn't come away empty handed either, arresting Guilfoyle and putting him behind bars. Based on a story by Arthur T. Horman, the serviceable screenplay (by Horman and J. Robert Bren) also had parts for June Johnson, Arthur Lake, Edythe Elliot, Alec Craig and Harry Hayden.

Maid's Night Out, felicitously adapted by Bert Granet from a story by Willoughby Speyers, told of a millionaire's son (Allan Lane, right) who becomes a milkman for a month to win a bet with his gruff, self-made father (George Irving). En route he meets Joan Fontaine (left) and, mistaking her for a servant girl, lays the foundation for a series of wild, mirth-provoking episodes. Director Ben Holmes piloted the film in energetic fashion, using Billy Gilbert, Cecil Kellaway, Hedda Hopper, William Brisbane, Hilda Vaughn, Frank M. Thomas, Solly Ward and Eddie Gribbon to fill out the cast. Robert Sisk produced this appealing 'B' comedy.

For years RKO had been trying to mount a film that would use the fabulous Radio City Music Hall (once the company's flagship theatre) as a backdrop. Producer Edward Kaufman finally put **Radio City Revels** together but, significantly, it opened at the Globe Theatre in New York, not the Music Hall. Blending together the comic talents of Milton Berle, Jack Oakie, Bob Burns, Helen Broderick and Victor Moore, director Ben Stoloff and four writers (Eddie Davis, Matt Brooks, Anthony Veiller and Mortimer Offner) concocted a jumbled mess that contained very little revelry. Oakie (left) and Berle played a couple of talentless songwriters who steal tunes from Burns (borrowed from Paramount), a composer able to function only while asleep. The plot would have been a trifle thin even for a programmer, but this was no such modest undertaking: final production costs added up to $810,000, dooming the movie to widespread critical opprobrium and a $300,000 loss at the box-office. Matt Brooks penned the original story, Joseph Santley directed the musical numbers, Hermes Pan staged the dances, and the less-than-fascinating songs were composed by Herb Magidson and Allie Wrubel. Also in the cast: Kenny Baker (centre), Ann Miller (right), Jane Froman, Buster West, Melissa Mason, Richard Lane, Marilyn Vernon and Hal Kemp and his orchestra. Songs included: 'Speak Your Heart', 'Take A Tip From The Tulip', 'I'm Taking A Shine To You', 'There's A New Moon Over The Old Mill', 'Swingin' In The Corn'.

Crashing Hollywood was one of an epidemic number of show biz spoofs emanating from the film capital during this period. An above-average example of its type, the film featured Lee Tracy (centre right) as a budding screenwriter who collaborates with ex-con Paul Guilfoyle (left) on a robbery story. Not having much imagination, Guilfoyle bases the plot on a real bank job in which he participated and, in no time, fact and fiction, true identity and false, become wildly jumbled up. Director Lew Landers kept it churning along at such a rapid pace that all the complications sorted themselves out in an hour. The lively script was written by Paul Yawitz and Gladys Atwater (from a play by Paul Dickey and Mann Page). The supporting cast included Joan Woodbury, Lee Patrick (centre left), Bradley Page, Tom Kennedy, George Irving, Frank M. Thomas, Jack Carson, Alec Craig and James Conlin (right). The Cliff Reid production also showcased Richard Lane's wildly ingratiating impersonation of a producer who signs up practically everyone he meets to fantastic contracts. Crashing Hollywood was a remake of a 1923 FBO picture called *Lights Out*, which was also the title of the original play.

The Rat was a poorly made romantic melodrama produced in Britain by Herbert Wilcox's Imperator Film Productions for RKO distribution. Jack Raymond's murky direction cast a pall over the story of a cunning Parisian jewel thief (Anton Walbrook, centre) who becomes romantically involved with society woman Ruth Chatterton and with Rene Ray (centre right), an underworld gamin left in Walbrook's custody by her condemned father. When Ray commits a murder, the protagonist's code of honour dictates that he must take the blame for it. Also shouldering a substantial portion of the blame for this feeble package were Ivor Novello and Constance Collier who wrote the original play, Marjorie Gaffney who provided the scenario, Miles Malleson who wrote dialogue, and Hans Gulder Rameau who penned the final screenplay. Others cast included: Beatrix Lehmann, Mary Clare (right), Felix Aylmer, Geraldine Hislop (left), Hugh Miller, Gordon McLeod, Frederick Culley, Nadine March, George Merritt and Leo Genn. The play had been filmed by Gainsborough in Britain in 1925, starring author Novello and Mae Marsh.

An office romance, stimulated by a nation-wide ▷ puzzle contest and complicated by the designs of a group of racketeers, formed the basis of Everybody's Doing It. Preston Foster (centre) and Sally Eilers (right) top-lined as a pair of commercial artists in the advertising department of a big breakfast food corporation who originate the idea of the contest, and then have to deal with crooks who attempt to sell lists of the correct answers to the public. J. Robert Bren, Edmund Joseph and Harry Segall's screenplay (story George Beck) was topical, but so overloaded with knock-about gags that it fell apart in short order. Also cast: Cecil Kellaway, William Brisbane, Richard Lane, Guinn Williams (left), Arthur Lake, Frank M. Thomas and newcomer Lorraine Kreuger, who warbled 'Put Your Heart Into Your Feet And Dance' (by Hal Borne and Mort Greene). Christy Cabanne directed for producer William Sistrom.

Bringing Up Baby, arguably the finest screwball comedy ever made, was looked on as an unmitigated disaster in its own day. Producer-director Howard Hawks allowed the film to run far over budget and its loss to RKO was $365,000. Already embattled by vicious exhibitor attacks *vis à vis* her lack of box-office pull, Katharine Hepburn proved she could be a first-rate comedienne – to no avail. The collapse of the film brought an end to her RKO career and also aborted Hawks' brief tenure, costing him an opportunity to make *Gunga Din*. Perhaps Bringing Up Baby was just ahead of its time, for it is received with delight by present-day audiences. Its story of a stuffy palaeontologist (Cary Grant, right) whose life is turned topsy-turvy by a giddy heiress (Hepburn, left) literally defies synopsis. But some of its delectable ingredients include a hyperactive dog named George, a mistaken identity plot involving two leopards (one of whom is the Baby of the title), a pompous big-game hunter (Charlie Ruggles, borrowed from Paramount) who specializes in loon calls, and a priceless fossilized bone which disappears, setting much of the insanity in motion. All these elements were moulded together by Hawks' seamless direction into a veritable treasure trove of comic moments which filmmakers have been plundering ever since. Peter Bogdanovich's *What's Up Doc?*, for example, was both an homage to and a sly plagiarism of Bringing Up Baby. Dudley Nichols and Hagar Wilde wrote the exuberant screenplay from an original story by Wilde. They fashioned memorable characters for all the cast members, including Walter Catlett, May Robson, Barry Fitzgerald, Fritz Feld, Leona Roberts, George Irving, Tala Birell, Virginia Walker and John Kelly. Associate producer Cliff Reid's main task was to hurry the imperturbable Hawks along; he didn't enjoy much success at it.
▽

Producer Sol Lesser and his Principal Productions delivered another syrupy Bobby Breen vehicle for RKO release, Hawaii Calls. Part travelogue, part Ned Sparks comedy, part drama about stolen Navy plans, and part musical with a Polynesian flavouring, the picture was all hokum. Wanda Tuchock's script, based on Don Blanding's novel *Stowaways in Paradise*, traced the adventures of a bootblack (Breen, illustrated) and a newsboy (Pua Lani) who stow away on a liner bound for Hawaii. The boys are caught, but escape with Sparks' assistance and eventually take refuge with Pua's relatives in the island paradise. Other plot points were introduced but never allowed to infringe on the obligatory musical numbers. Edward F. Cline's directorial gifts were equal to his task, providing an above-average cordial for Breen's loyal followers. Irwin S. Cobb, Mamo Clark, Warren Hull, Gloria Holden, Herbert Rawlinson, Juanita Quigley, and Raymond Paige and his orchestra played supporting parts. Songs included: 'That's The Hawaiian In Me' Johnny Noble; 'Hawaii Calls', 'Down Where The Trade Winds Blow' Harry Owens.

An odd mixture of elements that never managed to cohere, **Night Spot** walked the tightrope between serious crime melodrama and slapstick comedy. Parkyakarkas (real name Harry Einstein, right), who had gained a small measure of fame as a stooge on Eddie Cantor's radio programme, received top-billing. His job involved injecting as much comedy as possible into the story of an undercover policeman out to prove that a night club is the headquarters of a gang of gem thieves. Allan Lane played the detective with Gordon Jones as his pal and co-worker, Joan Woodbury as a singer in the club who cultivates a romance with Lane, and Bradley Page as the chief crook. Robert Sisk produced, Christy Cabanne directed and Lionel Houser wrote the script from a story by Anne Jordan. Lee Patrick, Jack Carson, Frank M. Thomas, Joseph Crehan, Crawford Weaver, Cecil Kellaway (left) and Rollo Lloyd were also in it. Song: 'There's Only One Way To Say "I Love You"' Sam H. Stept, Herman Ruby.

Paul Yawitz and Bert Granet (working from a story by Walter O'Keefe) finally manufactured a plot that suited Joe Penner's comic abilities. **Go Chase Yourself** featured Penner (right) as a goofy bank clerk who wins a swanky auto trailer in a lottery. The trailer is soon hijacked by bankrobbers, with Penner going along for the ride. And what a ride it was, culminating in a rip-roaring, out-of-control descent down the side of a mountain. Director Edward F. Cline kept the slapstick events on track and wheedled zany performances from a group of stalwarts that included Richard Lane, Tom Kennedy and Bradley Page (left) as the crooks, June Travis (centre) as a copper magnate's daughter, Fritz Feld a count wooing her for her millions, and Jack Carson as a radio news broad-caster. Most importantly, Lucille Ball (who would one day buy the studio) proved she could handle lead roles with her portrayal of Penner's hard-boiled wife. Robert Sisk produced this hit example of Penner's patented comedy of stupidity, with Granville Bates, George Irving, Arthur Stone and Frank M. Thomas cast in supporting parts. Song: 'I'm From The City' Hal Raynor.

The amazingly prolific Lew Landers directed no less than eight of the studio's 1938 releases. One of the best was **Condemned Women**, a vigorous prison drama that transcended its potboiler title. Centre stage among a welter of plot strands was the burgeoning love affair of a sympathetic psychiatrist (Louis Hayward, borrowed from Universal) and an embittered inmate (Sally Eilers, right). Fine ensemble performances came from Esther Dale (left) as a brutish matron who believes in old-school methods of rehabilitation, her nemesis George Irving as the enlightened and compassionate prison warden, and Anne Shirley as a naïve young girl taking the rap for her lover. Unlike most RKO films, this one had a sociological point to make – about the necessity of humane treatment for public offenders – though it was almost swamped by an overabundance of story material. Still, the film's atmospheric detail, taut direction and convincing performances attracted considerable interest and acclaim. Lionel Houser's story and screenplay also gave roles to Lee Patrick (centre), Leona Roberts, Richard Bond, Netta Packer, Rita LaRoy and Florence Lake. Robert Sisk produced.

Publicity and politics, flavoured with romance, were the concerns of **This Marriage Business**, another minor Victor Moore comedy. Moore (right) played a small town marriage licence clerk made famous by newspaperman Allan Lane (left) who discovers that not one of the marriages sanctioned by Moore over a 20-year period has ever ended in divorce. The ensuing publicity brings a flood of the matrimonially-inclined to Moore's doorstep and prompts Lane to push the purveyor of the 'Lucky Licence' into a mayoralty race. Featured as Moore's daughter and Lane's sweetheart was Vicki Lester, an actress who had derived her name from the character played by Janet Gaynor in David O. Selznick's *A Star Is Born*. It was Lester's first important role; she was then under exclusive contract to producer-director Mervyn LeRoy, from whom RKO borrowed her services. The Gladys Atwater–J. Robert Bren screenplay (story by Mel Riddle and Alex Ruben) was ticketed for neighbourhood theatres in the American heartland, where it succeeded on its own modest terms. Christy Cabanne directed for producer Cliff Reid, utilizing Cecil Kellaway, Jack Carson (centre), Richard Lane, Kay Sutton, Paul Guilfoyle, Jack Arnold, Frank M. Thomas, Leona Roberts and George Irving in secondary parts.

Director Lew Landers and writers Bert Granet and Edmund L. Hartmann did their best with **Law Of The Underworld**, but it still emerged as only a lukewarm remake of *The Pay-Off* (1930), a Lowell Sherman production that had not been especially memorable in its initial incarnation. The big problem was the soupy, sentimental narrative. Adapted from John B. Hymer and Samuel Shipman's story and stage play, it focused on sophisticated gang leader Chester Morris (left) who chivalrously trades his own life for the freedom of innocent love birds Anne Shirley (centre) and Richard Bond (right). Landers' direction proved to be a good deal more muscular than Sherman's original flaccid stab at the material, but Morris' gentleman thief was a pale shadow compared to Sherman's world-weary impersonation of the same character. Producer Robert Sisk's cast also included Eduardo Ciannelli, Walter Abel, Lee Patrick, Paul Guilfoyle, Frank M. Thomas, Eddie Acuff, Jack Arnold and Jack Carson.

The comic abilities of Ginger Rogers and director George Stevens were prominently displayed in **Vivacious Lady**, a sparkling piece of slapstick about a clash of cultures. P. J. Wolfson and Ernest Pagano's screenplay (story I. A. R. Wylie) related the saga of a young botany professor (James Stewart, left, borrowed from MGM) who impulsively marries a New York nightclub singer (Rogers, right) and then returns to his small college town to face another kind of music. The major impediment to the couple's happiness is Charles Coburn, an erudite and formal gentleman who happens to be the groom's father as well as the president of Old Sharon University. Stewart's inability to break the news to dad leads to a welter of predicaments and embarrassing situations, including a classic no-holds-barred brawl between Ginger and Stewart's former fiancée (Frances Mercer) at the college prom. The additional contributions of secondary players James Ellison, Beulah Bondi, Phyllis Kennedy, Franklin Pangborn, Grady Sutton, Jack Carson, Alec Craig and Willie Best helped to make **Vivacious Lady** one of RKO's finest comedies of the decade. George Stevens also earned his first credit as producer with Pandro S. Berman listed as 'in charge of production' (which he was by this time). Song: 'You'll Be Reminded Of Me' George Jessel, Jack Meskill, Ted Shapiro.

The Saint In New York was a delight for fans of Leslie Charteris' popular fictional detective; it also marked the auspicious beginning of RKO's most important series since the Astaire–Rogers movies. Louis Hayward (centre, borrowed from Universal) played the hero – a role that would be taken by George Sanders in most of the subsequent editions. In this one, the Saint leaves South America for New York on a mission to halt the Machiavellian activities of the 'Big Fellow', the kingpin of the metropolitan underworld. The Saint's methods are stylish, witty and consistently successful (he takes care of one gangster while garbed as a nun), and the same adjectives were applicable to the William Sistrom production. Sharply directed by Ben Holmes from a Charles Kaufman–Mortimer Offner screenplay that remained faithful to the Charteris novel, **The Saint In New York** was a winner, and resulted in immediate negotiations for the purchase of Charteris' other 'Saint' stories. Also cast: Kay Sutton, Sig Rumann, Jonathan Hale, Jack Carson (left), Paul Guilfoyle (right), Frederick Burton, Ben Welden, Charles Halton and Cliff Bragdon.

Pleased by the success of the independently produced George O'Brien films which it had released in 1937, RKO launched a new series of low-budget O'Brien westerns with **Gun Law**. The picture was full of barking guns and daredevil riding, and even contained one or two interesting variations on its formula plot. O'Brien (illustrated) acted the role of a US marshal masquerading as a bad guy in order to infiltrate the desperado element in a small frontier town. The clean-up campaign climaxes with the revelation that the town mayor is the instigator of the evil. O'Brien, closely associated with the genre since his starring performance in John Ford's silent epic, *The Iron Horse*, restored order with verve and determination. Newcomer Rita Oehmen as the daughter of a travelling preacher, Paul Everton as the mayor, and Ray Whitley as a singing waiter who doubles as an undercover aide to the hero, were the other featured performers. Oliver Drake's screenplay also provided roles for Robert Gleckler, Ward Bond, Francis MacDonald and Edward Pawley. Bert Gilroy produced and David Howard directed this remake of *When The Law Rides* (FBO, 1928), which had starred Tom Tyler. Songs included: 'Breezy Whiskers' Ray Whitley; 'So Long Old Pinto' Oliver Drake; 'Pappy Was A Gun Man' Whitley, Drake.

The studio's prodigal son, Richard Dix, returned to RKO after an absence of two years, to star in **Blind Alibi**. Dix's reputation was now in partial eclipse, and it was hoped that this Cliff Reid-produced programmer would return him to public favour. Indeed, Dix (centre) managed to deliver a credible performance as a man who adopts the disguise of a blind sculptor in order to foil a blackmail scheme, but the script impaired his comeback efforts. The team of Lionel Houser, Harry Segall and Ron Ferguson, working from William Joyce Cowan's original story, fabricated a melo that smouldered a little, but never caught fire. The writers' best role went to Ace the Wonder Dog (right), who upstaged Dix at every turn. Whitney Bourne, Eduardo Ciannelli, Frances Mercer, Paul Guilfoyle (left), Richard Lane, Jack Arnold, Walter Miller, Frank M. Thomas, Solly Ward, Tommy Bupp and George Irving were also in it. Lew Landers directed – not his best effort.

Joan Fontaine (right) was poorly served by the five writers whose misguided efforts created **Blond Cheat**. Aladar Laszlo (story) and Charles Kaufman, Paul Yawitz, Viola Brothers Shore and Harry Segall (screenplay) constructed this farce-comedy with British audiences in mind, and director Joseph Santley cast English actors in most of the major parts. Nevertheless, the tale of a London millionaire (Cecil Kellaway) who offers to back actress Fontaine's new musical show if she can break up the romance between his daughter Lilian Bond and prominent social lion Derrick de Marney (centre) was an affront to lovers of comedy of all races, creeds and nationalities. Cecil Cunningham, Robert Coote, Olaf Hytten, John Sutton, Gerald Hamer and Charles Coleman (left) also participated for producer William Sistrom. Song: 'It Must Be Love' Dave Dreyer, Herman Ruby.

In a year overloaded with RKO misfires, **Joy Of Living** was one of the most badly off-target. Dorothy and Herbert Fields cooked up its familiar plot about the liberation of a repressed musical comedy performer (Irene Dunne, centre), and Gene Towne, Graham Baker and Allan Scott collaborated on the rather juvenile screenplay. Miss Dunne's major problem turns out to be her over-protective and over-acquisitive family, who keep the singer under wraps but live off her ample salary. Douglas Fairbanks Jr (right), a ship owner, sweeps in from the South Seas to release the lady from bondage and, according to the film's advertising catch-phrase, teach her that 'it's fun to be foolish'. The movie's only saving grace was its Jerome Kern–Dorothy Fields score, with some good numbers capably sung by Miss Dunne. Director Tay Garnett worked hard to inject numerous slapstick gags into the affair, but also succeeded in running the budget up to an absurd level. Final negative cost for this trifle came to $1,086,000, and RKO was fortunate to escape with only a $314,000 loss. Felix Young produced with a cast that included Alice Brady, Guy Kibbee, Lucille Ball and Frank Milan (all members of the grasping family), plus Eric Blore, Warren Hymer, Jean Dixon, Billy Gilbert, Dorothy Steiner, Estelle Steiner, Phyllis Kennedy, Franklin Pangborn, James Burke, John Qualen and Spencer Charters. Songs: 'What's Good About Goodnight?', 'You Couldn't Be Cuter', 'Just Let Me Look At You', 'A Heavenly Party'.

A tip that large shipments of guns, ammunition, horses and men are being smuggled out of the country in violation of the neutrality act, brought special agent George O'Brien (left) to Texas in **Border G-Man**. There, he not only smokes out the malevolent arms-traffickers but falls in love with a young girl whose brother is innocently involved with the nefarious goings-on. Laraine Johnson (right, soon to be known as Laraine Day) – still a Long Beach high school student – stood out as the heroine of this razor-sharp modern western. Oliver Drake wrote the screenplay, based on a story by Bernard McConville, and David Howard provided the energetic direction. The Bert Gilroy production also employed Ray Whitley, John Miljan, Rita LaRoy, Edgar Dearing, William Stelling, Edward Keane, Ethan Laidlaw, Hugh Sothern and Bobby Burns in supporting roles. Songs: 'To Watch The Settin' Sun', 'Back In The Saddle Again' Ray Whitley.

A momentary snag in Ginger Rogers' steadily spiralling career, **Having Wonderful Time** was Arthur Kober's misconceived adaptation of his own stage hit. Originally a gently satiric look at a Jewish summer resort, the tale was transformed by its author into a romantic and decidedly *goyish* film enterprise. With most of the ethnic flavour and dialogue excised, it concentrated on the growing amour between Rogers (left) and Douglas Fairbanks Jr (right), in amongst a group of madcap souls, thrown together by fate, and forced to knock heads in the hope that loads of laughs will emanate from the concussions. The movie largely wasted the talents of Lucille Ball and Eve Arden, along with an impressive group of similarly gifted performers which included Peggy Conklin, Lee Bowman, Dorothea Kent, Red Skelton (his film debut), Donald Meek, Jack Carson, Clarence H. Wilson, Allan Lane, Grady Sutton, Shimen Ruskin, Dorothy Tree, Leona Roberts, Harlan Briggs, Inez Courtney and Juanita Quigley. Alfred Santell received directorial credit, though producer Pandro S. Berman found a number of scenes wanting, and called on George Stevens to reshoot them. **Having Wonderful Time** had its moments, but they were pathetically few and far between. It finished $276,000 in the red. Songs: 'My First Impression Of You', 'Nighty Night' Sam Stept, Charles Tobias.

Corporate president Leo Spitz encouraged 'B'-unit head Lee Marcus to produce some 'exploitation' pictures – films dealing with subject matter of a topical and slightly sensational nature. Marcus' initial response was **Smashing The Rackets**, a melo that had everything Spitz was looking for. Lionel Houser's screenplay (original story by Forrest Davis) was certainly inspired by the career of New York district attorney Thomas E. Dewey. Playing special prosecutor Jim Conway (the Dewey counterpart), Chester Morris (centre left) blasted his way through a morass of skulduggery and corruption, sweeping the big city clean in 80 minutes of screen time. Conway's achievements came a trifle too easily, but Lew Landers' airtight direction made the story so dynamic that no one noticed. With a capable supporting cast that included Frances Mercer (centre right), Rita Johnson, Bruce Cabot, Edward Pawley, Joseph de Stefani, Kay Sutton, Ben Welden, Paul Fix, Edward Acuff, George Irving and Frank O'Connor (left), **Smashing The Rackets** was a breathless, pugnacious entertainment, bursting with a vitality often lacking in programme pictures. B. P. Fineman, former production topper of FBO, was the producer. ▷

Painted Desert was one of George O'Brien's most disappointing westerns. Though the story itself contained enough gunplay, dirty dealing and wild riding for half-a-dozen outdoor adventures, the production made for 59 minutes of monotony, relieved only by some of the worst dialogue ever heard west of the Rio Grande. All about O'Brien's (left) determination to prevent crook Fred Kohler Sr from getting his greedy fingers on a piece of valuable property, the screenplay by John Rathmell and Oliver Drake, based on Jack Cunningham's story, suffered from major construction weaknesses, and David Howard's direction was no help. The beauty, and developing talent, of Laraine Johnson (Day), playing O'Brien's romantic partner for the second consecutive time, provided some small compensation for the overall inadequacies of this Bert Gilroy-produced oater. A remake of a 1931 RKO Pathé picture in which Bill Boyd had starred, it also cast Ray Whitley, Stanley Fields (right), Maude Allen, Lloyd Ingraham, Harry Cording, Max Wagner, Lee Shumway and William V. Mong in supporting roles. Songs: 'Moonlight On The Painted Desert' Oliver Drake; 'My Days Are Through On The Range', 'Painted Desert' Ray Whitley.

Katharine Hepburn's refusal to appear in **Mother Carey's Chickens** terminated her RKO career. As produced by Pandro S. Berman and directed by Rowland V. Lee, the completed picture was a pleasant diversion: sentimental, funny and 'wholesome' through and through. In the tradition of *Little Women* and *Anne Of Green Gables*, the novel by Kate Douglas Wiggin, play by Wiggin and Rachel Crothers, and screenplay by S. K. Lauren and Gertrude Purcell, charted the development of the Carey brood, left in desperate circumstances when their father fails to return from the Spanish-American War. There is no time for self-pity, however, as sisters Ruby Keeler (centre, in the role planned for Hepburn) and Anne Shirley (right) adeptly solve the financial problems while causing several local males to swoon. Performances in the 'adorable' vein were contributed by three-year-old Donnie Dunagan as little brother Carey and Virginia Weidler as a neighbouring girl whose mother makes her wear her shoes on the wrong feet three days a week so they will wear down evenly. Fay Bainter made an endearing Mother Carey, and Walter Brennan's portrayal of a crusty New Englander was laced with affectionate humour. James Ellison (left), Frank Albertson, Alma Kruger, Jackie Moran, Margaret Hamilton and Ralph Morgan were also among the cast. RKO later sold its story rights to Walt Disney Productions which released a remake in 1963 entitled *Summer Magic*, starring Hayley Mills, Burl Ives and Dorothy McGuire.

First-time feature director Leslie Goodwins coped well with the implausible plot of **Crime Ring**. Reginald Taviner's story, written for the screen by J. Robert Bren and Gladys Atwater, concerned the operations of a bunch of phony fortune-tellers who work hand-in-hand with stock-swindlers, and lead their customers to believe they are guided by the spirits when making their unsound speculations. Newspaperman Allan Lane (centre) and out-of-work actress Frances Mercer (left) offer themselves as decoys in an elaborate scheme to demolish the racket. Though the film offered little to sophisticated viewers, it emerged as a solid programmer. Clara Blandick, Inez Courtney (right), Bradley Page and Ben Welden were featured, with Frank M. Thomas, Jack Arnold, Morgan Conway, George Irving, Leona Roberts, Charles Trowbridge, Tom Kennedy, Paul Fix and Jack Mulhall also taking part. Cliff Reid produced.

Richard Dix scored a victory in **Sky Giant**, an airborne adventure undoubtedly inspired by the MGM blockbuster, *Test Pilot*. All about a pilot training school run by dependable Harry Carey, the picture's two major plot components were a love triangle featuring Dix (right), Joan Fontaine (centre) and Chester Morris (left), and an Arctic survival drama in which a plane containing Morris, Dix and Paul Guilfoyle goes down in the frozen wasteland while the three are charting a new route to the Orient. Dix's relaxed handling of the kind of *macho* role that had been his speciality in earlier years, Lew Landers' potent direction, and the first class aerial footage of cinematographer Nicholas Musuraca and special effects expert Vernon Walker, made for bracing entertainment. It was also a stirring tribute to the brave lads who made the airways safe. Robert Sisk produced and Lionel Houser wrote the story and screenplay. Also cast: Robert Strange, Max Hoffman Jr, Vicki Lester, James Bush and Edward Marr.

Bobby Breen (left) always seemed to be running away from something or somebody in his movies. **Breaking The Ice** found him forsaking his Pennsylvania Dutch relatives for the big city of Philadelphia where he becomes an entertainer in an ice-skating rink. There he meets six-year-old Irene Dare (billed as the world's youngest ice skater), and they show off for the rest of the picture – no doubt to deflect attention away from its undernourished plot. On hand to provide momentary respites from the skating and warbling were Charlie Ruggles (right), Dolores Costello, Robert Barrat, Dorothy Peterson, Billy Gilbert, Charlie Murray, John King, Margaret Hamilton, Jonathan Hale, Spencer Charters and Maurice Cass. Directing the Mary McCall Jr–Manuel Seff–Bernard Schubert screenplay (story by Fritz Falkenstein and N. Brewster Morse) was Edward Cline. Sol Lesser produced for his Principal Productions banner. Songs included: 'Tellin' My Troubles To A Mule' Victor Young, Paul Webster; 'Happy As A Lark', 'Put Your Heart In A Song', 'The Sunny Side Of Things' Frank Churchill, Webster.

Another pedestrian vehicle for Joe Penner, **I'm From The City** featured the comedian as a circus bareback rider who is mortally frightened of horses, but who performs like Buffalo Bill when hypnotized. This situation leads predictably to his participation in a cowboy obstacle race – without benefit of hypnosis. Essentially a one-joke movie stretched far beyond its limits, it featured Lorraine Krueger (right) as the dizzy blonde with whom Penner (left) ends up, and the rest of the cast included Richard Lane, Kay Sutton, Paul Guilfoyle, Kathryn Sheldon, Ethan Laidlaw, Lafayette McKee, Edmund Cobb and Clyde Kinney. Screenwriters Nicholas T. Barrows, Robert St Clair and John Grey were able to cultivate very few laughs from Ben Holmes' original story. Holmes also directed for producer William Sistrom. Songs: 'I'm A Tough Coyote', 'I'm From The City' Hal Raynor.

Fred and Ginger's **Carefree** (the stars illustrated) had much to recommend it. The script (by Allan Scott, Ernest Pagano, Dudley Nichols and Hagar Wilde, based on an original idea by Marian Ainslee and Guy Endore) was a clever spoof on psychiatry, the Irving Berlin score was classy and infectious, and the dance routines (choreographed by Astaire and Hermes Pan) were as fresh as ever. One of them in particular – a solo number which combined Astaire's dancing and golfing abilities – was dazzling almost beyond belief. In a general departure from the usual plot formula, Astaire portrayed a follower of Dr Freud who agrees to psychoanalyze Ginger in an attempt to uncover why she has broken her engagement to Ralph Bellamy (borrowed from Columbia) three times. Ginger falls for Fred, forcing him to hypnotize her and impress on her subconscious the notion that she hates him and loves her fiancé. When, however, the doctor realizes that he is reciprocating his patient's feelings for him, his former suggestion has to be erased … Mark Sandrich directed with his customary finesse and Pandro S. Berman produced. Other cast members included Luella Gear, Jack Carson, Clarence Kolb, Franklin Pangborn, Walter Kingford, Kay Sutton, and Robert B. Mitchell and his St Brendan's Boys Choir. However, although **Carefree** was not unsuccessful (it attracted $1,731,000 in film rentals), it became the first Astaire–Rogers musical to post a box-office deficit ($68,000), and forced the studio heads to recognize that Fred and Ginger were no longer the sure-fire ticket-sellers they once had been. Songs included: 'I Used To Be Color Blind', 'Change Partners', 'Since They Turned "Loch Lomond" Into Swing', 'The Yam'.

Who killed movie executive Maurice Tenwright and why? The rather unabsorbing answer was to be found in **Fugitives For A Night**, a low-octane, inside-Hollywood mystery produced by Lou Lusty and directed by Leslie Goodwins. The Richard Wormser story centred on Frank Albertson (left), a frustrated thespian who becomes the stooge for a rising star and another actor on the way down. When big shot Tenwright (Russell Hicks) is bumped off, the poor stooge becomes a suspect and flees with his publicist girl friend (Eleanor Lynn, borrowed from MGM), thus providing the picture with its title. Dalton Trumbo wrote the prosaic, unimaginative screenplay as his first assignment for RKO; it contained not a hint of the narrative excellence that would soon become a Trumbo hallmark. Also cast: Allan Lane, Bradley Page, Adrianne Ames, Jonathan Hale, Paul Guilfoyle, Ward Bond (centre) and Cornelius Keefe (right).

Hoping to launch Lucille Ball in a 'B' comedy series, Lee Marcus assigned Bert Granet and Paul Yawitz to write **The Affairs Of Annabel** from a story by Charles Hoffman. They came up with a breezy farce that included plenty of local colour, and aimed its affectionate potshots directly at Hollywood. Miss Ball (right) played a scatter-brained actress in thrall to her Svengali-like press agent (Jack Oakie, left, in a familiar role). His obsession with publicity stunts lands her in a bizarre family situation, into the clutches of a pair of 'most wanted', and in prison. The screwball stuff was not especially fresh, but Ben Stoloff's stopwatch direction and the inspired performances of the principals and bit-players (especially Ruth Donnelly, Bradley Page, Fritz Feld and Granville Bates) called for an encore. Lou Lusty, a former aide to Samuel Briskin, produced, and Thurston Hall, Elisabeth Risdon, James Burke, Lee Van Atta, Anthony Warde, Edward Marr and Leona Roberts were also cast.

Chief among the virtues of **The Renegade Ranger** was the performance of Rita Hayworth as the feminine lead. Hayworth (left, borrowed from Columbia), accused of murdering a shady tax collector, is befriended by Texas Ranger captain George O'Brien (right). O'Brien and young hot-head Tim Holt (the renegade of the title) root out the real villains, making Miss Hayworth and her questionable cohorts respectable again. Oliver Drake's screenplay (story by Bennet Cohen) contained the usual ingredients of such shenanigans, but was spiced with above-average dialogue, and a fiesta sequence that featured O'Brien's singing sidekick, Ray Whitley. Atoning for the lamentable *Painted Desert* were producer Bert Gilroy and director David Howard. Lucio Villegas, William Royle, Cecilia Callejo, Neal Hart, Monte Montague, Robert Kortman, Charles Stevens, James Mason and Tom London appeared in minor roles. Songs included: 'Move Slow, Little Doggie' Willie Phelps; 'Senorita' Albert Hay Malotte.

RKO spent $255,000 for the rights to **Room Service** by John Murray and Allen Boretz – a Broadway hit that became a Hollywood flop. The decision to cast the Marx Brothers as three crazy and thoroughly unscrupulous dramatic producers was a lethal mistake. Instead of a fresh new comedy, the film version emerged as just another Marx Brothers picture with everything tailored by scenarist Morrie Ryskind to the well-established *personae* of the threesome. All that the Pandro S. Berman production retained from the original were the outlines of classic farce. Groucho (left), the scheming bankrupt producer, is aided by Chico (foreground centre) and Harpo (centre) in his imaginative attempts to get a play off the ground and avoid the hotel supervisor's endeavours to evict them and their troupe for nonpayment of an incredible backlog of charges. Even though Groucho's one-liners were not up to their usual incisive standard and Chico was given little to do throughout, the performances of the *freres* certainly surpassed those of supporting characters Donald MacBride, the hotel supervisor who shambles about muttering 'jumping butterballs', and Frank Albertson (right), a neophyte playwright whose histrionic endeavours were a textbook example of bad acting. Unfortunately Albertson became the focal point of the wild climax – a fake suicide ploy devised by Groucho. Appearances by Lucille Ball, Ann Miller, Cliff Dunstan, Philip Loeb, Philip Wood, Alexander Asro and Charles Halton didn't help much either and neither did William Seiter's stagey, claustrophobic direction. The most expensive property ever purchased by RKO (although the budget was reasonable) resulted in a net loss of $340,000. It was just a poor show. The studio re-cycled it as *Step Lively* (1944), a musical starring Frank Sinatra.

The best RKO cowboy yarn of the year was **The Law West Of Tombstone**, a comedy that brought together a cluster of characters bearing more than a coincidental resemblance to such legendary figures as Judge Roy Bean, Calamity Jane, Billy the Kid and the Clanton family. John Twist and Clarence Upson Young's screenplay, based on a story by Young, featured Harry Carey (centre) as the Bean surrogate, dispensing justice from a barroom in the frontier town of Martinez, Arizona. He and the trigger-happy Tonto Kid join forces to subdue the dastardly McQuinn gang with the Kid filing a claim on Carey's daughter (Jean Rouverol, right) at the fade-out. Glenn Tryon's routine direction prevented the film from being as exciting or as funny as it could have been, but it was still a notch above the George O'Brien efforts. Tim Holt (left, borrowed from Walter Wanger) portrayed the Tonto Kid; he would soon be starring in his own series of 'B' westerns for the studio. The rest of producer Cliff Reid's cast included Evelyn Brent, Clarence Kolb, Allan Lane, Esther Muir, Bradley Page, Paul Guilfoyle, Robert Moya, Ward Bond and George Irving.

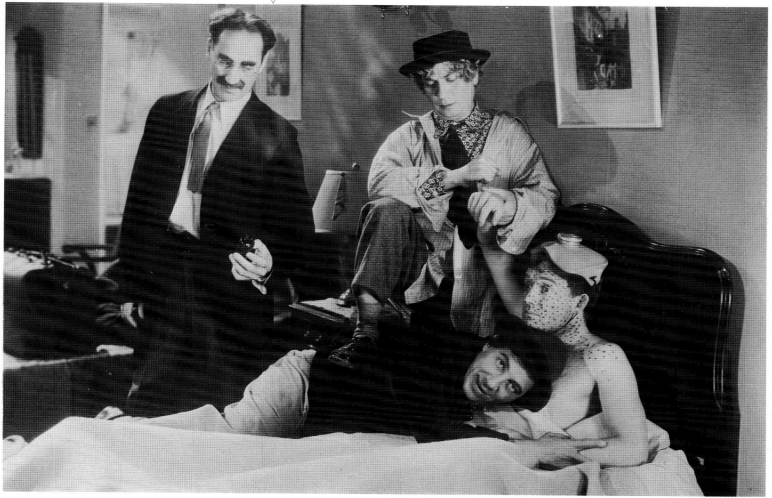

Another fumbled attempt to make Joe Penner (illustrated) palatable to movie audiences, **Mr Doodle Kicks Off** was a woeful example of the 'college comedy'. The story (by Mark Kelly, screenplay Bert Granet) had Penner as the victim of his wealthy father's determination to turn his son into a football star. Naturally he ends up running the wrong way in the big game (a metaphor for Mr Penner's movie career, perhaps?). William B. Davidson as the tycoon father, June Travis as the daughter of the college president, and Richard Lane and Frank M. Thomas as the pigskin coaches, did their best to cull a few laughs from the dreary enterprise for producer Robert Sisk and director Leslie Goodwins. The supporting cast included Ben Alexander, Billy Gilbert, Jack Carson, Alan Bruce, George Irving, Pierre Watkin, Wesley Barry (a former Warner Bros. child star of the silent era) and Robert Parrish (who would later become a prominent director). Songs: 'My All American Band', 'It's A Mystery To Me' Hal Raynor.

On rare occasions, a remake may actually surpass the original in quality, and **A Man To Remember** was one such triumph. Based on a story by Katharine Haviland-Taylor which had been produced in 1933 as *One Man's Journey*, the picture was a collaboration between two up-and-coming Hollywood talents: screenwriter Dalton Trumbo and director Garson Kanin. It was the first assignment for Kanin, a man with a Broadway background but no real film knowledge except odds and ends picked up during apprenticeships with Samuel Goldwyn and Pandro Berman, and the second for Trumbo, a former baker. In fact, the studio took no real gamble on the neophytes: **A Man To Remember** had no stars (Anne Shirley was the major name in the cast) and was made in 15 days for $118,000. Utilizing a flashback structure, it surveyed the life of deceased small-town doctor Edward Ellis (illustrated), who slowly emerges as the epitome of selflessness, always ready to sacrifice himself to the demands of others. A testament to the accomplishments of one small human being, the film was both dignified and amiable, and never lapsed into the sentimentality invited by the material. Robert Sisk produced this critically acclaimed sleeper with Lee Bowman, William Henry, John Wray, Granville Bates, Harlan Briggs, Frank M. Thomas, Dickie Jones, Carole Leete, Gilbert Emery and Joseph de Stephani also cast.

Tarnished Angel, the studio's second foray into the field of exploitation movies, fell well short of *Smashing The Rackets*. This time the focus was on a charlatan evangelist (Sally Eilers, left) whose true calling entails separating members of the flock from their precious jewellery. Alas, instead of following through on the exposé, screenwriter Jo Pagano (story and adaptation by Saul Elkins) and director Leslie Goodwins allowed Miss Eilers to 'get religion', whereupon she actually heals a cripple and is soon completely regenerated. The career of flamboyant Los Angeles evangelist Aimee Semple McPherson undoubtedly influenced the proceedings, but as an exploitation film, **Tarnished Angel** was sheer drivel. Producer B. P. Fineman's cast also featured Lee Bowman, Ann Miller (right), Alma Kruger, Paul Guilfoyle, Jonathan Hale, Jack Arnold, Cecil Kellaway, Janet Dempsey, Hamilton MacFadden and Byron Foulger. Song: 'It's The Doctor's Orders' Lew Brown, Sammy Fain.

The Mad Miss Manton starred Barbara Stanwyck (left) as a screwball socialite who sets about solving murders and enjoys a success that even the Saint would envy. Teamed with Henry Fonda (right, borrowed from Walter Wanger), as a newspaperman with a special interest in homicide, Stanwyck's portrayal of Melsa Manton stood out among an ensemble of capable performances. Sam Levene as a police lieutenant; Whitney Bourne, Frances Mercer and Vicki Lester as three of Stanwyck's society pals; Hattie McDaniel once again essaying the maid's role; and Stanley Ridges as the superbly sinister heavy, all sparkled when director Leigh Jason gave them their opportunities. The Philip G. Epstein screenplay, based on a story by Wilson Collison, was an astute blend of mystery and mirth, and took satirical swipes at everything from capitalism and communism, to baseball. All in all, it was a quality accomplishment for associate producer P. J. Wolfson and his team. Also cast: Ann Evers, Catherine O'Quinn, Linda Terry, Eleanor Hansen, James Burke, Paul Guilfoyle, Penny Singleton, Leona Maricle, Kay Sutton, Miles Mander, John Qualen, Grady Sutton and Olin Howland.

George O'Brien's efforts to clear his dead father's name, as well as his own, and to marry the girl he loves were on view in **Lawless Valley**. How O'Brien (right) defies the most powerful rancher in the country, outmanoeuvres a series of traps laid for him, finds the evidence that proves his father was murdered, forces a confession from the crooked sheriff and then wins the girl, formed the backbone of W. C. Tuttle's story and Oliver Drake's action-plus screenplay. David Howard directed and Bert Gilroy produced, with Kay Sutton (the girl), Fred Kohler Sr (the rancher), Earle Hodgins (the sheriff), Walter Miller, Fred Kohler Jr, Lew Kelly, George MacQuarrie, Chill Wills and Dot Farley in the cast.

Before the year ended, Lucille Ball (right) and Jack Oakie (centre left) returned for another instalment in the projected 'Annabel' series. Though running just one minute over an hour, **Annabel Takes A Tour** (scripted by Bert Granet and Olive Cooper from a story by Granet and Joe Bigelow based on characters created by Charles Hoffman) dawdled along, failing to recapture the non-stop wackiness of *The Affairs Of Annabel*. It was all about a public appearance jaunt designed by press agent Oakie to revitalize Annabel's flagging career. Oakie plumbs his bottomless well of outrageous ideas, but Ball gets sidetracked by Ralph Forbes (left), a viscount, and an author of amorous novels, whom the actress hopes will woo her into an early retirement. Just in time the nobleman's wife and children show up, and Annabel's castle in the air topples down to earth. Lew Landers directed what was his only 1938 picture to lose money. Producer Lou Lusty's cast also included Ruth Donnelly, Bradley Page (centre right), Frances Mercer, Donald MacBride, Alice White, Pepito, Chester Clute and Jean Rouverol. Noting that 'Annabel' seemed to be going nowhere, RKO cancelled the remainder of the series. No one was giving up on Lucille Ball, however; she remained a major asset in the studio's stock company.

Picking up where Jackie Coogan and Jackie Cooper had left off some years before, Tommy Kelly (left) played **Peck's Bad Boy With The Circus**. The lad's fun-making pranks, his youthful adulation of a 10-year-old bareback riding star, and his discovery of nefarious activities behind the big top, were woven into a cheery screenplay by Al Martin, David Boehm and Robert Neville (adaptation by Neville, based on the character created by G. W. Peck). Producer Sol Lesser and director Edward F. Cline made sure that audiences who had enjoyed Kelly's debut performance in *The Adventures Of Tom Sawyer* found the same kind of entertainment in this picture. Also cast: Ann Gillis (who had also appeared in *Tom Sawyer*) as the bareback rider, Edgar Kennedy, Benita Hume, 'Spanky' McFarland (centre), Louise Beavers, Grant Mitchell, Nana Bryant, William Demarest, Wade Boteler, Harry Stubbs, Fay Helm and Mickey Rentschler. Leonard Fields was associate producer for Lesser's Principal Productions.

The last release of the year, **Next Time I Marry** was the studio's best programme comedy of 1938. Screenwriters John Twist and Helen Meinardi (story by Thames Williamson) collaborated with director Garson Kanin and performers Lucille Ball (right) and James Ellison (left, borrowed from Harry Sherman) to generate the zany saga of a slap-happy heiress and a pick-and-shovel hero. Ball marries government-projects worker Ellison

to make herself eligible for a $20 million inheritance, then flies off to Reno so she can get a divorce, wed titled foreigner Lee Bowman and squander the inheritance on him. The frantic battling of the newlyweds eventually leads to real romance and to a whimsical cross-country diversion in the vein of *It Happened One Night*. Granville Bates, Mantan Moreland, Elliott Sullivan and Murray Alper also appeared for producer Cliff Reid.

★★★★★★★★★★★★★★★★★

1939

★★★★★★★★★★★★★★★★★

One of George J. Schaefer's initial decisions as RKO president was to revive unit production. The concept of contracting independent producers to make films for distribution by RKO had been introduced during the Selznick era, but the studio had never really capitalized on its possibilities.

Among the independents signed by Schaefer in 1939 were Broadway impresarios Max Gordon and Harry Goetz, screenwriting team Gene Towne and Graham Baker, and Stephens-Lang, an organization set to provide RKO with films based on a popular radio character, 'Doctor Christian'. Schaefer also signed Orson Welles and his Mercury Production Company, giving the young genius a near-unique contract which allowed him enormous creative freedom – as long as his films did not exceed $500,000 in budget.

Pandro S. Berman resigned as production head and ended his long association with RKO during the year. Berman was annoyed by Schaefer's determination to have final say in all important decisions, including the creative ones that normally fell within Berman's domain, and he was also offended by the wholesale signing of independents. Pandro Berman was not basically antagonistic to the unit concept but he resented Schaefer's failure to discuss the deals with him. Berman continued to work to the end of the year, completing **The Hunchback Of Notre Dame** and **Vigil In The Night** before departing for MGM. Harry Edington, a former agent with limited production experience, was named chief of 'A' production in late December.

The outbreak of World War II in September caused George Schaefer and the other executives a great deal of concern. Schaefer believed that the loss of key foreign markets would almost certainly lead to a cutback in production, a curtailment of big-budget films and a return to the penny-pinching policies of the early thirties. His initial response was to impose salary cuts on all employees earning $4500 per year or more.

It was both appropriate and unfortunate that RKO enjoyed its greatest production year in 1939. Certainly, better individual films had been made by the company in other years, but taken as a whole, the 49 releases were unrivalled. Unfortunately, the other studios were also enjoying an extraordinarily creative year, so that RKO's 1939 product which, at any other time, would have been the envy of the industry, was the victim of substantial competition.

The box-office winners were **Bachelor Mother, Fifth Avenue Girl, Five Came Back, Love Affair, That's Right—You're Wrong, In Name Only** and **The Saint In London**. Despite the profitability of the production arm, the corporation showed a net loss of $185,495 for the year.

John Barrymore (centre left, borrowed from Paramount) returned to RKO after a long absence to make **The Great Man Votes**. His career was in decline, and his physical condition had deteriorated enormously in only a few years which, ironically, made him the perfect actor to play the role of Gregory Vance in this Cliff Reid production. Vance is a former Harvard educator and a published scholar, whose ambition has dissolved since the death of his wife, and who has become a lush. He works as a night watchman and takes care of his two extraordinary children (Peter Holden, left, and Virginia Weidler, centre right). Assisted by their teacher, Katharine Alexander (right), the pair inspire their father to regain his self-respect by casting the decisive ballot in the mayoralty election. With this film, Garson Kanin again demonstrated that he deserved recognition as RKO's most promising young director. The suspenseful and heartwarming screenplay was written by John Twist from a story by Gordon Malherbe Hillman. Donald MacBride, Bennie Bartlett, Brandon Tynan, Elisabeth Risdon, Granville Bates, Luis Alberni, J. M. Kerrigan, William Demarest and Roy Gordon were also featured.

Twelve Crowded Hours proffered Richard Dix (left) as an underworld-shaking reporter who nimbly unmasks the local villain (Cyrus W. Kendall) and explodes his numbers racket. Observing one night in a reporter's life, the audience also met the ubiquitous Lucille Ball (right), who functioned as the romantic interest, Allan Lane as her misguided brother, Donald MacBride as a rather obtuse detective, and Murray Alper, Bradley Page, Joseph de Stephani, John Gallaudet and Addison Richards who portrayed Kendall's henchmen. Robert Sisk produced this passable 'B', with Lew Landers in the director's chair and John Twist providing the screenplay (story by Garrett Fort and Peter Ruric). John Arledge, Granville Bates and former Wheeler–Woolsey regular Dorothy Lee played small parts.
▽

Pacific Liner, originally intended as one of Leo Spitz's exploitation pictures, didn't turn out that way. All about the ill-fated *S.S. Arcturus* which sails from Shanghai with Asiatic cholera as one of its passengers, it starred Victor McLaglen (right), as chief engineer Crusher McKay, who leads a diverse group into battle against the plague. The ship's doctor and nurse, played by Chester Morris (left) and Wendy Barrie (centre), performed more than their share of heroics, while stock actors Alan Hale, Barry Fitzgerald, Allan Lane, Halliwell Hobbes, Cyrus W. Kendall, Paul Guilfoyle, John Wray, Emory Parnell, Adia Kuznetzoff and John Bleifer also had their moments. Director Lew Landers translated the Anthony Coldeway–Henry Roberts Symonds story (screenplay John Twist) to the screen with his usual feeling for action, and attention to narrative development. Although no masterpiece, the Robert Sisk production was an exciting yarn and a money maker.
▽

One of RKO's oddest pictures, **Boy Slaves** was a lurid tale that reeked of exploitation. But despite the fact that it originated in response to Leo Spitz's call for sensationalist material, the final film proved to be an angry, unrelieved indictment of peonage on the turpentine farms of the South. Some of the events were unquestionably melodrama of the lowest order, but producer-director P. G. Wolfson never compromised his grisly image of a brutal world of exploiters and their prey. Anne Shirley (third from left) turned in an affecting performance as a female victim of the system, while James McCallion (second from left) and Roger Daniel were standouts among the dead-end chattels of the title. The balance of the cast included Alan Baxter, Johnny Fitzgerald, Walter Ward, Charles Powers, Walter Tetley, Frank Malo, Paul White, Arthur Hohl, Charles Lane, Norman Willis and Roy Gordon. The depressing subject matter of Albert Bein and Ben Orkow's screenplay, doomed **Boy Slaves** to commercial failure, but the writers and Wolfson deserved better – if only for daring to be different.
▽

Almost A Gentleman (GB: **Magnificent Outcast**) may have demonstrated the intelligence of canines, but didn't say much for Hollywood big shots responsible for its utter triviality. The David Silverstein–Jo Pagano screenplay, written from a story by Harold Shumate, dealt with a neighbourly feud which degenerates into an argument over the merits of purebred dogs versus mongrels. Ace the Wonder Dog (right), playing the mongrel in question, proves his worth, thereby ironing out the bitter feelings between the opposing sides. With the possible exception of Ace, all the characters were mistreated by the puny story and Leslie Goodwins' dreary direction. James Ellison (centre) and Helen Wood were the most prominent martyrs, with Robert Kent, June Clayworth, Robert Warwick, Leonard Penn, John Wray, Brandon Tynan, Earle Hodgins (left) and Harlan Briggs also suffering. Producer Cliff Reid should have known better.
▽

△
In the dead of night a handful of brave men swear an oath that lawlessness must perish, and the Arizona Rangers, secret agents in the old west, are born. At their head rode George O'Brien (centre), the sagebrush hero of **Arizona Legion**. The film's plot, requiring O'Brien to lie to his sweetheart Laraine Johnson (Day, left) and ally himself with the bandits in order to bring them to justice, was hardly new or unusual, but Oliver Drake's crisp screenplay (original story by Bernard McConville), and David Howard's vigorous direction, gave the events a feeling of spontaneity. It was O'Brien's 6oth film, and one of his best 'B' efforts. Producer Bert Gilroy's cast also featured Chill Wills (right) and Carlyle Moore, with Tom Chatterton, Edward LeSaint, William Royle, Harry Cording, Glenn Strange, Monte Montague and Bobby Burns lending support. Song: 'I'd Rather Be Footloose Than Free' Oliver Drake.

George Sanders (illustrated, borrowed from 20th Century-Fox) took over from Louis Hayward and became the definitive Simon Templar, the Saint, in **The Saint Strikes Back**. With able support from Wendy Barrie, Barry Fitzgerald and Jonathan Hale, Templar tackles the San Francisco underworld, solving a series of ingenious homicides and proving that Barrie's dead father did not commit a crime of which he had been accused. John Farrow's taut direction of an uncompromising screenplay by John Twist, based on Leslie Charteris' novel *Angels Of Doom*, made it a hard-hitting (and profitable) mystery entertainment and guaranteed the future return of the character to theatres everywhere. Robert Sisk produced, and Jerome Cowan, Neil Hamilton, Robert Elliott, Russell Hopton, Edward Gargan, Robert Strange, Gilbert Emery, James Burke and Nella Walker filled secondary roles.
▽

The RKO advertising department called **Gunga Din** 'too big for words!', and, for once, the hyperbole was only slightly inflated. The studio had been endeavouring to make the film since 1936. Howard Hawks was originally scheduled to direct but casting difficulties postponed production, and Hawks lost out when company executives came to the conclusion (during the filming of *Bringing Up Baby*) that the director was too slow and too expensive for this epic undertaking. The dependable George Stevens inherited the project and, to the astonishment of producer Pandro S. Berman, was even slower and more painstaking than Hawks had ever been. When the dust settled, the final cost was a staggering $1,915,000, making **Gunga Din** the most expensive film RKO had ever made. Thankfully, it proved to be worth every cent. Composed of equal parts spectacle, adventure, suspense, humour and action, the picture remains one of the prime examples of the cinema of exhilaration. Its story seems remarkably coherent when one considers how many different writers contributed (final script credit was shared by Joel Sayre and Fred Guiol, based on a story by Ben Hecht and Charles MacArthur and inspired by Rudyard Kipling's poem). The story told of sergeants McChesney (Victor McLaglen, centre) and Cutter (Cary Grant, left) of the Royal Sappers who are faced with the loss of their closest fighting and drinking pal, Ballantine (Douglas Fairbanks

Jr, right), who is determined to marry Emmy Stebbins (Joan Fontaine) and quit the military. Interfering with Ballantine's plans is the revolt of the Thuggees, a murderous sect of religious fanatics, which threatens the safety of the British regiment, the surrounding area and, indeed, all of India itself. At the climax, Gunga Din (Sam Jaffe), a native water boy, blows a warning signal on his bugle, thus saving the lives of the three heroes as well as their regiment, but losing his own. Ballantine decides to remain in the army with his friends, and Gunga Din is made a posthumous corporal and buried with full military honours. A list of the important contributors to this film could go on forever, but a few names must be singled out: Henry Berman and John Lockert, whose dynamic editing (especially of the battle scenes) heightened the intoxicating excitement; Joseph August, whose superior photography transformed the area around Lone Pine, California, into authentic-looking Indian settings; and Alfred Newman, who composed the stirring musical score. Also cast: Eduardo Ciannelli, Montagu Love, Robert Coote, Abner Biberman and Lumsden Hare. The script was remade (without permission) as *Sergeants Three* in 1961. The Frank Sinatra–Dean Martin–Sammy Davis Jr film was released through United Artists after the production company (Essex Productions) purchased RKO's story rights to stop a plagiarism suit.

Bobby Breen's appeal was almost exclusively to juvenile audiences, and **Fisherman's Wharf** made no attempt to broaden the pint-sized crooner's box-office base. Leo Carrillo (left), Henry Armetta and Breen (right) played a trio of San Francisco fishermen who are perfectly happy until Carrillo's widowed sister-in-law (Lee Patrick) comes to live with them, her obnoxious offspring (Tommy Bupp) in tow. The pair upset the fish cart, forcing Bobby to run away from home (for the umpteenth time in his movies) and Carrillo, the kid's foster father, to mount a desperate drive to set things right. Why it required so many writers to concoct the formularised Breen vehicles must forever remain a mystery; Bernard Schubert, Ian McLellan Hunter and Herbert Clyde Lewis earned screen credit this time around. Bernard Vorhaus directed for Sol Lesser's Principal Productions. Slicker, a seal, received (and earned) fifth billing in the picture, ahead of Bupp, Rosina Galli, George Humbert, Leon Belasco, Pua Lani, Leonard Kibrick, Jackie Salling, Ronnie Paige and Milo Marchetti Jr. Songs included: 'Sell Your Cares For A Song' Victor Young, Charles Newman; 'Songs Of Italy' Frank Churchill, Paul Webster; 'Fisherman's Chantie' Farlan Myers, William Howe.

◁ Originally intended as an exposé of the 'beauty racket', **Beauty For The Asking** quickly abandoned this approach in favour of a routine love triangle featuring Lucille Ball (right), Patric Knowles (left) and Frieda Inescort. The writing credits (screenplay by Doris Anderson and Paul Jarrico, story by Edmund L. Hartmann based on an original idea by Grace Norton and Adele Buffington) suggest that there was considerable energy being expended in opposing directions by the various scribes, and the trite and clumsy outcome betrayed this lack of creative cohesion. The story centred on beautician Ball who, after being jilted by Knowles, develops a million dollar formula for facial cream which, coincidentally, is backed by Knowles' rich new wife (Inescort). Glenn Tryon's lumbering direction failed to smoothe out the jagged edges in the narrative, which producer B. P. Fineman should have rectified before allowing it to go before the cameras in the first place. Also cast: Donald Woods, Inez Courtney, Leona Maricle, Frances Mercer, Whitney Bourne, George Andre Beranger, Kay Sutton and Ann Evers.

The team of producer Bert Gilroy, director David Howard and star George O'Brien came up with another above-average 'B' western with **Trouble In Sundown**. The Oliver Drake–Dorrell McGowan–Stuart McGowan screenplay (story Charles F. Royal) made O'Brien (left) into a cowboy sleuth, running down a gang of bank robbers and, in the process, saving the father of his sweetheart from a prison term. Rosalind Keith (the girl), Howard Hickman (her banker father) and Chill Wills (right, O'Brien's comic sidekick) topped the supporting players, who also included Ray Whitley, Ward Bond, Cyrus W. Kendall, Monte Montague, John Dilson and Otto Yamaoka. Songs: 'Prairie Winds', 'Home On The Prairie' Ray Whitley.

Sensitive, poignant, heartbreaking and heartening at the same time, **Love Affair** was one of the finest romantic dramas in Hollywood history. It was also something of a miracle: working without a finished script, producer-director Leo McCarey, several writers and the principal actors put the picture together on a day-to-day basis. When it was finished, however, there was no hint of an 'off the cuff' job. A familiar plot had been infused with an extraordinary amount of freshness and energy. The film focused on two jaded people, American Terry McKay (Irene Dunne, right) and Frenchman Michel Marnet (Charles Boyer, left) who meet on a ship bound for New York. Despite their resolve not to become involved, they fall hopelessly in love and agree to meet at the top of the Empire State Building in six months if both still feel their love is alive. On her way to keep the appointment, Terry is struck down by a car and, not wanting her lover to pity her for her crippled condition, refuses to get in touch with him. Marnet

is embittered by this, but they are finally reunited, he comprehends what has happened, and Terry expresses her determination to walk again. Sentimental it certainly was, but the picture managed to rise above the treacle through its deft comic touches, fully-developed characters, and superb acting. The transformation from romantic comedy to tragic pathos was handled with consummate skill by McCarey and received much praise in critical circles. Other cast members included Maria Ouspenskaya (centre, giving a sublime performance as Marnet's perceptive grandmother), Lee Bowman, Astrid Allwyn and Maurice Moscovitch. The final screenplay credit belonged to Delmer Daves and Donald Ogden Stewart from a story by Mildred Cram and Leo McCarey. McCarey remade the picture for 20th Century-Fox in 1957 as *An Affair To Remember*, starring Cary Grant and Deborah Kerr. Songs: 'Wishing' B. G. DeSylva; 'Sing My Heart' Harold Arlen, Ted Koehler.

The theme of 'Americanism' may be found in a remarkable number of Hollywood films produced in 1939 and the early 1940s. This was, of course, a response to the totalitarian threats in Europe and the Far East, and an attempt to inspire patriotism in the face of the growing probability that the US would soon become involved in global hostilities. **They Made Her A Spy**, for example, contained a good deal of blatant propaganda for American freedom, opportunity and stability. Fittingly, the climactic action occurred at the top of the Washington Monument. The story by George Bricker and screenplay by Michael Kanin and Jo Pagano featured Sally Eilers (left) as an innocent damsel recruited by the Intelligence Corps to trap a foreign agent and, thereby, gain a measure of revenge for the murder of her brother, a US Army officer. Also cast: Allan Lane (right), Fritz Leiber, Frank M. Thomas, Theodore von Eltz, Addison Richards, Larry Blake, Pierre Watkin, Louis Jean Heydt, Spencer Charters, Leona Roberts, Charles Halton and Alec Craig. Jack Hively (a former film editor) made his directorial debut for producer Robert Sisk.

Fixer Dugan (GB: **Double Daring**) was a compendium of circus film clichés, vapidly written by Bert Granet and Paul Yawitz and apathetically directed by Lew Landers. Lee Tracy played the 'fixer', a fast-talking diplomat who spends most of his time smoothing arguments with local sheriffs and patrons, as well as patching up internal difficulties among the show's personnel. One such difficulty involves the future of Virginia Weidler (right, borrowed from MGM), an orphan girl whose highwire artist mother has fallen to her death. Another special problem concerns lion tamer Peggy Shannon (left), whose 'cats' are coveted by the unscrupulous showmen of a rival circus. Tracy succeeds in rectifying all the difficulties, but very few movie customers paid to see him do it. Bradley Page, William Edmunds, Edward Gargan, Jack Arnold, Rita LaRoy, Irene Franklin, John Dilson and Edythe Elliott also appeared for producer Cliff Reid. Screenwriters Granet and Yawitz based their script on a play by H. C. Potter entitled *What's A Fixer For?* ▷

The Flying Irishman turned out to be a very expensive publicity stunt. The promotion department worked overtime when Douglas 'Wrong-Way' Corrigan (left) was signed to star in a movie based on his famous flight from New York to California via Ireland. Ernest Pagano and Dalton Trumbo's screenplay also dealt with Corrigan's barnstorming days and his inability to secure a pilot's job due to his lack of a college degree. The story had an engaging, tall-tale quality about it, but unfortunately could not obscure the performance of neophyte 'star' Corrigan who proved manifestly incapable of playing himself. Leigh Jason's perfunctory direction did not help much either. Paul Kelly, Robert Armstrong, Gene Reynolds, Donald MacBride, Eddie Quillan (right), J. M. Kerrigan, Dorothy Peterson, Scotty Beckett, Joyce Compton, Dorothy Appleby, Minor Watson, Cora Witherspoon, Spencer Charters and Peggy Ryan also participated in this aerial misfire. Needless to say, it was 'Wrong-Way's' solitary screen excursion for RKO.

The Story Of Vernon And Irene Castle brought down the curtain on the most remarkable series of pictures in RKO history. The last of the studio's Astaire–Rogers (both illustrated) collaborations, it featured immaculate production values, masterfully choreographed dance sequences (dance director Hermes Pan) and a nostalgic and appealing musical score. Nonetheless, the magic that had touched the team's earlier triumphs was missing here. Part of the difficulty lay with the plot – a thorough departure from the regular formula. Based on stories by Irene Castle, this biography of a famous husband and wife dance team emerged as a stereotyped show business success story, without combustion or electricity. Irene (Ginger Rogers) persuades Vernon (Fred Astaire) to give up his 'hammy' vaudeville clowning and cultivate his dancing abilities. After some lean years, agent Edna May Oliver sponsors the pair, and their rise to the top is meteoric. World War I intervenes, forcing Vernon to enter the service where, just before he is due for release, he is killed in a foolish training accident. For the first time, one of the stars had died in an Astaire–Rogers picture and so

had their RKO partnership. They would dance together once more – for MGM – in the disappointing *Barkleys Of Broadway* (1949). **The Story Of Vernon And Irene Castle** was produced by George Haight (Pandro S. Berman took his 'in charge of production' credit) and directed by H. C. Potter (on loan from Samuel Goldwyn). Richard Sherman wrote the screenplay from an adaptation, by Oscar Hammerstein II and Dorothy Yost, of Mrs Castle's book. Roles were also provided for Walter Brennan, Lew Fields (as himself), Etienne Girardot, Janet Beecher, Rolfe Sedan, Leonid Kinskey, Robert Strange, Douglas Walton, Clarence Derwent, Sonny Lamont, Frances Mercer, Victor Varconi and Donald MacBride. The film lost $50,000 at the box office. Songs included 'Only When You're In My Arms' by Con Conrad, Herman Ruby and Bert Kalmar, and approximately 40 familiar tunes from the time period covered by the picture including 'By The Light Of The Silvery Moon', 'The Yama Yama Man', 'Waiting For The Robert E. Lee', 'Rose Room', 'Little Brown Jug', 'Too Much Mustard' and 'Missouri Waltz'.

Dalton Trumbo was responsible for the proficient script for **Sorority House** (GB: **That Girl From College**) which featured a well-tailored performance by lovely Anne Shirley. Miss Shirley (left) played a small town grocer's daughter who goes to college certain that her life will be ruined if she is rejected for membership in the Gamma sorority, a residential and social club for ambitious young women. Following the rigors of running a dispiriting social gauntlet while trying to qualify for membership, she realizes the superficiality of the enterprise and rips up her treasured invitation. Her good sense also helps her win the heart of collegiate hero James Ellison (centre). J. M. Kerrigan (as Shirley's father), Barbara Read, Adele Pearce, Helen Wood, Doris Jordan, June Storey, Elisabeth Risdon, Margaret Armstrong, Selmer Jackson, Chill Wills and Dick Hogan (right) also put in appearances. John Farrow directed the Robert Sisk production with solid professionalism. Trumbo based his scenario on *Chi-House*, a story by Mary Coyle Chase.

In **The Girl From Mexico**, producer Robert Sisk brought Lupe Velez back to American screens after an absence of 18 months. The temperamental Miss Velez (illustrated) was cast to type as a fiery Latin entertainer who turns Manhattan topsy-turvy with her madcap activities. Donald Woods as a bewildered ad-man who has little chance against the heroine's romantic onslaught, and Leon Errol as Woods' shiftless uncle who eggs the female whirlwind on, flourished in their supporting roles. Directing this berserk comedy was Leslie Goodwins, who was intelligent enough not to take one frame of the film seriously. Linda Hayes, Donald MacBride, Edward Raquello, Elisabeth Risdon and Ward Bond were also cast, and the screenplay was by Lionel Houser and Joseph A. Fields, from a story by Houser. Though not planned as such, **The Girl From Mexico** became the 'pilot' for the studio's 'Mexican Spitfire' series.

One of the very best programme melodramas in RKO history, **Five Came Back** was a precursor of the *Airport*-formula 'disaster' films. Twelve unlucky passengers are on board the 'Southern Star', a clipper plane that crashes into the dense South American jungle. Exacerbating the numerous conflicts among the survivors is the malignant presence of a tribe of headhunters. The native threat looms ever larger and more frightening as the pilot and his assistant work feverishly to repair the craft. Since the title indicated how many would make it out alive, audience members were kept on the edge of their seats, speculating whether Lucille Ball (left), Chester Morris (right), Joseph Calleia (centre left), C. Aubrey Smith (centre right), Allen

Jenkins (centre, reclining), Wendy Barrie, John Carradine or one of their other favourites would be a member of the lucky quintet. Another fine effort from producer Robert Sisk and director John Farrow, the major accolades belonged to Dalton Trumbo, Nathanael West and Jerry Cady who prepared the lively script, using a story by Richard Carroll as their point of departure. **Five Came Back**, which cost a mere $225,000 to make, eventually earned $262,000 in profits and collected substantial critical praise. Kent Taylor, Patric Knowles, Elisabeth Risdon, Casey Johnson and Dick Hogan completed the cast. RKO remade it as *Back From Eternity* in 1956 with Robert Ryan and Anita Ekberg.

The romantic triangle of a cabaret girl marooned in the tropics, an independent oil prospector and a gun-running aviator, furnished the dramatic launching pad for **Panama Lady**, a dreary remake of *Panama Flo*, an even drearier 1932 RKO Pathé release. Lucille Ball (centre) as the lady of the title, Allan Lane (left) as the oil man who virtually shanghais Ball to his wilderness camp, and Donald Briggs as her criminally-inclined former suitor all worked hard to pump some voltage into this hokum (story by Garrett Fort, screenplay by Michael Kanin). Their efforts were not noticeably successful, but Steffi Duna (right), playing a jealous native girl who resents Lane's attentions to Miss Ball, and Evelyn Brent as the operator of a Panamanian dive, contributed juicy supporting performances. Jack Hively directed for producer Cliff Reid. Bernadene Hayes, Abner Biberman, William Pawley and Earle Hodgins were also in it.

Ostensibly based on a novel by Phil Stong, **Career** was quite obviously constructed to cash in on the success of *A Man To Remember*. In the latter, Edward Ellis had played a saintly country doctor whose many sacrifices aided the lives of an entire community. Here, Ellis (right) is a storekeeper with remarkably similar instincts: he saves the local banker from ruin, protects an invention made by the town drunk, and advises and consoles his wife and son when life deals them problematic hands. In case anyone should miss the similarities between the two pictures, *A Man To Remember* co-star Anne Shirley (centre) put in an appearance as the daughter of the banker. **Career** was simply and piously, but unpretentiously, designed to tug gently at the heart strings of middle America. Still, there was something shoddy about RKO's rush to 'clone' one of its recent triumphs. Leigh Jason directed for producer Robert Sisk. Dalton Trumbo's screenplay (based on Bert Granet's adaptation of the Stong novel) also contained roles for Samuel S. Hinds, Janet Beecher, Leon Errol, Raymond Hatton, Maurice Murphy, Harrison Greene, Charles Drake, Hobart Cavanaugh and two newcomers, John Archer (left, real name Ralph Bowman) and Alice Eden (real name Rowena Cook). The pair had been winners of Jesse Lasky's 'Gateway to Hollywood', and **Career** was supposed to lift them to stardom. It did not accomplish its mission.

Dog pictures were always good for a few juvenile thrills, and that's about all **The Rookie Cop** (GB: **Swift Vengeance**) offered. Tim Holt played the hero who attempts to convince the commissioner that police dogs should be used in the solving of crimes. After disgracing himself through neglect of duty, Holt (centre) enlists the aid of Ace the Wonder Dog (right), and together they round up a gang of criminals who have been terrorizing the community. David Howard directed this $77,000 'quickie' from a story by Guy K. Austin and Earl Johnson and script by Morton Grant and Jo Pagano. Other members of producer Bert Gilroy's cast: Virginia Weidler (borrowed from MGM), Janet Shaw (left), Frank M. Thomas, Robert Emmett Keane (the police commissioner), Monte Montague, Don Brodie, Ralf Harolde and Muriel Evans.

Set in modern-day Arizona, **Racketeers Of The Range** featured George O'Brien (left foreground) waging a one-man war to protect his cattle herd against a large, unscrupulous meat-packing organization. Certain sequences in this oater were pretty farfetched – some chase scenes had men on horseback duelling against motorized vehicles and freight trains – but there were enough gun fights and two-fisted brawls to make action-freaks forgive the implausibilities. Director D. Ross Lederman kept everything moving, and Oliver Drake's screenplay (story Bernard McConville) also gave roles to Chill Wills (centre background), Marjorie Reynolds (right foreground), Gay Seabrook, Robert Fiske, John Dilson, Monte Montague, Bud Osborne, Ben Corbett, Ray Whitley, Cactus Mack and Frankie Marvin. Bert Gilroy was the producer. Songs: 'Sleepy Wrangler', 'Caboose On The Red Ball Train' Ray Whitley, Fred Rose.

George O'Brien (right) was back in action in ▷ **Timber Stampede**, fighting a land grab instituted by robber barons seeking to despoil a rich timber country. Newspaperwoman Marjorie Reynolds, hired by the crooked ring to spread their propaganda, learns she is being duped when she falls in love with O'Brien. The pair join forces with O'Brien's tall-tale spouting pal, Chill Wills, to subvert the racketeers. The production values, action elements and dramatic conflicts were on a par with other O'Brien adventures, but the film lacked box-office magnetism and became the first of the star's RKO vehicles to lose money. Perhaps the absence of singing cowboy Ray Whitley accounted for its loss of popularity, though it is more likely that the plot (story by Bernard McConville and Paul Franklin; screenplay by Morton Grant) was too derivative to hold much interest. David Howard directed, Bert Gilroy produced and Morgan Wallace, Robert Fiske, Guy Usher, Earl Dwire, Frank Hagney, Bob Burns, Monte Montague and Bud Osborne also participated in the theatrics.

Producer William Sistrom and star George Sanders (centre, borrowed from 20th Century-Fox) went to England and returned with the further adventures of RKO's colourful lone avenger: **The Saint In London**. Crackling with wit and suspense, the Lynn Root–Frank Fenton screenplay, from a story by Leslie Charteris, dealt with international currency fraud. Sally Gray, playing a society girl enamoured of the Saint and tagging along for the thrill of it all, headed a superlative British supporting cast that also included David Burns, Gordon McLeod, Athene Seyler, Henry Oscar, John Abbott, Ralph Truman, Charles Carson, Carl Jaffe, Norah Howard, Ballard Berkeley and Charles Paton. John Paddy Carstairs directed for RKO Radio Pictures Limited as part of a quota plan arrangement. And a happy arrangement it proved to be, earning profits of $140,000 for the studio.

Retribution came to brilliant, tricky and unscrupulous criminal lawyer Lee Tracy (left) in **The Spellbinder**. The shyster sows the seeds of his own dramatic come-uppance by defending men he knows are guilty. Misled by Tracy's eloquence in the courtroom, his precious daughter (Barbara Read) marries a murderer (Patric Knowles) whom her father has saved from the electric chair. Some form of retribution should also have been exacted against the makers of this banal rubbish. Atop the 'most wanted' list were writers Thomas Lennon and Joseph A. Fields (story Joseph Anthony) who constructed the wishy-washy and muddled screenplay, and Jack Hively who directed it with an erratic touch. The film's only compensations were the high-energy performance of Tracy, and Russell Metty's well-crafted cinematography. Allan Lane, Linda Hayes, Morgan Conway (right), Robert Emmett Keane, Roy Gordon, Robert Strange, Elliott Sullivan and Leonid Kinskey were among those present. Cliff Reid produced. ▷

Another RKO retread, **The Girl And The Gambler** was based on Willard Mack's play *The Dove* which the studio had filmed in 1932 as *Girl Of The Rio*. Leo Carrillo (right) reprised his original role as a Mexican Robin Hood who interrupts a romance between a cabaret dancer (Steffi Duna, left) and her naïve young beau (Tim Holt, centre). Lew Landers' direction was below par on this outing, which turned out to be a torpid melodrama, full of hackneyed dialogue and strained performances. Joseph A. Fields and Clarence Upson Young collaborated on the screenplay for producer Cliff Reid. Also cast in this 'B'-grade fizzle: Donald MacBride, Chris-Pin Martin, Edward Raquello, Paul Fix, Julian Rivero, Frank Puglia, Esther Muir, Paul Sutton, Charles Stevens and Frank Lackteen. Songs included: 'La Gunga Timbalero', 'Mi Ultimo Adios' Aaron Gonzales.

George O'Brien (right) headed up a band of tough, bullet-happy trouble-shooters in **The Fighting Gringo**. The feeble plot required the hero and his friends to take sides with Lupita Tovar and her father Lucio Villegas, whose ranch is being stolen out from under them by dastardly LeRoy Mason. A formula western with a Mexican flavour, the picture contained enough action to please the juvenile audience, but no special ingredients for more seasoned western tastes. Producer Bert Gilroy and director David Howard again formed the creative team, working from Oliver Drake's story and screenplay. Also in it: William Royle, Glenn Strange, Slim Whittaker, Mary Field, Martin Garralaga, Dick Botiller, Bill Cody Sr (left), Cactus Mack and Chris-Pin Martin. ▽

The class 'A' melodrama of the year was **In Name** ▷ **Only**, a screen adaptation, by Richard Sherman, of Bessie Breuer's novel *Memory Of Love*. John Cromwell returned to RKO to handle the direction for producer George Haight. Given a sterling cast topped by Cary Grant (right), Carole Lombard (left) and Kay Francis, Cromwell was able to transform a clichéd story about a loveless marriage into a poignant drama of emotional torment. The plot was well-worn: Francis has married Grant only for his wealth and position, an intolerable arrangement which drives him into the arms of widow Lombard. Francis agrees to divorce her husband, but changes her mind, and threatens to sue Lombard for alienating Grant's affections. Not surprisingly, all the problems were resolved in the end. The picture succeeded largely because of Cromwell's discreet handling of the material. Even Kay Francis, cast as a domestic monster, underplayed admirably, and the overall result was a mature study of love, and of passions both happy and unhappy. Charles Coburn, Helen Vinson, Katharine Alexander, Jonathan Hale, Nella Walker, Alan Baxter, Maurice Moscovich, Peggy Ann Garner (centre) and Spencer Charters were also cast.

◁ RKO's most extraordinary 'sleeper' of the decade was **Bachelor Mother**. A remake of *Kleine Mutti*, a 1935 Universal production filmed in Hungary, this moderately budgeted comedy realized profits of $827,000. Its star, Ginger Rogers, had strong reservations about the Norman Krasna screenplay (original story by Felix Jackson) and tried to get out of making the picture. Executive producer Pandro S. Berman strong-armed Ginger (centre right) into the role of store clerk Polly Parrish who is mistaken for the mother of an abandoned baby. After trying furiously and futilely to explain that the child is not hers, she finally accepts the youngster, and the proposal of the store owner (David Niven, right, borrowed from Samuel Goldwyn) who has fallen for the 'little mother' in the course of the picture's many hilarious complications. Much of the credit for the film's success belonged to Krasna, author of the exceptional script that Ginger disliked so intensely, and director Garson Kanin, whose splendid handling of the material established him as the studio's resident *wunderkind*. But Pandro Berman also deserved to take a bow for realizing the potential of the project and forcing Ginger to do it. Since **Bachelor Mother** was considered a 'solo' vehicle (co-star Niven had not, as yet, gained top box-office status), it boosted Rogers' career more dramatically than any picture since her early musicals with Astaire. B. G. DeSylva produced with a supporting cast that included Charles Coburn (left), E. E. Clive, Elbert Coplen Jr (centre, the baby), Frank Albertson, Ferike Boros, Ernest Truex, Leonard Penn, Paul Stanton, Frank M. Thomas, Edna Holland, Dennie Moore, June Wilkins and Donald Duck (appearing by courtesy of Walt Disney). *Bundle Of Joy*, starring Eddie Fisher and Debbie Reynolds, was a 1957 remake.

△ Producer Sol Lesser veered away from the usual Bobby Breen recipe somewhat in **Way Down South**. Though no great artistic achievement, the results were definitely better than usual. The Clarence Muse–Langston Hughes story and screenplay, set in pre-Civil War Louisiana, centred on Breen's battle with crooked lawyer Edwin Maxwell, who is determined to fleece the young master of his rightful inheritance. Aided by New Orleans innkeeper Alan Mowbray, Breen (centre right) seeks assistance from judge Robert Greig and rids himself of the unprincipled attorney. The picture still came straight from fantasy land (slavery, for example, is viewed as a potentially pleasant condition in which to spend one's life), but at least it had some dramatic punch and a tolerable sense of place and period. Bernard Vorhaus directed for Lesser's Principal Productions, with Ralph Morgan (centre left), Clarence Muse (left), Steffi Duna, Sally Blane, Charles Middleton, Lillian Yarbo, Stymie Beard (right), Jack Carr and Marguerite Whitten in secondary roles. The Hall Johnson Choir also appeared to complement Breen's vocal renditions. Songs included: 'Louisiana', 'Good Ground' Clarence Muse, Langston Hughes.

Bad Lands was *Lost Patrol* (1934) all over again, but transposed to a western setting, and certainly not competing with the John Ford picture for quality. In this instance a posse, headed by sheriff Robert Barrat, is pinned down by an Apache war party. One by one, its members are killed by the unseen enemy, just as Victor McLaglen's Legionnaires had been decimated by Arab sharpshooters in the earlier movie. To heighten the suspense and add a touch of irony, screenwriter Clarence Upson Young included the discovery of a natural vein of silver ore worth a fortune in the oasis where the men are trapped. Barrat (foreground centre) becomes the sole survivor, rescued in predictable fashion by the cavalry just as he is about to rush out to certain death. Decidedly mediocre in every sense, the picture also featured Noah Beery Jr (foreground left), Guinn Williams (prone), Addison Richards (foreground right), Andy Clyde, Paul Hurst, Robert Coote, Douglas Walton, Francis Ford and Francis McDonald as the members of the doomed law and order troop. Lew Landers directed and Robert Sisk produced for the 'B' unit.

Anti-fascist sentiments were at the core of **Conspiracy** (not in any way to be confused with the 1930 RKO release of the same name). The movie depicted a mythical Central American country run by a totalitarian dictator and swarming with secret police. Heroine Linda Hayes (foreground left) commits herself to the revolutionary cause, a sure signal that freedom and justice will eventually be reinstated. Hardly propaganda of the first order, the picture contained so much confusing intrigue, so many melodramatic plot conventions, and so many characters speaking in bewildering accents, that it burst the boundaries of cinematic poppycock. Miss Hayes was tolerable in her first leading role, but didn't get much help from Lew Landers' overstated direction or the haphazard performances of Allan Lane (foreground right), Robert Barrat, Charley Foy, Lionel Royce, J. Farrell MacDonald, Lester Matthews, Henry Brandon and William von Brincken. Cliff Reid produced and Jerome Chodorov churned out the wildly improbable screenplay from a story by John McCarthy and Faith Thomas. Song: 'Take The World Off Your Shoulders' Lew Brown, Sammy Fain.

Full Confession had much in common with *The Informer*. As in RKO's award-winning 1935 picture, Victor McLaglen played a man who cannot escape the fury of his conscience. McLaglen, (left) who has committed a murder and told his priest of the deed during confession, watches in agony while another man is convicted of the crime and sentenced to die for it. The film even contains an equivalent of the wake scene in *The Informer* when McLaglen is introduced into the home of the innocent victim bound for the electric chair. Jerry Cady's screenplay, based on a story by Leo Birinski, added a subplot involving the priest (Joseph Calleia, right) and his own struggle with the inviolable sanctity of the confessional, but the story failed to generate either the dramatic or psychological intensity of *The Informer* and critics were quick to point out all the 'borrowings' from the earlier John Ford production. Robert Sisk produced, John Farrow directed and J. Roy Hunt managed the first-rate photography. Also cast: Barry Fitzgerald (the falsely accused man), Sally Eilers, Elisabeth Risdon, Adele Pearce, Malcolm McTaggart, John Bleifer, William Haade and George Humbert.

Fifth Avenue Girl was a pleasant bon-bon of a movie that secured Ginger Rogers' reputation as one of Hollywood's foremost comediennes. Rogers (left) played a girl who is jobless and broke, but happy nonetheless. She runs into a miserable millionaire (Walter Connolly, right) in Central Park, and is subsequently installed as a member of the tycoon's household. This causes plenty of eruptions among the members of his spendthrift family, all of whom suspect the worst about the May–December relationship. Nothing original here, and yet the crisp screenplay by Allan Scott, the mellow direction by Gregory LaCava, and fine ensemble performances from the supporting players, coalesced in diverting fashion. Only Tim Holt was miscast – as Connolly's polo-playing son who is also supposed to be running a giant corporation. Also in it: Verree Teasdale, James Ellison, Kathryn Adams, Franklin Pangborn, Ferike Boros, Louis Calhern, Theodore von Eltz and Alexander D'Arcy. LaCava doubled as producer, giving the studio one of its sizeable hits of the year.

Joe Penner actually made good in **The Day The Bookies Wept**. Daniel Fuchs' story, about an alcoholic racehorse called Hiccup (out of Bourbon, by Distillery!), whose love of beer motivates him to win the big race, did not sound very promising, but a crackling script by Bert Granet and George Jeske, and amiable direction by Leslie Goodwins made this a showpiece among the year's 'B'-grade farces. And Penner (centre) proved he could be funny – not merely goofy – in his role as the trainer of the thirsty nag. Betty Grable (left) received second billing as Penner's heart-throb, and supporting troupers Richard Lane (right), Tom Kennedy, Thurston Hall, Bernadene Hayes, Carol Hughes and Jack Arnold were all on target in their performances. Robert Sisk was the producer.

George O'Brien took charge in **The Marshal Of Mesa City**. O'Brien (centre left) was centre stage as a skilled lawman who decides to clean up Mesa City, Arizona after its renegade sheriff tells him to leave town. The presence of Virginia Vale (centre right) has something to do with O'Brien's decision to hang around and, in concert with two-gunned Henry Brandon (left), he has the entire community behaving with remarkable decorum inside 61 minutes. Naturally, it takes a few arrests and killings along the way, to bring about this tranquil state of affairs. Jack Lait Jr wrote the screenplay for producer Bert Gilroy, and David Howard directed a cast that also included Leon Ames as the villain, Harry Cording, Lloyd Ingraham (right), Slim Whitaker, Joe McQuinn, Mary Gordon and Frank Ellis. The film was a remake of *The Arizonian*, a 1935 Richard Dix vehicle, but Warner Bros.' Technicolor spectacular, *Dodge City*, released earlier in 1939, was similar in plot.

Despite the efforts of producer Robert Sisk, director John Farrow and screenwriter John Twist (story Ellis St Joseph), **Reno** emerged as a limp Richard Dix programmer. A 'tragedy' about a man (Dix, right) accused of cheating by his own daughter (who is unaware she is prosecuting her father), the preposterous tale tried but failed to delineate the growth of the gambling capital and to expose its devastating impact on family relationships. Anita Louise was cast as the daughter, Gail Patrick (left) as Dix's socially ambitious wife and Paul Cavanagh as an eastern socialite who becomes Miss Patrick's second husband. Laura Hope Crews, Louis Jean Heydt, Hobart Cavanaugh, Charles Halton, Astrid Allwyn, Joyce Compton, Frank Faylen and William Haade had secondary roles, and Carole Landis, who would later become a prominent actress, played a bit part.

△

Producer-director Herbert Wilcox's first Hollywood film was **Nurse Edith Cavell**. Having already completed a 1928 silent version of the biography which caused controversy in Great Britain due to its ugly portrayal of war, Wilcox resurrected the pacifist drama in response to the darkening world situation. His timing proved impeccable: a few days before the picture opened at Radio City Music Hall, World War II was declared. The Michael Hogan screenplay (based on the story *Dawn* by Captain Reginald Berkeley) presented Anna Neagle (centre left) as Cavell, a saintly woman who works to transport refugee soldiers out of German-occupied Belgium during World War I. Though Miss Cavell is eventually executed by the Germans, the treatment was more anti-war than anti-Deutschland. At times the film seemed a bit overbearing and didactic, but few could argue with the sentiments expressed, or with Neagle's intense performance. Assisted by a supporting cast that included Edna May Oliver (centre right), George Sanders, May Robson (left), ZaSu Pitts (right), H. B. Warner, Sophie Stewart, Mary Howard, Robert Coote, Martin Kosleck, Gui Ignon, Lionel Royce, Jimmy Butler, Rex Downing, Fritz Leiber and Henry Brandon, the star delivered the movie's message in dramatically satisfying fashion. The picture (a co-production deal between RKO and Wilcox's Imperadio Pictures company) was not a major success; still, company executives counted it among the films that brought a new stamp of prestige and seriousness to RKO in 1939.

Sol Lesser decided to give another youngster a crack at stardom in **Everything's On Ice**. Six-year-old Irene Dare (illustrated) had cavorted previously in the Bobby Breen special, *Breaking The Ice*; here, she played a pint-sized skating sensation hauled off to a Florida resort by her uncle (Roscoe Karns) who believes he can cash in on the child's novel abilities. The little actress glided through her routines with ease, but the film's reception was considerably bumpy, thanks to the witless Adrian Landis–Sherman Lowe screenplay and Erle C. Kenton's pedestrian direction. Edgar Kennedy was featured as the girl's father, Lynne Roberts as her 19-year-old sister and Eric Linden as a millionaire suitor of Miss Roberts. Also cast: Mary Hart, Bobby Watson, George Meeker, Mary Currier, Maxine Stewart, Wade Boteler and Paul Winchell. Lesser produced for his Principal Productions outfit. Songs: 'Birth Of A Snowbird' Victor Young, Paul Webster; 'Everything's On Ice' Milton Drake, Fred Stryker.

Independent producer Boris Morros made a deal to release his first effort, **The Flying Deuces**, through RKO distribution channels. The agreement was a felicitous one for the studio as the film became a hit and upgraded the level of comedy on the studio's programme. The picture starred Stan Laurel (left) and Oliver Hardy (centre) as two fishmongers from Des Moines who enlist in the French Foreign Legion and spend the rest of the picture trying to get out of it. They finally escape via a runaway airplane, in a Keystone Kops-inspired sequence which director A. Edward Sutherland realized in suitably wild and zany fashion. Laurel and Hardy, the screen's longest

running comedy duo (13 years together) responded well to the sportive story and screenplay by Ralph Spence, Alfred Schiller, Charles Rogers and former silent comedy star Harry Langdon. Jean Parker, Reginald Gardiner, Charles Middleton (right), Jean Del Val, Clem Wilenchick and James Finlayson completed the cast. Morros produced for Boris Morros Productions.

Escape To Paradise, the last Bobby Breen RKO release, was also the least appealing. Its muddled Weldon Melick screenplay (from an original story by Ian McLellan Hunter and Herbert C. Lewis) presented Breen (left) as a South American cupid supposedly helping playboy Kent Taylor (right) to woo the local beauty (Marla Shelton, centre), but mostly fouling up the wealthy Romeo's every move. The final solution had ne'er-do-well Mr Taylor agreeing to go to work to win the girl's love. Erle C. Kenton's lackadaisical direction added nothing to the plot, and all the involved parties somnambulated their way through the mess. Principal Productions chief Sol Lesser kept his name off this bust, giving Barney Briskin associate producer credit. The other players were Joyce Compton, Pedro De Cordoba, Robert O. Davis, Rosina Galli, Frank Yaconelli and Anna Demetrio. Songs included: 'Tra-La-La', 'Rhythm Of The Rio' Nilo Menendez, Eddie Cherkose.

George J. Schaefer made a deal during 1939 with Stephens-Lang Productions whereby they were contracted to provide RKO with six films about 'Dr Christian', a humble, self-sacrificing country physician, who had become a favourite of radio listeners. Jean Hersholt (left), the broadcasting voice of the good doctor, also played him on-screen in **Meet Doctor Christian**. Its plot, forged from Harvey Gates' original story by scriptwriters Ian McLellan Hunter, Ring Lardner Jr and Gates, relied on a proven formula structured around a number of medical crises which are all magically dispatched by the talents of the kindly physician. Dorothy Lovett (right) appeared as the doctor's faithful nurse with whom the town druggist (Robert Baldwin) becomes romantically involved. Other members of director Bernard Vorhaus' cast included Enid Bennett, Paul Harvey, Marcia Mae Jones, Jackie Moran, Maude Eburne, Frank Coghlan Jr, Patsy Lee Parsons, Sarah Edwards, John Kelly and Eddie Acuff. William Stephens was the producer.

A perfunctory remake of *Sweepings* (1933), **Three Sons** told the story of a department store owner who is disappointed by his children's disinclination to take over the business. Edward Ellis (left) portrayed the merchant originally impersonated by Lionel Barrymore with Kent Taylor (right), Virginia Vale (centre right), Robert Stanton (centre) and Dick Hogan (centre left) as the uninterested offspring. William Gargan, who had played one of the sons in the original, now appeared as Ellis' liberal and perspicacious brother. As written for the screen by John Twist and directed by Jack Hively, the film choked on its own sentimental goo. Episodic, maudlin and consistently heavy handed, it never came to grips with its inherent dramatic tensions. Also cast: J. Edward Bromberg, Katharine Alexander, Grady Sutton, Adele Pearce, Alexander D'Arcy and Barbara Pepper. A novel by Lester Cohen provided the basis for this Robert Sisk production. Virginia Vale (real name Dorothy Howe) and Robert Stanton (real name Kirby Grant) won their roles through Jesse L. Lasky's 'Gateway to Hollywood' talent search.

Allegheny Uprising (released in Britain under its original title, **The First Rebel**) was one colossal *faux pas* in an otherwise vintage year for the studio. Basing his script on a story by Neil H. Swanson, P. J. Wolfson wrote and produced this tale of James Smith and his 'Black Boys' who defy the mandates of the British king (in the mid-1700s), thereby asserting the pre-eminence of liberty, justice and fairplay. The local tyrant is Captain Swanson (George Sanders, borrowed from 20th Century-Fox), an English officer who places half the region in chains – without warrant and without trial – in an attempt to stifle the uprising. The rather obvious parallel between Swanson's tactics and those of Hitler and his minions was not much appreciated by the inhabitants of Great Britain, who had just gone to war with Germany when the picture was released. This diplomatic blunder aside, the lukewarm direction of William Seiter and lacklustre performances of John Wayne (centre, borrowed from Republic) and Claire Trevor (left) dashed any hopes of success. RKO had teamed Wayne and Trevor to try to recapture the electricity generated by the pair in *Stagecoach*. Alas, they couldn't work up a single volt. Playing Janie, Wayne's love-sick devotee, Miss Trevor was forced to follow her man around like a starving puppy throughout, and Wayne himself was depressingly wooden. Other actors included Brian Donlevy, Wilfrid Lawson, Robert Barrat, John F. Hamilton, Moroni Olsen, Eddie Quillan, Chill Wills, Ian Wolfe, Wallis Clark, Monte Montague, Olaf Hytten, Eddy Waller, Clay Clement and Forrest Dillon (right). At the request of corporate president George J. Schaefer, Herbert Wilcox offered some editorial suggestions in an attempt to make the film more palatable to British viewers.

Sued For Libel was an efficient programmer produced by Cliff Reid and directed by Leslie Goodwins. Jerry Cady's melodramatic screenplay (story Wolfe Kaufman) concerned the efforts of a young radio broadcaster (Kent Taylor, left), a newspaper girl (Linda Hayes), and a reporter (Richard Lane) to solve a triple murder and thus avert two crushing libel suits. The backfiring of a supposedly harmless joke causes the broadcaster to announce over the air that a prominent broker (Morgan Conway) has been found guilty of murder when, in truth, he has been acquitted. The broker promptly slaps libel suits on the radio station and the newspaper that owns it, and the three principals, facing the loss of their jobs unless they can do something about the suits, frantically seek a solution. Lilian Bond, Roger Pryor, Thurston Hall, Emory Parnell, Roy Gordon, Keye Luke, Edward Earle, Jack Arnold, Leona Roberts and Solly Ward (right) also appeared.

Another radio personality arrived to launch a new film series. Bandleader Kay Kyser introduced his musicians and his 'Kollege of Musical Knowledge' in an addle-brained production called That's Right – You're Wrong. Kyser (right) had gained fame by combining a slapstick quiz show with swing music in a fashion that appealed to numerous disciples of the airwaves. The film had little in the way of plot; in fact, it presented Kyser and his band going to Hollywood to make a picture but never getting one off the ground because of the inability of two screenwriters to invent a suitable story. Mostly the movie was a pretext to exhibit Kyser and friends playing music, asking questions and generally making fools of themselves. Real-life scripters William Conselman and James V. Kern (story David Butler and Conselman) included a few satirical jabs at Hollywood with Adolphe Menjou (typecast as a producer), Lucille Ball, May Robson, and Edward Everett Horton and Hobart Cavanaugh, the two writers, representing the movie colony. Producer-director David Butler's picture would be totally forgettable except for one fact: it earned a profit of $219,000, thereby guaranteeing that RKO would sponsor more product starring Professor Kyser. Dennis O'Keefe, Roscoe Karns, Moroni Olsen, Ginny Simms (centre right), Harry Babbitt (centre left), Ish Kabibble, Sully Mason (left), Dorothy Lovett, Lillian West and Denis Tankard were other members of the cast. Songs included: 'The Little Red Fox' James V. Kern, Lew Porter, Johnny Lange & Hy Heath; 'Fit To Be Tied' Walter Donaldson; 'The Answer Is Love' Sam Stept, Charles Newman; 'Happy Birthday To Love' Dave Franklin; 'Chatterbox' Jerome Brainin, Allan Roberts.

Two Thoroughbreds, a warm and affecting small-scale picture, was written with charming simplicity by Joseph A. Fields and Jerry Cady from a story by Fields. Jimmy Lydon (illustrated) topped the cast as an orphaned farm boy who finds a stray colt, raises it against his greedy uncle's objections and then discovers that his sweetheart's father – a wealthy rancher – really owns the animal. The young man's struggle with his own conscience, and the girl's efforts to help him, nourished the moving and dramatically satisfying results. Jack Hively's sensitive direction of Lydon, Joan Brodel (to become better known as Joan Leslie) who played the sweetheart, Arthur Hohl and Marjorie Main as the boy's miserly uncle and aunt, and J. M. Kerrigan who portrayed a rugged groom, kept the film from falling into the trap of sentimentality. Selmer Jackson and Spencer Charters also had feature roles in this seasoned Cliff Reid production.

The studio's last release of the decade was also ▷ one of the biggest and best films in RKO history. Victor Hugo's The Hunchback Of Notre Dame, as adapted by Bruno Frank and scripted by Sonya Levien, painted the world of King Louis XI in broad strokes, emphasizing the contrast between rich and poor, freedom and repression, and medievalism and enlightenment that marked the era. Producer Pandro S. Berman and director William Dieterle spurned any romantic or soft-headed approach to the material; indeed, the realism bordered on a grotesquerie at times especially in its ugly portrayal of human nature, its unrelieved depiction of torture and suffering, and its incredibly misshapen Quasimodo (Charles Laughton, illustrated). Few pictures from this period would have dared show men being boiled alive by scalding oil, much less the appalling pillory scene in which the hunchback is whipped unmercifully, his hump exposed for all to see. Charles Laughton's superlative performance as the doomed outcast who falls in love with a gypsy girl (Maureen O'Hara) and twice saves her from death, overshadowed the other first-rate performances of Cedric Hardwicke, Thomas Mitchell and Hollywood newcomers O'Hara and Edmond O'Brien. Laughton – almost impossible to recognize beneath the heavy distortion of his make-up – still managed to convey Quasimodo's natural humanity. Though by no means a cheerful divertissement, The Hunchback pulsed with passion and vigour (abetted by Alfred Newman's bravura score) and audiences responded in kind to its gripping theatricality. Costing $1,826,000 to make, this spectacular brought in $3,155,000 in film rentals. It opened at about the same time as Gone With The Wind and was overshadowed by the more famous and profitable Selznick-MGM blockbuster; still, The Hunchback Of Notre Dame provided a suitable conclusion to the best production year the studio would ever have. The gigantic cast also included Alan Marshal, Walter Hampden, Harry Davenport, Katharine Alexander, George Zucco, Fritz Leiber, Etienne Girardot, Helene Whitney, Minna Gombell, Arthur Hohl, George Tobias, Rod La Rocque and Spencer Charters. A remake of the classic 1923 version starring Lon Chaney, the film was made again in 1956 with Anthony Quinn.

1940-

The ongoing drama of endless change at RKO continued to unfold throughout the new decade. Sandwiched in between the early and late years – which were marked by even greater turbulence and trauma than usual – was a tranquil middle period that represented the most euphoric juncture in the annals of the organization.

Radio-Keith-Orpheum finally freed itself from receivership in January 1940. Studio publicity made much of the event, heralding a 'new RKO' that would finally fulfil its destiny. President George J. Schaefer backed up the boast by spending $390,000 in a seven-day period for important literary properties, luring more independent outfits into the fold, and signing both single- and multiple-picture arrangements with several name stars.

Former agent Harry Edington was nominal head of production, but Schaefer continued to run things like a potentate, insisting on final say with regard to all important studio decisions. Though he adopted the slogan 'Quality Pictures at a Premium Price' to characterize RKO's filmmaking philosophy, the Schaefer approach was oddly schizophrenic. On the one hand, he cultivated prestige

Citizen Kane (1941)

offerings such as **Abe Lincoln In Illinois, They Knew What They Wanted, Citizen Kane** and **The Magnificent Ambersons**. On the other, he approved a giddy collection of 'B' efforts for the hoi polloi, including series built around The Mexican Spitfire, The Falcon and radio personalities Kay Kyser, Dr Christian, Scattergood Baines, and Lum and Abner. The lamentable fact was that Schaefer's amalgam of the high and the low didn't work – mostly because the majority of the 'A' specials were paybox failures.

The saga of Orson Welles' Mercury Productions sums up the nature of Schaefer's reign. Welles joined RKO to a tremendous fanfare in 1939; his unprecedented contract, his much bally-hooed belief that he could handle four creative areas on a single picture (writing, directing, producing, acting), and his reputation as a theatre and radio genius, generated both a surplus of publicity and an abundance of ill will. Many old Hollywood pros were offended by the audacity of the young Welles, and by what they judged to be Schaefer's foolishness in giving an untested filmmaker a virtually *carte blanche* contract.

After more than a year of false starts, Welles finally completed a film that stunned the nay-sayers: **Citizen Kane**. In addition to proving that Welles could back up his bluster, **Kane** represented a personal vindication for Schaefer, suggesting that his controversial policies were not insane after all. Regrettably, neither Welles nor his boss were able to savour the victory. Gossip hen Louella Parsons was given an advance peek at the picture and immediately began to squawk that it was a repulsive biography of her boss, William Randolph Hearst. In actuality, **Kane** was a fictionalized tale which incorporated elements from the lives of several different tycoons, Hearst included. There was, however, nothing libellous about it. Hearst, who hadn't seen the picture himself, accepted Miss Parsons' rantings at face value and began to put the thumb screws on RKO. His agents delivered an ultimatum to George Schaefer – shelve **Citizen Kane**, or the full weight of the Hearst newspaper empire would come crashing down on Hollywood in general and RKO in particular.

For the first several months of 1941, the RKO president worked feverishly to ensure the release of the film, fighting battles with certain members of his own board of directors as well as with industry moguls (including Louis B. Mayer) who were intimidated by Hearst's threats. The picture was finally offered to the public, though RKO's distribution arm had terrible problems persuading theatres to book it. Hearst made good his promise: his papers boycotted all copy concerning RKO, but were full of allegations that Welles was a Communist and a draft dodger.

The box-office proceeds of Welles' great film were sorely damaged by Hearst's bullying tactics and the ugly controversy that surrounded its release. But RKO was hurt in other ways as well. The **Citizen Kane** convulsion came at a time of acute internal instability and made the company appear to be a magnet that attracted all manner of troubles. Staff were shuffled in and out of important studio jobs so rapidly that one needed a scorecard to keep up with the RKO executive positions. Without doubt, George Schaefer's most unbelievable decision was the hiring of Joseph Breen to replace Harry Edington as production chief in 1941. Breen had been the industry's chief censor since 1934, a job he handled with fervour and reasonable tact. He definitely knew what couldn't go into pictures, but there was no assurance that he understood what should be put into them (i.e. what would be good *and* commercial). He had never developed a property or produced a picture, much less superintended the output of an entire studio. Thus, Schaefer's resolve to hire him bordered on the outlandish.

Apart from **Citizen Kane**, Schaefer's other 1941 coup was to sign the titan of the independents, Samuel Goldwyn. But even this arrangement was a mixed blessing. In order to get Goldwyn's product for RKO, Schaefer allowed him a very small distribution fee (17.5%), as well as other favourable concessions that made it impossible for the company to realize profits on the handling of the Goldwyn pictures.

By the time the US entered World War II in December 1941, the company was in woeful shape. The root cause of its difficulties was simple and obvious – despite considerable outlays of cash the studio had not produced a sufficient number of commercial films since the departure of Pandro Berman.

Early in 1942, Orson Welles went to Brazil to make a film called **It's All True**. This never-to-be-released picture would be a major factor in the ruination of George Schaefer's presidency. Before Welles left, he and Schaefer agreed that the picture should cost no more than $600,000. Even at that figure, the omnibus film could hardly be expected to break even, but it appeared viable because the Office of Inter-American Affairs had pledged to

protect RKO against losses of up to $300,000. One of Welles' well-known characteristics was that he never paid much attention to expenditure; he had gone over budget on both **Citizen Kane** and **The Magnificent Ambersons** and, before long, hair-raising reports from **It's All True** production manager Lynn Shores began to filter back to Hollywood. According to Shores, the film was being shot in a haphazard, off-the-cuff manner, causing discontent almost to the point of mutiny among the crew. Schaefer's consternation mounted when the studio started receiving footage that was, to put it mildly, disappointing. In mid-May, the Hollywood budget department forwarded the president a report indicating that $526,867 had been expended on **It's All True** and at least $595,000 more would be needed to complete the film.

In addition to this sobering news, and the painful realization that **The Magnificent Ambersons** was going to be another costly flop, Schaefer was handed financial projections that showed his company would not have enough cash on hand to meet its studio payroll in the middle of June.

Unless more capital could be raised quickly, there seemed to be only two possibilities – either the

The Best Years Of Our Lives (1946)

Cary Grant and Ingrid Bergman in **Notorious** (1946)

Journalists' accounts of the Welles and Lorentz altercations brought a substantial outcry against RKO. Koerner was attacked for his brutal treatment of creative talent, and held guilty of suffering from Hollywood money-mania. He abetted the criticism by ruling prestige films and artistic endeavours out of RKO's future plans and adopting 'Showmanship in the Place of Genius' as the keynote of his production philosophy.

Koerner managed to complete his own version of the raising of Lazarus by the end of 1942. The years which followed were the direct antithesis of the Schaefer period – happy, tranquil and prosperous. A rounded program included horror pictures (**Cat People, I Walked With A Zombie**), exploitable potboilers (**Hitler's Children, Behind The Rising Sun**), star vehicles (**Mr Lucky, Show Business**), war films (**Bombardier, Back To Bataan**), musicals (**The Sky's The Limit, Higher And Higher**) and comedies (**Government Girl, Bride By Mistake**). Koerner fed war- and movie-obsessed audiences a steady diet of palatable motion pictures. His efforts helped the company post record profits from 1943–46.

But wartime restrictions on rubber, gasoline, building materials and raw film stock forced the company to cut back on the number of its productions. Another exasperating difficulty was the manpower shortage. With more aggressive studios (especially MGM) swallowing up the available talent, Koerner constantly had to scramble to line up competent writers and directors and to cast his films with recognized players.

Although Charles Koerner began his tenure on a note of hard-nosed commercial film-making, he abandoned his philistine posture when the studio was back on firm financial ground. Artistically ambitious productions, such as **None But The Lonely Heart, Days Of Glory**, and **Sister Kenny** appeared under the RKO logo beginning in 1944. Each lost money, but proved that Koerner was no anti-intellectual boor.

Ironically, the production chief's most lasting contribution to film art came from the Val Lewton-produced horror films rather than from more aesthetically-oriented ventures. Made quickly on miniscule budgets, these pictures are now recognized as the first truly original horror formula since Frankenstein. They enriched the psychological underpinnings of the genre, building suspense through suggestion and brooding anticipation. Lewton's taste and intelligence were evident in his films, despite their lurid titles and sensationalistic advertising campaigns, and also enabled him to entice young, talented people into his circle. Two former RKO editors 'graduated' from the Lewton unit and later became prominent directors: Robert Wise and Mark Robson.

The first full year after the end of the war was a charmed one for RKO (and for the business at large). Hollywood film companies grossed $1,700,000,000 in 1946 alone, and RKO reported its best profits in history (more than $12 million). It was also a superior year for quality production, with **Notorious, The Spiral Staircase, It's A Wonderful Life** and Academy Award winner **The Best Years Of Our Lives** on the RKO distribution slate.

The attendant euphoria was substantially tempered by Charles Koerner's death in February 1946. Corporate president N. Peter Rathvon took over the production reins until a first-class studio topper could be found. Rathvon's job was made easier by a solid group of pictures that were in pre-production when Koerner died, and the contracts which the former helmsman had negotiated with stars of the stature of Joan Fontaine, Henry Fonda, Rosalind Russell, Cary Grant, Susan Hayward, John Wayne, Shirley Temple and Loretta Young.

Rathvon eventually settled on Dore Schary, placing him in charge of RKO filmmaking in January 1947. Schary's credentials included an Oscar for writing the original story that became MGM's *Boy's Town*, a period of running the 'B'-unit at MGM, and the production of **The Spiral Staircase, Till The End Of Time** and **The Farmer's Daughter** for RKO. He believed that Hollywood films should confront social issues head-on – without sacrificing entertainment values, of course.

studio would be closed, or it would fall, once again, into receivership. Possibilities for new funding were not promising because the major owners (Floyd Odlum of Atlas Corp., David Sarnoff of RCA and the Rockefellers) were feuding among themselves. The only thing they seemed to agree on was that George J. Schaefer had plunged RKO into the divisive controversy with Hearst, had failed to control profligate filmmakers like Welles and famed documentarian Pare Lorentz, whose **Name, Age And Occupation** had a production history similar to **It's All True**, and had sunk the corporation to its lowest point since the Depression. There was no way out for Schaefer; he resigned in June 1942.

Although the house of RKO was in a terrible state, there was a light glimmering in its window. A few months before Schaefer's resignation, the board directed that Charles Koerner replace Joseph Breen who had, predictably, fallen flat on his face as pilot of RKO production. Like his predecessor, Koerner lacked production experience. But he did have a long background in theatre operations (he was in charge of RKO exhibition when he moved to the west coast), and he possessed good instincts for guaging public taste.

As soon as Schaefer was gone, Floyd Odlum asserted himself. He arranged various loans to keep the cameras turning for the rest of the year, and saw to it that N. Peter Rathvon succeeded Schaefer as corporate president. Ned Depinet became president of RKO Radio Pictures.

The great plus in Charles Koerner's favour was that both Rathvon and Depinet intended to give him a free hand in production decisions. He wielded that hand in a realistic and tough-minded fashion. One of Koerner's most controversial actions was to evict the Mercury Productions team from its RKO Pathé offices and to put a stop to **It's All True**. Orson Welles, still in South America when he heard the news, wired his associates: 'Don't get excited. We're just passing a rough Koerner on our way to immortality'. Officials at the studio countered with 'All's well that ends Welles'. In addition, Koerner cancelled **Name, Age And Occupation**, Pare Lorentz's first Hollywood production, which had been shooting for several months.

Schary demonstrated this conviction immediately by sponsoring **Crossfire**, a hard-hitting and financially successful murder mystery whose real subject was anti-semitism.

Unfortunately for Schary, he began his RKO employment during the year in which the entire industry did an about-face. After a prolonged term of expanding audiences and easy profits, the studios began to experience setbacks. The first came from abroad where the British slapped a 75% tax on all foreign earnings. After prolonged negotiations, a settlement was reached abolishing the tax but limiting the amount of money American motion picture companies could withdraw to $17 million per year. Other countries also began imposing similar measures to protect their economic well-being, thereby reducing the foreign market capital which had contributed substantially to the record earnings of 1946. On the home front, the House Un-American Activities Committee's investigation of questionable loyalties among members of the film capital's intelligentsia provoked bitter factionalism. The unity that had existed during the war years dissolved into hysterical howls of 'Commie', 'Pinko' and 'Witchhunt'. Two of RKO's top staff members, producer Adrian Scott and director Edward Dmytryk, became members of the so-called 'Hollywood Ten', a group of left-wing sympathizers who defied the Congressional committee and ended up in jail. Ironically, Scott and Dmytryk had been the principal members of the creative team that made **Crossfire**, RKO's outspoken attack on intolerance. But the big problem was television, which started to make inroads into the studios' monopoly on visual entertainment. Theatre attendances dropped off substantially and so did RKO's corporate profits – down $7 million from the previous year.

Floyd Odlum had become controlling owner and chairman of the board of directors in 1943 by buying out the RCA (Sarnoff) and Rockefeller interests in RKO. Odlum surveyed the dismaying signs of 1947 and decided it was time to get out of the movie business. In May 1948, he found a buyer for his 929,000 shares of company stock – Howard R. Hughes. Odlum received several offers for the stock, but sold to Hughes because he felt the famed tycoon was more likely than other bidders to make a success of the enterprise.

Indeed, Hughes was famous for his remarkable Midas touch. His multi-faceted business ventures were highly profitable and he was no stranger to Hollywood, having produced *Two Arabian Knights, Hell's Angels, Scarface, The Outlaw* and other pictures. Still, the announcement that Hughes would take over RKO did not bring a universal chorus of hosannas from the film community. Past history suggested that Hughes, like George Schaefer and other former RKO leaders, was a 'meddler', who would not allow talented people their necessary freedom.

The Hughes situation was of special concern to Dore Schary, whose contract stipulated that he could terminate his relationship with RKO if the studio changed management. Hughes, however, promised to give Schary complete freedom, claiming he would be too busy attending to his other interests to devote much time to RKO.

On 1 July 1948 Dore Schary quit his job. Hughes had decided that two of Schary's pet projects, *Battleground* and *Bed Of Roses*, were not to his liking and postponed both. Angered by the top man's failure to keep his oath of non-interference, Schary left for MGM where he made *Battleground* the number two box-office success of the following year.

This was the beginning of the plague years for RKO. In the name of economy, Hughes cut studio personnel by 75%. Though embarrassed by the fact that he had assured RKO's employees that their jobs were safe only a short time before, N. Peter Rathvon agreed to replace Schary as production head. His own tenure under Hughes lasted slightly less than two weeks. By the time Rathvon quit, RKO was in chaos – production had dwindled to an absolute minimum and a skeleton staff of 600 was running the plant. A ruling triumvirate of Sid Rogell and two Hughes men, Bicknell Lockhart and C. J. Tevlin, took control of Hollywood operations. Rogell, an RKO executive of

Ethel Barrymore (left) and Loretta Young in **The Farmer's Daughter** (1947)

long standing, would manage production, while Lockhart and Tevlin took on the business affairs.

Ned E. Depinet became corporate president in New York after the Hughes takeover, but he was powerless to do anything about the actions of his inscrutable boss. Depinet also had another problem: late in the decade, government pressure forced the major studios to agree to divest themselves of their theatre chains. The impact of the loss of RKO exhibition – an essential component of corporate operations through the years – gave Depinet plenty to ponder. The theatres were eventually sold to Albert A. List and integrated into List Industries.

Production picked up somewhat in 1949. A report in late October claimed that the new, 'streamlined' RKO had shaved $30,000 off the weekly operating costs of the 1947–48 period. The company also promised to put 23 films in front of the cameras in the next three months.

As per usual, Howard Hughes failed to honour his promises. For some reason, he never moved to an office on the Gower Street lot, but remained cloistered at the Goldwyn Studios about a mile away, making his wishes known by telephone and messenger. He became notoriously difficult to reach when vital decisions had to be made, while continuing to insist that he and he alone would pass judgment on all important projects. In a business where split-second action is often imperative, Hughes would mull things over for weeks. Frustration reigned, and several RKO producers began looking for more fruitful employment. However, those fortunate enough to receive a green light on a project had plenty of contact with their boss. He called them all the time (usually in the middle of the night) to interfere in their labours. 'Working for Hughes', said one veteran, 'was like taking the ball in a football game and running four feet, only to find the coach was tackling you from behind'.

As the forties ended, industry specialists realized that RKO was once again in fearful trouble. Though the corporation claimed small profits for both 1948 and 1949, RKO Radio Pictures posted losses of $5,288,750 for the first year and $3,721,415 for the second. A film studio run on the lines of RKO could not survive for long, no matter how rich the madman in charge happened to be.

On 26 January 1940 – exactly seven years less a day since the corporation had filed its first petition in a federal court – Radio-Keith Orpheum officially emerged from receivership. During the period administered by Irving Trust Co, RKO and its subsidiaries reduced their fixed debt by more than $11 million and gross income rose from $44 m. in 1933 to $52 m. in 1939. The new company was starting fresh with no outstanding debts and a working capital of more than $8 m.

World War II continued to have an impact on the motion picture business. During the year, Denmark, Norway, Holland, Belgium and France fell to the Germans and heavy aerial bombardment closed many theatres in Great Britain. Since RKO was now increasingly dependent on domestic earnings, it focused on films that had always fared well with American audiences: comedies, musicals, escapist melodramas and more pictures highlighting 'Americanism'. In accordance with the general industry trend, RKO eschewed any stories based on contemporary world problems. Thus, even though the European conflict was wreaking havoc on company commerce, the production philosophy was to pretend that World War II did not exist.

RKO distributed 53 pictures during 1940 – 15 of these were either independently made, or the result of co-production deals.

In November, a 'consent decree' ended the government's anti-trust suit against RKO and the other majors. Executives could breathe easier, knowing that their theatres were not in immediate danger of forced sale, but they also had to face the fact that, beginning in fall 1941, each new picture would have to be shown to exhibitors before it was booked. The era of 'blind selling' was over.

George Schaefer continued his wholesale recruitment of independents. Voco Productions (Jack Votion, president), Pyramid Pictures (Jerrold T. Brandt, president), Vogue Pictures (Lou Ostrow, president), Franklin-Blank Productions (Harold B. Franklin, president) and Frank Ross-Norman Krasna Productions (Frank Ross, producer) all signed deals during the year. The studio also engaged Erich Pommer, producer *extraordinaire* from the famous German studio UFA, to handle three or four films a year. George Stevens represented the biggest loss; Schaefer decided not to exercise his option on Stevens' services following an altercation between the two men and the disappointing performance of Stevens' **Vigil In The Night**.

Despite all the receivership-related brouhaha about a 'new' RKO, the corporate loss for the year was $998,191. **Kitty Foyle, My Favorite Wife** and **Irene** were the biggest hits with **Lucky Partners, You'll Find Out** and **Primrose Path** also posting very satisfactory returns.

The feminine firecracker Lupe Velez exploded ▷ once more in **Mexican Spitfire**, a knockabout farce culminating in a custard-tossing party that would have made Mack Sennett grin. Joseph A. Fields' story, scripted by Fields and Charles E. Roberts, revolved around the efforts of Linda Hayes and Elisabeth Risdon to break up Donald Woods' marriage to Latin singer Velez (right). Playing the dual role of the groom's uncle who attempts to straighten out the marital and business problems of the newlyweds, and of a British whisky baron who is a client of advertising man Woods, Leon Errol (centre) practically pilfered the film from its irrepressible star. Director Leslie Goodwins sustained such a high level of energy throughout that it would be uncharitable to criticize the elemental mindlessness of the undertaking. Certainly the RKO brass found nothing to decry about its financial performance: made for $106,000, **Mexican Spitfire** earned $102,000. Producer Cliff Reid's cast also included Cecil Kellaway, Charles Coleman and Lester Dorr (left).

The Marines Fly High was a routine programmer, marred by the tragic death (in an automobile accident) of director George Nicholls Jr in the middle of production. Ben Stoloff took over, and completed the formula yarn in undistinguished fashion. Richard Dix (right) and Chester Morris (left) topped the cast as two leathernecks stationed in a Central American state who both fall in love with Lucille Ball (centre). Miss Ball can't get workers for her cocoa plantation because a mysterious outlaw named The Vengador is pillaging the country. When she is captured by the bandit (John Eldredge) and his motley army, Morris, Dix and a column of Marines rescue the girl and wipe out the evil-doers, thereby restoring peace and safety to the little nation. Jerry Cady and Lieutenant Commander A. J. Bolton wrote the dull and contrived screenplay from a story by A. C. Edington. Other participants in the luckless Robert Sisk production included Steffi Duna, Paul Harvey, Horace MacMahon, Dick Hogan, Robert Stanton, Ann Shoemaker and Nestor Paiva.
▽

Legion Of The Lawless contained a sober warning against vigilantism. Originally dedicated to the maintenance of justice and order, the vigilante organization in the frontier village of Ivestown (circa 1870) has become an instrument to terrorize the poor settlers of East Ivestown and keep them out of Ivestown proper. Young lawyer George O'Brien (illustrated) soon rallies to the defence of the victims and, swinging the town's honest citizens behind him, smashes the vigilante gang in a bullet-filled finale. Director David Howard squeezed a good deal of virile excitement out of Doris Schroeder's script (story Berne Giler). One fist fight between O'Brien and Monte Montague lasted over two minutes. Others cast in the Bert Gilroy production: Virginia Vale, Herbert Heywood, Norman Willis, Hugh Sothern, William Benedict, Edwin Waller, Delmar Watson, Bud Osborne, Slim Whitaker and Mary Field.
▽

Vigil In The Night was the getaway production for two major RKO names, Pandro Berman and George Stevens, who both departed the studio following clashes with president George Schaefer. Sadly, their last picture at RKO was not worthy of their substantial talents. The sober adaptation (by Fred Guiol, P. J. Wolfson and Rowland Leigh) of A. J. Cronin's novel presented Carole Lombard (illustrated) as a gallant nurse who takes responsibility for her sister's severe negligence which results in the death of an infant. She then withstands the most severe pressure, working to make sure physician Brian Aherne gets a new hospital unit that is desperately needed. Rather than the uplifting story of love and sacrifice that everyone assumed it would be, **Vigil In The Night** was laboured, uneven and lacking in a central point of view. Lombard, Aherne, Anne Shirley, Julien Mitchell, Robert Coote, Brenda Forbes, Rita Page, Ethel Griffies, Doris Lloyd, Emily Fitzroy and newcomer Peter Cushing all did their best under the circumstances. Audiences, however, found nothing attractive about the picture; it lost $327,000. Stevens received producer-director credit and Berman his final 'in charge of production' recognition.

Swiss Family Robinson, Johann David Wyss' well-known novel about a shipwreck and the building of a new life on an uninhabited island, was the first film from The Play's The Thing Productions – and probably the best. The policy of production partners Gene Towne and Graham Baker was to make films based on well-known stories that were in the 'public domain' (thus saving story costs). Directed by Edward Ludwig and written for the screen by Walter Ferris, Towne and Baker, the film boasted excellent production values and a capable cast headed by Thomas Mitchell (centre left) as William Robinson, the patriarch of the castaway family. Set during the Napoleonic Wars, it also whispered a contemporary message about the evils of civilization and progress, but patrons of popcorn entertainment didn't hear, and RKO's net loss amounted to $180,000. Also cast: Edna Best (centre foreground), Freddie Bartholomew (left), Terry Kilburn (right), Tim Holt (centre background), Baby Bobby Quillan (centre right, child in arms), Christian Rub, John Wray and Herbert Rawlinson. Both Bartholomew and Kilburn were borrowed from MGM. Walt Disney produced a remake in 1960.

RKO's most popular series kicked off in the new decade with **The Saint's Double Trouble**. Ben Holmes' screenplay (from a story by Leslie Charteris) was built around the striking resemblance between Simon Templar and The Boss, a notorious jewel thief whom Templar has sworn to dispatch. With the able assistance of George Sanders (centre left, borrowed from 20th Century-Fox) who played both roles, director Jack Hively mined plenty of humour and suspense from the circumstances. In one delirious scene, Sanders The Saint, impersonating Sanders The Boss confronts Sanders The Boss impersonating Sanders The Saint! The schizophrenia was healed agreeably in the end, enabling fans of the urbane crimefighter to prepare for the next instalment. Also cast: Helene Whitney (right), Jonathan Hale (left), Thomas W. Ross (centre right), Bela Lugosi, Donald MacBride, John F. Hamilton and Elliott Sullivan. Cliff Reid was the producer.

'A man's past catches up with his present and threatens his future', read one of the publicity catch-phrases for **Married And In Love**, a brittle domestic drama that attracted good critical reports but minimal consumer interest. John Farrow directed S. K. Lauren's story and screenplay about a selfish, pleasure-seeking woman (Helen Vinson, right) who decides to elope with her former college sweetheart (Alan Marshal, left, borrowed from David O. Selznick). The problem is that both Marshal and Vinson are already married – to Barbara Read and Patric Knowles respectively. Using flashbacks to fill in the exposition and increase suspense, Farrow unearthed a good deal of thought-provoking drama from the tired 'other woman' premise. He also extracted strong performances from the four principals, who were given nearly all of the screen time. Hattie Noel, Frank Faylen and Carol Hughes had bit parts in the Robert Sisk production.

Once again Walt Disney and his talented collaborators worked for three years to complete an animated feature, and their painstaking craftsmanship was evident in every frame of **Pinocchio**. The film was based on the Collodi morality tale about a kindly old woodcarver named Geppeto who creates a little puppet boy of pine (see illustration). Because the old man loves children and has never had any of his own, the Blue Fairy brings the marionette to life to be a son to him. But Pinocchio must prove himself worthy, and the bulk of the story concerned the adventures he undergoes before this is accomplished. **Pinocchio** revealed notable technical advances over *Snow White*: more refined drawing, richer Technicolor hues, a more fluid camera style. Dickie Jones was heard as Pinocchio, and other voices were supplied by, among others, Christian Rub, Cliff Edwards, Evelyn Venable, Walter Catlett and Frankie Darro. It was another hit ($3,600,000 in film rentals), though not the quantum smash that its predecessor had been. Based on the studio's complicated formula for computing profits on the distribution of the Disney films, it actually showed a loss to RKO of $94,000. Still, product of this quality upgraded RKO's offerings to exhibitors, and company executives were delighted to have the rights to it. Ted Sears, Webb Smith, Joseph Sabo, Otto Englander, William Cottrell, Erdman Penner and Aurelius Battaglia wrote the screenplay, and the supervising directors were Ben Sharpsteen and Hamilton Luske. Other major credits: Bill Roberts, Jack Kinney, Norman Ferguson, Wilfred Jackson and T. Hee (sequence directors); Fred Moore, Milton Kahl, Ward Kimball, Eric Larson, Franklin Thomas, Vladimir Tytla, Arthur Babbitt and Wolfgang Reitherman (animation directors); and Charles Philippi (art director). Songs included: 'When You Wish Upon A Star', 'Turn On The Old Music Box', 'Give A Little Whistle', 'I've Got No Strings', 'Little Wooden Head', 'Three Cheers For Anything', 'Hi-Diddle-Dee-Dee' Leigh Harline, Ned Washington, Paul J. Smith.

Seven years after *Chance At Heaven*, Ginger ▷
Rogers and Joel McCrea were reunited in
Primrose Path. Producer-director Gregory
LaCava's film pushed Joseph Breen's censorship
office to the limits with its realistic portrayal of the
heroine's mother as a practitioner of the world's
oldest profession, and its use of naturalistic language. Still, the plot was basically a girl-gets-
boy, girl-loses-boy, girl-wins-boy-again fantasy.
Desperately ashamed of her dissolute family and
determined to keep decent herself, Ginger (left)
meets McCrea (2nd left) and persuades him to
marry her. He is unaware of the unsavoury
reputation of her relatives until confronted with
the reality of the drink-sodden father (Miles
Mander), easy-going mother (Marjorie Rambeau)
and viperish grandmother (Queenie Vassar, 2nd
right). The shock is so great that it tears the
marriage asunder. The return of the unhappy girl
to her family and the temptations which confront
her when her mother dies and she is faced with
becoming the breadwinner of the motley group
formed the dramatic substance which screenwriters Allan Scott and LaCava used to build
towards an inevitable reconciliation between the
lovers. Though the romanticised elements and the
realistic approach never quite meshed, this was
still one of the studio's most daring and interesting
films of the year. Also cast: Joan Carroll (right),
Vivienne Osborne and Carmen Morales. The
credits stated that the picture was based on a play
by Robert L. Buckner and Walter Hart. It was also
based on *February Hill* by Victoria Lincoln, but
the novelistic source could not be listed due to
legal complications.

The presence of tough Marines William Gargan
(centre) and Wallace Ford in **Isle Of Destiny**
guaranteed they would rescue someone before this
South Sea island jungle farrago ran its course. The
someone turns out to be June Lang (right), a
round-the-world society aviatrix kidnapped by
baddie Gilbert Roland (left) whose principal
pastime is running guns to the Chinese. Adding to
the picture's laughable exoticism was the standard
catalogue of tropical birds, crocodiles, native
drums a-beating, and a wild creature of the jungle
(Katherine DeMille) who prowls about, armed
with a lethal blow gun. The wretched screenplay
by Arthur Hoerl, M. Coates Webster and Robert
Lively (original story by Allan Vaughn Elston),
exacerbated by Elmer Clifton's frenzied direction
and the inept performances of the lead actors,
made it a fizzle on all counts. Franklyn Warner's
production (for the independent Fine Arts
Pictures) was shot in Cosmocolor and also utilized
Etienne Girardot, Grant Richards, Tom Dugan,
Harry Woods and Ted Osborne in its cast. Song:
'Moonlight Magic' Irving Bibo, Eddie Cherkose.
▽

Millionaire Playboy (GB: **Glamour Boy**) unleashed daffy Joe Penner (centre) as a timid youth
who goes into a hiccuping frenzy whenever a
young woman kisses him. Joe's father pays a
psychologist $5000 to cure the lad of his affliction,
and doctor and patient end up at a summer resort
filled with lovely young girls. There, the film's best
gags were played out, including Penner's tussle
with a runaway outboard motor, which was a
slapstick gem. Engaged with the comedian in his
mad flight from the hiccup jinx were Linda Hayes
(right) as the prime reason Joe wants to be cured,
Russ Brown as his suave paid escort, Arthur Q.
Bryan as the wealthy father (named J. B. Zany)
and Fritz Feld (left), Tom Kennedy, Granville
Bates, Adele Pearce, Diane Hunter, Mary Milford
and Mantan Moreland. Bert Granet and Charles
E. Roberts wrote the cockeyed script from a story
by Granet; Leslie Goodwins directed and Robert
Sisk produced. **Millionaire Playboy** was Joe
Penner's final picture for RKO.
▽

With its plot based on the notion that overnight
success often spells ruin for the one who achieves
it, **Beyond Tomorrow** used the intervention of
three ghostly spirits who return from the grave to
straighten out the problems of Richard Carlson
and Jean Parker (centre) as its set piece. Carlson
and Parker are engaged until he becomes a
sensation as a radio singer and falls under the spell
of Broadway actress Helen Vinson. It is at this
point that Charles Winninger, Harry Carey and C.
Aubrey Smith come back to prevent Carlson from
abandoning Miss Parker. As written for the screen
by Adele Comandini (who was also associate
producer) from a story by Comandini and Mildred
Cram, and directed by A. Edward Sutherland, the
picture was unusual, but sluggish and lifeless in
spite of its supernatural aura. Highly respected
cinematographer Lee Garmes produced for his
own independent Academy Productions company.
Maria Ouspenskaya, Alex Melesh, Rod La Rocque,
J. Anthony Hughes, Robert Homans, Virginia
McMullen, James Bush and William Bakewell
were other members of the cast. Song: 'It's
Raining Dreams' Harold Spina, Charles Newman.
▽

Robert E. Sherwood's Pulitzer Prize play **Abe
Lincoln In Illinois** (GB: **Spirit Of The People**)
was purchased by George Schaefer despite his
knowledge that 20th Century-Fox was already
making a film about the revered president (John
Ford's *Young Mr Lincoln*) and would have it in
theatres before RKO's production could be
finished. Tracing Lincoln's career from its backwoods beginnings to his election to the White
House, the RKO effort was an object lesson in
Americanism and patriotism (popular themes as
war drew inexorably closer to US shores) and a
lionization of the Great Emancipator. Nevertheless, the work of director John Cromwell, screenwriter Sherwood, adaptor Grover Jones, cinematographer James Wong Howe and producer
Max Gordon proved singularly disappointing.
Episodic and colourless, the drama was diffuse and
unaffecting, and the picture chalked up a blistering
loss of $745,000 despite an avalanche of critical
encomia. Though a 'non-personality' in the star-
oriented parlance of Hollywood, Raymond Massey
(illustrated), playing the title character as he had
on stage, was not to blame for the failure. His
performance was majestic and precisely modulated
– a clear triumph given that he was forced to orate
almost as much as talk. Therein lay the crux of the
film's problems, for there was more vitality in one
minute of the amiable John Ford-Henry Fonda
collaboration than in the full 110 of stodgy **Abe
Lincoln In Illinois**. Gene Lockhart appeared as
Stephen Douglas, Ruth Gordon as Mary Todd
Lincoln, and Mary Howard as Ann Rutledge. Also
included in the huge cast: Minor Watson, Alan
Baxter, Harvey Stephens, Howard da Silva,
Dorothy Tree, Aldrich Bowker, Maurice Murphy,
Louis Jean Heydt, Clem Bevans, Harlan Briggs,
Herbert Rudley, George Rosener and Elisabeth
Risdon. The film was a co-production between
RKO and the Max Gordon Plays and Pictures
Corporation. ▷

Booth Tarkington's **Little Orvie**, the story of a
small boy, forbidden to own a dog, who adopts a
stray canine for a day and then can't get rid of it,
was transferred to the screen by producer William
Sistrom and director Ray McCarey. The result
was wholesome and unpretentious, but ploddingly
dull. John Sheffield (left), who had had better luck
in his debut role as Tarzan's offspring in MGM's
Tarzan Finds A Son, played Orvie, with Dorothy
Tree as the mother whose pseudo-psychological
primer is 'How to Raise a Son in Three Easy
Lessons', and Ernest Truex (right) as the lad's old-
fashioned father. The Lynn Root-Frank Fenton-
Robert Chapin script also contained roles for Ann
Todd, Emma Dunn, Daisy Mothershed, Fay
Helm, Virginia Brissac, Paul Burns, Del
Henderson, Fern Emmett, Edgar Dearing and Ray
Turner.

Curtain Call was the slightly mouldy story of two snake-eyed Broadway veterans who attempt to exploit a neophyte female playwright. Dalton Trumbo's script, based on a story by Howard J. Green, was not one of his highest achievements. It had some amusing moments – and many tedious ones. Alan Mowbray (centre) and Donald MacBride (left) hammed away as the two Broadway pirates, while Barbara Read (right) was given little to do as the callow author of the appropriately titled *The End Of Everything*. Former press agent Howard Benedict and former Broadway and radio director Frank Woodruff made their Hollywood debuts as producer and director respectively. Helen Vinson, John Archer, Leona Maricle, Frank Faylen, Tom Kennedy, Ralph Forbes, J. M. Kerrigan, Ann Shoemaker and Tommy Kelly also took part in this uneven comedy.

◁ There was nothing new in Bullet Code. Set during the days when cattle rustlers were driving their herds to Mexico where they could get a good price and no questions asked, the tale featured George O'Brien (centre right) as an honest rancher who mistakenly believes he has killed one of his own cowboys during a rustler attack. In attempting to make amends for the shooting, O'Brien meets the cowboy's cattleman father who is being harassed by a mysterious assailant determined to drive the old man off his property. O'Brien steps in, untangles the mystery, discovers that he is innocent of the cowboy's death and develops a romantic attachment to the cattleman's daughter. The team of Bert Gilroy (producer) and David Howard (director) mounted the picture from a story by Bennett Cohen and screenplay by Doris Schroeder. Other cast members included Virginia Vale (centre left), Slim Whitaker, Howard Hickman (left), Harry Woods (right), William Haade, Walter Miller and Robert Stanton.

Jean Hersholt (right) continued his humanitarian operations in The Courageous Dr Christian. In the course of an hour or so of screen time, the saintly physician managed to cure an epidemic of spinal meningitis, demonstrate benevolence towards the disenfranchised, set an example for wayward youth, and calm the passions of an amorous old maid. Ring Lardner Jr and Ian McLellan Hunter wrote the original screenplay, Bernard Vorhaus directed it and Dorothy Lovett, Robert Baldwin, Tom Neal, Maude Eburne, Vera Lewis, George Meader, Bobby Larson, Bobette Bentley, Reginald Barlow, Jacqueline de River, Edmund Glover, Mary Davenport, Earle Ross and Sylvia Andrew played supporting roles. William Stephens produced for Stephens-Lang Productions. ▷

Lucille Ball (left) and James Ellison (right) co-starred in You Can't Fool Your Wife, a dreary domestic comedy about a young couple who find five years of marriage disillusioning and separate, much to the delight of mother-in-law Emma Dunn who is responsible for a good percentage of the trouble in the first place. How the two attempt to get together again at a masquerade party was the central concern of Jerry Cady's insipid screenplay (from a story by Richard Carroll and Ray McCarey). The less said about the acting the better, though the picture's chief deficiencies rested in the script and in Ray McCarey's torpid direction. Also cast: Robert Coote, Virginia Vale, Elaine Shepard, William Halligan and Oscar O'Shea. Cliff Reid produced.

RKO's 1940 musicals hardly suggested that, only a few years before, some of the best song-and-dance pictures in the world had been sent out under the studio's logo. There was one surprise, however: Irene. The studio had bought the property (originally made by First National in 1926) years earlier with Astaire and/or Rogers in mind. When neither would tackle it, the James H. Montgomery–Harry Tierney–Joseph McCarthy stage show was turned over to producer-director Herbert Wilcox, who cast Anna Neagle and Ray Milland (borrowed from Paramount) in the top roles. Irene was quite a change of pace for Miss Neagle (right) who had recently played Queen Victoria and Nurse Cavell. Now she metamorphosed into a resourceful modern Cinderella surrounded by Prince Charmings and enjoying the world of Long Island society to the full. Though

Neagle's modest singing and dancing talents were acceptable, the film was so innocuous and dated that its amazing success serves as a barometer of the public's need for escapist fantasy during this tension-filled period in history. Earning profits of $364,000, it was the studio's third most financially successful picture of the year. Alice Duer Miller's screenplay also gave roles to Roland Young, Alan Marshal (left, borrowed from David O. Selznick), May Robson, Billie Burke (borrowed from MGM), Arthur Treacher, Marsha Hunt, Isabel Jewell, Doris Nolan, Stuart Robertson, Ethel Griffies and Tommy Kelly. Wilcox's company, Imperator Pictures Ltd., and RKO combined to produce the picture, one sequence of which was shot in Technicolor. Songs included: 'Alice Blue Gown', 'Out On A Limb', 'Castle Of Dreams', 'Irene' Harry Tierney, Joseph McCarthy.

A modern version of the 'Enoch Arden' story, Leo ▷
McCarey's production of **My Favorite Wife** was
RKO's second biggest hit of the year, earning
$505,000 in profits. Following a near-fatal auto-
mobile accident, McCarey relinquished the directorial reins to Garson Kanin. Still, the resulting
infectious tale clearly bore the McCarey imprint.
As scripted by Bella and Samuel Spewack (story
by McCarey and the Spewacks), the plot had Irene
Dunne (centre) returning home, after being shipwrecked for seven years, on the day her husband
(Cary Grant, left) is having her declared legally
dead and marrying another woman. Grant's
'quick' decision to remarry causes sparks to fly,
though the two are obviously still in love. The
sparks turn to thunderbolts when Grant discovers
that his wife spent those seven years on a desert
island with muscular Randolph Scott (right). Both
in theme and execution, **My Favorite Wife** was a
quasi-sequel to McCarey's earlier Dunne-Grant
blockbuster *The Awful Truth* (Columbia, 1937).
The film peaked about two-thirds of the way along
and began to wear thin near the end, yet still
contained a number of inspired scenes: two
separate sessions in court with irascible judge
Granville Bates; a droll but ultimately side-
splitting reunion between husband and wife at the
lodge in Yosemite National Park, where Grant has
taken his new bride (Gail Patrick) for their
honeymoon; and a carefully constructed 'moment
of truth' when Grant first encounters the supposedly prim Scott entertaining two nubile beauties beside the pool of a fancy hotel. Also cast:
Ann Shoemaker, Scotty Beckett, Mary Lou
Harrington, Donald MacBride, Hugh O'Connell
and Pedro De Cordoba. The top talents on the
picture (McCarey, Kanin, Dunne, Grant) had
been associated with a number of recent winners;
My Favorite Wife continued the hot streak for all
of them. 20th Century-Fox remade the story in
1963 as *Move Over Darling*, starring Doris Day
and James Garner.

The Saint Takes Over was the first movie in the
series not based on a story by Leslie Charteris.
Scenarists Frank Fenton and Lynn Root fashioned
the plot this time round, taking into account the
special traits of the protagonist as well as those of
such regular participants as Inspector Fernack
(Jonathan Hale). They succeeded nicely in con-
cocting a story – about a group of gamblers
specializing in race track fixes who frame Fernack
– which lovers of the private eye could believe to
have come straight from Charteris' pen. George
Sanders (left, on loan from 20th Century-Fox)
again performed flawlessly, rescuing his friend the
Inspector and getting the goods on the heavies.
Jack Hively directed a cast that also included
Wendy Barrie (right), Paul Guilfoyle, Morgan
Conway, Robert Emmett Keane, Cyrus W.
Kendall, James Burke, Robert Middlemass,
Roland Drew, Nella Walker and Pierre Watkin.
Howard Benedict was the producer for Lee
Marcus' 'B'-unit.
▽

Writer Dalton Trumbo and director John Farrow
worked hard on the remake of **A Bill Of
Divorcement** (1932), but to no avail. The
Clemence Dane play had somewhat yellowed with
age, and audiences evinced little interest in its
melodramatic rendering of Victorian taboos about
mental disease. Maureen O'Hara (left), playing the
part that had launched Katharine Hepburn's
career, and Adolphe Menjou (right) in John
Barrymore's role as the unbalanced father, were
inevitably and unfavourably compared to their
predecessors. Despite Trumbo's lucid script,
Farrow's delicate direction and an excellent support troupe that included Fay Bainter, Herbert
Marshall, Dame May Whitty, Patric Knowles, C.
Aubrey Smith, Ernest Cossart, Kathryn Collier
and Lauri Beatty, the Robert Sisk production
flopped ($104,000 loss).
▽

Another uniform, unexceptional George O'Brien
western, **Prairie Law** required the efforts of the
hero to restore order to a community mesmerized
by an unscrupulous promoter. Paul Everton, a
slick land-shark, sells worthless lots and farm
acreage to settlers on the false promise of unlimited
water from wells he will dig, thereby precipitating
a war between local cattlemen and the fast-arriving
settlers. O'Brien (right) assumes the leadership of
the cowmen and, after numerous battles with
guerillas hired by the malefactor, succeeds in
exposing him and bringing his hirelings to justice.
Virginia Vale (centre) once again added the
romantic sparkle and Slim Whitaker provided
comedy relief. Bernard McConville's story, and
the screenplay by Doris Schroeder and Arthur V.
Jones, also spotlighted Dick Hogan, J. Farrell
MacDonald, Cyrus W. Kendall, Henry Hall,
Monte Montague and Quen Ramsey. As always,
Bert Gilroy was the producer and David Howard
the director.   ▷

△

Dr Christian Meets The Women was more than
just a Hollywood entertainment; it was also a
sermon on a subject near and dear to millions of
American women: weight loss. Serious problems
face Dr Christian (Jean Hersholt, right) when the
female contingent of River's End succumb to the
silver-tongued sales pitch of an itinerant physical
culturist peddling a strenuous reducing plan.
Seeing the danger, the all-knowing physician takes
it upon himself to offer a sane and sensible
reducing system which was, supposedly, derived
by the production company from the suggestions
of 100 doctors around the country. The picture
had some value as health education, but it was
strictly no-go as a cinematic diversion. Marion
Orth wrote the original screenplay, William
McGann directed, and William Stephens pro-
duced for the Stephens-Lang production outfit.
Also cast: series regulars Dorothy Lovett and
Maude Eburne, plus Edgar Kennedy (left), Rod
LaRocque (centre), Frank Albertson, Marilyn
Merrick, Veda Ann Borg, Lelah Tyler, William
Gould, Phyllis Kennedy, Bertha Priestley, Diedra
Vale and Heinie Conklin.

Following his marriage to Jeanette MacDonald, Gene Raymond (right) took a two year sabbatical from the screen. He returned in **Cross-Country Romance**, a breezy and popular comedy about a young doctor who gets involved with a runaway heiress after she stows away in his trailer during a New York to San Francisco trip. Jerry Cady and Bert Granet did a bang-up job of translating Eleanor Browne's novel *Highway To Romance* to the screen, and Frank Woodruff directed its open road hi-jinx, properly balancing romance and farce. Wendy Barrie (centre) gave one of her finest performances as the spoiled heiress, and the rest of the cast, including Hedda Hopper, Billy Gilbert (left), George P. Huntley, Berton Churchill, Tom Dugan, Edgar Dearing, Frank Sully, Cliff Clark and Dorothea Kent, shared in the general success. The producer was Cliff Reid.

Tom Brown's School Days was the second letdown from Gene Towne and Graham Baker's The Play's The Thing Productions. It is easier to understand why this film fared poorly than why *Swiss Family Robinson* flopped. The scenario (adaptation and screenplay by Walter Ferris, Frank Cavett and the two producers, with additional dialogue by Robert Stevenson) applied a liberal sugar coating to the classic Thomas Hughes novel about education at Rugby in the 19th century. It shifted the focus away from Tom (Jimmy Lydon, left) and onto schoolmaster Thomas Arnold (Sir Cedric Hardwicke) who was presented as a magician capable of transforming savage barbarians into courteous, God-fearing gentlemen. In brief, the plot held little interest for a 1940 audience, and the blatant attempts to sentimentalize the events in order to captivate the emotions of American moviegoers failed. Robert Stevenson's direction was passable, but the performances of some of the pupils came dangerously close to the 'Dead End Kids' school of dramatic arts. Freddie Bartholomew (right), Josephine Hutchinson, Billy Halop, Polly Moran, Hughie Green, Ernest Cossart, Alec Craig, Gale Storm, Barlowe Borland, Forrester Harvey, Leonard Willey, Ian Fulton, Charles Smith, Dick Chandler, Paul Matthews, John Collum and Harry Duff rounded out the sizable cast. A remake was produced in Britain in 1951 with Robert Newton and John Howard Davies.

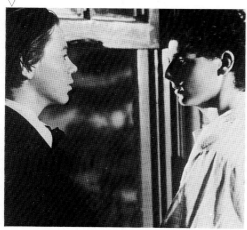

Leon Errol (centre) pranced away with **Pop Always Pays**, a B-plus loony comedy which also featured Dennis O'Keefe (borrowed from MGM), Adele Pearce and Walter Catlett. Pop's (Errol's) problems arise from his decision to allow daughter Pearce to marry O'Keefe if the spendthrift youth can save $1000, and Pop's rash offer to match the thousand with an equal amount, never imagining he will have to keep the promise. Complications soon come in chucklesome waves as the boy nears his goal and Errol finds he can't raise the pledged sum. Arthur J. Beckhart (story) and Charles E. Roberts (screenplay) furnished the narrative which Leslie Goodwins directed to a fare-thee-well. Marjorie Gateson, Tom Kennedy, Robert Middlemass, Effie Anderson (left), Erskine Sanford and Max Wagner (right) also appeared in the Bert Gilroy production.

Anne Shirley the actress was reunited with Anne Shirley the character in **Anne Of Windy Poplars** (GB: **Anne Of Windy Willows**). Using another of L. M. Montgomery's novels as their source, screenwriters Michael Kanin and Jerry Cady thrust Anne (left) into the role of schoolteacher beset by the Pringle clan, a hardy bunch of yahoos determined to make her life hellish. Armed with her innate goodness and a never-ending reservoir of homey platitudes, the dedicated educator eventually won the hearts of everyone except theatre patrons. The mawkish sentimentality and tedious construction of **Anne Of Windy Poplars** backfired in the faces of producer Cliff Reid, director Jack Hively, poor Anne Shirley and RKO. Made on a reasonable budget, the picture lost $176,000. Other casualties included James Ellison (right), Henry Travers, Patric Knowles (centre), Slim Summerville, Elizabeth Patterson, Louise Campbell, Joan Carroll, Katharine Alexander, Minnie Dupree, Alma Kruger, Marcia Mae Jones, Ethel Griffies, Clara Blandick, Gilbert Emery, Wright Kramer and Jackie Moran.

Millionaires In Prison was a real howler – an absurd trifle so bad that it had a certain surreal attractiveness. The penitentiary of the title turned out to be a pseudo-country club filled with kindly, intelligent tenants presided over by humanitarian convict Lee Tracy (left). One almost expected to find Dr Christian among the pinstripes. In between various stabs at humour, emanating from the antics of two irresponsible millionaires (Raymond Walburn and Thurston Hall), scenarists Lynn Root and Frank Fenton (original story Martin Mooney) manoeuvred the plot so that inmate Truman Bradley could continue his research on deadly Malta fever. Only in the never-never land of Hollywood 'B' filmmaking could such a preposterous tale unfold. Ray McCarey's half serious-half silly direction served the Howard Benedict production well. In support: Linda Hayes, Morgan Conway (right), Virginia Vale, Cliff Edwards, Paul Guilfoyle, Chester Clute (centre), Shemp Howard, Horace MacMahon, Thomas E. Jackson, Elliott Sullivan, Selmer Jackson and Jack Arnold.

Competition between rival stage lines put frontier postal inspector George O'Brien on the **Stage To Chino**. Virginia Vale (who had portrayed the heroine in each of O'Brien's last four films) owns one of the lines which is being sabotaged by her shifty uncle (Carl Stockdale) and the crooked owner of the other line (Roy Barcroft). Keeping his identity a secret, O'Brien (illustrated) takes a job as a driver for the crippled outfit and soon learns who the crooks are and what they are up to. Morton Grant and Arthur V. Jones scripted this action-loaded sagebrush saga from a story by Norton S. Parker. Former RKO assistant director Edward Killy was promoted to full-fledged solo pilot by producer Bert Gilroy. Hobart Cavanaugh, William Haade, Glenn Strange, Harry Cording, Martin Garralaga, Ethan Laidlaw and The Pals of the Golden West were also in it, plus four bit players who had been big names during the silent era: Elmo Lincoln (the original Tarzan), Billy Franey (one of the original Keystone Kops), Tom London (a Universal Pictures star) and Bruce Mitchell (a top director for Thomas Ince). Song: 'Riding On The Stage To Chino' Fleming Allen.

Queen Of Destiny (GB: **Sixty Glorious Years**) was producer-director Herbert Wilcox's second biopic about Queen Victoria. For some reason, Wilcox decided he had omitted too much of the monarch's story from *Victoria The Great*, so he included some of the neglected material in this 'sequel'. The filmmaker should have left well enough alone, for this episodic, patriotic homage to a dead leader proved a very dull affair indeed. The participation of Anna Neagle (right), Anton Walbrook, C. Aubrey Smith, Walter Rilla, Charles Carson, Greta Wegener, Felix Aylmer, Lewis Casson, Pamela Standish, Gordon McLeod, Stuart Robertson, Olaf Olsen, Henry Hallatt, Wyndham Goldie, Malcolm Keen (as Gladstone, left), Frederick Leister, Derrick de Marney, Marie Wright, Joyce Bland, Frank Cellier, Harvey Braban, Aubrey Dexter and Laidman Browne, plus Technicolor, failed to animate the ponderous Charles de Grandcourt-Miles Malleson-Robert Vansittart script and dialogue. The film was independently produced by Imperator Film Productions Ltd. in England, where it was first shown in 1938.

The Ramparts We Watch was the first feature-length production to come from Time Inc. Combining newsreel footage (see illustration) with the March of Time's practice of personalizing world events, it centred on a typical US town and the people in it from 1914 to 1918. The impact of World War I on these Americans was offered on the premise that one must remember the past in order to understand the present. Producer-director Louis de Rochemont and writers Robert L. Richards and Cedric R. Worth emphasized the similarities between the problems of preparedness facing the nation during the earlier period and those which it confronted in 1940. De Rochemont also incorporated scenes from *Baptism Of Fire*, a Nazi propaganda film, to demonstrate what a highly mechanized and carefully trained army could do to an unprepared foe. The message was clear and straightforward: America must provide for its own protection and security. Most of the docudrama was shot in New London, Connecticut, whose 1400 residents (none of them professional actors) played the various roles. Thomas Orchard was the associate producer, Westbrook Van Voorhis the narrator and Major George Fielding Eliot contributed the title, used initially for his 1938 book, *The Ramparts We Watch: A Study Of The Problems Of American Defense.*

One of RKO's most interesting 'B'-unit curiosities, **Stranger On The Third Floor** was a premature *film noir*, a picture that should, by all historical rights, have been produced in 1944 or 1945 – not 1940. Set in a claustrophobic urban milieu, it told the story of a newspaper reporter (John McGuire) who gives courtroom testimony which sends a young man to the electric chair. Tortured by uncertainty and guilt, McGuire suddenly finds himself enmeshed in a web of circumstantial evidence, accused of the murder of his detestable next-door neighbour. Creeping around the edges of the drama is the real killer, Peter Lorre (left), playing one of his patented psychopaths. Former writer Boris Ingster made his directorial bow, shooting Frank Partos' intriguing screenplay for producer Lee Marcus. The moody lighting of Nicholas Musuraca and an extraordinary, expressionistic dream sequence with special effects by Vernon L. Walker combined to visualize the protagonist's paranoia. Also cast: Margaret Tallichet (right), Charles Waldron, Elisha Cook Jr, Charles Halton, Ethel Griffies, Cliff Clark, Oscar O'Shea, Alec Craig and Otto Hoffman.

◁ **One Crowded Night** contained more cheap plot contrivances than a half dozen usual 'B's. At a tourist camp on the edge of the Mojave Desert, we find a young woman being reunited with her escaped convict husband, two mobsters in hot pursuit of the jailbird, a woman who just happens to be an acquaintance of one of the underworld types, a young mother-to-be who runs into her long-lost husband (in the custody of two law officers) and so on. Scenarists Richard Collins and Armand D'Usseau (working from a story by Ben Holmes) must have worked overtime to dredge up the incredible coincidences needed to fasten the lid on this Hollywood can of worms. Cliff Reid produced, and Irving Reis directed a cast that included Billie Seward (right), Gale Storm (left), William Haade, Charles Lang, Adele Pearce, J. M. Kerrigan, Paul Guilfoyle, Anne Revere, Dick Hogan, Don Costello, Gaylord Pendleton, Emma Dunn, George Watts, Casey Johnson, Harry Shannon and Ferris Taylor.

Recently rediscovered and championed by critics who admire its feminist sentiments, **Dance, Girl, Dance** took a severe drubbing from reviewers and audiences alike when it was first released. Roy Del Ruth directed the film for two weeks, then quit because of creative differences with producer Erich Pommer. Dorothy Arzner took over, tossed out Del Ruth's footage and began anew. She was powerless, however, against the inadequacies of Tess Slesinger and Frank Davis' tepid formula script (story by Vicki Baum). Lucille Ball (illustrated) and Maureen O'Hara, playing dancers with criss-cross ambitions and loves, delivered feeble performances, with Ball's coming off marginally better. The rest of the cast members seemed strangely fatigued throughout. Among them: Louis Hayward, Virginia Field, Ralph Bellamy, Mary Carlisle, Katharine Alexander, Edward Brophy, Walter Abel, Harold Huber, Maria Ouspenskaya, Ernest Truex, Chester Clute, Lorraine Krueger, Lola Jensen, Emma Dunn, Vivian Fay, Sidney Blackmer, Ludwig Stossel and Erno Verebes. The picture did spring briefly to life during Miss Ball's Breen Office-approved strip-tease and again during a brutal cat fight between the two principals, but the rest was soporific in the extreme. It lost $400,000 for RKO. Songs included: 'Morning Star', 'Jitterbug Bite' Edward Ward, Chet Forrest, Bob Wright; 'Mother What Do I Do Now?' Forrest, Wright.

Radio personalities Lum (Chester Lauck, centre) and Abner (Norris Goff, right) made their first movie appearances in **Dreaming Out Loud**. With the Jot-Em-Down store (of which they are the proprietors) as the hub of operations, they quietly but efficiently influence the lives of the citizens of Pine Ridge, Arkansas, stimulating charities by being the most charitable, encouraging progressiveness by being the most progressive and inspiring trust by being the most trustful. Combining their altruistic impulses with cracker-barrel humour and backwoods philosophizing, the pair evolve a plan to raise funds for a mobile hospital unit, straighten out a love affair between Frances Langford (left) and Robert Wilcox, and aid Irving Bacon in tracking down a murderous hit-and-run driver. The Howard J. Green-Barry Trivers-Robert D. Andrews screenplay (original story by Trivers and Andrews) was sufficiently amiable and diverting to enjoy a modest success which launched a new series for the studio. Frank Craven, Bobs Watson, Phil Harris, Clara Blandick, Donald Briggs, Robert McKenzie, Sheila Sheldon and Troy Brown Jr were also involved in the Harold Young-directed picture. Jack Votion and Sam Coslow produced for their independent Voco Productions banner. Song: 'Dreaming Out Loud' Sam Coslow.

▽

Fay Wray (centre) returned to RKO for **Wildcat Bus**, a sour little programmer about the hunt for racketeers whose sabotage of a reputable bus line has caused so many accidents and resulted in so many damage suites that the line is near bankruptcy. Lou Lusty's story and screenplay cast Wray as the daughter of the line's owner Oscar O'Shea, Charles Lang (right) as a playboy who becomes the hero in the end, Paul Guilfoyle (left) as a bus driver and Don Costello as the stock villain. Of the aforementioned, only Guilfoyle emerged from the preposterous carryings on with his actor's card intact. Paul McGrath, Joseph Sawyer, Roland Drew, Leona Roberts, Frank Shannon and Warren Ashe were others in director Frank Woodruff's cast. Cliff Reid produced.

▽

△

Ginger Rogers was the last important star under exclusive contract to RKO; the box-office muscle of her films made her value to the company almost incalculable at this juncture. **Lucky Partners** was a case in point – a cute cinematic cream puff that earned profits of $200,000. Adapted from Sacha Guitry's story *Bonne Chance* by screenwriters Allan Scott and John Van Druten, the film dealt with a Greenwich Village sketch artist (Ronald Colman, right, borrowed from United Producers Corporation) who wishes a passing errand girl (Rogers, left) good luck, whereupon all manner of favourable things begin to happen to her. Romantic complications come into play when the girl repairs to Niagara Falls with her good luck charm (Colman) and falls in love with him, despite her engagement to a lad from Poughkeepsie (Jack Carson). Veteran director Lewis Milestone blended Miss Rogers' exuberant charm with Mr Colman's debonair stylishness and came up with the ideal combination for this mellow, fanciful and, at times, racy comedy. Dimitri Tiomkin contributed the buoyant musical score and George Haight produced. Also cast: Spring Byington, Cecilia Loftus, Harry Davenport, Hugh O'Connell, Brandon Tynan, Billy Gilbert, Leon Belasco, Edward Conrad, Walter Kingsford, Lucile Gleason, Helen Lynd, Olin Howland and Benny Rubin. Sacha Guitry wrote, directed and starred in a French version around 1935.

George O'Brien rode off into the sunset following the completion of **Triple Justice**. The studio had decided to replace O'Brien with youngster Tim Holt and, thus, his tenure as RKO's resident sagebrush hero was over. It would be pleasant to report that O'Brien exited with a bang, and in one sense he did, for **Triple Justice** had more than the normal amount of thundering hoofbeats and exploding six-guns. Otherwise, it was the strictly conventional tale of rancher O'Brien (right) who inadvertently gets involved with a trio of bank robbers and is blamed for their latest crime. He tracks them down, recovers the $30,000 they have stolen, exposes a crooked deputy sheriff as their ringleader and, following formula to the end, finds romance in the arms of comely Virginia Vale. Bert Gilroy produced and David Howard directed. The story by Arnold Belgard and Jack Roberts and screenplay by Arthur V. Jones and Morton Grant also had roles for Peggy Shannon, Harry Woods, Paul Fix, LeRoy Mason, Glenn Strange, Malcolm McTaggart, Robert McKenzie, Wilfred Lucas and the Lindeman Sisters. Song: 'Lonely Rio' Fred Rose, Ray Whitley.

▽

'You are cordially invited', says Billy Gilbert, the antiquated m.c. of **The Villain Still Pursued Her**, 'to applaud the noble characters and to hiss the villain.' Former RKO theatre chief Harold B. Franklin formulated the idea to restage a famous Victorian melo called *The Fallen Saved*, feeling that the changing times would turn it from a serious drama into an uproarious comedy. The experiment failed miserably, attracting only $96,000 in total film rentals. Its story depicted the downfall of Richard Cromwell (back centre left) who is led into the evils of drink by villain Alan Mowbray. He plunges to the brink of suicide, but is miraculously rescued by his friends, and a reforming philanthropist (Hugh Herbert, back left) who has a sure-fire cure for inebriates. Anita Louise (front right) was the object of the black-beetled Mowbray's pursuit. Harold Franklin produced, Elbert Franklin authored the screenplay and Edward Cline directed. Also cast: Buster Keaton (back right), Joyce Compton (back centre right), Margaret Hamilton, William Farnum, Franklin Pangborn, Diane Fisher (front left) and Charles Judels. RKO distributed for Franklin-Blank Productions, Inc.

▽

△

The efforts of a discredited flyer to bring happiness to his sister and the man she loves formed the core of Nathanael West's screenplay (story by John Twist) for **Men Against The Sky**. Venerable Richard Dix (right), returning once more to the realm of sky-high adventure, topped the cast as the over-the-hill flyer who designs a new plane, then allows sister Wendy Barrie (centre) to take credit for it. Suspense mounts during the testing period, with the climax designed to allow the old-timer to go out in a blaze of glory. Leslie Goodwins' direction was on automatic pilot throughout, and the results were smooth but average. Howard Benedict produced, using Kent Taylor (left), Edmund Lowe, Granville Bates, Grant Withers, Donald Briggs, Charles Quigley, Selmer Jackson and Terry Belmont (later known as Lee Bonnell) in secondary spots. Note: The studio publicity department made much of the motion picture 'debut' of Howard Hughes' record-breaking transcontinental aircraft (Burbank to Newark in seven hours, 28 minutes, 25 seconds) in the picture.

△

Tim Holt tried George O'Brien's boots on for size and strode manfully into his own cowboy series with **Wagon Train**. Departing somewhat from standard 'B' western ingredients, Morton Grant's screenplay (story Bernard McConville) presented Holt (centre) as the leader of a supply train, battling Indians, outlaws and the rugged terrain to deliver life's necessities to the frontier's hard-pressed settlers. Martha O'Driscoll (left) as Holt's romantic target, Ray Whitley as a tuneful driver, Emmett Lynn as Holt's corny sidekick and Ellen Lowe as Lynn's hatchet-faced paramour all scored under Edward Killy's confident direction. Malcolm McTaggart (right), Cliff Clark, Wade Crosby, Ethan Laidlaw, Monte Montague, Carl Stockdale, Bruce Dane and Glenn Strange also appeared in the Bert Gilroy production. Songs included: 'Wagon Train', 'A Girl Just Like You', 'Why Shore', 'Farewell' Ray Whitley, Fred Rose.

They Knew What They Wanted, Sidney Howard's Pulitzer Prize-winning play, was purchased by RKO for $50,000 in the studio's continuing effort to raise the quality and eminence of its product. It was a drama about a waitress (Carole Lombard), who agrees, by mail, to marry an Italian grape grower (Charles Laughton) in California's Napa Valley. When she arrives at the vineyard, it is to discover that he had won her by sending a photograph of his handsome hired man (William Gargan), who later seduces her. A long and debilitating battle with the Breen office ensued before the censors finally agreed to allow RKO to use the title and the essential plot, provided it met Production Code requirements. When the picture was finally finished, George Schaefer, Harry Edington and other company executives probably wished Joseph Breen had stopped them from making it in the first place. The casting was one obvious drawback: the beautiful Miss Lombard (left), in the guise of a destitute waitress willing to do anything to escape poverty, strained credulity; Charles Laughton's impersonation of Tony Patucci (right) was a near-caricature of vociferous Italians, and William Gargan scowled and skulked his way through the action. He was not in the same league as the two stars and seemed to know it. At some point, director Garson Kanin lost control of the action, allowing it to degenerate into bathos and mangling the message of Howard's play, which concerned the necessity of tolerance. The movie was quite a departure for Kanin, who had hitherto more or less confined himself to comedy, and the rest of the acting ranged from acceptable to awful (Frank Fay as Father McKee was incredibly bad). There were rumours of constant turmoil on the set – of irreparable conflicts among cast and crew. If true, that may explain why everyone in the picture seemed to be working earnestly but without any conviction or enthusiasm. Another stab at culture exploded in George Schaefer's face; the eventual loss was $291,000. Erich Pommer produced, Robert Ardrey wrote the screenplay and Harry Stradling shot the footage which John Sturges edited. Also cast: Harry Carey, Joe Bernard, Janet Fox, Lee Tung-Foo, Karl Malden and Victor Kilian. The play had been filmed twice before under different titles: *The Secret Hour* (Paramount, 1928) with Pola Negri and Jean Hersholt and *A Lady In Love* (MGM, 1930) with Vilma Banky and Edward G. Robinson.

▷

Whirling dervish Lupe Velez (right) took off for Reno in **Mexican Spitfire Out West**. Written by Charles E. Roberts and Jack Townley (from Roberts' original story) in the venerable tradition of wild and woolly slapstick farce, and directed with knockabout effortlessness by Leslie Goodwins, the tale revolved around Lupe's craving for more attention from hubby Donald Woods and the threatened divorces she employs to get it. Leon Errol (left) showed off his multiple abilities, playing Uncle Matt, Woods' British client Lord Epping and the nobleman's cockney valet Higgins. Elisabeth Risdon, Cecil Kellaway, Linda Hayes, Lydia Bilbrook, Charles Coleman, Charles Quigley, Eddie Dunn, Grant Withers and Tom Kennedy also dropped in for the Cliff Reid-produced tomfoolery.

Tim Holt played the title role in the third cinematic incarnation of **Laddie**. Though less beguiling than George Stevens' 1935 version, the film's nostalgic, sentimental plot still had ample homey appeal. All about the romance of a sturdy Indiana farmer (Holt, left) and a spirited English girl (Virginia Gilmore) with the former's adoring kid sister (Joan Carroll, right) playing Cupid, the Gene Stratton-Porter novel used the plot device of a family scandal to bring the lovers together. Spring Byington, Robert Barrat, Miles Mander, Esther Dale, Sammy McKim, Joan Brodel (Leslie), Martha O'Driscoll, Rand Brooks and Peter Cushing had the other significant roles in Cliff Reid's production. Bert Granet and Jerry Cady joined forces on the screenplay, which Jack Hively directed.

Vogue Productions brought Al Capp's Dogpatch inhabitants to life (though just barely) in **Li'l Abner** (GB: **Trouble Chaser**). Charles Kerr and Tyler Johnson's screenplay was a choppy pastiche of Capp's comic strips, more or less tied together by Abner's continual attempts to elude the matrimonial snares of Daisy Mae and other hillbilly sirens. The cast featured Granville Owen (Li'l Abner, centre right), Martha O'Driscoll (Daisy Mae, centre left), Mona Ray (Mammy Yokum, right), Johnnie Morris (Pappy Yokum, left), Buster Keaton (Lonesome Polecat), Billie Seward (Cousin Delightful), Kay Sutton (Wendy Wilecat), Maude Eburne (Granny Scraggs), Edgar Kennedy (Cornelius Cornpone), Charles A. Post (Earthquake McGoon), Bud Jamison (Hairless Joe) and Dick Elliot (Marryin' Sam). Johnny Arthur, Walter Catlett, Lucien Littlefield, Frank Wilder, Chester Conklin, Mickey Daniels and Doodles Weaver were in it too, adding to the comedy. Director Albert S. Rogell sealed the picture's fate by allowing the actors to babble in a variety of stupefyin' accents. Herman Schlom was the associate producer for the independent Vogue organization. Song: 'Li'l Abner' Ben Oakland, Milton Drake, Milton Berle. Paramount released a musical version, from the later Broadway stage show, in 1959.

Broadway grandee George Abbott conveyed his stage hit **Too Many Girls** to Hollywood, where it was transformed into an innocuous musical comedy. The cast came mainly from RKO's stock company, although Eddie Bracken, Desi Arnaz, Hal LeRoy, Libby Bennett, Ivy Scott, Byron Shores and bit-player Van Johnson were allowed to reprise their original stage roles. Lucille Ball was top-cast as Connie Casey, a beautiful, madcap heiress who goes away to college shadowed by four unsuspecting body-guards, who also happen to be ace football players. Though expressly forbidden to display their skills, the four put the jerk-water school on the gridiron map. Producer-director Abbott's lack of cinematic training was evident throughout; though supposedly a light-hearted college romp, the picture sagged at important moments due to poor camera work, sluggish editing and inconsistent performances, and even the Richard Rodgers-Lorenz Hart score was below par. The large cast also included Richard Carlson, Ann Miller (centre with Desi Arnaz), Frances Langford, Harry Shannon, Douglas Walton, Chester Clute and Tiny Person. John Twist provided the screenplay based on George Marion Jr's stage original. Songs included: 'Heroes In The Fall', 'Pottawatomie', 'Cause We All Got Cake', 'Spic And Spanish', 'Love Never Went To College', 'I Didn't Know What Time It Was'.

Kent Taylor, who played second-string to Richard
Dix in *Men Against The Sky*, was given the lead in
another aviation fable called **I'm Still Alive**. The
Edmund North story and screenplay narrated the
problems of thrill flyer Taylor (right) after he
marries movie queen Linda Hayes (left). The
romance cracks up with the death of one of
Taylor's fellow stunt men, but the efforts of Hayes
and some of Taylor's pals bring the couple back
together. At one point, the hero espouses the
following philosophy: 'Risking your life for a
movie isn't as silly as starving to death'. Maybe so
– but it was certainly silly for director Irving Reis
and producer Frederic Ullman Jr to make a movie
as trite and joyless as this one turned out to be.
Also cast: Howard da Silva, Ralph Morgan, Don
Dillaway, Clay Clement and famous silent film
director Fred Niblo. Note: Former RKO Pathe
star Helen Twelvetrees sued RKO, claiming the
picture was based on her life with her ex-husband,
stunt man Jack Woody. The suit was settled for
$1100 in January 1943.

Comedy took precedence over drama in **Remedy
For Riches**, the fourth instalment of the Dr
Christian series. Jean Hersholt (left) applied his
stethoscope to the economic rather than physical
heartbeat of his River's End patients, who are
seduced into buying shares in a worthless piece of
property on the assumption that it is rich in oil. In
addition to exposing the fraudulent scheme and
saving the locals from financial ruin, the wily
physician finds time to chuckle at the antics of the
town's prominent folk, and to enter into a few
comic situations himself. Dorothy Lovett (right),
Edgar Kennedy, Jed Prouty, Walter Catlett,
Robert Baldwin, Maude Eburne, Margaret
McWade, Warren Hull and Renie Riano were also
among those cast, and Erle C. Kenton's jolly
direction of Lee Loeb's original screenplay resulted in one of the most attractive of the Dr
Christian pictures. William Stephens produced for
Stephens-Lang.

The Fargo Kid, a remake of *Man In The Rough*
(FBO, 1928) and *The Cheyenne Kid* (RKO, 1933)
presented two-fisted cowpuncher Tim Holt
(centre) riding into an Arizona town where he is

immediately mistaken for a notorious gunman.
Not pleased with what he finds, the hero decides to
assume the bad guy's identity long enough to
expose the activities of two mining crooks. W. C.
Tuttle's original fiction, capably scripted by
Morton Grant and Arthur V. Jones, also accom-
modated the tunesmanship of Ray Whitley (right),
the comedy relief of Emmett Lynn (left) and the
comeliness of Jane Drummond. Edward Killy
handled the workaday direction for producer Bert
Gilroy, using Cyrus W. Kendall, Ernie Adams,
Paul Fix, Paul Scardon, Glenn Strange and Mary
MacLaren in secondary parts. Songs: 'Crazy Ole
Trails', 'Twilight On The Prairie' Ray Whitley,
Fred Rose.

Producer-director David Butler stacked the deck
by rounding up Boris Karloff, Bela Lugosi (right)
and Peter Lorre (left) in an attempt to inject a few
chills into the Kay Kyser vehicle, **You'll Find
Out**. James V. Kern's screenplay (story by Butler
and Kern, with special material by Monte Brice,
Andrew Bennison and R. T. M. Scott) unravelled
a murder plot in a forbidding old Massachusetts
manse, where Kyser (centre) and his hepcat band
got in the way of the villains, and provided
scattered moments of nervous laughter in a total
package largely devoid of true wit and thrills.
Helen Parrish (borrowed from Universal), Dennis
O'Keefe, Alma Kruger and Joseph Eggenton were
also involved in the sinister carryings on, together
with Ginny Simms, Harry Babbitt, Ish Kabibble,
Sully Mason, and other regulars from the Kyser
entourage. Just why audiences found the bandleader and his shows so appealing is difficult to
fathom, but they did ($167,000 profit) and RKO
was not about to argue with success. Songs
included: 'I'd Know You Anywhere', 'You've Got
Me This Way', 'The Bad Humor Man', 'Like The
Fella Once Said', 'I've Got A One-Track Mind'
Jimmy McHugh, Johnny Mercer.

No, No, Nanette, another Herbert Wilcox-Anna
Neagle nostalgia musical, was RKO's Christmas
gift to movie customers depressed by a world
coming apart at the seams. One of the strengths of
Irene had been its supporting cast, so producer-
director Wilcox again surrounded Miss Neagle
with a solid contingent of character actors: Roland
Young, Helen Broderick, ZaSu Pitts, Eve Arden
and Billy Gilbert. They added exuberance to the
production, but Wilcox's decision to downplay the
Vincent Youmans score emphasized certain plot
inadequacies. Another saccharine fable, the Frank
Mandel-Otto Harbach-Vincent Youmans-Emil
Nyitray musical comedy (screenplay by Ken
Englund) proffered Miss Neagle (centre) as a busy
'Miss Fixit' seeking to pry her wealthy uncle
(Roland Young) out of the financial jam into which
he has been manoeuvred by some gold-diggers.
Neagle's solution involves an artist (Richard
Carlson, right) and a theatrical producer (Victor
Mature, left, borrowed from 20th Century-Fox),
both of whom promptly fall in love with her.
Though the romantic and gold-digger troubles
were sorted out in reasonably satisfactory fashion,
Wilcox's stodgy direction weighed down the
story's grace and gaiety. Audiences did not clasp
No, No, Nanette to their bosoms in the way they
had *Irene*, and RKO's ultimate loss was $2000.
Merrill G. White was the associate producer,
Anthony Collins the musical director and decorat-
ive supporting performances were supplied by
Tamara, Stuart Robertson (Miss Neagle's
brother), Dorothea Kent, Aubrey Mather, Mary
Gordon and Russell Hicks. A remake of a 1930
First National picture which starred Bernice
Claire, the film was a co-production between RKO
and Suffolk Productions (Wilcox's company).
Songs included: 'I Want To Be Happy', 'Tea For
Two' Vincent Youmans, Irving Caesar; 'No, No,
Nanette' Youmans, Otto Harbach.

Kitty Foyle took audiences for a satisfyingly emotional roller coaster ride. The lugubrious saga of a Philadelphia girl who gets mixed up with one of the 'Main Liners', suffers the indignant snobbery of his family, loses her baby and finally summons the wherewithal to leave her lover behind at the end, it burrowed its way into the hearts of American filmgoers, pulling in an amazing $869,000 profit. Dalton Trumbo's screenplay (additional dialogue by Donald Ogden Stewart), based on a novel by Christopher Morley, gave Ginger Rogers an opportunity to 'go straight', dramatically speaking, after years of comedy and musical roles. Academy members were so impressed that they voted her Best Actress of 1940. It was RKO's first major Academy Award since 1935. One of the most imaginative publicity campaigns in studio history emphasized that the picture was about an ordinary working girl, and created an enormous amount of empathy and sympathy for the character; Ginger (right) even changed her hair colour from blonde to brunette to 'de-glamourize' her image. By today's standards, the direction of Sam Wood and the performances of James Craig, Dennis Morgan (borrowed from Warner Bros.), Eduardo Ciannelli, Ernest Cossart (left), Gladys Cooper and even Rogers herself seem bland, and lacking any emotional wallop. The David Hempstead production opened many a tear duct in its own day, however. Also cast: Odette Myrtil, Mary Treen, Katharine Stevens (Sam Wood's daughter), Walter Kingsford, Cecil Cunningham, Nella Walker, Edward Fielding, Kay Linaker, Richard Nichols and Florence Bates.

This year is best remembered for the release of **Citizen Kane**. The resemblance between Orson Welles' fictional Charles Foster Kane and newspaper tycoon William Randolph Hearst fuelled the nastiest controversy that had ever involved the company.

The poor performances of 1940 features caused continuing upheaval at the studio. Though production chief Harry Edington kept working, he was *persona non grata* and George Schaefer finally turned over the job to Joseph Breen, the former director of the Production Code Administration. J. R. McDonough replaced Lee Marcus as head of the 'B'-unit; Joseph Nolan resigned from his post as vice-president in charge of the studio, and Sol Lesser joined as executive producer in charge of the 'A' product. In the theatre division in New York Charles Koerner took over John J. O'Connor's job.

Floyd Odlum watched these dizzying transformations and began purchasing RKO stock again. N. Peter Rathvon, an Odlum man, was elected to a corporate vice-presidency in December.

Schaefer's biggest publicity coup was an agreement with Samuel Goldwyn. The distribution of his prestigious, independently financed pictures seemed very promising, but Schaefer allowed Goldwyn such attractive terms that it was almost impossible to make a profit on any of his pictures.

Ginger Rogers' seven-year contract expired in May. Schaefer, desperate to retain her exclusive services, offered her $390,000 per year on a three-year basis. Rogers, however, insisted on being free to make pictures for other companies; she finally signed a non-exclusive pact and by year's end had already agreed to make three pictures for 20th Century-Fox.

The studio also lost Garson Kanin, who was drafted, Robert Sisk, who became fed up with George Schaefer's meddling in his productions and quit, and Erich Pommer, who was fired rather cruelly after he suffered a heart attack. New pacts were made with Broadway producer Jed Harris; Gabriel Pascal, a Hungarian producer-director who controlled film rights to Shaw's plays; famous documentary filmmaker Pare Lorentz; and former Warner Bros.' ace director William Dieterle. Foreign actresses Michele Morgan and Signe Hasso were also signed to agreements that George Schaefer would soon regret.

Of the 46 films released, 33 were normal studio products and 13 were products of various independent deals. The most profitable pictures were **Suspicion, Look Who's Laughing, Tom, Dick And Harry, Parachute Battalion, The Devil And Miss Jones** and **The Gay Falcon**. A corporate profit of $538,692 was claimed for 1941, though many insiders considered this the product of creative bookkeeping.

After the success of *Rebecca* (United Artists, 1940), RKO leaders aggressively pursued the services of Alfred Hitchcock and finally cornered him for two films. The arrangement was actually concluded with former production chief David O. Selznick who held an exclusive contract with Hitchcock, although the director had veto power and came to RKO because he wanted to direct the two stories he was offered. The first of these was **Mr And Mrs Smith**, a quasi-screwball comedy starring Carole Lombard (right) and Robert Montgomery (left). Hitchcock was not altogether comfortable with the material, a Norman Krasna contrivance about a couple who learn that their marriage is void because of a shifting state boundary line. After Lombard and Montgomery discover their 'freedom', the picture degenerated into a tiresome parade of misunderstandings and arguments, diluting much of the audience's affection for the characters. Though deprived of the thrills and suspense which he always manipulated so skilfully, Hitchcock still enlivened the situations with a technical mastery not usually found in such domestic trivia. Also cast: Gene Raymond, Jack Carson, Philip Merivale, Lucile Watson, William Tracy, Charles Halton, Esther Dale, Emma Dunn, Patricia Farr, William Edmunds, Adele Pearce and former RKO queen bee Betty Compson. This was Lombard's last film for the studio; following the completion of *To Be Or Not To Be* for Ernst Lubitsch and United Artists, she was tragically killed in an air crash.

◁Filmed in cooperation with the British Admiralty, and with a British cast, **Convoy** depicted life aboard an English cruiser on convoy duty in the North Sea. The climax to the plot was a confrontation between the cruiser and a German battleship. Though outgunned by her formidable adversary, the little vessel holds out until a friendly battle squadron arrives and chases the intruder away. Clive Brook (left), John Clements, Edward Chapman and Judy Campbell played the chief dramatic parts in this sporadically interesting propaganda adventure, whose background was the reality of the European war. Patrick Kirwan and Pen Tennyson wrote the screenplay, which Tennyson directed for producer Michael Balcon. Other cast members included: Penelope Dudley Ward, Edward Rigby, Charles Williams, Allan Jeayes (right), Michael Wilding, Stewart Granger, John Laurie, George Benson, Hay Petrie, Mervyn Johns and Albert Lieven. The picture was made at Ealing Studios in Great Britain by Associated British Film Distributors.

△
George Sanders (left) played Simon Templar for the fifth and final time in **The Saint In Palm Springs**. A mildly pleasurable whodunit about rare stamp snitching, the film featured three murders, an attempted kidnapping and a number of attempts on the modern-day Robin Hood's own life. Series regulars Wendy Barrie, Jonathan Hale and Paul Guilfoyle (right) also appeared, along with Linda Hayes, Ferris Taylor, Harry Shannon and Eddie Dunn. Jerry Cady drafted his screenplay from a Leslie Charteris story; Jack Hively added the suspenseful direction. Producer Howard Benedict toted up another Saint success: $90,000 net profit.

Little Men had been on the minds of RKO executives ever since the success of *Little Women* in 1933. Compared to the George Cukor-Katharine Hepburn gold mine, however, this Gene Towne-Graham Baker effort was pure bust. Louisa May Alcott's novel about a school managed by Jo (the Hepburn role in *Little Women*, now played by Kay Francis) contained a wealth of homespun charm and unalloyed sentiment which screenwriters Mark Kelly and Arthur Caesar negated by cheap jokes, anachronistic dialogue and maudlin plot manipulations. Producers Towne and Baker, who took an uncredited hand in the writing, deserved most of the blame, though Norman Z. McLeod's direction and the histrionic endeavours of such cast members as Miss Francis (left), George Bancroft (centre right) and Jimmy Lydon (centre) were decidedly second-rate. Only Jack Oakie (right), playing an ingratiating thief called Willie the Fox, contributed value beyond the call of duty. Ann Gillis, Charles Esmond (centre left), Richard Nichols, Casey Johnson, Francesca Santoro, Johnny Burke, Lillian Randolph, Sammy McKim, Edward Rice, Anne Howard, Jimmy Zaner, Bobbie Cooper, Schuyler Standish, Paul Matthews, Tony Neil, Fred Estes, Douglas Rucker, Donald Rackerby, William Demarest, Sterling Holloway, Isabel Jewell and Elsie the Cow filled out the cast. A $214,000 paybox loser, it was the final effort of The Plays The Thing Productions. An earlier version of the Alcott novel was released by the Mascot organization in 1934.

An old-fashioned gold-digger story starring Kay Francis, **Play Girl** was another in a long line of lightweight, irksome RKO comedies. In this one, a fortune hunter (Francis, left), who is now losing her charms, decides to pass on the tricks of the trade to a young novice (Mildred Coles) who soon finds herself the victim of an age-old conflict between love and her 'career'. Fortunately, the object of her affections (James Ellison, centre) turns out to have $11 million in addition to his other attractions, and thus Mildred's dilemma is solved. Jerry Cady's overwritten story and screenplay and Frank Woodruff's listless direction were good for one or two laughs. Cliff Reid produced with Nigel Bruce, Margaret Hamilton, Katharine Alexander (right), George P. Huntley, Charles Quigley, Georgia Carroll, Kane Richmond, Stanley Andrews and Selmer Jackson completing the cast.

Along The Rio Grande was the story of a young cowhand and his two pals who join a bandit gang in order to avenge the murder of their former boss. Tim Holt (illustrated) played the hero, Emmett Lynn and Ray Whitley his cronies, and Betty Jane Rhodes provided the feminine icing. Morton Grant and Arthur V. Jones' screenplay (story by Stuart Anthony) also contained roles for Robert Fiske, Hal Taliaferro, Carl Stockdale, Slim Whitaker, Monte Montague, Ruth Clifford and Harry Humphrey. Edward Killy furnished the competent direction, and Bert Gilroy produced. Songs included: 'Along The Rio Grande', 'My Grandpap', 'Old Monterey Moon' Fred Rose, Ray Whitley.

RKO began distributing another radio-inspired series with **Scattergood Baines**. Guy Kibbee (left) appeared as Clarence Budington Kelland's mellow country philosopher, a veritable encyclopedia of sensible advice and old-fashioned maxims. For dramatic purposes, scriptwriters Michael L. Simmons and Edward T. Lowe forced Scattergood to deal with an iniquitous group determined to separate the hero from his holdings and, thereby, disrupt the pastoral harmony of the community of Coldriver. Scattergood nimbly outwits the culprits, saving his possessions, and rescuing the surrounding area from their corrupting influence. Carol Hughes, John Archer, Francis 'Dink' Trout (right), Emma Dunn, Lee 'Lasses' White, Willie Best, Paul White, Fern Emmett, Edward Earle, Bradley Page and Joseph Crehan were others involved for director Christy Cabanne and producer Jerrold T. Brandt (a Pyramid Pictures Corporation film.)

Bob Crosby, Bing's younger brother, made his motion picture debut in **Let's Make Music**, a well-intentioned but inconsequential diversion produced by Howard Benedict and directed by Leslie Goodwins. Nathanael West's screenplay (with special dialogue for Crosby by Helen Phillips and Bernard Dougall) traced the night life adventures of an elderly spinster (Elisabeth Risdon, right) whose corny song is bought by a New York publisher and subsequently used as a freak novelty number by bandleader Crosby (left). The song meets with instant success and makes its composer famous overnight – both as a songwriter and as an entertainer with the band. Playing himself, Crosby gave a confident and energetic performance, but the sheer inanity of the tale diminished the actor's impact. Jean Rogers (centre left, borrowed from 20th Century-Fox), Joseph Buloff (centre right), Joyce Compton, Bennie Bartlett, Louis Jean Heydt, Bill Goodwin, Frank Orth, Grant Withers, Walter Tetley, Benny Rubin, Jacqueline Nash, Donna Jean Dolfer and Bob Crosby's Orchestra, featuring the Bobcats, also appeared. Songs included: 'Central Park' Johnny Mercer, Matt Malneck; 'Fight On For Newton High' Roy Webb, Dave Dreyer & Herman Ruby; 'The Big Noise From Winnetka' Bob Crosby, Ray Haggart, Gil Rodin & Ray Bauduc; 'You Forgot About Me' Richard Robertson, Jimmy Hanley.

It Happened To One Man (GB: **Gentleman Of Venture**) was one of several pictures made in Great Britain during this period with RKO's 'frozen funds' – monies earned by the company which could not be removed from the country due to wartime restrictions. The picture suffered from a hackneyed, outdated story and a lack of name actors with marquee drawing power and, consequently, Victor Hanbury's British Eagle production, directed by Paul L. Stein, received limited distribution in the US. Wilfrid Lawson (left) starred as a financial manipulator whose exposure by his treacherous partner Reginald Tate (right) leads to a four-year prison term and the collapse of his family life. Roland Pertwee and John Hastings Turner wrote the original play which Paul Merzbach and Nina Jarvis re-scripted for the screen. Also cast: Nora Swinburne, Marta Labarr (centre), Ivan Brandt, Brian Worth, Edmund Breon, Patricia Roc, Athole Stewart, Thorley Walters, Ruth Maitland and Ian Fleming.

Former silent comedy star Harold Lloyd supervised **A Girl, A Guy And A Gob** (GB: **The Navy Steps Out**), a slapstick excursion in which a wealthy snob (Edmond O'Brien, right) and a boisterous sailor (George Murphy, left) vie for the affections of pert stenographer Lucille Ball (centre). As scripted by Frank Ryan and Bert Granet from a story by Grover Jones, and directed by Richard Wallace, the film exhibited the same bounce, breakneck pace and variety of gags which had contributed to Lloyd's success as a performer. Although not a giant hit, **A Girl, A Guy And A Gob** was one of the year's top comedy offerings. Henry Travers, Franklin Pangborn, George Cleveland, Kathleen Howard, Marguerite Chapman, Lloyd Corrigan, Mady Correll, Frank McGlynn, Doodles Weaver, Frank Sully, Nella Walker, Richard Lane, Irving Bacon and Rube Demarest were other cast members in this co-production between RKO and Harold Lloyd's company.

Although Herbert Wilcox's **Sunny** was the best RKO musical of 1941, that didn't say much for it. After *Irene* and *No, No, Nanette*, Wilcox and star Anna Neagle might have been wiser to avoid a third consecutive sentimental journey, particularly as this revival (originally filmed by First National in 1930 with Marilyn Miller) remained true to the old-fashioned pleasantries and mannerisms of the other pictures. Another Cinderella fable, it presented Miss Neagle (left) as a circus performer who falls in love with a New Orleans aristocrat (John Carroll, right) and marries him in the end, despite the protests of his stiffnecked family. The plot and songs by Otto Harbach, Oscar Hammerstein II and Jerome Kern (screenplay by Sig Herzig) retained a certain congeniality and the dancing of Neagle and co-star Ray Bolger was presentable, but Wilcox's flat and colourless direction kept the merriment to a minimum. Helen Westley, cast as Carroll's harridan aunt and playing the part to the hilt, seemed to be the only character having a good time. Edward Everett Horton, Grace and Paul Hartman, Frieda Inescort, Benny Rubin, Muggins Davies, Richard Lane and Martha Tilton were also in it. RKO co-produced with Wilcox's Suffolk Productions. Songs included: 'Sunny', 'Who?', 'Two Little Bluebirds', 'D'ya Love Me?'

Teamed romantically for the third time, Wendy Barrie (right) and Kent Taylor (left) played an impulsive heiress and a young tie salesman in **Repent At Leisure**. Their messy marital life provided the springboard for an indoor romp that tried every ingratiating trick in the book, but succeeded in provoking only an occasional grin. James Gow and Arnaud D'Usseau dreamed up the original story which Jerry Cady transformed into a wordy and wooden screenplay. Cliff Reid produced and Frank Woodruff directed, with George Barbier, Thurston Hall, Charles Lane, Nella Walker, Rafael Storm, Ruth Dietrich, Cecil Cunningham and 'Snowflake' Toones also cast.

With behind-the-scenes RKO power Nelson Rockefeller holding the title of 'Coordinator of Commercial and Cultural Relations Between the American Republics' and the company growing more dependent on earnings from the South American countries, it was logical that the studio would begin to produce films with Latin American themes and settings. Lou Brock, the driving force behind *Flying Down To Rio*, returned to RKO and assumed production responsibility on one of the first of these pictures, **They Met In Argentina**. The embarrassing result was closer to Brock's calamitous *Down To Their Last Yacht* than to *Rio*. An aimless script by Jerry Cady (story by Brock and Harold Daniels) about the amorous jousting between a young man who doesn't want to love and a girl accustomed to having her own way, inept direction by Leslie Goodwins and Jack Hiveley, absurd casting (Maureen O'Hara, right, as an 'Irish senorita'!), and arguably the worst score ever composed by Richard Rodgers and Lorenz Hart, combined to make **They Met In Argentina** a messy spectacle sure to offend Spanish-speaking viewers and leave domestic audiences in a dander. Made for less than $500,000, the picture lost $270,000 and ended Brock's RKO career forever. James Ellison (left), Alberto Vila, Buddy Ebsen (centre), Robert Barrat, Joseph Buloff, Diosa Costello, Victoria Cordova, Luis Alberni, Paul Ellis, Fortunio Bonanova, Carlos Barbe, Francisco Maran and Antonio Moreno were other melancholy members of the cast. Songs included: 'North America Meets South America', 'You've Got The Best Of Me', 'Never Go To Argentina', 'Cutting The Cane'. Note: The co-direction credit came about when Jack Hively replaced Leslie Goodwins, who became ill during the production. One certainly understands why.

The adventures of Scattergood Baines (Guy Kibbee, left), Hollywood's walking 'Poor Richard's Almanac', continued in **Scattergood Pulls The Strings**. Ironing out double troubles, Scattergood helps a pair of young lovers realize their life's dream and brings about the reunion of a 10-year-old boy and his estranged father, who has been unjustly accused of murder. Susan Peters and James Corner (right) played the lovers, struggling against an ample supply of inane dialogue handed them by the Christy Cabanne-Bernard Schubert script. Young Bobs Watson and veteran actor Monte Blue fared somewhat better as the lad and his unlucky sire. Cabanne also directed, utilizing Emma Dunn, 'Dink' Trout, Carl Stockdale, Paul White, Fern Emmett, Lee 'Lasses' White, Ann Shoemaker, Gordon Hart, Howard Hickman, Earle Hodgins and a dog named Rex to complete the cast. Jerrold T. Brandt produced for Pyramid Pictures Corporation.

After completing *The Saint In Palm Springs*, George Sanders surrendered the Leslie Charteris character to Hugh Sinclair. Sinclair (centre) starred in **The Saint's Vacation**, produced in England by William Sistrom with RKO's frozen funds. Sinclair lacked the polish and professional finesse of Sanders, but still managed a worthy performance in a mystery revolving around a small and innocent looking music box. Mail robbery, torture and murder are employed by a band of international crooks seeking the box, which contains the key to a valuable code. Leslie Fenton's kinetic direction captured the essence of the Leslie Charteris-Jeffrey Dell screenplay (story by Charteris). Also cast: Sally Gray (right), Cecil Parker, Arthur Macrae, Leueen MacGrath, Gordon McLeod, John Warwick, Manning Whiley, Felix Aylmer and Ivor Barnard (left). This was the seventh and final instalment of the current series, though the avenging detective would make his screen comeback soon enough.

Sentiment, romance, humour and music were the basic ingredients in Dr Christian's entertainment prescription entitled **Melody For Three**. The beneficiaries of the doctor's good will on this occasion were a child prodigy and his divorced parents. Departing somewhat from the usual formula, screenwriters Lee Loeb and Walter Ferris concentrated on the domestic predicament of 12-year-old violinist Schuyler Standish, his music teacher mother (Fay Wray) and orchestra conductor father (Walter Woolf King, left). Christian (Jean Hersholt, centre) eventually finds a way to reunite the parents and, at the same time, give the young man a chance to exhibit his abundant talent. Erle C. Kenton directed this adroit chapter in the ongoing series. Astrid Allwyn, Andrew Tombes (right), Maude Eburne, Patsy Lee Parsons, Toscha Seidel, Irene Ryan, Elvia Allman, Irene Shirley, Donnie Allen, Leon Tyler and Cliff Nazarro were also present in William Stephens' production for Stephens-Lang.

The chief miscreants in **Robbers Of The Range** ▷ were land agents working in advance of the railroad for their own greedy interests. In Morton Grant and Arthur V. Jones' screenplay, Tim Holt (right) played a rancher framed on a murder charge by the crooks. In his battle to clear his name and bring the dastards to justice, Holt is helped by his regular comrades, Emmett Lynn and Ray Whitley. Virginia Vale (left), formerly George O'Brien's leading lady in six episodes of the O'Brien series, portrayed the romantic heroine for producer Bert Gilroy and director Edward Killy. Helping to make Oliver Drake's original story exciting were LeRoy Mason, Howard Hickman, Ernie Adams, Frank LaRue, Ray Bennett, Tom London, Ed Cassidy, Bud Osborne, George Melford, Malcolm McTaggart and Harry Harvey. Song: 'The Railroad's Coming To Town' Fred Rose, Ray Whitley.

Robert de Grasse's superior photography, the excellent art direction of Van Nest Polglase and Carroll Clark and a clever script by Ian McLellan Hunter and Bert Granet (story by Granet) were all chewed to pulp by the egregious overacting of Alan Mowbray (left) and Donald MacBride (right) in **Footlight Fever**. As always-busted but always-optimistic theatrical producers in the throes of mounting a Broadway show, Mowbray and MacBride spent more time mugging in the 70 minute picture than the Three Stooges did in a lifetime of similar activity. The pair, who had created the characters in *Curtain Call*, laid them to rest permanently in this $40,000 loser. Irving Reis' direction of the other players, especially Elisabeth Risdon, Elyse Knox (centre), Lee Bonnell and Charles Quigley was quite satisfactory, but he merited hearty censure for allowing the two principals to run wild. Bradley Page, Chester Clute, Jane Patten and Georgia Backus took secondary roles in the Howard Benedict ◁ production.

The Devil And Miss Jones, RKO's foremost comedy of 1941, was based on a witty Norman Krasna screenplay about the world's richest man (Charles Coburn, centre) who takes a lowly job in one of his own department stores and learns a good deal more than he expected in the process. Producer Frank Ross' wife, Jean Arthur (right), played a sincere shop girl who teaches Coburn a lesson in basic humanity, while Spring Byington (left) succeeds in awakening long-dormant romantic impulses in the tycoon. Sam Wood's spirited direction lost its punch during the last half hour, which was composed mostly of an unfocused melodramatic sub-plot centring on Robert Cummings' attempts to organize the store-workers into a union. Some judicious editing would have strengthened **Miss Jones**, but allowances must be made for a picture that contained as many superlative moments as this one did. Edmund Gwenn, S. Z. Sakall, William Demarest, Walter Kingsford, Montagu Love, Richard Carle and Charles Waldron gave bite to the character roles, and William Cameron Menzies supplied the stylish production design. Also cast: Edwin Maxwell, Edward McNamara, Robert Emmett Keane, Florence Bates, Charles Irwin, Matt McHugh, Julie Warren, Ilene Brewer, Regis Toomey and Pat Moriarty. Another co-production arrangement, the film made partners of RKO and Frank Ross-Norman Krasna Inc. ▽

While reminding its audience that love is more important than money, **Tom, Dick And Harry** earned profits of $234,000 – mainly thanks to the popularity of its leading lady, Ginger Rogers. Paul Jarrico wrote the cream puff script about a small-town Cinderella (Rogers, right) who cannot decide which of three attractive suitors – George Murphy (borrowed from MGM), Alan Marshal (borrowed from David O. Selznick) or Burgess Meredith – she should choose. She finally decides on the wealthy Prince Charming (Marshal) but changes her mind and takes off with Meredith (left), who makes bells ring (literally) when he kisses her. Director Garson Kanin, tongue firmly in cheek, decided to have some fun with cinematic fantasy, and the picture – overall a rather sickly sweet contrivance – did contain several finely etched moments of satire. Joe Cunningham, Jane Seymour, Lenore Lonergan, Vicki Lester, Phil Silvers and Betty Breckenridge filled out the cast. The picture, sadly, represented a triple *vale* for the studio: it was the last RKO film for 'B'-unit whiz producer Robert Sisk, who departed for Paramount following its completion; it was Garson Kanin's final picture before he entered military service; and it marked the end of Ginger Rogers' exclusive contract to the studio. With Ginger now entering the freelance market, RKO was in the disadvantageous position of having to compete with other powerhouse studios without a single important star under term contract. Jane Powell starred in a musical remake of the picture, called *The Girl Most Likely*, in 1956.

Cyclone On Horseback revealed the nefarious methods used by outlaws to sabotage a young contractor (Dennis Moore) attempting to complete a telephone line through wild, mountainous country. Young cattleman Tim Holt (right) comes to the aid of the beleaguered contractor, setting himself up for a series of the usual battles with fists, six-guns and dynamite. Bert Gilroy produced and Edward Killy directed this 'B'-level hymn to communications progress. Norton S. Parker's screenplay (original story by Tom Gibson) also gave employment to Marjorie Reynolds (left), Ray Whitley, Lee 'Lasses' White, Harry Worth, Eddie Dew, Monte Montague, Slim Whitaker, Max Wagner, John Dilson and Lew Kelly. Songs included: 'Bangtail', 'Tumbleweed Cowboy', 'Blue Nightfall' Fred Rose, Ray Whitley.

Walt Disney's **The Reluctant Dragon**, part live-action and part animation (illustrated), was basically a feature-length advertisement for the new Disney studio in Burbank, California. Robert Benchley conducted a tour of the facility for the cameras, with help from Donald Duck and others. Appended to the expedition was a silly animated tale about a pacifistic, tea-sipping dragon and his faint-hearted adversary, Sir Giles. Unlike Disney's previous undertakings, this *pot-pourri* had the look and feel of a 'quickie' churned out to help finance the expanding organization. Other human performers were Frances Gifford, Buddy Pepper, Nana Bryant, Claud Allister, Barnett Parker, Billy Lee, Florence Gill, Ward Kimball, Clarence Nash, Alan Ladd, Norm Ferguson, Hamilton MacFadden, Jimmy Luske and Maurice Murphy. Alfred Werker directed the live action from a screenplay by Ted Sears, Al Perkins, Larry Clemmons, Bill Cottrell and Harry Clork (the cartoon segment was adapted from a story by Kenneth Grahame). Frank Churchill and Larry Morey composed the musical score, and Technicolor was used for certain sequences. Song: 'The Reluctant Dragon' Charles Wolcott, Ed Penner & T. Hee.

The excitement of an elephant hunt, a close call with a man-eating tiger, battles with giant pythons and scraps between a wide variety of marauding beasts were on view in **Jungle Cavalcade**. Compiling the highlights of *Bring 'Em Back Alive*, *Wild Cargo* and *Fang And Claw*, great white hunter Frank Buck (illustrated) took audiences on a nostalgia safari back to the Malayan wilds. For those unfamiliar with the earlier pictures, this Best-of-Buck show was stimulating fare. Jay Bonafield edited the footage together, Nathaniel Shilkret was responsible for the musical direction and Phil Reisman Jr prepared the script. The narration was, of course, by Mr Buck.

Dr Christian turned amateur sleuth in **They Meet Again**. Spurred on by his instinctive feeling that a man who has been sent to prison for embezzlement is innocent, and his concern for the convict's opera-singing daughter who has a breakdown because of his absence, the River's End physician takes it upon himself to expose the real culprit. In spite of the inclusion of several songs, the un-original story by Peter Milne and screenplay by Milne and Maurice Leo, made this final edition of the Stephens-Lang chapter-play one of the most sluggish and uninvolving. As usual, Erle C. Kenton occupied the director's chair, Jean Hersholt (right) played the doctor, Dorothy Lovett his nurse Judy and Maude Eburne his astrologically-minded housekeeper. Robert Baldwin, Neil Hamilton, Anne Bennett (left), Barton Yarborough (centre), Arthur Hoyt, John Dilson, Frank Melton, Leon Tyler, Milton Kibbee, Gus Glassmire, Patsy Lee Parsons and Meredith Howard also appeared for producer William Stephens. Songs included: 'When Love Is New' Jack Owens, Claude Sweeten; 'In The Make Believe Land Of Dreams', 'Get Alive' Jack Owens; 'The Rhythm Is Red An' White An' Blue' David Gregory, Al Moss.

RKO's association with famed producer Samuel Goldwyn began on a high note with distribution of **The Little Foxes**, a picture meriting consideration as one of the finest adaptations of a stage play ever committed to celluloid. The source was Lillian Hellman's brooding, malignant drama of greed and treachery eating away at a genteel Southern family. William Wyler's impeccable direction gave free rein to the talents of Herbert Marshall (left), Teresa Wright, Richard Carlson, Dan Duryea and, especially, Bette Davis (right), who jolted Miss Hellman's characters to life in brilliant fashion. Although Tallulah Bankhead had created the central role of Regina Giddens on Broadway, the part seemed written for Davis, and she performed it with a relentless iciness that was heartstopping – and appropriate to the portrayal of a woman who, when her husband (who has refused her the money for a sordid business arrangement) has a coronary, stands back and allows him to die rather than fetch his medicine. It was one of the greatest achievements of a great actress. Patricia Collinge, Charles Dingle, Carl Benton Reid, John Marriott and Duryea all repeated their stage roles, and Jessie Grayson, Russell Hicks, Lucien Littlefield, Virginia Brissac, Terry Nibert, Henry 'Hot Shot' Thomas and Charles R. Moore were other cast members. Miss Hellman wrote the sulphuric screenplay with additional scenes and dialogue by Arthur Kober, Dorothy Parker and Alan Campbell, and Gregg Toland's deep-focus camerawork facilitated the stage to screen translation. Inspired by the Biblical reference to 'the little foxes which spoil the vines', the tale was cruel, cold and cynical but extraordinarily vivid and compelling. It towered above most of the other stabs at drama that issued from Hollywood studios during the year.

United Producers, an independent company set up by William Hawks and Ronald Colman, co-sponsored **My Life With Caroline** with RKO. Sadly, the finished film was a disappointment to both organizations. Based on a featherweight French play by Louis Verneuil and Georges Berr, the story required wealthy publisher Colman (left) to chase after dizzy Anna Lee (right, a British actress making her Hollywood film debut) who happens to be his wife. Her nincompoop logic suggests that Reginald Gardiner or Gilbert Roland may be a preferable mate, thus impelling the suave hero to woo her constantly while fending off Gardiner and Roland in what is supposed to be a battle of wits. It was, however, uniformly witless. Producer-director Lewis Milestone merited a substantial portion of the culpability, though writers John Van Druten and Arnold Belgard also deserved their fair share for a verbose and idiotic script. Charles Winninger, Katherine Leslie, Hugh O'Connell, Murray Alper and Matt Moore were also in it.

◁ **Hurry, Charlie, Hurry** was a string of two-reel comedy gags, loosely patched together by Luke Short's story and Paul Gerard Smith's screenplay. A henpecked husband involves himself in complications when he sneaks away on a fishing trip, but tells his wife that he will be visiting the vice-president of the US. Leon Errol (right), who had tried out every gag known to man (and then some) during his career, played the husband with Cecil Cunningham as the wife, Mildred Coles as their daughter, Kenneth Howell as a bakery wagon driver she wants to marry, George Watts as Errol's fishing companion and Eddie Conrad (centre left), Noble Johnson (left) and Lalo Encinas (centre right) as a trio of Indians he meets on the expedition. They show up later in his home, embarrassing their 'blood brother' in a variety of ways. Howard Benedict produced and Charles E. Roberts directed this demented nonsense. Also cast: Douglas Walton, Renee Haal and Georgia Caine.

The corn was as high as an elephant's eye in **Scattergood Meets Broadway**, the third of the Scattergood Baines movies. Scattergood (Guy Kibbee, left) goes to the big city when a young neighbour (William Henry) with playwriting ambitions finds himself the victim of White Way confidence men. The sage of Coldriver is almost trapped by the serio-comic slickers himself, but his old fashioned horse sense pulls him through and saves the young lad as well. Ethel B. Stone and Michael L. Simmons' screenplay was handled in wry, sympathetic fashion by director Christy Cabanne, who coaxed jocular performances from Kibbee, Frank Jenks and Bradley Page (as the unscrupulous Broadway producers), Joyce Compton (as a showgirl siren on the make) and Chester Clute (her 'sugar daddy'). The Pyramid Pictures production also featured Mildred Coles (right), Emma Dunn, Morgan Wallace, Carl Stockdale, Charlotte Walker, Paul White, Donald Brodie and Herbert Rawlinson. Jerrold T. Brandt was the producer. ▷

△ Just before the outbreak of World War II, Time Inc. was given permission to bring its 'March of Time' cameras into Vatican City. More than 30,000 feet of film were shot, yielding a feature-length documentary entitled **The Story Of The Vatican** (see illustration). Produced by Richard de Rochemont and written and narrated by noted Catholic churchman Fulton J. Sheen, the film depicted the ecclesiastical and civil life inside the tiny Papal state. The picture's biggest scoop was its intimate study of Pope Pius XII, but it also unveiled the palaces, halls and corridors of the Holy See, the Vatican library and Sistine Chapel, the Cathedral of St Peter's and the low vaulted crypts in which most of the Popes were buried. Though its box-office performance was diminutive, **The Story Of The Vatican** proved educational, reverent, and entertaining as well.

Now fully ensconced as the major-domo of RKO's outdoor pictures, producer Bert Gilroy steered another Tim Holt vehicle, **Six-Gun Gold**, to success. Tom Gibson's story and Norton S. Parker's screenplay opened with Holt (left), Ray Whitley and Lee 'Lasses' White riding into Placer City to surprise the hero's brother, who is the town marshal. They find a tough-looking gunman masquerading as the lawman, and no sign of the brother. Concealing his identity, Holt smokes out the bad guys, who are pilfering gold from the local miners, and rescues his sibling during the lead-slinging climax. Jan Clayton (right), LeRoy Mason, Eddy C. Waller, Fern Emmett, Davison Clark, Harry Harvey, Slim Whitaker, Lane Chandler and Jim Corey played other roles in the David Howard-directed oat-opera. Song: 'Six-Gun Gold' Fred Rose, Ray Whitley.

Gloria Swanson (left) returned to the screen, after ▷
a seven-year absence, in **Father Takes A Wife**, a
threadbare comedy produced by Lee Marcus and
scripted by Dorothy and Herbert Fields. Adolphe
Menjou (right), who had been a bit player at
Paramount when Miss Swanson was the queen of
the studio, received first billing as an aging
widower who falls head-over-heels in love with a
famous actress (Swanson). Menjou's big dilemma
is how to break the news to his stuffy, serious-
minded son (John Howard). Swanson showed no
signs of rustiness in her performance, but the
usually polished Menjou's impersonation of a man
entering his second childhood was lamentable, and
Jack Hively's plodding direction took the edge off
much of the intended humour. The silent film
star's choice for a comeback was ill-considered; its
box-office loss came to $104,000. Desi Arnaz,
Helen Broderick, Florence Rice, Neil Hamilton,
Grady Sutton, George Meador, Mary Treen and
Ruth Dietrich led the supporting cast.

After many months of pretending that all was
tranquil in the world, RKO finally faced the
realities of international trauma and began to make
war films and films dealing with national defence.
Parachute Battalion succeeded both as an educational and an inspirational study of airborne
training. With help from the Army, producer
Howard Benedict and director Leslie Goodwins
included authentic footage of the entire process –
from the careful folding of chutes to the actual
jumps. The plot, a superficial melo about recruits
who battle over the sergeant's daughter but
become loyal buddies in the air, provided the
fulcrum around which the documentary-style
footage revolved. Audiences did not seem to
mind; their curiosity about all things 'military'
brought in profits of $128,000. The original
screenplay by John Twist and Major Hugh Fite
gave Robert Preston, Nancy Kelly, Edmond
O'Brien (centre) and Harry Carey (right) the main
parts, and also required Buddy Ebsen, Paul Kelly
(left), Richard Cromwell, Robert Barrat, Edward
Fielding, Erville Alderson, Selmer Jackson, Grant
Withers, Jack Briggs, Walter Sande, Kathryn
Sheldon, Lee Bonnell, Robert Smith, Gayne
Whitman, Douglas Evans and Eddie Dunn to
complete the cast. Song: 'Parachute Battalion' Roy
Webb, Herman Ruby.
▽

◁**Lady Scarface** starred Judith Anderson (illustrated) of *Rebecca* fame, as a gang leader known
only as Slade and believed to be responsible for a
series of sensational robberies and murders in
metropolitan cities. The police have no suspicion
that Slade is a woman, who has turned master
criminal as a result of her bitterness over the
hideous scar which disfigures her face. Armand
D'Usseau and Richard Collins partially based their
screenplay on *Wanted! Jane Turner* (1936), and
director Frank Woodruff kept it hurtling along at
such a rapid pace that only the critically minded
noticed its complete lack of originality – the
novelty of a female Edward G. Robinson figure
notwithstanding. Also cast in the Cliff Reid
production: Dennis O'Keefe, Frances Neal,
Mildred Coles, Eric Blore, Marc Lawrence,
Damian O'Flynn, Andrew Tombes, Marion
Martin, Rand Brooks, Arthur Shields, Lee
Bonnell, Harry Burns and Horace MacMahon.

△

The Bandit Trail, an exceedingly inexpensive
Tim Holt western ($45,000 negative cost), still
contained the requisite amount of riding, fighting
and gunsmoke. Holt (right) played a youthful
cattleman who helps to rob a bank in order to gain
revenge on the unscrupulous banker who had
slapped a chiselling mortgage on his father's ranch.
Determined to make amends for his misstep, he
restores the stolen money and becomes a hero in
the little town of Remington, where he is elected
marshal. As usual, the Bert Gilroy production also
featured the comedy routines of Lee 'Lasses'
White and the cowboy warbling of Ray Whitley.
Norton S. Parker's script (story by Arthur T.
Horman) also gave roles to Janet Waldo (left),
Morris Ankrum, Roy Barcroft, J. Merrill Holmes,
Eddie Waller, Glenn Strange, Frank Ellis, Joseph
Eggenton, Guy Usher, Jack Clifford and Bud
Osborne. Director Edward Killy managed to cram
the action efficiently into the brief hour of screen
time usually allocated to this particular series.
Song: 'Outlaw Trail' Fred Rose, Ray Whitley.

The biggest programme-unit surprise of 1941 was **Look Who's Laughing**. Produced and directed by Allan Dwan, the film brought together several radio comedians – Edgar Bergen (right) with Charlie McCarthy (left), Fibber McGee and Molly (Jim and Marian Jordan), and J. Throckmorton Gildersleeve (Harold Peary) – in a nonsensical story about a small-town entrepreneur and his scheme to lure an aircraft factory into the vicinity. Released just after the Japanese bombing of Pearl Harbor, it had a certain topicality and lunatic attractiveness, but the precise reasons for the picture's sizeable box-office success must forever remain a mystery. Lucille Ball gave a standout performance as Bergen's secretary, and Lee Bonnell, Dorothy Lovett, Isabel Randolph, Walter Baldwin, Neil Hamilton, Charles Halton, Harlow Wilcox, Spencer Charters, Jed Prouty and George Cleveland completed the cast. James V. Kern typed out the story and screenplay, to which Don Quinn and Leonard L. Levinson contributed material for Fibber McGee and Molly, and Zeno Klinker and Dorothy Kingsley added material for Edgar Bergen.

Another Tay Garnett-produced bomb, **Weekend For Three** narrated the frustrations of a pair of newlyweds (Dennis O'Keefe, right, and Jane Wyatt, centre right) who are imposed upon by a playboy guest in no hurry to depart. Dorothy Parker and Alan Campbell, taking off from Budd Schulberg's original story, contributed a jocular parodic screenplay which Irving Reis nullified by his static and enervated direction. The final product had a few moments of high hilarity but too many others of leaden monotony. Philip Reed's (left) hyper-exaggerated performance as the obnoxious pest sealed the picture's doom. Also cast: Edward Everett Horton (centre left), ZaSu Pitts, Franklin Pangborn, Marion Martin, Hans Conried and Mady Lawrence. The waggish musical score by Roy Webb was deserving of a better picture.

World War II effectively put an end to the ▷ screwball comedy, making **Ball Of Fire** the last classic example of the genre. A riotous cultural collision about dead languages and live dishes, its script by Billy Wilder and Charles Brackett (based on a story by Wilder and Thomas Monroe) called on Gary Cooper to portray stuffy Bertram Potts, a linguistics professor involved with seven (dwarfish) colleagues in the preparation of an encyclopedia. During his research on modern expressions, he runs into hot-cha dancer Sugarpuss O'Shea (Barbara Stanwyck), a yum-yum type with underworld connections. She teaches him about slanguage and a few other things as well. Under the gung-ho direction of Howard Hawks, Cooper and Stanwyck were wonderful and the supporting players were equally fine – especially Dana Andrews as a gangster desperately needing to tie the knot with Stanwyck, Allen Jenkins as a chatty garbage man and Oscar Homolka, Henry Travers, S. Z. Sakall, Tully Marshall, Leonid Kinskey, Richard Haydn and Aubrey Mather as the seven academic colleagues. In addition to all the fun they were having, audiences learned the contemporary meanings of such phrases as 'hoytoytoy', 'hit the jiggles', 'jabber-wacky', 'squirrel fever', 'cooking with gas', 'chop-chop', 'smackeroo' and 'sucker for succotash'. What a way to get an education! Gregg Toland shot it, Alfred Newman composed the musical score and Edith Head designed Miss Stanwyck's striking costumes. Other members of independent producer Samuel Goldwyn's cast included Dan Duryea, Ralph Peters, Kathleen Howard, Mary Field, Charles Lane, Charles Arnt, Alan Rhein and Gene Krupa and his Orchestra. Song: 'Drum Boogie' Krupa. Illustration L to R: Henry Travers, Oscar Homolka, Gary Cooper, Leonid Kinskey (upper), Aubrey Mather, S. Z. Sakall, Richard Haydn, Tully Marshall, Barbara Stanwyck.

George Sanders (illustrated, borrowed from 20th Century-Fox) embarked on a new mystery series with **The Gay Falcon**. Leslie Charteris sued RKO after the picture's release, claiming that the Falcon was really the Saint with a few minor changes. He was not far off base, for screenwriters Lynn Root and Frank Fenton (story by Michael Arlen) incorporated many of the traits of Sanders' former persona in the new character, as well as adding touches of Don Juan and Philo Vance. Stylish, fast-paced and very funny, the film centred on the operations of a gang of jewel thieves, who are in collusion with some impoverished socialites to defraud insurance companies. The Falcon, who can't resist a pretty woman or an intriguing crime problem, unravels the mystery and rounds up the leader of the gang. Howard Benedict produced and Irving Reis directed with a supporting cast that included Wendy Barrie, Allen Jenkins, Anne Hunter, Gladys Cooper, Edward Brophy, Arthur Shields, Damian O'Flynn, Turhan Bey, Eddie Dunn, Lucile Gleason and Willie Fung. The film brought home profits of $108,000.

Bernard Herrmann's ominous music begins as the camera ventures past a wire fence complete with 'NO TRESPASSING' sign, across the grounds of a darkly imposing mansion and into the room of an exhausted old man who utters one cryptic word ('Rosebud') – and dies. A boy is seen through a closed window, playing with his sled in the snow while his parents and a lawyer cement the arrangement that will transfer responsibility for the child's upbringing from the mother and father to a financial concern. In a series of breakfast table vignettes, the growing gulf between a newspaper tycoon and his wife is shown, the couple moving further and further apart physically until they sit at opposite ends of a huge table, she reading a rival newspaper. These are among the scenes one remembers from **Citizen Kane**. There are dozens of others, equally memorable; taken together, they comprise the most audacious, iconoclastic jigsaw puzzle of a movie ever produced in Hollywood. Though he had many talented collaborators, Orson Welles was the major creative force behind the production. Recklessly combining expressionistic, deep-focus photography (by Gregg Toland), a complex plot structure that utilized five narrators, the most inventive manipulation of sound heretofore attempted in a motion picture and a cluster of radio and stage actors, most of whom had never performed in front of a camera, Welles made a film about egomania and unnatural obsession that stripped bare the American love affair with power and materialism, and revealed the emptiness within. Gossip columnist Louella Parsons believed that Charles Foster Kane, the protagonist, was just a thinly-veiled, slanderous portrait of her boss, William Randolph Hearst. As a consequence, the Hearst newspapers declared war on RKO, disrupting the film's release and damaging its box-office performance. Critics tried to help, working overtime to come up with proper words of appreciation for the extraordinary achievement, but it still ended up a $160,000 loser (subsequent re-issues brought it into the black). However, no American motion picture (with the possible exception of *The Birth Of A Nation*) has had more lasting influence; indeed, a poll of international critics conducted by the highly-respected British film journal *Sight and Sound* in 1971 named it the best picture of all time. Besides producing, directing and playing the role of Kane, Welles (illustrated) deserved his co-authorship credit (with Herman J. Mankiewicz) on the screenplay. Film critic Pauline Kael argues otherwise in a 50,000 word essay on the subject, but her case against Welles is one-sided and unsupported by the facts. Also cast: Joseph Cotten, Dorothy Comingore, Agnes Moorehead, Ruth Warrick, Ray Collins, Erskine Sanford, Everett Sloane, William Alland, Paul Stewart, George Coulouris, Fortunio Bonanova, Gus Schilling, Philip Van Zandt, Georgia Backus, Harry Shannon, Sonny Bupp and Buddy Swan. Robert Wise edited, Vernon L. Walker supervised the special effects, Van Nest Polglase and Perry Ferguson designed, and John Aalberg took charge of sound. RKO co-produced with Welles' Mercury Productions company. 'It's Terrific!' boasted the ads for **Citizen Kane**; for once, the hype was an understatement. ▷

All That Money Can Buy, based on Stephen Vincent Benet's *The Devil And Daniel Webster*, was the first fruit of an independent deal between RKO and William Dieterle Productions. Working with a moderate budget and no major stars, producer-director Dieterle turned out a sly and provocative tall tale featuring a bravura performance by Walter Huston (replacing Thomas Mitchell who was injured at the beginning of production). Huston (left) played Mr Scratch, the seductive devil who gets his hooks into the soul of a countrified Faust (James Craig, right, as Jabez Stone. Coming to the rescue at the last moment is Daniel Webster (Edward Arnold, centre), whose oration about freedom, suffering and American ideals wins over a jury of treacherous ghosts, thus saving Jabez and underscoring the general mood of the nation in 1941. Visually the film was a feast, with Joseph August's chiaroscuro camerawork and Vernon L. Walker's stunning special effects combining to suggest a demonic underbelly to the stolid New England setting. Dan Totheroh and Benet wrote the eloquent screenplay, Bernard Herrmann composed the Oscar-winning score, and Charles L. Glett laboured as Dieterle's associate producer. Helping to make it altogether satisfying (although it lost $53,000 on its initial run) were Jane Darwell, Simone Simon, Gene Lockhart, John Qualen, Anne Shirley, H. B. Warner, Frank Conlan, Lindy Wade and George Cleveland.

◁ As dictated by the fractured logic that governed the entire series, **The Mexican Spitfire's Baby** turned out to be voluptuous Marion Martin, a French war orphan imported by Uncle Matt (Leon Errol, centre) in an attempt to calm the discord between his nephew (Charles 'Buddy' Rogers, left, replacing Donald Woods who had played the role in previous editions) and explosive niece (Lupe Velez, right). In due course, Miss Martin's jealous and belligerent fiancé (Fritz Feld) arrives on the scene, anxious to fight a duel with all comers. Director Leslie Goodwins piloted this scrambled domestic farce, resisting the temptation to slow it down to even a moderate pace. Jerry Cady and Charles E. Roberts dreamed up the zany screenplay for producer Cliff Reid. Also cast: ZaSu Pitts, Elisabeth Risdon, Lloyd Corrigan, Lydia Bilbrook and Jack Arnold.

Tay Garnett, whose luck at RKO had always been bad and showed no signs of improving, produced **Unexpected Uncle**. A Capraesque fable about a former tycoon (Charles Coburn, right) who forsakes his millions in order to preach the gospel of happiness, it zig-zagged back and forth between farce and pathos to confusing and tedious effect. The Delmer Daves-Noel Langley screenplay, based on a novel by Eric Hatch, was the main problem, but Peter Godfrey's jagged direction compounded the crime. Others martyred by this $195,000 loser: Anne Shirley (left), James Craig, Ernest Truex, Renee Haal, Russell Gleason, Astrid Allwyn and Jed Prouty.

Unlike *The Reluctant Dragon*, **Dumbo** (see illustration) had the wit, polish and visual panache one expected from a Walt Disney production. Based on the book by Helen Aberson and Harold Pearl, the story of the baby pachyderm born with sail-like ears was populated with a plethora of memorable characters: Dumbo's gentle mother, Mrs Jumbo; the addle-pated stork who delivers Dumbo; the formidable social leaders of the elephant clique, including the Matriarch, Giggles, Prissy and Catty; the raggle-taggle crows who teach Dumbo to use his ears for flying; the bellowing, pompous ringmaster; and a mighty mite known as Timothy Q. Mouse who befriends the title character after he has been deserted by his own kind. The film contained several dazzling sequences. Among them was the justly famous 'Pink Elephants on Parade', a champagne-induced nightmare nearly unmatched as a piece of native American surrealism. Ben Sharpsteen was the supervising director and Joe Grant and Dick Huemer wrote the screenplay. Norman Ferguson, Wilfred Jackson, Bill Roberts, Jack Kinney and Sam Armstrong served as sequence directors; Vladimir Tytla, Fred Moore, Ward Kimball, John Lounsbery, Art Babbitt and Wolfgang Reitherman were the animation directors. Oliver Wallace contributed to the musical score. Songs included: 'When I See An Elephant Fly', 'Look Out For Mr Stork', 'Baby Mine', 'Song Of The Roustabouts', 'Pink Elephants' Ned Washington, Frank Churchill.

The kidnapping of a US government engraver by counterfeiters who force him to print illegal money, catapulted Tim Holt back into action in **Dude Cowboy**. With the aid of buddies Lee 'Lasses' White and Ray Whitley, Treasury agent Holt (right) eventually locates the missing man, who has been imprisoned in an abandoned mine, and discovers that the gang is using the gambling tables of a dude ranch to unload the phony money on unsuspecting tourists. Byron Foulger as the engraver, Marjorie Reynolds as Foulger's daughter and Holt's romantic foil, and Eddie Kane and Eddie Dew as the major felons turned in solid work in support of the series regulars. Bert Gilroy produced and David Howard directed from Morton Grant's story and screenplay, and Louise Currie (left), Helen Holmes, Tom London, Lloyd Ingraham and Glenn Strange were also in it. Songs included: 'Silver Rio', 'Dude Cowboy', 'End Of The Canyon Trail', 'Echo Singing In The Wild Wind' Fred Rose, Ray Whitley.

After sitting on a studio shelf for six years, *Before The Fact*, an unusual novel by British author Francis Iles (a pseudonym for Anthony Berkeley Cox) was taken down, dusted off, and became Alfred Hitchcock's **Suspicion**. The story – of a woman (Joan Fontaine, borrowed, with Hitchcock, from David O. Selznick) who surmises that her ne'er-do-well husband (Cary Grant) is a murderer plotting her own demise – provided Hitchcock with ample opportunities to put audiences through his suspenseful wringer. Indulging in flashy, expressionistic lighting effects, the director created a spider's web of paranoia and helplessness, placing his heroine directly in the centre. The screenplay by Samson Raphaelson, Joan Harrison and Alma Reville (Hitchcock's wife) changed the novel's ending, making the husband a villain only in his wife's imagination. This was done at the director's insistence, though in later years he often protested that the RKO brass had forced him to employ this decidedly unconvincing coda. Though **Suspicion** was a flawed work from a generally brilliant filmmaker, its ripple-effects were significant: it won Joan Fontaine (right) an Oscar as Best Actress of 1941 (some said she received the award because the Academy had passed over her performance in *Rebecca* the years before); it began a long and fertile association between Hitchcock and Cary Grant (left); and it earned a profit of $440,000, which was a great relief to company executives fearful that the picture's high negative cost could never be recouped. Sir Cedric Hardwicke, Dame May Whitty, Heather Angel, Isabel Jeans, Auriol Lee, Reginald Sheffield, Leo G. Carroll, and Nigel Bruce (as the irresistible Beaky) comprised the distinguished supporting cast. Franz Waxman composed the menacing music, and Harry Stradling was responsible for the provocative cinematography.

The final impudent gesture of the 1941 cinema was **Playmates**. Essentially a Kay Kyser vehicle, the film exploited poor John Barrymore who was nearing the end. Barrymore bellowed and hammed throughout, caricaturing himself pathetically as a has-been actor making a comeback through the adaptation of Shakespeare to swing music. As if the sad spectacle of a burned-out Barrymore (right) and the vulgarization of the Bard were not enough, Lupe Velez (centre) dropped by to add her manic slapstick to Kyser's (left) patented buffoonery. Mortifying mishmash are the only words that come close to describing the final result. David Butler produced and directed, using Ginny Simms, May Robson, Patsy Kelly, Peter Lind Hayes, George Cleveland, Alice Fleming and Kyser's Band, featuring – as was usual in Kyser movies – Harry Babbitt, Ish Kabibble and Sully Mason, to fill out the cast. James V. Kern wrote the screenplay from a story by himself and M. M. Musselman, with additional dialogue by Arthur Phillips. Songs included: 'Romeo Smith And Juliet Jones', 'Thank Your Lucky Stars And Stripes', 'Que Chica', 'Humpty Dumpty Heart', 'How Long Did I Dream?' Jimmy Van Heusen, Johnny Burke.

For RKO, 1942 was a dizzying and dramatic year; for president George J. Schaefer, the first half of it was a long and relentless nightmare. Beginning with the institution of trade show selling of motion pictures in August 1941, the production arm of the corporation lost money every month until Schaefer tendered his resignation in June of 1942. Incredibly, the entire company was close to receivership by that time. Only the intervention of Floyd Odlum and one of the fastest turnarounds in the annals of show business kept the enterprise afloat.

The man responsible for the turnaround was Charles Koerner, who replaced Joseph Breen as production head in March. Koerner's background in exhibition gave him a firm sense of what the public wanted to see. Under his aegis, RKO pictures prospered as never before (and never again) in the studio's history.

The revolving door on Gower Street whirled at a giddy pace throughout the year. Before Schaefer departed, long-time studio manager Sid Rogell was fired, and J. R. McDonough ('B'-unit supervisor) and Sol Lesser (in charge of 'A' pictures) both quit. Producers Cliff Reid, Howard Benedict, William Hawks, Gabriel Pascal and Jed Harris also exited; the last two had not gotten a picture off the ground during their abbreviated stay at RKO. Even more controversial was Koerner's dismissal of Orson Welles' Mercury Theatre contingent, and his decision to scrap a film by Pare Lorentz called *Name, Age and Occupation* in mid-production. Though film historians have often vilified Koerner for his treatment of these two men, he had little choice in his actions. If RKO was to survive, Koerner had to think commercially.

Lou Ostrow was employed to superintend the 'B' pictures, and Koerner brought Joe Nolan back to handle talent commitments, rehired Sid Rogell, and engaged Val Lewton, formerly David O. Selznick's story editor, to produce a series of low-budget horror films. Odlum representative N. Peter Rathvon succeeded Schaefer as president of Radio-Keith-Orpheum, and Ned Depinet was rewarded for years of diligent service with the presidency of RKO Radio Pictures.

By the end of the year, the financial crisis was over. Odlum had secured a $3 million loan to pull the studio through its zero hour and Koerner's pictures were already beginning to show exceptional profits. Thanks to excellent earnings from its theatre subsidiary, the corporation was able to report a profit of $736,241 for the year, despite $2,340,617 in losses posted by RKO Radio Pictures.

Seven Days Leave and **The Navy Comes Through** were the top earners. Goldwyn's **Pride Of The Yankees** and Disney's **Bambi** brought in even more box office, but were distributed at a loss by RKO. Thirty nine films were released that year.

The Pride Of The Yankees was precisely the type of picture on which Samuel Goldwyn had built a reputation as Hollywood's top prestige producer. Eloquently written by Herman J. Mankiewicz and Jo Swerling (from a story by Paul Gallico), beautifully photographed by Rudolph Maté, tastefully designed by William Cameron Menzies, movingly directed by Sam Wood and superbly acted by Gary Cooper (right), Teresa Wright, Walter Brennan, Dan Duryea and others, the film was a major league effort from first frame to last. This sweetly sentimental biography chronicled the life of New York Yankee first baseman Lou Gehrig from its homey beginnings through his awkward – but ultimately lovely – romance with his wife Eleanor, to the enormously moving day in 1939 when, knowing that his life was almost over because of an incurable disease, Gehrig stood at home plate and spoke to his fans: 'People all say I've had a bad break. But today – today I consider myself the luckiest man on the face of the earth'. The message was inspirational to Americans filled with tension over their own uncertain futures. One element that may have annoyed diehard fans was the relative paucity of baseball footage in a story about a man who played 2130 consecutive big league games. But this was necessitated by Cooper's limited ability with bat and glove, and partially compensated for by the appearances of real-life ball players Babe Ruth (left), Bill Dickey, Mark Koenig and Bob Meusel. Also cast: Veloz and Yolanda, Elsa Janssen, Ludwig Stossel, Virginia Gilmore, Ernie Adams, Pierre Watkin, Harry Harvey, Bill Stern, Addison Richards, Hardie Albright, Edward Fielding, George Lessey, Edgar Barrier, Douglas Croft, Gene Collins, David Holt and Ray Noble and his Orchestra. Song: 'Always' Irving Berlin.

△

Call Out The Marines reunited Victor McLaglen (left) and Edmund Lowe (right) in a frolicsome service comedy. Years before, McLaglen and Lowe had played a pair of rowdies named Flagg and Quirt in a series of pictures with a World War I backdrop. Howard Benedict's production was simply an updated version of the old films, using the second global conflict as the setting and new names (McGinnis and Curtis) for the characters. Though ostensibly topical, the Frank Ryan-William Hamilton screenplay had nothing to do with the real military or the real war, being a spy romp about the sergeants' involvement with a waterfront Mata Hari (Binnie Barnes), enlivened by plenty of cussing and brawling and a few Mort Greene-Harry Revel songs. The studio contemplated this as the first of a new series, but abandoned the idea even though the picture made a small profit. Scripters Ryan and Hamilton co-directed, utilizing Paul Kelly, Robert Smith, Dorothy Lovett, Franklin Pangborn, Corinna Mura, George Cleveland, The King's Men, and Six Hits and a Miss in support. Songs included: 'Zana Zaranda', 'Call Out The Marines', 'The Light Of My Life', 'Beware', 'Hands Across The Border'.

George Sanders (right, borrowed from 20th ▷
Century-Fox) left his bride-to-be Wendy Barrie
(first centre right) fuming while he investigated the
kidnapping of a brilliant scientist in **A Date With
The Falcon**. The scientist has invented a process
for making synthetic diamonds, badly needed in
defence manufacturing; a gang of crooks has
abducted him in order to obtain the formula and
reap a fortune. Lynn Root and Frank Fenton's
screenplay determined that the suave sleuth would
allow himself to be captured by the gang, working
out the rescue of the scientist and the collaring of
the lawbreakers from there. RKO veteran James
Gleason (first centre left) played police lieutenant
O'Hara, a character similar in nature to Inspector
Oscar Piper of the now defunct Hildegarde
Withers series. Other notable performances were
rendered by Allen Jenkins (second centre right) as
the Falcon's jittery handyman, Alec Craig (left) as
the inventor and Mona Maris and Victor Kilian as
the villains. Howard Benedict produced, Irving
Reis directed and Frank Moran, Russ Clark,
Edward Gargan (second centre left), Eddie Dunn,
Frank Martinelli and an unbilled Hans Conried
were also cast.

△
Valley Of The Sun, RKO's first major western in
many years, was big only in terms of budget
($646,000). Screenwriter Horace McCoy (basing
his scenario on a *Saturday Evening Post* story by
Clarence Budington Kelland) and director George
Marshall seemed unable to decide if the film
should be serious or frivolous. As it turned out, it
was merely silly. Marshall had done a masterful
job of marrying farce to the classical conventions
of the genre in Universal's *Destry Rides Again*
(1939), but this time his attempts went awry. The
plot brought 'discredited' Army scout James Craig
(centre left) into conflict with evil government
agent Dean Jagger over the wooing of Arizona
maiden Lucille Ball (centre right), and over
Jagger's treatment of the local Indians. The main
actors, plus Sir Cedric Hardwicke, Peter Whitney,
Billy Gilbert (left), George Cleveland, Hank Bell,
Tom Tyler as Geronimo and Antonio Moreno as
Cochise, appeared to be constantly off balance in a
saga that contained bloody action on the one hand
and Kay Kyser-ish japes on the other. This
Graham Baker production lost $158,000 at the
paybox window.

An updated remake of *Street Girl* (1929) and *That* ▷
Girl From Paris (1937), **Four Jacks And A Jill**
found Ray Bolger, Eddie Foy Jr, Jack Briggs and
William Blees as nightclub musicians who are left
without a singer when torchy June Havoc retires at
the behest of gangster Jack Durant. Bolger (centre
right) digs up Anne Shirley (left) as a substitute,
leading to laboured complications created primarily by Shirley admirer Desi Arnaz's masquerade
as a fugitive king. Shirley, Bolger, Havoc and
Arnaz (centre left) all had moments of distinction,
but the picture was rather dismal on the whole.
Audiences failed to be diverted by this undistinguished musical, and it finished its run
$113,000 in the red. Producer John Twist based
his screenplay on a story by Monte Brice which
was, in turn, suggested by W. Carey Wonderly's
The Viennese Charmer. Director Jack Hively also
cast Fritz Feld, Henry Daniell (right), Robert
Smith and Fortunio Bonanova. Songs included:
'I'm In Good Shape For The Shape I'm In', 'You
Go Your Way And I'll Go Crazy', 'I Haven't A
Thing To Wear', 'Wherever You Are', 'Boogie
Woogie Conga' Mort Greene, Harry Revel.

Paul Henreid (left) and Michele Morgan (right)
made their American film debuts in **Joan Of
Paris**, an anti-Nazi drama that was one of RKO's
best efforts of the year. The story focused on a
Parisian barmaid (Morgan) who sacrifices her life
to aid a Free French flyer (Henreid) and his four
RAF companions in their escape from Gestapo-
controlled France. The girl's patron saint who
guides and moulds her destiny is, of course, Jeanne
D'Arc. Director Robert Stevenson handled
Charles Bennett and Ellis St Joseph's screenplay
(story Jacques Thery and Georges Kessel) with
discretion, using a realistic approach without
compromising the romantic and suspenseful thrust
of the action. Michele Morgan gave a poignant
performance, and Thomas Mitchell (as a French
priest) and May Robson (a British agent) also
contributed adroit characterizations. Although the
work of the Paris Underground remained largely
a mystery to Americans at this point in the war,
Joan Of Paris grasped what was going on and
dramatized it in moving fashion. Laird Cregar,
Alexander Granach, Jack Briggs, James Monks,
Richard Fraser, Paul Weigel, John Abbott, and
Alan Ladd (in a small role as an RAF flyer)
completed producer David Hempstead's cast. At
$666,000, the picture's cost was an inflated one,
◁ but it still managed a respectable profit.

Sing Your Worries Away was 80 minutes of
moth-eaten nonsense, awkwardly constructed
around a goofy songwriter (Bert Lahr, left) who
receives the big heat from mobsters bent on
appropriating his inheritance. The injection of
tunes by Mort Greene and Harry Revel, and
singing and dancing by the talented Buddy Ebsen
(right), June Havoc, Patsy Kelly and others failed
to raise this conglomeration above the incompetence level. Cliff Reid produced, A. Edward
Sutherland directed and Monte Brice penned the
screenplay from a story by Erwin Gelsey and
Charles E. Roberts (based on an idea by Charles S.
Belden). Dorothy Lovett, Sam Levene, Margaret
Dumont, Morgan Conway, Fortunio Bonanova,
Don Barclay, Russ Clark, Sammy Stein, and
Alvino Rey and his Orchestra with the King
Sisters, also put in appearances. The title was
perversely ironic; pictures like this one (company
loss $255,000) were causing president George J.
Schaefer nothing but worry. Songs included
'Cindy Lou McWilliams', 'It Just Happens To
Happen', 'Nothing Can Change My Mind', 'Sing
Your Worries Away'.
▽

Set in the Pacific southwest in 1890, **Riding The Wind** chronicled the plight of a group of ranchers faced with ruin when a land owner builds a dam across a river and shuts off the water supply to the grazing land. Tim Holt (left) led the fight against the unscrupulous schemer who demands an exorbitant price for the water rights. Morton Grant and Earle Snell's trite script (based on a story by Bernard McConville), and Edward Killy's boring direction made this one of the least inspiring of the Bert Gilroy-produced Holt adventures. Ray Whitley and Lee 'Lasses' White were again in attendance, with Mary Douglas, Eddie Dew (the man with the dam), Ernie Adams, Earle Hodgins, Kate Harrington, Charles Phipps, Bud Osborne, Karl Hackett, Hank Worden and Larry Steers also cast. Songs included: 'Ridin' The Wind', 'I'll Live Until I Die', 'Goin' On A Hayride Tonight' Fred Rose, Ray Whitley.

RKO began to distribute **Fantasia** in 1942, though there had been roadshow engagements handled by the Walt Disney organization beginning in 1940. The picture was an audacious experiment – the attempt by an innovative American genius to wed his art to the music of such masters as Bach, Tchaikovsky, Stravinsky, Beethoven, Mussorgsky and Schubert. It grew out of Disney's decision to make a version of 'The Sorcerer's Apprentice' (by Paul Dukas) featuring Mickey Mouse (illustrated) in the title role, and also contained portions of Tchaikovsky's 'Nutcracker Suite', brought to life by fairies and all manner of animated flora and fauna, Stravinsky's revolutionary 'Rite of Spring' interpreted as the creation and evolution of the world, and Mussorgsky's 'Night On A Bald Mountain', an orgy of Satanic creatures that is snuffed out by the ringing of church bells and the strains of Schubert's 'Ave Maria'. The critical appraisal of the film remains as divided today as it was when it first appeared. One camp accepts the picture as a major work of art, pointing to its continuous rediscovery as evidence of its aural and graphic dynamism. The other side believes that Disney's prancing toadstools and other 'cute' creations are an insult to the classical music which they illustrate – an appropriate example of American philistinism and corruption of the arts. The Philadelphia Orchestra (conducted by Leopold Stokowski, who also appeared in the film) performed the music. Ben Sharpsteen was the production supervisor; Joe Grant and Dick Huemer took charge of story direction; and Samuel Armstrong, James Algar, Bill Roberts, Paul Satterfield, Hamilton Luske, Jim Handley, Ford Beebe, T. Hee, Norm Ferguson and Wilfred Jackson worked as animation directors. It was shot in multiplane Technicolor and recorded with the advanced RCA Fantasound System, under the supervision of William E. Garity, C. O. Slyfield and J. N. A. Hawkins. Musical selections also included Bach's Toccata And Fugue In D Minor, Beethoven's Sixth Symphony and Ponchielli's 'Dance Of The Hours'.

Provoking another unanimous yawn at the box-office was **Obliging Young Lady**, produced by Howard Benedict from Arthur T. Horman's story. Nine-year-old Joan Carroll (left) played the pivotal role of a child who is spirited away by secretary Ruth Warrick (centre) who hopes the disappearance will reunite the precocious youngster's divorcing parents (John Miljan and Marjorie Gateson). Frank Ryan and Bert Granet's screenplay soon bogged down into one long, extended chase, ornamented with numerous romantic complications. Director Richard Wallace was more attentive to camera gimmickry than to the performances of his actors; these varied from pleasing (Edmond O'Brien and Eve Arden having fun as two rival newspaper reporters) to wooden (Miss Warrick, a *Citizen Kane* discovery, seemed a veritable oak plank). Also cast: Robert Smith (right), Franklin Pangborn, George Cleveland, Luis Alberni, Charles Lane, Fortunio Bonanova, Andrew Tombes, Almira Sessions, Pierre Watkin, Florence Gill, Sidney Blackmer, Virginia Engels, George Watts, Jed Prouty and George Chandler.

◁**Mexican Spitfire At Sea** was set on an ocean liner bound for Hawaii. Otherwise it was just a worn out rehash of stock Spitfire situations with advertising executive Charles 'Buddy' Rogers (right) trying to land a contract from a wealthy passenger. En route he has to reckon with his jealous, choleric wife (Lupe Velez, left), his blundering uncle (Leon Errol, again finding an excuse to masquerade as a British nobleman), and a bunch of madcap relatives who have accompanied him on what they imagine will be a lovely vacation. Cliff Reid produced and Leslie Goodwins directed, with ZaSu Pitts, Elisabeth Risdon, Florence Bates, Marion Martin, Lydia Bilbrook, Eddie Dunn, Harry Holman and Marten Lamont also on board. Jerry Cady and Charles E. Roberts wrote the redundant screenplay.

In **Land Of The Open Range**, Tim Holt played a deputy sheriff faced with maintaining order when an old scoundrel leaves a will stipulating that his 64,000 acre ranch will be open for homesteading by men who can prove they are ex-convicts. The town is soon full of plug-uglies, keeping Holt (centre), Ray Whitley (left) and Lee 'Lasses' White (right) busy sorting out the 'honest' crooks from the troublemakers. Producer Bert Gilroy and director Edward Killy took the opportunity to insert some of the out-takes shot for the famous landrush sequence in *Cimarron*, thereby upgrading the production values of this $49,000 programmer immensely. Cinematographer Harry Wild and editor Frederic Knudtson also deserved plaudits for cleverly blending new footage with old. Morton Grant's screenplay, based on Lee Bond's story *Homesteads Of Hate*, also spotlighted Janet Waldo, Hobart Cavanaugh, Lee Bonnell, Roy Barcroft, John Elliott, Frank Ellis, Tom London and J. Merrill Holmes. Songs included: 'Land Of The Open Range', 'KI-O' Fred Rose, Ray Whitley.

Made in England by RKO Radio British Productions, **Suicide Squadron** (GB: **Dangerous Moonlight**) starred Anton Walbrook as a Polish composer-pianist tricked into fleeing his native land by comrades who remain behind to die. Walbrook (right) meets and falls in love with American journalist Sally Gray (left), but decides to enlist in a Polish air squadron in England following a hectic honeymoon with her. Director Brian Desmond Hurst's most exciting sequences were aerial in nature, filmed from the noses of fighter planes in actual combat. Otherwise, the film was a routine drama in which Walbrook weighed the relative importance of music, patriotism and love in his life, and made his decisions accordingly. The screenplay was by director Hurst, Shaun Terence Young and Rodney Ackland, from a story by Young. Among the large cast were Derrick de Marney, Cecil Parker, Percy Parsons, Kenneth Kent, Guy Middleton, John Laurie, Frederick Valk, Marion Spencer, Lesley Gordon, Philip Friend, Bob Beatty, Conway Palmer, Cynthia Heppner, Alan Keith and Michael Rennie. RKO officials felt that producer William Sistrom's picture had very limited domestic potential and leased American distribution rights to Republic Pictures for a restricted period ending in 1947. The most enduring element in the film was Richard Addinsell's score which included the famous 'Warsaw Concerto'.

Scattergood Baines (Guy Kibbee, right) bet on ▷ human nature and won in **Scattergood Rides High**. The object of the Coldriver wizard's venture is the orphaned son of an old friend. Deprived of his inheritance – the racing stable and farm which his family had operated for years – the boy is still determined to pursue a career with trotting champions. Scattergood backs him, noting that he would rather invest in human nature than in anything else. RKO's investment in this series was another matter altogether, for audiences were turning off to Scattergood and his ever-bubbling cauldron of wise and wonderful advice. Michael L. Simmons wrote the screenplay which Christy Cabanne directed for producer Jerrold T. Brandt. Charles Lind (as the plucky orphan), Jed Prouty, Dorothy Moore (left), Kenneth Howell, Regina Wallace, Frances Carson, Arthur Aylesworth, Paul White, Philip Hurlic, Walter S. Baldwin Jr and Lee Phelps were Kibbee's main supporters. RKO distributed for the Pyramid Pictures Corporation.

The principal strength of **The Falcon Takes Over** came from its source – the Raymond Chandler classic *Farewell, My Lovely*. Working on a limited budget and shooting schedule, producer Howard Benedict and director Irving Reis were unable to do full justice to the ingenious tale of Moose Malloy and his quest for his beloved Velma. As the man who decides to help Moose locate his lost love, the Falcon (George Sanders, left, borrowed from 20th Century-Fox) made an acceptable substitute for Chandler's Philip Marlowe, and Ward Bond provided an appropriately goonish Moose Malloy; still, much of the resonance of the story got lost in the rush to tie everything up neatly in 67 minutes. Lynn Root and Frank Fenton wrote the serviceable screenplay, and Lynn Bari (also borrowed from 20th Century-Fox), James Gleason, Allen Jenkins (right), Helen Gilbert, Edward Gargan, Anne Revere, George Cleveland, Harry Shannon and Hans Conried were other cast members. The private eye tale proved itself in two later, more expensive and better known versions under the original title. One, starring Dick Powell and made in 1945, was also known as *Murder My Sweet*; the ◁ other, made in 1975, starred Robert Mitchum.

◁ **The Bashful Bachelor**, the second Lum and Abner vehicle, contained no youthful romance and no serious drama of any kind – nothing but running gags developed around the two Ozark storekeepers. Chandler Sprague's screenplay, based on an original story by the two stars, found Lum (Chester Lauck, right) attempting to become a hero in the eyes of ZaSu Pitts (centre) by using Abner (Norris Goff, left) as the victim of a series of incidents designed to demonstrate Lum's bravery. Director Malcolm St Clair coped well enough with the asinine plot, manufacturing more guffaws out of it than anyone could have reasonably expected. Grady Sutton, Oscar O'Shea, Louise Currie, Constance Purdy, Irving Bacon, Earle Hodgins and Benny Rubin also performed in the Voco Production, supervised by Jack William Votion.

◁ **The Tuttles Of Tahiti** was reminiscent of Kaufman and Hart's *You Can't Take It With You*. Charles Laughton received top billing as the patriarch of an improvident, prolific part-Tahitian family who eat, drink and make merry – for tomorrow they can always borrow from a friend. Among the sources of Tuttle woe are cock fights, checking accounts and a fishing boat that always runs out of gas just as they are about to haul in a stupendous catch. The rivalry between Laughton (left) and Florence Bates, the head of a prosperous neighbouring clan, motivated much of the action, while Laughton's son (Jon Hall, right, borrowed from Samuel Goldwyn) and Bates' daughter (Peggy Drake) furnished the romance. Though congenial in a trifling sort of way, the film's swollen cost ($847,000) doomed it to commercial failure. *No More Gas*, a novel by *Mutiny On The Bounty* authors Charles Nordhoff and James Norman Hall, supplied the basic story which James Hilton adapted and S. Lewis Meltzer and Robert Carson scripted. The director was Charles Vidor (on loan from Columbia), and it was produced by Sol Lesser, who stayed on at RKO to complete the film after handing in his resignation as executive producer for 'A'-budget films. Also in the cast: Victor Francen, Gene Reynolds, Curt Bois, Adeline de Walt Reynolds, Mala, Leonard Sues, Jody Gilbert, Tommy Cook and Jack Carr.

Victor McLaglen, Edmond O'Brien, June Havoc and Dorothy Lovett were the chief inhabitants of **Powder Town**. Based on an original idea by Vicki Baum and a novel by Max Brand, the David Boehm screenplay placed moony scientist O'Brien (left) in the employ of a giant munitions enterprise honeycombed with saboteurs. After McLaglen (centre right) is assigned to guard him, O'Brien falls foul of all manner of fiends interested in a formula he has developed which can blow an army into atoms. Rowland V. Lee directed this confusing box-office misfire for producer Cliff Reid. Also cast: Eddie Foy Jr (centre left), Damian O'Flynn, Marten Lamont, Roy Gordon, Marion Martin, Mary Gordon, Frances Neal, Julie Warren, Jane Woodworth, George Cleveland, John Maguire (formerly McGuire) and Frank Mills (right). 'B'-unit head J. R. McDonough, who launched the production, had exited from RKO by the time it was released.

Except for its title, **Syncopation** had nothing whatever in common with RKO's premiere 1929 release. Utilizing a story about a gal from New Orleans (Bonita Granville, left) and a guy from Chicago (Jackie Cooper, centre) who are obsessed with jazz, producer-director William Dieterle attempted to dissect that American musical phenomenon during its formative period. The endeavour was surprisingly unsuccessful; slow, stiffly formal and uneven, the picture completely missed the rhythmical spirit promised by its title. Adolphe Menjou received first billing as Miss Granville's architect father, and the supporting performances came from George Bancroft, Ted North, Todd Duncan, Connie Boswell, Frank Jenks (right), Jessie Grayson, Mona Barrie, Lindy Wade, Peggy McIntyre, the Hall Johnson Choir and the All-American Dance Band featuring Benny Goodman, Harry James and Gene Krupa. Philip Yordan and Frank Cavett collaborated on the screenplay, which used an original story by Valentine Davies as its basis. Charles F. Glett functioned as associate producer for this co-production between William Dieterle's company and RKO. Songs included: 'Goin' To Chicago' Leith Stevens; 'Under A Falling Star' Stevens, Rich Hall.

My Favorite Spy, Harold Lloyd's final co-production with RKO, blended tripe with topicality. The script (by Sig Herzig and William Bowers from a story by M. Coates Webster) required bewildered bandleader Kay Kyser (left) to join Army intelligence and play espionage games that make him the target of accomplished assassins. Evidently they are not accomplished enough, for Kyser avoids their bullets, rounds up a pack of spies, sorts out his romantic entanglements with Jane Wyman (right, borrowed from Warner Bros.) and Ellen Drew (borrowed from Paramount) and still finds time to lead his band in a few snappy tunes before the end credits roll. Tay Garnett directed this wartime lark. Robert Armstrong, Helen Westley, William Demarest, Una O'Connor, Lionel Royce, Moroni Olsen, George Cleveland, Vaughn Glaser, Hobart Cavanaugh, Chester Clute, Teddy Hart and Kay Kyser's Band, featuring Harry Babbitt, Ish Kabibble, Sully Mason, Trudy Irwin and Dorothy Dunn, also appeared. Songs included 'Just Plain Lonesome', 'Got The Moon In My Pocket' Jimmy Van Heusen, Johnny Burke.

Leon Errol's inspired impersonations were the only thing keeping the Mexican Spitfire series alive. In **Mexican Spitfire Sees A Ghost**, Errol (centre left) again portrayed henpecked Uncle Matt, rubber-legged Lord Epping and the Lord's cockney valet. Script authors Charles E. Roberts and Monte Brice set much of their film in a phony haunted house which is the secret hideout of enemy aliens engaged in the manufacture of nitroglycerin. 'It's Wild! It's Weird! It's Wacky!' read the studio publicity. But it wasn't much fun, except when Errol was carrying on. Regular participants Lupe Velez (centre right), Charles 'Buddy' Rogers (right) and Elisabeth Risdon (left) headed a cast that also embraced Donald MacBride, Minna Gombell (centre), Don Barclay, John Maguire, Lillian Randolph, Mantan Moreland, Harry Tyler and Marten Lamont. Leslie Goodwins directed and Cliff Reid, after many years with the company, picked up his final producer credit.

Little Pinks (Henry Fonda, left, borrowed from 20th Century-Fox), Professor B (Ray Collins), Horsethief (Sam Levene), Violette Shumberger (Agnes Moorehead), Nicely Nicely Johnson (Eugene Pallette) and a host of Damon Runyon's other kindly gamblers, lowlifes and con-men were on hand to minister to abrasive, selfish nightclub singer Gloria Lyons (Lucille Ball, right) in **The Big Street**. Leonard Spigelgass' screenplay, based on a *Collier's* magazine fable by producer Runyon, was all about busboy Fonda's selfless devotion to Ball after she is crippled by gangster Barton MacLane. Fonda even pushes her (in her wheelchair) to Florida in the hope that the tropical sunshine will speed her recovery. Runyon's standard brew of pathos, comedy, action and drama was ultimately swamped by a tidal wave of sentimentality, and yet this film had its special pleasures. Chief among them was the performance of Lucille Ball, playing an unsympathetic character for one of the few times in her career and endowing that character with depth and convincing verisimilitude. As Ball's 'Little Weasel', Fonda brought genuine compassion to his portrait of a man who believes no sacrifice is too great to make for his beloved idol. Irving Reis' heady direction and Russell Metty's sensitive cinematography were also distinguishing features. Other actors having a go at Runyon's patented 'Big Stem' dialogue included Marion Martin, William Orr, George Cleveland, Louise Beavers, Millard Mitchell, Juan Varro, Hans Conried, Vera Gordon, Harry Shannon, William Halligan, John Miljan, Don Barclay, Julius Tannen, Eddie Dunn, Bert Hanlon, Bob Perry, Anthony Blair, Art Hamburger and Addison Richards. Ozzie Nelson and his Orchestra were also on hand. Song: 'Who Knows?' Mort Greene, Harry Revel.

Come On Danger was a toothless remake of a 1932 Tom Keene oater about a Texas ranger's attempts to solve a murder allegedly committed by a woman rustler and her renegade gang. Ranger Tim Holt (right) soon discovers that the woman (Frances Neal, left) and her followers are innocent, and that county official Karl Hackett and his minions are the true lawbreakers. Bennett Cohen wrote the original story and Norton S. Parker the screenplay which Edward Killy directed in un-illuminating fashion. Other actors in producer Bert Gilroy's cast included Ray Whitley, Lee 'Lasses' White, Malcolm 'Bud' McTaggart, Glenn Strange, Davison Clark, John Elliott, Slim Whitaker, Kate Harrington and Henry Rocquemore. Songs: 'Come On Danger', 'On The Trail Again', 'Old Bow-legged Jones' Fred Rose, Ray Whitley.

The fate of **The Magnificent Ambersons** was sealed one evening in March 1942 when the film had its first preview at a theatre in Pomona, California. President George J. Schaefer attended and, in a confidential letter to Orson Welles who was then in South America working on *It's All True*, Schaefer described the experience as being 'like getting one sock in the jaw after another for over two hours'. The Pomona audience kidded the picture, laughed in the wrong places and talked back to the performers. Flabbergasted by the crowd reaction and sickened by the knowledge that $1,125,000 of the studio's money was tied up in the film, the president ordered editor Robert Wise to cut approximately 40 minutes out of it. It seemed to play better at this length, but preview audiences still complained about the downbeat ending so a new, more positive finish was filmed. Though Orson Welles was understandably outraged by the emasculation of his masterpiece, what remains is still enormously impressive. Using a novel by Booth Tarkington as his basis, producer-

director-writer Welles was able to objectify major changes in the social and economic fabric of twentieth century American life through the deterioration of the proud but moribund Amberson family. Welles' cinematic technique was again striking, though more subtle and controlled than in *Citizen Kane*. Long takes, composition in depth, overlapping dialogue, elliptical editing and extreme contrasts of light and shadow enriched the story without damaging the naturalistic tone that was necessary to its development. Certainly one feels the gaps in the narrative (especially towards the end when the plot lurches from one crisis to the next), and the syrupy denouement is out of place with all that comes before, but many film critics and historians still regard **Ambersons** as one of the great works of the American cinema. Welles extracted richly shaded performances from Joseph Cotten, Dolores Costello, Anne Baxter, Agnes Moorehead (illustrated), Ray Collins, Erskine Sanford, Richard Bennett and Don Dillaway. The biggest surprise in the cast was Tim Holt (il-

lustrated), playing the key role of George Amberson Minifer. RKO's resident cowboy gave an expert performance as the spoiled scion of the Amberson dynasty who finally gets his 'come-uppance', exposing the character's personality in revelatory flashes such as the way he eats strawberry shortcake during an intense conversation with his aunt. Other important members of the filmmaking team were Stanley Cortez (cinematography), Bernard Herrmann (musical score), Mark-Lee Kirk (art direction) and Bailey Fesler and James G. Stewart (sound recording). The RKO-Mercury Productions co-venture was released in August, two months after George Schaefer's departure. It was not handled gently by the distribution arm, playing in some theatres on a double-bill with one of the Mexican Spitfire comedies. RKO's ultimate loss came to $624,000. A silent version of the Tarkington novel had been released by Vitagraph in 1925 featuring Cullen Landis and Alice Calhoun. It was called *Pampered Youth*.

If RKO executives had had any choice in the matter, **Scattergood Survives A Murder** would have had a different title and denouement, for the brass was anxious to be rid of Coldriver's leading citizen and his consistently third-rate pictures. But the Pyramid Pictures Corporation contract called for one more Scattergood picture, and one more there had to be. Michael L. Simmons' screenplay, directed by Christy Cabanne, was an enervated whodunit requiring the protagonist (Guy Kibbee, right) to shed his guise as a storekeeper and have a go at amateur detective work. The strange deaths of two spinsters who leave their fortune to a house cat is his provocation and, after determining that the old ladies' demise was not accidental, he baits a trap which snares the murderer. John Archer played a rural newspaperman, Margaret Hayes a metropolitan reporter who becomes romantically involved with Archer, and Wallace Ford the skulking villain, with other parts going to, among others, Spencer Charters (left), John Miljan, Willie Best, Eily Malyon, George Chandler, Dick Elliott and Florence Lake. Jerrold T. Brandt again produced.

Producer-director Herbert Wilcox returned to war-torn England to make films with RKO's frozen monies. His homecomng picture was **Wings And The Woman** (GB: **They Flew Alone**) a biography of Amy Johnson Mollison, Britain's pioneer woman flyer. Beginning with Amy's rebellion against the strictures of English society, it covered her first amazing flights, her marriage to daredevil pilot Jim Mollison, their solo and joint record-breaking feats and, finally, her death while ferrying a fighter plane from factory to airfield for the RAF. This gave Wilcox the opportunity to pay tribute to the patriotic work being done by British women, releasing male pilots for more dangerous duties. Which, of course, was the film's underlying message – the necessity to live and die for the rights of all people in a world of peace. The strongest areas of Miles Malleson's screenplay (from a story by Viscount Castlerosse)

actually dealt with the *terra firma* relationship between Amy (Anna Neagle, centre) and Jim (Robert Newton), two celebrities who had the world at their feet yet completely failed to safeguard their own personal happiness. Their flesh-and-blood domestic problems made the film something more than just a patriotically inspired tribute to a remarkable woman. Victor Hanbury was the associate producer, and the large supporting cast included Edward Chapman, Nora Swinburne, Joan Kemp-Welch, Brefni O'Rorke, Charles Carson, Martita Hunt, Anthony Shaw, Eliot Makeham, David Horne, Miles Malleson, Aubrey Mallalieu, Charles Victor, Hay Petrie, John Slater, Perry Parsons, Cyril Smith, George Merritt, Muriel George, Ian Fleming, Billy Hartnell, MacDonald Park, Ted Andrews, Arthur Hambling, Peter Gawthorne, Ronald Shiner and Margaret Halston.

For the first time, Walt Disney chose a current best-selling novel as the subject for an animated feature. Author Felix Salten created **Bambi**, a story of birth, love, tragedy and triumph in the forest kingdom. Besides Bambi, the tiny fawn who grows up to be the prince of the woodlands (see illustration), the talented Disney pens breathed life into Flower, the 'twitterpated' skunk, Thumper, the Mickey Rooney of rabbitdom, the crotchety and sarcastic Friend Owl, and a host of other anthropomorphized critters. Perhaps the film's finest achievements were its mature rendering of the forest's changing seasons and the dramatic depiction of a forest fire which threatens the lives of all the lovable animals. Once again, the Disney organization had produced a Technicolor celebration for the young-at-heart. David D. Hand was the supervising director; Perce Pearce was responsible for story direction and Larry Morey for story adaptation; and James Algar, Bill Roberts, Norman Wright, Sam Armstrong, Paul Satterfield and Graham Heid worked as sequence directors. Franklin Thomas, Milton Kahl, Eric Larson and Oliver M. Johnston Jr were the supervising animators, while Sidney A. Franklin, who brought the story to Walt Disney's attention in the first place, received a special word of thanks in the picture's credits. Songs included: 'Love Is A Song', 'Little April Shower', 'Let's Sing A Gay Little Spring Song' Frank Churchill, Larry Morey.

Richard Carlson (left) played an indolent millionaire who decides to learn how the other half lives in **Highways By Night**. It turns out that they live very dangerously for Carlson, who intrudes on a gangland murder and is soon hunted by the police on one hand, and marked for extermination by the racketeers on the other. Clarence Budington Kelland's *Saturday Evening Post* serial *Silver Spoon* provided the basic plot, which screenwriters Lynn Root and Frank Fenton fleshed out with all the usual clichés. Roy Webb's music and Robert de Grasse's cinematography were plus factors in an otherwise uninspired melo. Jane Randolph (right), Jane Darwell, Barton MacLane, Ray Collins, Gordon Jones, Renee Haal, George Cleveland, Marten Lamont, Jack LaRue, John Maguire, James Seay, Cliff Clark and Paul Fix took their direction from Peter Godfrey. Herman Schlom produced, but received no screen credit.

Stage holdups, gun fights, a fire and some ripsnorting chases provided the predictable action highlights of **Thundering Hoofs**, produced by Bert Gilroy and directed by RKO newcomer Lesley Selander. Paul Franklin's original screenplay was built around the attempts of a crooked attorney (Archie Twitchell) to buy out a stage line for a rival operator while milking the deal on both ends. The son of the buyer (Tim Holt, left) and the daughter of the seller (Luana Walters, right) uncover the conniving, inspiring Holt to bring to light the lawyer's trickery and help the heroine obtain a fair price for her father's business. Ray Whitley, Lee 'Lasses' White, Gordon DeMain, Charles Phipps, Monte Montague, Joe Bernard, Frank Fanning, Fred Scott and Frank Ellis were among those present. Songs: 'Ramble On', 'As Along The Trail I Ride' Fred Rose, Ray Whitley.

Lupe Velez changed husbands for the second time in **Mexican Spitfire's Elephant**. With Charles 'Buddy' Rogers entering the service, young RKO contract player Walter Reed inherited the role. He was at a loss to cope with the nutty plot about a smuggled toy elephant used as a hiding place for a valuable gem, but Leon Errol (left) and Velez (centre left) took it in their stride. Lupe, in fact, seized the opportunity to introduce a live pink elephant with green polka dots into the slapstick spree. Charles E. Roberts' screenplay (story by Roberts and director Leslie Goodwins) also gave parts to Elisabeth Risdon, Lydia Bilbrook, Marion Martin, Lyle Talbot, Luis Alberni (right), Arnold Kent, George Cleveland, Marten Lamont, Jack Briggs, Max Wagner and Don Barclay (centre right). The producer was Bert Gilroy.

Bandit Ranger was the first of six Tim Holt westerns hammered out between 11 May 1942 and 17 July 1942. The mad rush was necessitated by Holt's induction into the Air Corps – a wartime reality that robbed RKO of one of its few rising stars. Weaving its action around the adventures of a Texas ranger (Holt, right) endeavouring to bring a passel of cattle thieves to justice, the picture was standard sagebrush escapism pepped up by the substitution of Cliff 'Ukelele Ike' Edwards for Lee 'Lasses' White as Holt's sidekick 'Whopper'. Ray Whitley was also among the missing, though two of his songs made the final cut. Bennett R. Cohen and Morton Grant wrote the screenplay from a story by Cohen; Lesley Selander gave it sturdy direction and Bert Gilroy produced. Joan Barclay played the stock damsel in distress, with Kenneth Harlan, LeRoy Mason, Glenn Strange, Jack Rockwell, Frank Ellis, Bob Kortman, Bud Geary, Dennis Moore (left) and Russell Wade also contributing. Songs included: 'Musical Jack', 'Move Along' Fred Rose, Ray Whitley.

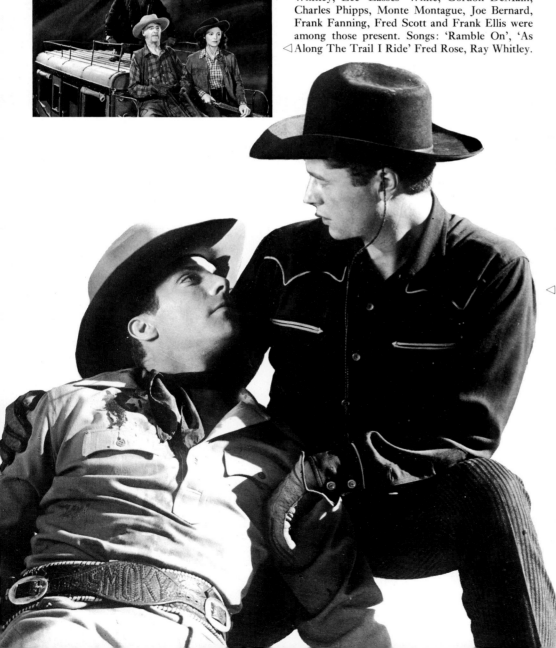

The **Falcon's Brother** introduced Tom Conway ▷
as George Sanders' brother (which he was in real
life as well) and arranged its incidents so that he
could take over the series. Sanders (borrowed from
20th Century-Fox) was fed up with playing urbane
sleuths, but agreed to make one final appearance to
smooth the transition. Stuart Palmer and Craig
Rice's screenplay found Sanders (right) sniffing
out some murders when Conway (left) arrives from
Latin America. After his brother is temporarily
put out of commission, Conway follows the clues
to the editor of a fashion magazine which is being
used to transmit Nazi messages throughout the
US. Conway is trapped, but Sanders recovers in
time to rejoin the action and die while saving a
Southern diplomat from an Axis death plot. R.I.P.
Gay Falcon. Stanley Logan's sluggish direction
and the convoluted script added up to a pretty
lame detective yarn; nevertheless, audiences accepted Conway as Sanders' replacement, thereby
justifying the *raison d'être* of Maurice Geraghty's
production. Also cast: Jane Randolph, Don
Barclay, Cliff Clark, Edward Gargan, Eddie Dunn,
Charlotte Wynters, James Newill, Keye Luke,
Amanda Varela, George Lewis, Gwili Andre,
Andre Charlot, Mary Halsey and Charles Arnt.

The follow-up to *Look Who's Laughing*, **Here We
Go Again** provided sorely needed profits for the
beleagured studio. Its hodge-podge plot used
Fibber McGee and Molly's twentieth wedding
anniversary as its basis, and incorporated Edgar
Bergen's twin search for romance and for a rare
American moth, as well as the schemes of get-rich-
quick promoter Gale Gordon to sell interests in
synthetic gasoline. Jim Jordan (left) and Marian
Jordan (right) played Fibber McGee and spouse,
and Harold Peary (also known as The Great
Gildersleeve), 'Charley McCarthy', Ginny Simms,
Bill Thompson, Isabel Randolph, 'Mortimer
Snerd' and Ray Noble and his Band were also on
hand. Faced with dreaming up a story that would
make use of the various comedians and other
divergent talents, Paul Gerard Smith gave in to his
most preposterous impulses, which was just fine
with audiences who made the film a $228,000
winner. Screenwriters Smith and Joe Bigelow had
help from Don Quinn who typed out material for
Fibber McGee and Molly, and Zeno Klinker,
Dorothy Kingsley and Royal Foster who followed
suit for Edgar Bergen and his knotheaded friends.
Allan Dwan produced and directed. Songs included: 'Delicious Delirium', 'Until I Live Again'
Mort Greene, Harry Revel.

One of Cliff Reid's last RKO productions, **The
Mayor Of 44th Street** starred George Murphy
(centre) as the operator of a dance band booking
agency. The agency is being watched closely by the
cops, thanks to the racketeering tactics of its
former proprietor. With Anne Shirley (right) as his
confidential aide, Murphy is making a success of
the business until juvenile thug Rex Downing
threatens to muscle in with his predatory band of
street urchins. The situation is further complicated
by the parole of gangster Richard Barthelmess (left)
who seeks to regain control of the agency and
resume his blackmailing operations. Scriptwriters
Lewis R. Foster and Frank Ryan attempted to mix
a raw underworld melodrama with bandleader
Freddy Martin's 'sweet swing' music; the outcome
was about as involving and stimulating as a game
of solitaire. Alfred E. Green directed, bringing
William Gargan, Joan Merrill, Millard Mitchell,
Mary Wickes, Eddie Hart, Roberta Smith, Marten
Lamont, Walter Reed, Robert Smith, Lee Bonnell,
Kenneth Lundy, Esther Muir and John H. Dilson
into the action at various points. The picture was
based on Robert D. Andrews' story, which was, in
turn, suggested by a *Collier's* magazine article by
Luther Davis and John Cleveland. Songs in-
cluded: 'Heavenly Isn't It?', 'You're Bad For Me',
'There's A Breeze On Lake Louise', 'A Million
Miles From Manhattan' Mort Greene, Harry
Revel.

The **Pirates Of The Prairie** were crooked
members of a vigilante committee who use their
power to terrorize ranchers and drive them off
their property. Deputy marshal Tim Holt (centre),
disguised as a gunsmith, discovers that the object
of the land grab is to hold up the railroad for right-
of-way when a line is put through the territory.
With the help of the despoiled ranchers, Holt
wipes out the gang in a well-staged street battle
which provided the picture's climax. Bert Gilroy
produced, Howard Bretherton directed and Doris
Schroeder and J. Benton Cheney wrote the screenplay, based on a story by Berne Giler. Cliff
'Ukelele Ike' Edwards, Nell O'Day, John H.
Elliott, Roy Barcroft, Karl Hackett, Edward
Cassidy and Charles King completed the cast.
Songs: 'Grandpop', 'Where The Mountain Meets
The Sunset' Fred Rose, Ray Whitley.
▽

A happy portent of the prosperous days ahead,
The Navy Comes Through was an unexceptional military fantasy which earned eye-opening
profits of $542,000. Pat O'Brien (right), George
Murphy, Jackie Cooper (left), Max Baer, Desi
Arnaz (centre left) and Carl Esmond (centre right)
comprised the chief crew members of captain Ray
Collins' dirty old freighter which blows German
bombers to smithereens, dispatches U-boats to the
bottom and, when it seems that the Atlantic must
be cleansed of these pests, captures a Nazi supply
ship and uses it against the enemy with devastating
effect. In the foreground action, Murphy and Jane
Wyatt played out a boy meets-loses-meets-wins
girl plot to add spice to the combat pyrotechnics.
Borden Chase wrote the original story, Earl
Baldwin and John Twist adapted it and Roy
Chanslor and Aeneas MacKenzie completed the
screenplay. A. Edward Sutherland's smooth direction enlisted capable supporting performances
from Lee Bonnell, Frank Jenks, John Maguire,
Frank Fenton, Joey Ray, Marten Lamont and
◁ Cyril Ring. The producer was Islin Auster.

Producer-director Tim Whelan crammed **Seven** ▷
Days Leave with enough entertainers to carry on
for seven years. Its screenplay by William Bowers,
Ralph Spence, Curtis Kenyon and Kenneth Earl
concerned the trials and tribulations of a recent
enlistee (Victor Mature, right, borrowed from 20th
Century-Fox) who has one week to marry a girl he
has never met (Lucille Ball) in order to fulfil the
stipulations of a will leaving him $100,000. The
story line was, of course, just a pretext to showcase
Ginny Simms singing 'Can't Get Out Of This
Mood' with Freddy Martin's Band; torrid
Mexican entertainer Mapy Cortes dancing rumbas
and congas, and Les Brown's 'hottest white band'
dishing them out; puckish 16-year-old Marcy
McGuire intoning 'I Get The Neck Of The
Chicken'; Ralph Edwards broadcasting his *Truth
Or Consequences* radio programme; the Great
Gildersleeve (Harold Peary) belching forth with
his infamous giggle and much, much more.
Though just another in the long line of lumpy
musical comedy goulashes prepared by RKO over
the years, audiences gobbled it up with incredible
gusto. Arnold Stang (left), Peter Lind Hayes,
Walter Reed, Wallace Ford, Buddy Clark, King
Kennedy, Charles Andre, Harry Holman, Addison
Richards, Lynn, Royce and Vanya, and *The Court
Of Missing Heirs* radio show with announcer
Charles Victor were also part of it. Charles
Walters, who would soon become one of MGM's
top musical directors, staged the dance ensembles;
it was his first Hollywood assignment. Other songs
included: 'Touch Of Texas', 'Please Won't You
Leave My Girl Alone', 'You Speak My Language'
Frank Loesser, Jimmy McHugh.

△
Once Upon A Honeymoon was a prosaic
comedy about a girl who sets her cap at a titled
gentleman and discovers in the end that it's far
better to love and be loved by a news reporter.
Unfortunately that was only part of the story.
Producer-director Leo McCarey played out the
love chase against the devastation of Czecho-
slovakia, Poland and France, which turned the
frivolous premise into an odd and singularly
tasteless comedy drama. Ginger Rogers (left)
starred as an American dancer who succumbs to
the blandishments of a German baron (Walter
Slezak, right) and marries him, despite the efforts
of reporter Cary Grant to dissuade her. The
reporter understands what the dancer does not –
that her husband is a Nazi agent paving the way for
the invasion of the aforementioned countries.
Grant follows the honeymooning couple to keep an
eye on the girl. In the course of the action an
attachment forms between them, complete with
flirting, trifling and burlesque humour while the
world goes up in flames around them. Grant,
Rogers and Slezak carried out their roles with
hard-nosed professionalism, though no amount of
excellence in performance could have redeemed
the stupidity and callousness of this very expensive
undertaking. The screenplay by Sheridan Gibney
(story Gibney and McCarey) also contained parts
for Albert Dekker, Albert Basserman, Ferike

Boros, Harry Shannon and Natasha Lytess. It
seems genuinely incredible that the man who made
The Awful Truth, *Love Affair*, and a number of
other exceptionally intelligent and witty pictures
could have been responsible for this fiasco. Note:
The foolishness even permeated the picture's
credits. Since neither Rogers nor Grant would
agree to give the other top billing, half of the
advertising featured Ginger's name first and the
other half had Cary's name first.

Set against a World War I backdrop, **Army
Surgeon** centred on a banal triangle featuring a
military doctor (James Ellison, right), a courageous
nurse (Jane Wyatt, centre) and a dashing aviator
(Kent Taylor, left). However, the movie didn't
pass muster either as romantic drama or as
patriotic acknowledgement of the contributions of
the Army Medical Corps. Barry Trivers and
Emmet Lavery's heavy-handed screenplay (based
on a story by John Twist), and A. Edward
Sutherland's murky direction combined to make
the final release of 1942 a characteristic epilogue to
a year of general mediocrity. Walter Reed, James
Burke, George Cleveland, Lee Bonnell, Jack
Briggs, Cyril Ring, Cliff Clark, Dick Hogan, Eddie
Dew, Ann Codee, Russell Wade and Richard
Martin were other members of producer Bert
Gilroy's cast. Since the wartime picture boom was
now in full swing and nearly every film was making
money, the $46,000 loss incurred by **Army
Surgeon** was indicative of its thoroughgoing
◁ wretchedness.

☆☆☆☆☆☆☆☆☆☆☆☆☆☆

1943

☆☆☆☆☆☆☆☆☆☆☆☆☆☆

1943 saw an extraordinary run of money-making pictures. Of the 50 films released, only four posted losses and two of those were Goldwyn productions subject to special distribution terms. **Mr Lucky**, **Hitler's Children** and **Behind The Rising Sun** were blockbusters, bringing in more than $1 million each in profits, and **Tender Comrade**, **The Fallen Sparrow**, **Government Girl**, **The Sky's The Limit**, **Bombardier** and **A Lady Takes A Chance** also socked home runs at the box office. Radio-Keith-Orpheum profits for the year soared to $6,964,005.

Though the prosperous business climate made Charles Koerner's job a good deal easier than it had been the year before, he still had plenty of headaches. Chief among them was a manpower shortage produced by the war, and exacerbated by the omnivorous talent round ups of other studios, particularly MGM. As a consequence, the production head had immense difficulty in casting his films with name performers, and finding above-average scribes to write them. Koerner also faced a crisis in his 'B' department where films began to go consistently over budget, and **Petticoat Larceny**, **Ladies' Day** and several other programmers proved major embarrassments to the company. He remedied this situation by replacing Lou Ostrow with former studio manager Sid Rogell, and axing Bert Gilroy who produced several of the offending pictures.

It was a quiet year on the executive front, Floyd Odlum's election as chairman of the RKO board of directors being the only noteworthy event. At the studio, Frank Sinatra and Gregory Peck signed contracts to appear in RKO pictures, editor Mark Robson was promoted to the directorial ranks by horror film producer Val Lewton, and Edward Dmytryk rose very rapidly to the top level of company helmsmen, directing five films including **Hitler's Children**, **Behind The Rising Sun** and **Tender Comrade**.

△ Awakening patriotism was the subject of **Seven Miles From Alcatraz**, a topical melo climaxed by a rousing, hand-to-hand fight on the circular staircase of a west coast lighthouse. James Craig (right) and Frank Jenks escape from the famous island penitentiary of the title and end up at the lighthouse, which has become a haven for Nazi spies. Though cynical at first, the two convicts are eventually won over by the honesty and bravery of the lighthouse keeper (George Cleveland) and his daughter (Bonita Granville, left). Knowing that it will cost them their freedom, Craig provokes the big fight, allowing Cleveland a chance to send an SOS and save San Francisco from a U-boat attack. Cliff Edwards (centre), Erford Gage, Tala Birell, John Banner and Otto Reichow played other characters in the Joseph Krumgold screenplay (story by John D. Klorer). Herman Schlom produced, giving Edward Dmytryk his first RKO directorial assignment. Dmytryk would soon become one of the company's premier filmmakers.

Renowned French director Jean Renoir joined forces with screenwriter Dudley Nichols and actor Charles Laughton to create **This Land Is Mine**, a moving and inspirational drama set in an unnamed country in occupied Europe. Laughton (left) played a mother-fixated schoolteacher, so cowardly that his own pupils laugh at him during an air raid. It is the Nazis, of course, who provoke him to develop a backbone; he puts it on display in court, delivering an impassioned speech about liberty during his trial for a murder he did not commit. What distinguished the film from the general run of World War II melodramas was its feeling for character. Rather than the standard collection of good guys and bad, it went to great lengths to demonstrate how the unnatural world situation affected a wide variety of personalities. There was compassion for George Sanders, a railroad superintendent who collaborates with the enemy under the mistaken notion that appeasement is the way to peace and security, as well as for Maureen O'Hara who understands that the concept of freedom can only remain alive through education of the youth, and her brother Kent Smith who surreptitiously perpetrates acts of sabotage against the Nazis. In short, the film offered honest insights into human nature, coupled with an appreciation of each person's strengths and frailties – elements rarely present in typical Hollywood flights of fancy. Also cast: Walter Slezak, Una O'Connor (right), Philip Merivale, Thurston Hall, George Coulouris, Nancy Gates, Ivan Simpson, John Donat, Frank Alten, Leo Bulgakov, Wheaton Chambers and Cecil Weston. Renoir and Nichols co-produced.
▽

Producer Val Lewton had no interest in shuffling ▷
monsters, spooky haunted houses or giant gorillas
running amok. What intrigued him were the
psychodramatic possibilities of the horror genre,
and his first RKO production, **Cat People**, was an
apt demonstration of this fascination. A Serbian
girl who believes that if her passions are aroused
she will turn into a panther and slay her lover, was
the central figure in DeWitt Bodeen's intriguing
screenplay. Played by Simone Simon (illustrated)
with sincerity and restraint, the girl becomes a
pathetically tortured creature – as terrifying to
herself as to others. The tale derived its power
from the imaginations of the audience, forcing
each viewer to fill in the horrific elements in his
own mind. A swimming pool scene in which the
cat woman stalks (or does she?) her rival (Jane
Randolph) was a *tour de force* of suggestive camera
angles, nerve-tingling sound effects and shadowy
lighting – the very essence of the Lewton style.
Miss Randolph, Kent Smith as a Manhattan ship
designer who marries Simon and thereby primes
the pump for disaster, and Tom Conway as a
lecherous psychoanalyst gave adequate performances, but the real stars were Lewton, Bodeen,
director Jacques Tourneur (also beginning his
RKO career), cinematographer Nicholas
Musuraca and Roy Webb, who composed the
subtle musical score. RKO's new horror cycle was
launched and launched most profitably; **Cat
People** completed its run $183,000 in the black.
Also cast: Jack Holt, Alan Napier, Elizabeth
Dunne and Elizabeth Russell.

△

Having put in an appearance in *Look Who's
Laughing*, *Here We Go Again* and *Seven Days
Leave*, comedian Harold Peary (right) unleashed a
series of his own with **The Great Gildersleeve**.
According to the 'conservative' estimates of
RKO's publicity staff, Throckmorton P.
Gildersleeve had a radio following of 17 million
listeners, some of whom might care to see the
rotund, moustachioed humourist and his
Summerfield environs in the flesh. Certainly,
enough of them turned out to make the Herman
Schlom production a hit. Jack Townley and Julien
Josephson's screenplay presented Gildy as the
custodian of his young niece (Nancy Gates) and
nephew (Freddie Mercer), and the victim of a
matrimonial ambush laid by spinster Mary Field.
How he eluded Miss Field and kept custody of the
children filled out 62 minutes of uniformly puerile
screen time. Gordon Douglas directed, and Jane
Darwell, Charles Arnt, Thurston Hall, Lillian
Randolph (left) and George Carleton were also
involved.

Hope was in the air and on the screen in **They Got
Me Covered** – Bob Hope, that is. Cast as the
Moscow correspondent for Amalgamated News,
the comedian is so busy eating caviar that he
neglects to report Hitler's invasion of Russia.
Amalgamated's apoplectic boss (Donald Mac-
Bride) recalls his employee and fires him, whereupon Hope (right) decides that the only way to
win his job back is to get the goods on some Nazi
agents. With long-suffering sweetheart Dorothy
Lamour (left) in tow, he accomplishes his mission,
leaving a trail of snappy wisecracks and burlesque
gags in his wake. The team of Leonard Q. Ross
and Leonard Spigelgass (story), Harry Kurnitz
(screenplay), Frank Fenton and Lynn Root (additional dialogue) and David Butler (direction)
assembled this lively and topical entertainment,
garnished with lavish production values which
were *de rigueur* in any Samuel Goldwyn production. Otto Preminger played the chief Nazi malefactor, and Eduardo Ciannelli, Marion Martin,
Donald Meek, Lenore Aubert, Phyllis Ruth,
Philip Ahn, Mary Treen, Bettye Avery, Margaret
Hayes, Mary Byrne, William Yetter, Henry
Guttman, Florence Bates, Walter Catlett, John
Abbott and Frank Sully completed the cast. Song:
◁ 'Palsy Walsy' Johnny Mercer, Harold Arlen.

Set in the Mother Lode country, **Fighting
Frontier** surprised Tim Holt's fans by presenting
him as a wild and reckless bandit running with a
gang of very nasty villains. *Mais non*, it all turns
out to be a ruse dreamed up by Holt and the
governor to catch the secret leader of the marauders. Working with Cliff 'Ukelele Ike' Edwards
(right), Holt (left) gets his man and squares himself
with girl friend Ann Summers before hanging up
his pistol belt. J. Benton Cheney and Norton S.
Parker wrote the screenplay from a story by
Bernard McConville. Lambert Hillyer directed for
producer Bert Gilroy, and Eddie Dew, William
Gould, Davison Clark, Slim Whitaker, Tom
London, Monte Montague and Jack Rockwell
played secondary roles. Songs: 'On The Outlaw
Trail', 'The Edwards And The Drews' Fred Rose,
Ray Whitley.

▽

You may have thought that darkest Africa was uncontaminated by the Nazi menace, but **Tarzan Triumphs** proved otherwise. When a bunch of German paratroops descend on the monosyllabic hero's jungle territory to plunder raw materials, Tarzan (Johnny Weissmuller, right) routs them easily, with some help from a perceptive elephant who shoves one storm trooper over the edge of a cliff, and Cheeta the chimpanzee who wields a devastating tommy gun at the height of the action. The ever-present Jane was missing from this one, but there was Zandra, white princess of a lost civilization, played by Frances Gifford (left). Directed by William Thiele from a story by Carroll Young and screenplay by Young and Roy Chanslor, the picture inaugurated a pleasant and profitable run of ape man pictures made by producer Sol Lesser's Principal Artists Productions Company and released through RKO. Also cast: Johnny Sheffield (as Boy), Stanley Ridges, Sig Rumann, Philip Van Zandt, Rex Williams and Pedro De Cordoba. Edgar Rice Burroughs, creator of the Tarzan characters, received prominent credit, though he certainly did not write this particular story.

Saludos Amigos was the product of a trip made by Walt Disney and his staff to South America in 1941. Hundreds of sketches and recordings collected en route were later reworked in Hollywood to produce this part live action–part animated travelogue. The highlights were the cartoon segments: Donald Duck (left) as a Yankee tourist in Peru, marvelling at Lake Titicaca and making the acquaintance of a supercilious llama; Goofy riding the pampas as an Argentinian gaucho; Donald learning the samba from a Brazilian jitterbird named Joe Carioca (right). Better relations between the Americas were on everyone's mind during this period, and Walt Disney led the way in fostering them. The picture was initially released south of the border, where it became a rousing success. Norman Ferguson supervised the production, making use of Homer Brightman, Ralph Wright, Roy Williams, Dick Huemer, Harry Reeves and Joe Grant to fashion the story and Bill Roberts, Jack Kinney, Hamilton Luske and Wilfred Jackson to serve as sequence directors. The human voices behind the characters included Clarence Nash (Donald), Aloysio Oliveira (Joe Carioca) and Pinto Colvig (Goofy). Charles Wolcott was the musical director, and the songs included: 'Saludos Amigos' Ned Washington, Charles Wolcott; 'Brazil' Ary Barroso, English lyrics by S. K. Russell. ▷

Convinced that Scattergood Baines was now box-office cyanide, the RKO brass changed the title of his last picture from *Scattergood Swings It* to **Cinderella Swings It**. No title change, however, could obscure Michael L. Simmons' hapless plot or the desultory direction of Christy Cabanne. For the record, the story concerned Scattergood's campaign to make singer Gloria Warren (right) a star, and the USO benefit show he mounts to unveil her talents. The show itself turns out to be one of the most agonizing parades of amateur talent ever committed to celluloid. Guy Kibbee (centre right) gave Scattergood one last try, supported by Helen Parrish (left), Dick Hogan (centre left), Leonid Kinskey, Billy Lenhart, Kenneth Brown, 'Dink' Trout, Willie Best, Pierre Watkin, Lee 'Lasses' White, Fern Emmett, Ed Waller, Kay Linaker, Christine McIntyre and Grace Costello. Jerrold T. Brandt produced for Pyramid Pictures Corporation. Songs included: 'The Flag's Still There, Mr Key' George Jessel, Ben Oakland; 'I Heard You Cried Last Night' Ted Grouya, Jerrie Kruger.

The Lum and Abner series continued with **Two Weeks To Live** in which Abner (Norris Goff, right), believing his days are numbered, agrees to pilot a rocket ship to Mars. Michael L. Simmons and Roswell Rogers' gingerbread screenplay worked in plenty of other gags including some Jekyll and Hyde potion-taking, a haunted house, a bomb in a violin case and the by now almost obligatory foiling of a Nazi spy plot. The star, of course, eventually learns that he is in perfect health. Director Malcolm St Clair kept the wild events spinning along at a heady pace. Chester Lauck (left) was featured as Lum, and the cast was completed by Franklin Pangborn, Kay Linaker, Irving Bacon, Herbert Rawlinson, Ivan Simpson, Rosemary LaPlanche, Danny Duncan, Evelyn Knapp, Charles Middleton, Luis Alberni (centre), Jack Rice, Tim Ryan, Oscar O'Shea and Edward Earle. Ben Hersh produced for Jack William Votion Productions.

One of the strangest multi-national human cargoes ever assembled on a movie ship sailed for Batumi in Orson Welles' **Journey Into Fear**. Joseph Cotten (left) topped the passenger list as an American gunnery engineer pursued by Gestapo agents. Also on board: a worldly-wise adagio dancer and her gigolo partner, a refugee Greek widow and her son, a querulous French woman and her long-suffering British husband, a grandiloquent German archaeologist and a grimy old Greek sea captain. Welles himself showed up as Colonel Haki, the head of the Turkish secret police. Uneven, confusing, and with stylized and low-key photography (by Karl Struss), the picture nonetheless offered thrills, suspense, and moments of typically Wellesian cinematic brilliance, in the course of which, after a series of perilous (if illogical) adventures, Cotten tires of running, and gets rid of the most dangerous of the Nazi hit men. Charles Koerner, viewing it as a tedious jumble, had editor Mark Robson work over the footage for almost a year after principal photography was completed, and allowed some extra material to be shot in an effort to give the story coherence. No miracles were forthcoming, though the finished product was well worth seeing. Norman Foster directed under Welles' general supervision, working from Joseph Cotten's screen adaptation of a novel by Eric Ambler. Also cast: Dolores Del Rio (right), Ruth Warrick, Agnes Moorehead, Jack Durant, Everett Sloane, Eustace Wyatt, Frank Readick, Edgar Barrier, Stefan Schnabel, Hans Conried, Robert Meltzer, Richard Bennett and Welles' business partner Jack Moss, who played a pudgy-faced Nazi hit man. **Journey Into Fear** was the last cooperative venture to come from the stormy alliance between Mercury Productions and RKO. A Canadian remake was released in 1975 by New World Pictures.

A son's desire to clear his dead father's name was the familiar foundation of **Sagebrush Law**, directed by Sam Nelson from a Bennett R. Cohen screenplay. In it, star Tim Holt (right) eventually comes to grips with the crooks who stole funds from the local bank and pointed the finger of guilt towards Holt's father who was president of the bank. Cliff 'Ukulele Ike' Edwards was again on hand to provide comedy and music, and Joan Barclay (left) made an appealing romantic heroine. However, a pitifully undernourished script and flaccid direction ensured that this was one of Holt's most anaemic outdoor efforts. Producer Bert Gilroy populated his cast with John H. Elliott, Roy Barcroft, Ernie Adams, Edward Cassidy, John Merton, Bud McTaggart, Karl Hackett, Edmund Cobb and Otto Hoffman. Songs: 'Crazy Old Trails', 'Rockin' Down The Cherokee Train' Fred Rose, Ray Whitley. ▷

Sensational in both content and box-office performance, **Hitler's Children** was the champion sleeper in RKO history. Made for a slender $205,000, the picture attracted $3,355,000 in film rentals – more than *Top Hat, King Kong, Little Women* and other famous blockbusters from the studio's past. Emmet Lavery's screenplay, based on a book by Gregor Ziemer entitled *Education For Death*, purported to be an authentic picture of Nazism in action. Mostly, it was an excuse to film a catalogue of horrors visited upon girls – married or not – who refused to bear children for the Fuehrer. Bonita Granville (left) was the main victim, an Aryan lass ticketed for sterilization and publicly flogged for failing to discern the wisdom in Deutschland Uber Alles. Tim Holt (right), the girl's naive lover, signs his own death warrant by stopping the whipping. In truth, the film was little more than a violent potboiler that played fast and loose with the censorship office because of its subject matter. And therein lay the key to its enormous popular success. Both writer Lavery and director Edward Dmytryk were given $5000 bonuses for their work. Kent Smith, Otto Kruger, H. B. Warner, Lloyd Corrigan, Erford Gage, Hans Conried, Gavin Muir and Nancy Gates were also featured, and the film was a co-production between RKO and producer Edward A. Golden.

'There'll always be an England,' was the theme of ▷ **Forever And A Day**, an unusual Anglo-American production which boasted the largest cast of notables ever assembled for one picture. Seventy-eight name actors, seven leading directors and 21 well-respected writers contributed their services (most of them without pay) to the first war charity film ever offered to the public. RKO agreed to distribute the picture at cost, with profits to be divided among various charities having to do with the Allied war effort. The story centred on a London house, built in 1804, and the generations of men and women who had lived in it during critical moments in the recent history of England. Standout cast members were C. Aubrey Smith as the fire-breathing admiral who builds the house, Charles Laughton (left) as a comic butler, Sir Cedric Hardwicke and Buster Keaton as a pair of Dickensian plumbers, and Gladys Cooper and Roland Young as the parents of a flying ace killed in World War I. Though some of the sequences were naturally stronger than others, this was more than just a charity stunt; it was an estimable piece of entertainment also. René Clair, Edmund Goulding, Cedric Hardwicke, Frank Lloyd, Victor Saville, Robert Stevenson and Herbert Wilcox were the directors; C. S. Forester, James Hilton, Donald Ogden Stewart, John Van Druten, Christopher Isherwood, Alice Duer Miller and Alan Campbell were among the writing contingent, and Merle Oberon, Ray Milland, Anna Neagle, Ida Lupino, Herbert Marshall, Brian Aherne, Robert Cummings, Donald Crisp, Nigel Bruce, Wendy Barrie, Eric Blore, Jessie Matthews (right), Claude Rains, Gene Lockhart, Kent Smith and Elsa Lanchester were included in the vast cast. Lloyd Richards served as production co-ordinator for this mammoth undertaking, which required more than a year to complete and fared well enough at the box-office to help out a large number of worthy causes.

Ladies' Day teamed Lupe Velez (foreground right) and Eddie Albert (foreground centre right) in a baseball comedy-romance that attempted to utilize Miss Velez's continual shrieking and bounding about as a substitute for humour. Charles E. Roberts and Dane Lussier's script, based on a play by Robert Considine, Edward Clark Lilley and Bertrand Robinson, concerned the efforts of star pitcher Albert's teammates, manager, and even the teammates' wives, to break up the romance between him and Velez, because the young man is worthless to the ball game when in the throes of a love affair. Bert Gilroy produced and Leslie Goodwins directed, with more misses than hits. Also cast: Patsy Kelly (second row, left), Max Baer (foreground centre left), Jerome Cowan, Iris Adrian (second row, centre), Joan Barclay (second row, right), Cliff Clark (foreground left), Carmen Morales, George Cleveland, Jack Briggs, Russ Clark, Nedrick Young, Eddie Dew, Tom Kennedy and Ralph Sanford. ▽

◁ Cary Grant (illustrated) played a role tailor-made for George Raft in **Mr Lucky**, a David Hempstead production that became an enormous hit ($1,603,000 net profit). An ice-cold sharpie determined to duck the draft and scrape up enough cash to launch his gambling ship, Grant decides to fleece the American War Relief society to raise the necessary bankroll. From the moment that Laraine Day (borrowed from MGM) flitted across the screen, it was obvious that she would thaw him out and bring about his patriotic reformation. She does, and his vessel eventually becomes a transporter of medical supplies rather than slot machines. Though H. C. Potter's direction was noticeably uneven, and the wartime propaganda stifled much of the film's humour, it was the right picture at the right moment for RKO, the charming Mr Grant, and Miss Day, whose Hollywood star status received a huge boost from the film's success. Paul Stewart as the ex-partner who tries to force Grant to go through with the double-cross, Charles Bickford as the captain of the gambling boat, Alan Carney as Grant's bodyguard, and Kay Johnson and Gladys Cooper as society women at work for war relief all delivered superior performances against a backdrop of wonderfully conceived production designs by William Cameron Menzies. The Milton Holmes-Adrian Scott screenplay (based on Holmes' story *Bundles For Freedom*) also contained parts for Henry Stephenson, Walter Kingsford, J. M. Kerrigan, Edward Fielding, Vladimir Sokoloff and Erford Gage. The picture inspired a television series which starred John Vivyan and ran on the CBS network in 1959-60.

Dramatic choices had to be made by Eric Portman (illustrated) and Ann Dvorak in **Squadron Leader X**. Portman, a Nazi pilot at bay in war-torn London, finds himself hunted by British intelligence and marked for death by his own treacherous comrades, the Gestapo. Dvorak, a young girl of German extraction, is faced with betraying England, her adopted country, or facing almost certain imprisonment and dishonour. Just another excuse to reiterate the arrogance and ruthlessness of the Nazi mentality, the picture completed its propaganda mission successfully, then quickly faded into oblivion. Emeric Pressburger's story *Four Days In A Hero's Life* provided the basic plot which screenwriters Wolfgang Wilhelm and Miles Malleson, and director Lance Comfort translated to the screen. Also cast: Fredric Richter, Barry Jones, Henry Oscar, Martin Miller, Beatrice Varley and Walter Fitzgerald. Victor Hanbury produced in England for RKO Radio British Productions.

The comedy team of Wally Brown and Alan Carney (illustrated) was cemented in **The Adventures Of A Rookie**. Both graduates of the night club circuit, Brown and Carney whooped it up as a pair of nitwit recruits running afoul of Army regulations. On leave, they attend a party in a girls' boarding house and are trapped there, along with six gorgeous females, by a scarlet fever quarantine. William Bowers and M. Coates Webster (original story and adaptation) and Edward James (screenplay) concocted this routine GI wish fulfilment which Leslie Goodwins directed without much enthusiasm. Omnivorous moviegoers didn't mind about the quality – they gave a $198,000 profit to RKO. Others cast for producer Bert Gilroy were Richard Martin, Erford Gage, Margaret Landry, Patti Brill, Rita Corday, Robert Andersen, John Hamilton, Ruth Lee, Lorraine Krueger, Ercelle Woods, Toddy Peterson and Byron Foulger.

Take *Jane Eyre*, transpose it to the West Indies, mix in a healthy dose of voodoo mysticism and a soupçon of scientific scepticism and you have the recipe for **I Walked With A Zombie**. Frances Dee (centre) played a trained nurse brought to the tropics by Tom Conway (right) to care for his ill wife, a woman who walks and breathes but cannot speak or think. Amid the barbaric rhythm of voodoo drums, Dee learns the truth – her patient is a zombie, one who is dead but has been brought back to life by native sorcerers. The most amazing thing about this outrageous *pot-pourri* was that it worked. Jacques Tourneur's direction, Curt Siodmak and Ardel Wray's screenplay (based on an original story by Inez Wallace), the expressionistic photography of J. Roy Hunt and the evocative art direction of Albert D'Agostino and Walter Keller, combined to create the most challenging and poetic of the Val Lewton-produced horror pictures. Also cast: James Ellison, Edith Barrett, James Bell, Christine Gordon (left, the zombie), Theresa Harris, Jeni LeGon, Sir Lancelot and Darby Jones.

The public's insatiable appetite for moving picture entertainment boosted **Gildersleeve's Bad Day** to success, even though it was a dull and corny fribble without a single redeeming virtue. The high point of this 'comedy-drama' came when Gildersleeve (Harold Peary, centre), trapped by two gangsters and forced to drive them away from the scene of the crime, crashes the automobile into a tree, thereby saving his own life and capturing the crooks. The responsible parties included Jack Townley (screenwriter), Herman Schlom (producer) and Gordon Douglas (director). Jane Darwell, Nancy Gates, Charles Arnt, Freddie Mercer, Russell Wade, Lillian Randolph, Frank Jenks, Douglas Fowley (right), Alan Carney (left), Grant Withers and Richard LeGrand were also in it. The best thing about **Gildersleeve's Bad Day** was that it lasted only 63 minutes.

Producer Bert Gilroy used Harry O. Hoyt's story *The Five Of Spades* as the basis for **The Avenging Rider**. The tale concerned the efforts of cowboy Tim Holt (left) to clear himself of the murder and robbery of his partner in a gold claim. The real black hats use a five of spades, torn in five pieces, as a claim check to the stolen gold. Holt eventually catches up with four of the robbers, but each is murdered before he can prove his innocence. Finally, he runs down the brains behind it all – a crooked banker who has the gold and is trying to escape. Morton Grant and Harry O. Hoyt wrote the screenplay, Sam Nelson directed it and Cliff 'Ukelele Ike' Edwards (right), Ann Summers, Davison Clark, Norman Willis, Karl Hackett, Earle Hodgins, Edward Cassidy, Kenneth Duncan, Bud McTaggart, Bud Osborne and Bob Kortman were also in it. Song: 'Minnie, My Mountain Moocher' Cliff Edwards.

Edgar Kennedy, the comic who made the 'slow burn' famous, fooled his followers by playing a sinister puppeteer in **The Falcon Strikes Back**. Implicated in the crimes of a gang of war bond thieves, the Falcon (Tom Conway, right) accumulates evidence until it points to ruthless killer Kennedy. Also enmeshed in the treacherous events were Harriet Hilliard (left), Jane Randolph, Cliff Edwards, Rita Corday, Erford Gage, Wynne Gibson, Andre Charlot, Richard Loo, Cliff Clark and Edward Gargan. Edward Dmytryk directed this intermittently exciting programmer from a story by Stuart Palmer and screenplay by Edward Dein and Gerald Geraghty. Maurice Geraghty (Gerald's brother) was the producer.

RKO board chairman Floyd Odlum, who rarely involved himself in the affairs of the studio, took a special interest in **Flight For Freedom**. Though the film was a highly fictionalized biography of Amelia Earhart, it also contained incidents that paralleled the career of Odlum's aviatrix wife Jacqueline Cochran; thus, the tycoon wanted to make certain it did justice to the subject of women's aviation and to the two special ladies as well. Horace McCoy's story, adapted by Jane Murfin and scripted by Oliver H. P. Garrett and S. K. Lauren, was a contemporary-minded speculation on the disappearance of Earhart during her final around-the-world hop. It proposed that the famous flyer crashed her plane into the Pacific on purpose, in order to give the US Navy an excuse to search the area thoroughly, photographing Japanese military fortifications in the process. With Rosalind Russell (illustrated) cast as 'lady Lindbergh' Tonie Carter and Fred MacMurray (borrowed from Paramount) as ace pilot Randy Britton, most of the screen time was taken up by a rather prosaic love drama. Carter's flying teacher (Herbert Marshall) tells her not to get involved with pilots because 'they live at 10,000 feet' – advice which she forgets altogether as soon as she meets Randy. The romance between the two flyers sputtered along and the film's premise was more than slightly preposterous, yet it still provided a solid measure of entertainment thanks to the jaunty performance of Miss Russell and the high-octane direction of Lothar Mendes. Floyd Odlum found nothing to grumble about in the final product. Eduardo Ciannelli, Walter Kingsford, Damian O'Flynn, Jack Carr, Matt McHugh, Richard Loo and Charles Lung also appeared in the David Hempstead production. Note: George Palmer Putnam, Amelia Earhart's widower, allowed **Flight For Freedom** to be made on the condition that his former wife's name would not be mentioned.

Bombardier was in production for three months and in pre-production for three years. The story of men who drop explosives with uncanny accuracy from way upstairs, it was postponed by Pearl Harbor, the loss of several members of the production staff to the armed forces, and the rapidly changing shape of military realities. The film did receive a gleeful greeting when it finally arrived in neighbourhood theatres, earning a net profit of $565,000 despite the fact that it was a veritable catalogue of war-film clichés. Among them: Major Pat O'Brien (right) and Captain Randolph Scott (left) who argue over the relative importance of pilots versus bombardiers, and compete for the romantic favours of Anne Shirley, plus a boom-boom finale in which Scott martyrs himself to assure the success of a big bombing raid on Tokyo. Producer Robert Fellows and future star Robert Ryan made their RKO bows on this picture; other members of the cast included Eddie Albert, Walter Reed, Barton MacLane, Leonard Strong, Richard Martin, Russell Wade, James Newill, John Miljan and Charles Russell. Richard Wallace directed and John Twist penned the screenplay from a story by himself and Martin Rackin. Song: 'Song Of The US Bombardiers' M. K. Jerome, Jack Scholl.

'Never has so much been owed by so many to so few', stated Winston Churchill after British Spitfires took apart the Nazi Luftwaffe over English skies in 1940. Behind that feat was the story of R. J. Mitchell, the inventor of the magnificent fighter plane, which reached American theatre screens under the title **Spitfire** (GB: **The First Of The Few**). Obviously, the film bore no relation to the Katharine Hepburn vehicle of 1934. According to the screenplay by Anatole De Grunwald and Miles Malleson (original story by Henry C. James and Kay Strueby), Mitchell got his design ideas from watching the flight of sea gulls. He was also one of the first to perceive the malevolent plans of Hitler and worked himself to death developing the formidable fighting machines that would frustrate those plans. Producer-director-star Leslie Howard (right) eschewed the melodramatic temptations of the material, and kept the film sober and straightforward. As such, it was a bit on the dull side, though its well-expressed appreciation of Mitchell and his convictions made **Spitfire** a moving achievement. Major David Niven, then serving in the British Army, was given leave to play a test pilot in the picture and, thanks to his presence, Samuel Goldwyn gained US rights to the British-made picture and released it through RKO. Rosamund John (left), Roland Culver, Anne Firth, David Horne, J. H. Roberts, Derrick de Marney, Rosalyn Boulter, Herbert Cameron, Gordon McLeod, Tonie Edgar Bruce, George Skillan and Erik Freund completed the cast. Note: By the time the picture was shown in American theatres, Leslie Howard was dead, having perished in a plane shot down between London and Lisbon. Rumours persist that Howard's aircraft was a decoy, used to divert attention from Churchill who was flying on the same day.

Deciding to upgrade the romantic appeal of the Falcon series, producer Maurice Geraghty surrounded Tom Conway (right) with Rosemary LaPlanche (Miss America of 1941), Jean Brooks (left), Amelita Ward, Elaine Shepard and Joan Barclay in **The Falcon In Danger**. Screenwriters Fred Niblo Jr and Craig Rice did a fairly smooth job of working the beauties into their story, an otherwise standard whodunit involving a double murder and the theft of $100,000 in securities. Before the murderer is captured, the Falcon is naturally suspected of the crime and nearly killed twice while trailing the varlets. Director William Clemens drove the action along at an accelerated pace, and Cliff Clark, Edward Gargan, Clarence Kolb, Felix Basch, Richard Davies, Richard Martin, Erford Gage and Eddie Dunn completed the cast. ▷

Except for one really frightening (and cinematically inspired) sequence in which a young girl (Margaret Landry) is clawed to death outside her own home, **The Leopard Man** was a flat, undistinguished thriller, lacking the fresh and penetrating approach that producer Val Lewton and director Jacques Tourneur had exercised in their two previous collaborations. One of the problems existed in the source material, Cornell Woolrich's novel *Black Alibi*, which was a hackneyed man-or-beast teaser about a series of murders committed in a sleepy New Mexico village. Another was the decision by Lewton and screenwriter Ardel Wray (additional dialogue by Edward Dein) to dispense with a central character. This caused the diffuse film to meander from one screen personage to the next and prevented it from developing more than a dab of dramatic tension. Though well made, with clever editing by Mark Robson and atmospheric photography by Robert de Grasse, **The Leopard Man** was a misfire. Dennis O'Keefe (right) topped the cast, with Margo, Jean Brooks (left), Isabel Jewell, James Bell, Abner Biberman, Richard Martin, Talu Parma, Ben Bard, Ariel Heath and Fely Franquelli also appearing.

The eighth and final movement of the Mexican Spitfire's symphony of sledgehammer slapstick recycled many of the gags and situations used before in the series. **Mexican Spitfire's Blessed Event** rested on a garbled telegram which indicated the birth of a baby spitfire to Lupe Velez (centre right). In fact, she has acquired a baby ocelot. Lord Epping's announcement that he will award a big business contract to the 'baby's' father (Walter Reed, right) opens the floodgates, prompting Lupe to 'borrow' a baby, and giving Leon Errol's (left) Uncle Matt another opportunity to impersonate his Lord Epping. Thanks to the near total lack of originality in Charles E. Roberts and Dane Lussier's script (story by Roberts) and Leslie Goodwins' direction, the time had finally come to lay the Spitfire's unbridled adventures to rest. Elisabeth Risdon (centre left), Lydia Bilbrook, Hugh Beaumont, Aileen Carlyle, Alan Carney, Marietta Canty, Ruth Lee and Wally Brown also performed for producer Bert Gilroy.

RKO should have been prosecuted for child abuse following the production of **Petticoat Larceny**. The victim was 11-year-old Joan Carroll (centre left) and the chief troublemakers were scribes Jack Townley and Stuart Palmer. Their screenplay presented Miss Carroll as a brash radio star, dissatisfied with her material, who involves herself with a trio of dumb burglars who she hopes will give her some fresh ideas. Meanwhile, both her aunt (Ruth Warrick) and the police are convinced that the young lady's disappearance is a publicity gag engineered by the aunt's fiancé (Walter Reed). After the requisite number of difficulties, Reed rescues the girl from a real kidnapper who has arrived on the scene in the meantime. The lovers are reconciled, and the starlet returns to the air with new – and better – material. One could only hope that junior Miss Carroll would merit something superior to this laboured and transparent burlesque in her next screen outing. Director Ben Holmes' supporting cast included Wally Brown, Tom Kennedy (centre right), Jimmy Conlin (left), Vince Barnett (right), Paul Guilfoyle, Grant Withers, Earl Dewey, Charles Coleman and Cliff Clark. The producer was Bert Gilroy.

The real prototype for **Red River Robin Hood** was not the legendary bandit of Sherwood Forest, but Zorro. Whitney J. Stanton's story and Bennett R. Cohen's screenplay concerned ranchers threatened with eviction when a crook claims title to their property through a phony Spanish land grant. Two brave cowboys (Tim Holt, foreground centre, and Cliff 'Ukulele Ike' Edwards, foreground left), dressed in black robes and hoods, foil the land grabber and his henchmen. The fist fights, gun battles, hell-for-leather riding and expert roping left time for 'Ukulele Ike' to sing only one song (Fred Rose and Ray Whitley's 'Twilight On The Prairie') – which was just as well because his yodelling style was beginning to grate on even the staunchest horse opera fans. Bert Gilroy produced, Lesley Selander directed and Barbara Moffett, Eddie Dew, Otto Hoffman, Russell Wade, Tom London, Earle Hodgins, Bud McTaggart (foreground right), Reed Howes and Kenneth Duncan also contributed. This would be the last Tim Holt western until the war came to an end.

Hugh Sinclair (centre) who had played the Saint in *The Saint's Vacation*, returned to impersonate Leslie Charteris' hero in the last chapter of the present series – **The Saint Meets The Tiger**. Produced in England in 1941 by William Sistrom for RKO Radio British Productions, the film was considered so pallid by company executives that they turned it over to Republic for US distribution. The laugh-provoking acting, British accents often impenetrable to American audiences, and a ridiculous plot line (screenplay by Leslie Arliss, Wolfgang Wilhelm and James Seymour from a novel by Charteris) were the chief liabilities. The Tiger in the case is an underworld smoothie trying to smuggle gold ingots out of England, as well as peddling interests in a phony gold mine. The Saint becomes involved when a man is killed on his doorstep and he is suspected of the crime. More murders come in giddy waves via bullets, knives and stranglings, but our hero survives, and dispatches the gangster in customary fashion. Paul L. Stein directed with a cast that included John Slater, Gordon McLeod, Clifford Evans, Wylie Watson, Dennis Arundell, Charles Victor, Louise Hampton, John Salew, Arthur Hambling, Amy Veness, Claude Bailey, Noel Dainton, Eric Clavering, Ben Williams and Jean Gillie (centre left). RKO released one more *Saint* movie, *The Saint's Girl Friday*, in 1954, with Louis Hayward in the title role.

'SEE captive women treated with unspeakable barbarity! SEE girls forced into gilded Geisha palaces! SEE cruel acts of war committed against even babes in arms! SEE helpless prisoners tortured until they're willing to say or do ANYTHING! SEE children driven to slave labor under the lash of hunger!' To be sure, **Behind The Rising Sun** contained all these elements, but the film was a notch above the purple potboiler that its advertising suggested. Written by Emmet Lavery and directed by Edward Dmytryk (the *Hitler's Children* team), it attempted to show the forces that led to Japanese militarism and aggression, and even dared to suggest that there might be a few 'sons of heaven' who were decent human beings unsympathetic to their government's quest for world domination. The main plot was the story of a Japanese diplomat (J. Carrol Naish) who forces his American-educated son (Tom Neal) to join the Nipponese army with tragic consequences. Robert Ryan also appeared, playing an American boxer who bests Japanese jiu-jitsu expert Mike Mazurki in the film's most rousing action sequence. Margo (left), Gloria Holden (right), Don Douglas (centre) and Adeline DeWalt Reynolds were also featured, and the rest of the cast included Leonard Strong, Iris Wong, Wolfgang Zilzer, Shirley Lew, Benson Fong and Lee Tung Foo. James R. Young's book of the same title provided Lavery with the basic material for his screenplay and RKO with another stupendous box-office bonanza (net profit $1,480,000).

Coastal Command, a one hour documentary from Britain, put audiences in the front seat of a Sunderland flying boat. Patrolling thousands of miles of ocean off the British coast, the Sunderland (illustrated) observes and guards the great convoys below, and intercepts and attacks enemy submarines and raiding battleships attempting to wreak havoc on England's Atlantic lifeline. The J. B. Holmes-directed picture contained a number of revelations about the war at sea, but it was compromised by obviously staged battle footage which cast doubt on the veracity of the documentary material. Supervisor Ian Dalrymple enjoyed the full cooperation of the Royal Air Force and Royal Navy in this Crown Film Unit production for the Ministry of Information. RKO distributed in the US.

Based on Dorothy B. Hughes' best-seller of the same title, **The Fallen Sparrow** was an exhilarating cloak-and-dagger melo featuring John Garfield (right, borrowed from Warner Bros.) and Maureen O'Hara (centre). Richard Wallace's stylish, suspenseful direction and Garfield's powerhouse performance kept audiences riveted to the saga of a Spanish Civil War veteran (Garfield) who returns to America after enduring two years of torture in a fascist prison. In New York, the hero's trials begin anew as Nazi agents use a beautiful woman (O'Hara), drugs and psychological warfare to make him divulge the secret he held fast to during those two years of hell. What the enemy doesn't count on is that the torture made their target as ruthless as they are, and provided him with the determination to outwit and smash them. Also cast: Walter Slezak (left), Patricia Morison, Martha O'Driscoll, Bruce Edwards, John Banner, John Miljan, Hugh Beaumont and Sam Goldenberg. Warren Duff wrote the screenplay and Robert Fellows produced.

Lum (Chester Lauck, left) and Abner (Norris Goff, right) set up shop on a park bench in **So This Is Washington**; before long, senators and congressmen are standing in line to consult the pair on legislative matters. The idea is that the yokels from Pine Ridge have a scarce commodity to offer the lawmakers and they aren't rationing it – common sense. Films of this kind were sincere, humorous in a simple-minded way, and so completely a product of the wartime mentality that they literally defy criticism. Alan Mowbray, Mildred Coles, Roger Clark, Sarah Padden, Minerva Urecal, Don Duncan, Matt McHugh and Barbara Pepper also had roles in the Leonard Praskins-Roswell Rogers script, which was based on an original story by Rogers and Edward James. Ray McCarey directed and Ben Hersh produced for Jack William Votion Productions.

Devil-worship was the subject of **The Seventh Victim**, another experiment in psychological terror from the fertile imaginations of Val Lewton and his 'B'-unit cohorts. The Charles O'Neal-DeWitt Bodeen screenplay called for neophyte Kim Hunter to stumble upon a satanic cult while searching for sister Jean Brooks (illustrated), who has disappeared into the bowels of Greenwich Village. Former editor Mark Robson, boosted into the director's chair by producer Lewton, displayed a flair for suspense and a feel for shuddery atmosphere, but revealed his inexperience by muddying the narrative with multiple confusions. Befuddled audiences decided the picture was horrible rather than horrific and made it the least successful of Lewton's initial cycle (they probably didn't even notice the staircase from *The Magnificent Ambersons* used in the first scene). Tom Conway again received top billing, in the familiar guise of a psychiatrist, while Isabel Jewell, Evelyn Brent, Erford Gage, Ben Bard, Hugh Beaumont, Chef Milani, Marguerita Sylva, Mary Newton, Wally Brown and Feodor Chaliapin had supporting roles.

Fred Astaire came home to RKO for **The Sky's The Limit**, a pleasant but rather poky musical that paired him with Joan Leslie (formerly Brodel). Miss Leslie had come into her own opposite Gary Cooper in *Sergeant York* and James Cagney in *Yankee Doodle Dandy*, following her apprenticeship in such RKO films as *Two Thoroughbreds* and *Laddie*. Frank Fenton and Lynn Root's original screenplay arranged for Flying Tiger pilot Astaire (right) to take a short leave in Manhattan, where he decides to avoid hero-worship by posing as a civilian idler. He meets Leslie (left), a photographer for a picture magazine, and mounts a high pressure campaign to capture her heart. She, however, is anxious to do her part for the war effort and has little use for the apparent ne'er-do-well. On this wafer-thin foundation, director Edward H. Griffith shot a series of song and dance routines (staged by Astaire) that gave the picture its few moments of intoxication. Producer David Hempstead's cast also featured Robert Benchley as Joan's magazine publisher boss, Elizabeth Patterson as a landlady, Clarence Kolb as an industrialist, Robert Ryan and Richard Davies as two of Astaire's fellow Flying Tigers plus Marjorie Gateson, Eric Blore, Peter Lawford and Freddie Slack and his Orchestra with Ella Mae Morse. Sherman Todd was the associate producer. Songs included: 'My Shining Hour', 'One For My Baby And One For The Road', 'I've Got A Lot In Common With You' Johnny Mercer, Harold Arlen. Note: In order to acquire Miss Leslie's services, and those of John Garfield for *The Fallen Sparrow*, RKO was forced to trade Warner Bros. the rights to *The Animal Kingdom* and *Of Human Bondage*. ▷

A bucking bronco conveniently deposited John Wayne in Jean Arthur's lap during **A Lady Takes A Chance**. From this point forward, it was simply a matter of time before Molly (Miss Arthur, right) put her New York City brand on Duke (Mr Wayne, left, borrowed from Republic), a cowboy wolf who claims not to be the marrying kind. Robert Ardrey's screenplay, based on a story by Jo Swerling, was a wild west variation on *It Happened One Night*, complete with well-observed spoofs of a barroom brawl, a crooked dice game and an evening on the lone prairie. It was also a bundle of fun, thanks mainly to the infectious performance of comedienne Arthur. William Seiter directed, giving orders to a large cast that included Charles Winninger, Phil Silvers, Mary Field, Don Costello, John Philliber, Grady Sutton, Grant Withers, Hans Conried, Peggy Carroll, Ariel Heath, Nina Quartaro, Alex Melesh, Cyrus W. Kendall, Paul Scott, Charles D. Brown, Butch and Buddy and The Three Peppers. Frank Ross produced with Richard Ross as his associate; the picture was a co-production between RKO and Frank Ross, Inc.

Aimed at the kiddies rather than their parents, **Gildersleeve On Broadway** found Harold Peary (left) playing Romeo to a man-hungry widow and a high-powered Broadway gold-digger in an attempt to salvage his niece's happiness. During the film's 64 lunatic minutes, Gildersleeve becomes the target of a maniac with a bow-and-arrow complex, is forced to escape the police by tight-roping along the window ledges of a skyscraper and is almost compelled to marry a woman he hardly knows. Gildy eventually accomplishes his goal and is happy to get out of New York; even the youngsters were pleased to get out of theatres that presented this Herman Schlom-produced and Gordon Douglas-directed buffoonery. Robert E. Kent's screenplay also employed Billie Burke (right), Claire Carleton, Richard LeGrand, Freddie Mercer, Hobart Cavanaugh, Margaret Landry, Leonid Kinskey, Ann Doran, Lillian Randolph and Michael Road.

The formidable team of producer Samuel Goldwyn, associate producer William Cameron Menzies, director Lewis Milestone and writer Lillian Hellman created **The North Star**, a drama about the Nazi invasion of Russia. Stressing the triple themes of romance, patriotism and revenge, the film focused on one small village whose farmers are expecting bountiful harvests, and whose young people are thinking of love and marriage, when the Stukas roar out of the western sky. Forty casualties are the result – and the rallying point for revenge. How the villagers exact their reprisals formed the basis of this uneven but nonetheless stirring tribute to our Russian allies. The all-star cast featured Anne Baxter (left) as a high school girl swept up in the tide of war, Dana Andrews as a heroic Soviet bombardier, Walter Huston as the vengeful village doctor, Walter Brennan as an elderly peasant and Erich von Stroheim as the chief Nazi vampire. Farley Granger (right) made his screen debut as Miss Baxter's lover, and Ann Harding, Jane Withers, Dean Jagger, Eric Roberts, Carl Benton Reid, Ann Carter, Esther Dale, Ruth Nelson, Paul Guilfoyle, Martin Kosleck, Tonio Selwart, Peter Pohlenz, Robert Lowery, Gene O'Donnell, Frank Wilcox, Loudie Claar, Lynn Winthrop and Charles Bates completed the cast. The striking photography was by James Wong Howe and Aaron Copland wrote the music. Songs included: 'No Village Like Mine', 'Younger Generation', 'Song Of The Guerillas' Aaron Copland, Ira Gershwin. The film, re-edited to become anti-Communist propaganda, was shown on American television in 1957, re-titled *Armoured Attack*.

The Iron Major was the story of Frank Cavanaugh, family man, World War I hero and one of the most successful football coaches in the nation at Dartmouth, Boston College, Fordham and other colleges. Screenwriters Aben Kandel and Warren Duff, working from an original story by Florence E. Cavanaugh (the Major's wife) left nary a cliché untapped in their depiction of this All-American maker of men whose last words to his boys were, 'fight for what you believe in and believe in three things – love of God . . . love of country . . . and love of family'. Who in America could argue with that? Pat O'Brien (right), who warmed up for the role by playing the famed Notre Dame coach in *Knute Rockne – All American* (Warner Brothers, 1940), was the chief inducement for seeing the picture. He gave the Cavanaugh character a solidity and magnetism that held this episodic and none-too-exciting biopic together. Ray Enright provided the lukewarm direction for producer Robert Fellows. Ruth Warrick as the Major's wife, Robert Ryan as his priest and former teammate, and Leon Ames as his lifelong friend and adviser led the supporting cast, with Russell Wade, Bruce Edwards, Richard Martin and Bob Thom (left) also appearing.

Around The World was a make-believe version of a globe-trotting entertainment tour put on by Kay Kyser (centre) and friends to lift the spirits of US fighting troops. The film was overloaded with songs by Jimmy McHugh and Harold Adamson that were not up to their best, stagy production numbers, comic volleys launched by Mischa Auer, Alan Carney, Wally Brown, Joan Davis and Kyser himself. There was also a cloak-and-dagger subplot mixing Kay and Mischa up with omnipresent Nazi spies, and a sentimental denouement in which Marcy McGuire receives the Purple Heart won by her dead father. It was hardly surprising that the film proved too bloated and frenetic to win applause from either soldiers or civilians, and it put an end to Kyser's RKO career. Ralph Spence stitched together the story and screenplay with the help of Carl Herzinger, who added special material. Producer-director Allan Dwan's cast also included Kay Kyser's Band, featuring Ish Kabibble, Georgia Carroll, Harry Babbitt (centre left), Sully Mason (left), Julie Conway, Diane Pendleton and Jack and Max. Songs included: 'Don't Believe Everything You Dream', 'Candlelight And Wine', 'He's Got A Secret Weapon', 'They Just Chopped The Old Apple Tree', 'Great News In The Making', 'Roodle-eedoo', 'The Moke From Shamokin'.

Bert Gilroy's prolific RKO career ended with **Rookies In Burma**. Charles Koerner decided that Gilroy, producer of many shorts, the George O'Brien and Tim Holt westerns, and a number of other assorted 'B's during his 11-year tenure, had gone stale and gave him the pink slip in September 1943. Gilroy's final picture provided ample justification for Koerner's views. Wally Brown (right) and Alan Carney (left) continued their impersonations of a couple of scatterbrained army privates who double-talk their way out of a Japanese concentration camp, blunder through the Burmese jungle via jeep and elephant, and finally return to the American lines in a stolen enemy tank. Scenarist Edward James even managed to work in a pair of stranded American showgirls (Joan Barclay and Claire Carleton) for the chumps to fool around with. Leslie Goodwins' dizzying direction could not hide the excruciating inanity of the undertaking. Erford Gage and Ted Hecht played the other significant roles.

Government Girl provided famed writer Dudley Nichols with his first opportunity to direct. Since Nichols also produced and penned the screenplay (based on Budd Schulberg's adaptation of a story by Adela Rogers St John), he had no one to blame but himself for the picture's inadequacies, which were legion. The story of a Detroit automobile expert (Sonny Tufts, borrowed from Paramount) who is brought to Washington to speed up the bomber programme, and the secretary (Olivia de Havilland, left) who takes him in hand and tries to guide his impetuous footsteps, it was a silly mishmash of *The More The Merrier* and half a dozen other topical plots, exacerbated by amateurishly staged comic sequences and one of the worst performances ever delivered by Miss de Havilland. She had not wanted to do the picture in the first place, but was forced into it by an arrangement whereby Warner Bros. loaned her services to David O. Selznick, who turned her over to RKO. Her distaste for the arrangement was evident in the wide variety of grimaces, mugs, smirks and other expressions she used to avoid creating a character of any depth or credibility. Though the film was dismissed as gruel by critics everywhere, theatre patrons embraced it and made it a $700,000 paybox hit. Charles Koerner deserved the bonanza more than anyone; he suffered a great deal at the hands of his intransigent female star before the film ever went before the cameras. The associate producer was Edward Donahoe, and Anne Shirley (right), Jess Barker, James Dunn, Paul Stewart, Agnes Moorehead, Harry Davenport, Una O'Connor, Sig Rumann, Jane Darwell and George Givot (centre) were also in it.

The dramatic highlights in the lives of five people – a French refugee girl (Margo, right), a race driver (Robert Ryan), a beauty contest winner (Amelita Ward), a prison warden (James Bell) and a hobo (John Carradine) – were chronicled in novel fashion by producer-director John H. Auer in **Gangway For Tomorrow**. The quintet, now working shoulder to shoulder in a defence plant, reveal the key chapters of their past as they ride to their jobs in a car owned by Charles Arnt, who has formed very different ideas about each one of them. Using flashbacks, flashbacks within flashbacks and off-screen narration, Auer succeeded in making each story distinct while still blending them into a coherent movie. And his twin themes – the deceptive nature of appearances and the unusual human connections brought about by the war effort – came through loud and clear. Also cast: William Terry, Harry Davenport, Alan Carney, Wally Brown, Erford Gage, Richard Ryen (left), Warren Hymer, Michael St Angel, Don Dillaway, Sam McDaniels and John Wald. Arch Oboler wrote the complex screenplay, based on an original story by Aladar Laszlo.

The fox turned loose in the chicken coop was a favourite plot during the war when Hollywood overflowed with female talent but had a scarcity of male performers. Tom Conway acted out a thriller variation in **The Falcon And The Co-eds**, which was set in motion by the murder of a professor in a girls' seminary. Conway (left) arrives on the scene and soon has the case wrapped up, though just exactly how he does it remained a mystery to scripters Ardel Wray and Gerald Geraghty (original story by Wray), and thus to audiences. Those viewers distracted by a bevy of delectable students didn't seem to mind, but there could be no denying that the twisting and turning narratives – formerly the essence of these pictures – were getting downright sloppy. William Clemens directed, Maurice Geraghty produced, and the cast included Jean Brooks, Rita Corday, Amelita Ward (right), Isabel Jewell, George Givot, Cliff Clark, Edward Gargan, Barbara Brown, Juanita Alvarez, Ruth Alvarez, Nancy McCollum, Patti Brill, Olin Howland and Ian Wolfe.

Writers Edward T. Lowe (screenplay) and Carroll Young (story) gave their imaginations free rein and came up with the ridiculous but diverting **Tarzan's Desert Mystery**. Rousting Tarzan (Johnny Weissmuller, left) out of the jungle and onto the fringes of the Sahara desert, the two authors had him encounter a handsome stallion named Jaynar, a beautiful American chorus girl named Connie Bryce (Nancy Kelly, right), a throng of Nazi secret agents, two Arab sheiks and their followers, prehistoric monsters and giant spiders with a special appetite for the minions of Hitler. William Thiele directed with appropriate verve and a good time was had by all – especially Cheeta the chimp who, given enough time at a typewriter, might have come up with a script like this himself. Also cast: Johnny Sheffield (centre), Otto Kruger, Joe Sawyer, Lloyd Corrigan, Robert Lowery, Frank Puglia and Phil Van Zandt. Sol Lesser produced, with Kurt Neumann as his associate, for Principal Artists Productions.

Tender Comrade should be enshrined in some World War II museum; it is one of the true historical artifacts of the war years. Producer David Hempstead, director Edward Dmytryk and writer Dalton Trumbo overlooked nothing in their story of a 'chin-up' girl (Ginger Rogers, illustrated) whose husband (Robert Ryan) dies on the battlefield shortly after a son, unknown to him, is born. In addition to its portrayal of the problems of women bereft of their loved ones and the contributions these women were making to the war effort, the picture contained sermon after sermon on the glories of America and freedom, admonitions about the danger of violating rationing restrictions, etc. All this was tied together by the most sentimental twine imaginable and shored up by the remorseless strings of Leigh Harline's musical score. The picture would soon come to be regarded as one of the most blatant examples of Communist propaganda ever put on an American screen, with Ginger and several of her co-workers at Douglas Aircraft pooling their salaries, renting a house together and sharing everything in a collective fashion. Its covert implications returned to haunt Trumbo and Dmytryk during the McCarthy period when both became members of the famous 'Hollywood Ten'. Ruth Hussey (borrowed from MGM), Patricia Collinge, Kim Hunter (borrowed from David O. Selznick) and Mady Christians played Ginger's 'share and share alike' roommates, and Jane Darwell, Richard Martin, Mary Forbes and Richard Gaines filled out the cast. A genuine three handkerchief weeper, the film hypnotized female film patrons to the tune of $843,000 in profits. Sherman Todd was the associate producer.

Val Lewton put his unique horror formula aboard **The Ghost Ship** and produced another tightly coiled and penetrating study of psychological impairment. Slightly reminiscent of *The Sea Wolf*, Donald Henderson Clarke's screenplay (from a story by Leo Mittler) focussed on freighter captain Richard Dix (right) who is gradually going insane, and third mate Russell Wade who is the only crew member perceptive enough to realise it. Wade's mates think he is the madman and laugh at his pleas for assistance, while the captain remorselessly plots a campaign of sadistic terror against the young seaman. In his final role for the studio, Richard Dix played a heavy for the first time in his career and contributed a potent, unnerving performance under Mark Robson's controlled direction. The supporting cast included Edith Barrett, Ben Bard, Edmund Glover, Skelton Knaggs, Tom Burton, Steve Winston, Robert Bice, Lawrence Tierney, Dewey Robinson, Charles Lung, George de Normand, Paul Marion, Sir Lancelot and Boyd Davis. Note: The film has not been legally screened in many years because of a plagiarism suit brought by Samuel R. Golding and Norbert Faulkner, who claimed that Lewton based **The Ghost Ship** on a play they had written and produced in 1942. RKO lost the case in trial court, the judgment was affirmed on appeal and no one could thenceforward distribute the picture.

Although Michele Morgan (left), Jack Haley, Leon Errol, Marcy McGuire, Victor Borge, Mary Wickes, Elisabeth Risdon, Barbara Hale, Mel Torme, Paul and Grace Hartman, Dooley Wilson and Ivy Scott were also in it, **Higher And Higher** was billed as 'The Sinatra Show!' Swooner-crooner Frank Sinatra (right), given his first major Hollywood vehicle, emerged with his teenage following intact, despite the film's murky plot and less-than-scintillating musical score. Based on a play by Gladys Hurlbut and Joshua Logan and scripted by Jay Dratler and Ralph Spence (additional dialogue William Bowers and Howard Harris), the story had something to do with a group of servants facing the loss of their back wages due to their employer's imminent bankruptcy. The busted employer (Errol) forms a corporation headed by his valet (Haley); the corporation's goal is to pass off scullery maid Morgan as Errol's debutante daughter and marry her off to a rich man, thereby saving the lot of them. Sinatra played the boy next door who popped up whenever it seemed appropriate to pause for a tune. Tim Whelan added the artless direction, doubling as producer with George Arthur as his associate. Rex Evans, Stanley Logan, Ola Lorraine, King Kennedy and Robert Andersen also played bit parts, and Constantin Bakaleinikoff functioned as musical director. Songs included: 'A Most Important Affair', 'The Music Stopped', 'Today I'm A Debutante', 'A Lovely Way To Spend An Evening', 'I Couldn't Sleep A Wink Last Night', 'I Saw You First', 'You're On Your Own' Jimmy McHugh, Harold Adamson; 'Disgustingly Rich' Richard Rodgers, Lorenz Hart.

☆☆☆☆☆☆☆☆☆☆☆☆☆☆
1944
☆☆☆☆☆☆☆☆☆☆☆☆☆☆

Charles Koerner realigned studio operations during the year, creating various units within the overall production framework. These units were headed by Jack J. Gross, whom Koerner lured away from Universal, Robert Fellows and Sid Rogell. Each of these gentlemen would be accorded executive producer status and supervise a slate of pictures under the general administration of Mr Koerner. Koerner also employed William Dozier as his executive assistant; Dozier would work closely with various writers and producers.

Another powerful independent organization entered the fold. International Pictures, the brainchild of William Goetz and Leo Spitz, began to make pictures and release them via RKO. **Casanova Brown** was their first production.

One of RKO's major stars of later years, Robert Mitchum, began his studio career with a minor role in **Girl Rush**, then received top billing in the Zane Grey western **Nevada**. Gregory Peck also made his film debut, in **Days Of Glory**. Three screenwriters entered the field of directing – Clifford Odets (**None But The Lonely Heart**), Howard Estabrook (**Heavenly Days**) and Herbert Biberman (**The Master Race**).

Thirty-three films were released in 1944. There were no $1 million-plus profit-makers, though **Show Business, Tall In The Saddle** and **Bride By Mistake** posted very strong earnings. The year's corporate net profit was $5,206,378 – down slightly from the year before. Nevertheless, the RKO board of directors and stockholders were so delighted that they voted approval of a pension trust plan for the employees of the company and its affiliates.

Escape To Danger was another routine espionage titillation, full of narrative surprises but not much trenchant drama. An English teacher in Denmark (Ann Dvorak, left) appears to be working for the Axis but is really doing her duty for the Allies. The Nazis send her to England on a spying mission where she is trailed and exposed by unconventional secret agent Eric Portman (right). The information at stake in this picture turned out to be the invasion plans of the Allies which, at least, made it a well-timed if lacklustre diversion. Lance Comfort and Mutz Greenbaum co-directed for producer Victor Hanbury. Wolfgang Wilhelm and Jack Whittingham's screenplay (story by Patrick Kirwan) gave roles to Karel Stepanek, Ronald Ward, Felix Aylmer, David Peel, Ronald Adam, Marjorie Rhodes, Hay Petrie, Lilly Kann, Charles Victor, George Merritt, Brefni O'Rorke, Frederick Cooper, Anthony Shaw, John Ruddock, A. E. Matthews, Ivor Barnard, Richard George, D'Oyley John, James Pirrie, Ian Fleming, George Woodbridge and Norman Whitcomb. **Escape To Danger** was made in England by RKO Radio British Productions.

The search for a killer who murders with rattlesnake venom took **The Falcon Out West**. Produced by Maurice Geraghty and directed by William Clemens, the story mixed the sleuthing with standard horse-opera clichés including ambushes, runaway stagecoaches and chase scenes. Appearing in his fifth Falcon picture, Tom Conway (right) now seemed bored instead of nonchalant as he moved automatically through another exercise in detection. The Billy Jones-Morton Grant screenplay gave him plenty to be bored about. Harry Wild's first-rate photography of several interesting western locations was the best thing in the picture. Also in the cast: Carole Gallagher, Barbara Hale (left), Cliff Clark, Edward Gargan, Minor Watson and Lyle Talbot.

The talents of producer-writer Nunnally Johnson, director Sam Wood and star Gary Cooper were not shown to good advantage in **Casanova Brown**. Based on the play *Little Accident* by Floyd Dell and Thomas Mitchell (filmed by Universal in 1930 and again in 1939), the trifling story focused on 'Caz' Brown (Cooper, left) who is about to marry for the second time when he learns that he is the father of a child born to his first wife (Teresa Wright, right) and that she is offering the baby for adoption. Aghast at this possibility, he spirits the child from the maternity hospital, takes her to a cheap hotel and settles down to baby-tending. Most of the humour in the film emanated from the sight of the man who had played the Virginian, Wild Bill Hickok and Sergeant York coo-cooing, clowning and behaving in a manner more infantile than the baby. Anita Louise, Frank Morgan, Patricia Collinge, Edmond Breon, Jill Esmond, Mary Treen, Emory Parnell, Isobel Elsom, Halliwell Hobbes, Charles Cane, Larry Olsen, Irving Bacon, Dorothy Tree and Robert Emmett Keane were also in it. **Casanova Brown** was the first production from International Pictures, a potent new independent company formed by William Goetz and former RKO corporate president Leo Spitz.

George Sanders (left, borrowed from 20th Century-Fox) made himself at home in treacherous surroundings in **Action In Arabia**. Cast as a resourceful American newspaperman on the prowl in Damascus, Sanders set about unravelling the murder of a reporter colleague. Displaying wits and daring, and aided by good luck and a female secret agent (Virginia Bruce), he solved the homicide and sabotaged a Nazi scheme to destroy the Suez Canal. Critics regarded the film as a thoroughly routine piece of wartime intrigue, but were puzzled by one element: how did producer Maurice Geraghty, working on what looked to be a 'B' budget, manage to include an action-filled desert climax involving more Arabs, horses and camel caravans than the mind could count? What they didn't know was that the spectacular material was really stock footage, shot in 1933 by director Ernest B. Schoedsack, for an abortive RKO film about Lawrence of Arabia. Also cast: Lenore Aubert (right, borrowed from Samuel Goldwyn), Gene Lockhart, Robert Armstrong, H. B. Warner, Alan Napier, Andre Charlot, Marcel Dalio, Robert Andersen, John Hamilton and Mike Ansara. Leonide Moguy directed from an original screenplay by Philip MacDonald and Herbert Biberman.

The performance of Elsa Lanchester made **Passport To Destiny** almost worth seeing. Cockney scrubwoman Lanchester (right), convinced that a snake-eye charm owned by her late husband will keep her out of danger, goes trooping off to Berlin to kill Hitler. Though she never comes near him, she does get mixed up in the German underground and is arrested, before returning to England in a German plane piloted by an underground officer. Val Burton and Muriel Roy Bolton's screenplay was quintessential tommyrot, undiluted by even the smallest amount of intelligence or common sense, but Miss Lanchester made it bearable with her unique histrionic abilities. Ray McCarey directed, Herman Schlom produced and Gordon Oliver (on loan from David O. Selznick), Lenore Aubert (on loan from Samuel Goldwyn), Lionel Royce (centre left), Fritz Feld, Joseph Vitale (centre right), Gavin Muir (left), Lloyd Corrigan, Anita Bolster, Lumsden Hare and Hans Schumm supported.

Contrary to expectations raised by its title, **The Curse Of The Cat People** was not really a sequel to *Cat People* or, indeed, a horror picture at all. It did have one scary sequence but, otherwise, the film was a journey into the fertile realm of a child's imagination. Six-year-old Ann Carter (right) played the protagonist whose loneliness provokes her to create a dream world of her own. Her father, Kent Smith (the cat woman's husband in the first picture), is afraid the youngster will grow up to be obsessed by weird ideas like his first wife and tries to guide her away from her supernatural preoccupations. Soon, however, she has manufactured an imaginary friend (Simone Simon, left, the original cat woman) who becomes her adviser and protector against the unpleasant realities of the human condition. Dissatisfied with the work of director Gunther Von Fritsch, producer Val Lewton decided to replace him with Robert Wise, thereby launching the career of one of Hollywood's major directors. Wise shared the final credit with Fritsch, though the former *Citizen Kane* editor directed most of the picture. Jane Randolph, Elizabeth Russell, Eve March, Julia Dean, Sir Lancelot, Joel Davis and Juanita Alvarez also played roles in DeWitt Bodeen's screenplay. RKO definitely should have been sued for false advertising on this movie. 'The Beast-Woman Haunts The Night Anew!' and 'Strange Adventures In Evil' hardly captured the essence of this wistful and ambiguous fable.

When one doughboy in **Up In Arms** spies a bevy of Goldwyn girls romping on the deck of his troop ship, he exclaims, 'We didn't have anything like this in the last war!' A fellow soldier retorts, 'We don't have anything like it in this one, either.' Thanks to the presence of Danny Kaye, most audiences were willing to suspend disbelief and play along with the movie's total implausibility. Kaye (centre left) made his screen debut as a hypochondriac elevator operator who cannot understand it when he is drafted into the Army. Indulging in his own unique brand of double-talk, burlesquing the movies in a hilarious musical number set in the lobby of Radio City Music Hall, singing a jive duet with Dinah Shore (left) and rounding up a troop of Japanese soldiers in a Mack Sennett-inspired finale, Kaye became the screen's newest original and Mr Goldwyn's newest star. Director Elliott Nugent possessed the good sense to stand back and let the comedian mimic his way into the public's good graces. An old chestnut called *The Nervous Wreck* by Owen Davis provided the inspiration for the Don Hartman-Allen Boretz-Robert Pirosh screenplay. Goldwyn produced (associate producer Don Hartman) and his cast also included Dana Andrews (right), Constance Dowling (centre right), Louis Calhern, George Mathews, Benny Baker, Elisha Cook Jr, Lyle Talbot, Walter Catlett, George Meeker, Margaret Dumont (centre), Charles Arnt, Sig Arno and Rudolf Friml Jr. Songs included: 'Now I Know', 'Tess', 'Torch Song', 'All Out For Freedom' Harold Arlen, Ted Koehler; 'Melody In 4-F' Sylvia Fine, Max Liebman. ▷

What's this? Anna Neagle (centre) playing a Nazi sympathizer in **Yellow Canary**? Not to worry – the Miles Malleson-DeWitt Bodeen screenplay eventually divulges that the heroine's pro-Nazi tendencies are just a ploy to infiltrate an Axis spy ring headquartered in Canada and prevent the Germans from blowing up the harbour in Halifax, Nova Scotia. She accomplishes her mission, with some assistance from British intelligence officer Richard Greene (left). Producer-director Herbert Wilcox handled the plot in such a slow, cautious style that much of its force evaporated before the action-filled climax. P. M. Bower wrote the original story and Nova Pilbeam, Albert Lieven (right), Lucie Mannheim, Margaret Rutherford, Marjorie Fielding, Valentine Dyall, David Horne, Claude Bailey and Cyril Fletcher were also in the cast. The picture was made by Imperator and RKO Radio British Productions.

Show Business, suggested by incidents in the career of Eddie Cantor, chronicled the fortunes of a small group of stage folk from 1914 to 1929 and, in the process, reviewed the changes that occurred in American variety entertainment during that era. Breezy, lavish and nostalgic, the Edwin L. Marin directorial effort pleased both the average person looking for 90 minutes of fun, and the dyed-in-the-wool theatrical buffs. Cantor produced the movie and topped the cast; highlights included George Murphy (left), Constance Moore (centre left), Cantor (centre right) and Joan Davis (right) doing a side-splitting travesty of Grand Opera, Cantor singing 'Dinah' in blackface, and Cantor performing the famous title song from the Ziegfeld Follies production, *Whoopee*. Bert Granet wrote the original story, Joseph Quillan and Dorothy Bennett the screenplay and Irving Elinson penned additional dialogue. Nancy Kelly and Don Douglas also had feature roles. Songs: 'You May Not Remember Me' George Jessel, Ben Oakland; and a number of old standards including 'Alabamy Bound' Ray Henderson, Buddy De Sylva, Bud Green; 'I Want A Girl (Just Like The Girl Who Married Dear Old Dad)' Harry von Tilzer, Will Dillon; 'They're Wearing Them Higher In Hawaii' Halsey K. Mohr, Joe Goodwin; 'It Had To Be You' Gus Kahn, Isham Jones.

Casey Robinson, the writer of scripts for *Dark Victory, Now Voyager, Kings Row* and other major Warner Brothers pictures, turned producer with **Days Of Glory**, casting his picture with actors and actresses never before seen on theatre screens. This daring experiment was intended to give the film a sense of realism that would be lost if familiar faces appeared. Gregory Peck represented the major unknown, playing the leader of a handful of Soviet patriots hiding inside Nazi lines south of Moscow and waging guerrilla warfare against the enemy. A romance blossoms between Peck (left) and a dancer (Tamara Toumanova, right, former premier ballerina of the Ballet Russe de Monte Carlo and now Mrs Casey Robinson); both earn their glory by dying during the big Russian counteroffensive against the Nazis. The film garnered considerable praise for its low-key intensity and humanistic spirit, but flopped for several reasons: the absence of marquee names, the uniformly stiff acting of the neophytes, the grim and depressing ending and screenwriter Robinson's long-winded dialogues about heroism, poetry and death. Jacques Tourneur did a satisfactory job directing his first 'A' picture, and Lowell Gilmore, Maria Palmer, Alan Reed, Hugo Haas, Igor Dolgoruki, Edward Durst, Glenn Vernon and Dena Penn also appeared. Melchior Lengyel wrote the original story which Robinson used as the basis of his $958,000 production.

Gordon Oliver (right) needed plenty of salesmanship to convince Elaine Shepard (left) that she was the only girl for him in **Seven Days Ashore**, a well-flavoured musical comedy produced and directed by John H. Auer. Oliver's troubles begin when his ship docks in San Francisco and three girls (Miss Shepard, Amelita Ward and Virginia Mayo) are waiting to greet him. The sailor escapes from this ticklish situation temporarily by roping in two shipmates (Alan Carney and Wally Brown) as dates for the extra girls. A couple of breach-of-promise suits and the efforts of the two pals to extricate philanderer Oliver from his problems kept it moving along to a merry, musical climax. Edward Verdier, Irving Phillips and Lawrence Kimble wrote the screenplay (based on a story by Jacques Deval), which also gave opportunities to spotlight Marcy McGuire, Dooley Wilson, Marjorie Gateson, Alan Dinehart, Miriam La Velle, Margaret Dumont, Emory Parnell, Ian Wolfe, Freddie Slack and his Orchestra and Freddie Fisher (Colonel Corn) and his Band. Songs included: 'The Poor Little Fly On The Wall', 'Improvisation In B Flat' Freddie Fisher; 'Apple Blossoms In The Rain', 'Hail And Farewell', 'Sioux City Sue', 'Ready, Aim, Kiss' Mort Greene, Lew Pollack.

The aptly titled **Gildersleeve's Ghost** was RKO's last film starring Harold Peary (left), who had the ability to transport audiences rather quickly to slumberland but not to make them laugh. In a desperate attempt to wake up the patrons, scenarist Robert E. Kent uncorked a wild plot about the efforts of two of Gildy's ancestral ghosts to make him a town hero and thus ensure his election as police commissioner. They lead him to a haunted house where a pair of scientists (Frank Reicher and Joseph Vitale) are carrying out invisibility experiments with a gorilla and a kidnapped girl (Marion Martin, right). According to form, the great one stumbles and fumbles before capturing the ape, freeing the girl, bringing the sinister scientists to justice and more or less proving he is not insane. Gordon Douglas handled the perfunctory direction for producer Herman Schlom. Also cast: Richard LeGrand, Amelita Ward, Freddie Mercer, Margie Stewart, Marie Blake, Emory Parnell, Lillian Randolph, Nicodemus Stewart and Charles Gemora.

Scenarists Warren Duff and Peter Milne and songwriters Sammy Cahn and Jule Styne embroidered *Room Service* with singing, dancing and romancing and gave birth to **Step Lively**. Frank Sinatra (foreground left) received first billing as a determined young playwright seeking to recover the money he has loaned fast-talking Broadway producer George Murphy (foreground right, borrowed from MGM). Murphy has other ideas, involving Sinatra in a series of stratagems designed to stall eviction from his hotel and to coax financial support from a reluctant backer. With Murphy in top form and Walter Slezak, Adolphe Menjou, Wally Brown, Alan Carney and Eugene Pallette also contributing, the farcical horseplay was generally superior to that of the 1938 Marx Brothers version. Though the musical numbers tended to break the comic momentum on occasion, Tim Whelan's pacey direction brought the events back to high gear in a remarkably short time. Sinatra received his initial screen kisses from Gloria de Haven (foreground centre, borrowed from MGM) and Anne Jeffreys, causing thousands of young, female Frankie-philes to swoon. Grant Mitchell, Frances King and Harry Noble also appeared in the Robert Fellows production, based on the slightly whiskered Broadway play by John Murray and Allen Boretz. Songs included: 'Some Other Time', 'As Long As There Is Music', 'Ask The Madam', 'Where Does Love Begin?', 'Why Must There Be An Opening Song?'

A routine bombardment from Hollywood's propaganda howitzer, complete with action, romance and a conflict between two he-man officers, **Marine Raiders** fell into step with dozens of other accounts of America's devil-dogs in action. Pat O'Brien (right) and Robert Ryan (left) played Marines who survive the Guadalcanal affair and are sent to Australia for a respite from battle. Ryan meets Ruth Hussey (borrowed from MGM), they fall in love but are prevented from marrying by O'Brien who orders his fellow officer back to California to help train a new invasion force. Bitter over O'Brien's action, Ryan refuses to speak to him other than officially, and the feud continues until they are sent back to Australia. There, the friendship and the romance are rekindled prior to the departure of the two leathernecks on another dangerous mission. Harold Schuster directed from a story by Martin Rackin and Warren Duff and screenplay by Duff. Others cast for producer Robert Fellows were Frank McHugh, Barton MacLane, Richard Martin (centre), Edmund Glover, Russell Wade, Robert Andersen, Michael St Angel, Martha MacVicar (later Vickers) and Harry Brown.

Producer Maurice Geraghty and director Gordon Douglas teased Tom Conway (centre) with a series of filmland murders in **The Falcon In Hollywood**. The murderer in this case is picking off various people connected with the production of a certain motion picture, a premise that provided the opportunity to take audiences on a tour of the various departments of a movie studio (guess which one?), plus side trips to Hollywood Park race track and the Hollywood Bowl. This was the tenth edition of the Falcon series, and its hackneyed Gerald Geraghty script suggested it might be wise to give the whole production team some time off. Film consumers still relished the heavy-handed carryings on, however; they made **The Falcon In Hollywood** a $115,000 winner. Also cast: Barbara Hale and Rita Corday (right) as two actresses, Konstantin Shayne as a temperamental director, John Abbott as a Shakespearean producer, plus Veda Ann Borg (left), Sheldon Leonard, Emory Parnell, Frank Jenks, Jean Brooks, Walter Soderling, Useff Ali and Robert Clarke.

Shades of Wheeler and Woolsey at their lowest ebb, **Girl Rush** presented Alan Carney and Wally Brown as vaudeville troupers stranded in San Francisco by the 1849 Sutter's Mill gold strike. Following an unsuccessful round of prospecting, the two clowns decide to bring a revue, featuring lots of girls, to the mining camps and strike paydirt that way. Robert E. Kent wrote it from a story by Laszlo Vadnay and Aladar Laszlo, Gordon Douglas directed it and Sid Rogell produced (uncredited). Except for the appearance of future RKO heavy weight Robert Mitchum (centre) in a secondary role, the picture was forgettable. Frances Langford (right), Paul Hurst (left), radio's Vera Vague (Barbara Jo Allan), Patti Brill, Sarah Padden, Cyrus W. Kendall and John Merton were also cast. Songs included: 'Annabella's Bustle', 'Rainbow Valley', 'If Mother Could Only See Us Now', 'Walking Arm In Arm With Jim' Harry Harris, Lew Pollack.

In **Goin' To Town**, Lum (Chester Lauck, centre) and Abner (Norris Goff, left) persuade the natives of Pine Ridge to mortgage their property so they can drill for oil around the Jot-Em-Down store. When all the money is spent and there is no black gold, the two storekeepers head for Chicago where they have the time of their lives dancing with chorus girls, then take advantage of the greedy impulses of various wheeler-dealers and return home with $80,000 to rescue their neighbours. Frank Melford produced, Leslie Goodwins directed and Charles E. Roberts and Charles R. Marion wrote the screenplay. Also cast in this mediocre comedy: Barbara Hale, Florence Lake, Grady Sutton, Dick Elliott (right), Herbert Rawlinson, Dick Baldwin, Ernie Adams, Jack Rice, Sam Flint, Andrew Tombes, George Chandler, Ruth Lee, Danny Duncan, Marietta Canty and Nils T. Granlund. The film was made by Jack William Votion Productions.

Howard Estabrook had been a top RKO writer ▷ during the LeBaron era, with the prestigious *Cimarron* to his credit. Now he returned to the studio as director and co-author of **Heavenly Days**. A failed kettle of Capra-corn in the *Mr Smith Goes To Washington* vein, the story used Fibber McGee and Molly to represent the desires of the common man before Congress in Washington. At first ridiculed for his efforts, Fibber is eventually chosen as Mr Average Man by the Gallup Poll and uses this position to awaken his fellow Americans to their civic responsibilities. The propagandistic sorghum proved too thick for most filmgoers to stomach, causing the picture to bomb ($205,000 loss). Domestic audiences obviously preferred Fibber the comedian to Fibber the patron saint of American virtues. Jim Jordan (right) and Marian Jordan (centre right) played Fibber and Molly, with Eugene Pallette, Gordon Oliver, Raymond Walburn, Barbara Hale, Don Douglas, Irving Bacon, the King's Men, Frieda Inescort (left) and Charles Trowbridge (centre left) also cast. Don Quinn collaborated with Estabrook on the screenplay, which was based on an original story by the director. Robert Fellows produced.

Tall In The Saddle was a rip-roaring mystery romance with a western setting, involving two murders, several gun fights, three bare-knuckle brawls, two beautiful gals and a tough, misogynistic cowhand. John Wayne (centre) played the taciturn woman-hater in his first RKO film under a new, multiple-picture deal with the studio. Screenwriters Michael Hogan and Paul P. Fix (who also appeared in it) adapted Gordon Ray Young's story about two villains (Don Douglas and Ward Bond) who cook up a land grab scheme which Wayne eventually demolishes. In the process, Ella Raines (left, borrowed from Universal) and Audrey Long (right) change his attitude towards the fair sex. George 'Gabby' Hayes supplied the comedy relief as a cantankerous stage driver, and Elisabeth Risdon, Russell Wade, Emory Parnell, Raymond Hatton, Harry Woods, Wheaton Chambers, Frank Puglia and Bob McKenzie were in it too. Robert Fellows produced and Edwin L. Marin directed this ten-gallon hit; former studio editor Theron Warth received his initial credit as associate producer. ▽

Nevada, the first of a new series of westerns based on the novels of Zane Grey, cast Robert Mitchum (left) in the role of Jim 'Nevada' Lacy, a cowpoke who heads for the Comstock Lode to try and strike it rich. Instead, he taps into a vein of trouble. Suspected of having murdered a homesteader, Mitchum narrowly escapes being lynched, then hangs around long enough to romance the homesteader's daughter (Nancy Gates) and unmask the real killers (Craig Reynolds, right, and Harry Woods). Norman Houston's screenplay also provided featured roles for Anne Jeffreys, Guinn 'Big Boy' Williams, Richard Martin, Edmund Glover, Alan Ward, Harry McKim, Larry Wheat, Jack Overman, Emmett Lynn, Wheaton Chambers and Philip Morris. It was well-directed by Edward Killy, who was particularly good on the action scenes, and the Herman Schlom production (executive producer Sid Rogell) looked much more expensive than it really was. Paramount had already made two versions of Grey's novel; the first starred Gary Cooper and Thelma Todd in 1927 and the second featured Larry 'Buster' Crabbe and Kathleen Burke in 1936. ▽

Echoing the plot of *Gaslight*, **Experiment Perilous** presented Hedy Lamarr (left, on loan from MGM) as the hauntingly beautiful wife of Paul Lukas, a jealous maniac who is terrorizing her to the brink of insanity and turning their son into a neurotic wreck. Psychiatrist George Brent (right) comes to the rescue, frustrating the madman and winning the love of Miss Lamarr. Warren Duff's screenplay, based on a novel by Margaret Carpenter, was excessively verbose and unnecessarily complicated by multiple flashbacks, but the superlative acting of Lukas and Lamarr and the supple, probing direction of Jacques Tourneur created a psychological thriller of absorbing quality. Also cast: Albert Dekker, Carl Esmond, Olive Blakeney, George N. Neise, Margaret Wycherly, Stephanie Bachelor, Mary Servoss, Julia Dean, William Post Jr and Billy Ward. Under Charles Koerner's new unit arrangements, Robert Fellows received executive producer credit and writer Warren Duff was the producer. ▽

None But The Lonely Heart was a daring and unusual film, written and directed for the screen by Clifford Odets from a novel by Richard Llewellyn. Cary Grant (right), cast against type as a restless cockney resident of the London slums reaching out towards a better life, delivered a restrained, exemplary performance, matched by Ethel Barrymore's (left) moving portrayal of his cancer-stricken mother. Resolutely downbeat and depressing, the picture never compromised in its glum portrait of shattered dreams in a sordid and indifferent world. This was not the uplifting escapism that audiences were accustomed to seeing in 1944, and it understandably lost money at the box-office (though not a huge amount). Mr Odets' stage background was evident in the picture's major weakness – his extended use of long, static, conversational scenes that communicated the thematic content but were not cinematically satisfying. Still, this was a respectable job by a first-time director. Barry Fitzgerald, June Duprez, Jane Wyatt, George Coulouris, Dan Duryea, Roman Bohnen, Konstantin Shayne, Eva Leonard Boyne, Morton Lowry, Helene Thimig and William Challee also appeared for producer David Hempstead. It was Hempstead's final RKO production. Note: To secure the services of Ethel Barrymore, the studio had to pay the expenses involved in temporarily closing her play, *The Corn Is Green*. ▷

★★★★★★★★★★★★★★★★★★★

1945

★★★★★★★★★★★★★★★★★★★

An eight-month strike of disenchanted office employees and technicians slowed down production throughout Hollywood, but the studio was still able to put 32 pictures into theatres by the end of the year. The last of these, **The Bells Of St Mary's**, raked in enough profits throughout the following year to become the biggest smash in RKO history. Other top money-spinners were **The Spanish Main, Johnny Angel, The Enchanted Cottage, Those Endearing Young Charms** and **Murder, My Sweet**. Corporate profits totalled $6,031,085.

Charles Koerner continued to set up deals with powerhouse independents. An agreement between the studio and Leo McCarey's Rainbow Productions gave RKO **The Bells of St Mary's**, and Liberty Productions (Frank Capra-William Wyler-George Stevens-Sam Briskin) also signed to release through RKO. Koerner showed his faith in the star system by arranging for Bing Crosby, Ingrid Bergman, Cary Grant, Joan Fontaine, Claudette Colbert, John Wayne, Rosalind Russell, George Raft, Paul Henreid, Robert Young, Ginger Rogers and other top people to appear in future RKO releases.

World War II finally ended in August; RKO geared itself to the reopening of various foreign markets by quickly establishing a field exploitation staff for European sales. Production chief Koerner made a trip to Europe in the fall to survey company prospects and discuss a joint production arrangement with J. Arthur Rank and the Rank group in the United Kingdom.

Raymond Chandler regarded **Murder, My Sweet** (GB: **Farewell, My Lovely**, the title of the original novel) as the best film adaptation of any of his works, and considered Dick Powell the nearest cinematic equivalent to his own conception of Philip Marlowe. Powell (right) was surprisingly good in the role, abandoning his cheery song-and-dance man persona to become one of the classic hard-boiled heroes. Director Edward Dmytryk explored the full vocabulary of film to convey the descent of private eye Marlowe into a nether world of homicide, blackmail, charlatanism, thievery, sadistic violence, sexual enslavement and, above all else, mystery. The film's dream and drug sequences (cinematography by Harry J. Wild; special effects by Vernon L. Walker) were especially effective in their visualization of Marlowe's confused and paranoiac state of mind. One of the refreshing aspects of **Murder, My Sweet** was its notable lack of clean-living, soft-spoken heroes and heroines. Here we find two-faced Claire Trevor, cretinous giant Mike Mazurki (centre, playing Moose Malloy who sets the plot in motion), boozy old floozy Esther Howard, psychoanalytic blackmailer Otto Kruger (left) and angry and scornful Anne Shirley. It was some cross-section of *homo sapiens*, performed wholeheartedly by the leading actors, and supported by equally impressive characterizations from Miles Mander, Douglas Walton, Don Douglas and Ralf Harolde. John Paxton's screenplay remained reasonably faithful to its source and preserved a fair dose of Chandler's exceptional dialogue. Adrian Scott produced, working with executive producer Sid Rogell. Elements of the basic story had been used in *The Falcon Takes Over* (1942); it would be remade as *Farewell, My Lovely* in 1975 with Robert Mitchum playing Marlowe in the Avco-Embassy release.
▽

△
Director Max Nosseck and actor John Loder squeezed a full measure of chills out of the intriguing premise of **The Brighton Strangler**. Thespian Loder (right) has been on the London boards with a play about a murderer for over a year when a Nazi bomb destroys his theatre. Though the actor is only stunned, he begins to confuse his true identity with that of the character he has been impersonating. Wandering into Victoria Station, he overhears a remark made by a complete stranger which is an exact cue from the play; this sends him off to Brighton where he starts to enact, for real, the drama's brutal plot points. June Duprez, Michael St Angel, Miles Mander (left), Rose Hobart, Gilbert Emery, Rex Evans, Matthew Boulton, Olaf Hytten, Lydia Bilbrook and Ian Wolfe added strong support in the Herman Schlom production (executive producer Sid Rogell). Arnold Phillips collaborated with director Nosseck on the original screenplay (additional dialogue by Hugh Gray). Director George Cukor, writers Garson Kanin and Ruth Gordon and star Ronald Colman probed roughly the same phenomena with considerably more psychological depth in *A Double Life* (1948), but this modest RKO programmer aimed only to frighten, and succeeded very nicely as a spine-tingler.

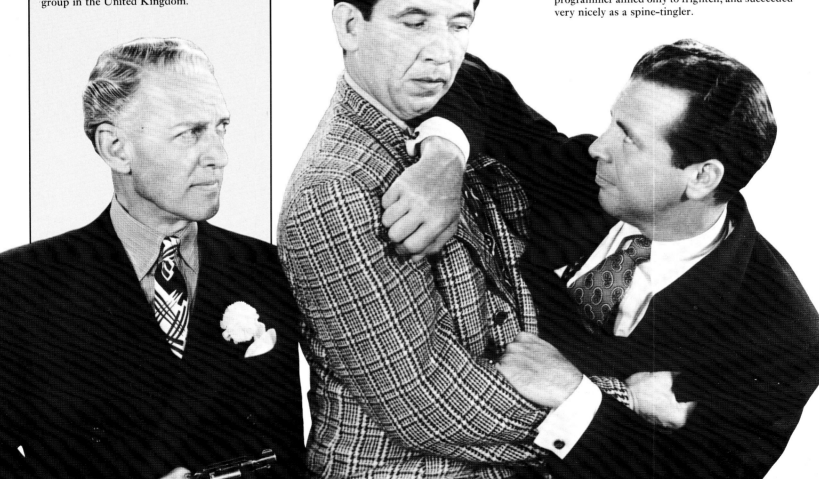

The first feature comedy based on gas rationing, **What A Blonde** had funny moments, but it was hardly the 'mirthquake' that the studio advertised. Director Leslie Goodwins used Leon Errol (left) as the lingerie tycoon who has run out of gas coupons. Errol orders butler Richard Lane to drum up riders so that he can secure extra coupons from the ration board. The roguish Lane finds a group of out-of-work showgirls, parks them in Errol's mansion and stands back to watch the domestic fireworks which inevitably erupt. Veda Ann Borg (right) played the blonde of the title, Lydia Bilbrook was Errol's not-so-understanding wife and Clarence Kolb a highly moralistic business rival. Charles E. Roberts' screenplay (story Oscar Brodney) also gave work to Michael St Angel, Elaine Riley, Ann Shoemaker, Chef Milani, Emory Parnell, Larry Wheat, Dorothy Vaughan and Jason Robards. Ben Stoloff produced; Sid Rogell was the executive producer.

Constructed to showcase the talents of various Latin-American performers, **Pan-Americana** followed the adventures of the editorial staff of *Western World* pictorial magazine who head south of the border to research a feature story. They stop off in such countries as Cuba, Mexico and Brazil just long enough for producer-director John H. Auer to punch in a quick musical number, then hurry on. Told in flashback style and narrated by Robert Benchley (courtesy of Paramount), who is one of the members of the journeying party, the film was frenetic, synthetic and mediocre. Its one moment of electricity was furnished by Harold and Lola, who contributed a smoldering snake dance. Also cast: Phillip Terry (right), Audrey Long (left), Eve Arden, Ernest Truex, Marc Cramer, Isabelita, Rosario and Antonio, Miguelito Valdes, Louise Burnett, Chinita Marin, Chuy Castillon, the Padilla Sisters, Chuy Reyes and his Orchestra and Nestor Amaral and his Samba Band. Sid Rogell supervised and Lawrence Kimble wrote the screenplay from a story by Frederick Kohner and Auer. Songs included: 'Rumba' Bobby Collazo; 'Guadalajara' Pepe Guizar; 'Babalu' Margarita Lecuona; 'Negra Leona' A. Fernandez; 'Baramba' Margarita Lecuona, English lyrics Mort Greene.

Comedy and thrills competed for first position in **Having Wonderful Crime**, but neither crossed the finishing line. Pat O'Brien (left) played a lawyer constantly embroiled in murder mysteries because of his zany friends Carole Landis (centre, borrowed from 20th Century-Fox) and George Murphy (right, on loan from MGM) who have a passion for crime detection. The amateur sleuths get in over their heads while investigating the disappearance of a magician. So did director A. Edward Sutherland and screenwriters Howard J. Green, Stewart Sterling and Parke Levy, whose indecisive and sluggish collaboration produced plenty of empty seats in theatres that played it. Based on a novel by Craig Rice, it also featured Lenore Aubert (borrowed from Samuel Goldwyn), Anje Berens (to be better known as Gloria Holden), George Zucco, Richard Martin, Charles D. Brown, William 'Wee Willie' Davis, Blanche Ring, Josephine Whittell and Chili Williams. Theron Warth worked as associate to producer Robert Fellows.

A recommendation by executive producer Jack J. Gross that the employment of well-known horror film actors would boost the box-office of the Val Lewton series brought Boris Karloff and Bela Lugosi to RKO for **The Body Snatcher**. The setting was Edinburgh in 1831 where cab-driver Karloff (left) lines his pockets by supplying corpses to one of the city's eminent medical professors (Henry Daniell). Karloff takes a satanic delight in taunting his patron, constantly reminding the doctor of the hold he enjoys over him by reason of their ghastly transactions. Lewton's preference for psychological horror asserted itself at the end when Daniell, who has killed the grave robber in a desperate fight, is hounded to his own death by his guilty conscience. Thanks to Robert Wise's firm direction, the superb period recreation of art directors Albert S. D'Agostino and Walter E. Keller and set decorators Darrell Silvera and John Sturtevant, and the exemplary adaptation of Robert Louis Stevenson's original story by Philip MacDonald and Carlos Keith (a nom-de-plume for producer Lewton), Val Lewton finally gained a measure of critical acceptance for one of his 'shudder' shows. Edith Atwater, Russell Wade (right), Rita Corday, little Sharyn Moffett and Donna Lee also appeared. Lugosi received second-billing, but his role was just a bit. Playing a blackmailer, the screen's original Dracula died at the hands of its prototypal Frankenstein around the mid-point in the ghoulish drama.

American ne'er-do-well Lee Tracy (left) was employed by Japanese agents to get hold of military plans for the defence of the Panama Canal in **Betrayal From The East**. He reports the arrangement to Army Intelligence and is ordered to play along until he discovers all of the enemy's intentions. Secret dictaphones, faked messages, false clues, a bit of jiu-jitsu and a whale of a fight between Tracy and the Japanese leader, raised this cat-and-mouse yarn one notch above the standard espionage dramas so plentiful during this period. Aubrey Wisberg adapted Alan Hynd's novel and Kenneth Gamet and Wisberg completed the final script for producer Sid Rogell. William Berke directed a cast that included Nancy Kelly, Richard Loo, Abner Biberman, Regis Toomey, Philip Ahn, Addison Richards, Bruce Edwards, Hugh Hoo (right), Sen Young, Roland Varno, Louis Jean Heydt and Jason Robards. Journalist Drew Pearson narrated the prologue and epilogue, designed to fool audiences into believing that the on-screen melodramatics bore some relation to reality.

It's A Pleasure presented Sonja Henie prancing and pirouetting on ice in glorious Technicolor. Director William Seiter should have kept his camera glued to the frosty gymnastics for, whenever the Lynn Starling-Elliot Paul plot intruded, the film instantly self-destructed. An old saw about the romantic ups and downs of skating whiz Henie (illustrated) and hockey champion Michael O'Shea, it proceeded by numbers through all the intrinsic clichés before arriving at its obligatory reconciliation scene. The flaccid dialogue and limited acting abilities of Henie and O'Shea were other liabilities. Also cast: Bill Johnson, Marie McDonald, Gus Schilling, Iris Adrian, Cheryl Walker, Peggy O'Neill, Arthur Loft, Alyce Fleming, George Brown, Jack Chefe and Don Loper. Loper was also associate producer for producer David Lewis and International Pictures. Song: 'Romance' Edgar Leslie, Walter Donaldson.

Tarzan's ape call echoed through the jungle once again in **Tarzan And The Amazons**. John Jacoby and Marjorie L. Pfaelzer's fanciful screenplay determined that the hero (Johnny Weissmuller, right) would protect a tribe of Amazons from archaeologists whose scientific curiosity is overcome by their lust for the gold possessed by the female warriors. Producer Sol Lesser made certain the production values were first-class, employing Kurt Neumann to direct, Archie Stout to handle the lucid cinematography and Walter Koessler to furnish the lush art direction. Brenda Joyce (left) played Jane, Johnny Sheffield (centre) was Boy, and Henry Stephenson, Maria Ouspenskaya, Barton MacLane, Don Douglas, Stephen Geray, J. M. Kerrigan and Shirley O'Hara were also cast. Director Neumann also served as associate producer for Lesser's new company, Champion Productions.

Hands – or, in this case, feathered wings – reached across the border in friendship in **The Three Caballeros**. A quasi-sequel to *Saludos Amigos*, the movie combined live action and animated footage into a delightful amalgam that proved a boon to Nelson Rockefeller's Good Neighbour policy. Donald Duck, Joe Carioca the Brazilian parrot, and a Mexican rooster named Panchito were the title characters, visiting beautiful Latin-American locations and interacting with such human performers as Aurora Miranda of Brazil (illustrated) and Carmen Molina and Dora Luz of Mexico. There were also cartoon episodes about a penguin who grows tired of the frigid Antarctic and emigrates to the tropics, and an Argentine boy and his flying donkey. Norman Ferguson supervised and directed the production; Homer Brightman, Ernest Terrazzas, Ted Sears, Bill Peet, Raph Wright, Elmer Plummer, Roy Williams, William Cottrell, Del Connell and James Bodrero worked on the story; Clyde Geronimi, Jack Kinney and Bill Roberts were the sequence directors, and Charles Wolcott, Paul J. Smith and Edward H. Plumb served as music directors. Songs included: 'The Three Caballeros' Manuel Esperon, Ray Gilbert, Ernesto Cortezar; 'Baia' Ary Barroso, Gilbert; 'You Belong To My Heart' Agustin Lara, Gilbert; 'Mexico' Charles Wolcott, Gilbert. RKO, once again, were distributing for Walt Disney Productions.

This Alan Carney-Wally Brown comedy of blunders deserved a prize for its title alone – **Zombies On Broadway** (GB: **Loonies On Broadway**). Alas, its possibilities were in no way realized by the combined efforts of writers Robert Faber and Charles Newman (original story), Robert E. Kent (adaptation) and Lawrence Kimble (screenplay). All they managed was a collection of turgid gags based on the necessity of press agents Brown (left and Carney (centre right) to provide a real zombie for a new night club. During their quest they bump into mad scientist Bela Lugosi (right) with predictable results. Anne Jeffreys dressed up the proceedings as a café singer and constant companion-in-distress to the two leads, and Sheldon Leonard, Frank Jenks, Russell Hopton, Joseph Vitale (centre left), Ian Wolfe, Louis Jean Heydt and Darby Jones also took part. Gordon Douglas directed, Ben Stoloff produced and Sid Rogell was the executive producer.

The Enchanted Cottage was a beautiful film about ugliness. Acting out its age-old theme that beauty is in the eye of the beholder, Dorothy McGuire (left, borrowed from David O. Selznick) and Robert Young (right, borrowed from MGM) portrayed two of society's outcasts whose drabness and disfigurement vanish after they marry and begin to inhabit the magical cottage of the title. Only for a moment – when the unthinking cruelty of Young's mother (Spring Byington, borrowed from MGM) drags them back to reality – do they again see one another as the rest of the world sees them. But even this is not enough to destroy their illusions or to ruin their new life. John Cromwell directed the 'tone-poem' (as narrator Herbert Marshall calls it) with a mellow touch that made the film shimmer and glow, and caused audiences to embrace its unadulterated sentimentality with open arms. Jack J. Gross was executive producer, Harriet Parsons produced and DeWitt Bodeen and Herman J. Mankiewicz wrote the script from Sir Arthur Wing Pinero's stage play. Also cast: Mildred Natwick, Hillary Brooke, Richard Gaines, Alec Englander, Robert Clarke and Eden Nicholas. First National released a 1924 version of the Pinero play, starring Richard Barthelmess and May McAvoy.

Producer Ben Stoloff and supervisor Sid Rogell cast Tom Conway as an amnesia victim in **Two O'Clock Courage**, a passable remake of *Two In The Dark* (1936). Conway (centre), suffering from loss of memory after being slugged, finds himself involved in a murder investigation with all the evidence pointing towards him as the culprit. Aided by lady taxi driver Ann Rutherford (right) and a bullet that stuns him but also rewires his memory, Conway discovers the truth about the bewildering events. Robert E. Kent's run-of-the-mill screenplay was based on a story by Gelett Burgess and contained additional dialogue by Gordon Kahn. Also cast: Richard Lane, Lester Matthews, Roland Drew, Emory Parnell, Bettyjane Greer (her screen debut; she would soon dispense with the 'Betty'), Jean Brooks, Edmund Glover, Bryant Washburn and Sarah Edwards (left). Anthony Mann, who would become one of Hollywood's top directors of 'A' westerns in the 1950s, earned his first RKO credit as helmsman.

Pearl S. Buck's **China Sky** inspired another unoriginal and over-stated triangle film set, this time, in a remote village under constant pressure from Japanese soldiers. Randolph Scott (left) and Ruth Warrick (right) played conscientious American doctors helping the cause of guerrilla leader Anthony Quinn (borrowed from 20th Century-Fox). However, Miss Buck's message about the beauty of friendship and cooperation between Americans and Chinese was shoved into the background as soon as Ellen Drew entered the picture as Scott's selfish and jealous wife. From that point on, the Brenda Weisberg-Joseph Hoffman screenplay recycled all the threadbare melodramatic conventions, presenting them like flashcards for programmed audience response. And respond they did. The film was a hit, despite white hot volleys of abuse launched by the critical establishment. Ray Enright directed a cast that also included Carol Thurston, Richard Loo, 'Ducky' Louie, Philip Ahn, Benson Fong, H. T. Tsiang and Chin Kuang Chow. Maurice Geraghty produced; Jack J. Gross was the executive producer. Note: The film was originally intended as an 'A' special to star Claudette Colbert, but Miss C. did not care for the script and said no.
▽

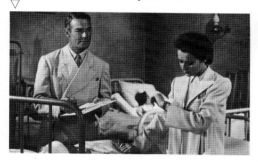

A double helping of Danny Kaye (left) was served up by producer Samuel Goldwyn in **Wonder Man**. One Kaye persona is Buzzy Bellew, a brash nightclub entertainer who specializes in such impudent novelties as translating Balinese dancing into Basin Street jive. The other is his twin, Edwin Dingle, more mouse than man, a grown up whiz-kid with a vast fund of tongue-twisting erudition. Each character has his own leading lady – played by Vera-Ellen (right) and Virginia Mayo respectively. A platoon of writers (Arthur Sheekman wrote the original story, Jack Jevne and Eddie Moran adapted it and Don Hartman, Melville Shavelson and Philip Rapp completed the screenplay) came up with a vehicle that effectively displayed Kaye's comic versatility, as well as allowing plenty of Goldwyn pageantry (including the Goldwyn Girls). Director Bruce Humberstone coaxed choice performances out of a cast that included Donald Woods, S. Z. Sakall, Allen Jenkins, Edward Brophy, Otto Kruger, Steve Cochran, Virginia Gilmore, Richard Lane, Natalie Schafer, Alice Mock, Huntz Hall, Edward Gargan and Gisela Werbiseck. The Technicolor production contained some specialty musical numbers by Sylvia Fine (Mrs Danny Kaye) and 'So In Love', a song written by Leo Robin and David Rose.
▽

Gary Cooper (left) turned producer for **Along Came Jones**, a delicious spoof that poked fun at the stereotyped western and at Cooper's own well-established cowboy persona. Nunnally Johnson's screenplay, based on a novel by Alan LeMay, presented the producer-cum-star as Melody Jones, a whimsical and inglorious range rider who can't hit the side of a barn with his six-gun but is human enough to want people to respect him. The script arranged to introduce Melody to Cherry DeLongpre (Loretta Young, right) who is as proficient with a weapon as Melody is not. The spontaneous combustion created by the two characters, plus a mistaken identity plot that gives the hero – for a while at least – the deferential treatment his wryly quixotic trail. Stuart Heisler directed for International Pictures, with William Demarest, Dan Duryea, Frank Sully, Russell Simpson, Arthur Loft, Willard Robertson, Don Costello, Ray Teal and Erville Alderson also cast.

Keyed to the sentiment of an old favourite song, **Those Endearing Young Charms** told the story of a love-'em-leave-'em smoothie brought to bay by a Snow White of a heroine. The team of executive producer Sid Rogell, producer Bert Granet, screenwriter Jerome Chodorov, director Lewis Allen and stars Robert Young (right) and Laraine Day (both borrowed from MGM) was able to perform a magical transfusion on the humdrum plot, endowing it with a sufficient number of laughs and tears to make the film a huge draw at the box-office. Ann Harding (centre) returned to her old studio after a nine year absence and contributed a beguiling performance as Day's sagacious mother, while Bill Williams (left) gave a good account of himself as Young's earnest fellow GI – his first film role. The studio had high hopes of building Williams into a leading man, but he never really lived up to their expectations. Also cast: Marc Cramer, Anne Jeffreys, Glenn Vernon, Norma Varden, Lawrence Tierney and Vera Marshe. Samuel Goldwyn sold RKO the rights to the Edward Chodorov play on which the picture was based.
▷

In Zane Grey's **West Of The Pecos**, Robert Mitchum (left) made up his mind to teach a young punk the rough and ready ways of Texas cowboys. The punk turns out to be lovely Barbara Hale (right), a sensitive lass from Chicago who has adopted a male disguise for purposes of safety. Boy falls for girl and she falls right back, but our hero must prove his worth by cleaning up the lawless country before settling down to his new-found happiness. A thoroughly respectable 'B' oater, strengthened by its casting and the no-nonsense direction of Edward Killy, **West Of The Pecos** earned $151,000 in profits. It was also Mitchum's final acting job for a while; he entered military service after its completion. Herman Schlom produced, Sid Rogell supervised and Norman Houston wrote the screenplay, providing roles for Richard Martin, Thurston Hall (centre), Rita Corday, Russell Hopton, Bill Williams, Bruce Edwards and Harry Woods. The film was a remake of a 1935 Richard Dix vehicle.

Back To Bataan was a perfect specimen of what Hollywood producers felt a war film should be. On the one hand, its informative narration, episodic structure, use of documentary footage, and the re-enactment of certain historical highlights suggested that here was a true account of the guerrillas who played a crucial role in the liberation of the Philippines. On the other, screenwriters Ben Barzman and Richard H. Landau (original story by Aeneas MacKenzie and William Gordon), executive producer Robert Fellows, associate producer Theron Warth and director Edward Dmytryk made sure they worked in all the stock characters and situations that Americans expected to find in gun-and-glory epics. Colonel John Wayne (right) was there to teach the natives how to fight 'guerrilla style', Beulah Bondi to educate them about freedom before the Japanese come to take it away and Anthony Quinn (left, borrowed from 20th Century-Fox) to lead them to victory following a period of equivocation about the role thrust upon him by his lineage (he is the grandson of a great Filipino patriot). To make certain the heartstrings were not neglected, there was also the martyrdom of 'Ducky' Louie (borrowed from Monogram), Miss Bondi's favourite pupil, who dies but takes a truckload of Japanese soldiers along with him. Omitting nothing, the picture added a stirring roll call finale which audiences answered in stentorian tones: total film rentals amounted to $2,490,000. Also cast: Fely Franquelli, Richard Loo, Philip Ahn, J. Alex Havier, Lawrence Tierney, Leonard Strong, Paul Fix, Abner Biberman, Vladimir Sokoloff and a dozen members of the Army, Navy and Marine Corps who were prisoners of war held at Cabanatuan prison camp outside Manila. The liberation of the prison camp was, of course, repeated in the film.

Isle Of The Dead combined vampire mythology, premature burial, grave robbery and plague-induced insanity. The time was 1912 and the setting a tiny island off the coast of Greece where Boris Karloff (left), Marc Cramer, Jason Robards, Alan Napier, Katherine Emery (right), Ernest Dorian, Skelton Knaggs, Helene Thimig and Ellen Drew are trapped by an outbreak of the plague. Heroic Greek general Karloff leads the battle against the disease but, when attacked by it himself, falls victim to an ancient superstition which convinces him that Ellen Drew is a 'vrykolaka' (vampire) and responsible for the deaths. Mark Robson directed from Ardel Wray and Josef Mischel's hodge-podge of a script, and Jack J. Gross was the executive producer. It was one of the poorest of producer Val Lewton's horror movies, although it did contain a few startling moments. Note: Boris Karloff's real-life serious illness and subsequent operation forced a four-month suspension in the filming.

One of the quaint conventions of the Falcon series was that whenever Tom Conway (left) embarked on a vacation, a corpse would pop up to interrupt his relaxation. A murder on a train in **The Falcon In San Francisco** catapults him into an investigation of a gigantic silk-smuggling operation. Other featured performers included Fay Helm as the head of the smugglers, Rita Corday (right) as a lady suspected of being involved with them, Sharyn Moffett (centre) as a little girl befriended by the hero after her nurse is killed, and Edward S. Brophy as the Falcon's dumb but faithful friend who spends most of his time trying to find a wife in order to lessen his income tax payments. Joseph H. Lewis directed, Maurice Geraghty produced and Robert E. Kent and Ben Markson wrote the screenplay from an original story by Kent. Robert Armstrong, Carl Kent, George Holmes and John Mylong also appeared, and Sid Rogell was the executive producer.

Another grab-bag musical with a programmer budget, **Radio Stars On Parade** centred on the efforts of Frances Langford (centre right) to break into radio with the bumbling help of Wally Brown (centre left) and Alan Carney who act as her agents. The popular *Truth Or Consequences* radio show with host Ralph Edwards also figured prominently in the action, as did Skinnay Ennis (right) and his Band, Don Wilson (left), Tony Romano, the Town Criers, the Cappy Barra Boys, Rufe Davis, Robert Clarke, Sheldon Leonard, Max Wagner and Ralph Peters. Robert E. Kent and Monte Brice penned the screenplay from a story by Kent; Leslie Goodwins directed for producer Ben Stoloff and executive producer Sid Rogell. Since the studio did not want to spend the money to have special musical numbers written for the picture, it recycled several songs from previous RKO films, including Jimmy McHugh and Frank Loesser's 'Can't Get Out Of This Mood', and McHugh and Harold Adamson's 'Don't Believe Everything You Dream' and 'I Couldn't Sleep A Wink Last Night'.

The first mistake RKO made with **Mama Loves Papa** was to pay Paramount $8500 for the rights to such a property. The second mistake occurred when the studio assigned Charles E. Roberts and Monte Brice to prepare an original script that would use the aforementioned title. And the third mistake was to put said screenplay into production. A dreary fable about a mollycoddled clerk who becomes a playground commissioner and gets involved with a crooked manufacturer of recreational equipment, it featured Leon Errol (right) and Elisabeth Risdon as the title characters, and Edwin Maxwell, Emory Parnell, Charles Halton, Paul Harvey (left), Charlotte Wynters, Ruth Lee and Lawrence Tierney in secondary parts. Leon Errol toiled extra hard to bring the movie to life, but it was clearly a corpse from the start. The producer was Ben Stoloff, the executive producer Sid Rogell and the ineffectual director Frank Strayer.

Director Gordon Douglas, writer-producer J. Robert Bren and executive producer Jack J. Gross made **First Yank Into Tokyo** (GB: **Mask Of Fury**) another highly exploitable war era melodrama. By rewriting and reshooting a couple of sequences after the end of principal photography, they turned the Bren-Gladys Atwater story about an American soldier smuggled into Japan to make contact with an imprisoned American scientist into the first Hollywood feature dealing with the atomic bomb. The original plot called for scientist Marc Cramer to hold the key to a new gun which the Army needs as an invasion weapon. The revised version traded A-bomb for gun, instantly transforming a run-of-the-mill melo into a hot box-office performer. Tom Neal played the soldier whose face has been transformed by plastic surgery so he can pass smoothly through enemy territory, and Barbara Hale (left) acted the role of Neal's pre-war fiancée who (gulp!) turns up in the same prison camp as the atomic brain. Also cast: Richard Loo (right), Keye Luke, Leonard Strong, Benson Fong, Clarence Lung, Keye Chang and Michael St Angel. This film was released approximately one month after the destruction of Hiroshima and Nagasaki.

Johnny Angel was the year's major surprise package. Production chief Charles Koerner had no great enthusiasm for it, calling the picture 'routine' and something that 'won't set the world on fire'. Consumers, however, did a war dance to plunk their admission fees down at the box office, and the mystery thriller eventually earned profits of $1,192,000. Some of Koerner's misgivings were undoubtedly based on the tangled plot strands and clumsy flashbacks that infected Steve Fisher's screenplay (adapted by Frank Gruber from Charles Gordon Booth's *Mr Angel Comes Aboard*), but these deficiencies were ameliorated by the moody and suspenseful direction of Edwin L. Marin, the atmospheric photography of Harry J. Wild and the forceful performances of Claire Trevor (left), Signe Hasso, and George Raft (right) as the titular hero. Sea captain Raft sets out to track down unknown mutineers who killed his father and hijacked gold bullion from his father's vessel. He is aided by French refugee Hasso who was on board the ill-fated ship and witnessed the murderous events. Architect William L. Pereira, winner of an Oscar for his special effects work on C. B. DeMille's *Reap The Wild Wind*, made an auspicious debut as producer. Jack J. Gross was the executive producer, and Lowell Gilmore, Hoagy Carmichael, Marvin Miller, Margaret Wycherly, J. Farrell MacDonald and Mack Gray were also cast. Hoagy Carmichael and Paul Webster wrote 'Memphis In June', a song used in the picture. Note: Signe Hasso was borrowed from MGM; she had spent a year under contract to RKO during the Schaefer period but had never been used in a picture.

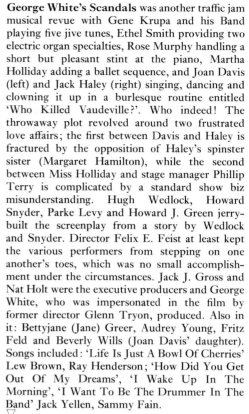

With Robert Mitchum away in the service, six-foot-four-inch James Warren (left) took over as top cowboy in the Zane Grey series. Warren's narrow acting range was plenty expansive for **Wanderer Of The Wasteland**, a dehydrated tale of revenge with complications arising from the fact that the man who killed Warren's father is also the uncle of the girl he loves (Audrey Long, right). Warren's Irish-Spanish sidekick Richard Martin (now a continuing character in the series) stole the film from the two principals, but it was, at best, petty larceny. Producer Herman Schlom's cast also included Robert Barrat, Robert Clarke, Harry Woods, Minerva Urecal, Harry D. Brown, Tommy Cook, Harry McKim and Jason Robards. Norman Houston typed out the screenplay, Edward Killy and Wallace Grissell co-directed and Sid Rogell was the executive producer. Paramount had released earlier versions of the novel in 1924 (with Jack Holt and Billie Dove) and in 1935 (with Larry 'Buster' Crabbe and Gail Patrick).

George White's Scandals was another traffic jam musical revue with Gene Krupa and his Band playing five jive tunes, Ethel Smith providing two electric organ specialties, Rose Murphy handling a short but pleasant stint at the piano, Martha Holliday adding a ballet sequence, and Joan Davis (left) and Jack Haley (right) singing, dancing and clowning it up in a burlesque routine entitled 'Who Killed Vaudeville?'. Who indeed! The throwaway plot revolved around two frustrated love affairs; the first between Davis and Haley is fractured by the opposition of Haley's spinster sister (Margaret Hamilton), while the second between Miss Holliday and stage manager Phillip Terry is complicated by a standard show biz misunderstanding. Hugh Wedlock, Howard Snyder, Parke Levy and Howard J. Green jerry-built the screenplay from a story by Wedlock and Snyder. Director Felix E. Feist at least kept the various performers from stepping on one another's toes, which was no small accomplishment under the circumstances. Jack J. Gross and Nat Holt were the executive producers and George White, who was impersonated in the film by former director Glenn Tryon, produced. Also in it: Bettyjane (Jane) Greer, Audrey Young, Fritz Feld and Beverly Wills (Joan Davis' daughter). Songs included: 'Life Is Just A Bowl Of Cherries' Lew Brown, Ray Henderson; 'How Did You Get Out Of My Dreams', 'I Wake Up In The Morning', 'I Want To Be The Drummer In The Band' Jack Yellen, Sammy Fain.

Jack Haley (illustrated) played a war correspondent with a swelled head and an urge to return to America for a series of lecture dates, forced to take charge of a group of young entertainers in order to secure a berth on a ship from Cherbourg to New York. The juvenile affairs of the youngsters, Haley's own romance with Anne Jeffreys and plenty of high C's on the high seas were stressed in **Sing Your Way Home**, a Bert Granet production based on an absurd but diverting William Bowers screenplay (original story by Edmund Joseph and Bart Lytton). The film was directed by Anthony Mann, supervised by Sid Rogell and featured Marcy McGuire, Glenn Vernon, Donna Lee, Patti Brill, Nancy Marlow, James Jordan Jr (son of 'Fibber McGee and Molly'), Emory Parnell, David Forrest and Edward Gargan. Songs included: 'Heaven Is A Place Called Home', 'Who Did It?', 'Seven O'Clock In The Morning', 'I'll Buy That Dream' Herb Magidson, Allie Wrubel.

Following its release of the first feature in three-strip Technicolor (*Becky Sharp*, 1935), RKO seemingly lost interest in the production of colour films. Charles Koerner decided to remedy this situation by signing a deal with Technicolor; the first fruit of the arrangement was **The Spanish Main**. The George Worthing Yates-Herman J. Mankiewicz screenplay, based on a story by Aeneas MacKenzie, was warmed-over swashbuckle, containing not a single character or situation that audiences hadn't glimpsed many times before. And yet Paul Henreid (centre), cast against type as the athletic hero, Maureen O'Hara (left) as the ravishing heroine and Walter Slezak as the treacherous villain attacked their roles with such obvious relish that they prodded the tired script to pulsating life. Frank Borzage also had much to do with the film's giant success (profit $1,485,000), directing the tale of Spanish grandee Slezak's downfall at the hands of 'honest' Dutch pirate Henreid with all the gusto and attention to detail that successful romantic action-adventures demand. Executive producer Robert Fellows spared no expense on the sets, costumes, scenic backgrounds and action sequences, making it a first-cabin production all the way. Also cast: Binnie Barnes (right), John Emery, Barton MacLane, J. M. Kerrigan, Fritz Leiber, Nancy Gates, Jack LaRue, Mike Mazurki, Ian Keith, Victor Kilian, Curt Bois and Antonio Moreno. George Barnes photographed the beautiful colour imagery, and Stephen Ames gained associate producer credit as part of the contractual arrangement with the Technicolor organization.

Robert Wise directed **A Game Of Death**, an above-average remake of *The Most Dangerous Game* (1932). Norman Houston's screenplay, based on Richard Connell's famous short story, had John Loder (right) and Audrey Long (left) as the quarry of maniac hunter Edgar Barrier. (Fay Wray and Joel McCrea had duelled with Leslie Banks in the original). Loder pits his own stalking skill against that of the homicidal madman and triumphs inside 72 screen minutes. The fluid cinematography of J. Roy Hunt, the tight editing of J. R. Whittredge and the imaginative art direction of Albert S. D'Agostino and Lucius Croxton helped make this one of the year's best detours into the world of the macabre. Sid Rogell was the executive producer, Herman Schlom produced and Russell Wade, Russell Hicks, Jason Robards, Gene Stutenroth, Noble Johnson and Robert Clarke also appeared. A partial remake, entitled *Run For The Sun*, starring Richard Widmark, Trevor Howard and Jane Greer was released by United Artists in 1956.

'A Comedy with Hex Appeal' read one of the publicity mats for **Man Alive**; hex was the only operative word in the phrase, for the picture contained neither comedy nor appeal and was thoroughly hexed from beginning to end. The Jerry Cady-John Tucker Battle story and Edwin Harvey Blum screenplay had possibilities, but they were wrecked by Ray Enright's woeful direction and the surprisingly deficient performances of Pat O'Brien, Adolphe Menjou, Ellen Drew and Rudy Vallee in the main roles. O'Brien (right) played Speed McBride who gets plastered after he learns that wife Drew (left) has invited her old admirer (Vallee) for a visit. Speed's binge results in an auto crash and an erroneous report of his demise. At the urging of Kismet (Menjou), a magician of sorts, the protagonist decides to masquerade as a ghost and haunt his wife, which provided the only flashes of humour in this muddle. Fortunio Bonanova, Joseph Crehan, Jonathan Hale, Minna Gombell, Jason Robards and Jack Norton were also employed by executive producer Robert Fellows and his associate Theron Warth. Films of this type which cost much too much ($738,000) and entertained less than a little suggested just how lackadaisical the Hollywood studios had become, thanks to the all-devouring movie audiences of the war years.

RKO saw out 1945 with **The Bells of St Mary's**, the year's top box-office picture throughout the entire industry and the biggest hit (net profits $3,715,000) in the company's history. A sequel to *Going My Way* (Paramount, 1944), the film narrated the further adventures of Father O'Malley (Bing Crosby, left) in his new job as parish pastor of St Mary's, a proud but decrepit parochial school in danger of being condemned. With the aid of Sister Superior Ingrid Bergman (right, borrowed from David O. Selznick), the priest convinces a local skinflint (Henry Travers) to deed the school his newly constructed building, taking time out at various points in the drama to lift the spirits of a confused young pupil (Joan Carroll), bring about a reconciliation between the girl's long-separated parents (Martha Sleeper and William Gargan), and decide on the best course of action regarding an attack of tuberculosis suffered by the Sister Superior. Needless to say, Bing also managed to croon a few songs in the inimitable Crosby manner. The film was obviously contrived to strike all the sentimental chords to which audiences had responded in *Going My Way*, but it accomplished its goals with a sincerity of conviction, and a highly professional finesse that was undeniable. Leo McCarey deserved most of the credit; he wrote the original story, as well as producing and directing. The Dudley Nichols screenplay also gave featured roles to Ruth Donnelly, Rhys Williams, Dickie Tyler and Una O'Connor. RKO co-produced with Rainbow Productions, a company recently formed by McCarey. Songs included: 'Aren't You Glad You're You' Johnny Burke, Jimmy Van Heusen; 'The Bells Of St Mary's' Douglas Furber, A. Emmett Adams. Note: One could almost have predicted that this would be a smash. McCarey, Crosby and Bergman had won Academy Awards the year before, and Bing Crosby was, at the time, the most popular star in the entire business.

☆☆☆☆☆☆☆☆☆☆☆☆☆☆☆

1946

☆☆☆☆☆☆☆☆☆☆☆☆☆☆☆

RKO's mightiest year generated a record-shattering $12,187,804 in net profits, $72,966,727 in gross film rentals and such well-remembered releases as **Notorious, The Spiral Staircase, The Best Years Of Our Lives** and **It's A Wonderful Life**.

Regrettably, the man most responsible for this bounty did not live to receive the plaudits he so richly deserved. Studio chief Charles Koerner contracted leukemia in late 1945 and died on 2 February. To minimize the turmoil caused by Koerner's death, corporate president N. Peter Rathvon took over production, while a survey was conducted to find a qualified successor to the most successful executive producer in company annals. The only other important management change was the mid-year departure of executive assistant William Dozier, who left to enter independent production.

Two of Rathvon's biggest headaches were continued labour unrest, which caused some production slowdowns, and a concomitant rise in filmmaking costs. 'B' pictures were now almost twice as expensive as they had been before the war, and some of the 'A' films were nosing up to and beyond the $2 million mark. Still, with business so prosperous there seemed no reason for alarm. One group of films was phased out – the horror pictures. Along with them went producer Val Lewton who had provided the most interesting cluster of programmers in RKO history.

With the company enjoying an unprecedented number of commitments from name stars, Rathvon began concentrating on the development of young actors into box-office names. Barbara Bel Geddes was signed during the year, and Robert Mitchum, Bill Williams, Barbara Hale, Jane Greer, Lawrence Tierney, Anne Jeffreys and other hopefuls received exceptional opportunities to demonstrate their talents.

Of the 34 releases, RKO made its heftiest profits from **Notorious, The Spiral Staircase, Badman's Territory, Till The End Of Time** and **Cornered**.

Dick Tracy (GB: **Splitface**) added another ▷ famous name to RKO's stable of crime investigators. Followers of Chester Gould's popular comic strip were delighted by Morgan Conway's impersonation of the square-jawed detective and by the Eric Taylor screenplay which pitted Conway (left) against psychotic Mike Mazurki as a thug (called Splitface) who is bumping off the members of a jury that once convicted him. Anne Jeffreys (right) played Tess Trueheart, the hero's best gal, Lyle Latell was Pat Patton, his right-hand man, and Mickey Kuhn was Junior, his adopted son; other support troops included Jane Greer, Joseph Crehan, Trevor Bardette, Morgan Wallace, Milton Parsons, William Halligan, Edythe Elliott, Mary Currier, Ralph Dunn, Edmund Glover and Bruce Edwards. William Berke directed, Herman Schlom produced and Sid Rogell was executive producer of the studio's newest series.

A murderous African secret society, dedicated to massacre and torture, staged its reign of terror in **Tarzan And The Leopard Woman**. The pagan fanatics come to the attention of Tarzan (Johnny Weissmuller, right) when they wipe out a peaceful caravan and leave clues indicating a pack of leopards has committed the attack. Tarzan, Jane (Brenda Joyce) and Boy (Johnny Sheffield) are captured by the cult members, who plan to sacrifice the trio at a ceremony in their cavern headquarters. Thanks to Cheeta, the king of the jungle is released from his bonds, saves his wife and son and pays back the spotted society for their hospitality. Sultry Acquanetta (left) portrayed the high priestess of the leopard cult, Edgar Barrier was their half-breed leader, Tommy Cook played a vindictive juvenile member of the group, and Dennis Hoey and Anthony Caruso also found roles in Carroll Young's screenplay. Director (and associate producer) Kurt Neumann squeezed a fair amount of excitement out of the formularized tale; Sol Lesser produced for his own independent banner. ▽

Riverboat Rhythm featured Leon Errol (right) as a Mississippi River showboat captain who stages his entertainment without a licence, and tangles with a local sheriff as a result. Escaping from the law, Errol becomes embroiled in an ancient feud and soon finds a whole family of Southern gentlemen out for his blood. The stodgy Charles E. Roberts screenplay (story Robert Faber), enervated Leslie Goodwins direction and penny-pinching Nat Holt production made this movie about as welcome as a case of poison ivy on a humid bayou day. Glenn Vernon, Walter Catlett (left), Marc Cramer, Jonathan Hale, Joan Newton (centre), Ben Carter, Mantan Moreland and Frankie Carle and his Orchestra completed executive producer Jack J. Gross's cast. ▽

Ding Dong Williams (GB: **Melody Maker**) was a musical conglomeration dealing with the efforts of a 'hot lick' clarinettist to compose a blues symphony for a motion picture. It turns out that Ding Dong (Glenn Vernon, left) doesn't know one note from another; he just lugs his instrument around and plays as the spirit moves him. This situation is solved when two music arrangers (Cliff Nazarro and Tom Noonan) agree to follow him and write down everything he plays, but they discover that the clarinettist's music is dependent on his mood, and they must resort to various strategies to put him in a creative frame of mind. Besides Ding Dong's jazz, Brenda Weisberg and M. Coates Webster's screenplay (based on *Collier's* magazine stories by Richard English) also worked in classical interpretations and the western specialties of Bob Nolan and the Sons of the Pioneers. Battling against the all-embracing inanity of the production were Marcy McGuire (right), Felix Bressart, Anne Jeffreys, James Warren, William Davidson, Ruth Lee, Jason Robards, Richard Korbel and director William Berke. They came up losers, as did producer Herman Schlom and executive producer Sid Rogell. Songs included: 'Candlelight And Wine', 'I Saw You First' Jimmy McHugh, Harold Adamson; 'Cool Water' Bob Nolan.

Victor Hanbury, Lance Comfort and Max Greene all appear to have produced and directed **Hotel Reserve**, a trivial spy melodrama starring James Mason. The time was 1938 and the setting a French coastal inn where medical student Mason (left) faces a charge of espionage. In order to clear himself and become a full-fledged French citizen (he is Austrian born), he is forced to run down the real spy. The fact that this film came near the end of a long series of war-related cloak-and-dagger dramas and was paced like the world chess championship resulted in pitiful US box-office returns. John Davenport's screenplay was based on Eric Ambler's novel *Epitaph For A Spy*. Among the large cast were Lucie Mannheim, Raymond Lovell, Julien Mitchell, Herbert Lom, Martin Miller, Clare Hamilton (also known as Flory Fitzsimmons), Frederick Valk (right), Patricia Medina, Valentine Dyall and Patricia Hayes. **Hotel Reserve** was filmed by RKO Radio British Productions in England (where it was released in 1944).

Tom Conway (right), by now one of the deans of filmland detection, went through the motions once more in **The Falcon's Alibi**. Dane Lussier and Manny Seff's story and Paul Yawitz's screenplay were all about the theft of costly pearls and the plight of pretty secretary Rita Corday who fears she will be accused of stealing them. The Falcon locates the jewels, but has to cope with the murders of a waiter, a hotel guest and a young singer before he traps the villain. The usual stock characters supported Conway; they included Vince Barnett as his feeble-minded assistant, Emory Parnell as an ineffectual insurance investigator, Esther Howard as an apparently victimized dowager and Al Bridge as a pushy police inspector. Given a bit more to work with were Elisha Cook Jr as a menacing radio disc jockey and Jane Greer (left, formerly Bettyjane) playing a vivacious orchestra singer who becomes one of the victims. Jean Brooks, Paul Brooks, Jason Robards, Morgan Wallace and Lucien Prival completed the cast for producer William Berke and director Ray McCarey. Sid Rogell was executive producer.

Producer Adrian Scott, director Edward Dmytryk and star Dick Powell followed *Murder, My Sweet* with **Cornered**, a seething man-hunt drama about a demobilized Canadian airman who vows to track down the Nazi collaborators who murdered his French wife. Close-cropped and saturnine Mr Powell (left) follows a trail from France to Switzerland, then to the hothouse atmosphere of Buenos Aires where a colony of corrupt Europeans are living in splendour. There, after being wined, dined, seduced, beaten and nearly killed, Powell finds the malefactors and exacts his revenge. One could quibble with certain narrative confusions in John Paxton's screenplay (story and adaptation by John Wexley) and a few dull spots that firmer editing would have cured, but this was, nonetheless, an edge-of-the-seat thriller whose violent climax left viewers gasping for breath. Also cast: Walter Slezak, Micheline Cheirel (right), Nina Vale (also known as Anne Hunter), Morris Carnovsky, Edgar Barrier, Steven Geray, Jack LaRue, Gregory Gay and Luther Adler.

The action in **Deadline At Dawn** took place during the last seven hours of sailor Bill Williams' shore leave in New York. Williams spends his final evening in the company of Lola Lane who slips him a 'Mickey Finn' and is subsequently murdered while the midshipman is out cold. When he recovers consciousness, Williams (left) believes he must have killed her, but is persuaded by cab driver Paul Lukas and dancer Susan Hayward (right, borrowed from Paramount) to join them in the search for the real killer. Clifford Odets' script and Harold Clurman's direction combined to create another muscular mystery thriller that fizzled out due to its contrived and anticlimactic ending. Also cast: Joseph Calleia, Osa Massen, Jerome Cowan, Marvin Miller, Roman Bohnen, Steven Geray, Joe Sawyer, Constance Worth and Joseph Crehan. Odets based his screenplay on a novel by William Irish (also known as Cornell Woolrich), and Adrian Scott was the producer for executive producer Sid Rogell. Note: This was the only celluloid collaboration between Clurman and Odets, the famous director-writer partnership of The Group Theatre.

The distinguished trio of Orson Welles, Claudette Colbert and George Brent were undoubtedly maltreated by Lenore Coffee's trite adaptation of Gwen Bristow's novel **Tomorrow Is Forever**. Miss Colbert (right) portrayed a Baltimore bride whose husband (Welles, left) is reported missing in action in 1918. Twenty years later, her second husband (Brent) employs an Austrian chemist whom Colbert begins to suspect is really husband number one. He is, of course – come back to resolve a conflict between his former wife and their son (Richard Long) who has a burning desire to involve himself in World War II. Welles played his part in a Ulysses S. Grant beard, which was symbolically appropriate to this tedious, old-fashioned and emotionally desiccated melodrama. Irving Pichel directed as if it were *War And Peace*, and Max Steiner flooded the film with a soggy musical score. David Lewis produced for International Pictures, hiring Jean Louis to design the glamorous Miss Colbert's eighteen changes of wardrobe. Lucile Watson, Sonny Howe, Ian Wolfe, Douglas Wood, Joyce MacKenzie, Henry Hastings, Lane Watson and a cute little six-year-old Natalie Wood, making her film debut, were also in it.

Based on Ethel Lina White's novel *Some Must Watch*, **The Spiral Staircase** was a superb thriller in the Hitchcockian tradition. Dorothy McGuire (illustrated) played the central figure, a mute companion-servant to bedridden Ethel Barrymore. McGuire suspects that one of her employer's sons is a maniac who has been murdering young girls who don't measure up to his ideas of physical perfection. Unaware that she is making a hideous mistake, the girl locks up her suspect (Gordon Oliver), only to discover that he is innocent while the real madman (George Brent) is closing in for the kill. Director Robert Siodmak, cinematographer Nicholas Musuraca, special effects expert Vernon L. Walker, art directors Albert S. D'Agostino and Jack Okey, and soundmen John L. Cass and Terry Kellum pulled out all the stops to make this a traumatic knockout, a film that was as intimidating and nightmarish as the Gothic mansion where the bulk of the action took place. Miss McGuire delivered a dexterous performance that had audiences agonizing over her safety; she received firm support from Barrymore, Brent, Oliver, Kent Smith, Rhonda Fleming, Elsa Lanchester, Sara Allgood, Rhys Williams and James Bell. Dore Schary produced and Mel Dinelli wrote the tightly constructed screenplay. Note: **The Spiral Staircase** was the first fruit of a unique co-production venture between RKO and David O. Selznick's Vanguard Films. In this instance, Selznick furnished the basic novel, the screenplay and the services of Schary, Siodmak, McGuire and Barrymore, while RKO added all the remaining elements and profits were split fifty-fifty. RKO's share of the earnings came to $885,000. The film was remade in Britain (badly) almost 30 years later, with Jacqueline Bisset and Christopher Plummer. There is no record of an American release, though Warner's released it in Britain.
▽

RKO purchased Thomas Bell's novel *All Brides Are Beautiful* in 1940, but could never quite cope with its story about a brave young couple who get married in the tenement district of New York just in time to face the rigours of the Depression. Executive producer Jack J. Gross and producer William L. Pereira retitled it **From This Day Forward**, updated the material and turned its protagonist Mark Stevens (left, borrowed from 20th Century-Fox) into a returned war hero who recalls the agonies and ecstasies of his married life with Joan Fontaine (right, borrowed from David O. Selznick) between 1937 and the present. Though Hugo Butler's screenplay (adapted from Bell's novel by Garson Kanin, with additional scenes by Edith R. Sommer and Charles Schnee) touched on the problems of post-war unemployment, it was mainly a love story complicated by ill luck, in-law troubles, poverty and a brush with the law. Many critics despised the film, blasting its episodic monotony and lack of a central point of view, but audiences snuggled up to it and made it a hit. Director John Berry's cast also included Rosemary DeCamp (on loan from Warner Bros.), Henry Morgan (on loan from 20th Century-Fox), Wally Brown, Arline Judge, Renny McEvoy, Bobby Driscoll, Mary Treen, Queenie Smith, Doreen McCann and Erskine Sanford. Song: 'From This Day Forward' Mort Greene, Leigh Harline.

A proletarian equivalent of *Fantasia*, Walt Disney's **Make Mine Music** contained both popular songs and a few classical numbers, illustrated with varying degrees of imagination by the Disney animators. The best sections were 'The Whale Who Wanted To Sing At The Met', a charming fable for which Nelson Eddy provided *all* the voices; 'After You've Gone' (by Henry Creamer and Turner Leighton), played by Benny Goodman and his quartet and surrealistically illustrated by a clarinet, a bass, a piano and a set of drums that pass through a remarkable series of transformations; and 'Johnny Fedora and Alice Blue Bonnet' (by Allie Wrubel and Ray Gilbert), the story of two hats who fall in love in a department store window, sung by the Andrews Sisters. Its excellent animation (see illustration) notwithstanding, the film had as many minuses as plusses, with the biggest disappointment an over-emphatic rendition of Prokofiev's 'Peter And The Wolf'. Nonetheless, filmgoers all found something to treasure among the ten separate sequences. Joe Grant supervised the production, with no less than 11 writers working on the story: Homer Brightman, Dick Huemer, Dick Kinney, John Walbridge, Tom Oreb, Dick Shaw, Eric Gurney, Sylvia Holland, T. Hee, Dick Kelsey, Jesse March, Roy Williams, Ed Penner, James Bodrero, Cap Palmer and Erwin Graham. Jack Kinney, Clyde Geronimi, Hamilton Luske, Robert Cormack and Joshua Meador shared directorial credit. Other songs in the Technicolor production included: 'Blue Bayou' Bobby Worth, Ray Gilbert; 'Two Silhouettes' Charles Wolcott, Gilbert; 'All The Cats Join In' Alec Wilder, Gilbert, Eddie Sauter; 'The Martins And The Coys' Al Cameron, Ted Weems; 'Without You' Osvaldo Farres, English lyrics Ray Gilbert.
▽

Executive producer Sid Rogell brought Lew Landers, former 'B'-unit whiz director, back to RKO to handle **The Truth About Murder** (GB: **The Lie Detector**). The Lawrence Kimble-Hilda Gordon-Eric Taylor screenplay hardly provided Landers with cause for celebration, being a nondescript whodunit about a woman lawyer (Bonita Granville, right) who undertakes to defend a man whom her boyfriend (Morgan Conway, left) is prosecuting for homicide. Figuring that the only defence is to find the real murderer, the heroine sets out on an investigation of her own that meanders along to a climax (of sorts) in which a lie detector plays an important part. Also cast: Rita Corday, Don Douglas, June Clayworth, Edward Norris, Gerald Mohr, Michael St Angel and Tom Noonan. The producer was Herman Schlom.
▽

Pantomaniac Danny Kaye chalked up another triumph in **The Kid From Brooklyn**. Against a kaleidoscopic backdrop of Technicolor settings, Goldwyn girls and sumptuous production numbers, Kaye (left) acted out the adventures of a mild-mannered milkman who, quite accidentally, wins a world championship fight. Lynn Root and Harry Clork's play *The Milky Way* (filmed by Leo McCarey with Harold Lloyd for Paramount in 1936) provided the narrative spine for Don Hartman and Melville Shavelson's adaptation of the 1936 *Milky Way* screenplay by Grover Jones, Frank Butler and Richard Connell. Samuel Goldwyn produced, Norman Z. McLeod directed and Virginia Mayo (right), Vera-Ellen, Steve Cochran, Eve Arden, Walter Abel, Lionel Stander, Fay Bainter, Clarence Kolb, Victor Cutler, Charles Cane, Jerome Cowan, Don Wilson, Knox Manning, Kay Thompson and Johnny Downs lent high-calibre support. Songs included: 'You're The Cause Of It All', 'I Love An Old Fashioned Song', 'The Sunflower Song', 'Josie' Jule Styne, Sammy Cahn; 'Pavlova' Sylvia Finè, Max Liebman.

For the first time, Lum (Chester Lauck, right), and Abner (Norris Goff, centre left) appeared on screen as young men in **Partners In Time**. Director William Nigh and scriptwriter Charles E. Roberts turned the clock back to 1904 when Abner first breezed into Pine Ridge in a brand new Flanders automobile. He meets Lum, they romance the town belles, go to all the dances and drive the fire horses to the town's first fire. Then they form a partnership to operate the Jot-Em-Down store which is opened with great fanfare. The nostalgic remembrances were bracketed by a modern story which showed the two comedians in their more familiar guises, battling with Dick Elliott and Charles Jordan to save their property and working to reconcile a pair of young lovers (John James, left, and Teala Loring, centre right) whose engagement is on the rocks. Also cast: Pamela Blake, Danny Duncan, Grady Sutton, Ruth Lee and Ruth Caldwell. Ben Hersh produced for Jack William Votion Productions; the picture was the sixth and final edition of the Lum and Abner chapter-play.

Any resemblance between *It Happened One Night* and **Without Reservations** was strictly intentional. As well as chronicling a cross-country journey made by a famous woman travelling incognito, it depicted her infatuation with a cool, strong-willed man, and even included a scene between them played in a haystack! Claudette Colbert (who else?) essayed the role of a best-selling authoress on her way to Hollywood to see about the filming of her latest novel. On the train she meets Marine flyer John Wayne (centre right) and his comrade-in-arms Don DeFore (centre left, borrowed from Hal Wallis). Even though Wayne ridicules her book unmercifully, he strikes Colbert (centre) as the ideal hero for the picture, so she determines to keep him in her sights until they arrive in California. The adventures of the trio become increasingly hectic (but, alas, not increasingly humorous) as they head westward. Andrew Solt's screenplay, based on Jane Allen and Mae Livingston's novel *Thanks God, I'll Take It From Here*, was aggressively bland, relying on threadbare gags and seen-it-all-before romantic situations. The actors acquitted themselves well, but considering the cost ($1,683,000) and the talent involved, one certainly expected a more bracing entertainment. Jesse L. Lasky produced, Mervyn LeRoy directed with Anne Triola, Phil Brown, Frank Puglia, Thurston Hall, Dona Drake, Fernando Alvarado, Charles Arnt and, as themselves, Louella Parsons, Cary Grant, Jack Benny and Dolores Moran. **Without Reservations** was a co-production between RKO and Jesse L. Lasky Productions.

William Hogarth's famous series of satirical paintings, 'The Rake's Progress', provided thematic and visual inspiration for **Bedlam**, and was also used as transition material between major scenes. A Val Lewton production directed by Mark Robson, the film presented Boris Karloff (right) as Sims, the sadistic head of St Mary's of Bethlehem Asylum in 1761. Sims, who owes his job to the patronage of fat and foolish Lord Mortimer (Billy House), looks upon his charges as animals, but treats them much worse. When Nell Bowen (Anne Lee, left), a protégé of Mortimer, attempts to do something about the horrors of Bedlam, Sims has her declared insane and committed to the madhouse. Justice inevitably triumphs in a clever scene lifted from Edgar Allan Poe. Lewton desperately wanted to graduate to 'A' productions and succeeded in shoring up his plot with an exceptional amount of period detail. Critics noticed and voiced their approval, but the audience for horror pictures had gone soft. **Bedlam** lost money at the box office, sabotaging Lewton's hopes and ending his career at the studio. Director Robson and Carlos Keith (Lewton using his pen name once again) wrote the screenplay. Also cast: Richard Fraser, Glenn Vernon, Ian Wolfe, Jason Robards, Leyland Hodgson, Joan Newton and Elizabeth Russell. Jack J. Gross was the executive producer.

Having languished almost three years without a Ginger Rogers picture, RKO finally got one from independent producers Robert and Raymond Hakim entitled **Heartbeat**. The bloom, however, was definitely off the peach – not off peachy Ginger, but off the patchwork script, a flaccid imitation of dozens of superior French film comedies. Writers Morrie Ryskind (adaptation) and Rowland Leigh (additional dialogue) stitched together this bagatelle about a French reform school escapee (Miss Rogers, left) who is indoctrinated into the fine art of picking pockets by Basil Rathbone (right) and subsequently assigned by ambassador Adolphe Menjou to pilfer a watch from dashing Jean Pierre Aumont. One way or another, it all leads to a marriage between Rogers and Aumont. Sam Wood directed as if his mind were far, far away from the project – which is precisely where his body should have been. Melville Cooper, Mikhail Rasumny, Eduardo Ciannelli, Mona Maris and Henry Stephenson also appeared, and RKO distributed for the Hakims' New World Productions. The film was a remake of a French picture, *Battement De Coeur* (1939), written by Hans Wilhelm, Max Kolpe and Michel Duran. These gentlemen here received credit for the original screenplay on which Ryskind based his adaptation.

Badman's Territory turned out to be the Quinto strip along Oklahoma's panhandle – supposedly the last bandit stronghold of the old west. Working from the theory that a western can't have too many bad guys, screenwriters Jack Natteford and Luci Ward arranged to introduce US marshal Randolph Scott (left) and crusading newspaper editor Ann Richards to Jesse James (Lawrence Tierney), Frank James (Tom Tyler), Bob Dalton (Steve Brodie), Grat Dalton (Phil Warren), Bill Dalton (William Moss), Sam Bass (Nestor Paiva), Belle Starr (Isabel Jewell, right), plus other assorted horse thieves, sidewinders and enraged Indians. The whole fandango was hopelessly contrived, but action-loving patrons swallowed it whole (net profit $557,000). Clarence Upson Young and Bess Taffel wrote additional sequences, Nat Holt produced and Tim Whelan called the shots. Others in executive producer Jack J. Gross's picture were George 'Gabby' Hayes, Ray Collins, James Warren, Virginia Sale, John Halloran, Andrew Tombes, Richard Hale, Harry Holman and Chief Thundercloud.

With the exception of Frances Langford's musical numbers, **The Bamboo Blonde** was tedium all the way, drearily scripted by Olive Cooper and Lawrence Kimble (from a story by Wayne Whittaker) and colourlessly directed by Anthony Mann. In it, Ralph Edwards, who has made a fortune selling 'Bamboo Blonde' products, recalls the story of how the name became famous on an American bomber. Russell Wade (right), it seems, spent his last night in New York with Miss Langford (left), a singer in Edwards' nightclub, before embarking for overseas duty. His crew spotted the blonde with their captain and painted her likeness on the side of their B-29, after which the plane became the scourge of the Pacific, dunking Japanese ships like doughnuts and swatting Zero fighters like so many harmless gnats. The attendant publicity naturally propelled the heroine into a big-time singing career and led Edwards into the merchandizing business. Iris Adrian, Richard Martin, Jane Greer, Glenn Vernon, Paul Harvey, Regina Wallace, Jean Brooks, Tom Noonan and Dorothy Vaughn had other feature roles in the Herman Schlom production (executive producer Sid Rogell). Songs: 'Moonlight Over The Islands', 'Right Along About Evening', 'Good For Nothing But Love', 'I'm Dreaming Out Loud' Mort Greene, Lew Pollack.

In **Genius At Work**, a deranged expert on crime gives clues about each of his murders to two unbelievably dumb radio sleuths and the girl who writes their material. The accuracy of the clues brings a pair of real cops into the case and, after an avalanche of outrageous puns and a wild scramble around the window ledges of a tall building, the egomaniac criminologist and his sinister assistant are brought to justice. Producer Herman Schlom and director Leslie Goodwins populated the Robert E. Kent-Monte Brice screenplay with Alan Carney and Wally Brown (centre and right, the broadcasting team), Anne Jeffreys (left, their writer), Marc Cramer and Ralph Dunn (the two policemen), Lionel Atwill (the criminologist) and Bela Lugosi (Atwill's aide-de-crime). Sid Rogell was the executive producer of this ragged but giggle-provoking farce.

Crack-Up opened with Pat O'Brien's fist smashing through the door of a museum and never slowed its action-packed pace until the end credits crawled across the screen. Still, action was not enough as far as movie customers were concerned; they never could make much sense of the contrived and disjointed plot and left the film swaying pitifully in the box-office breeze, unappreciated and unattended. Writers John Paxton, Ben Bengal and Ray Spencer worked on Frederic Brown's story *Madman's Holiday*, which had something to do with the forgery and theft of priceless paintings by a group of international crooks. O'Brien (left) is an art expert and lecturer who treads upon the villains' carefully laid plans and pays for his clumsiness by suffering what appears to be a violent mental breakdown. Also cast: Claire Trevor (right) as O'Brien's supportive fiancée, Herbert Marshall (centre) as a Scotland Yard man posing as a visiting art expert, Wallace Ford as a hard-nosed police lieutenant, Erskine Sanford as the head of the museum, plus Ray Collins, Dean Harens, Damian O'Flynn and Mary Ware. Irving Reis, making his first film after being discharged from the Army, displayed real directorial flair in several brilliantly executed scenes, but he clearly didn't give much thought to the logic of his narrative. Jack J. Gross was the executive producer.

Transporting its audience to the midst of the English countryside, **Great Day** told how a small community overcomes its internal feuds and romantic problems while preparing to greet the arrival of American first lady Eleanor Roosevelt. Eric Portman was top-billed as a maladjusted World War I veteran who clings to the weary remnants of his pride, although his wife (Flora Robson, right) and daughter (Sheila Sim, left) frequently pay for his alcoholic follies. The daughter has other problems generated by her indecision regarding the marriage proposals of young military officer Philip Friend and her middle-aged employer Walter Fitzgerald. These and other plot lines were unravelled by screenwriters John Davenport, Lesley Storm and Wolfgang Wilhelm, though American audiences couldn't have cared less. They gave the film a wide berth and it ended up a $232,000 loser despite tolerable foreign rentals. Lance Comfort directed, Lesley Storm wrote the play on which the film was based, and Victor Hanbury produced in England for RKO British Productions. In support were Isabel Jeans, Marjorie Rhodes, Maire O'Neill, John Laurie, Kathleen Harrison, Leslie Dwyer, Margaret Withers, Beatrice Varley, Irene Handl, Patricia Hayes, Jacqueline Clarke, Norman Pierce, Pauline Tennant, John McLaren, Ivor Barnard, Valentine Dunn, O. B. Clarence, Jean Shepherd, David Ward and Ray Malcolm.

Orson Welles left some of his cinematic tricks on the shelf, and directed **The Stranger** in what was, by his standards, a restrained fashion. Welles (right) also starred in the film. Billed as 'the most deceitful man a woman ever loved', he portrayed a Nazi mass-murderer who has escaped the Allied net and taken up residence in a small Connecticut village. There, he meets and marries Loretta Young (centre). An investigator from The Commission for War Crimes (Edward G. Robinson, left) comes to town, picks up the scent, and begins using psychological warfare to make the guilty man admit his identity. Young, in the meantime, slowly discovers her husband's true nature but cannot bring herself to betray him until he attempts to kill her. The final battle between hunter and hunted, in which the Nazi rat is symbolically impaled, was heavy-handed but electrifying, and the film itself was a top-notch thriller. Victor Trivas and Decla Dunning's story and Anthony Veiller's screenplay also gave parts to Philip Merivale, Richard Long, Byron Keith, Konstantin Shayne, Billy House, Martha Wentworth, Pietro Sosso and Irving Pichel. S. P. Eagle (Sam Spiegel) produced the final International Picture distributed by RKO.

Notorious was one of those rare cinematic masterworks that casts a spell over audiences. Ben Hecht's vibrant screenplay, the exquisite performances of Cary Grant (left) and Ingrid Bergman (right), and Alfred Hitchcock's mesmeric direction had filmgoers abandoning themselves completely to the story of the daughter of a convicted spy who atones for her father's treason by helping to expose a group of enemy plotters in South America. Besides the suspense elements which producer-director Hitchcock manipulated like a silken cord around each viewer's neck, the film contained some of the most inflammatory love scenes ever put on the screen during the Production Code era. No film chefs ever blended espionage and sex into a more potent Molotov cocktail than this particular team. Other significant contributions were made by Claude Rains, delivering one of many exceptional performances as a sympathetic Nazi villain; Madame Konstantin, playing Rains' suspicious and dominating mother with calculated iciness; and Louis Calhern, adding vivid nuances to his stock G-man role. Reinhold Schunzel, Moroni Olsen, Ivan Triesault, Alex Minotis, Wally Brown, Sir Charles Mendl, Ricardo Costa, Eberhard Krumschmidt and Fay Baker also appeared. Ted Tetzlaff was responsible for the daring cinematography, including a justifiably famous crane shot that begins at the top of a grand staircase, then swoops down to the foyer below where a party is in progress, ending in close up on a key clutched in Bergman's hand. Roy Webb composed the insinuating musical score, and RKO made $1,010,000 profit on this co-production with Vanguard Films which furnished the screenplay, and the services of Hitchcock, Grant and Bergman. Note: The story was suggested by John Taintor Foote's *Song Of The Dragon*, a magazine story that had been written in 1921 and filmed under the title *Convoy* in 1927 with Dorothy Mackaill. Since Hecht's final script was so far removed from the basic material, Mr Foote received no screen or advertising credit.

A casino full of amusing characters popped up in **Lady Luck**, a high stakes comedy directed by Edwin L. Marin from Lynn Root and Frank Fenton's screenplay (story by Herbert Clyde Lewis). The story concerned a gambler (Robert Young, centre), and his bride (Barbara Hale, right) who is descended from a long line of gents who bet their shirts and lost them. An hour after the hero promises his new spouse that he is reformed and will never risk another dollar on anything, she catches him at the crap table and sets out after a divorce. Complications proliferate when the girl's grandpa (Frank Morgan, borrowed from MGM) and the boy's pals endeavour to patch up the embattled couple. Executive producer Robert Fellows and producer Warren Duff also utilized the talents of James Gleason (borrowed from 20th Century-Fox), Don Rice, Harry Davenport, Lloyd Corrigan, Teddy Hart, Joseph Vitale and Douglas Morrow (left). Although the picture was a pleasant trifle, good for 97 minutes of effortless diversion, its outlandish $877,000 production cost was an indicator of the way filmmaking costs had escalated in a few short years and an omen of big problems to come.

Post-war readjustment was the subject of **Till The End Of Time**, a surprisingly realistic and often compelling drama produced by Dore Schary and directed by Edward Dmytryk. Allen Rivkin's screenplay, based on Niven Busch's novel *They Dream Of Home*, focused on three ex-Marines: Guy Madison (left) whose parents want to settle him into a job and get him married almost before he takes off his uniform; Robert Mitchum whose plans to buy a little ranch are smashed by a disastrous trip to Las Vegas; and Bill Williams, an ex-boxer who has lost both legs and maintains a thoroughly hopeless outlook on life. Dorothy McGuire (right) also figured prominently in the action, portraying an emotionally ravaged war widow who helps Madison to find himself.

Schary's preference for message-oriented entertainment was evident in the film's most famous scene – a barroom brawl between the veterans and members of a racist, Klan-like group called the American War Patriots. Needless to say, the good guys win, with Williams even getting in a few good licks. Tom Tully, William Gargan, Jean Porter, Johnny Sands, Loren Tindall, Ruth Nelson, Selena Royle, Harry von Zell and Richard Benedict completed the cast. The novel, screenplay and services of Schary, McGuire and Madison were supplied by David O. Selznick in another co-production venture between RKO and Vanguard Films. Song: 'Till The End Of Time' Buddy Kaye, Ted Mossman, based on Chopin's 'Polonaise In A Flat Major'.

Step By Step was a 'B'-level chase film that ground to a halt long before its seemingly interminable 62 minutes elapsed. Anne Jeffreys (left) and Lawrence Tierney (right) zoom up and down the California countryside, pursued by Nazis determined to rebuild their country's lost pride, and similarly determined to relieve Tierney of certain incriminating papers which have innocently fallen into his possession. The unfortunate couple are also being hunted by the police, who believe that naive Mr Tierney has murdered a federal agent. All in all, it was a shameful waste of petroleum and celluloid. Stuart Palmer wrote the unfocused screenplay, based on a story by George Callahan, and Phil Rosen provided the consistent misdirection. Lowell Gilmore, George Cleveland, Jason Robards, Myrna Dell, Harry Harvey, Addison Richards, Ray Walker and John Hamilton also participated for executive producer Sid Rogell.

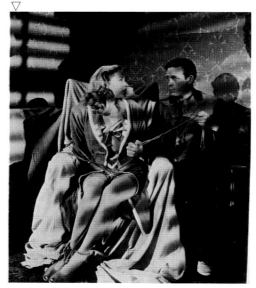

Samuel Goldwyn's The Best Years Of Our Lives became the most honoured release in RKO history, winning seven Academy Awards (including Best Picture) and innumerable other accolades. The picture weighed in at two hours and 50 minutes — a hefty dosage of moral uplift deftly written by Robert E. Sherwood from a novel by MacKinlay Kantor, and masterfully directed by William Wyler. Fredric March (seated right), Dana Andrews (centre) and Harold Russell (left) were three military veterans who meet on a plane taking them back to their home town. Each is returning to a woman he loves — March to his wife, Myrna Loy (centre right); Andrews to Virginia Mayo, his bride whom he left years before (after only a few weeks of marriage) when he departed overseas; Russell (an actual veteran who lost both hands during the war), maimed and handicapped by combat, to his childhood sweetheart Cathy O'Donnell. Each faces a crisis upon his arrival, and each crisis is a microcosm of the experiences of many American warriors who found an alien world awaiting them when they came marching home. This film had everything: laughs, tears, romance, anger, compassion, steadfast love, wrenching drama, social message. In short, it was emotional dynamite and audiences were emotionally shattered by it. Others fortunate enough to be associated with producer Goldwyn, for whom The Best Years was the apogee of a long and distinguished show business career, were director of photography Gregg Toland, art directors Perry Ferguson and George Jenkins, film editor Daniel Mandell, music composer Hugo Friedhofer, and supporting players Teresa Wright (centre left), Hoagy Carmichael (standing right), Gladys George, Roman Bohnen, Ray Collins, Minna Gombell, Walter Baldwin, Steve Cochran, Dorothy Adams, Don Beddoe, Victor Cutler, Marlene Aames, Charles Halton, Ray Teal, Howland Chamberlin, Dean White, Erskine Sanford and Michael Hall.

With the divorce rate in America totalling more than 250,000 annually in 1946, RKO decided to dust off *Wednesday's Child* (1934) and film it again, changing the title to Child Of Divorce. First-time producer Lillie Hayward handled the picture under the tutelage of executive producer Sid Rogell; she also wrote the screenplay (based on a play by Leopold L. Atlas) about a hypersensitive little girl (Sharyn Moffett, centre) who can't reconcile herself to the breakup of her parents. Richard O. Fleischer, another newcomer, directed with a probing eye that was sympathetic to his characters without patronising them. Pint-sized Miss Moffett clearly dominated the picture, although Regis Toomey and Madge Meredith (right) as the mother and father, and Walter Reed (left) and Doris Merrick as the 'other man and other woman' also stood out. In the end the girl finally accepts the reality that her parents will never get back together, and the inevitability of life in a boarding school. This unusually downbeat denouement hurt the popular appeal of the film, but it is seldom that one finds an RKO picture whose only flaw was an excess of artistic integrity. Una O'Connor, Harry Cheshire, Selmer Jackson, Lillian Randolph, Pat Prest, Gregory Muradian, George McDonald, Patsy Converse and Ann Carter were others in the cast.

Serious, sincere, reverent and, alas, excruciating, **Sister Kenny** came to the screen under the supervision of producer-director-writer Dudley Nichols. Rosalind Russell (right) gave a commendable performance as the fighting nurse who achieved fame with her treatment for infantile paralysis, but it was not enough to redeem the film's landslide of biopic clichés and its snail-like pace. The plot, disregarding historical accuracy, read like a blueprint for such films. It chronicled Elizabeth Kenny's activities in the Australian bush where she first encounters a case of the crippling disease; the sacrifice of romantic happiness for her work; the bitter battle she must wage for recognition by the medical community, including heart-breaking rebuffs which stifle many of her efforts; and finally her breakthrough to victory, symbolized by the establishment of the Kenny Institute in Minneapolis, Minnesota. Hagiography had never been a big seller at the box-office, and the **Sister Kenny** audiences manifested no inclination to make it one; the eventual loss to RKO was $660,000. Alexander Knox and Mary McCarthy worked with Nichols on the screenplay, which was based on *And They Shall Walk* by Elizabeth Kenny (in collaboration with Martha Ostenso). Alexander Knox (borrowed from Columbia) also co-starred, with Dean Jagger, Philip Merivale, Beulah Bondi, Charles Dingle, John Litel, Doreen McCann (left), Fay Helm, Charles Kemper and Dorothy Peterson completing the cast. Edward Donahoe was the associate producer.

A train holdup, a bank robbery and a bandit ambush were about the only highlights of **Sunset Pass**, a mediocre Zane Grey western produced by Herman Schlom and directed by William Berke. Rangy James Warren played a frontier detective assigned to break up an outlaw band preying on trains along the Arizona border. John Laurenz helped out as Warren's Spanish-Irish sidekick and Nan Leslie and Jane Greer added the romantic interest. Also cast: Robert Clarke (left), Steve Brodie (centre), Harry Woods (right), Robert Barrat and Harry Harvey. Norman Houston hammered out the screenplay for executive producer Sid Rogell. Two earlier film versions had been made by Paramount in 1929 starring Jack Holt and Nora Lane, and in 1933 with Randolph Scott and Tom Keene.

RKO offered an embarrassment of riches for the 1946 Christmas season. On the heels of *The Best Years Of Our Lives* came **It's A Wonderful Life**, Frank Capra's personal favourite and one of the enduring achievements of the studio era. Philip Van Doren Stern's *The Greatest Gift* was a short story originally mailed to his friends as a Christmas card. It received such a favourable reception that Stern had it published, whereupon RKO bought the rights with the idea of developing it into a starring vehicle for Cary Grant. Capra, a member of the new Liberty Films team, read it, purchased it from RKO, worked with Frances Goodrich and Albert Hackett on the screenplay (plus Jo Swerling who wrote additional scenes) and then produced and directed the picture. Its fantasy plot centred on James Stewart (right) who is about to commit suicide when a kindly angel (Henry Travers, left) shows him a vision of the world as it would have developed had he never been born. He learns that his mother would be running a boarding house, his brother would have died as a child, his friends

One of the year's top programme pictures, **Criminal Court** featured Tom Conway (left) as a cocksure young attorney who accidentally kills a crooked saloon owner and then – in an unusual switch – must prove his guilt to a jury when his lady love (Martha O'Driscoll, right) is put on trial for the murder. Former crime journalist Martin Mooney produced his first film for RKO, making certain that this 62-minute effort had the punch and compression of a hard-hitting newspaper exposé. Lawrence Kimble's screenplay (based on a story by Earl Felton) was directed by Robert Wise who used June Clayworth, Robert Armstrong, Addison Richards, Pat Gleason, Steve Brodie, Robert Warwick, Phil Warren, Joe Devlin, Lee Bonnell and Robert Clarke to round out the cast. Sid Rogell was once again the executive producer.

would be living in a slum and his wife would be a soured spinster. Only one person could have transformed this treacly premise into a moving statement on the human condition and, fortunately, that man was in the director's chair. Not that Capra did it alone – Stewart delivered one of his best-remembered performances, receiving superlative backing from Donna Reed, Lionel Barrymore and Gloria Grahame (all three borrowed from MGM), Thomas Mitchell (borrowed from 20th Century-Fox), Beulah Bondi, Frank Faylen, Ward Bond, H. B. Warner, Todd Karns, Samuel S. Hinds, Mary Treen, Frank Albertson, Virginia Patton, Carol Coombes, Jimmy Hawkins, Larry Simms, Karolyn Grimes and Sarah Edwards. Sadly, the postwar atmosphere was not conducive to Capra's unique blend of love, humour and pathos, and the film lost $525,000 at the box-office for RKO. Although the studio had a releasing contract with Liberty Films for a number of pictures, this was the only co-production ever consummated between the two organizations.

★★★★★★★★★★★★★★★★★★★
★★★★★★★★★★★★★★★★★★★

Dore Schary assumed charge of studio production early in the year, succeeding N. Peter Rathvon who returned to his duties as corporate president. An award-winning writer and producer, Schary came to RKO from the Selznick organization after demonstrating his abilities on such films as **The Spiral Staircase** and **The Farmer's Daughter**. Schary brought in William J. Fadiman, former head of the MGM story department, and Edgar Peterson, Frank Capra's civilian associate during the war years, to be his chief assistants.

The new executive would need plenty of help, for the motion picture industry was entering a prolonged period of crisis. Production costs had nearly doubled since 1944, and the amount of capital needed to run the RKO studio alone had increased by more than $2 million during those three years. Meanwhile, the period when almost anything on celluloid could be sold for a profit had come to an abrupt end. A confiscatory tax slapped on the earnings of American pictures in Great Britain, and similar measures introduced in other countries, cut foreign revenues by more than a third, while domestic box-office income declined by approximately 20%. RKO did report corporate profits of $5,085,847, but this was far below the record earnings of 1946. The studio also sold the RKO Pathé newsreel to Warner Bros.

1947 brought the debilitating storm known as McCarthyism. J. Parnell Thomas' House Un-American Activities Committee began its investigation into Hollywood Communism, provoking an atmosphere of fear and splitting the film capital into several different camps. Eight writers, one producer and one director (the so-called 'Hollywood Ten') refused to cooperate with the Committee and were cited for contempt of Congress. The producer was Adrian Scott and the director Edward Dmytryk, two of RKO's top talents. Both were subsequently fired and blacklisted, along with many others accused of having the 'Red' tinge. Ironically, the studio's biggest financial, as well as critical, success was the Scott–Dmytryk **Crossfire**. **The Bachelor And The Bobby-Soxer**, **Nocturne** and **Trail Street** also performed well at the box office.

RKO released 40 pictures in 1947, including the usual number of independent features and co-productions. In the acting arena, Robert Mitchum was upgraded to an 'A' film star; Robert Ryan and Tim Holt returned from the service and distinguished themselves in their respective pictures; Barbara Bel Geddes made her debut in **The Long Night**; and Gloria Grahame's impressive work in **Crossfire** was rewarded with a long-term contract.

Joan Harrison, who learned the fine art of filmic suspense as one of Alfred Hitchcock's scenarists, gave RKO a solid hit (profits $568,000) with **Nocturne**, her first production for the studio. The story turned on ten beautiful women who are all suspected of murder. When the police are called in to investigate the death of a Hollywood composer, it looks like an open-and-shut case of suicide, but hard-boiled detective George Raft (centre) judges it to be murder. The photographs of the ten women – all known as Delores to the dead Don Juan – launch Raft on an investigation that costs him his job but leads to a romantic relationship with Lynn Bari (borrowed from 20th Century-Fox). Although Jonathan Latimer's screenplay (based on a story by Frank Fenton and Rowland Brown) contained a number of annoying narrative fissures, Edwin L. Marin's practised direction was admirable in plastering them over, and, of course, hero Raft nails the killer (Joseph Pevney) in the end. Virginia Huston, Myrna Dell, Edward Ashley, Walter Sande, Mabel Paige (right), Bernard Hoffman, Queenie Smith, Mack Gray and Virginia Edwards (left) were cast for executive producer Jack J. Gross. Songs included: 'Nocturne' Leigh Harline, Mort Greene; 'Why Pretend', 'A Little Bit Is Better Than None' Eleanor Rudolph.

Never one to cold-shoulder a damsel in distress, ▷ Tom Conway (right) postponed his vacation once again and rescued Madge Meredith from a kidnapper in **The Falcon's Adventure**. Miss Meredith has been entrusted with a formula for synthetic diamonds, drawing Conway into a continuing battle with thieves determined to possess the formula. After meeting the usual challenges in the usual fashion, the Falcon finally earned his vacation – a permanent one. This Herman Schlom-produced and William Berke-directed film was the series finale, leaving Dick Tracy as RKO's only continuing whodunit hero. Aubrey Wisberg's screenplay (additional dialogue Robert E. Kent) also employed Edward S. Brophy (left), Robert Warwick, Myrna Dell, Steve Brodie, Ian Wolfe, Carol Forman, Joseph Crehan, Phil Warren, Tony Barrett, Harry Harvey and Jason Robards.

The Freudian stew pot bubbled merrily in **The Locket**, an absorbing *film noir* detailing how the life of a beautiful woman, and those of the men who love her, are ruined as a result of her traumatic childhood experience. Using flashbacks, director John Brahm (on loan from 20th Century-Fox) told a story of progressive insanity which began at age ten when Laraine Day (borrowed from MGM) was accused of stealing a locket by a cruel and vicious woman. The psychological cancer created by this experience becomes manifest in adult life when her compulsive kleptomania leads to murder, the execution of an innocent man, suicide, and the complete mental collapse of the protagonist. The men unfortunate enough to fall under Miss Day's (right) charming spell were Robert Mitchum, Brian Aherne (left) and Gene Raymond (centre). Sharyn Moffett, Ricardo Cortez, Henry Stephenson, Katherine Emery, Reginald Denny, Fay Helm, Helene Thimig, Nella Walker, Queenie Leonard, Myrna Dell, Johnny Clark and Lilian Fontaine (mother of Joan Fontaine and Olivia de Havilland) were also cast. Sheridan Gibney wrote the formidable screenplay for producer Bert Granet and executive producer Jack J. Gross.
▽

Despite an acrobatic performance by Douglas Fairbanks Jr (right) in the type of role his father patented, **Sinbad The Sailor** was two hours of Technicolor wallow – a very long and very disgruntling Arabian night. Screenwriter John Twist, who also worked on the story with George Worthing Yates, was chiefly at fault. His tale of Sinbad's eighth voyage in search of Deryabar, the island where Alexander the Great supposedly hid his treasure, made all the mistakes that Yates and Herman J. Mankiewicz's script for *The Spanish Main* had scrupulously avoided; it was convoluted and fatuously verbose, and scrimped on the action. The costumes, sets and performers were all pleasant to look at, but they couldn't clear away the murkiness of the plot which was almost beyond the comprehension of adults, let alone the kiddies who were supposed to be the target audience for the fanciful adventures. Director Richard Wallace and producer Stephen Ames should have paid more attention to the story problems and less to the splashy logistics of their $2,459,000 production. Walter Slezak, as a treacherous barber aboard Sinbad's vessel, emerged as the most interesting character, and Maureen O'Hara, Anthony Quinn, George Tobias (left), Jane Greer, Mike Mazurki, Sheldon Leonard, Alan Napier, John Miljan and Barry Mitchell also set sail. Though the film made a small profit, **Sinbad The Sailor** would surely have cost Scheherazade her head if she had tried it out as one of her hypnotic narratives.
▽

Walt Disney's **Song Of The South** embedded Joel Chandler Harris' 'Uncle Remus' stories in a comedy-drama about a young boy who runs away from home because of a rift between his parents. Trudging along, the forlorn lad encounters Uncle Remus whose fables about Brer Rabbit, Brer Fox, Brer Bear, and their antic kin of the briar patch, cause the runaway to change his mind about deserting his family. The Disney staff again combined animated footage (the fables) with live-action photography; predictably, the sketched material (see illustration) outclassed the Bobby Breen-like story and the human performers who acted it out. Bobby Driscoll played the boy, James Baskett was Uncle Remus, and Erik Rolf and Ruth Warrick were the feuding parents, with Luana Patten, Mary Field, George Nokes, Gene Holland, Glenn Leedy, Hattie McDaniel and Lucile Watson also cast. Dalton Reymond, Maurice Rapf and Morton Grant wrote the screenplay from a story by Reymond; Wilfred Jackson was the cartoon director, Harve Foster the photoplay director and Perce Pearce the associate producer. Songs included: 'Song Of The South' Arthur Johnston, Sam Coslow; 'Zip-A-Dee-Doo-Dah' Allie Wrubel, Ray Gilbert; 'How Do You Do?' Robert MacGimsey; 'Let The Rain Pour Down' Ken Darby, Foster Carling; 'Sooner Or Later' Charles Wolcott, Ray Gilbert.
▽

Lawrence Tierney starred in **San Quentin**, a throbbing exploitation item cooked up by screenwriters Lawrence Kimble, Arthur A. Ross and Howard J. Green. The 'Inmate's Welfare League', an organization composed of San Quentin inmates devoted to maintaining discipline and preparing lawbreakers for useful lives after parole, nearly receives its death blow when trusted convict Barton MacLane (left) stages a break and embarks on a crime spree. Tierney (right), the ex-con who originated the League, feels honour-bound to collar the fugitive in the hope that this will prevent his rehabilitation concept from being scrapped. The picture had just enough social message to satisfy the critics, and plenty of action to please audiences looking for a red-blooded manhunt saga. It was one of Gordon Douglas' most accomplished directorial jobs for RKO. Also cast: Marian Carr, Harry Shannon, Carol Forman, Joe Devlin, Tony Barrett, Lee Bonnell, Robert Clarke, Raymond Burr and Richard Powers (RKO's old cowboy star Tom Keene, using another of his movie monikers). Martin Mooney was the producer and Sid Rogell the executive producer.

Frances Langford, Ralph Edwards and Phillip Terry were top-cast in **Beat The Band**, a witless trifle directed by John H. Auer that contained enough sour notes to dampen half-a-dozen 'B' musicals. Returning from the war, band leader Terry (centre) discovers that his manager (Edwards) has frittered away their joint savings account. In order to earn sufficient money to reassemble his band, Terry impersonates a middle-aged voice teacher whose notions of operatic training are more than slightly unorthodox. His pupil is, of course, Miss Langford (left). The Broadway musical play by George Abbott, John Green and George Marion Jr, adapted by Arthur A. Ross and Lawrence Kimble and written for the screen by Kimble, ultimately climaxed in a hotel boiler room where Gene Krupa and his band (background) get really 'hot' when the steam is turned on. Michel Kraike received his first RKO credit as producer, working under the aegis of executive producer Sid Rogell and using June Clayworth, Mabel Paige, Andrew Tombes, Donald MacBride, Mira McKinney, Harry Harvey and Grady Sutton to complete the cast. Songs included: 'Kissin' Well', 'I'm In Love', 'I've Got My Fingers Crossed' Leigh Harline, Mort Greene.

Producer Herman Schlom and director Felix Feist defied the old Hollywood maxim that the audience demands a sympathetic hero when they cast Lawrence Tierney as a satanic menace in **The Devil Thumbs A Ride**. Director Feist's script, based on a novel by Robert C. DuSoe, centred on Tierney (left), a swaggering hold-up man who kills a theatre manager in San Diego and makes his getaway by hitching a ride with naive motorist Ted North. Soon afterwards, North picks up Nan Leslie (right) and Betty Lawford, setting the stage for three more deaths, two injuries, and plenty of standard melodramatics as the police net closes around the killer. Also cast: Andrew Tombes, Harry Shannon, Glenn Vernon, Marian Carr, William Gould, Josephine Whittell, Phil Warren and Robert Malcolm. Tierney, who seemed to attack villainous roles with substantially more gusto than he did heroic parts, had first gained prominence as the title character in *Dillinger* (Monogram, 1945).

Set in the Arizona strip around 1880, Zane Grey's **Code Of The West** was all about a gang of desperadoes who gain political control of a small town, and the plucky settlers who wage war against them. James Warren (left) represented the major challenge to town boss Raymond Burr and his minions, with John Laurenz chipping in to trouble Burr, and Debra Alden (right) waiting for the shooting to end and the romance to begin. Steve Brodie, Rita Lynn, Robert Clarke, Carol Forman, Harry Woods, Harry Harvey, Phil Warren and Emmett Lynn were also featured for producer Herman Schlom, director William Berke and screenwriter Norman Houston. Song: 'Rainbow Valley' Lew Pollack, Harry Harris. Paramount produced two earlier versions of the story; the first, in 1925, featured Owen Moore and Constance Bennett; the second, released in 1934 under the title *Home On The Range*, starred Randolph Scott and Evelyn Brent.

An expeditionary party intent on trapping animals wholesale for the world's zoos caused all the trouble in **Tarzan And The Huntress**. Having already dealt with such formidable nuisances as Nazis and leopard cultists, early ecologist Johnny Weissmuller (right) hardly worked up a sweat in defeating the despoilers, led by Patricia Morison and Barton MacLane. In fact, he allowed his animal friends to exact appropriate retribution in the form of a thunderous elephant stampede which drove out the invaders permanently. The creative team, which included director and associate producer Kurt Neumann, scriptwriters Jerry Gruskin and Rowland Leigh, cinematographer Archie Stout and production designer Phil Paradise, also rested on their laurels, making this a rather lukewarm adventure in darkest Africa. Series regulars Brenda Joyce (left) and Johnny Sheffield were also cast, plus John Warburton, Charles Trowbridge, Ted Hecht and Wallace Scott. Sol Lesser produced for Sol Lesser Productions Inc.

Could anyone take seriously a film with characters named Cueball, Vitamin Flintheart, Filthy Flora of the Dripping Dagger Inn, Jules Priceless and Tess Trueheart? Certainly not – and that was the salvation of **Dick Tracy vs Cueball**. Screenwriters Dane Lussier and Robert E. Kent (original story by Luci Ward) and director Gordon Douglas tackled the project with their tongues firmly in their cheeks, and succeeded in creating a picture with plenty of humour and lots of action. Cueball (Dick Wessel, right) played the bald-headed trigger man for a trio of jewel thieves who engineer the theft of $300,000 worth of diamonds. He murders thrice by strangulation before super-sleuth Tracy chases him to a railroad yard where the mug is killed by a speeding train. Anne Jeffreys played Tess and Lyle Latell was Tracy's thick-headed assistant, Pat Patton. Portraying the other colourful characters were Esther Howard (Flora), Douglas Walton (Priceless) and Ian Keith (Flintheart). Morgan Conway (left) played Tracy for the second and final time, and Rita Corday, Joseph Crehan, Byron Foulger, Jimmy Crane, Milton Parsons and Skelton Knaggs were in it too. Herman Schlom was the producer and Sid Rogell the executive producer.

Trail Street was a traditional western built around the exploits of US marshal Bat Masterson who, according to Norman Houston and Gene Lewis' script (based on a novel by William Corcoran) believed in 'shooting first and shooting straight'. Sodbusters in Liberal, Kansas, appeal to Masterson (Randolph Scott, left) to come and help them in their fight against the lawless, hard-drinking trail drivers who ruin crops by driving their herds across the farmlands. The situation builds to a rousing climax in which cowmen and ploughmen meet in a pitched battle that re-establishes law and order. Robert Ryan came home to RKO after completing his contract with Uncle Sam, and played a young land agent who believes in the future of Kansas despite the chaos. The rest of producer Nat Holt's superior cast included Anne Jeffreys (right), George 'Gabby' Hayes, Madge Meredith, Steve Brodie, Billy House, Virginia Sale, Harry Woods, Phil Warren, Harry Harvey and Jason Robards. Ray Enright directed. Supervisor Jack J. Gross's film had absolutely nothing to do with the historical Mr Masterson, but it was a rip-snorter at the box office (profit $365,000). Songs included: 'You May Not Remember' Ben Oakland, George Jessel; 'You're Not The Only Pebble On The Beach' Stanley Carter, Harry Braisted.

Anne Jeffreys was the only virtue of **Vacation In Reno**, an otherwise stupefying farce, written by Charles E. Roberts and Arthur A. Ross, and indifferently directed by Leslie Goodwins. The story (by Charles Kerr) had Jeffreys (left) becoming suspicious when she discovers that her husband (Jack Haley, right) has gone to Nevada to search for an old-time outlaw's hidden loot. She wonders if he isn't really seeking a divorce and follows, locating him at a dude ranch near Reno where he is involved with blundering bank robbers Morgan Conway and Alan Carney and their accomplice Iris Adrian. From this point onwards, the picture spewed forth a collection of shop-worn gags that provoked considerable off-screen movement towards movie house exits. The beautiful and talented Miss Jeffreys had been around RKO long enough to merit something a whole lot better than this fatuity. Goodwins also produced, using Wally Brown, Myrna Dell, Matt McHugh, Claire Carleton and Jason Robards in secondary roles. The executive producer was Sid Rogell.

Ethically-minded critics sharpened their talons and attacked **Born To Kill** (GB: **Lady Of Deceit**) with a vengeance, flaying its indulgent treatment of 'bullet-man' Lawrence Tierney (right) and 'silken savage' Claire Trevor (left). Eve Greene and Richard Macaulay's screenplay, based on James Gunn's novel *Deadlier Than The Male*, narrated the sordid adventures of killer Tierney whose ambition is to 'fix it so's I can spit in anybody's eye'. Mercenary divorcee Trevor cannot resist the brutal appeal of Tierney, leading to the film's climax in which both are snuffed out. This was supposed to prove – once and for all – that crime doesn't pay, but it failed to pacify the arbiters of public morality. Much of their discomfort was based on the fact that director Robert Wise made this descent into the human cesspool damned exciting, drawing powerfully candid performances from the two stars and solid supporting work from Walter Slezak, Phillip Terry, Audrey Long, Elisha Cook Jr, Isabel Jewell, Esther Howard, Kathryn Card, Tony Barrett and Grandon Rhodes. Sid Rogell was the executive producer and Herman Schlom produced.

Anthony Mann's trigger-finger direction turned **Desperate** into a harrowing programmer that more than lived up to its melodramatic title. Steve Brodie essayed his first major role, playing a newly-married trucker who becomes innocently involved in a fur robbery in which a policeman is killed. Taken hostage by the gang members, Brodie (left) is told that they will mutilate his wife unless he confesses to the murder and clears the guilty man. Brodie pretends to agree but makes his escape, gathers up his wife (Audrey Long) and begins a wild flight, with cops and gangsters in relentless pursuit. Dorothy Atlas and director Mann wrote the original story which Harry Essex scripted with additional dialogue by Martin Rackin. Producer Michel Kraike also cast Raymond Burr (right), Douglas Fowley, William Challee, Jason Robards, Freddie Steele, Lee Frederick, Paul E. Burns and Ilka Gruning.

David O. Selznick purchased a play with a Swedish setting, *Hulda, Daughter Of Parliament* (by Juhni Tervataa), intending to film it with Ingrid Bergman. When that idea fizzled out, his Vanguard Films organization entered into another arrangement with RKO, providing the studio with the property, an Americanized screenplay by Allen Rivkin and Laura Kerr, and the services of Joseph Cotten and producer Dore Schary (before he became RKO production chief) in exchange for a partial ownership in the picture. Eventually called **The Farmer's Daughter**, this delightful comedy-romance starred Loretta Young (left) as a Swedish lass fresh off the Minne-so-ta farm who becomes politically aware when she takes a job in the household of forthright and urbane Congressman Glenn Morley (Cotten, right). She eventually wins the heart of the legislator and a congressional seat of her own in this happy mixture of Frank Capra, Horatio Alger and Cinderella. Though the Oscar Young won for her performance was considered an upset (insider betting favoured Rosalind Russell for her work in *Mourning Becomes Electra*), she richly deserved the award. Excellent support was given by Cotten, by Ethel Barrymore as Cotten's mother who is also the brains behind his political machine, by Charles Bickford as his easy-mannered butler, and a group of fine secondary players that included Rose Hobart, Rhys Williams, Harry Davenport, Tom Powers, William Harrigan, Lex Barker, Harry Shannon, Keith Andes, Thurston Hall, Art Baker, Don Beddoe, James Aurness (later Arness), Anna Q. Nilsson, John Gallaudet, William B. Davidson, Cyrus W. Kendall, Frank Ferguson and William Bakewell. Director H. C. Potter turned in one of the most cogent and impressive efforts of his career.

Barbara Hale (centre) and Bill Williams (right) announced their engagement during the filming of **A Likely Story**. Their glowing faces lit up the screen, but they couldn't redeem Bess Taffel's cliché-packed script (suggested by Alexander Kenedi's story) about an ex-GI (Williams) who erroneously believes he is going to die of a heart ailment, and a young girl from the midwest (Hale) who comes to New York to carve out an art career. Fishing for laughs with every extant comedy approach from subtlety to slapstick, this H. C. Potter-directed effort remained stubbornly unfunny throughout its 88 minutes. Also cast: Lanny Rees (left), Sam Levene, Dan Tobin, Nestor Paiva, Max Willenz, Henry Kulky, Robin Raymond and Mary Young. Richard H. Berger, former manager-director of the highly successful St Louis Municipal Opera Company, produced his first picture for RKO, working under the general supervision of executive producer Jack J. Gross.

Banjo was one of those homespun, human interest movies about a misunderstood child (Sharyn Moffett, centre) and her beloved dog, who are transplanted from a carefree life in the South to the restrictions of a strange home in the North. The disconsolate girl's efforts to adjust, and her ultimate victory over her circumstances were shamelessly designed to pluck the heartstrings of middle American filmgoers. Its mission accomplished in gingerly fashion, the film faded quickly into oblivion. Lillie Hayward wrote and produced and Richard O. Fleischer directed with a cast that included Jacqueline White (right), Walter Reed (left), Una O'Connor, Herbert Evans, Louise Beavers, Ernest Whitman, Theron Jackson and Howard McNeely. RKO still had notions of turning 10-year-old Sharyn Moffett into a child star in the Margaret O'Brien mould, but the studio staff couldn't seem to come up with the right vehicle to thrust her into the limelight.

Jean Renoir's final American film was **The Woman On The Beach**. A stormy drama of isolation, characterized by striking imagery, poetic symbolism and rampant thematic metaphors, it was crammed with such an excessive variety of riches that they couldn't really quite cohere. The screenplay, by Renoir and Frank Davis, was based on Mitchell Wilson's novel *None So Blind*, adapted by Michael Hogan. It concerned a triangle between a Coast Guard lieutenant (Robert Ryan, centre) who suffers from terrible nightmares caused by his combat experience, a bored and beautiful housewife (Joan Bennett, right) harbouring a terrible secret, and her blind, embittered artist husband (Charles Bickford, left). Renoir kept the events pitched at a high level of emotional intensity, yet the film gradually came apart at the seams. The main reason for this rested in the motivations of the characters, which became increasingly muddy and ill-defined as the action homed in on its fiery climax. The director must have realized the problems, for he shot extensive retakes, but was unable to get it right. Despite its weaknesses, however, the picture was obviously the work of a cinematic arist and well worth seeing. Also cast: Nan Leslie, Walter Sande, Irene Ryan, Glenn Vernon, Frank Darien and Jay Norris. Leo Tover and Harry Wild were responsible for the moody, stylized photography, and Jack J. Gross was executive producer with Will Price as his associate.

RKO had always played fast and loose with Zane Grey's western novels; films made from them often bore little or no resemblance to the basic literary material. A case in point was **Thunder Mountain**, made under the working title *To The Last Man*. When the studio had trouble clearing that appellation because of a proposed Liberty Films project called *The Last Man*, it simply affixed the title of one of Grey's other sagebrush tales to the finished picture. Obviously, what the studio wished to exploit was the fame of the author, and the well-known titles of his books. In this movie, Tim Holt (left) demonstrated that he had not forgotten the proper demeanour of a cowboy hero during his years in the Air Corps. He played Marvin Hayden, who finds himself battling against crooks who are seeking control of his land and feuding with a pretty girl (Martha Hyer, right, her RKO debut) and her two brothers. Spanish-Irish Chito Rafferty, the only continuing character in the series, was played by Richard Martin, and the cast was completed by Steve Brodie, Virginia Owen, Harry Woods, Jason Robards, Robert Clarke, Richard Powers and Harry Harvey. Norman Houston wrote the screenplay for director Lew Landers and producer Herman Schlom. Two earlier versions of *To The Last Man* were released by Paramount: in 1923 starring Richard Dix and Lois Wilson, and 1933 with Randolph Scott and Esther Ralston.

Ralph Byrd (left), who had formerly appeared in Republic's 'Dick Tracy' serial, took over the title role from Morgan Conway in **Dick Tracy's Dilemma** (GB: **Mark Of The Claw**). When a trio of thugs headed by The Claw (Jack Lambert), a gangster whose right hand has been replaced by a heavy steel hook, steals a valuable shipment of furs and murders the night watchman, Tracy charges into action. He believes some 'higher-up' is behind the villainy and stalks the meanies until he discovers who the big-shot really is. Audience members fascinated by the outrageous violence in Chester Gould's comic strip loved the finale, where The Claw is electrocuted when his steel mitt comes in contact with a live trolley wire. Otherwise, it was both a literal and figurative flatfoot adventure, slackly directed by John Rawlins from Robert Stephen Brode's feeble screenplay. Also cast: Lyle Latell (right), Kay Christopher, Ian Keith, Bernadene Hayes, Jimmy Conlin, William B. Davidson, Tony Barrett and Richard Powers. Herman Schlom produced.

Honeymoon (GB: **Two Men And A Girl**) was a fluffy little farce made on a very substantial budget ($1,739,000). Predictably, it proved a major league disaster (RKO loss $675,000). Vicki Baum's original story and Michael Kanin's screenplay were all about grown-up Shirley Temple's elopement to Mexico City to meet and marry soldier boy Guy Madison (left). Complications multiply as soon as she arrives and finds that Corporal Madison, stationed in the Canal Zone, is having trouble making his way northward for the rendezvous. Miss Temple (right) enlists the aid of American consul Franchot Tone, who is soon enveloped in a maelstrom of vexations stirred up by the impetuous young lady. Director William Keighley never came close to giving it either comic or romantic life, and wasted a cast that also included Lina Romay, Gene Lockhart, Corinna Mura, Grant Mitchell, Julio Villareal, Manuel Arvide and Jose R. Goula. Robert Sparks was the executive producer and Warren Duff produced this co-venture with Vanguard Films, which furnished the services of Temple and Madison. Songs included: 'I Love Geraniums', 'Ven Aqui' Leigh Harline, Mort Greene.

'When a man goes to the devil he usually takes a woman with him . . . this man took THREE!' RKO publicity for **They Won't Believe Me** left no doubt that this was the story of a heel, and it was. Robert Young (right) starred as a man who sponges off his rich wife (Rita Johnson), loves and deserts another woman (Jane Greer), runs off with yet another (Susan Hayward, left, borrowed from Walter Wanger), killing her in a car accident, and then returns home to murder his wife for her money. He arrives to find she has committed suicide, but he is arrested for the crime anyway. Thus, the title. Told in fashionable flashback style, Jonathan Latimer's screenplay (story by Gordon McDonell) was cunningly contrived in the *Double Indemnity* (Paramount, 1944), tradition, and directed in tough but shrewd fashion by Irving Pichel. The top-line actors all gave outstanding performances; they were supported by Tom Powers, George Tyne, Don Beddoe, Frank Ferguson and Harry Harvey. Joan Harrison produced, and Jack J. Gross served as executive producer.

The Long Night was a grim, uninvolving remake of Marcel Carné's *Le Jour se Lève* (1939). In it, a demobilised soldier (Henry Fonda, right) is goaded by jealousy into shooting a philandering magician (Vincent Price, borrowed from 20th Century-Fox) on the top floor of a tenement building. While the police besiege the house and a crowd gathers, Fonda's mind recalls the events that led up to the tragedy. Though realism was supposedly the foremost intent of screenwriter John Wexley (story by Jacques Viot) and director Anatole Litvak, they compromised themselves at every turn, even to tacking on an unconvincing happy ending. Dimitri Tiomkin's bombastic score didn't help things either. Audience members, most of whom found the film's title ironically appropriate, advised their friends to stay away. They did, and RKO had to absorb a stinging loss of $1,000,000. Screen tyro Barbara Bel Geddes (left) gave a good account of herself as Fonda's girl friend, and the star, as well as featured Ann Dvorak were likewise blameless for the failure; Price, however, contributed heavily to the picture's lack of credibility with a bad John Barrymore imitation in place of a real performance. Also cast: Howard Freeman, Moroni Olsen, Elisha Cook Jr, Queenie Smith, David Clarke, Charles McGraw, Patty King and Robert A. Davis. Robert and Raymond Hakim and director Litvak were the producers for Select Productions, which co-sponsored the film with RKO.

Stage line owner Tim Holt (right) went on the warpath when robbers raided one of his coaches and killed the driver in **Under The Tonto Rim**. Posing as an outlaw himself, he gets the information needed for a sheriff's posse to take over. Norman Houston's over-familiar screenplay and Lew Landers' enervated direction made this the year's most negligible cowpoke adventure. Nan Leslie, Richard Martin, Richard Powers, Carol Forman, Tony Barrett, Harry Harvey, Jason Robards, Robert Clarke (left), Jay Norris, Lex Barker and Steve Savage also appeared in the Herman Schlom production. Paramount's two earlier translations of this Zane Grey novel featured Richard Arlen and Mary Brian (in 1928) and Stuart Erwin and Verna Hillie (in 1933).

Cute was the word for **The Bachelor And The Bobby-Soxer** (GB: **Bachelor Knight**). Indeed, Sidney Sheldon's screenplay about 17-year-old Shirley Temple's (right) relentless pursuit of Cary Grant (left) contained so many cute moments that it sucked in $5,550,000 in film rentals. Among the chief endearments were visions of suave Mr Grant caught up in a dizzying round of juvenile rituals, including jitterbugging, rah-rahing, ingesting ice cream sodas and running obstacle races. This is all the idea of Temple's older sister (Myrna Loy), a judge who sentences Grant to become the bobby-soxer's constant escort until the girl's crush wears off. Producer Dore Schary ensured the production values were uniformly top-drawer, employing Irving Reis to direct, Robert de Grasse to pilot the camera, Albert S. D'Agostino and Carroll Clark to provide the art direction and Leigh Harline to compose the musical score. Also cast: Rudy Vallee, Ray Collins, Harry Davenport, Johnny Sands, Don Beddoe, Lillian Randolph, Veda Ann Borg, Dan Tobin, Ransom Sherman, William Bakewell, Irving Bacon, Ian Bernard, Carol Hughes, William Hall and Gregory Gay. Another co-operative arrangement between RKO and Vanguard Films (which provided the screenplay, producer, Shirley Temple and Johnny Sands), the comedy was Dore Schary's last personal production before he took over as filmmaking chief of RKO.

The fifth film treatment of **Seven Keys To Baldpate** offered Phillip Terry (right) as the author who retires to the shuttered and snow-bound New England inn to write a mystery story, only to find himself in on a rendezvous of murderous criminals. Screenwriter Lee Loeb spruced up the Earl Derr Biggers novel and George M. Cohan dramatization, and the picture played as a middling programmer. Terry was ably supported by phony caretaker Eduardo Ciannelli, insurance company investigator Arthur Shields, hermit Jimmy Conlin, gang moll Margaret Lindsay, and heroine Jacqueline White (left), plus Tony Barrett, Richard Powers and Jason Robards. Lew Landers directed as if the rather threadbare story were freshly woven, and Herman Schlom handled the producer's chores. RKO's two earlier versions were released in 1930 and 1935 respectively. Note: Jack Haley refused to play the writer in the film, a decision that brought about the cancellation of his RKO contract.

Set in the Utah mountains during the 1880s, **Wild Horse Mesa** dealt with cowboys who round up wild mustangs for a living. Tim Holt (right) locates a valuable band of the animals and then helps to fight off a raid by a rival gang. The horses are finally driven to market and sold, but Holt's boss is robbed and murdered on his way back to camp with the money. The hero and his amigo Richard Martin (centre) then flush out the killer and bring him to justice. Norman Houston wrote the screenplay, Wallace A. Grissell directed it, Herman Schlom produced, and Nan Leslie (left), Richard Powers, Jason Robards, Tony Barrett, Harry Woods, William Gould, Robert Bray, Richard Foote and Frank Yaconelli completed the cast. **Wild Horse Mesa** was the eighth and last of the Zane Grey westerns; the story had been filmed by Paramount in 1925 with Jack Holt and Billie Dove and again in 1933 by the same company with Randolph Scott and Sally Blane.

Crossfire was RKO's most controversial (and most lucrative) film of 1947. A *film noir* with a message, it was based on Richard Brooks' novel *The Brick Foxhole*. The novel focused on a vicious soldier whose violent hatred of homosexuals leads him to murder one, but with homosexuality still totally taboo as a screen subject, producer Adrian Scott, director Edward Dmytryk and screenwriter John Paxton changed the victim to a Jew. The result was a potent – though rather superficial – indictment of anti-Semitism. Robert Ryan (left) was appropriately chilling as Montgomery, the rabid Jew-hater whose unprovoked murder of Sam Levene (right) is ultimately exposed by fellow GI Robert Mitchum and clever police captain Robert Young. Other outstanding cast members were George Cooper as an innocent victim of the eruption of hate, Gloria Grahame (borrowed from MGM) as a cheap dance hall doll who meets Cooper on the fateful night, and Paul Kelly, a bizarre hanger-on who may or may not be in love with Miss Grahame. Jacqueline White, Steve Brodie, Richard Benedict, Richard Powers, William Phipps, Lex Barker and Marlo Dwyer also appeared. Dore Schary took his first executive producer credit on this smash hit which earned $1,270,000 in profits for his new company. Note: Although *So Well Remembered* was released later, **Crossfire** was the last film made by Scott and Dmytryk before each became embroiled in the Communist witchhunt. It was, therefore, their final picture for RKO.

Ace cinematographer Ted Tetzlaff (he photographed *Notorious*, 1946) directed **Riff-Raff**. Predictably, the most interesting thing about the picture was the camerawork (supervised by George E. Diskant), full of unusual angles and suggestive lighting. As for Martin Rackin's screenplay, it was standard rough-and-tumble melodrama documenting the deadly competition between Panama-based adventurer Pat O'Brien and a group of sinister opponents to gain possession of a map showing valuable oil concessions. O'Brien (right) surrendered the acting honours to Anne Jeffreys (left), who finally won a lead (as a nightclub singer) in an 'A' picture and made the most of it – even if she didn't quite live up to her titular description. The supporting players, who included Walter Slezak, Percy Kilbride, Jerome Cowan, George Givot, Jason Robards and Marc Krah, were uniformly good. Nat Holt produced for the Jack J. Gross unit. Song: 'Money Is The Root Of All Evil' Joan Whitney, Alex Kramer. Note: This film was *not* a remake of the 1936 MGM release of the same title.

A film still largely underappreciated, **Out Of The Past** (GB: **Build My Gallows High**, the title of the original novel) was one of the masterworks of *film noir*, a hard boiled drama of double-crossing, back-sliding and revenge that was also a piercing emotional journey. Producer Warren Duff and director Jacques Tourneur gave Robert Mitchum his first starring role after both John Garfield and Dick Powell turned the picture down. Playing a gas station owner in a small mountain community whose love for pretty local girl Virginia Huston is doomed by an earlier liaison with 'black widow' Jane Greer (left), Mitchum (right) carved out the cynical, laconic, droopy-lidded screen persona on which he would play variations for the rest of his career. And almond-eyed Jane Greer passed directly into the *femme fatale* hall of fame with this one performance. Other important cast members were smiling rattlesnake Kirk Douglas, voluptuous and dangerous Rhonda Fleming, and deaf-mute Dickie Moore who was both essential to the plot and its most arrestingly symbolic character. Geoffrey Homes (a pseudonym for Daniel Mainwaring), working from his own novel, dealt out a rough, tough, thrill-packed hand with the best dialogue heard west of Chandler and the most alluringly diabolical characters south of Hammett. The picture was a major victory for director Tourneur, whose rich visual style added a crucial dimension to the story, and long-time RKO employee Nicholas Musuraca whose hypnotic cinematography was always in sync with the psychological zig-zags inherent in the plot. Executive producer Robert Sparks also cast Richard Webb, Steve Brodie, Paul Valentine and Ken Niles. 'A man . . . trying to run away from his past. A WOMAN . . . trying to escape her future! When they clash it's *WILDFIRE!*' For once, the studio hyperbole came close to capturing the essence of a picture.

Fun And Fancy Free, a Walt Disney Technicolor novelty, combined actors Edgar Bergen and Luana Patten, cartoon characters Mickey Mouse, Donald Duck and Goofy, and mannikin performers Charlie McCarthy and Mortimer Snerd into a musical *mélange* that was undistinguished – by Disney standards. Jiminy Cricket served as co-ordinator of the merriment, introducing the one truly beguiling section of the film – the story of Bongo, a runaway circus bear who encounters love and shivery freedom in a wilderness of pines. The adventures of Bongo originated in a Sinclair Lewis story and were narrated by Dinah Shore, who also sang three of the songs. Homer Brightman, Harry Reeves, Ted Sears, Lance Nolley, Eldon Dedini and Tom Oreb worked on the story; William Morgan directed the live-action sequences and Jack Kinney, W. O. Roberts and Hamilton Luske handled the animated sections (see illustration) for production supervisor Ben Sharpsteen. Songs included: 'My Favorite Dream' William Walsh, Ray Noble; 'Too Good To Be True' Buddy Kaye, Eliot Daniel; 'Say It With A Slap' Eliot Daniel; 'Lazy Countryside' Bobby Worth; 'Fun And Fancy Free' Bennie Benjamin, George Weiss.

9780517546567

Robert Riskin, long time collaborator with Frank Capra, wrote and produced **Magic Town**. The material would have been just right for Riskin's former partner, but this time William A. Wellman occupied the director's chair and the results were deflating. Wellman's heavy hand (always more profitably applied to action pictures) turned this delicate fable into an indigestible lump of mush that even James Stewart couldn't rescue. Stewart topped the cast as a poll taker who happens upon a small village that miraculously reflects the opinions of the entire nation. However, as soon as the town finds out how ideal it is, it immediately goes 'boom' crazy. Stewart (right) and heroine Jane Wyman then get to work saving the local citizens from their various follies. Joseph Krumgold collaborated with Riskin on the original story, and Kent Smith, Ned Sparks (left), Wallace Ford, Regis Toomey, Ann Doran, Donald Meek, E. J. Ballantine, Ann Shoemaker and Mickey Kuhn were the other featured players. Songs included: 'My Book Of Memory' Edward Heyman; 'Magic Town' Mel Torme, Bob Wells. The picture was a co-production between RKO and Robert Riskin Productions.

Shamelessly constructed to mine the same mother lode as *Going My Way* and *The Bells Of St Mary's*, Samuel Goldwyn's **The Bishop's Wife** cast devilish Cary Grant (left) in the unlikely role of an angelic Mr Fixit named Dudley. Dudley shows up in response to the prayers of Protestant bishop Henry Brougham (David Niven, centre) whose obsession with the raising of money for a new cathedral has erected barriers between himself and his old friends, his wife (Loretta Young, right) and his child. Although the clergyman resents the stranger's interference, the rest of the household quickly falls under his spell and, before long, he has straightened out the financial troubles, won the bishop's parishioners back to him, and reunited husband and wife in a Christmas Eve climax. Manipulative fantasy from first to last, the film still left a sweet taste in viewers' mouths thanks to the airy Robert E. Sherwood-Leonardo Bercovici screenplay (based on a novel by Robert Nathan), the spritely acting of Grant in particular and the cast in general, and the shining direction of Henry Koster. Also cast: Monty Woolley, James Gleason, Gladys Cooper, Elsa Lanchester, Sara Haden, Karolyn Grimes, Tito Vuolo, Regis Toomey, Sara Edwards, Margaret McWade, Ann O'Neal, Ben Erway, Erville Alderson, Bobby Anderson, Teddy Infuhr, Eugene Borden, Almira Sessions, Claire DuBrey, Margaret Wells, Kitty O'Neill, Isabel Jewell, David Leonard, Dorothy Vaughn, Edgar Dearing, and the Mitchell Boys' Choir.

Man About Town (French title: **Le Silence Est D'Or**) was a film of firsts: it was the first Franco-American co-production following the war; it was René Clair's first French film in a dozen years; and it was Maurice Chevalier's first picture in seven years. Sadly, it was not first-rate. Chevalier (left) played a turn-of-the-century film director who falls in love with a pretty starlet (Marcelle Derrien, right), but loses her to a younger man (François Perier). Even though the picture received the Grand Prize at the 1947 Brussels World Film Festival, it fell short of Clair's best work, being rather simple-minded on the whole and lacking the satiric bite of *Le Million* and *À Nous La Liberté*. To avoid dubbing or the use of printed sub-titles for American audiences, Chevalier spoke an English narration. The effect was supposed to be like having the actor seated beside you in the theatre, interpreting the action as the story unfolded, but it proved cumbersome and the film did minimal business in the US. Shot at the Joinville Studios in Paris, it was a co-production between RKO and Pathé Cinema of France. Clair wrote, produced and directed, working with Robert Pirosh who penned the English adaptation and received an 'associate in production' credit on the American version. Dany Robin, Robert Pizani, Raymond Cordy, Paul Olivier and Roland Armontel were also in it. Songs included: 'Place Pigalle' M. Alstone, Maurice Chevalier. The English version was cut to 89 minutes from the original 106-minute French release.

Writers William H. Graffis and Robert E. Kent (story), and Robertson White and Eric Taylor (screenplay), banged their heads together and came up with a wild premise for **Dick Tracy Meets Gruesome** (GB: **Dick Tracy's Amazing Adventure**). It was all about a drug that will freeze human movement for several minutes. A gang of thieves gets hold of the substance and begins using it to rob banks until Tracy puts Gruesome, the principal culprit, on ice permanently. Boris Karloff (right) played Gruesome in a manner befitting both the character's name and the actor's reputation, with Ralph Byrd as Tracy. Anne Gwynne, Edward Ashley, June Clayworth, Lyle Latell, Tony Barrett, Skelton Knaggs (left), Jim Nolan, Joseph Crehan and Milton Parsons were others in the cast. Herman Schlom produced and John Rawlins directed this final chapter in an abbreviated series. Note: The film was originally titled *Dick Tracy Meets Karloff*, but the craggy-faced actor objected to the use of his name. No one dared argue.

One of the epic landmarks in the history of the American theatre, Eugene O'Neill's **Mourning Becomes Electra** came to the screen through the efforts of producer-director-writer Dudley Nichols and star Rosalind Russell. They convinced N. Peter Rathvon that a three-hour film could be made from Eugene O'Neill's six-hour Freudian drama without sacrificing either artistic or commercial considerations. The green light which Rathvon gave them was arguably the largest mistake of his RKO career. O'Neill had used the tragic story of Agamemnon, commander of the Greek armies at the siege of Troy, as the foundation for his play. Returning home after the victory, he found his wife Clytemnestra in love with a younger man. The events which followed – the poisoning of Agamemnon by his wife; the vengeance visited on her and her paramour by her daughter and son, Electra and Orestes; and the suicidal madness that descended on the youthful murderers thereafter – were woven by the playwright into the passionate tale of Ezra Mannon whose return after the end of the American Civil War precipitates the tragic drama. The problem with the picture was not the inevitable cuts Nichols had to make; in fact, he telescoped the action very skilfully, remaining faithful to O'Neill's conception throughout. Rather, he failed the test of his own medium, directing the picture in such an unimaginative, anti-cinematic fashion that the inherent power of the mythically-charged tale simply vanished. With its big moments all unfolding in static confrontation scenes, **Mourning Becomes Electra** became the epitome of that oft-used, derogatory term 'the photographed stage-play'. The Theatre Guild handled special road show engagements late in 1947. It flopped miserably, then was cut and released on a general basis by RKO in 1948. This didn't help either; a pathetic sum of $435,000 in film rentals eventually came in, making RKO's loss a record-shattering $2,310,000. The many filmgoers who shied away from the picture did miss several fine performances – most notably, Rosalind Russell (right) as the malignantly righteous Electra figure, Katina Paxinou as her weak, lovelorn mother, Raymond Massey as the soldier father who has lived with death too long and is anxious to taste the joys of life again, and Michael Redgrave (left, borrowed from J. Arthur Rank) as the confused brother inflamed by his sister's barbaric notions of justice. Other capable acting came from Leo Genn, Kirk Douglas (his first for RKO), Nancy Coleman, Henry Hull, Sara Allgood, Thurston Hall, Walter Baldwin, Elisabeth Risdon, Erskine Sanford, Lee Baker, Emma Dunn, Nora Cecil and Marie Blake. Edward Donahoe was the associate producer.

Protean Danny Kaye played James Thurber's ▷ famous milquetoast with the overripe imagination in **The Secret Life Of Walter Mitty**. Caught in the trap of his own inferiority complex, Mitty daydreams his way out, projecting himself into all manner of heroic guises including a miracle-working Viennese surgeon, a fearless cowboy (right) and an icy-nerved Mississippi gambler. Ken Englund and Everett Freeman's screenplay, based on Thurber's short story, included a melo-dramatic adventure plot that detracted from the reveries by suggesting that proof reader Mitty's life was anything but dull. Still, this Samuel Goldwyn Technicolor production offered a good measure of pleasurable escape, and provided a superb vehicle for its star's uniquely agile comic gifts. Norman Z. McLeod tendered the capable direction, with Virginia Mayo (the romantic interest, left), Boris Karloff, Fay Bainter, Ann Rutherford, Thurston Hall, Florence Bates, Gordon Jones (centre), Konstantin Shayne, Reginald Denny, Henry Corden, Doris Lloyd, Fritz Feld, Frank Reicher, Milton Parsons and the Goldwyn Girls also cast. Songs included: 'Symphony For Unstrung Tongue', 'Anatole Of Paris' Sylvia Fine.

'How To Avoid World War III' would have been an apt title for **Design For Death**. Assembled from captured Japanese film, this 48-minute documentary traced the development of Japanese militarism back to feudal nobles whose lust for power turned a peaceful people into a formidable fighting machine and led directly to Pearl Harbor. The message, according to Oriental expert Theodore S. Geisel and his wife Helen who wrote the commentary, was simple – only if the inhabitants of every nation learn to understand one another and keep power-mad 'racketeers' from manipulating their governments can another global conflict be prevented. Though it was advertised in the sensationalistic vein of *Hitler's Children* and *Behind The Rising Sun* and won the Oscar for best documentary feature of 1947, the picture did very little business on its general release the following year. Audiences obviously had minimal interest in another exploration of the Japanese mind. Theron Warth and Richard O. Fleischer produced, Kent Smith and Hans Conried narrated and editors Elmo Williams and Marston Fay pieced together the footage from eight million feet of captured celluloid (see still). ◁ Sid Rogell was the executive producer.

△
Made in garish Technicolor on the largest budget thus far expended by RKO ($3,209,000), **Tycoon** was a full-blown stinker, hamstrung by a ridiculous plot, artificial conflicts, romance without passion and atrocious acting. Borden Chase and John Twist's screenplay, adapted from a novel by C. E. Scoggins, concerned a feud between engineer John Wayne (left), who is attempting to build a railroad through the Andes Mountains, and his haughty employer Sir Cedric Hardwicke. Hardwicke played the tycoon of the title – a financial big shot who objects to Wayne's methods and, even more so, to the roughneck's romance with his daughter Laraine Day (right). As the film unfolds, Wayne's mad obsession with his dangerous job sends everyone diving for cover, including his associates and the beloved Miss Day. And yet, the star's overblown performance never succeeded in making the character either titanic or believable, a feat he would accomplish magnificently when portraying similar individuals in Howard Hawks' *Red River* (1948) and John Ford's *The Searchers* (1956). Since the other characters were also generally unconvincing, the finger of guilt pointed in the direction of the writers, and of director Richard Wallace, who must have been concentrating on the spectacular action scenes while everything else siphoned down the drain. RKO's money went along as well; the final loss was $1,035,000. Judith Anderson, James Gleason, Anthony Quinn, Grant Withers, Paul Fix, Fernando Alvarado, Harry Woods, Michael Harvey, Charles Trowbridge and Martin Garralaga had the other significant roles. The producer was Stephen Ames.

☆☆☆☆☆☆☆☆☆☆☆☆☆☆

1948

☆☆☆☆☆☆☆☆☆☆☆☆☆☆

In a move labelled the 'biggest motion picture transaction since Twentieth Century took over Fox Films', Howard R. Hughes purchased 929,000 shares of RKO stock from Floyd Odlum in May for $8.8 million – and ushered in the most insane era in the company's history.

The Hughes purchase touched off a flurry of rumours, prompting N. Peter Rathvon to issue a statement assuring all employees that their jobs were safe, and Dore Schary to inform the press that he intended to stay on and continue his duties as head of production. Their words turned to ashes in July when Schary quit because of interference from Mr Hughes, three-fourths of the studio work force was laid off, and production was cut to an absolute minimum. Rathvon again became filmmaking boss, but lasted less than two weeks in the job.

In late July, Bicknell Lockhart, C. J. Tevlin and Sid Rogell were placed in charge of studio operations, with Rogell concentrating on production matters. Ned E. Depinet became corporate president in early September. Though a backlog of completed pictures enabled the company to continue releasing on a regular basis, the new leadership faced plenty of problems. One was how to meet star commitments, given the near-total reduction in production activities. RKO had deals with 25 actors for 43 pictures – most were 'pay or play' arrangements with rigid expiry dates. Studio publicity constantly emphasized that RKO film production would soon return to pre-Hughes levels, but a general statement sent to all Hollywood agencies that RKO was no longer in the market for story material put a damper on the hopeful pronouncements.

The discord that was shaking the company as a whole was mirrored in the acting arena where Robert Mitchum became the industry's number one bad boy of 1948. The 31-year-old performer was arrested in late summer for smoking marijuana, precipitating a 'dope' scandal that became headline news and many outraged letters to his company when it decided to continue Mitchum's employment. Mitchum was judged guilty and served 60 days in jail (in 1949) and two years on probation; the incident did not, however, ruin his career as many (including the actor himself) had predicted. Indeed, the notoriety may even have helped him, for he became RKO's most important star by the end of the decade.

Thirty films were handled by RKO distribution in 1948. Most were financially unprofitable due to a continuing decline in theatre attendance. The year-end financial statement reported profits of $504,044, which took into account $3,357,371 in losses on 'investments in productions, stories and continuities'. Top money-earning pictures were **Every Girl Should Be Married**, **Fort Apache** and **Rachel And The Stranger**.

So Well Remembered opened shortly after the first wave of Communist paranoia crashed on Hollywood shores. Several critics, noting that tainted director Edward Dmytryk, tainted producer Adrian Scott and tainted musical composer Hanns Eisler were involved, interpreted the film as a Marxist tract and branded it a pure example of subversive propaganda. Those audiences unaware of these hysterical rantings witnessed an altogether different film – a social problem saga of unexpected emotional depth. John Mills (right) topped the cast as a newspaper editor and town councillor in Bowdley, England, who campaigns for the rights of local mill workers. His grasping, ambitious wife (Martha Scott, left) badgers him into running for Parliament, but Mills neglects his campaign to help overworked doctor Trevor Howard when an epidemic of diphtheria strikes. The hero withdraws from candidacy after losing his child in the epidemic, owing to his wife's negligence. Years later he finally earns some measure of happiness by preventing Scott from destroying the love relationship of her son (Richard Carlson) by a second marriage and the daughter of the doctor (Patricia Roc). The film was drama of the first order, examining human values in depth, and effectively acted by an Anglo-American cast that also included Reginald Tate, Beatrice Varley, Frederick Leister, Ivor Barnard, Julian D'Albie, Roddy Hughes, John Turnbull, Lyonel Watts, Kathleen Boutall and Juliet (aged five) and Hayley Mills (an infant), the daughters of the star. John Paxton's screenplay was based on a novel by James Hilton, who also narrated the picture. It was filmed in rural England and at Denham Studios near London. The film was produced by Alliance, a company set up by RKO and British mogul J. Arthur Rank; although the two organizations were supposed to join forces on a number of productions, this was the only project that actually came to fruition.

▽

△

The Miracle Of The Bells was the hopelessly mushy and graceless story of a Hollywood press agent (Fred MacMurray, right) arranging the funeral of his deceased love, an actress played by Alida Valli (left, borrowed from David O. Selznick), and simultaneously attempting to convince film producer Lee J. Cobb to release her final picture. Frank Sinatra played a hard-working priest in the small Pennsylvania coal town where MacMurray brings Valli to be buried and where the 'miracle' of the title occurs. Ben Hecht and Quentin Reynolds' screenplay, based on Russell Janney's bestseller, was a lachrymose pomposity that director Irving Pichel handled in clumsy, mirthless fashion. The actors – none of whom were shown to good advantage – also included Harold Vermilyea, Charles Meredith, Jim Nolan, Veronica Pataky, Philip Ahn, Frank Ferguson and Frank Wilcox. Jesse L. Lasky and Walter MacEwen produced for Jesse L. Lasky Productions which co-sponsored the film with RKO. A song, 'Ever Homeward', was adapted from an old Polish folk song by Jule Styne and Sammy Cahn.

Based on Kathryn Forbes' novelistic reminiscences of growing up with her Norwegian family in San Francisco, **I Remember Mama** came to the screen five years after RKO purchased the original property. In the intervening period, Richard Rodgers and Oscar Hammerstein II had produced a successful stage version (with dramatization by John Van Druten) which stimulated interest in the story and raised its status to that of a major production. Star Irene Dunne and director-executive producer George Stevens (borrowed from Liberty Films) returned to their old studio, and it was a happy homecoming for both. Working with screenwriter DeWitt Bodeen and producer Harriet Parsons, Stevens guided Dunne (seated centre) through an honest and tender portrayal of the indomitable Norwegian housewife who schemes and struggles to bring up her family in the alien atmosphere of turn-of-the-century San Francisco. The charmingly episodic saga also featured Barbara Bel Geddes (2nd left) as the eldest daughter who recalls the events, Philip Dorn (left) as the placid papa, Oscar Homolka as a boisterous but kindly uncle, Edgar Bergen as a mild-mannered undertaker, Sir Cedric Hardwicke as a hammy thespian whose rent is always unpaid, and Ellen Corby, Hope Landin and Edith Evanson as three whimsical aunts. Bright with human interest, congeniality and the quaint appeal of a bygone era, **I Remember Mama** came close to duplicating the magic of the studio's classic *Little Women* (1933). Despite glowing critical plaudits and the best preview reponses given an RKO film in years, it failed to turn a profit because of the excessive negative cost ($3,068,000). Rudy Vallee, Barbara O'Neil, Florence Bates, Peggy McIntyre (right), June Hedin, Steve Brown (centre) and Tommy Ivo also appeared. The film inspired a television series which starred Peggy Wood and ran on the CBS network from 1949 through 1957.

Producer Bert Granet and director Jacques Tourneur took their cameras to Europe, making **Berlin Express** the first American picture filmed (in part) inside Germany since before the war. Using Curt Siodmak's story and Harold Medford's screenplay as a point of departure, they turned out a satisfying mystery-adventure which stressed the need for unity among the peoples of the war-torn continent. The villains were a group of underground Nazi fanatics seeking to prevent the unification of Germany, the heroes a trio of American, British and Russian officers, a French girl secretary and a couple of 'good' Germans. Working together (often reluctantly), they save the life of a German statesman who is the one man in the world with a feasible plan for unifying Germany. Robert Ryan (centre) delivered a low-key and well-observed performance as the American, with Robert Coote (left) and Roman Toporow (right) portraying his uneasy fellow officers, Merle Oberon (2nd left) the secretary and Paul Lukas the anti-Nazi statesman. The film's most extraordinary aspect was its vivid sense of place; cinematographer Lucien Ballard photographed the action against backdrops in bombed out Frankfurt and Berlin which served as visual reminders of war's total devastation. Also cast: Charles Korvin (centre right), Reinhold Schunzel, Peter von Zerneck, Otto Waldis, Fritz Kortner, Michael Harvey and Richard Powers.

Perceptive reviewers of **Tarzan And The Mermaids** pointed out that the characters in the film looked more Mexican than African. This was unquestionably the case, for producer Sol Lesser made his independent feature at RKO's Churubusco Studios in Mexico City. Most of the action in Carroll Young's original screenplay took place around the coastal village of the Aquatanians, a tribe of pearl divers under the brutal rule of white trader Fernando Wagner, who is posing as a tribal god. When Wagner orders the clan's prettiest girl (Linda Christian, left, in her first film appearance) to marry him, she runs away and appeals to Tarzan (Johnny Weissmuller, right) for help. He battles against a giant octopus and husky armed natives in underwater fights before rescuing Christian and his own Jane (Brenda Joyce), and overthrowing the evil potentate. Cheetah wandered in and out of the story, contributing a modicum of amusement to its exotic foolishness. Director Robert Florey also employed George Zucco, Andrea Palma, Edward Ashley, John Laurenz, Gustavo Rojo and Matthew Boulton in character parts. Joseph Noriega was the associate producer. The movie was Weissmuller's last appearance as the ape-man hero.

The oft-encountered phony Spanish land grant showed up again as the plot fulcrum of **Western Heritage**, the first of a new group of horse operas starring Tim Holt (centre). With his pal Chito Rafferty (Richard Martin, right) carrying over from the Zane Grey series, Holt spearheaded the battle between a group of honest ranchers and a nest of outlaws who use the forged land grant as a pretext to steal the ranchers' cattle and burn their homes. Nan Leslie was Holt's leading lady for the third consecutive time, and Lois Andrews, Tony Barrett, Walter Reed (left), Harry Woods, Richard Powers, Jason Robards, Robert Bray and Perc Launders were also in it. Herman Schlom produced, Wallace A. Grissell directed and Norman Houston wrote the original screenplay.

Graham Greene's *The Power And The Glory* (published in the US as *The Labyrinthine Ways*) came to the screen as **The Fugitive**. The story of a priest on the run in an anti-clerical Central American country, who determines to honour his religious duties while battling with both the oppressive military regime and his own fall from holy grace, it starred Henry Fonda (right). Directed by the now-hallowed John Ford, the film was – and is – regarded by Greene's admirers as a travesty of the fine novel from whence it sprang. Nonetheless, some of Ford's devotees see it as a major work of cinematic art that is, to quote Bosley Crowther, 'a symphony of light and shade, of deafening din and silence, of sweeping movement and repose'. Either way, it was not a financial success. Shot wholly in Mexico from a screenplay by Dudley Nichols the movie also featured Pedro Armendariz (on loan from Mary Pickford) as the military adversary in ruthless pursuit of the priest, and Dolores Del Rio (left) as a beautiful native woman who gives Fonda sanctuary and places temporal temptation in his way. Also cast for associate producer Emilio Fernandez, were J. Carrol Naish, Leo Carrillo, Ward Bond, Robert Armstrong, Fortunio Bonanova, Chris-Pin Martin, Miguel Inclan and Fernando Fernandez. The film was the first joint venture of RKO and Argosy Pictures, a company formed by Ford and former studio head Merian C. Cooper. Ford and Cooper co-produced. Note: The novel was later filmed under the title *The Power And The Glory* with Laurence Olivier as the priest, but was shown only on US television.

Covering the limited emotional spectrum from mawkish to maudlin, **Night Song** was a calamity starring Dana Andrews as a blind pianist whose bitterness over his condition causes him to abandon the brilliant concerto he had been composing before his accident. Enter millionairess Merle Oberon (right) who gains his sympathy by pretending to be blind and poor, then puts up a prize for the best musical composition and persuades Andrews (left, borrowed from Samuel Goldwyn) to compete. He wins the money, uses it to regain his eyesight and immediately takes up with benefactress Oberon until he remembers the poor little blind girl and decides he really loves her best. Imagine his surprise (and relief) when he discovers that rich girl and poor inhabit the same attractive body! Writers Dick Irving Hyland (story), DeWitt Bodeen (adaptation) and Frank Fenton and Hyland (screenplay) were responsible for this ludicrous hokum, which managed to showcase Arthur Rubinstein and the New York Philharmonic, conducted by Eugene Ormandy, playing the finished concerto (actually written by Leith Stevens) in Carnegie Hall. Maestro Rubinstein performed with a sternness of visage that no doubt reflected his opinion of the piece itself and the picture that surrounded it. Director John Cromwell, whose talent seemed largely absent from this venture, gave roles to Ethel Barrymore, Hoagy Carmichael, Jacqueline White, Donald Curtis, Walter Reed and Jane Jones. Jack J. Gross worked as executive producer and Harriet Parsons as producer of this $1,040,000 box-office loser. Song: 'Who Killed 'Er?' Hoagy Carmichael, Fred Spielman & Janice Torre.

Western stars of two generations locked horns in **The Arizona Ranger**. Tim Holt and his father Jack acted together for the first time in Norman Houston's screenplay about the emergence of law and order in the Arizona cattle country, *c.* 1900. As a two-fisted rancher who favours 'rope-and-gun' justice, the elder Holt (centre) conflicts with his son (left) who joins the local rangers to pursue lawbreakers in legal fashion. When the boy rescues a rustler whom the older man is about to hang and sends him off to jail, the gap between father and son widens, but subsequent events convert Jack to Tim's point of view. John Rawlins directed, Herman Schlom produced and Nan Leslie (right), Richard Martin, Steve Brodie, Paul Hurst, Jim Nolan, Robert Bray, Richard Benedict, William Phipps and Harry Harvey completed the cast.

As its title intimated, **If You Knew Susie** was a dated, nondescript pastiche of songs and comedy 'shtiks' made famous by Eddie Cantor. Producer Cantor (left) teamed with Joan Davis (right) as married ex-vaudevillians who discover a document signed by George Washington awarding $50,000 to one of Cantor's ancestors during the Revolutionary War. They take the document to the nation's capital to get it authenticated, where they find that the government owes the pop-eyed comedian several billion dollars in accrued compound interest. Cantor's patriotic gesture in refusing the money makes him a national hero and the darling of a bunch of New England blue bloods who had formerly snubbed him and his wifey. Oscar Brodney and associate producer Warren Wilson authored his charade, which included additional dialogue by Bud Pearson and Lester A. White, and was directed by Gordon Douglas. Allyn Joslyn, Charles Dingle, Bobby Driscoll (borrowed from Walt Disney), Phil Brown, Sheldon Leonard, Joe Sawyer, Douglas Fowley, Margaret Kerry, Dick Humphreys, Howard Freeman, Mabel Paige, Sig Rumann, Fritz Feld and Isabel Randolph were in it, too, for executive producer Jack J. Gross. Songs included: 'If You Knew Susie' B. G. DeSylva, Joseph Meyer; 'My Brooklyn Love Song' George Tibbles, Ramez Idriss; 'What Do I Want With Money', 'We're Living The Life We Love', 'My, How The Time Goes By' Jimmy McHugh, Harold Adamson.

The first film in director John Ford's 'cavalry trilogy', **Fort Apache** was a stirring meditation on the George Armstrong Custer legend. Embittered cavalry colonel Henry Fonda (the Custer surrogate, 2nd left) is sent out to take charge of a lonely outpost on the Arizona desert. Unversed in the ways of the Indians, the colonel ignores the advice of experienced frontier fighter John Wayne (foreground right) and endeavours to make a name for himself by tricking and capturing the elusive band of Apache warriors led by Cochise (Miguel Inclan). The attempt is stupid and suicidal, but Wayne, for the good of the service and the memory of his fallen comrades, covers up the colonel's blunder, allowing his name to live on in the Army's annals of heroism. Given our post-Vietnam, post-Watergate attitudes, it is now pretty difficult to swallow this denouement, but audiences of the time had no problems with it and the film earned $445,000 in profits. Ford's practised eye filled the broad canvas with breathtaking compositions and gripping action sequences. Former *New York Times* film critic Frank Nugent began a long association with the director, writing the screenplay from James Warner Bellah's story *Massacre*. Also cast: John Agar (4th left), Shirley Temple, (both borrowed from David O. Selznick), Pedro Armendariz, Ward Bond, George O'Brien, Victor McLaglen, Anna Lee, Irene Rich, Dick Foran, Guy Kibbee, Grant Withers, Jack Pennick, Ray Hyke, Movita Castaneda, Mary Gordon, Philip Keiffer and Mae Marsh. Argosy Pictures co-sponsored with RKO; again, Ford and Merian C. Cooper shared the producer credit.

Observing the premise that anything worth doing is worth overdoing, RKO unleashed another 'super-western' – a slam-bang epic oater with hordes of miscreants and enough gunsmoke to enshroud the North American continent. In **Return Of The Badmen**, marshal Randolph Scott (right) faced up to the Sundance Kid (Robert Ryan), Cheyenne McBride (Anne Jeffreys), Cole Younger (Steve Brodie), Jim Younger (Richard Powers), John Younger (Robert Bray), Emmett Dalton (Lex Barker), Bob Dalton (Walter Reed), Grat Dalton (Michael Harvey), Billy the Kid (Dean White), Wild Bill Doolin (Robert Armstrong), Wild Bill Yeager (Tom Tyler) and the Arkansas Kid (Lew Harvey). Unfortunately, the gunmen galore were all as helpless as babes against the banal and commonplace screenplay by Charles O'Neal, Jack Natteford and Luci Ward (story by Natteford and Ward). Their scenario, which was no better than an average Tim Holt script, received direction in kind from Ray Enright. Executive producer Jack J. Gross, producer Nat Holt and supporting players George 'Gabby' Hayes (left), Jacqueline White, Gary Gray, Walter Baldwin, Minna Gombell, Warren Jackson, Robert Clarke and Jason Robards also bit the dust. Song: 'Remember The Girl You Left Behind' Mort Greene, Harry Revel.

The Pearl was an uncompromisingly ironic and brilliantly photographed translation of John Steinbeck's fable about civilized greed and plunderlust. Producer Oscar Dancigers and director Emilio Fernandez cast Pedro Armendariz (left) as a pearl-fisher who finds a fabulous gem and rejoices in contemplation of the freedom it symbolizes. He envisions new clothes for his long-suffering wife (Maria Elena Marques, right), an education for his son, and the comforts of prosperity. Alas, the naive peasant misunderstands the venal world that surrounds him; instead of salvation, the gift from the sea brings disaster in the form of greedy vultures who cheat him, beat him, kill his child and turn him into a murderer. In a final act of cosmic disgust, he flings the cursed pearl back into the angry sea. Renowned cinematographer Gabriel Figueroa, who also photographed John Ford's *The Fugitive*, shot the picture in a classic style that underlined the violent, elemental qualities of the story. The script by Steinbeck, director Fernandez and Jack Wagner also contained roles for Fernando Wagner, Charles Rooner, Alfonso Bedoya, Gilberto Gonzalez, Juan Garcia and Maria Cuadros. Though it did not fare well at US box-offices, this was one of RKO's best pictures of 1948. The studio co-produced with Aguila Films and Films Asociados Mexico-Americanos, which shot the film at the Churubusco Studios and on location in Mexico.

Pat O'Brien was **Fighting Father Dunne**, a priest who struggles to found a home for underprivileged newsboys in St Louis, Missouri during the early years of the twentieth century. On the ten-point Richter scale of uplifting, religiously-inspired entertainment, this film rated a one. Afflicted with tear-jerking clichés, unimaginative stock characters, hackneyed situations and insufferably pompous effects, it was a thoroughgoing insult to the man it intended to honour. Even O'Brien (left), usually adept at capturing the essence of real-life characters, missed by a mile on this occasion. The army of the inept who lobbed this pious stink bomb at theatre patrons included Jack J. Gross (executive producer), Phil L. Ryan (producer), Ted Tetzlaff (director), William Rankin (story) and Martin Rackin and Frank Davis (screenplay). Darryl Hickman, Charles Kemper, Una O'Connor, Arthur Shields, Harry Shannon, Joe Sawyer, Anna Q. Nilsson, Donn Gift, Myrna Dell (right), Ruth Donnelly, Jim Nolan, Billy Cummings, Billy Gray, Eric Roberts, Gene Collins, Lester Matthews, Griff Barnett, Jason Robards and Rudy Whistler were members of the large but oh-so-forgettable cast.

Bad guy Lawrence Tierney (*The Devil Thumbs A Ride, Born To Kill*) returned to a sympathetic role in **Bodyguard**. The Fred Niblo Jr-Harry Essex screenplay (story by George W. George and Robert B. Altman) presented Tierney (left) as a Los Angeles plainclothes officer who resigns from the force and takes a job as protector of wealthy widow Elisabeth Risdon, only to find himself hunted by his former buddies on a murder charge. His efforts to avoid arrest and run down the actual criminal are aided by his fiancée Priscilla Lane (right), a clerk with access to the police files that provide the clues he needs. Director Richard O. Fleischer's crisp pictorial style zipped the melo along from one action scene to the next. Also cast: Philip Reed, June Clayworth, Steve Brodie, Frank Fenton and Charles Cane. The producer was Sid Rogell.
▽

Novelist Eric Hodgins and scriptwriters Norman Panama and Melvin Frank turned the American dream of home ownership into a satiric nightmare in **Mr Blandings Builds His Dream House**. Exasperated with his cramped New York flat, Jim Blandings (Cary Grant) is easy pickings for a shrewd real estate broker who sells him a ramshackle farmhouse in the country. Blandings and his wife (Myrna Loy) soon discover that their new home is on the verge of collapse, so they decide to tear it down and erect a dream castle of their own. That is the cue for an unending series of problems, ranging from windows that don't fit to a budget that fits even less. Warmed by the personalizing influence of the two stars (foreground left), plus Melvyn Douglas as their close friend and attorney, the film emerged as a fully constructed comic edifice – even though the events portrayed were a good deal more hair-raising then humorous. H. C. Potter directed, with Reginald Denny, Sharyn Moffett, Connie Marshall, Louise Beavers, Ian Wolfe (illustrated up centre), Harry Shannon, Tito Vuolo, Nestor Paiva, Jason Robards, Lurene Tuttle, Lex Barker and Emory Parnell providing the support. The film was a co-production between RKO and David O. Selznick's Vanguard Films, which provided the services of Cary Grant. Note: As part of the settlement with Selznick that allowed Dore Schary to take over as studio production head, RKO granted initial US and Canadian distribution rights to the Selznick Releasing Organization. Full distribution rights reverted back to RKO in July 1953.

◁ The wildest wooing in American legend – the conquest of Sluefoot by the redoubtable Pecos Bill – was the romantic highlight of Walt Disney's last (and arguably best) grab bag musical fantasy, **Melody Time**. The Disney animators (see illustration), working as always in Technicolor, made an irresistibly entertaining story out of Pecos Bill's prowess and perplexities, situating him alongside six other pieces of Americana. One of Pecos' companion heroes was Johnny Appleseed, the mild and modest planter of orchards in the new clearings of Ohio, Indiana and Pennsylvania. Roy Rogers and the Sons of the Pioneers, seen in a prologue with juveniles Bobby Driscoll and Luana Patten, narrated and sang the legend of Pecos Bill, and Dennis Day spoke and vocalized over the Johnny Appleseed tale. The Andrews Sisters, Fred Waring and the Pennsylvanians, Frances Langford, Ethel Smith, and the Dinning Sisters were among the other background musical performers. Buddy Clark narrated for production supervisor Ben Sharpsteen who utilized Winston Hibler, Harry Reeves, Ken Anderson, Erdman Penner, Homer Brightman, Ted Sears, Joe Rinaldi, Art Scott, Bob Moore, Bill Cottrell, Jesse Marsh and John Walbridge to develop the various stories, and Clyde Geronimi, Wilfred Jackson, Hamilton Luske and Jack Kinney to direct the cartoon sections. Songs included: 'Melody Time' George Weiss, Bennie Benjamin; 'Little Toot' Allie Wrubel; 'Apple Song', 'The Pioneer Song' Kim Gannon, Walter Kent; 'Once Upon A Wintertime' Bobby Worth, Ray Gilbert; 'Blame It On The Samba' Ernesto Nazareth, Gilbert; 'Blue Shadows On The Trail', 'Pecos Bill' Eliot Daniel, Johnny Lange.

Made at about one-tenth the cost of *Blood On The Moon* (see facing page), **Indian Agent** also dealt with the conniving of a government agent (Richard Powers), who has been selling the Indians' food supplies to outside interests. Tim Holt (left) uncovers the duplicity, convinces chief Noah Beery Jr (right) not to go on the war path, then cleans out the crooks and brings peace to the reservation. Lesley Selander directed this non-stop action programmer from Norman Houston's original screenplay. Also cast: Richard Martin, Nan Leslie, Harry Woods, Claudia Drake (centre), Robert Bray, Lee 'Lasses' White, Bud Osborne and Iron Eyes Cody. Herman Schlom produced.
▽

▷

William Lundigan (right) and Jacqueline White (left) were given top billing in **Mystery In Mexico**. Lawrence Kimble's screenplay (story by Muriel Roy Bolton) gave Lundigan the role of an insurance company detective dispatched to Mexico City to investigate the disappearance of another company agent. Miss White portrayed the missing man's sister, who also heads south to find out what happened to him. The dangers faced by the pair include a murder and a kidnapping, before they and the local police find the missing man and round up a gang of jewel thieves. Ricardo Cortez was also featured, plus Tony Barrett, Jacqueline Dalya, Walter Reed, Jose Torvay, Jaime Jimenez, Antonio Frausto, Dolores Camerillo, Eduardo Casado and Thalia Draper. Robert Wise directed at the Churubusco Studios for producer Sid Rogell and associate producer Joseph Noriega.

One searched in vain for a whit of originality in **Race Street**. Martin Rackin's trite screenplay (suggested by a story by Maurice Davis) was set in San Francisco. There, big time bookie George Raft (left) goes through the motions of avenging a pal's murder and resisting a gang of Eastern crooks who try to muscle in on his business. Marilyn Maxwell played Raft's treacherous sweetheart, William Bendix (centre) a friendly police officer, and Frank Faylen the chief heavy. Henry Morgan, Gale Robbins, Cully Richards, Mack Gray, Russell Hicks, Richard Powers (right), William Forrest, Jim Nolan, George Turner, Richard Benedict, Dean White and Freddie Steele were also in it. Nat Holt produced and Edwin L. Marin sleep-walked through the direction. Songs included: 'Love That Boy' Don Raye, Gene De Paul; 'I'm In A Jam With Baby' Ray Heindorf, Moe Jerome, Ted Koehler.

Similar in pattern to previous Tim Holt vehicles, **Guns Of Hate** revolved around the efforts of a pair of cowpunchers to clear themselves of a wrongful murder charge. Holt (left) and Richard Martin (right), arrested as the culprits when an elderly prospector is murdered in the desert, know that the old man had just re-discovered the fabulously rich Lost Dutchman gold mine, which explains why he was killed and why they have been framed for the murder. They break out of jail and set about exposing the real assassins. Norman Houston and Ed Earl Repp's screenplay, based on a story by Repp, was confidently directed by Lesley Selander, who brought out good things in a cast that also included Nan Leslie, Steve Brodie, Myrna Dell, Tony Barrett, Jim Nolan, Jason Robards, Robert Bray and Marilyn Mercer (plucked out of the studio messenger department). Herman Schlom produced.

Should stage star Rosalind Russell (left) be allowed to play Ibsen's Hedda Gabler? That was the first issue of concern in **The Velvet Touch**, a passable drama of conscience directed by John Gage. When Russell's theatrical producer (Leon Ames, borrowed from MGM) tries to prevent her from essaying the role and threatens to sabotage her forthcoming marriage, she flies into a rage, hits him with a statuette and kills him. No one suspects Miss Russell of the crime, but then fellow thespian Claire Trevor is accused and the actress' conscience begins to gnaw away at her. Leo Rosten's screenplay, based on Walter Reilly's adaptation of a story by William Mercer and Annabel Ross, was over-long and over-emphatic, but Miss Russell's many-layered performance kept it alive. Sydney Greenstreet (right), Leo Genn, Frank McHugh, Walter Kingsford, Dan Tobin, Lex Barker, Nydia Westman, Theresa Harris, Russell Hicks, Irving Bacon, Esther Howard, Harry Hayden, William Erwin, Martha Hyer, Steven Flagg (formerly known as Michael St Angel), Louis Mason, James Flavin, Charles McAvoy and Don Foster were others in the cast. Miss Russell's husband Frederick Brisson produced for Independent Artists, the company that co-sponsored the film with RKO. Song: 'The Velvet Touch' Mort Greene, Leigh Harline.

Scriptwriter Waldo Salt and director Norman Foster mixed comedy, drama, action, spectacular scenery and a number of incidental songs in a pleasant historical fabrication called **Rachel And The Stranger**. Loretta Young (right) was especially effective as an 1820 bondswoman purchased by backwoodsman William Holden (left, borrowed from Paramount) so that his motherless son (Gary Gray) may be properly cared for. Neither father nor boy finds much to appreciate in the woman until happy-go-lucky Indian scout Robert Mitchum visits them and falls in love with her. Violent jealousy soon erupts between the two men; it is not settled until they are forced to fight together to save the home from an Indian attack. The Richard H. Berger production, based on Howard Fast's stories *Rachel* and *Neighbor Sam*, was one of the year's top box-office performers, earning profits of $395,000. Jack J. Gross was the executive producer, and Tom Tully, Sara Haden, Frank Ferguson, Walter Baldwin and Regina Wallace completed the cast. Songs included: 'Rachel', 'Tall, Dark Stranger', 'Foolish Pride', 'Summer Song', 'Just Like Me' Waldo Salt, Roy Webb.

Blood On The Moon was a class 'A' western. Capably written by screenwriter Lillie Hayward and adaptors Harold Shumate and Luke Short from Short's novel, it was given spectacular treatment by director Robert Wise. Set on an Indian reservation shortly after the Civil War, it featured Robert Mitchum (illustrated) as a wandering cowpuncher, Barbara Bel Geddes as the daughter of wealthy cattlemen Tom Tully, and Robert Preston as a ruthless adventurer who plots with crooked Indian agent Frank Faylen to get the cattleman's herds away from him. Mitchum hires himself out as a gunman on Preston's payroll, but the more he sees of his employer's methods the less he likes them. He decides to quit and leave the country, but Preston prevents him, thereby causing Mitchum to ally himself with the cattleman and his daughter. Walter Brennan, Phyllis Thaxter, Charles McGraw, Clifton Young, Tom Tyler, George Cooper, Richard Powers, Bud Osborne, Zon Murray and Robert Bray also appeared for executive producer Sid Rogell and producer Theron Warth.

Dick Powell found himself riding the range in **Station West**, but the hard-boiled gumshoe persona he had established in *Murder, My Sweet* was still in evidence in his portrayal of a military intelligence officer. Assigned to clear up the murder of two soldiers killed while guarding a gold shipment, Powell (left) runs head on into beautiful but ruthless gambling house owner Jane Greer (right), who is the brains behind the bandits terrorizing the region. The hero whips Miss Greer's husky bouncer, wins a job from her and then gathers the evidence that will bring about her demise. Both stars delivered superior performances under the watchful eye of director Sidney Lanfield. Producer Robert Sparks employed Frank Fenton and Winston Miller to script Luke Short's exciting novel, and also cast Agnes Moorehead, Burl Ives (borrowed from 20th Century-Fox), Tom Powers, Gordon Oliver, Steve Brodie, Guinn 'Big Boy' Williams, Raymund Burr, Regis Toomey, Olin Howlin and John Berkes. Songs included: 'The Sun Shining Warm', 'Sometime Remind Me To Tell You' Mort Greene, Leigh Harline.
▽

Benevolence nearly wrecked the fortunes of an average American family in Leo McCarey's **Good Sam**. Gary Cooper (centre left) was the good samaritan manager of a department store, whose generous impulses play havoc with his family's resources. His wife Ann Sheridan (centre right) has no quarrel with charity; she just thinks that it ought to begin at home. Her plans for a new house are torpedoed whenever Sam's latest philanthropic escapade comes to light. The premise might have served as a springboard for a satisfying satirical comedy in the Capra vein, but producer-director McCarey bungled almost everything. He coached Cooper to deliver one of the most dopey, insipid performances of his long career, squelched many genuinely funny moments with direction so wobbly it could best be described as geriatric, and drowned the proceedings in a lethal dose of sentimentality. Miss Sheridan emerged unscathed from this catalogue of missed opportunities, creating a vital, believable character who gave evidence of what the film could have been. The screenplay, based on a story by McCarey and John Klorer, was by Ken Englund. Also cast: Ray Collins, Edmund Lowe, Joan Lorring, Clinton Sundberg, Minerva Urecal, Louise Beavers, Dick Ross, Bobby Dolan Jr (left), Lora Lee Michel (right), Matt Moore, Netta Packer, Ruth Roman, Carol Stevens, Todd Karns, Irving Bacon, William Frawley and Harry Hayden. Rainbow Productions co-produced with RKO.
▽

In New York seven academics have worked for ▷ years piecing together a history of music. Professor Frisbee (Danny Kaye, foreground left), in charge of the American section, feels confident that ragtime is right up to the minute. But when two window washers introduce him to swing and jive and boogie-woogie, Frisbee decides he had better explore the world of jazz for himself. Sound familiar? It should, because **A Song Is Born** was a musicalized remake of Samuel Goldwyn's *Ball Of Fire* (1941). Goldwyn again produced and Howard Hawks again directed, but the film was more jam session than comedy. The presence of Benny Goodman (left), Tommy Dorsey (2nd left), Louis Armstrong (2nd right), Lionel Hampton (right), Charlie Barnet (centre), Mel Powell, Buck and Bubbles, The Page Cavanaugh Trio, The Golden Gate Quartet, and Russo and The Samba Kings all performing their specialities, clogged up the madcap plot (story by Billy Wilder and Thomas Monroe, screenplay by Harry Tugend) and even forced the irrepressible Kaye to slide somewhat into the background. Virginia Mayo tried out the Barbara Stanwyck role, and Hugh Herbert, Steve Cochran, J. Edward Bromberg, Felix Bressart, Ludwig Stossel, O. Z. Whitehead, Esther Dale, Mary Field, Howland Chamberlin, Paul Langton, Sidney Blackmer, Ben Welden, Ben Chasen, Peter Virgo, Harry Babasin, Louie Bellson and Alton Hendrickson also earned performer credits. Songs included: 'A Song Is Born', 'Daddy-O' Don Raye, Gene De Paul; 'Blind Barnabus' Willie Johnson; 'I'm Gettin' Sentimental Over You' George Bassman, Ned Washington; 'Flying Home' Benny Goodman, Lionel Hampton, Sig Robinson; 'Redskin Rhumba' Dale Bennet.

Billed as 'vaudeville-come-to-the-screen', **Variety Time** was an incredibly cheap (negative cost $51,000) compilation of skits, dance routines and other acts clipped from other RKO features, plus two shorts in their entirety. The only new footage was of master of ceremonies Jack Paar delivering the connecting patter and teaming with Hans Conried for a French comedy song routine. Among the highlights: Frankie Carle and his Orchestra doing the 'Carle Boogie' from *Riverboat Rhythm*; Jesse and James dancing a blackface routine shot for *Show Business* which was cut out of the release versions of that picture; Lynn, Royce and Vanya dancing their comedy adagio number from *Seven Days Leave*; and Miguelito Valdes and His Orchestra with dancers Harold and Lola performing the 'Babalu' number from *Pan-Americana*. The two very funny shorts were Leon Errol in *Hired Husband* and Edgar Kennedy (centre) in *I'll Build It Myself*. Jack Rice (left), Dot Farley (centre left), Florence Lake (centre right), Jason Robards (right), Pat Rooney, Dorothy Granger, Jack Norton and Minerva Urecal also appeared. George Bilson, who formulated the recycling concept, was the producer. Hal Yates directed the two shorts and wrote the one starring Edgar Kennedy; Hal Law authored the Leon Errol screenplay and Leo Soloman and Joseph Quillan typed out Jack Paar's material. How could you lose on this one? Final profits were $132,000.

Every Girl Should Be Married, the company's 1948 Christmas release, became the most lucrative film of the year with $775,000 in eventual profits. Don Hartman produced, directed, and co-wrote (with Stephen Morehouse Avery) the screenplay, introducing Betsy Drake (right) as a salesgirl who mounts an elaborate campaign to win the attention and affections of baby doctor Cary Grant (left). The first part comes easily, but it takes a full measure of predatory wiles to manoeuvre the wily doctor into a matrimonial corner. Though the title alone would raise the hackles of modern-day feminists, it served audiences the always welcome tonic of innocent and generous laughter. Grant was his usual bemused and polished self, while Miss Drake carried off her role with the aplomb of an established star rather than a screen neophyte. Eleanor Harris wrote the original story, and Franchot Tone, Diana Lynn, Alan Mowbray, Elisabeth Risdon, Richard Gaines, Harry Hayden, Chick Chandler, Leon Belasco, Fred Essler and Anna Q. Nilsson completed the cast. Note: Some sort of variation on the film's plot was evidently played out in real life, for Betsy Drake soon became Mrs Cary Grant.
▽

Producer Walter Wanger, director Victor Fleming and star Ingrid Bergman formed Sierra Pictures for the sole purpose of making **Joan Of Arc**, a handsomely mounted, beautifully photographed (in Technicolor) exercise in *ennui*. Miss Bergman (illustrated) fought gallantly to carry the weight of the film, but the cast of thousands and the never-ending parade of sumptuous but static set pieces was simply too heavy for her to bear. Maxwell Anderson and Andrew Solt's script, based on Anderson's play *Joan of Lorraine*, focused on the last two years of the martyr's life, detailing her attempts to win the confidence of the weak-willed Dauphin (Jose Ferrer), her stubborn reorganization of the French army, her flaming victory over the British at Orleans, and then her betrayal, trial and execution on a charge of heresy. It was oh-so sincere, oh-so serious and oh-so boring – a forerunner of the overstuffed, wide-screen spectaculars that would glut theatre screens in the 1950s. Francis L. Sullivan, J. Carrol Naish, Ward Bond, Sheppard Strudwick, Hurd Hatfield, Gene Lockhart, John Emery, George Coulouris, John Ireland and Cecil Kellaway were the featured members of the giant supporting cast. RKO distributed for Sierra, offering the two hour, 25 minute film for road show engagements in 1948, then marketing a shortened version for general release in 1949.
▷

In March, RKO stockholders approved a plan to split the theatre organization off from the production-distribution business. This came as a result of a 'consent decree' between the government and the vertically-integrated (i.e. having production, distribution and exhibition capabilities) motion picture companies: MGM, Paramount, Warner Bros., Twentieth Century-Fox and RKO. One of the most momentous decisions in the history of the film industry, the move proved to be a prime factor in the eventual collapse of the studio system.

RKO would not actually dispose of its exhibition arm until the early 1950s. This was fortunate, for the theatres were the only corporate component making money at the time. Radio-Keith-Orpheum reported profits of $1,710,944 for the year, despite losses by RKO Radio Pictures of $3,721,415. Theatre operations accounted for $6,986,385 in earnings.

The doldrums continued inside the Hollywood studio. More than 30 films were announced during the year, but only 12 actually went into production. Howard Hughes was supposed to be concentrating on **Jet Pilot**, a John Wayne picture designed to rekindle the magic of his **Hell's Angels** (1930), but he found the time to handcuff production chief Sid Rogell and constantly meddle in his producers' efforts. Two of them – Nat Holt and Richard Berger – grew exasperated and checked out of RKO permanently. Long-time vice-president Joseph Nolan also left, although for health reasons; he was replaced by another battle-scarred veteran, Gordon Youngman.

The company did release 36 films in 1949, but most were carry-overs from the Schary period, independent pictures and co-production deals. Financially, they harvested a woeful crop, with **Savage Splendor** (profit $250,000) being the top money-maker and **The Window** and **The Big Steal** also posting small profits.

Tim Holt (left) was so well established as a cowboy ▷ hero that he simply played himself – rather than a fictional character – in **Gun Smugglers**. This ripsnorting, 60-minute oater presented Holt and Richard Martin as rangers on the trail of a gang that steals weapons from the Army and then sells them to some unnamed foreign power. The twist in Norman Houston's screenplay was that one of the gang members is a small boy (Gary Gray) who serves as a decoy during the holdups. Holt eventually traps the bad guys and brings about the reformation of the youngster. Beautiful Martha Hyer (right) added to the interest, and Paul Hurst, Douglas Fowley, Robert Warwick, Don Haggerty, Frank Sully and Robert Bray led the support. Frank McDonald directed for producer Herman Schlom.

Ebenezer Scrooge would have had plenty to bah and humbug about had he seen **Holiday Affair**. Garnished with treacly sentiment, the Isobel Lennart screenplay (based on *Christmas Gift*, a story by John D. Weaver) told of a tow-headed, gap-toothed youngster (Gordon Gebert) whose widowed mother Janet Leigh (left, borrowed from MGM) is too poor to buy him the electric train he wants for Christmas. This gives Robert Mitchum (right) a chance to play Santa Claus by spending his last few dollars on the toy and sets the stage for a tepid competition between Mitchum and solemn attorney Wendell Corey (borrowed from Hal Wallis) for the lady's affections. Producer-director Don Hartman stuffed this holiday turkey with secondary players Griff Barnett, Esther Dale, Henry O'Neill, Larry J. Blake, Helen Brown and Henry Morgan. A $300,000 box-office loser, it was Hartman's second and last picture for RKO. ▽

The old story of white men despoiling an Eden-like wilderness was told once again in **Tarzan's Magic Fountain**. Tall, muscular Lex Barker (right) took on the mantle that Johnny Weissmuller had worn for so long, and opposed the incursions of a group of avaricious traders intent on commercializing a jungle spring that has remarkable powers of rejuvenation. Director Lee Sholem did screenwriters Curt Siodmak and Harry Chandlee the service of making their silly story move briskly across the forested landscape. He was also able to draw personable performances from the new king of the jungle and secondary performers Brenda Joyce (left), Albert Dekker, Evelyn Ankers, Charles Drake, Alan Napier, Ted Hecht and Henry Brandon. Sol Lesser produced for his own independent company.

Dore Schary's determination that motion pictures should inform and educate the public at large was most blatantly revealed in **The Boy With The Green Hair**. Dean Stockwell (left, borrowed from MGM) played the title role, a war orphan who sets out on a solo crusade against war. His hair miraculously turns green (with Technicolor assistance) as a symbol of the cruelty of warfare, which brings nothing but suspicion, hostility and intolerance his way. The visual message was abundantly clear – until people learn to love one another in spite of their myriad differences, the threat of murderous hostility will always be strong. The film was certainly right-thinking and worthwhile, but presented in such heavy-handed fashion by screenwriters Ben Barzman and Alfred Lewis Levitt (story by Betsy Beaton), and so ponderously directed by Joseph Losey (his first Hollywood film) that it only achieved its ambitions sporadically. Pat O'Brien (right), Robert Ryan and Barbara Hale were featured, and Richard Lyon, Walter Catlett, Samuel S. Hinds, Regis Toomey, Charles Meredith, David Clarke, Billy Sheffield, John Calkins, Teddy Infuhr, Dwayne Hickman, Eileen Janssen, Curtis Jackson and Charles Arnt also appeared for producer Stephen Ames. Song: 'Nature Boy' (by eden ahbez, who believed that capital letters for names should be restricted to the word 'GOD').

Walt Disney's **So Dear To My Heart** was the cheerful, down-to-earth saga of Jeremiah Kincaid (Bobby Driscoll, right), a country lad locked in a spirited contest of wills with his austere grandmother (Beulah Bondi). The battle involves the whole neighbourhood and the fate of a rumbustious black ram foundling. Live action predominated for the first time in a Disney film, though cartoon sequences were used to represent the scrapbook fantasies of the boy. Burl Ives was on hand as the village smith who champions the lad in times of stress, Luana Patten (centre right) played a loyal comrade, and Harry Carey was seen as a sage judge of livestock and of human nature. John Tucker Battle's script, adapted by Maurice Rapf and Ted Sears from a novel by Sterling North, had its cloying moments, but its crackerbarrel humour and pleasing nostalgic aura gave the film plenty of appeal. Harold Schuster directed in Technicolor, using Raymond Bond, Walter Soderling, Matt Willis and Spelman B. Collins in secondary roles. Perce Pearce was associate producer and Hamilton Luske the cartoon director. Songs included: 'So Dear To My Heart' Ticker Freeman, Irving Taylor; 'Country Fair' Robert Wells, Mel Torme; 'Ol' Dan Patch', 'Lavender Blue (Dilly Dilly)', 'Stick-To-It-Ivity' Eliot Daniel, Larry Morey.

Enchantment told of two love affairs that burgeoned – half a century apart – in a stately old London mansion. A young British subaltern (David Niven, right) and his father's pretty ward (Teresa Wright, left) were the principals in the earlier romance, which is snuffed out by family jealousy. By the time Niven has become a retired and cynical general, he finds himself a spectator to the second amour between his American grand-niece (Evelyn Keyes) and the nephew (Farley Granger) of his old fiancée. At the crucial moment, Niven intercedes to prevent the pair from suffering the same frustration that he had. Rumer Godden's novel *Take Three Tenses* provided the raw material that John Patrick mined to provide a rather arch and colourless screenplay. Independent mogul Samuel Goldwyn produced, using Hugo Friedhofer to write the musical score, Gregg Toland to photograph and Irving Reis to direct. 'Just About the Most Wonderful Love Story Ever Filmed' was the blatant hyperbole trumpeted by Goldwyn's publicity department. Jayne Meadows, Leo G. Carroll, Philip Friend, Shepperd Strudwick, Henry Stephenson, Colin Keith-Johnston, Gigi Perreau, Peter Miles, Marjorie Rhodes, Edmond Breon, Gerald Oliver Smith and Melville Cooper were among those also involved. Song: 'Enchantment' Don Raye, Gene De Paul.

The Clay Pigeon was the first picture produced under the Howard Hughes regime at RKO. Bill Williams (illustrated) starred as a seaman who spends months in a coma in a Naval hospital, then regains consciousness only to learn that he is to be court-martialled for treason. Shocked and confused, he seeks out a former friend, only to find that his pal was killed by a brutal guard in a Japanese prison camp and that he himself is accused of having brought about the death. Carl Foreman's story and screenplay were partially based on an actual incident in which an American soldier recognized his former Japanese prison guard in Los Angeles. Richard O. Fleischer's taut direction turned the events into gripping melodrama; he cast Barbara Hale to good advantage as the suspicious wife of Williams' dead buddy, and also featured Richard Quine, Richard Loo, Frank Fenton, Frank Wilcox, Marya Marco, Robert Bray, Martha Hyer, Harold Landon, James Craven and Grandon Rhodes. Herman Schlom produced.

Director Lesley Selander never allowed Norman Houston's plot to interfere with the wall-to-wall action in **Brothers In The Saddle**. The efforts of Tim Holt (centre right) to keep younger brother Steve Brodie (centre left) out of trouble were the pretext for all sorts of pugilistic encounters and gun melées. Richard Martin (right) reprised his Chito Rafferty character, Virginia Cox (left, her screen debut) portrayed Brodie's slightly bewildered but attractive fiancée, and Richard Powers and Robert Bray were the mandatory black hats. Producer Herman Schlom's cast also included Carol Forman, Stanley Andrews, Francis McDonald, Emmett Vogan and Monte Montague.

A Woman's Secret was hardly the high-water mark for director Nicholas Ray or producer-screenwriter Herman J. Mankiewicz. Mankiewicz imposed a *Citizen Kane* structure on Vicki Baum's novel *Mortgage On Life* with results that were confusing and mundane. It all began when singer Gloria Grahame was shot and her benefactress Maureen O'Hara (left) confessed that she was responsible. In criss-cross flashbacks, the true story of the accidental wounding is revealed. Miss O'Hara, it seems, was a prominent singer who began grooming the coarse and sluttish Grahame as her protégé after her own voice gave out. Grahame soon rebelled against the attempts to turn her into a lady as well as a singer, causing the philanthropic O'Hara an abundance of pain. This idea – of a person trying to push someone else to fame as a replacement for her own unfulfilled dreams – was intriguing, but the filmmakers shredded their premise with the unnecessarily convoluted structure and a welter of soap-opera clichés. Audiences responded to it intelligently – by staying away, and RKO's deficit amounted to $760,000. Melvyn Douglas (right), Bill Williams, Victor Jory, Mary Philips, Jay C. Flippen, Robert Warwick, Curt Conway, Ann Shoemaker, Virginia Farmer, Ellen Corby and Emory Parnell wandered in and out of the proceedings. Songs included: 'Estrellita' Manuel Ponce; 'Paradise' Nacio Herb Brown, Gordon Clifford. Note: *A Woman's Secret* was shot after, but released before, Ray's first film *They Live By Night*.

Back in 1905, when votes for women were just a ▷
gleam in the eyes of a few zealots, a suffragette was
coming of age in Miss Ingraham's Exclusive
School for Girls. The story of the lively female was
supposed to be 'warm, wonderful and completely
delightful', but **Adventure In Baltimore** (GB:
Bachelor Bait) was, instead, flaccid, unengaging
and completely dispensible. Shirley Temple
(centre right, borrowed from David O. Selznick)
played the lady in question, employing her usual
repertoire of pouts, dimple twitches and wide-eyed
expressions to characterize the minister's daughter
whose militant ideas scandalize her home town and
immerse her family and friends in continual hot
water. The influence of Dore Schary, who launched the film before leaving RKO, was evident in a
speech delivered by minister Robert Young (left)
about tolerance; the oratory was, however, a good
deal less stirring than his sermon on bigotry in
Crossfire. Also cast: John Agar (also borrowed
from Selznick), Josephine Hutchinson (centre
left), Charles Smith (right), Albert Sharpe,
Charles Kemper, Johnny Sands, John Miljan,
Norma Varden, Carol Brannan, Josephine
Whittell, Patti Brady, Gregory Marshall and Patsy
Creighton. Lionel Houser wrote it from a story by
Lesser Samuels and Christopher Isherwood,
Richard H. Berger produced, and Richard Wallace
directed it. The box-office loss was $875,000.

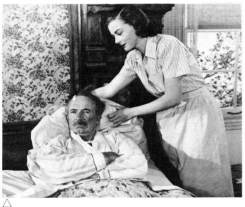

△
The Green Promise (GB: **Raging Waters**) was
a feature length advertisement for America's 4-H
clubs, enclosed in a wretched cornball drama by
Monty F. Collins. Walter Brennan played a
suspicious and domineering farmer of the old
school, a man who has ruined one farm by his
ignorance and is starting all over again in a new
place. Ruling his four motherless children with an
iron hand, he tries to break up his eldest
daughter's romance with the country agricultural
agent, scorns the agent's suggestions for improving
the farm, and blocks his youngest daughter's
efforts to join the local 4-H club. Predictably,
mother nature intervenes through an accident that
puts Brennan (left) out of commission, allowing the
oldest girl to take over and set everything right.
Marguerite Chapman (right) played the big sister,
Robert Paige the agricultural agent and Natalie
Wood the moppet who ultimately finds happiness
in 4-H. Ted Donaldson, Connie Marshall, Robert
Ellis, Irving Bacon, Milburn Stone, Jeanne La
Duke and Geraldine Wall also laboured in the
fields for director William D. Russell and producers Robert Paige and Monty F. Collins.
Howard Hughes' crony Glenn McCarthy, a Texas
hotel and oil man, backed the film through his own
independent company; it was McCarthy's first and
last picture for RKO release. Note: 4-H clubs are
yough organizations which offer instruction in
agriculture and home economics. The name
signifies the primary goal of improving each
member's head, heart, hands and health.

Jack Natteford and Luci Ward's script for
Rustlers focused on the activities of the Salt River
gang, a bunch of thugs who drive off cattle and
then demand ransom money for the return of the
stock. Tim Holt (left) and his sidekick Richard
Martin (centre) are arrested by crooked sheriff
Harry Shannon; he plans to frame them for the
robberies, but they break out of jail and prove their
innocence by wiping out the rustler ring. Director
Lesley Selander and producer Herman Schlom
again teamed to mount this routine 'B', which also
spotlighted Martha Hyer, Steve Brodie, Lois
Andrews (right), Addison Richards, Frank
Fenton, Robert Bray, Don Haggerty, Monte
Montague and Stanley Blystone.
▽

One of the finest fight films ever made, **The Set-
Up** covered 80 minutes in the life of third-rate
palooka Stoker Thompson. Just before leaving for
a bout, Stoker has a quarrel with his wife over his
refusal to abandon his hopeless career in the ring.
Later, in the stadium dressing room, he watches
ring-scarred battlers return from their matches,
recognizing in them phases of his own unhappy
life. In the meantime, unknown to Stoker, his
manager has made a deal with a gambler to throw
the fight. During one of the most brutal ring
encounters ever filmed, Stoker learns that he is
supposed to take a dive. His pride surfaces; he
knocks out the opponent, then must pay the piper
for his act of rebellion. Everyone associated with
this searing screen experience deserved the highest
plaudits. Robert Ryan (left), who was himself an
undefeated pugilist during his four years at
Dartmouth College, made Stoker a wholly believable character – a weary, inarticulate bum who
gains heroic stature in the course of the events.
Audrey Totter (right, borrowed from MGM) as
the wife, George Tobias as the manager, Alan
Baxter as the gambler and Hal Fieberling as the
opponent all played their roles with remarkable
acuity, while Wallace Ford, Percy Helton, Darryl
Hickman, Kenny O'Morrison, James Edwards,
David Clarke, Phillip Pine and Edwin Max added
to the local colour. Robert Wise, in one of his finest
directorial efforts, demonstrated an extraordinary
eye for detail, exploring the dark and dingy world
of tank-town boxing with withering verisimilitude;
Art Cohn wrote the screenplay from Joseph
Moncure March's famous narrative poem, and
Milton Krasner was responsible for the highly-
charged photography. The producer was Richard
Goldstone.
▽

◁ Don Siegel, who would become one of the best action directors in Hollywood history, worked all the pressure points in **The Big Steal**, one of his early efforts based on Richard Wormser's story and a Geoffrey Homes-Gerald Drayson Adams screenplay. All about an extended chase through Mexico (where filming took place), it had Jane Greer (left) and Robert Michum (right) pursuing Patric Knowles and being dogged, in turn, by William Bendix (borrowed from Hal Roach Studios). The goal is a $300,000 Army payroll pilfered from Mitchum by Knowles. Although the story contained more potholes than the primitive roads over which the characters travel, Siegel maintained such a full head of steam that audiences were never bothered by the confusions. Indeed, most viewers were draped limply in their seats by the time it was over, thanks to the pulsating energy of this first-rate thriller. Jack J. Gross produced for the Sid Rogell unit, giving secondary roles to Ramon Novarro, Don Alvarado, John Qualen and Pascual Garcia Pena.

△ Though television would ultimately kill off the 'B' western, **Stagecoach Kid** hastened the funeral. Norman Houston's screenplay was a hotbed of clichés about two owners of a stage line (Tim Holt, right, and Richard Martin, left) who ride to the rescue of a millionaire landowner being swindled by his foreman. Thurston Hall impersonated the absentee owner, Jeff Donnell his strong-willed daughter and Joe Sawyer the crooked overseer. Herman Schlom produced, Lew Landers directed and Carol Hughes (centre), Robert Bray, Robert B. Williams, Kenneth MacDonald and Harry Harvey also appeared.

A wistful and congenial romantic comedy, **The Judge Steps Out** (GB: **Indian Summer**) starred Alexander Knox (right, borrowed from Columbia) as a Boston jurist who tires of his harassed life and disappears, leaving his selfish wife (Frieda Inescort) and wilful daughter (Martha Hyer) to their own devices. In the course of his wanderings, he becomes a cook at a wayside cafe, whose attractive owner (Ann Sothern, left, borrowed from MGM) provides him with the understanding and sympathy that was so completely absent at home. Boris Ingster wrote the story, co-authored the screenplay (with actor Knox) and directed, giving birth to a perceptive study of the frustrations and yearnings of middle-aged men. Producer Michel Kraike's cast also included George Tobias, Sharyn Moffett, Florence Bates, Myrna Dell, Ian Wolfe, H. B. Warner, James Warren, Whitford Kane, Harry Hayden and Anita Bolster. The executive producer was Sid Rogell. Note: This picture was finished approximately two years before its American release.

△ **The Window** was a well-crafted, high tension *film noir*, claustrophobic in tone and harrowing in its impact. Bobby Driscoll (centre, borrowed from Walt Disney) represented the eye of the storm, a youngster in the habit of spinning wild tales who goes out on the fire escape of his Manhattan tenement one evening and spots a murder being committed in an adjoining flat. Since he has 'cried wolf' so often, no one will believe his story – no one but the killers, that is, who realize that the boy is a menace to their safety, and they launch a plot to do away with him. Director Ted Tetzlaff squeezed a full measure of suspense out of Mel Dinelli's screenplay (based on a story by Cornell Woolrich). As usual in a Tetzlaff film, the cinematography (by William Steiner) was outstanding, and so was Roy Webb's taut musical score. The only sad thing about this $210,000 paybox hit was that its producer Frederick Ullman Jr (executive producer of RKO Pathé News for many years) died before the picture was released. Other important cast members were Barbara Hale (left) and Arthur Kennedy (right) as the boy's parents, and Paul Stewart and Ruth Roman as the murderous couple. Philip N. Krasne produced a remake of the film under the title *The Boy Cried Murder* in Europe; it was released by Universal in the US in 1966.

Lacking the incendiary magnetism of *The Big Steal*, **Follow Me Quietly** was a leaden melo directed by Richard O. Fleischer and produced by Herman Schlom. In it, detective Harry Grant (William Lundigan, left) sluggishly tracks down a metropolitan strangler known as 'the Judge'. From scraps of evidence and a partial description of the murderer, Grant constructs a dummy resembling the criminal to use as a guide in his painstaking search for suspects. More emblematic than convincing, the dummy nonetheless eventually leads the cop to his quarry. Lillie Hayward's screenplay, based on a story by Francis Rosenwald and Anthony Mann, had no sense of urgency, making the one hour film seem like an epic. Also cast: Dorothy Patrick (right), Jeff Corey, Nestor Paiva, Charles D. Brown, Paul Guilfoyle, Edwin Max, Frank Ferguson, Marlo Dwyer, Michael Branden and Douglas Spencer.

An above-average western with *Stagecoach* overtones, **Roughshod** revolved around the adventures of a young stock-raiser, his kid brother, and four dance hall girls travelling together across Sonora Pass. The rancher is being stalked by an ex-convict who has sworn to kill him, and is faced with saving his own life, his stock, and the women whom he has unwillingly agreed to take along. A further conflict in Geoffrey Homes and Hugo Butler's screenplay (story Peter Viertel) arises when the hero finds himself falling in love with one of the girls, despite his puritanical standards regarding women. Robert Sterling (left) played the rancher, Claude Jarman Jr (right, borrowed from MGM) his brother, John Ireland the menacing do-badder and Gloria Grahame (centre) the object of Sterling's affections, with Myrna Dell, Martha Hyer and Jeff Donnell as the other problematic entertainers. Director Mark Robson handled the piece in clear, direct and bracing fashion, although he could have done with a stronger leading man. George Cooper, Jeff Corey, Sara Haden, James Bell, Shawn McGlory, Robert B. Williams, Steve Savage and Edward Cassidy were also involved in the Richard H. Berger production. The executive producer was Jack J. Gross.

Producer Samuel Goldwyn decided to turn the hillbilly feud between the Hatfields and the McCoys into a rustic equivalent of the strife between the Montagues and Capulets in *Romeo and Juliet*. His effort, entitled **Roseanna McCoy**, failed for obvious reasons: tissue-thin characterizations, ineffectual direction, uneven performances. Joan Evans (left) and Farley Granger (right) were adequate as the young lovers whose romance fans the smoldering feud into open and sustained violence, but Richard Basehart's portrayal of a goonish member of the Hatfield clan was right out of *Li'l Abner* and Raymond Massey and Charles Bickford, the patriarchs of the opposing families, were never afforded the opportunity to build their characters beyond stereotype. Also cast: Gigi Perreau, Aline MacMahon, Marshall Thompson, Lloyd Gough, Peter Miles, Arthur Franz, Frank Ferguson, Elisabeth Fraser, Hope Emerson, Dan White, Mabel Paige, Almira Sessions and William Mauch. Irving Reis directed and John Collier wrote the screenplay from Alberta Hannum's novel.

Tarzan was nowhere to be found in **Savage Splendor**. An arresting Technicolor documentary, the film recorded the Armand Denis-Lewis Cotlow African expedition, capturing many rare insights into the Dark Continent. Among them: Pygmies of the Belgian Congo slaying an elephant that outweighted two score of them; the spectacular coronation of his majesty Mbofe Mabinshe of the Bakuba tribe, a 300 pound precursor of Idi Amin whose several hundred wives hover in the background during the ceremony; the Manbetu who bind fibre tightly around the heads of their babies, causing a long, narrow skull to develop which is regarded as the height of beauty and elegance; and some exciting animal footage including a battle between maddened hippopotami. Denis functioned as producer and Cotlow as associate producer, while Jay Bonafield received credit as supervisor. Richard Hanser wrote the narration for Armand Denis Productions, which co-produced with RKO. The 60-minute film was both educationally sound and visually stimulating (African tribesman illustrated); however, the fact that it represented RKO's most profitable release of the year ($250,000 in box-office earnings) was indicative of how rapidly the company's economic fortunes were plummeting.

Another 'clip show' produced by George Bilson and directed by Richard O. Fleischer, **Make Mine Laughs** called upon master of ceremonies Gil Lamb to introduce the Leon Errol comedy *Beware of Redheads*, Frances Langford singing 'Moonlight Over The Islands' (from *The Bamboo Blonde*), Anne Shirley and Dennis Day crooning 'If You Happen To Find A Heart' (from *Music In Manhattan*), Jack Haley and Joan Davis collaborating on the 'Who Killed Vaudeville?' number (from *George White's Scandals*), Ray Bolger doing his humorous prizefighter routine (from *Four Jacks And A Jill*), and much, much more. Frankie Carle and His Orchestra, Robert Lamouret (illustrated), Manuel and Marita Viera, Rosario and Antonio, Freddy Fisher and His Schnickelfritz Band, The Titans, Myrna Dell and Dorothy Granger were also featured, and Hal Yates wrote and directed the Errol short. Though it made for a breezy 63 minutes of simulated vaudeville, neither Ray Bolger nor Jack Haley found any humour in the novelty. Both sued RKO for the illegal use of their names and performances, winning cash settlements and forcing withdrawal of the picture from distribution in 1951.

Easy Living was a football picture that managed to side-step routine situations and shake off the usual clichés in its realistic description of pigskin politics. Charles Schnee's screenplay (story by Irwin Shaw) centred on Victor Mature (left, borrowed from 20th Century-Fox), the star halfback of the New York Chiefs, who finally realizes that being a gridiron big shot does not make either himself or his wife (Lizabeth Scott, borrowed from Hal Wallis) happy. He receives more jolts when he learns that a college coaching job he'd hoped for has been offered to Sonny Tufts instead, and that he has a heart condition which makes it dangerous for him to play any more football. Former RKO 'B' queen Lucille Ball (right) returned to her old home after a seven-year absence, playing the team secretary who carries a torch for Mature but unselfishly helps him resolve his problems, including the domestic difficulties with Miss Scott. Jacques Tourneur provided adroit direction for producer Robert Sparks. The large cast also included Lloyd Nolan, Paul Stewart, Jack Paar, Jeff Donnell, Art Baker, Gordon Jones, Don Beddoe, Dick Erdman, William 'Bill' Phillips, Charles Lang, Kenny Washington, Julia Dean, Everett Glass, Jim Backus, Robert Ellis, Steven Flagg, Alex Sharp, Russ Thorson, June Bright, Eddie Kotal, Audrey Young and the Los Angeles Rams professional football squad. Note: This was not a remake of Paramount's *Easy Living* (1937).

Masked Raiders was a galloping western programmer brought to the screen by the team of Norman Houston (scriptwriter), Lesley Selander (director) and Herman Schlom (producer). Texas rangers Tim Holt (left) and Richard Martin learn that a bunch of masked outlaws are harassing the Big Bend country. Posing as cowpokes, they ride out to investigate and discover that the outlaws are Robin Hood types stealing money to help ranchers pay off their mortgages to an unscrupulous banker. The topper is that their leader, the Diablo Kid, is really lovely Marjorie Lord (right). The two white hats teach her that she can't take the law into her own hands, bringing banker Frank Wilcox and scheming marshal Harry Woods to justice at the same time. Gary Gray, Charles Arnt, Tom Tyler, Houseley Stevenson, Clayton Moore and Bill George led the support.

Farley Granger (left) and Cathy O'Donnell (right), ▷ both borrowed from Samuel Goldwyn, played Bowie and Keechie, the doomed lovers in Nicholas Ray's justifiably famous first feature, **They Live By Night**. Charles Schnee's screenplay (based on Ray's adaptation of Edward Anderson's novel *Thieves Like Us*) was a 'Bonnie and Clyde'-type story, filmed in such an expressionistic, claustrophobic style that it managed to be intensely romantic and nearly suffocating at the same time. According to the title credits, this was the tale of a boy and a girl who 'were never properly introduced to the world we live in'. As the pair attempt to escape from their pasts, from unwanted criminal associates and from the impending vengeance of the law, they construct their own fantasy world, fabricating it from a well-spring of naiveté and forcing the audience to participate in their entrapment and share in their tragedy. Ray was brought to RKO by producer John Houseman, a former Orson Welles associate who had handled two of the director's plays on Broadway and worked with him in the Office of War Information. Their film was a critical success in Europe (where it was first released) and in the US, but it lost $445,000 at the box-office. Also cast: Howard Da Silva, Jay C. Flippen, Helen Craig, Will Wright, Marie Bryant, Ian Wolfe, William Phipps and Harry Harvey. Song: 'Your Red Wagon' Richard M. Jones, Don Raye & Gene De Paul. Robert Altman remade the story as *Thieves Like Us*, released by United Artists in 1974.

△

Purchased outright by RKO from Plymouth Productions, **Arctic Fury** was a synthetic, unconvincing drama of survival. Norman Dawn's story, adapted by Charles F. Royal with dialogue by Robert Libbot, Frank Burt and Norton S. Parker, re-enacted the story of Dr Thomas Barlow whose converted amphibian plane crashes while he is on a mission to aid a colony of Eskimos. Trekking through snow, marshes, glaciers and forests, eating fish and rabbits to stay alive and eluding polar bears, wolves and other dangerous animals, he finally makes it back to civilization. Del Cambre played the doctor, and Merril McCormick (left), Fred Smith (centre), Eve Miller (right) and Gloria Petroff were also cast. Don Riss narrated the story; author Dawn co-directed with Fred R. Feitshans Jr who was also the production supervisor and film editor. Boris Petroff produced, stretching out his picture with sequences from *Tundra*, a photographic record filmed within the Arctic circle by Burroughs-Tarzan Pictures for 1936 release.

Tim Holt (right) and his pal Chito (Richard Martin) found trouble a-plenty waiting for them in **The Mysterious Desperado**. Arriving in the little town of Santo Domingo, California, where Chito is to inherit the estate of his uncle, they soon learn that the uncle was murdered, his son (Edward Norris), who should by all rights inherit the ranch, is accused of the crime, and public administrator Frank Wilcox and two crooked real estate promoters (Robert Livingston and William Tannen) are the low-down coyotes who orchestrated the events in order to steal the ranch. Screenwriter Norman Houston and director Lesley Selander blended mystery, comedy, action and romance into a fair-to-middling 'B' oater, with Movita Castaneda (left), Robert B. Williams, Kenneth MacDonald, Frank Lackteen and Leander De Cordova also appearing for producer ◁ Herman Schlom.

◁ Walt Disney's first all-cartoon feature since *Bambi* (1942), **The Adventures of Ichabod And Mr Toad** combined two famous stories into a zesty 68-minute Technicolor diversion. Basil Rathbone narrated the story of Mr Toad from Kenneth Grahame's *The Wind In The Willows*. The erratic owner of Toad Hall, J. Thaddeus Toad must rely on his long suffering friends MacBadger, Mole and Water Rat to get him out of jail, help him recover the castle he traded for a gaudy red automobile and restore his good name after a series of damn-the-torpedoes adventures. Bing Crosby sang and spoke the tale of Ichabod Crane (from Washington Irving's *The Legend of Sleepy Hollow*), a smug and stuffy school teacher who covets the hand of vivacious Katrina Van Tassel. Slow-witted bully Brom Bones loses every round for the affections of Katrina to Ichabod except the devastating final one in which, disguised as the ghostly Headless Horseman, he runs his rival out of the district (see illustration). Ben Sharpsteen supervised the production, employing Erdman Penner, Winston Hibler, Joe Rinaldi, Ted Sears, Homer Brightman and Harry Reeves to work on the stories and Frank Thomas, Ollie Johnston, Wolfgang Reitherman, Milt Kahl, John Lounsbery and Ward Kimball to serve as animation directors. Songs: 'Merrily On Our Way' Frank Churchill, Charles Wolcott, Larry Morey & Ray Gilbert; 'Ichabod', 'Katrina', 'The Headless Horseman' Don Raye, Gene De Paul.

Strange Bargain was a cheaply made but off-beat and suspenseful mystery drama. White-collar worker Jeffrey Lynn (left) goes to the senior partner of his firm (Richard Gaines) to ask for a desperately needed raise. He is, instead, handed his notice and told the company is nearly bankrupt. But Gaines also tells the bookkeeper that he intends to kill himself and presses him to remove the gun afterward, promising that there is $10,000 in it for Lynn. The idea is to convince the police that Gaines has been murdered so that Gaines' insurance company will pay off on a large policy to his wife and son. Needless to say, the plan goes awry, thrusting Lynn into multiple complications that lead to a surprising climax. Lillie Hayward's screenplay (based on a story by J. H. Wallis) abounded with satisfying narrative twists and was carefully translated to the screen by first-time director Will Price. Martha Scott (right) delivered a polished performance as Lynn's sensible and devoted wife, and Henry Morgan, Katherine Emery, Henry O'Neill, Walter Sande, Michael Chapin, Arlene Gray, Raymond Roe and Robert Bray supplied added lustre to the cast. This was one 'B' of which producer Sid Rogell could be justifiably proud.

Co-producer and story author Merian C. Cooper, director Ernest B. Schoedsack, screenwriter Ruth Rose, actor Robert Armstrong and technical creator Willis O'Brien attempted to recapture the magic of *King Kong* with **Mighty Joe Young**. They were sporadically successful, thanks to the spectacular visual effects created by O'Brien, Ray Harryhausen, Peter Peterson, George Lofgren, Marcel Delgado, Fitch Fulton, Harold Stine, Bert Willis and Linwood Dunn. Unhappily, the plot was not worthy of their efforts. Entrepreneur Armstrong (a character obviously modelled on his Carl Denham role in *Kong*) discovers the eponymous hero (illustrated) in Africa, where he is the happy and docile pet ape of Terry Moore (borrowed from Columbia). Transporting them to Hollywood, he bills the ten-foot simian as 'Mr Joseph Young of Africa' and makes him and his diminutive keeper the star attraction in a 'supercolossal' nightclub. After a floor-show-to-end-all-floor-shows, drunken patrons give the gorilla liquor which goads him into a rampage of destruction. Later, the animal redeems himself during an orphanage fire in a scene straight out of the 'Fireman, Save My Child' tradition. There were clever touches (Joe indulging in a tug-of-war with Primo Carnera, Man Mountain Dean and eight other beefy strongmen), elements of high camp (the nightclub itself) and moments of high hilarity (Armstrong's roughnecks trying to lasso the ape, cowboy-style), but the final product was still closer to the disappointingly sentimental *Son of Kong* than to the boomingly original 1933 blockbuster. Ben Johnson was also featured, with Frank McHugh, Douglas Fowley, Denis Green, Paul Guilfoyle, Nestor Paiva, Regis Toomey, Lora Lee Michel and James Flavin playing secondary roles. John Ford co-produced with Cooper for Arko Inc., a company formed by Argosy Pictures and RKO for the purpose of making this one film.

The fact that even good 'B' westerns like **Riders Of The Range** now routinely lost money (in this case, $50,000) was another indicator of the deteriorating business climate that plagued the studios as their most profitable decade came to a close. Norman Houston's screenplay contained punch-packed brawls, exciting chases and blazing gun fights, but television was beginning to offer a steady diet of similar fare. This time Tim Holt (left) and Richard Martin (centre) were good samaritan cowboys employed by rancher Jacqueline White after they save her no-good brother from a crooked gambler. The heroes are once again framed for murder, but fight their way out of trouble and get the goods on the real killer. Reed Hadley, Robert Barrat, Robert Clarke (right), Tom Tyler and William Tannen also took part in the Lesley Selander-directed and Herman Schlom-produced picture.

Though designed for the lower half of neighbourhood double-bills, **The Threat** was tense melodrama crammed with surprises and breathless moments – a minor league *White Heat*. Vicious convict Charles McGraw (left) breaks jail, then kidnaps the police detective who caught him, the district attorney who convicted him, and a cafe singer whom he suspects of having squealed to the cops regarding his loot. The ensuing manhunt, the attempts of the trio to escape, and the cat-and-mouse tactics McGraw uses to torture them, piled on the thrills throughout 65 nervous-making minutes of screen time. Hugh King, who produced, wrote the story and co-authored the script (with Dick Irving Hyland), but director Felix Feist deserved the major plaudits. The cast included Michael O'Shea as the detective, Frank Conroy as the district attorney and Virginia Grey (right) as the girl, plus Julie Bishop, Robert Shayne, Anthony Caruso, Don McGuire, Frank Richards and Michael McHale.

A Dangerous Profession presented George Raft (right) and Pat O'Brien (left) as partners in a bail bond firm. Former police officer Raft makes use of the lessons of his uniform days when robbery suspect Bill Williams, who he has bailed out, is killed under peculiar circumstances. Raft is determined to clear up the mystery to justify his own actions and for the sake of the suspect's pretty widow (Ella Raines, centre). Ted Tetzlaff directed at a fast tempo, but he failed to enrich the film's conventional plot manipulations or clarify certain vague and confusing elements in the Martin Rackin-Warren Duff screenplay. Producer Robert Sparks and executive producer Sid Rogell also engaged Jim Backus, Roland Winters, Betty Underwood, Robert Gist and David Wolfe in supporting roles.

The triangle formed by two men and one woman is a geometrical figure well-known to Hollywood screenwriters. Scribes Bruce Manning and Islin Auster, working from a story by Joseph Fields and Frederick Kohner, pumped new comic adrenalin into the dehydrated formula, calling their effort **Bride For Sale**. The lady in question, Claudette Colbert (right), takes a job as office manager of an income tax firm in order to comb the files for a wealthy husband. Company owner George Brent gets wind of Miss Colbert's scheme and conspires with his wealthy pal Robert Young (left) to teach her a lesson. But everything backfires when both men fall for the mercenary heroine and end up fighting it out for her. William D. Russell's direction captured the slapstick spirit of the piece very nicely; he uncorked a sparkling performance from Colbert and coaxed good support from Max Baer, Gus Schilling, Charles Arnt, Mary Bear, Ann Tyrrell, Paul Maxey and Burk Symon. Jack H. Skirball was the producer for Crest Productions, an independent organization that co-produced the film with RKO.

An old-fashioned soaper of dubious merit, Samuel Goldwyn's **My Foolish Heart** surveyed a wartime love affair and its bitter aftermath. Dana Andrews (left) played a young-man-about-Manhattan who crashes parties and plays the wolf while waiting for the military to call. The central character, however, was Susan Hayward (right), a college girl from Boise who falls for Andrews, becomes pregnant and then marries a man she doesn't love after Andrews is killed in a training accident. Cynical, selfish and alcoholic, she almost loses her love child before finally waking up to the damage her self-pity has done to everyone around her. Even in the sections that were supposed to be bright and carefree, this film exuded a dull weariness that made it seem hollow and unappealing. Mark Robson's pedestrian direction was partially to blame; so was the acting of everyone (except Hayward) and the Julius J. and Philip G. Epstein screenplay (based on a *New Yorker* story by J. D. Salinger). Musical director Emil Newman made sure that the Academy Award-nominated title song (by Ned Washington and Victor Young) was much in evidence throughout. Also cast: Robert Keith, Kent Smith, Lois Wheeler, Jesse Royce Landis, Gigi Perreau, Karin Booth, Todd Karns, Philip Pine, Martha Mears, Edna Holland, Jerry Paris, Marietta Canty, Barbara Woodell and Regina Wallace.

Shot principally in John Ford's beloved Monument Valley, **She Wore A Yellow Ribbon** was the director's personal monument to the United States military. Frank Nugent and Laurence Stallings' nostalgic screenplay, based on *War Party* and *Big Hunt*, two stories by James Warner Bellah, focused on Nathan Brittles (John Wayne, centre), a cavalry captain facing retirement just when his vast knowledge of Indian tactics is most urgently needed. Taking technical advantage of his status, Brittles uses his last few minutes of regular service to thwart a massacre. Though the story was exciting and well-written – except for a lamentable love triangle featuring John Agar, Joanne Dru and Harry Carey Jr and some buffoonish Irish comedy turns by Victor McLaglen – it was really of minor importance. Much more significant was the breathtaking and evocative Technicolor photography of Winton Hoch, based to an extent on the western paintings of Frederic Remington, and the general atmosphere of pride, strength, dignity, compassion and love that surrounded all the main characters. Ford obviously felt these things about his frontier folk and about the armed forces, for whom he had served during the war. No one ever made a more attractive tribute to the professional soldier than **She Wore A Yellow Ribbon**. Wayne dominated the action, creating in Captain Brittles a tower of mythic strength who deserved to stand with Ringo (*Stagecoach*), Tom Dunson (*Red River*) and Ethan Edwards (*The Searchers*) in the actor's personal gallery of screen immortals. The other players included Ben Johnson (left), George O'Brien, Mildred Natwick, Frank McGrath (right), Arthur Shields, Michael Dugan, Fred Graham, Tom Tyler, Chief John Big Tree, Chief Sky Eagle and Noble Johnson, most of them members of the Ford stock company. Ford and Merian C. Cooper co-produced for Argosy Pictures, which joined with RKO to sponsor the film.

1950

The general trends that began when Howard R. Hughes took control of RKO Radio Pictures in 1948 escalated throughout the company's final decade so that, by 1957, RKO abandoned the field of motion picture production. In a relatively short period of time, RKO's central concerns changed from production to pandering, from creative endeavour to contention and conflict, from business to bombast, from a struggle for success to a profile of monomania. With Hughes at the wheel, the studio went careening around a number of sharp corners and finally landed in the ditch. The story of how it all happened is a story without a big finish – a sad soap opera full of infantilism, outrage, frustration, injustice and, above all else, broken dreams.

In 1950, Hughes appeared ready to relinquish some of his omnipotent control as managing director of production. Following the departure of executive producer Sid Rogell, who clashed with Hughes over the latter's fondness for routing him out of bed at two or three in the morning to discuss business, the RKO boss hired Samuel Bischoff to assume charge of the studio and, more importantly, cemented a deal with the independent team of Jerry Wald and Norman Krasna. Wald and Krasna were among Hollywood's most highly respected creative talents; they signed to produce 60 features within the next five and a half years. The $50 million deal was called 'the biggest independent transaction in industry history' by *The Hollywood Reporter*. At a mammoth press conference, Wald and Krasna promised to assemble 'the smartest people since the Greeks' and stated optimistically that Hughes would allow them 'even more autonomy than Zanuck'.

RKO's veteran employees and industry insiders greeted the news with enthusiasm. It was impossible to believe that even Hughes would pay $150,000 to buy out Jerry Wald's contract from Jack Warner and then refuse to allow him or Krasna to function freely. Once again, however, the inscrutable tycoon fooled the experts. He handcuffed Wald–Krasna by insisting that script and star approval on all major projects would be his prerogative. Reaching him was just as difficult for his new producers as it had been for the old ones, and the delays slowed production to an agonizing pace. Within a year, the Whiz Kids (as they were known in industry circles) were completely exasperated and looking for some means of escape.

Mr Hughes' outlandish *modus operandi* sent Samuel Bischoff packing in 1951 and continued to be a source of bewilderment to RKO's employees. An oft-repeated, perhaps apocryphal, story claimed that the mysterious leader visited his studio only once, in the middle of the night, and uttered two words after touring the plant: 'Paint it'. An authentic example of the mountain coming to Mohammed occurred during the preproduction phase of a film entitled **Two Tickets To Broadway**. After the sets for this musical extravaganza were constructed on the Gower Street lot, Hughes demanded that they be taken down, trucked two miles to the Samuel Goldwyn Studios (where he had offices) and reassembled there. He then inspected them and expressed his approval, whereupon they were struck once again, hauled back to RKO and put up for the actual shooting. Throughout 1950 and 1951, RKO continued to announce exciting production schedules but failed to meet them. More and more of the studio's releases evolved from distribution deals with independent producers, joint ventures with affiliated companies, and straight purchases of films produced outside the studio walls. RKO made only a few pictures of its own, and most fared poorly. Needless to say, the company's financial condition was deteriorating at an alarming rate.

On Dangerous Ground (1952)

In 1952, a fresh controversy rocked the shaky organization. The preceding year, a screenwriter under contract to RKO refused to inform the Congressional committee if he had ever been a member of the Communist party. Paul Jarrico was immediately fired by Hughes, who invoked the 'morals clause' – an infamous addendum to most Hollywood contracts which stipulated that an employee could be discharged if his personal conduct reflected disgrace on himself or his employer.

The Jarrico affair came to the surface in May 1952. The writer filed a suit demanding that RKO give him screen credit on **The Las Vegas Story**, a film he was working on when fired. Hughes claimed that Jarrico's script had been scrapped and completely rewritten by others. The case seemed rather insignificant in a Hollywood where credit disputes were commonplace, but Hughes turned it into a *cause célèbre*. He declared vehemently: 'As long as I am an officer or director of RKO pictures, this company will never temporize, conciliate with or yield to Paul Jarrico or anyone guilty of similar conduct.'

The Screen Writers Guild, which had jurisdiction in arbitration problems of this kind, concluded that Jarrico had written the necessary one-third of the script and was entitled to screenplay credit. Naturally, the Guild became Hughes' new enemy. He informed the press that he would not abide by the decision, dared the Guild to call a strike against RKO and smoothly suggested that the Guild should scrutinize the rest of its members to be sure it wasn't harbouring Communist sympathizers. Horrified by the mounting hysteria, Jarrico stated that Hughes had magnified matters in order to 'obtain wide-spread publicity with immunity by purporting to pose as a saviour of the morals of the American public'.

Hughes' war on the Reds shifted directly into high gear. He further reduced RKO production, placed numerous employees on 'leave of absence' status and set up a 'security office' whose job was to screen the backgrounds of all studio personnel for subversive inclinations. This Gestapo-like unit would also begin combing the credits of all company re-issues, excising the names of anyone suspected of Communist leanings. Thus, musical composer Hanns Eisler and featured player Victor Kilian disappeared from the credits of **The Spanish Main** when it was re-released; story author Howard Fast and screenwriter Waldo Salt received similar treatment *vis à vis* **Rachel And The Stranger**, and scriptwriter Josef Mischel's name was removed for the re-issue of

Isle Of The Dead.

Reactions to the dramatic events were mixed. W. R. Wilkerson, publisher of *The Hollywood Reporter*, applauded Hughes' actions in deafening fashion, and Senator Richard M. Nixon, after first branding the activity of Communists in the motion picture industry a matter of concern to Congress and to 'loyal Americans everywhere', declared that Hughes' stand was 'deserving of approval'. Others openly questioned the RKO chief's motives. Mary McCall Jr, president of the Screen Writers Guild, charged that Hughes had used the Communist issue as an excuse to cut back production at his financially plagued studio. 'Howard Hughes has thrown a mantle of Americanism over his own ragged production record', she said.

Hughes' legal combat with Paul Jarrico would drag on for more than two years before finally being settled in RKO's favour. It was, however, only one of many lawsuits that bedevilled the studio during the period. In June 1952, a contract dispute between Jean Simmons and RKO went to court. Hughes claimed he had an 'oral agreement' for exclusive rights to her services, while Miss Simmons and her husband, actor Stewart Granger,

Jet Pilot (1957)

stated that Hughes had refused to sign a written contract prepared after six months of negotiations and, therefore, had no claim on the actress at all. Hughes countered, saying he was unwilling to sign the contract because it contained elements of a 'tax bamboozle'. After several weeks of legal wrangling, an out-of-court settlement was reached. Miss Simmons agreed to star in three pictures for RKO at a salary of $66,666 each. One month later Martin Gang, who served as attorney for Simmons and Granger, filed an $800,000 libel and slander against Hughes, RKO and a publicity firm.

In September 1952, Hughes and corporate president Ned Depinet sold their RKO stock to a Chicago-based syndicate made up of Ralph Stolkin, Abraham Koolish, Ray Ryan, Edward G. Burke and Sherrill Corwin. Stolkin was the dominant force in the take-over. The purchase price was $7.35 million, and the group handed Hughes a $1.25 million check as down payment on his shares. They took control of the studio in early October.

Two weeks later, the *Wall Street Journal* began publishing a series of articles that shook Hollywood to the core. The stories exposed the dubious backgrounds of three of RKO's new owners. Part one concerned Koolish's gambling and mail order insurance schemes, which had earned him a Federal indictment charging fraudulent use of the mails and conspiracy to defraud. Ray Ryan's penchant for gambling and association with notorious racketeer Frank Costello were examined in the second instalment. The third and most damaging exposé dealt with Stolkin. It claimed he had made $3.5 million in eight years through highly suspicious mail-order operations.

Principals within the film industry were shocked by these disclosures. The House Un-American Activities Committee hearings had already done a thorough job of tarnishing Hollywood's image; the prospect of organized crime running a studio was too scandalous for words. In addition, RKO was awash in red ink, had not started a production in more than three months and was receiving danger signals from its valued independents, including Walt Disney and Sol Lesser.

Faced with an incredible mass of adverse publicity and an ailing motion picture company, the syndicate ostensibly re-linquished control. Ralph Stolkin resigned as president and member of the board of directors. Koolish and William Gorman (Ryan's representative) also vacated their chairs on the board. The resignations came one month after the original deal had been consummated in what was called, 'the speediest and most spectacular change in RKO history'. After recovering from their initial amazement, Jerry Wald and Norman Krasna realized this was the opportunity they had been awaiting. They asked for and received cancellation of their RKO contracts.

Arnold Grant, an ambitious young lawyer who had been named chairman of the board when the syndicate gained control, vowed to reorganize the company's studio and get it back into film production. He had an able assistant in Arnold M. Picker, whom Grant had lured away from a successful executive position at United Artists.

Within a month, both Grant and Picker resigned, and a minority stockholders' suit was filed asking that a temporary receiver be appointed for the company. An accompanying suit against Hughes called for an accounting of his stewardship of RKO. Grant claimed he resigned because the Stolkin syndicate, which still owned controlling stock interest, had 'manacled' him. RKO now had no president, no chairman, no production head, and was controlled by men who couldn't run it and wouldn't allow others to take charge.

Ralph Stolkin and his associates realized that their only hope of escaping the debacle without absorbing a huge loss was to sell the stock and sell it quickly. But no one leaped forward to bid for a million shares of that fiscal black hole called RKO. Finally, the syndicate's partners returned the stock to its former owner and forfeited their $1.25 million down payment. In February 1953, Howard R. Hughes was in charge once again, having made a healthy profit from the preceding turmoil.

Hughes named James R. Grainger president of the corporation. An industry veteran who came to RKO from Republic Pictures, Grainger radiated optimism. Ignoring the fact that RKO had made only one feature (**Split Second**) in seven months, Grainger stated that the company was 'in fine shape' and predicted that a steady stream of important pictures would be flowing out 'in six months'. Ironically, the first one put into production was called **Second Chance**.

In fact, 1953 produced an avalanche of law suits rather than a steady stream of important pictures. By April, Hughes had been named in five separate actions related to his personal profit on the Stolkin deal. The suits were filed by infuriated stockholders and, as the year drew on, RKO became so ensnared in legal entanglements that *Variety* reported, 'no litigation in recent motion picture history has created as much confusion'. Dick Powell quipped, only half-facetiously: 'RKO's contract list is down to three actors and 127 lawyers'. One suit charged that the company had lost $38.5 million during Hughes' tenure. Others enumerated more specific sins. The company's purchase and/or distribution of previously-made Hughes' pictures (**The Outlaw, Mad Wednesday, Vendetta**) was often mentioned, and there was even more outrage over Hughes' importation of a bevy of females (Gina Lollobrigida and other less famous names) at the company's expense, some of whom were never used in RKO films. The most mind-boggling story involved Renée (Zizi) Jeanmaire. In order to acquire the French ballerina's services, Hughes engaged her entire ballet troupe and brought its members to Hollywood from Paris. Miss Jeanmaire never appeared in a single RKO film (Hughes did loan her to Samuel Goldwyn for **Hans Christian Andersen**), resulting in a $750,000 loss to the company.

In early 1954, to silence his critics, Hughes offered to purchase all of the company's outstanding stock for $6 per share. In making the offer, he referred to the many lawsuits against him and stated that he wanted all stockholders to be able to obtain more for their stock than they could have through sale at the market value any time since he became associated with the company. In March, the announcement came that the sale of the company to Hughes for $23,489,478 had been over-whelmingly approved by the stockholders.

Some Wall Street experts were puzzled by Hughes' action. They wondered why he would pay so much to rid himself of legal nuisances. After all, RKO was a complete flop – Hollywood's resident studio *non grata*. Others, however, realized that Hughes had hardly forfeited his business acumen. *Newsweek* pointed out that a money-losing concern can be a valuable item, especially to someone like Hughes whose other enterprises were so profitable. If he could acquire 95 percent of the RKO stock, he could apply the picture company's losses against the earnings of Hughes Tool Co., et al., thereby gaining a substantial tax advantage.

But Hughes would never acquire the necessary percentage. Even before the share owners voted to accept the offer, someone else began buying huge blocks of RKO stock. When it came time to sell the stock for $6 a share, the new owner refused to part with his very substantial holdings. The obstructionist was none other than Floyd Odlum, president of Atlas Corporation, the man who had turned over control of RKO to Hughes in the first place by selling him 929,000 RKO shares in 1948. Odlum had held a grudge against his fellow tycoon for some time. He claimed Hughes had promised to give him first chance to buy the RKO theatres when divorcement proceedings were fina-lized. Hughes, however, gave him no opportunity at all, unloading the movie houses to Albert A. List in 1953. Odlum now repaid the favour by preventing Hughes from acquiring the necessary 95 percent. He believed Hughes would give up plenty to gain control of the precious shares. If not, Odlum indicated that his Atlas Corporation would be interested in purchasing RKO and its built-in tax advantages.

Negotiations between the two capitalist giants dragged on for months. In the meantime, RKO continued to produce few pictures and post large deficits. A tiny crew was running the lot, only one or two producers were still functioning, independents were making nearly all of the company's releases. The Odlum–Hughes dealings reached stalemate in July 1955, and Hughes exercised his only remaining option. He sold RKO for the second time.

The new owner was a subsidiary of the monolithic General Tire and Rubber Company. Known as General Teleradio Inc., the subsidiary controlled six television stations and a network of radio outlets that included 58 percent of the Mutual Broadcasting System, the Yankee Radio Network in New England and the Don Lee Network on the Pacific Coast. T. F. O'Neil, president of General Teleradio, was elected chairman of the RKO board when the $25 million sale was consummated.

Although his record at RKO was disastrous, Hughes came through it with his Midas image unblemished. He reportedly made a personal profit of $6.5 million, with most of it coming from the sale of the theatres, the syndicate forfeiture and the final transaction.

The company that Tom O'Neil purchased from Hughes was RKO Radio Pictures, a separate entity from RKO Pictures Corporation which had been reorganized as a holding company for the money earmarked to pay off stockholders at $6 per share. This administrative shell was the focus of the in-fighting between Howard Hughes and Floyd Odlum. Since the new owners had no interest in RKO Pictures Corp., they did not inherit any of the Odlum difficulties, which he settled with Hughes at a later date.

Many Hollywood experts believed RKO was now finished as a producer of theatrical motion pictures. It was hardly a secret that Tom O'Neil had bought the studio to gain control of its library of old feature films. He had tried to purchase the library separately, but Hughes insisted on an all-or-nothing proposition. O'Neil's interest in the backlog was simple: television. Hollywood's old guard continued to abide by their gentleman's agreement not to release features for video consumption, even though people were clamouring to see major studio movies on their home screens. O'Neil had discovered this a year and a half earlier when he paid $1.5 million for 30 pictures that were gathering dust in the vaults of the Bank of America, due to forfeited mortgages. He created a program called 'Million Dollar Movie' on his stations and played a film every night for a week. Response was so great that he eventually rented them to 95 other stations and made a substantial profit.

O'Neil announced, however, that his regime had no intention of eliminating film-making at RKO. On the contrary, he believed his new studio could be a 'successful business venture' and promised to increase activity in the production and distribution areas. Daniel T. O'Shea, a senior vice-president of the Columbia Broadcasting System, was named president to succeed James R. Grainger. Mr Grainger, who had held such high hopes, was allowed to continue for a few months 'in an advisory capacity'. Eight full-fledged RKO productions had been made during his two and one-half years at the helm.

By November 1955, it was obvious that O'Neil intended to keep his word. William Dozier had joined the company as vice-president in charge of production, and a contract had been signed to finance and distribute the pictures of former RKO production chief David O. Selznick, and to re-release some of Selznick's previous films, including *Rebecca*, *The Third Man*, *Spellbound* and *The Paradine Case*. *A Farewell To Arms* was scheduled as Selznick's first new production under the financing arrangement. Besides returning to a level of activity it had not approached in years, including signing new talent and re-hiring many old employees, the company acquired a new name. RKO Teleradio Pictures Inc. was born from a marriage of General Teleradio Inc. and RKO Radio Pictures Inc.

Late in the year, Matty Fox of C & C Corporation reached an agreement with Tom O'Neil for world-wide television rights in perpetuity to 740 old RKO pictures. Although the deal included complete copyright ownership in the RKO shorts, it granted C & C no theatrical rights to the features in the US and Canada, and prohibited showing of the films in New York, Los Angeles, and four other markets where RKO Teleradio owned TV stations. Thus, O'Neil was able to make a substantial amount of money ($15 million was the selling price) without sacrificing the new 'Million Dollar Movies' he had picked up for his own outlets.

Through the first half of 1956, RKO was probably the busiest lot in Hollywood, with thousands of employees turning out features, industrial films, television commercials and shorts. *Newsweek*, in a cover story on Tom O'Neil, called the about-face, 'one of the fastest and most supercolossal comebacks in Hollywood history'. Then, suddenly, everything fell apart.

President O'Shea, who had earlier promised to reconstruct the RKO trademark so that it would again mean 'the great things that the organization stood for in the past' announced that production would be cut drastically and that the studio was looking for some organization to take over its distribution operations. In January 1957, RKO stopped making movies and Universal-International began to handle its releases. One of the films that went to U-I was **Jet Pilot**. A symbolic vestige of the Hughes era, it had been shot years before at a cost of over $4 million, but never released.

A number of factors led to the studio's quick collapse. RKO was in wretched shape when O'Neil bought it: story properties were at a low point and production needed to be almost completely re-tooled. The deal with Selznick, much counted on by the RKO executives, fell apart. More than $2 million was paid for foreign distribution rights to *Oklahoma!*; it proved to be a commercial disappointment abroad. But the actual *coup de grâce* was the failure of RKO Teleradio's own productions. At a time when the industry's big money-makers were star-stuffed blockbusters (*Giant*, Warner Bros.), serious dramas with well-respected names (*I'll Cry Tomorrow*, MGM) and controversial pictures (*Baby Doll*, Warner Bros.), the new RKO tried to compete by producing expensive remakes of its old films that had neither big stars nor contemporary relevance. The result was a paybox blight that annihilated what was left of the studio's will to survive.

Stories circulated throughout 1957 that RKO would spring back to life. In the fall, Tom O'Neil put an end to the speculation by announcing that he intended to sell RKO's Gower Street and Culver City studios to Desilu at a price of $6,150,000 for the production of television programmes. The ending was doubly ironic: television's impact on the box office had, of course, been a major factor in the company's demise, and both Lucille Ball and Desi Arnaz, the owners of Desilu, had once been less-than-stellar contract performers at RKO during its more active and prosperous days.

Ball and Arnaz purchased only the RKO studio buildings, equipment and real estate. Upon the dissolution of their partnership, the original RKO studio at Melrose and Gower in Hollywood was sold to Gulf and Western and merged with the neighbouring Paramount Pictures lot. The famous Radio Tower symbol continues to flash across television and repertory cinema screens around the world.

These films are distributed in the United States by RKO General Pictures, an offshoot of RKO General which has, since 1959, been the name of the General Tire subsidiary owning RKO's residual assets. RKO General, through RKO Pictures Inc., recently re-entered the film production arena via partnerships with other major companies. **Dick Turpin**, made in conjunction with London Weekend Television and starring Richard O'Sullivan and Mary Crosby, is the first of these ventures. RKO also financed **Carbon Copy** with George Segal and Susan St James and has agreed to invest $25 million a year for three years into co-productions with Universal Studios. The initial Universal-RKO picture is **The Border**, starring Jack Nicholson and Valerie Perrine. It will be interesting to see how the new RKO pictures compare with its classics which have, thus far, been the highlights of the RKO story.

1950

For the first time in RKO history, not one release earned profits of $100,000 or more for the company. **The Capture** and **Outrage** each managed a $70,000 return on investment, leading the parade of mediocre to awful financial performers. Fewer than 15 of the 32 pictures handled by the distribution arm were outright RKO productions.

In May, Sid Rogell became fed up with Howard Hughes' wee hours phone calls and told his boss so in candid fashion. Rogell was fired the next day. Hughes brought in Samuel Bischoff, a Hollywood veteran who had spent much of his career at Warner Bros., to replace Rogell as executive producer. Administrative vice-president Gordon Youngman also said enough is enough and departed.

The most dramatic news came in the summer when the team of Jerry Wald and Norman Krasna agreed to a joint venture with RKO designed to yield 60 pictures during the next five years. Krasna was one of Hollywood's star writers, a man who had penned some of RKO's best and most lucrative comedy hits including **The Richest Girl In The World, Bachelor Mother** and **The Devil And Miss Jones**. Wald came to RKO after 18 years at Warner Bros. where he began as a junior writer and worked his way up to a top producer position. Among his notable credits were *Destination Tokyo* and *Mildred Pierce*. Known as the 'Whiz Kids' because of their initials and Wald's notorious exuberance, the pair would soon find themselves becalmed on the sea of Howard Hughes, who was reported to have paid Jack Warner $150,000 to release Jerry Wald from his contract.

The wheels of RKO production continued to turn slowly, despite the hiring of other talent such as Edmund Grainger, producer of John Wayne's Republic hit, *The Sands Of Iwo Jima*. By September, the studio was again losing $100,000 a week due to the infrequency of its releases. The final corporate net loss came to $5,832,000.

The Tattooed Stranger illustrated the methods used by New York's homicide squad in solving a baffling murder committed in the heart of the city. Producer Jay Bonafield and director Edward J. Montagne had made a documentary short called *Crime Lab* for RKO Pathé (now the documentary short subject arm of the company) in 1948; that two-reeler became a sketch for their feature, which contained the same sense of realism as the earlier effort. When an unknown girl is found murdered in Central Park, police lieutenant Walter Kinsella (right) and detective John Miles (left) slowly and scientifically begin to piece together her identity from one small clue – a Marine Corps emblem tattooed on her wrist. The audience is taken along on their step-by-step search, an excursion short on melodramatics but long on authenticity. Phil Reisman Jr's screenplay also gave roles to Patricia White, Frank Tweddell, Ron McLennan, Henry Lasko, Arthur Jarrett, Jim Boles and William Gibberson. RKO Pathé produced the picture for $124,000 in and around New York City.

Tim Holt (right) and Richard Martin played two roving cowboys who begin to court trouble when they break up a lynching in **Storm Over Wyoming**. Ed Earl Repp's screenplay told the story of a range war between cattlemen and sheepmen stirred up by thieving sheep owner Bill Kennedy to cover his crooked operations. After breaking up the 'necktie party', Holt and Martin continue their efforts to restore order until Kennedy is finally arrested. The Herman Schlom-produced, Lesley Selander-directed film was a feast for action addicts – in essence, a continuous 60-minute battle. Noreen Nash (left), Richard Powers, Betty Underwood, Kenneth MacDonald, Holly Bane, Leo McMahon, Richard Kean and Don Haggerty were also in the cast.

The City of Paris received fifth-billing in **The Man On The Eiffel Tower** and earned it, effortlessly stealing the thunder from fellow cast members Charles Laughton, Franchot Tone, Burgess Meredith, Robert Hutton, Jean Wallace, Patricia Roc, Belita, George Thorpe, William Phipps, William Cottrell, Chaz Chase and Wilfrid Hyde-White. Stanley Cortez's Ansco Color photography provided a scenic tour of the French capital, showing off its boulevards, sidewalk cafés, graceful bridges and famous landmarks in breathtaking fashion. Georges Simenon's story *A Battle of Nerves*, scripted by Harry Brown, was something else again. A prosaic thriller, it detailed the attempts of detective Laughton to break down maniacal killer Tone (illustrated) and force a confession. Continual application of psychological pressure by the sleuth gradually shatters his quarry's confidence and leads to the picture's one exciting sequence – a climactic chase atop the Eiffel Tower. The direction of Burgess Meredith was altogether better than his uneven portrayal of a half-blind knife-grinder who becomes a suspect in the case. Irving Allen and Franchot Tone produced for their own independent company, A & T Film Productions, with RKO serving as distributor.

Walt Disney attempted to surpass *Snow White And The Seven Dwarfs* with **Cinderella**. He failed, but his Technicolor effort was a near-miss. Charles Perrault's fairy tale about the beautiful commoner who captures the love of a prince (see illustration) with the aid of her fairy godmother was told with charm and humour by the Disney team. The main characters, including Cinderella's cruel stepmother and vicious stepsisters, were less interesting than the retinue of animal friends who watch out for the young lady, just as the godmother does. Jacques and Gus-Gus the mice, Bruno the dog, several bluebirds, and a selection of other anthropomorphic critters carried on in the tradition of the whimsical circus performers of *Dumbo*, and the amiable forest inhabitants of *Bambi*. Audiences loved them and responded fully to the oft-repeated story, contributing over $7 million in film rentals to the Disney organization. Ben Sharpsteen was again production supervisor, Wilfred Jackson, Hamilton Luske and Clyde Geronimi earned directional credits and Kenneth Anderson, Ted Sears, Homer Brightman, William Peet, Joe Rinaldi, Erdman Penner, Winston Hibler and Harry Reeves collaborated on the story. The actors' voices used included those of Ilene Woods (Cinderella), William Phipps (Prince Charming), Eleanor Audley (Stepmother), Verna Felton (Fairy Godmother) and James MacDonald (Jacques and Gus-Gus). Songs included: 'A Dream Is A Wish Your Heart Makes', 'Cinderella', 'So This Is Love', 'Sing, Sweet Nightingale', 'Bibbidi-Bobbidi-Boo' Mack David, Jerry Livingston, Al Hoffman.

Dynamite Pass was the bullet-filled drama of western pioneers who fought for free highways against the armed thugs who controlled the toll roads in New Mexico. Switching from their customary jobs of punching cattle, Tim Holt (centre) and Richard Martin (left) become road builders in league with construction engineer Regis Toomey and his wife Lynne Roberts (right). Their opposition is John Dehner, who operates a toll road and doesn't cotton to competition – especially of the *gratis* variety. Director Lew Landers bolstered the story's conventional plot manipulations with atmospheric detail and finely honed performances from a cast that also included Robert Shayne, Don Harvey, Cleo Moore, Don Haggerty, Ross Elliott and Denver Pyle. Norman Houston penned the screenplay for producer Herman Schlom.

Launched as the first volley in Howard Hughes' personal war on Communism, **The Woman On Pier 13** took place on the San Francisco waterfront, with the Marxist heavies conducting themselves just like Depression-era movie gangsters and wartime movie Nazis. It starred Robert Ryan as a shipping executive who, in his reckless younger days, was mixed up with radical politics, but who has long since turned away from his Red acquaintances and a murder case he was involved in at the time. So it comes as a shock when a man who knows all about him demands that Ryan (left) join in a plot to tie up shipping in the Bay Area. The situation is further complicated by an effort to involve Ryan's impressionable brother-in-law (John Agar, borrowed from David O. Selznick), and by the hero's inability to tell his wife (Laraine Day, right) the truth. Acting out the adage that 'it's better to be dead than Red', Ryan eventually sacrifices his life to halt the subversive activities. The film was red in more ways than one; audiences displayed a powerful resistance to its boneheaded melodramatics, and it finished its run with a box-office deficit of $650,000. Thomas Gomez, Janis Carter, Richard Rober, William Talman, Paul E. Burns, Paul Guilfoyle, G. Pat Collins, Fred Graham, Harry Cheshire and Jack Stoney also appeared for executive producer Sid Rogell, producer Jack J. Gross and director Robert Stevenson. Charles Grayson and Robert Hardy Andrews wrote the screenplay, based on a story by George W. George and George F. Slavin. Note: The picture had test runs as *I Married A Communist* in New York and San Francisco before its general release under the final title.

Stromboli the film was dwarfed by **Stromboli** the event – a gossip monger's dream-come-true, played out far from that Sodom and Gomorrah called Hollywood. It all began when Ingrid Bergman agreed to star in the film for Neo-realist master director Roberto Rossellini. Shortly after Miss Bergman arrived on the rocky, volcanic island of Stromboli where most of the filming was to take place, she and the director began a torrid love affair that made headlines in all the world's newspapers. Dr Peter Lindstrom, Miss Bergman's husband, contributed to the fireworks by flying to Italy, insulting Rossellini and refusing to give Ingrid a divorce. He finally relented when she gave birth to the director's child, but the scandal so inflamed American women's organizations that they mounted a well-organized campaign against RKO and against the picture. More contention surrounded the artistic integrity of the American release version, which Rossellini claimed had been butchered by the studio. Director Alfred Werker did, in fact, do extensive editing on the 43 cans of celluloid that made their way from Europe to 780 Gower Street; neither he nor RKO, however, was to blame for a dull, trite and crushingly anti-climactic film that could in no way live up to the pre-release publicity or the studio's ill-advised advertising campaign ('RAGING ISLAND ... RAGING PASSIONS! This is IT!'). In the story, to escape the dismal confines of a displaced persons' camp near Rome, refugee Bergman (left) marries a young Italian fisherman and accompanies him to his home on Stromboli. Resentful of the squalor and loneliness of her life there, she tries unsuccessfully to run away, ending up on the side of a live volcano where she is spiritually regenerated among the smoke and fumes. Striving for 'verismo' as the Italians called it, producer-director Rossellini surrounded his star with a cast of well-meaning but totally incompetent amateurs. This use of real people rather than actors had worked well in other Neo-realist films (including several by Rossellini himself), but it blew up more disastrously than the volcano on this occasion. The vague and monotonous script (story Rossellini; collaboration Sergio Amidei, G. P. Callegari, Art Cohn and Renzo Cesana) was the other dominant problem; it looked and sounded as if it were made up as filming went along, which was, in fact, pretty much the case. Mario Vitale (right), Renzo Cesana and Mario Sponzo also appeared for Bero Films, which co-produced with RKO.

The Secret Fury was an approximate description of viewers' reactions to this incredible, nearly unintelligible, mystery melodrama in which the wedding ceremony of a concert pianist is interrupted by an assertion that she is already married. Much to everyone's astonishment, the claim seems to be true; marriage licence records, witnesses, even the justice of the peace who performed the ceremony, confirm it. Determined to solve the puzzle, the heroine and her fiancé mount their own investigation, which eventuates in increasingly ridiculous plot manipulations including the lady's trial on a murder charge and her incarceration in a mental asylum straight out of *The Snake Pit*. As the principals, Claudette Colbert (centre right) and Robert Ryan (centre left) wandered through the film like two abandoned children in search of their father. Director Mel Ferrer was undoubtedly the man they were looking for, but he must have been out hunting screenwriter Lionel Houser who, no doubt, was tracking down story authors Jack R. Leonard and James O'Hanlon to find out what this nonsense was all about. Other lambs led to the slaughter by producer Jack H. Skirball included Jane Cowl (left), Philip Ober (right), Paul Kelly, Elisabeth Risdon, Doris Dudley, Dave Barbour and Vivian Vance. The film was a co-venture between RKO and the Loring Theatre Corporation (whose partners were Colbert, Skirball and Bruce Manning).

◁A master crook and his gang, a double-crossing stripteaser, a square-jawed police detective and a rookie cop were the *dramatis personae* of **Armored Car Robbery**, a *macho* action picture directed by Richard O. Fleischer and produced by Herman Schlom. Earl Felton and Gerald Drayson Adams' screenplay (story by Robert Angus and Robert Leeds) used William Talman as the bandit leader and Charles McGraw (centre right) as the patient detective who goes after him when Talman and his cohorts besiege an armoured car and loot it of a fortune. Other members of the gang are soon killed or captured, but Talman and his burlesque queen mistress (Adele Jergens) prove elusive, until the felon is cornered at the airport, where he is sent to perdition by an incoming airliner. Don McGuire played McGraw's assistant, adding a few laughs to the serious-minded proceedings, Douglas Fowley, Steve Brodie and Don Haggerty impersonated Talman's criminal accomplices and James Flavin (right) and Gene Evans were also featured.

John Ford directed **Wagonmaster**, a saga of a Mormon wagon train sent out to establish a new colony in an unexplored region of the West. After encountering a stranded troupe of patent-medicine peddlers, a murderous bandit gang and hostile Indians along the way, the religious pioneers finally make it to their destination with help from their rawboned frontier guide, Ben Johnson. This film was one of the director's personal favorites, combining the tense excitement of *Stagecoach*, the nostalgia of *She Wore A Yellow Ribbon* and the veneration of the family that infuses almost all of Ford's pictures with a sense of a romantic dream journey to the Promised Land. Frank Nugent and Patrick Ford's screenplay made full use of the stock company, including fiery-tempered Mormon elder Ward Bond, Johnson's sidekick Harry Carey Jr, medicine show performers Joanne Dru (right) and Alan Mowbray (centre), plus Jane Darwell, Hank Worden and Francis Ford; Charles Kemper, Ruth Clifford (left), Russell Simpson, Kathleen O'Malley, James Arness, Mickey Simpson, Jim Thorpe, Cliff Lyons, Fred Libby and Don Summers completed the cast. Bert Glennon shot the film in Monument Valley for co-producers Merian C. Cooper and Ford. It lost $65,000 and was the final co-production between Argosy Pictures and RKO. Songs: 'Rollin' Dust', 'Wagons West', 'Chuckawalla Song', 'Song Of The Wagonmaster' Stan Jones (sung by The Sons of the Pioneers).

The white-skinned, lion-worshipping Lionions caused all the trouble in **Tarzan And The Slave Girl**. A mysterious epidemic ravaging their population forces the tribe to begin kidnapping women from the surrounding regions. When his new Jane (Vanessa Brown, right) is hauled off by the Lionions, Tarzan (Lex Barker, left) roars into action to save her, all the while demonstrating his 'forgive and forget' philosophy by conveying a serum to prince Hurd Hatfield that saves Hatfield's son and promises to wipe out his people's malady. Except for Cheetah's rib-tickling encounter with a liquor bottle, this was no-nonsense action-adventure, efficiently directed by Lee Sholem from Hans Jacoby and Arnold Belgard's serviceable screenplay. Also cast: Robert Alda, Arthur Shields, Anthony Caruso, Denise Darcel and Robert Warwick. Sol Lesser produced for his own independent organization.

Niven Busch, author of *Duel In The Sun*, wrote and produced **The Capture** for his Showtime Properties company. Spun out against Mexican backgrounds, this dull and verbose melo starred Lew Ayres as the field boss of a small American oil company who shoots a man suspected of having stolen the organization's payroll. After discovering that the fellow was probably innocent, Ayres (centre left) falls in love with and marries the victim's widow Teresa Wright (right, who happened to be Mrs Niven Busch at the time). But Ayres' conscience moves him to clear up the puzzle – a decision that leads to a second accidental killing and makes him a fugitive from the law just as the first victim was. Former RKO editor John Sturges directed, endowing the pretentious script with a modicum of style, Edward Donahoe was associate producer, Edward Cronjager managed the skilful photography, and Victor Jory (centre right), Jacqueline White, Jimmy Hunt, Edwin Rand, Barry Kelley, Duncan Renaldo and William Bakewell were in it, too. RKO distributed for Showtime.

Shortly after taking charge of RKO in 1948, Howard Hughes sold **The Outlaw**, a film he had produced independently, to his new company. The transaction would become a matter of controversy in later years, partially because **The Outlaw** was already one of the most controversial films in Hollywood history. The film was actually finished in 1941, but its release was postponed while producer-director Hughes fought an acrimonious battle with Joseph Breen's Production Code Administration which refused to grant the movie a Code Seal. Hughes arranged a token San Francisco exhibition in February 1943, and United Artists handled limited bookings in 1946. The

RKO distribution was, in actuality, a re-release. All the *sturm und drang* revolved around the portrayal of the ample-bosomed Hughes discovery Jane Russell (illustrated). The picture's high-voltage scenes with Miss Russell, including one in which she got undressed and climbed into bed 'to warm' sickly Jack Buetel (his debut) had been excised by the time RKO became the distributor. This left a picture that was not very sexy, but was extremely bizarre. Jules Furthman's screenplay depicted the relationship between Billy the Kid and 'Doc' Holliday (Walter Huston). Before the story begins, Billy has stolen Holliday's horse, and the entire film becomes a contest between the two

men for possession of the animal. Though both characters have the advantage of Rio's (Miss Russell's) affections, they consider her much less important than the sacred steed. Overlong, disjointed, weirdly parodic in its approach to western movie conventions, and misogynistic to the core, **The Outlaw** was also visually stunning and eccentrically provocative. Gregg Toland shot the supple, mood-setting cinematography and Victor Young composed the generous musical score. Also cast: Thomas Mitchell as Sheriff Pat Garrett, Mimi Aguglia, Joe Sawyer and Gene Rizzi. Note: Howard Hawks directed the film for a short time before Hughes fired him and took over.

The **Golden Twenties** was a fascinating pictorial record covering the years between Armistice Day in 1918 and the Wall Street crash of 1929. Stringing together newsreel footage, the March of Time release captured the delirious aspects of the era (the Charleston – see illustration – , bathtub gin, flagpole sitting, marathon dancing and human flies), as well as more sobering events (the rise of the Ku Klux Klan, gangland violence, Sacco and Vanzetti, the Teapot Dome scandal, a roundup of Socialists that paralleled the contemporary Communist bloodsport). There were also sections on the heroes of the entertainment world (Garbo, Valentino, Chaplin, etc.), of athletics (Babe Ruth, Bobby Jones, Jack Dempsey, Red Grange and others) and of the newly emerging field of aviation (Charles A. Lindbergh). All in all, the Richard de Rochemont production covered a vast canvas in a little over an hour without a single lapse in entertainment value. Frederick L. Allen, Robert Q. Lewis, Allen Prescott, Red Barber and Elmer Davis narrated from Samuel Wood Bryant and Frederick L. Allen's story. RKO distributed for Time Incorporated.

Faith Domergue (who, like Jane Russell, was under personal contract to Howard Hughes) made her public motion picture debut in **Where Danger Lives** (she had completed the as yet unreleased *Vendetta* before this). A shapely, sultry woman whose acting talents were reminiscent of, but somewhat less accomplished than, those of Maria Montez, Miss Domergue (left) chewed the scenery to shreds, spoiling the more professional efforts of director John Farrow and star Robert Mitchum (centre). The plot had her as a definitely psychopathic lady, married to elderly millionaire Claude Rains (right), whom she detests. Domergue infatuates Mitchum, manoeuvres him into a violent quarrel with her husband, then convinces him that he has killed Rains in the fight that ensues. In reality, she smothered the man herself after Mitchum knocked him out. Later, the affectionate young lady also smothers Mitchum and leaves him for dead, but he catches up with her just before she is shot down while trying to cross the Mexican border. Charles Bennett's well-written screenplay, based on a story by Leo Rosten, deserved a better actress in the driver's seat. Maureen O' Sullivan, Charles Kemper, Ralph Dumke, Billy House, Harry Shannon, Philip Van Zandt, Jack Kelly and Lillian West were also featured for producer Irving Cummings Jr and his associate Irwin Allen.

Walt Disney's Technicolor version of Robert Louis Stevenson's **Treasure Island** took film adventurers on board the *Hispaniola* for 96 minutes of swashbuckling excitement. Bristol, England, was the point of departure for an expedition in search of buried pirate loot on a remote tropical isle, where the argonauts must battle for their lives with a mutinous pirate gang that has infiltrated the ship's crew. Bobby Driscoll (right) delivered an excellent performance as cabin boy Jim Hawkins, and Robert Newton (2nd right) became the screen's definitive Long John Silver, the one-legged rogue whose name and 'Yo-ho-ho' chant have fired the imaginations of myriads of boys, young and old. Adding to the exhilaration were a group of the finest character actors on land or sea, including Basil Sydney as Captain Smollett, Walter Fitzgerald as Squire Trelawney, Denis O'Dea as Doctor Livesey, Ralph Truman as George Merry, Geoffrey Keen as Israel Hands, Geoffrey Wilkinson as Ben Gunn, Francis de Wolff as Black Dog, John Laurie as Blind Pew and Finlay Currie as Captain Billy Bones. Lawrence E. Watkin's screenplay remained scrupulously faithful to the original, yielding one of Disney's finest live-action films, directed by Byron Haskin and photographed by Freddy Young. Perce Pearce produced at the D & P Studios in England. Also among the large cast: William Devlin, Diarmuid Kelly, Sam Kydd, Eddie Moran, Harry Locke, Harold Jamieson, Stephen Jack, Patrick Troughton, Leo Phillips, Fred Clark and John Gregson. Other cinematic versions of the Stevenson story included a 1918 silent directed by Maurice Tourneur for Paramount with a female (Shirley Mason) playing Jim Hawkins, and a 1934 MGM production starring Wallace Beery and Jackie Cooper.

Loyalty motivated the plot of **Rider From Tucson**, a deluxe 'B' culled from the script pile of writer Ed Earl Repp. Tim Holt (right) and Richard Martin (left), a pair of cowpunchers testing their skills in the Arizona rodeo, receive a telegram asking them to come to the aid of their old friend William Phipps. Phipps has found a rich gold vein and fears the worst from claim-jumpers. His fears prove well-founded, for a gang of desperadoes led by Robert Shayne and his greedy wife Veda Ann Borg kidnap the miner's bride-to-be Elaine Riley (centre) and hold her as barter for the valuable strike. Holt and Martin set things right in familiar but stirring fashion. Lesley Selander provided the high-powered direction for producer Herman Schlom. Also cast: Douglas Fowley, Harry Tyler, Luther Crockett, Dorothy Vaughn, Stuart Randall and Marshall Reed.

Producer Harriet Parsons was clearly asking for trouble when she called her latest film **Never A Dull Moment**. Bilious reviewers pumped the title full of sarcastic buckshot, savaging the movie for its tediousness, banality and overall humdrum. In all fairness, Lou Breslow and Doris Anderson's screenplay (based on a novel by Kay Swift) did have its antic moments and ingratiating characters. New York songwriter Irene Dunne marries a rodeo cowboy (Fred MacMurray) whom she meets at a charity performance. Transplanted to her husband's ranch, the Manhattan tenderfoot adapts to a bewildering life that includes bucking broncos, cougars and step-children. Miss Dunne (centre) took her required pratfalls with the grace and good spirits of a seasoned pro, but MacMurray (right) let down the good guys, playing her romantic foil in a smug, balmy fashion that robbed numerous scenes of their laughs. Likewise, director George Marshall was not in top form; his over-emphatic handling soured several potentially charming characters including MacMurray's kindly foreman (Andy Devine), his crusty neighbour (William Demarest) and his crafty youngsters (Gigi Perreau, borrowed from Samuel Goldwyn, and Natalie Wood). Philip Ober, Jack Kirkwood, Ann Doran and Jacqueline DeWit (left) also appeared. Songs included: 'Once You Find Your Guy', 'The Man With The Big Felt Hat', 'Sagebrush Lullaby' Kay Swift. Note: There was no relationship between this film and a Walt Disney film (starring Dick Van Dyke) released in 1968 under the same title.

It was man against nature, as well as against his ▷
own egomaniacal obsessions in **The White
Tower**, one of RKO's better 1950 productions.
American flyer Glenn Ford (illustrated), alluring
European Alida Valli (on loan from David O.
Selznick), disillusioned French author Claude
Rains, veteran Swiss guide Oscar Homolka, British
naturalist Sir Cedric Hardwicke and arrogant ex-
Nazi Lloyd Bridges join in an attempt to scale the
mountain peak that had killed Valli's father some
years before. Each climber's true character is
revealed by the rivalries that develop within the
group as they struggle to reach the top. Paul
Jarrico's screenplay, based on a best-selling novel
by James Ramsey Ullman, was originally designed
as an Adrian Scott-Edward Dmytryk project.
After their run-in with the House Un-American
Activities Committee, it was turned over to
producer Sid Rogell and director Ted Tetzlaff.
Ray Rennahan shot the arresting Technicolor
images on the slopes of Mont Blanc in the French
Alps, and June Clayworth, Lotte Stein, Fred
Essler and Edit Angold completed the cast.

Purchased by RKO from Prominent Pictures for
$131,250, **Destination Murder** was an appalling
programme-filler featuring Joyce MacKenzie
(left), Stanley Clements (right) and Hurd Hatfield. When a gambler is killed, his daughter
(MacKenzie) becomes irritated at the police
department's casual attitude and decides to find
the killer herself. She takes a job at the nightclub
run by the man she suspects, managing to become
romantically involved with Clements, Hatfield and
Albert Dekker, all of whom had a hand in the
murder. Don Martin's screenplay was so lamely
executed that it never even bothered to explain
why Miss MacKenzie's father was knocked off in
the first place. Myrna Dell, James Flavin and John
Dehner also took roles for director Edward L.
Cahn and producers Cahn and Maurie M. Suess.
Songs: 'Let's Go To A Party' James Springs,
Steve Gibson; 'Palace Of Stone' James Springs.

Always promising more than it ultimately delivered, **Edge Of Doom** (GB: **Stronger Than
Fear**) told the story (script by Philip Yordan) of a
moody slum youngster who, unable to persuade an
elderly priest to give his mother an elaborate
funeral, murders the cleric in a fit of rage. A
younger, more sympathetic priest tries to aid the
boy in his bereavement, begins to suspect him of
the crime and helps bring about his repentance.
Mark Robson's direction was cogent and powerful
in certain sections of the film, but he was unable to
coax more than adequate performances from
Farley Granger (centre) as the angry youth and
Dana Andrews (right) as the understanding priest.
Consequently, the psychological depths of Leo
Brady's novel were left mostly untapped. Joan
Evans, Robert Keith (left), Paul Stewart, Mala
Powers, Adele Jergens, Harold Vermilyea, John
Ridgely, Douglas Fowley, Mabel Paige, Howland
Chamberlin, Ellen Corby, Ray Teal, Mary Field
and Virginia Brissac were also in it. Samuel
Goldwyn produced for his own independent
banner.
▽

Our Very Own, another Samuel Goldwyn human
interest drama, tackled the subject of adoption, but
failed to cast any light on it. Ann Blyth (left)
played a high-school girl who is perfectly contented until she discovers that Jane Wyatt (2nd
right) and Donald Cook (right) are not her natural
parents. This precipitates an emotional crisis for
the young lady, who goes trooping off in search of
her real mother (Ann Dvorak) and receives an
indifferent reaction when she finally finds her.
Realizing that she is fortunate to have such
understanding foster parents, she incorporates her
new knowledge about life into her graduation day
speech. F. Hugh Herbert's paint-by-numbers
screenplay and David Miller's indifferent direction
made for an insufferably dishonest movie – smug,
self-important, tedious and sentimentally simplis-
tic about the problem it presented. Farley
Granger, Joan Evans (centre), Natalie Wood, Gus
Schilling, Phyllis Kirk and Jessie Grayson were
other members of the ill-used cast. Hedda Hopper
called it: 'The kind of picture America has been
screaming for!' 'Screaming about' would have
been more apt.
▽

Outrage was an intrepid, partially successful
attempt to deal with the psychological effects of
rape. Mala Powers (foreground centre) was the
victim, a perfectly happy young woman who is so
unstrung by the senseless attack that she runs away
from home and from her fiancé. Under an assumed
name and with the help of a concerned clergyman,
she endeavours to carve out a new life. But the fear
continues to haunt her until a moment comes when
she believes herself about to be victimized again.
Given the raw facts, it was impossible not to
sympathize with Miss Powers, but scenarists
Collier Young, Malvin Wald and Ida Lupino piled
on so many turbulent flourishes that some of the
impact drained out of their indictment of this
bestial social phenomenon. Miss Lupino directed,
Young produced and Wald was the associate
producer for their company, The Filmakers, which
co-sponsored the picture with RKO. Tod Andrews
(centre), Robert Clarke, Raymond Bond, Lilian
Hamilton, Rita Lupino, Hal March, Kenneth
Patterson, Jerry Paris, Angela Clarke, Roy Engel,
Tristram Coffin, Jerry Hausner, Bernie Marcus,
Joyce McCluskey, John Morgan and Victor Perrin
were among those also involved.
▽

Robert Sterling foiled confidence men determined to rob a widow of her fortune in **Bunco Squad**, a potboiler directed in semi-documentary fashion by Herbert I. Leeds. Sterling discovers the crooks have induced Elisabeth Risdon (left) to will them $2 million by delivering messages to her from her dead son in a phony seance. With the help of his sweetheart Joan Dixon (right), Sterling forces Ricardo Cortez and his fellow 'psychics' to close shop. There was nothing original here, but its simple plot (screenplay by George Callahan, suggested by Reginald Taviner's story) was enough to keep audiences attentive for 67 minutes. Producer Lewis J. Rachmil used Douglas Fowley, Marguerite Churchill, John Kellogg, Bernadene Hayes, Robert Bice, Vivien Oakland and Dante, a practicing magician, to complete the cast. The film was a partial remake of *Crime Ring* (1938).

Except for a head-knocking barroom fight, **Border Treasure** offered minimal action, adventure or diversion. Norman Houston's screenplay concerned the plans of an outlaw gang to steal a treasure collected for the relief of Mexican earthquake victims. Tim Holt (centre left) and Richard Martin (left) learn what the uncharitable miscreants are planning, but are lured away from the ambush by Jane Nigh, the girlfriend of one of the crooks. They are then accused of being in league with the robbers, but clear themselves in the usual fashion. Herman Schlom produced, with John Doucette, House Peters Jr, Inez Cooper (centre right), Julian Rivero, Ken MacDonald, Vince Barnett, Robert Peyton (formerly known as Lee Frederick), David Leonard, Tom Monroe and Alex Montoya (right) filling out the cast. George Archainbaud, a name much in evidence at RKO during the 1930s, was the director.

John Howard (left) played an earnest young doctor who develops a new treatment for radioactive poisoning in **Experiment Alcatraz**. When the drug is tested on a group of convict volunteers, a murder ensues and the doctor is faced with clearing up the homicide in order to prove the real worth of his discovery. The basic premise – of criminals who agree to serve as guinea pigs in exchange for freedom *if* they survive – was interesting, but scriptwriter Orville H. Hampton (working from a screenplay by George W. George and George F. Slavin) and producer-director Edward L. Cahn quickly churned it into hokum. Also cast: Joan Dixon (right), Walter Kingsford, Lynne Carter, Robert Shayne, Kim Spalding, Kenneth MacDonald, Dick Cogan, Frank Cady, Byron Foulger, Ralph Peters, Lewis Martin, Harry Lauter (centre) and Raymond Largay. RKO had nothing to do with the making of this 57-minute film, purchasing it outright from Crystal Productions for $100,000.

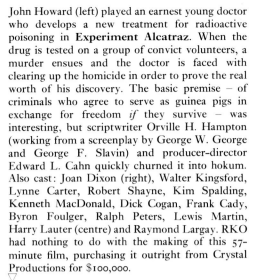

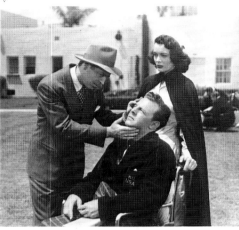

Set in San Francisco among such well-to-do types as socialities, book publishers and artists, **Born To Be Bad** chronicled the activities of Christabel Caine (Joan Fontaine), a woman described as being a 'cross between Lucrezia Borgia and Peg O' My Heart'. Cloaking her desire for wealth and power under a deceptively innocent facade, she traps a millionaire (Zachary Scott) for a husband, but is not satisfied and decides to enjoy extra romance with a rising novelist (Robert Ryan, right). Her plans are eventually shattered when both men discover her true nature. RKO publicity called the movie: 'The rare and racy adventures of a female savage in a jungle of intrigue!'. Most of it was as advertised, thanks to Nicholas Ray's vital direction, but an over-zealous desire to satisfy the censors led to a come-uppance finale that was sentimental, self-righteous and as phony as a glass eye. It ruined an otherwise admirable picture. Charles Schnee adapted Anne Parrish's novel *All Kneeling*, and Edith Sommer fashioned the screenplay with additional dialogue by Robert Soderberg and George Oppenheimer. Fontaine (left) was chillingly attractive as the ruthless lady, and Scott (borrowed from Warner Bros.) and Ryan were equally effective. Joan Leslie, Mel Ferrer, Harold Vermilyea, Virginia Farmer, Kathleen Howard, Dick Ryan, Irving Bacon and Gordon Oliver were also in producer Robert Sparks' cast. Note: This film was originally scheduled to be made in 1946 with Fontaine, Henry Fonda, John Sutton and Marsha Hunt, but was cancelled for a variety of reasons. It was again placed on the production docket under the title *Bed of Roses* in 1948 with Barbara Bel Geddes cast as Christabel Caine, but Howard Hughes decided he did not care for Miss Bel Geddes and postponed it. This interference by Hughes convinced Dore Schary to leave RKO.

Preston Sturges wrote, produced and directed ▷ **Mad Wednesday**, the film that welcomed Harold Lloyd back to the screen after a long absence from acting. One of the most uneven comedies ever made, it was a schizophrenic mixture of side-splitting sequences which recaptured the ingenuity of such Lloyd classics as *The Freshman* (1923), a clip from which served as the picture's prologue; and sections so leaden, dull and mirthless that it is hard to believe the same director-writer was calling the shots. Lloyd (front, right) played a bookkeeper who is dismissed after 20 years, goes on a binge and wakes up the owner of a bankrupt circus. He sets out to raise some money just to feed the hungry animals, eventually arriving at his trade-mark scene – a game of tag with a lion along the window ledges of a 15-story building. Lloyd proved that he was still in fine fettle while dangling from the tall building, but he was at a loss to pep up the numbing scenes that led to his patented thrill comedy. Jimmy Conlin (front, centre left), Franklin Pangborn (back, right), Arline Judge (front, centre right), Lionel Stander (back, left), Frances Ramsden, Raymond Walburn, Margaret Hamilton, Al Bridge, Edgar Kennedy, Frank Moran, Torben Meyer, Victor Potel, Jack Norton, Arthur Hoyt, Georgia Caine, Gladys Forrest, Max Wagner and Charles R. Moore (left) also appeared. Note: Howard Hughes financed this picture before he acquired RKO. United Artists, the original distributor, arranged token exhibitions under the title *The Sin Of Harold Diddlebock* in 1947, but the deal was cancelled and Hughes ended up having RKO distribute it, along with *The Outlaw* and *Vendetta*.

Like *The Outlaw* and *Mad Wednesday*, **Vendetta** was another Howard Hughes picture filmed before he made his RKO connection. Preston Sturges was the original director and adapter of Prosper Merimée's French novel *Colomba*. But after the Hughes-Sturges partnership blew sky-high, the picture found its way to theatre screens with Mel Ferrer credited as director, Peter O'Crotty as adapter and W. R. Burnett as scripter. Burnett, who wrote *Little Caesar* and *High Sierra*, would undoubtedly like to forget this one. A verbose, strident and uninspired period piece, it revolved around the Corsican code of honour which impels Faith Domergue (right) to avenge her father's murder. Although Domergue's brother George Dolenz (left) refuses to believe she knows the identity of the slayer, he is goaded into joining his sister's bloody quest. A good deal of plasma is ultimately spilled, but the result was still a wholly bloodless dramatic exercise. Miss Domergue was again the central problem; placed in the pivotal role, her atrocious acting continually undermined the picture's credibility. The other performers – including Hillary Brooke, Nigel Bruce, Joseph Calleia, Hugh Haas and Donald Buka – mostly stood around as if waiting for a train to pass by and spirit them away from this ludicrous enterprise.

Walk Softly, Stranger was the final co-production between RKO and Selznick's Vanguard Films, which provided the services of director Robert Stevenson and stars Alida Valli and Joseph Cotten; it was also the last RKO picture to carry a Dore Schary credit. The film first saw the light of day more than two years after it was finished, and in no way re-echoed the quality of *The Third Man* in which Valli and Cotten had first appeared together. The pre-eminent problem was Frank Fenton's clichéd screenplay (story by Manny Seff and Paul Yawitz) about a smooth crook (Cotten, left) who decides to lie low in a small Ohio town, but falls in love with a wealthy but bitter girl (Valli, right) who must spend the rest of her life in a wheelchair as the result of a skiing accident. After thumbing through his catalogue of melodramatic plot rudiments, Fenton ended it with the boy going off to pay his debt to society and the girl promising to wait for his release. Underwhelmed audiences caused the picture to be the year's biggest financial bust (RKO loss $775,000). Also cast: Spring Byington, Paul Stewart, Jack Paar, Jeff Donnell, John McIntire, Howard Petrie, Frank Puglia (who replaced Moroni Olsen during a period of retakes), Esther Dale, Marlo Dwyer and Robert Ellis. Robert Sparks produced.
▽

Rio Grande Patrol starred Tim Holt in another Saturday matinee western filled with plenty of noisy but harmless violence. Norman Houston's screenplay required Holt (right) and Richard Martin (centre) to portray border guards who uncover a plot to smuggle machine guns from the US to insurrectionists in Mexico. Tom Tyler, once the hero of many a similar sagebrush drama, played a vicious hired killer this time around, and Jane Nigh, Douglas Fowley, Cleo Moore, Rick Vallin (left), John Holland, Larry Johns and Harry Harvey were also in it. Herman Schlom produced and Lesley Selander directed.
▽

A desultory programmer made by Bel-Air Productions with the proviso that RKO would buy the completed picture, **Double Deal** told of two-fisted petroleum engineer Richard Denning (left) who accepts a rush job to bring in an oil well owned by driller Carleton Young. After the driller is killed, Denning decides to stay on and help Marie Windsor (centre), who inherits Young's oil lease, despite opposition from Young's rapacious sister (Fay Baker) and an innocent-seeming drunk (Taylor Holmes) who turns out to be the murderer. James Griffith, Tom Browne Henry and Paul E. Burns (right) were also cast. James T. Vaughn produced, employing Don McGuire to write the original story, Lee Berman and Charles S. Belden to turn it into a screenplay and Abby Berlin to add the tepid direction.
▽

The new year brought the creation of two new companies: RKO Pictures Corporation and RKO Theatres Corporation. This was the direct result of the consent decree accepted in the government's anti-trust suit against the major distributors, and made RKO the second company (after Paramount) to split its theatres off from its production-distribution operations. Although Radio-Keith-Orpheum Corporation was dissolved, Ned E. Depinet remained president of the picture concern, while Sol J. Schwartz was named president of the theatre company.

The studio continued to announce promising production schedules which failed to materialize. Major Hollywood talent agencies now routinely advised their important clients to steer clear of RKO, which had become the combination laughing stock and pariah of the entire industry. By year's end, there were strong rumblings of dissatisfaction from Jerry Wald and Norman Krasna, who were receiving the same sort of run-around from Howard Hughes that other producers on the lot routinely had to endure.

Samuel Bischoff left in November, shell-shocked after a year and a half of working for Howard Hughes. No one was signed to take Bischoff's place as executive producer. **The Blue Veil, Payment On Demand** and **The Racket** were the most successful of the year's 38 releases. A profit-generating RKO picture still remained an anomaly, however, and the corporation's claim that it made $334,627 in profits was one of the major miracles in bookkeeping history.

△ Made before but released after *All About Eve,* **Payment On Demand** was Bette Davis' first free-lance picture following 18 years of contract work for Warner Bros. Bruce Manning and Curtis Bernhardt's screenplay documented a divorce, *sans* weeping children, courtroom melodramatics and the other expected ingredients of such domestic tragedies. In flashback, it showed the mistakes leading to the rupture between Davis (right) and Barry Sullivan (left, borrowed from MGM), then focused on the vindictive retribution she exacts from her spouse for straying into the arms of Frances Dee. A trip to Port-au-Prince where Miss Davis visits Jane Cowl, a cynical former acquaintance now living with a gigolo, sobers and softens the protagonist up, forcing her to admit her own shortcomings and paving the way for a possible reconciliation. Though the film did not belong to the pantheon of Bette Davis' cinematic accomplishments, it afforded her marvellous opportunities to do all the things she did best. Director Bernhardt staged the story with style and energy, drawing deft performances from everyone in his cast. Among the actors were Kent Taylor, Betty Lynn, John Sutton, Peggie Castle, Otto Kruger, Walter Sande (centre), Richard Anderson and Natalie Schafer. Jack H. Skirball was the producer for Gwenaud Productions, which co-sponsored the film with the studio.

A compelling 68-minute whodunit, **Hunt The Man Down** starred Gig Young (centre) as a public defender who unravels a tangled web of clues to clear a man of a murder charge 12 years after the crime was committed. James Anderson played the penniless defendant, Lynne Roberts his loyal girlfriend, and Carla Balenda (another actress under personal contract to Howard Hughes), Mary Anderson, Gerald Mohr, John Kellogg, Cleo Moore and Christy Palmer the witnesses Young tracks down in order to piece the puzzle together. George Archainbaud supplied the crisp direction for producer Lewis J. Rachmil. DeVallon Scott's screenplay also gave roles to Willard Parker, Paul Frees, James Seay, Harry Shannon (left) and Iris Adrian (right).
▽

Independent producer Sol Lesser took cameras and crew to the jungles of British East Africa for the first time to film **Tarzan's Peril** (GB: **Tarzan And The Jungle Queen**). The flora, fauna and folk of the Dark Continent were used to good effect, without pushing the ape man's carryings-on too far in the direction of realism. George Macready impersonated the major villain, a gun-runner who stirs up the belligerent Yorango tribe in the knowledge that they will attack the peaceful Ashubas. Tarzan (Lex Barker, right) swings through the trees to liberate the innocent natives and their queen Dorothy Dandridge, then returns home in time to save another new Jane (Virginia Huston) from the menacing heavy. Karl Struss's practiced cinematographic eye captured the full flavour of the authentic locales, and Byron Haskin directed the Samuel Newman-Francis Swann screenplay (additional dialogue by John Cousins). The film also spotlighted Douglas Fowley, Glenn Anders, Frederick O'Neal, Alan Napier, Edward Ashley and Cheetah (left), who seemed somewhat chagrined to be so far from the comforts of Hollywood.

The Racket, based on a slightly dated play by Bartlett Cormack, picked up box-office momentum from a contemporaneous war on American lawlessness spearheaded by Chairman Estes Kefauver and his Senate Crime Investigating Committee. However, this Edmund Grainger production didn't have much going for it except timeliness and Robert Ryan's powerhouse performance. Its plot was the one about the incorruptible police officer (Robert Mitchum) and the brutal racketeer (Ryan, right) who go after each other with a vengeance. Mitchum played the cop role – a departure from his customary characterizations – without much enthusiasm; Ryan, on the other hand, strong-armed his way through the picture, re-moulding the stereotyped heavy into a figure who was repellent and magnetic at the same time. Lizabeth Scott (left, borrowed from Hal Wallis) had very little to do as a sultry torch singer, but did it well, and William Talman, Ray Collins, Joyce MacKenzie, Robert Hutton, Virginia Huston, William Conrad, Walter Sande, Les Tremayne, Don Porter, Walter Baldwin, Brett King, Richard Karlan and Tito Vuolo completed the cast. John Cromwell, who had worked for RKO on and off since 1932, directed his final assignment for the studio from a script by William Wister Haines and W. R. Burnett. Howard Hughes had made an earlier film version of the play, released in 1928 by Paramount, directed by Lewis Milestone, and starring Thomas Meighan and Louis Wolheim in the Mitchum and Ryan roles. Song: 'A Lovely Way To Spend An Evening' Jimmy McHugh, Harold Adamson.

Story author Erwin Gelsey and scriptwriters Marvin Borowsky and Allen Rivkin dredged up the old 'reformation of the gangster' plot and used it as the basis of **Gambling House**. Victor Mature (left, on loan from 20th Century-Fox), was a foreign-born gambler who has never bothered to take out naturalization papers, and finds himself facing deportation when his status is revealed during a murder trial. Pretty social worker Terry Moore (right, on loan from Columbia) awakens the mug to the values of citizenship, whereupon he strong-arms big-time underworld boss William Bendix (on loan from Hal Roach Studios) out of $50,000, donates it to Miss Moore's organization and is permitted to remain in the country by a sympathetic judge. Somehow this was supposed to represent a rousing salute to the American way, but it took a very distorted sense of logic to come up with that conclusion. Executive producer Sid Rogell, producer Warren Duff and director Ted Tetzlaff would have been better off hiring Francis the Talking Mule to sing 'The Star-Spangled Banner'. Zachary A. Charles, Basil Ruysdael, Donald Randolph, Damian O'Flynn, Cleo Moore, Ann Doran, Eleanor Audley, Gloria Winters and Don Haggerty completed the cast.

Making his directorial debut, Academy Award-winning editor Robert Parrish (*Body and Soul*, 1947) hammered out a class 'A' actioner called **Cry Danger**. Dick Powell put on his tough-guy hat once more, portraying an ex-convict determined to make the man who framed him pay for his five years behind bars. One-legged ex-Marine Richard Erdman and police detective Regis Toomey (centre) shadow Powell (right, standing), hoping he will lead them to the $100,000 he supposedly stashed after a robbery. Powell also bumps into Rhonda Fleming (right, seated) who tries to dissuade him from his efforts for her own selfish reasons. Parrish succeeded in welding his actors into a polished ensemble and transferring all the tough-gutted dramatics in William Bowers' script (story Jerry Cady) to the screen. William Conrad (left), Jean Porter, Jay Adler, Joan Banks, Gloria Saunders, Hy Averbach, Renny McEvoy, Lou Lubin and Benny Burt also appeared for producers Sam Wiesenthal and W. R. Frank. RKO functioned as distributor for Olympic Productions, an independent outfit that put the picture together. Song: 'Cry Danger' Hugo Friedhofer, Leon Pober.

Star Tim Holt (left) and his trusty pal Richard Martin (right) terrorized a bunch of counterfeiters in **Law Of The Badlands**. Posing as 'most-wanteds', the pair are hired by the gang's boss and are ready to tie up the case when Martin's ex-lady love (Joan Dixon) comes to town and innocently identifies them as Texas rangers. The criminals may deal in phony money, but they shoot real bullets, aiming a fusillade of them at our heroes before a troop of rangers rides to their rescue. The only distinguishing feature of this picture was its cost; at $98,000 it was the cheapest Tim Holt vehicle since the war years, yet still lost $20,000 at the box-office. The handwriting on the livery stable wall was growing quite distinct – the days of the 'B' western were almost over. Herman Schlom produced, Lesley Selander directed and Ed Earl Repp wrote the screenplay. Also cast: Robert Livingston, Leonard Penn (centre), Harry Woods, Larry Johns, Robert Bray, Kenneth MacDonald and John Cliff.

Sealed Cargo starred Dana Andrews (right, borrowed from Samuel Goldwyn) in a sporadically exciting World War II drama set along the coast of Newfoundland. The Dale Van Every-Oliver H. P. Garrett-Roy Huggins screenplay (based on Edmund Gilligan's novel *The Gaunt Woman*) assigned Andrews the role of fishing boat captain who comes to the rescue of a seemingly innocent square-rigger that turns out to be a mother-vessel for a wolf pack of Nazi submarines. Andrews tows the crippled ship into harbour, discovers that its hold is full of bombs, mines and torpedoes and then formulates a plan to destroy the death-carrier. Director Alfred Werker managed some good action scenes, but his work with the actors was only lukewarm. They included Carla Balenda (left) as an innocent caught up in the intrigue, Claude Rains as a Nazi naval officer and Philip Dorn, Onslow Stevens, Skip Homeier, J. M. Kerrigan, Arthur Shields, Morgan Farley, Henry Rowland, Charles A. Browne, Don Dillaway, William Andrews, Richard Norris and Kathleen Ellis. Warren Duff produced, with Samuel Bischoff receiving his first RKO credit as executive producer.

The **Company She Keeps** was the odd title of a triangle melo starring Lizabeth Scott (left, borrowed from Hal Wallis) as a parole officer, Jane Greer (right) as a distrustful parolee, and Dennis O'Keefe as a newspaper columnist loved by Scott who falls under the spell of Miss Greer. Brokenhearted but magnanimous, Scott steps aside and works to smooth the way for a marriage between Greer and O'Keefe. Screenwriter Ketti Frings made sure that O'Keefe warms to an appreciation of the fine woman he is leaving behind before the end credits roll. The laudable acting of the three principals, John Cromwell's solid direction and the superior technical values supplied by producer John Houseman were thoroughly sabotaged by the contrived and hackneyed story, which was not worth their attention in the first place. The movie ended up $315,000 in the red. Also cast: Fay Baker, John Hoyt, James Bell, Don Beddoe, Bert Freed, Marjorie Wood, Marjorie Crossland and Virginia Farmer. Sid Rogell was the executive producer.

▽

A science fiction film still much beloved by aficionados of the genre, **The Thing** was the first co-production between RKO and Howard Hawks' Winchester Productions. Former editor Christian Nyby received directorial credit but, without taking anything away from Nyby, it is only fair to say that the sensibility of producer Hawks, who was in and out constantly during the shooting, is manifest in every frame of the picture. The love of professionalism, of group effort, of facing danger with toughness and cynical detachment, represent a few of the Hawksian themes in this story of a vegetative space traveller who crash lands his saucer near the North Pole and becomes a major nuisance to the inhabitants of an Arctic research base. Chief among the corps of American scientists, military men and newspaper reporters who do battle with the alien behemoth were Kenneth Tobey (left), Douglas Spencer, James Young, Robert Nichols, Dewey Martin and William Self. Margaret Sheridan (right) furnished the romantic interest, playing a woman cast in the mold of such former Hawks' heroines as Lauren Bacall (*To Have And Have Not*) and Joanne Dru (*Red River*). She serves as secretary to Robert Cornthwaite, a scientist who tries to make friends with the monster and is gleefully torn apart for his gesture. Charles Lederer's screenplay, based on John W. Campbell Jr's story *Who Goes There?*, provided two or three of the most frightening moments in the annals of sci-fi, thanks partially to the film's brilliant editing (by Roland Gross) and the out-of-this-world performance by James Arness (best known as Marshal Matt Dillon of the long-running *Gunsmoke* TV series) as the huge and extremely belligerent celestial carrot. Edward Lasker functioned as associate producer, Dimitri Tiomkin composed the ominous music and Eduard Franz and Sally Creighton also appeared. For those who saw the picture in their youth, the tag line ('WATCH THE SKIES') remains a menacing reverberation from this unpretentious, superlative motion picture. Note: The actual title was *The Thing From Another World*, but the last three words were generally dropped on marquees wherever it played.

▷

△

The third of producer George Bilson's musical revues, **Footlight Varieties** featured the Leon Errol short *He Forgot To Remember* with Dorothy Granger, Elaine Riley, Harry Harvey, Byron Foulger, Emory Parnell and Patti Brill, plus The Sportsmen, Liberace, Red Buttons (right), Jerry Murad's Harmonicats, Inesita and Grace Romanos. To avoid lawsuits this time around, most of the material was actually shot for the picture by director Hal Yates, though it did include a song and dance routine from *Radio City Revels* featuring Buster West and Melissa Mason and a segment from the short *Carle Comes Calling* with Frankie Carle and his Orchestra. Master of ceremonies Jack Paar (left) also participated in several of the skits, while Felix Adler and director Yates authored the screenplay of the Leon Errol comedy.

△

When Tim Holt (right) and Richard Martin sign on with Cliff Clark as cowpunchers in **Saddle Legion**, they soon smell something odoriferous in their midst. The rotten egg turns out to be Robert Livingston, a counterfeit cattle inspector who condemns Clark's herd on the grounds that it is infected with blackleg disease. The rest of Livingston's gang plans to drive the cattle over the border into Mexico after pretending to kill them, but Tim and his pardner, with the assistance of woman doctor Dorothy Malone (left), toss a monkey wrench into their scheme. The usual team of Herman Schlom (producer), Lesley Selander (director) and Ed Earl Repp (screenplay) turned out this respectable oater. Also cast: Mauritz Hugo, James Bush, Movita Castaneda, Stanley Andrews, George Lewis, Dick Foote and Bob Wilke.

▷

Kon-Tiki was the name of the jaunty, diminutive raft (see illustration) that ferried six non-seafaring scientists more than 4000 nautical miles across the Pacific. The trip was organized by Thor Heyerdahl to test his theory that the Polynesian Islands were populated by natives from South America who – some 1500 years earlier – made similar journeys across the ocean on rafts built by lashing together logs cut from balsa trees. Heyerdahl took 16mm camera equipment along and shot a pictorial diary of the adventure. Though the film was crude by Hollywood standards, there was nothing phony about the drama that it captured. Through fair weather and foul, encountering good fortune and bad, escorted by friendly sea creatures (dolphins) and more threatening denizens (sharks and killer whales), the little craft and its resourceful passengers come to symbolize man's striving, questing spirit. Heyerdahl, Knut Haugland, Erik Hesselberg, Torstein Raaby, Herman Watzinger (all Norwegian) and Bengt Danielsson (a Swede) were the members of the expedition, and Olle Nordemar produced for Artfilm, A.B., a Swedish company. Heyerdahl, who had written a bestselling book about the voyage, also narrated, with Ben Grauer providing a short introduction. Sol Lesser purchased American rights to the film, then turned it over to RKO for distribution.

▽

My Forbidden Past was a typical Howard Hughes-era production with more sound and fury going on behind the scenes than in front of the cameras. The original deal called for Polan Banks and RKO to co-produce a film based on his novel *Carriage Entrance*, with Ann Sheridan in the lead. But Hughes decided that Miss Sheridan was not to his liking and stalled the picture until Banks finally filed suit. The upshot was that RKO took over (though Banks remained on the project as co-producer with Robert Sparks), and the story was finally made starring Ava Gardner (borrowed from MGM). Ann Sheridan, who was less than pleased by the turn of events, also sued, winning a settlement from RKO and employment in a later picture (*Appointment in Honduras*). Set in New Orleans in 1890, the movie was a soapy saga about a woman (Gardner, left) who unexpectedly inherits a fortune and uses the money in a cold-blooded scheme to win the affections of a married man (Robert Mitchum, right). Mitchum's wife is killed and he is accused of the crime, but Gardner clears him by revealing her own unsavoury ancestry. This, of course, earns her the rekindled love of her man. Despite lavish costumes and opulent sets, the film was quite abysmal – 71 minutes of vintage claptrap that chalked up $700,000 in losses for the studio. Leopold Atlas wrote the adaptation and Marion Parsonnet the script; Robert Stevenson directed and Sid Rogell acted as executive producer. Melvyn Douglas, Lucile Watson, Janis Carter, Gordon Oliver, Basil Ruysdael, Clarence Muse, Walter Kingsford, Jack Briggs and Will Wright were others in the cast.

▷

The trials and tribulations of a young tennis champion formed the dramatic core of **Hard, Fast And Beautiful**, produced by Collier Young and directed by Ida Lupino. Sally Forrest (centre) rockets to fame, due to the constant pressure of her greedy and ambitious mother (Claire Trevor, left) who intends to live high off her daughter's professional earnings. At the top of her game but in the depths of depression, Forrest rebels and quits to marry Robert Clarke. Martha Wilkerson's screenplay, based on a novel by John R. Tunis, was hardly the final word on maternal or sporting matters, being trite and predictable from first serve to last. Trevor was fine as the grasping mother, but naive Miss Forrest and the rest of the cast would have been better occupied elsewhere. In support were Carleton Young (right), Kenneth Patterson, Joseph Kearns, William Hudson, George Fisher, Arthur Little Jr, Bert Whitley, William Irving and Barbara Brier. The film was a co-production between RKO and The Filmakers.

'See Human Heads Shrunk To The Size Of Baseballs!' boomed the appetizing come-on for **Jungle Headhunters**. Filmed during an Amazonian expedition led by Lewis Cotlow (left), it documented such interesting tribes as the nearly extinct Colorados who paint themselves red believing this will make them live longer, the Vaguas whose fibre skirts caused early explorers to think them women and call them Amazons, and the headhunting Jivaros whose habitat is deep in the jungle adjacent to the Andes Mountains. The picture was hardly a purist's idea of documentary; punctuated with obviously staged sequences, it even included a wholly dramatized incident in which the drunken Jivaros descend on an enemy, lop off his head, shrink it and then dance the *tsantsa* around their war trophy. The escapade was about as convincing as one of Tarzan's more fantastic forays. Joseph Ansen and Larry Lansburgh received writing credits and Lansburgh was also listed as supervisor. RKO distributed the Thalia Productions release. Julian Lesser produced, and the prints were made by Technicolor.

Filmed entirely in Japan, **Tokyo File 212** contained a grimly determined US undercover agent, a seductive woman without a country, a Communist-inspired spy plot to sabotage the American war effort in Korea, plus geisha girls, kamakazi pilot rituals, underworld dens and a steamer trunk full of other exploitation clichés. Robert Peyton (right, formerly under contract to RKO as Lee Frederick) played the Army G-2 operative dispatched to ferret out the Red trouble-makers and Florence Marly (left) the footloose and dangerous Mata Hari who eventually sees the light regarding Communism, throwing herself out of a window to foil an assassination attempt. Herman Schopp's photography of Japanese backgrounds, including street scenes, cabaret life and a theatre performance, brought this potboiler as close to salvation as it ever came. Dorrell and Stuart McGowan directed and wrote the screenplay from a story by George Breakston. Katsuhaiko Haida, Reiko Otani, Tatsuo Saito, Satoshi Nakamura, Heihachiro Okawa, Suisei Matsui, Jun Tazaki, Dekao Yokoo, Hideto Hayabusa, Gen Shimizu, Major Richard W. N. Childs, Lieutenant Richard Finiels, Corporal Stuart Zimmerley, Private James Lyons and Byron Michie also appeared for executive producer Melvin Belli, co-producers George Breakston and Dorrell McGowan and associate producer C. Ray Stahl. RKO distributed the independent feature for Breakston-McGowan Productions. Song: 'Oyedo Boogie' Yasuo Shimizu, Shizuo Yoshikawa.

Roadblock was a febrile, unyielding *film noir* about a trusted insurance investigator (Charles McGraw, left) who plots a million dollar mail robbery in order to win the love of Joan Dixon (right), a lady with mink and caviar tastes. When it is too late for McGraw to pull out of the gambit, Miss Dixon marries him, but their happiness is short-lived. Making their getaway in a car, they find themselves checkmated at every turn until McGraw is finally gunned down by the cops in one of Los Angeles' famous concrete river beds. Director Harold Daniels, with the assistance of Nicholas Musuraca's admirable camerawork, created the feeling of a malignant world contracting to strangle the protagonist. Steve Fisher and George Bricker collaborated on the taut screenplay, using a story by Richard Landau and Geoffrey Homes as their launching pad. Producer Lewis J. Rachmil completed his cast with Lowell Gilmore, Louis Jean Heydt, Milburn Stone and Joseph Crehan. Song: 'So Swell Of You' Leona Davidson.

William Cameron Menzies designed and directed **Drums In The Deep South**, a vivid Civil War drama starring James Craig, Barbara Payton and Guy Madison. Hollister Noble's story, and the screenplay by Philip Yordan and Sidney Harmon, concerned the efforts of 20 rebel soldiers to delay General Sherman's march on Atlanta, Georgia. James Craig headed the unit, blasting Union supply trains from atop a mountain precipice and resisting the enemy's efforts to annihilate his natural fortress. Woven into the plot was a romance between Craig (left) and Payton (right) – who is married to another Confederate officer (Craig Stevens) – and the psychological ambivalence of Madison, the Northern officer who must dynamite the mountain even though Craig is his former West Point roommate. Menzies took the formula narrative elements and made them surprisingly cogent and vigorous. The major actors played off one another very well, and Barton MacLane, Tom Fadden, Robert Osterloh, Taylor Holmes, Robert Easton, Lewis Martin, Peter Brocco, Dan White and Louis Jean Heydt provided excellent support. Maurice and Frank King produced in Supercinecolor for their independent King Bros Productions, with RKO acting as distributor.

Another big-time western roundup, **Best Of The Badmen** featured Robert Ryan (left) as a Union officer who persuades a group of outlaws – formerly members of Quantrell's Confederate raiders – to surrender, take the oath of allegiance and get a fresh start on life. Unscrupulous detective Robert Preston has other ideas: he wants to collect the rewards offered for the capture of the bandits and, when Ryan interferes with his plans, has him framed on a murder charge and sentenced to death. Ryan escapes with the help of Preston's angry and disillusioned wife (Claire Trevor, right) and joins the outlaw band to strike back at his nemesis. Robert Hardy Andrews and John Twist's screenplay, based on a story by Andrews, featured snappy dialogue and gutsy characters and was energetically directed by William D. Russell. The register of sagebrush tough guys included Jack Buetel as Bob Younger, Walter Brennan as 'Doc' Butcher, Bruce Cabot as Cole Younger, John Archer as Curley Ringo, Lawrence Tierney as Jesse James, Tom Tyler as Frank James, Bob Wilke as Jim Younger and John Cliff as John Younger. Barton MacLane, Lee MacGregor, Emmett Lynn and Carleton Young also appeared for executive producer Samuel Bischoff and producer Herman Schlom. The Technicolor production wasn't exactly a classic western, but it was a bracing brew for lovers of America's mythic past.

N. P. Rathvon and Company, an independent production outfit set up by the former RKO president, co-produced **Happy Go Lovely** in England with Associated British Picture Corporation. A featherweight care-lifter, the Technicolor picture began to roll when dancer Vera-Ellen is seen arriving at the theatre in a car belonging to a Scottish millionaire. In truth, she simply thumbed a lift in the limo, but her arrival in state precipitates a flood of rumours regarding her relationship to the wealthy Scot. This leads inevitably to her becoming the star of the show and romancing David Niven who she thinks is a newspaper man but who, naturally, turns out to be the millionaire. Val Guest's screenplay, based on a story by F. Dammann and Dr H. Rosenfeld, played five times better than it sounds, thanks to Bruce Humberstone's light-fingered direction and the thespian efforts of Vera-Ellen (left) and David Niven (right). Cesar Romero, Bobby Howes, Diane Hart, Gordon Jackson, Barbara Couper, Henry Hewitt, Gladys Henson, Hugh Dempster, Sandra Dorne, Joyce Carey, John Laurie, Wylie Watson, Joan Heal, Hector Ross, Ambrosine Philpots and Molly Urquhart added strong support in the Marcel Hellman production. Songs included: 'One-Two-Three' Mischa Spoliansky; 'Would You-Could You?' Spoliansky, Jack Fishman. RKO distributed for Rathvon's Motion Picture Capital Corporation.

The first co-production between RKO and Wald-Krasna Productions, **Behave Yourself**! concerned a pair of newlyweds and their troubles with an unending herd of gangsters. The turmoil is brought about by a dog who has been trained by one underworld gang to act as a go-between with another. The hound gets away from his trainer and follows Farley Granger (left, on loan from Samuel Goldwyn) home. Granger's wife Shelley Winters (right) thinks the animal is a present, but the members of both hordes try frantically to retrieve the canine in order to go through with a million dollar smuggling scheme. Played strictly for laughs by writer-director George Beck, the film fell short of top-flight farce, but it was light, fast and foolish and didn't wear out its welcome. The director had the good sense to use an excellent group of character actors in supporting roles; they included William Demarest, Francis L. Sullivan, Margalo Gillmore, Lon Chaney Jr, Hans Conried, Elisha Cook Jr, Glenn Anders, Allen Jenkins, Sheldon Leonard, Marvin Kaplan and Archie the Dog. Beck collaborated with Frank Tarloff on the original story, Jerry Wald and Norman Krasna produced and Stanley Rubin was the associate producer. Lew Spence and Buddy Ebsen contributed a title song.

Costing approximately $5 million and requiring five years to complete, Walt Disney's **Alice In Wonderland** was both a critical and financial disappointment. Commentators felt that the film took too many liberties with Lewis Carroll's original story, undercutting the author's satirical intentions with 'enchanting' musical numbers and characters who were too 'picturesque'. Audiences found it a traffic jam of uneven episodes and did not support the picture with the enthusiasm to which Walt was accustomed. Most of the classic creations from Carroll's tale were on hand: Alice, the White Rabbit, the Caterpillar (spoken by Richard Haydn), the Mad Hatter, (spoken by Ed Wynn), the March Hare (Jerry Colonna), the Queen of Hearts (Verna Felton), etc. Alice herself was spoken by Kathryn Beaumont. But the only one that stood out was the Cheshire Cat, a brilliantly conceived surrealistic smiler with the distinctive voice of Sterling Holloway. Alice's journey down the rabbit hole contained some flashy sections, yet the animated film seemed somewhat fragmentary and didn't really add up to much (Mad Hatter's Tea Party illustrated). The Technicolor production was put together by production supervisor Ben Sharpsteen with directors Clyde Geronimi, Hamilton Luske and Wilfred Jackson; a regiment of story writers including Winston Hibler, Bill Peet, Joe Rinaldi, Bill Cottrell, Joe Grant, Del Connell, Ted Sears, Erdman Penner, Milt Banta, Dick Kelsey, Dick Huemer, Tom Oreb and John Walbridge; and a veritable army of directing animators, including Milt Kahl, Ward Kimball, Frank Thomas, Eric Larson, John Lounsbery, Ollie Johnston, Wolfgang Reitherman, Marc Davis, Les Clark and Norm Ferguson. Songs included: 'The Unbirthday Song' Mack David, Al Hoffman & Jerry Livingston; ''Twas Brillig' Don Raye, Gene De Paul; 'I'm Late', 'All In The Golden Afternoon', 'Very Good Advice', 'In A World Of My Own' Sammy Fain, Bob Hilliard.

Carefully prepared to be made on a $93,000 budget, **Pistol Harvest** presented Tim Holt (right) and Richard Martin as two cowboys whose elderly employer is killed by a robber. Suspicion falls on two other men, but Tim tracks down the real culprit after indulging in some tentative romantic interludes with the foster daughter of the dead man. Joan Dixon (centre) played the girl, and Robert Clarke, Mauritz Hugo, Robert Wilke, William Griffith, Guy Edward Hearn (left), Harper Carter, Joan Freeman and Herrick Herrick took supporting roles in Norman Houston's screenplay. The director was Lesley Selander and the producer Herman Schlom.

The running gag in **Flying Leathernecks** involved Jay C. Flippen as an army sergeant who steals anything and everything from other companies to make sure his own outfit is well supplied. The character must have been close to the hearts of story author Kenneth Gamet and screenwriter James Edward Grant who plundered scores of old war films to flesh out their saga with every cliché and stereotype in the military manual. Centring on the exploits of a fighter squadron during the World War II struggle for Guadalcanal, the Technicolor picture bogged down into a long and tedious argument between John Wayne (left) and Robert Ryan (right) on the subject of leadership. Commander Wayne is a rugged, no-nonsense martinet, while executive officer Ryan favours a less rigid, more open relationship with the troops. After the required amount of aerial action involving an American squadron of typically Hollywood ethnic balance, plus a plane load full of sentimental moments, Ryan perceives the wisdom in Wayne's approach and is ready for his own command. John Wayne's star power helped the film to break even despite its manifest deficiencies. Howard Hughes took his first RKO screen credit ('Howard Hughes Presents'), and Edmund Grainger, who had worked with Wayne on *Wake Of The Red Witch* and *Sands Of Iwo Jima*, served as producer. Director Nicholas Ray also cast Don Taylor, Janis Carter, William Harrigan, James Bell, Barry Kelley, James Dobson, Carleton Young, Steve Flagg and Gordon Gebert to fill out the cast.

Louella Parsons called Robert Mitchum (left) and Jane Russell (centre): 'The hottest combination that ever hit the screen!' Though one might quibble with her hyperbole, there was no denying the chemistry between the two in **His Kind Of Woman**. The Robert Sparks production offered Mitchum as a gambler who blindly accepts an offer of $50,000 to go to a Mexican resort for reasons to be explained later. There he finds sultry singer Russell, who claims to have a million dollars, but is really on the make for Hollywood star Vincent Price. Just about the time Mitchum and his co-star begin their fiery romance, he discovers that he is the fall guy in a plot to bring about the re-entry of a Lucky Luciano-type mobster into the US. A plastic surgeon will furnish the deported criminal (Raymond Burr) with Mitchum's face, whereupon Mitchum will be rubbed out and Burr will assume his identity. Government agent Tim Holt tips the hero off in time, and he fights his way out of the jam with the help of both Russell and Price. John Farrow directed this above-average melo from a screenplay by Frank Fenton and Jack Leonard. Also cast were Charles McGraw, Marjorie Reynolds, Leslye Banning, Jim Backus, Philip Van Zandt (right), John Mylong and Carleton Young. Songs: 'Five Little Miles From San Berdoo' Sam Coslow; 'You'll Know' Jimmy McHugh, Harold Adamson. ▷

△
Gunplay was the misleading title of a 60-minute programme western that contained only a smidgen of action. Scriptwriter Ed Earl Repp's plot hinged on a mysterious murder which makes an orphan of 11-year-old Harper Carter (centre left) and the subsequent efforts of Tim Holt (centre right) and Richard Martin (right) to find the killer and restore the youngster's inheritance. The two cowpokes flush out the black hat, and the boy gets what is rightfully his. One of the most listless, anaemic chapters of the entire Holt series, the Herman Schlom production generated only $145,000 in total film rentals. Lesley Selander was the director, and Joan Dixon (left), Mauritz Hugo, Robert Bice, Marshall Reed, Jack Hill, Robert Wilke and Leo McMahon were others in the cast.

Lilli Marlene was the story of a song that went around the world and of the woman who supposedly inspired it. Lisa Daniely (left) played the fictionalized heroine, a French girl working as a combination entertainer and waitress in North Africa during World War II. The lilting melody she sings appeals to a German propaganda officer who attempts to force her to make broadcasts for the Nazis. But American broadcaster Hugh McDermott (right) falls in love with the girl and whisks her off to Cairo to advertise for the Allies. Daniely's happiness, however, is short-lived: the Germans kidnap her and take her to Berlin where torture induces her to sing the praises of Hitler. It all ends happily when, after the war, she goes to London, is cleared of collaboration charges and falls safely back into the welcoming arms of Mr McDermott. Leslie Wood wrote the screenplay, Arthur Crabtree directed and William J. Gell served as executive producer. Their efforts were shockingly unsuccessful – amateurish and entirely lacking in entertainment value. Some of those included in the very large cast were Richard Murdoch, Leslie Dwyer, Estelle Brody, Stanley Baker, John Blythe, Cecil Brock, Kenneth Cleveland, Rufus Cruickshank, Barbara Cummings, Walter Gotell, Philo Hauser, Russell Hunter, Carl Jaffe, Arthur Lawrence, Stuart Lindsell, Richard Marney and Olaf Olsen. Monarch Film Corporation produced the picture at the Gate Studios, Elstree, England with RKO functioning as US distributor. The title song was written by Hans Leip, Norbert Schutze and ◁ Tommie Connor.

On The Loose confronted the problem of 'delinquent parents' rather than 'delinquent youth'. Melvyn Douglas (left) and Lynn Bari portrayed the irresponsible and thoughtless father and mother whose neglect causes Joan Evans (right, borrowed from Samuel Goldwyn) to become the local 'bad girl', misunderstood by her boyfriend and ostracized by her female peers. Her attempted suicide finally shocks Douglas and Bari into a realization of their own failings. The script by husband-and-wife team Dale Eunson and Katherine Albert (Joan Evans' real-life parents), based on a story by Collier Young and Malvin Wald, made for a schizoid mixture of sincere social statement and exploitative treatment that never managed to jell. Writer Charles Lederer, debuting as a director, didn't show any special aptitude for his new job. Also cast: Robert Arthur, Hugh O'Brian, Constance Hilton, Michael Kuhn, Susan Marrow, Lilian Hamilton, Elizabeth Flournoy, John Morgan, Lawrence Dobkin and Tristram Coffin. Collier Young produced for The Filmakers, which co-sponsored it with RKO.

Slaughter Trail had all the standard western equipment: badmen and law-and-order heroes, a stagecoach hold-up, a mail robbery, a rescue of a fair lady in distress, a tenderfoot from back East, a square dance and, oh yes, Indians on the warpath. One decidedly novel aspect, however, was a commentary delivered by toothy baritone Terry Gilkyson, via folk songs injected into the action to provide a musical narration. Gilkyson's continual interruptions induced many members of the audience to join the Indians in their fury; whoever thought up this 'unique' narrative device should have been summarily burned at the stake. Brian Donlevy (foreground, centre right) was top cast as Captain Dempster, a cavalry officer pitted against Gig Young (foreground, centre left), a frontier bandit whose wanton slaying of two Navajos arouses the entire tribe. Virginia Grey (foreground, right) portrayed the delicate damsel who happens to be in league with the crook, and Andy Devine, Robert Hutton, Lew Bedell, Myron Healey, Eddie Parks, Ralph Peters, Rick Roman and Lois Hall also put in appearances. Sid Kuller wrote the screenplay for producer-director Irving Allen. Songs included: 'Hoofbeat Serenade', 'Ballad Of Bandelier' Lyn Murray, Sid Kuller; 'The Girl In The Wood' Terry Gilkyson, Neal Stuart; 'Everyone's Crazy 'Ceptin' Me' Gilkyson, Kuller; 'Jittery Deer-Foot Dan' Gilkyson. Note: The completed Cinecolor picture, which RKO purchased from Justal Productions, included Howard Da Silva in the role of Captain Dempster. But since Da Silva was allegedly infected with the Communist malady, Howard Hughes insisted that all the scenes in which he appeared be re-shot. They were – with Donlevy.

Made in strict secrecy, **The Whip Hand** (originally titled *The Man He Found*) was supposed to be about the discovery of Adolf Hitler, alive and knowingly sheltered by the inhabitants of a small New England village. After the film was finished, Howard Hughes decided he didn't like the 'Hitler angle' and ordered most of it to be re-shot. The release version focused on villains much closer to the Hughes purview – the Communists, who have taken over a fortress-like lodge where they conduct germ-warfare experiments, and plot the destruction of the US populace through biological means. Elliott Reid (centre left) played a magazine writer whose snooping uncovers the germy Reds and brings the FBI a-calling for a shoot-'em-up finale. Mr Hughes' Communist obsession was evidently not shared by the average movie consumer, for the $376,000 production finished its run a $225,000 box-office loser. William Cameron Menzies designed and directed the Lewis J. Rachmil production from a story by Roy Hamilton and screenplay by George Bricker and Frank L. Moss. Carla Balenda (centre right), Otto Waldis, Michael Steele, Lurene Tuttle, Peter Brocco, Lewis Martin, Frank Darien, Olive Carey, Edgar Barrier (left) and Raymond Burr (right) were among those present.

The Blue Veil, a sopping-wet 'woman's' picture, sopped up a far from wet $3,550,000 in film rentals and $450,000 in profits for RKO. Covering a period of 30 years, Norman Corwin's screenplay (story François Campaux) presented Jane Wyman (borrowed from Warner Bros.) as a woman who loses her husband and baby in World War I and spends the rest of her life caring for other people's offspring. The lady with the blue veil (a traditional symbol of governesses) is finally left with nothing to show for her years of selfless devotion, but Corwin, producers Jerry Wald and Norman Krasna and director Curtis Bernhardt conspired to have her rescued from poverty and decrepitude by her now-mature charges. This denouement caused a veritable flood to burst loose from the tear ducts of viewers hypnotized by such artificial and sentimental diversions. In all fairness, it must be said that Miss Wyman brought conviction and great dignity to her role, and received sterling support from a cast that included Charles Laughton, Joan Blondell, Richard Carlson, Agnes Moorehead, Don Taylor, Audrey Totter, Cyril Cusack, Everett Sloane, Natalie Wood, Warner Anderson, Alan Napier, Henry Morgan, Vivian Vance, Les Tremayne, John Ridgely, Dan O'Herlihy, Carleton Young and Dan Seymour. A remake of the French film *Le Voile Bleu*, the picture was the second co-production between Wald-Krasna and the studio. Raymond Hakim was the associate producer.

◁ **Jungle Of Chang**, an unexceptional docudrama about life in Siam, was originally released in Sweden in 1940 under the title *Handful Of Rice*. But RKO needed product and picked it up for distribution from Films International of America and Thalia Productions. The story opened with the wedding of Po Chai and Me Ying, two impoverished youngsters who must build their own home and cultivate their own rice field by clearing a space in the jungle. After a series of backbreaking calamities, Po Chai gains employment as a 'mahout', an elephant driver in the teak forest (see illustration) earning enough money to begin work on the rice farm all over again. Though the Svensk Filmindustri Production did offer a few insights into South-east Asian culture, its awkward acting and sluggish pace caused spectators to edge away before the 68-minute film had run its course. Paul Fejos and Gunnar Skoglund co-directed, and Leonard Bucknall Eyre spoke the commentary. Note: Chang was the name of the renegade elephant that Po Chai succeeds in taming and riding.

△

Two Tickets To Broadway was a throwback to the old musicals about a cluster of young talents, hypnotized by the smell of grease paint and determined to make it their lives. Only the final objective was different – these troupers end up breaking into the world of television, rather than the theatre or the movies. Despite skilful dance direction by Busby Berkeley and energetic performances by most of the cast members, the only novel aspect of the film was the video angle; audiences gave it a collective yawn and it ended its runs $1,150,000 in the red. Janet Leigh (illustrated standing) and Ann Miller (foreground – both on loan from MGM), Tony Martin, Gloria De Haven (left centre) and Barbara Lawrence (left) played the budding show folk, with Eddie Bracken as a tricky booking agent whose manoeuvres to keep them as clients generate most of the complications in the Sid Silvers-Hal Kanter screenplay (story by songsmith Sammy Cahn). Director James V. Kern also featured Bob Crosby, comedy duo Smith and Dale, Taylor Holmes, Buddy Baer and The Charlivels to play other featured parts. The Technicolor musical carried no producer credit, though Jerry Wald and Norman Krasna actually supervised it for Howard Hughes. Songs included: 'Manhattan' Richard Rodgers, Lorenz Hart; 'There's No Tomorrow' Al Hoffman, Leo Corday, Leon Carr; 'Let's Make Comparisons' Sammy Cahn, Bob Crosby; 'The Closer You Are', 'Let The Worry Bird Worry For You', 'Are You A Beautiful Dream?', 'It Began In Yucatan', 'Baby, You'll Never Be Sorry' Jule Styne, Leo Robin.

Tim Holt galloped into action against train robbers in **Hot Lead**, an energetic oater that partially atoned for the wretched *Gunplay*. Holt (right) and his pal Richard Martin (left) swear revenge when one of their friends is killed during a train hold-up. They eventually trap the bandits with the help of telegrapher Ross Elliott, who joins the villains and then tips off the time and location of the next robbery. William Lively's screenplay lived up to his name; it was directed by Stuart Gilmore and produced by Herman Schlom. Also cast: Joan Dixon, John Dehner, Paul Marion, Lee MacGregor, Stanley Andrews, Paul E. Burns, Kenneth MacDonald and Robert Wilke.

▽

Completed three years before its release, **Double Dynamite** was another testament to the obsessions and vicissitudes of Howard Hughes. During the prolonged post-production period, Hughes dispensed with the original title (*It's Only Money*) and mounted an advertising campaign which left little doubt as to the meaning of the new heading. It showed Jane Russell, attired in a low-cut dress, with Groucho Marx leering over her shoulder and reacting in pop-eyed amazement at what he spies. Hughes also demoted Frank Sinatra from first to third billing in the intervening years, simply because he didn't like him. Writers Leo Rosten (story), Melville Shavelson (screenplay) and Harry Crane (additional dialogue) built their plot around a sober young bank clerk (Sinatra, centre), his impatient fiancée (Russell, right), and a carefree waiter (Marx, left), who pretends to be an expert on crime and the joys of living dangerously. An unexpected meeting between Sinatra and bookie Nestor Paiva results in the former winning a fortune, but he is unable to convince his sweetheart or the waiter that he didn't steal the money from the bank after it is learned that a $75,000 shortage has been found on the books. Publicized as 'Double Delicious', 'Double Delightful' and 'Double Delirious', the film might be more accurately described as double dumb and double dull. If Groucho had not been on hand, firing off some premium one-liners that provoked the only laughs in the show, it would have been a thoroughgoing mess. Irving Cummings directed and Irving Cummings Jr produced, with a supporting cast composed of Don McGuire, Howard Freeman, Frank Orth, Harry Hayden, William Edmunds and Russ Thorson. Songs included: 'It's Only Money', 'Kisses And Tears' Sammy Cahn, Jule Styne.

▽

Carroll Young's story and Adele Buffington's screenplay for **Overland Telegraph** concerned a plot to delay the completion of a trans-continental telegraph line. Cowhands Tim Holt (left) and Richard Martin (right) become detectives, following the clues to a storekeeper who sells supplies to frontier army posts and stands to lose his customers once the telegraph lines are finished. The heroes short-circuit the troublemakers with a minimum of effort, keeping the nation's galvanic lifeline intact. Another routine and nondescript 'B', the Lesley Selander-directed, Herman Schlom-produced effort also utilized the talents of Gail Davis, Hugh Beaumont, Mari Blanchard (centre), George Nader, Robert Wilke, Cliff Clark, Russell Hicks, Robert Bray and Fred Graham.

△

Having produced the definitive film on the re-adjustment problems of returning servicemen (*The Best Years Of Our Lives*), Samuel Goldwyn turned his attention to the ordeals of people facing war in **I Want You**. The time was 1950, the place a small Eastern town and the war – an event that alters the lives of Dana Andrews, Dorothy McGuire, Farley Granger, Peggy Dow, Robert Keith, Mildred Dunnock, Martin Milner and Walter Baldwin – Korea. For Andrews (left), a family man and World War II veteran, the struggle is with his conscience over the idea of re-enlistment, a notion that his wife Dorothy McGuire (right) finds disconcerting; for Granger, the prospects of the draft and its disruption of his romance with Miss Dow bring a considerable amount of angry and immature behaviour; for Mildred Dunnock, who has already lost one son in action, the possibility of losing another (Granger) causes her to attack her husband (Robert Keith) for his sham heroics and glorying in warfare; and for Milner, the problem is his frightened and possessive father (Baldwin) who cannot understand why his only son is not considered 'indispensable'. Though the contrivances of screenwriter Irwin Shaw (working from stories by Edward Newhouse published in *The New Yorker*) peeked through the plot on occasion, the film captured the hard crust of reality throughout. Mark Robson's direction illuminated all the conflicting emotional drives and provoked uniformly fine acting from a cast that also included Ray Collins, Jim Backus, Marjorie Crossland, Walter Sande, Peggy Maley, Jerrilyn Flannery and Erik Neilsen. In sum, this was a moving evocation of the impact of the famous finger-pointing Uncle Sam recruitment poster.

1952

1952

Without question, 1952 was the most tempestuous year in the history of an altogether tempestuous enterprise. The first half was marked by a series of well-publicized legal disputes. The first of these involved Paul Jarrico, a screenwriter caught up in the McCarthy witchhunt, who sued RKO for refusing to give him a writing credit on **The Las Vegas Story**. Howard Hughes turned the case into full-scale war against Jarrico in particular, and against anyone who challenged Hughes' authority to do anything in general. Chief among his antagonists was the Screen Writers Guild, an organization that attempted to force the RKO mogul into arbitration over the Jarrico credit. Other heated lawsuits involved a contract dispute between Jean Simmons and Hughes, and Miss Simmons' attorney, Martin Gang, who filed his own damage suit against Hughes, RKO, and a publicity firm, charging that they had acted to libel and slander him during the Simmons court action.

Perhaps tiring of their multiple headaches, Howard Hughes and corporate president Ned E. Depinet sold their RKO stock to a Chicago-based syndicate in September. The group consisted of Ralph Stolkin, Abraham Koolish (Stolkin's father-in-law), Ray Ryan, Edward G. Burke and Sherrill Corwin. The purchase price for Hughes' holdings was $7.35 million and included a down payment of $1.25 million. The new owners took control of the studio on 2 October, with Stolkin elected president and Arnold Grant named chairman of the board.

Two weeks later *The Wall Street Journal* began a series of articles probing the unsavoury backgrounds of three members of the syndicate. The stories exposed Koolish and Stolkin's mail-order shenanigans, Koolish's gambling schemes and Ryan's association with notorious racketeer Frank Costello. Hit by a blizzard of adverse publicity, the new executives backed away from RKO. Stolkin resigned as president and Koolish and William Gorman (Ryan's representative) vacated their positions on the board. Grant tried to reorganize the studio and get it rolling again, but he was forced to quit in November. A minority stockholders' suit filed at the same time asked that a temporary receiver be appointed. By year's end, the corporation was in complete limbo; no one had been found to purchase RKO from its disgraced owners and only one feature (**Split Second**) had gone before the cameras in the preceding five months. Jerry Wald and Norman Krasna gained cancellation of their contracts and slipped away from the company forever.

RKO's net loss for the year was $10,178,033. Financial data relating to individual pictures disappears mysteriously in 1952, though it is safe to say that very few of the 32 releases were profit-makers. Once again, fewer than half of them were full-fledged RKO productions.

On Dangerous Ground was the story of a thug cop – a man so dehumanized by his experience with the 'garbage' of the world that he takes pleasure in bashing suspects until they tell him what he wants to hear. Sent into the country on a case involving the murder of a schoolgirl, the man is slowly regenerated by his relationship with two people: the dead girl's father whose thirst for revenge provides a mirror image of the policeman's own brutality, and the neurotic killer's blind sister, a sensitive, perceptive woman who understands the cop's loneliness. The film's awkward, two-part structure, and its emphasis on mood and character rather than plot and action, failed to capture the fancy of audiences (box-office loss $425,000). Those who gave it a chance discovered an honest, probing and worthwhile experience, as gripping as it was intelligent and as emotionally involving as it was realistic. Robert Ryan (right) played the cop with his usual excellence, Ida Lupino (left) was the blind girl who 'sees' more than any of the other characters, and Ward Bond portrayed the bloodthirsty father who dreams of emptying his shotgun into the slayer of his daughter. Behind the camera were producer John Houseman, executive producer Sid Rogell and, most importantly, director Nicholas Ray. Bernard Herrmann composed the beautiful musical score and A. I. Bezzerides wrote the screenplay, based on an adaptation by himself and director Ray of Gerald Butler's novel *Mad With Much Heart*. Also cast: Sumner Williams (the killer), Charles Kemper, Anthony Ross, Ed Begley, Ian Wolfe, Gus Schilling, Frank Ferguson, Cleo Moore, Olive Carey, Richard Irving and Pat Prest.

One would think that producer Edmund Grainger and director Tay Garnett, given $2,181,000 to make **One Minute To Zero**, could have come up with at least one or two fresh angles on the war film *genre*. Alas, their picture was a cornucopia of nonsensical manoeuvres, stiff-upper-lip clichés and miniaturized effects, made to seem all the more artificial by the inclusion of real Korean War battle footage. Robert Mitchum (right) played a case-hardened colonel who must cope with the sneaky North Koreans on the one hand and stubborn United Nations official Ann Blyth (left) on the other. With the assistance of sergeant Charles McGraw and jet pilot William Talman, Mitchum toughs it out, whipping the Commies and winning the love of the toothsome Miss Blyth before the end credits mercifully arrive. Milton Krims and William Wister Haines typed out the shopworn script, and Margaret Sheridan, Richard Egan, Eduard Franz, Robert Osterloh and Robert Gist trooped through the other supporting parts. Song: 'Golden Moon' (also known as 'China Night') Norman Bennett & Nobuyuki Takeoka.

Audiences had chuckled when Tarzan confronted the Leopard Woman in 1946, but **Tembo** revealed there really was a tribe of hostile leopard men (so-named because of the metal claws they attach to their hands in order to kill their prey) in Africa. Archery expert Howard Hill (illustrated) took viewers along on his search for the little-known tribe. En route he had a close call with a maddened rhino, stalked lions and crocodiles with his bow, and was welcomed by the belles of the Rangubba tribe who staged a ceremonial dance for the cameras. Finally the leopard men were located and became friendly when Hill killed their foe, a giant elephant named Tembo. An appealing and instructive documentary, the film featured the authoritative voice of Westbrook Van Voorhis who narrated, and the Ansco Color photography of Arthur E. Phelps who captured some startling scenes of animals in their natural habitat. Hill produced and directed, with Bud McKinney and James Leicester as associate producers. RKO distributed for Howard Hill Productions.
▽

△

A Girl In Every Port blended gobs, nags and blondes into a lukewarm farce that contained the three or four giggles which now seemed a quota for one of RKO's feeble comedies. Acquiring twin race horses and the acquaintance of curvaceous carhop Marie Wilson (centre), seaman Groucho Marx (left) and his dim-witted mate William Bendix (right, his first film under a new multiple-picture contract with the studio) decide to make a bundle by racing one horse and selling the other. Through a series of predictable blunders, both horses are entered in the same race and finish in a dead heat for first place. But everything turns out peachey when the two Navy men are cited for distinguished service in unwittingly capturing a pair of saboteurs. Director-writer Chester Erskine's screenplay, based on Frederick Hazlitt Brennan's story *They Sell Sailors Elephants*, also gave roles to cover girl Dee Hartford, Don DeFore, Gene Lockhart, Hanley Stafford, Teddy Hart, Percy Helton and George E. Stone. The producers were Irwin Allen and Irving Cummings Jr.

Good, bad or so-so, the Tim Holt outdoor adventures continued to lose money. **Trail Guide**, one of the better segments in the series, cost only $89,000 to produce, but still ended up $20,000 in the hole. This time, the non-variation on a theme had Holt (centre) and Richard Martin (right) guiding a wagon train to its Arizona destination, and then defending the immigrants when they are robbed and evicted by land-grabbers. During the action, the heroes are charged with murder and almost lynched, but succeed in outwitting the villains and pinpointing the real killers. Linda Douglas (left, also known as Mary Jo Tarola) gave a fine performance as a ranch girl who hunts down her brother's slayers, and Frank Wilcox, Robert Sherwood, John Pickard, Kenneth MacDonald, Wendy Waldron, Patricia Wright, Tom London and John Merton had other significant roles. The usual team of producer Herman Schlom and director Lesley Selander mounted the film from William Lively's story and a screenplay by Arthur E. Orloff.
▽

Road Agent proved to be one of the most polite and civilized westerns ever made, with nary a blow struck by either Tim Holt or the heavies. Unfortunately for Holt, as well as writer Norman Houston, producer Herman Schlom and director Lesley Selander, sagebrush fans doted on bloody battle, and they felt severely short-changed by the one feeble gunfight that punctuated this oater. When Holt (left) and Richard Martin (right) are overcharged for the right to travel over a private road they become angry. Learning that ranchers in the area are being bankrupted by the exorbitant toll fees, they pose as masked bandits, rob the profiteer's safe, and return the money to the honest folk he has cheated. Rancher's daughter Noreen Nash and dance hall belle Dorothy Patrick supplied the romantic seasoning, while Mauritz Hugo played the owner of the toll road who is backed up by henchmen Bob Wilke and Tom Tyler. Also cast: Guy Edward Hearn, William Tannen, Sam Flint, Forbes Murray and Stanley Blystone.
▽

◁ Howard Hughes' refusal to give Paul Jarrico script credit on **The Las Vegas Story** because of the writer's alleged Communist sympathies led to a lengthy legal imbroglio between Jarrico and RKO, and open hostility between Hughes and the Screen Writers Guild. One can certainly understand Jarrico's outrage over Hughes' high-handed violation of his rights, but the writer was truly fortunate not to have his name affixed to this appallingly bad melodrama. Jane Russell (centre) played a cafe singer who marries Vincent Price because she thinks she has lost her true love, Victor Mature (left). Fate brings the three together in the Nevada gambling capital where they become involved in a robbery and murder plot containing about as much explosive power as a wet firecracker. In case anyone should miss the similarities to *Casablanca*, Hoagy Carmichael dropped in to play the piano, sing, and act as a sort of go-between for Russell and Mature. The three sides of the triangle one-upped each other to see who could deliver the worst performance, with Mature winning a narrow victory over Russell for top (or is it bottom?) honours. Robert Stevenson's rancid direction also had plenty to do with the final results (RKO loss $600,000). Brad Dexter, Gordon Oliver, Jay C. Flippen (right), Will Wright, Bill Welsh, Ray Montgomery, Colleen Miller and Robert Wilke were others in the cast. Final screenplay credit went to Earl Felton and Harry Essex (story by Jay Dratler), with Samuel Bischoff listed as executive producer and Robert Sparks as producer. Songs included: 'My Resistance Is Low' Hoagy Carmichael, Harold Adamson; 'I Get Along Without You Very Well', 'The Monkey Song' Carmichael.

△

Whispering Smith vs Scotland Yard (GB: **Whispering Smith Hits London**), a ghastly whodunit, suggested that stupidity is the key to successful sleuthing. American detective Smith (Richard Carlson, left) goes to England on vacation and soon becomes embroiled in a suicide case that he divines is really murder. Blundering along from one dangerous situation to the next, he finally unravels the mystery, though writers Frank H. Spearman (story), John Gilling (adaptation) and Steve Fisher (screenplay) provided the audience with a scant number of clues concerning how he figures it out. Francis Searle directed the picture in England, with an English cast that included Greta Gynt (right), Rona Anderson, Herbert Lom, Alan Wheatley, Reginald Beckwith, Dora Bryan, Daniel Wherry, Michael Ward, Danny Green and James Raglan. Julian Lesser produced in association with Exclusive Films and RKO distributed for Royal Productions Incorporated. Note: Curiously, Gilling received sole screenplay credit in England, and Fisher likewise in America.

Produced in Technicolor by Jerrold T. Brandt and directed by Lewis Allen, **At Sword's Point** (GB: **Sons Of The Musketeers**) was an enthusiastic, undemanding swashbuckler, full of flashing rapiers, reckless devilry and plenty of hard-charging on horseback. Story authors Aubrey Wisberg and Jack Pollexfen and screenwriters Walter Ferris and Joseph Hoffman took up where Alexander Dumas' *The Three Musketeers* left off: with the original defenders of the French throne too old to repeat their daring deeds, and their aging queen (Gladys Cooper) calling for help to defeat the machinations of the traitorous Duc de Lavalle (Robert Douglas), they send their offspring to save the day. Young d'Artagnan (Cornel Wilde, left), young Aramis (Dan O'Herlihy, standing centre) and young Porthos (Alan Hale Jr, right) willingly offer their services, as does the daughter of Athos (Maureen O'Hara, centre) who is just as adept with the blade as her male cohorts. Their failure to anticipate the bitter enmity of the queen's trusted lady-in-waiting (June Clayworth), who is actually a member of the enemy camp, nearly wrecks the mission, but they win through in the end, rescuing the royal prince (Peter Miles) and saving the princess (Nancy Gates) from a loveless marriage. There was not a single situation, character or idea here that had not been used (and abused) many times before, and yet the film still provided a reasonable measure of fun and diversion. Other members of the acting contingent were Blanche Yurka, Edmond Breon, George Petrie, Boyd Davis, Holmes Herbert, Lucien Littlefield, Claude Dunkin and Moroni Olsen who, as Porthos, played a role which he had first essayed in RKO's 1935 version of *The Three Musketeers*. Sid Rogell was credited as executive producer. Since he had long gone from the company, it indicated that this was another picture that had been languishing on the shelf for more than two years. During that time, Jerry Wald and Norman Krasna supervised re-takes and post-production work at the behest of Howard Hughes.

Norman Houston's screenplay for **Target** contained one interesting plot departure – a lady marshal who arrives in the troubled town of Pecos, Texas in place of her sick father. But Houston didn't give her a chance to be more than a decorative presence, dispatching Tim Holt (centre) and Richard Martin (left) to bring peace to the frontier town by rounding up a band of cut-throats who are tricking ranchers out of their lands. Linda Douglas (right) portrayed the substitute lawperson, with Walter Reed, Harry Harvey, John Hamilton, Lane Bradford, Riley Hill and Mike Ragan in support. Stuart Gilmore directed for producer Herman Schlom.

A delirious western that was half-serious and half-send-up, **Rancho Notorious** presented Marlene Dietrich (centre), glamorously attired in Don Loper gowns, as a former dance hall girl who operates a hideout for outlaws in exchange for ten percent of their take. As the theme ballad ('Legend of Chuck-a-Luck' by Ken Darby) constantly reminded the audience, Daniel Taradash's screenplay (story by Sylvia Richards) was a tale of 'hate, murder and revenge' in which Arthur Kennedy (left) trailed the man who raped and killed his sweetheart – all the way to Dietrich's ranch. There, among some of the gaudiest sets this side of *Johnny Guitar*, most of the seven deadly sins intermingle in magnified fashion. Fritz Lang directed what proved to be one of his most bizarre and unique creative efforts, with Mel Ferrer (right), Gloria Henry, William Frawley, Lisa Ferraday, John Raven, Jack Elam, George Reeves, Frank Ferguson, Francis McDonald, Dan Seymour, John Kellogg, Rodric Redwing, Stuart Randall, Roger Anderson, Charles Gonzales, Felipe Turich, Jose Dominguez, Stan Jolley and John Doucette also cast in Howard Welsch's Technicolor production. RKO was engaged to distribute for Fidelity Pictures, then gained full ownership of the film after its release. Other songs: 'Gypsy Davey', 'Get Away, Young Man' Ken Darby. Note: The killer who sets the revenge plot in motion was played by Lloyd Gough. Gough's refusal to answer questions before the House Un-American Activities Committee brought the standard Howard Hughes punishment – elimination from the screen credits.

⊲ In **Tarzan's Savage Fury** two crooks, posing as British agents, called on ape man Lex Barker (centre left) to guide them to the Wazuri country. The Wazuris have a horde of uncut diamonds which the rapscallions allege are needed by England for armament purposes, so Tarzan reluctantly agrees to help. He takes along his new Jane (Dorothy Hart, left) and a boy (Tommy Carlton) he had rescued from natives who were using him as crocodile bait. As soon as they arrive at their destination, 'agents' Patric Knowles (centre right) and Charles Korvin (right) attempt to steal the diamonds for themselves, but Tarzan puts the kibosh on their scheme. The flaccid screenplay by Cyril Hume, Hans Jacoby and Shirley White, lifeless direction of Cyril Endfield and sombre acting of the principal performers made this one of the least absorbing of the Tarzan episodes. Sol Lesser produced for his own company.

The first film to be made with English dialogue in the newly-born country of Israel, **Faithful City** was a poignant drama about children orphaned and victimized by World War II. From Hitler's Germany, from China and Morocco, and from every other place where death and destruction plunged them into lives of desperate opportunism, came the hostile, disillusioned youngsters. But the kindness and sympathetic handling by their elders eventually acts as a palliative to their emotional disturbances, and forges a path for their absorption into normal society. Producer-director Josef Leytes completed this inspiring film with a cast composed mainly of non-actors. Jamie Smith (right), Ben Josef, John Slater, Rachel Markus, Dina Peskin, Didi Ramati, Israel Hanin (left), Juda Levi and Amnon Lifshitz played the principal characters in the M. Yona Friedman presentation. There was no writing credit on this picture. RKO distributed for Moledeth Films.

A watershed in the artistic development of the cinema, **Rashomon** drew attention to the Japanese film industry by winning the Grand Prize at the 1951 Venice Film Festival and receiving a Special Award from the Hollywood Academy as the Best Foreign Film of 1951. The picture also brought international recognition to one of the world's great filmmakers, Akira Kurosawa, who directed and co-wrote the screenplay with Shinobu Hashimoto. The film's twin themes – the relativity of truth and the subjective nature of human perception – were brilliantly elucidated in a story of rape and murder told from four points of view, those of the three participants in the action and that of an onlooker. The three shape their versions of the events as favourably as possible to themselves and to the eyes of the court before whom they testify (the dead man testifies via a medium). The onlooker's version appears to be the correct one, but he, too, proves to be something less than an objective witness. Based on *In the Forest*, a novel by Ryunosuke Akutagawa who committed suicide in 1927 after declaring that he was hopelessly depressed by the moral problems of the world, the film housed a complex web of moral ambiguities and ironies that had barely been touched upon, much less dramatized, before on the screen. It would have been a stunning work in any year, from any studio, but offered by RKO among the flotsam and jetsam of its other releases, **Rashomon** seemed like a miracle. Jingo Minoru produced for Daiei Motion Pictures, from whom RKO secured American distribution rights. Toshiro Mifune (left), Machiko Kyo (right) and Masayuki Mori topped the cast, with Takashi Shimura, Minoru Chiaki, Kichijiro Ueda, Fumiko Homma and Daisuke Kato also appearing. In 1964 MGM remade the film as an American western called *The Outrage*, directed by Martin Ritt and starring Paul Newman, Claire Bloom and Laurence Harvey.

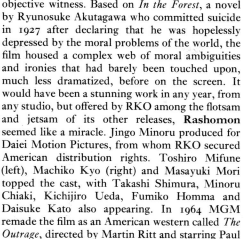

Robert Mitchum (left) and Jane Russell (right) continued their celluloid rapport in **Macao**, a hopelessly confused but visually dynamic and sexy *film noir*, directed by Josef von Sternberg. The story concerned a group of 'picturesque' characters, not one of whom is what he or she seems to be, who meet and act out a game of subterfuge in the gambling houses, hotels, streets and docks of the infamous Portuguese protectorate off the south coast of China. Attired in gowns that fitted like wallpaper, Miss Russell never looked more alluring, playing her role with the sullen indifference that was her primary thespian strength. The female members of the audience weren't short-changed either: they were given a peek at muscular Robert Mitchum without his shirt on! Other members of producer Alex Gottlieb's cast included the smouldering but under-used Gloria Grahame, William Bendix, Thomas Gomez, Brad Dexter, Edward Ashley, Philip Ahn, Vladimir Sokoloff and Don Zelaya. Bernard C. Schoenfeld and Stanley Rubin penned the screenplay from a story by Bob Williams, and Harry J. Wild shot the suggestive imagery, including one brilliant scene along the docks which used fish netting for metaphorical effect. Songs included: 'One For My Baby' Johnny Mercer, Harold Arlen; 'Ocean Breeze', 'You Kill Me' Jule Styne, Leo Robin. Note: Jerry Wald supervised and Nicholas Ray directed a series of retakes on this picture.

The Pace That Thrills purported to be an inside story of motorcycle racing, but it was bogged down by routine plot devices more worn than the grooves in the two-wheel raceway. DeVallon Scott and Robert Lee Johnson's screenplay concerned the rivalry between aggressive, dare-devil racer Bill Williams (left) and his best friend, motorcycle designer Steve Flagg, for the love of Carla Balenda, and also presented the efforts of Flagg to perfect a revolutionary motorcycle transmission. To prop up interest, director Leon Barsha and producer Lewis J. Rachmil included real-life footage of all the field events – passenger pick-up, drag-out and hill climb, as well as flat track contests. But only initiates into the cult of spill-a-second racing found anything to fancy here. Also cast: Cleo Moore (right), Robert Armstrong, Frank McHugh, Diana Garrett, John Hamilton and John Mallory (Robert Mitchum's younger brother).

Following the success and critical acclaim of Delmer Daves' *Broken Arrow* (20th Century-Fox, 1950), the Hollywood studios made a number of films dealing with the white man's inhuman treatment of the Indians in the Old West. One of those films, **The Half-Breed**, was a well-intentioned message picture that failed to connect because of its leaden, imitative screenplay (by Harold Shumate and Richard Wormser with additional dialogue by Charles Hoffman, based on a story by Robert Hardy Andrews) and the ineffectual acting of Jack Buetel (right) in the title role. Playing a half-breed Apache Indian, Buetel attempts to forge a common meeting ground for peace and understanding between the two races, but his efforts are undermined by local politician Reed Hadley who has found indications of gold on Apache land and foments trouble with the Indians in hope that the Army will drive them elsewhere. Robert Young (left) added a touch of professional finesse to the dreary enterprise as a gambler sympathetic to the Indian cause who expresses all the meaningful sentiments and thwarts the efforts of black-hearted Mr Hadley. Stuart Gilmore's direction was anaemic in spite of Technicolor, and Herman Schlom produced. Also cast: Janis Carter, Barton MacLane, Porter Hall, Connie Gilchrist, Sammy White, Damian O'Flynn, Frank Wilcox, Judy Walsh, Tom Monroe, Lee MacGregor and Charles Delaney. Songs included: 'I'm Walkin' Arm In Arm With Jim' Lew Pollack, Harry Harris; 'Remember The Girl You Left Behind' Harry Revel, Mort Greene.

The Tim Holt westerns finally fizzled out with **Desert Passage**. Having starred in 46 sagebrush sagas for RKO – many of them quite good by 'B' standards – Holt was forced to hang up his spurs by the encroachment of television, which made his type of theatrical actioner a financially unworkable anachronism. The final chapter was of only middling quality, with Norman Houston's screenplay featuring Holt (left) and Richard Martin (right) as operators of a stage coach line along the Mexican border. The two men are soon in jeopardy when former bank robber Walter Reed returns to the scene of the crime, digs up $100,000 in buried loot, and hires Holt and Martin to drive him south of the border. Not knowing the crook's identity, they protect him when the coach is attacked by former members of the robber's gang who want their share of the cash. Before long the heroes figure things out, round up the miscreants and return the money to Joan Dixon, the daughter of the bank president who was robbed. Also cast: Dorothy Patrick, John Dehner, Clayton Moore, Lane Bradford, Michael Mark and Denver Pyle. Herman Schlom produced and Lesley Selander directed; it was their final film for RKO.

A four star drama of emotional conflict, **Clash By Night** took place in a fishing village where life on the surface is simple and placid, but passions born of boredom and frustration run deep. Alfred Hayes' script, based on the stage play by Clifford Odets, centred on Barbara Stanwyck who returns to the village after ten years spent in futile attempts to find personal happiness. Tired and resigned, she marries fisherman Paul Douglas, but soon finds she cannot resist the physical appeal of shallow sophisticate Robert Ryan, who is her husband's best friend. The emotions come to a boil when Douglas discovers her infidelity. Receiving the most benefit from the picture was Marilyn Monroe (left, borrowed from 20th Century-Fox). Playing a girl as hungry for excitement as Stanwyck was when she first left her home town, Monroe showed she could act in, as well as adorn, a movie. Marilyn would soon be playing leads, but not in RKO pictures. Fritz Lang provided the penetrating direction for producer Harriet Parsons, whose cast also included J. Carrol Naish, Keith Andes (right) and Silvio Minciotti. The film was the third co-production between RKO and Wald-Krasna Productions. Song: 'I Hear A Rhapsody' George Fragas, Jack Baker & Dick Gasparre.

Following the success of *Treasure Island*, Walt Disney decided to make another live-action feature in Great Britain. The upshot was one of the finer versions of the Sherwood Forest legend, **The Story Of Robin Hood**. Unfolding with swashbuckling excitement, lavish pageantry and a generous helping of humour, the Technicolor production cast Richard Todd (right) as Robin, Joan Rice as Maid Marian, James Hayter (left) as Friar Tuck, Martita Hunt as Queen Eleanor, Peter Finch as the Sheriff of Nottingham, James Robertson Justice as Little John, Anthony Forwood as Will Scarlet, Elton Hayes as Allan-A-Dale, Hubert Gregg as Prince John and Patrick Barr as King Richard the Lionheart. Lawrence E. Watkin's screenplay and Ken Annakin's direction gave the actors *carte blanche* to create characters of full-blown mythic stature, and most were equal to the challenge. Guy Green supervised the stunning Technicolor cinematography, Perce Pearce produced, and Bill Owen, Michael Hordern, Reginald Tate, Hal Osmond, Clement McCallin, Louise Hampton and Anthony Eustrel had secondary roles. RKO distributed and co-financed the film with Walt Disney British Productions. Note: The seldom-used complete title was *The Story Of Robin Hood And His Merrie Men*.

Mel Dinelli, who had written screenplays for *The Spiral Staircase* and *The Window*, developed another tale of terror and mayhem for radio and the Broadway stage called *The Man*. It came to the screen as **Beware, My Lovely**, with Ida Lupino (right) as a widow who hires Robert Ryan (left) to clean her old-fashioned house. She is, of course, unaware that he is a mental case with a persecution complex. By the time she realizes the danger, he has made her a prisoner in her own home. Director Harry Horner kept the melodramatic air thick and threatening throughout, drawing coiled-spring performances from the two leads, and acute support from Taylor Holmes, Barbara Whiting, James Willmas, O. Z. Whitehead and Dee Pollack. Author Dinelli served as associate producer, and Collier Young produced for The Filmakers. RKO co-sponsored the film with the latter organization.

Under The Red Sea was an underwater documentary made by people with enough show business savvy to include an attractive blonde named Lottie Berl (illustrated) among the divers. If Miss Berl received a good deal more screen time than she actually deserved, at least she gave male audience members something to contemplate besides the barracuda, manta rays, giant groupers, fire fish, whale sharks and other deep-sea citizens on view. The latter were the ostensible subject of a scientific quest to discover whether fish will react to sounds, and whether they have a distinct language of their own. Gerald Weidler, Leo Rohrer, Edward Wawrowetz and Alfonso Hochhauser were the other members of the expedition, which was led by the film's producer Dr Hans Hass. Bill Park earned credits for narrative and supervision, while Les Tremayne recited the rather pompous commentary. RKO distributed for Thalia Productions, a company formed by Sol and Julian Lesser.

The Wild Heart (released in Britain under the title of Mary Webb's original novel **Gone To Earth**) featured a potent, dexterous performance by Jennifer Jones (illustrated) in a story that was not worthy of her efforts. Written, produced and directed by Michael Powell and Emeric Pressburger, this silly, old-fashioned film found Miss Jones racing about the English countryside rescuing a variety of woodsy critters from local hunters and simultaneously labouring to sort out her stormy romantic difficulties with virile squire David Farrar, and local minister Cyril Cusack to whom she happens to be married. It becomes clear early on that the heroine's fate is beyond her control, and all ends tragically when she plummets down a mine shaft while trying to save her pet fox. The plot was also evidently beyond the control of Powell and Pressburger, for they made of it a mine-field movie which blew up every ten minutes or so, due to a complete lack of credibility. Sybil Thorndike, Edward Chapman, Esmond Knight and Hugh Griffith were also in it. The film was photographed in Technicolor on locations along the Welsh border and in Hollywood; RKO distributed for independent David O. Selznick who co-financed it with Alexander Korda's London Films. Note: Selznick disliked the film as released in Britain in 1950. He employed no less than Rouben Mamoulian to direct additional footage in Hollywood, and also added an opening narration by Joseph Cotten. Even so, the American version ran only 82 minutes as against the original 110.

The Lusty Men dissected the world of the rodeo cowboy – a nomadic, dangerous, sleazy universe in which a man's greatest enemy is neither bucking broncos nor Brahma bulls, but his own ego. Robert Mitchum (centre) appeared as an ex-rodeo star who trains eager cowpoke Arthur Kennedy (left) in the fine arts of the arena. His protégé is soon hooked on the limelight, but Kennedy's wife (Susan Hayward, borrowed from 20th Century-Fox) gains no joy from her husband's triumphs; she realizes that her own longing for domestic tranquillity is imperilled by his growing thirst for glory, so she convinces Mitchum to help her pull Kennedy away from his obsession. Mitchum goes back into the arena to accomplish the goal and dies – after first proving that he really is the best of the rodeoers. The title was richly ironic, for the women are the lusty characters in the movie; the men are mostly broken and beaten, both physically and psychologically, by the rigours of life on the 'circuit'. The film was inspired by Claude Stanush's *Life* magazine story, and scripted by one-time cowboy David Dortort, and Horace McCoy, who spent several months following the rodeo tour to catch the flavour of the performers and their unique language. Nicholas Ray directed in uncompromising fashion for producer Jerry Wald and associate producer Thomas S. Gries. The movie was the final co-production between Wald-Krasna and RKO. Also cast: Arthur Hunnicutt (right), Frank Faylen, Walter Coy, Carol Nugent, Maria Hart, Burt Mustin, Karen King, Jimmy Dodd and Eleanor Todd.

Billed as 'duo-drama', **Face To Face** was an interesting experiment composed of two self-contained literary adaptations: Joseph Conrad's *The Secret Sharer* and Stephen Crane's *The Bride Comes To Yellow Sky*. The only common bond between the two stories was that, in each, a figure of authority must deal with a thorny problem. In *The Secret Sharer*, neophyte sea captain James Mason (illustrated) is torn between a longing to establish his credibility on his first voyage and a compulsion to mete out a merciful justice to a fugitive who swims to his ship. Turning away from the brooding ethical dilemmas of Conrad, the second featurette was a lighthearted meditation on the end of the Old West. Sheriff Robert Preston (left) has brought law and order to all the inhabitants of Yellow Sky except one unregenerate old-timer (Minor Watson) whose goal is to plug the sheriff because he is the only man left who Watson respects. When the confrontation comes, Watson is mortified to find his target without weapons and saddled with a new wife (Marjorie Steele, right). Realizing that civilization has beaten him to the draw, the grizzled gunfighter throws away his pistols and trudges wearily off down the dusty road. Each film was a small gem, and all the people associated with each of them deserved the highest respect. Aeneas Mackenzie wrote the screenplay for *The Secret Sharer* and John Brahm directed it, with Gene Lockhart, Michael Pate, Albert Sharpe, Sean McClory and Alec Harford in the cast. Bretaigne Windust directed *The Bride Comes To Yellow Sky*, based on James Agee's screenplay, with a cast that included Dan Seymour, Olive Carey and scripter Agee. George Tobin and Norman A. Manning were the associate producers, Huntington Hartford produced for his Theasquare Productions, and RKO was the distributor. Note: The studio later released the two films independently of one another.

Howard Hughes loaned Jane Russell to producer Howard Welsch's Fidelity Pictures in 1948 for **Montana Belle**. When the picture was finished, Hughes decided he wanted to control it, so he instructed RKO to purchase it outright from Fidelity who had intended to release it through Republic. After gathering dust for almost four years, the Trucolor picture finally emerged toward the end of 1952. Very few people would have been disappointed if the film had remained permanently under lock and key. Miss Russell (right) impersonated Belle Starr, the bandit queen saved from a lynching by the Dalton boys (Scott Brady, centre, and Ray Teal). In the movie, this touches off a hectic romance between Russell and Brady, and a series of episodes in which Belle and the Daltons double-cross one another. But Belle's true love is a gambler (George Brent) who ultimately sends her off to prison, promising to wait patiently for her release. Allan Dwan directed Horace McCoy and Norman S. Hall's trite screenplay, which was based on an original story by M. Coates Webster and producer Welsch. Forrest Tucker (left), Andy Devine, Jack Lambert, John Litel, Rory Mallinson, Roy Barcroft, Holly Bane, Ned Davenport, Dick Elliott, Eugene Roth and Stanley Andrews had the other featured roles, and Robert Peters was associate producer. Song: 'The Gilded Lily' Portia Nelson & Margaret Martinez.

Opening with a three-minute lecture on the apocalypse that lies ahead unless men curb their bellicose ways, **Captive Women** (GB: **3000 A.D.**) was a plodding, verbose and ineptly made science-fiction saga set in a bombed-out, post-atomic world. Writer-producers Aubrey Wisberg and Jack Pollexfen envisioned New York City as a rank garden of weeds where the Norms, a group living like cavemen, continue to wage war against the Mutates, the scarred and disfigured descendents of victims of centuries-old radiation. After an hour or so of unmotivated gesticulation and whopping bad dialogue, the future New Yorkers look with hope upon a marriage between a Mutate man and a Norm woman that will, presumably, produce a child of peace. Stuart Gilmore directed a cast composed of Robert Clarke (right), Gloria Saunders (centre right), Robert Bice (left), Eric Colmar (centre left), Margaret Field, Ron Randell, Stuart Randall, Paula Dorety, Chili Williams, William Schallert and Douglas Evans. Albert Zugsmith was the associate producer for his American Pictures Corporation, which co-produced the film with RKO.

A thriller set on a train, **The Narrow Margin** sizzled all the way from Chicago to Los Angeles, thanks to Earl Felton's crafty screenplay (based on a story by Martin Goldsmith and Jack Leonard) and the stimulating direction of Richard O. Fleischer. Charles McGraw played a hardened police detective trying to protect a gangster's widow who is scheduled to testify before a grand jury on the West Coast. Out to snuff her are a trio of gangsters who aren't sure which passenger is their target. The tension approaches the upper limits as the hoodlums eliminate various suspects before killing the woman whom McGraw thinks is the witness. In fact, the murder victim is an undercover police woman whose mission was to lead the thugs astray and to test McGraw's honesty. This sets up more suspense as both cop and killers discover the truth and begin their deadly conflict all over again. Marie Windsor (right), given some of the script's most pungent dialogue, was outstanding as the undercover police woman. Her performance was matched by McGraw's (left) and Jacqueline White's (the real widow), and the rest of the cast – including Gordon Gebert, Queenie Leonard, David Clarke, Peter Virgo, Don Beddoe, Paul Maxey and Harry Harvey – also attacked their roles with exceptional vigour. Produced by Stanley Rubin at a $230,000 negative cost, **The Narrow Margin** was a streamlined sleeper, one of the best in the studio's history.

RKO's 11-year relationship with Samuel Goldwyn ended after the distribution of **Hans Christian Andersen**, a captivating Technicolor children's story, scripted by Moss Hart (story by Myles Connolly) and directed by Charles Vidor. Danny Kaye (illustrated) played Andersen, a cobbler in the little town of Odense, Denmark, whose skill at spinning fantasy tales is such that he keeps many children mesmerized and out of school. To the relief of the local authorities, he goes off to Copenhagen where he mends the slippers of ballerina Jeanmaire and promptly falls in love with her. After his shy, fumbling attempts to win her heart come to naught, he returns to Odense where his fame as a writer is now well-established and where he soon regains happiness, entertaining both children and adults with his fanciful fictions. Kaye toned down his usual comic exuberance, playing Andersen in restrained and sympathetic fashion. The ballet sequences (choreographed by Roland Petit) and Frank Loesser's songs added extra dimensions to the entertainment, which also featured munificent art direction by Richard Day and Antoni Clavé, and beautiful colour photography by Harry Stradling. Farley Granger, Joey Walsh, Philip Tonge, Erik Bruhn, John Brown, John Qualen, and choreographer Petit had supporting parts. Songs included: 'No Two People', 'The King's New Clothes', 'Thumbelina', 'The Ugly Duckling', 'Wonderful Copenhagen', 'I'm Hans Christian Andersen'. ▷

A. B. Guthrie Jr's novel **The Big Sky** was a story of mountain men embarking on the first keelboat trip up the uncharted Missouri River and into the 1830 haunts of the Sioux, the Crow and the Blackfoot Indians. Dudley Nichols' episodic screenplay and Howard Hawks' direction made the cinematic journey awfully fatiguing. Kirk Douglas (centre) and Dewey Martin (right) were a pair of restless Kentuckians who join Martin's uncle (Arthur Hunnicutt, left) and an excitable Frenchman (Steven Geray) on the 63-foot, hand-operated boat. The task of hauling the heavy craft upstream, the efforts of Geray's fur-trapping rivals to incite the Indians to attack them, and the love-hate relationship between Martin and captured Blackfoot princess Elizabeth Threatt were supposed to keep viewers glued to their seats. They had just the opposite effect, mostly because of Hawks' uneven and unfocused direction, and his inability to spark better than mediocre performances from his cast. In fact, the only memorable character in the picture turned out to be Hunnicutt, a loquacious geezer whose tall tales were at least fun to listen to. Buddy Baer, Henri Letondal, Hank Worden, Jim Davis, Robert Hunter, Booth Colman, Paul Frees, Frank de Kova and Guy Wilkerson played supporting parts for producer Hawks and associate producer Edward Lasker, whose Winchester Pictures co-sponsored the film with RKO. Songs included: 'The Big Sky' Dimitri Tiomkin, Stan Jones; 'Brandy Leave Me Alone' Josef Marias; 'Buffalo Gal', 'Charlotte' Tiomkin, Gordon Clark.

In **Sudden Fear**, Joan Crawford (illustrated) ▷ portrayed a playwright who is also one of San Francisco's wealthiest heiresses. Jack Palance, an actor she fires but later marries, brings her perfect happiness until she discovers that he and a scheming blonde (Gloria Grahame) are plotting to kill her. Initial terror is replaced by Crawford's determination to thwart the plot, and she uses her dramatist's skill to design a scenario whereby the culprits will be caught in their own net. But her knowledge of the human equation proves faulty; by the time she discovers her own inability to carry through a key part of her plan, it is too late for anything except the most desperate sort of temporizing. It took too long for director David Miller to begin shoving his star toward the buzz saw, but once the suspense hooks took hold, they kept their grip through to the picture's rather contrived conclusion. Lenore Coffee and Robert Smith's screenplay (story Edna Sherry) also gave additional roles to Bruce Bennett, Virginia Huston and Touch Connors. Joseph Kaufman produced for his own independent company, with RKO distributing. Songs included: 'Afraid' Elmer Bernstein, Jack Brooks; 'Sudden Fear' Irving Taylor, Arthur Altman.

Macho director Raoul Walsh and screenwriter Alan LeMay (story by DeVallon Scott) packed **Blackbeard The Pirate** with gunplay, swordplay, lust, intrigue and a number of other action ingredients. Unfortunately, Walsh allowed Robert Newton (right) to play the man whose trade is 'sinkings, burnings, kidnaps, murder ... but larceny above all' in such hammy fashion that he seemed nothing more than a cackling caricature of his own impersonation of Long John Silver in Disney's *Treasure Island*. With the lead actor so out of control, the feud between Blackbeard and reformed pirate (or is he?) Sir Henry Morgan (Torin Thatcher) seemed pretty silly, and the romance between Linda Darnell (left) and physician-cum-swashbuckler Keith Andes generated minimal voltage. One interesting detail was the inclusion of Blackbeard's reputed fancy for wearing firecrackers in his abundant whiskers. But it was the actor's performance, not the fireworks, that blew up in the pirate's face and sent his Technicolor galleon plunging to the bottom rung on double bills. Also cast: William Bendix, Irene Ryan, Alan Mowbray, Richard Egan, Skelton Knaggs, Dick Wessel, Anthony Caruso, Jack Lambert, Noel Drayton and Pat Flaherty. Edmund Grainger was the producer. Note: The film was originally prepared by Val Lewton, who ◁ projected Boris Karloff for the Blackbeard role.

SF-7

1953

In February, 1953, the Chicago syndicate finally caved in. They returned Howard Hughes' stock and forfeited the $1.25 million down payment to him. Hughes was running RKO again (now as chairman of the board, as well as managing director of production) and had made a nice profit on the prior months of pandemonium.

Hughes named James R. Grainger (father of RKO producer Edmund Grainger) president of the company. He came to RKO from Republic, where he had been vice-president in charge of distribution. After surveying his new job, Grainger predicted that RKO was in for big business improvements, and would soon be turning out many fine productions. However, the organization continued to generate more law suits than completed pictures. By the end of the year, RKO was totally encrusted with legal barnacles, most of them originating with stockholders and attached directly to Captain Hughes and his unbridled piloting of the company ship.

Though it made half-hearted attempts to convince the world that RKO was 'The Showmanship Company', and even began making 3-D pictures in 1953, the studio experienced another cheerless year, continuing to lose massive amounts of money. Sadly, its famous location ranch in the San Fernando Valley near Encino – which had been in use since the early 30's – was sold to a real estate company to help defray the deficits. Controlling interest in the RKO theatres was also finally sold – to Albert A. List. In all, 24 pictures (plus a number of re-issues) were released. Of the 24 new films, only one-third were fully-fledged RKO productions.

In search of a jaunty lampoon of Communism ▷ along the lines of *Ninotchka* (MGM, 1939), producer Mort Briskin and director Don Siegel travelled to Austria where they tossed off a picture that was part-serious, part-silly and all bad. **No Time For Flowers** sorely tried the movie consumer's patience, as well as that of a fiercely loyal Czechoslovakian party member (Viveca Lindfors, left) who is the secretary to a wavy-haired comrade (Paul Christian, right) who has just returned from the United States. Unaware that she is being examined to see if she can withstand the temptations of the capitalist world, Miss Lindfors is shocked to find Christian grousing about the ill-groomed Iron Curtain women and offering her lipstick and a lovely evening gown. Before long, such gifts as nylons, bubble bath and champagne begin to appeal to the heroine, and she falls in love with the 'traitor'. At this point, the film did a *volte-face* from comedy to melodrama, with the lovers racing to escape the country before all is lost. They eventually make it to Germany, embracing in front of the American Zone sign for the delectation of the three or four patrons still in their seats. Laszlo Vadnay and Hans Wilhelm's misbegotten screenplay also gave parts to a large number of German actors, among them Ludwig Stossel, Adrienne Gessner, Peter Preses, Manfred Inger, Frederick Berger, Oscar Wegrostek, Helmut Janatsch, Karl Bachmann, Hilde Jaeger, Pepi Glockner-Kramer, Willi Schumann and Ilka Windisch. Maurie M. Suess worked as associate producer for Morjay Productions, which turned the film over to RKO for distribution.

Filmed largely at the Women's Army Corps training centre in Fort Lee, Virginia, **Never Wave At A WAC** (GB: **The Private Wore Skirts**) was a spicy service comedy written by Ken Englund (story by Frederick Kohner and Fred Brady) and directed by Norman Z. McLeod. Rosalind Russell (right) starred as a Washington socialite who joins the Army as a stepping stone to Paris, where her boyfriend (William Ching) is stationed as a general's aide. Russell's ex-husband Paul Douglas, and bouncy Broadway beauty Marie Wilson (left), who joins the WACs to escape the stage door wolves, also advance on Fort Lee for manoeuvres that were not to be found in any Department of Defence training manual. Adding to the fun were Arleen Whelan, Leif Erickson, Hillary Brooke, Charles Dingle, Lurene Tuttle, Regis Toomey, Frieda Inescort and Louise Beavers. Frederick Brisson produced for Independent Artists Pictures, a company bankrolled by former RKO board chairman Floyd Odlum. Song: 'WAC Song' Jane Douglass, Camilla Mays Frank.
▽

Hungarian producer Gabriel Pascal passed ▷ through RKO toward the end of George Schaefer's presidency, but was unable to launch any films due to the turmoil of the period. Pascal controlled the cinematic rights to Bernard Shaw's plays. He had produced *Pygmalion, Major Barbara* and *Caesar and Cleopatra* in Britain before returning to Hollywood and signing a co-production agreement with RKO for **Androcles And The Lion. Androcles** was an abbreviated drama, used by Shaw as a sounding board for his opinions on ancient Rome, Christianity, martyrdom, hypocrisy and lots more. In order to stretch out the picture to normal screen length, writers Chester Erskine and Ken Englund added additional material, including a sub-plot that suggested the dangers of a secret police force. The basic legend of Androcles (Alan Young), the henpecked tailor who proves to be the salvation of his Christian brethren because he once extracted a thorn from a lion's paw, remained the core of the film, but the entire production suffered from excessive verbosity, unimaginative staging and a crippling lack of pace. Jean Simmons (left, her debut in American pictures) played a valorous Christian girl who falls in love with stern Roman captain Victor Mature (right, borrowed from 20th Century-Fox), Maurice Evans made a suave and wily Caesar, and Robert Newton contributed a somewhat over-ripe portrayal of a stormy Christian giant. Elsa Lanchester, Reginald Gardiner, Gene Lockhart, Alan Mowbray, Noel Willman, John Hoyt, Jim Backus and Lowell Gilmore were also featured, under the direction of co-scenarist Chester Erskine. The associate producer was Lewis J. Rachmil. Note: after principal photography was completed, Howard Hughes decided the picture needed to be pepped up and had Nicholas Ray shoot a steamy 'Vestal Virgin Bathing Sequence' that ran into immediate trouble with the censors and outraged Pascal and other members of the team. The sequence was eventually deleted from release prints.

Ida Lupino, Hollywood's sole woman director at the time, tried her hand at a violent suspense drama and pulled it off in pungent, nerve-shattering fashion. **The Hitch-Hiker** concerned the attempts of a pair of vacationing fishermen to outwit a kill-crazy madman who holds them hostage during a dash across Mexico. Terror mounts as they near the gulf port from which the psycho plans to escape to Central America and where the two innocent men face certain death. William Talman (left) did justice to one of the best roles of his career as the vicious hitch-hiker, and received surefooted support from Edmond O'Brien (right) and Frank Lovejoy (centre) as the bystanders who become his means of escape and his source of sadistic amusement. The screenplay was by Lupino and producer Collier Young from an adaptation by Robert Joseph. Also among the cast were Jose Torvay, Sam Hayes, Wendel Niles, Jean Del Val, Rodney Bell, Nacho Galindo, Martin Garralaga, Jerry Lawrence, Felipe Turich, Rose Turich, and Joe Dominguez. Christian Nyby was associate producer for The Filmakers, whose fifth and final joint venture with RKO this was.

One searched in vain for a glimmer of intelligence, flair or competence in **Sword Of Venus** (GB: **Island Of Monte Cristo**), an American Pictures Corporation cheapie co-produced by RKO. Set in 1832, the Aubrey Wisberg-Jack Pollexfen screenplay dealt with a plot to put the Count of Monte Cristo's son (Robert Clarke, left) out of the way and seize his estate and vast fortune. Although the intended victim escapes the trap and turns the tables on his assailants, the sophomorically-plotted, fatuously-dialogued script and Harold Daniels' spiritless direction dealt the hero and the movie a succession of lethal blows. With the exception of Catherine McLeod (right), whom the heavies use as a pawn in their scheme against young Monte Cristo, the featured actors all turned in wooden performances. They included Dan O'Herlihy, William Schallert, Marjorie Stapp, Merritt Stone, Renee de Marco, Eric Colmar and Stuart Randall. Writers Wisberg and Pollexfen doubled as producers, with Albert Zugsmith receiving associate producer credit.

A reunion of RAF flyers set the stage for **The Big Frame** (GB: **The Lost Hours**). This listless melo focused on Mark Stevens (foreground, left) as a devil-may-care test pilot from Texas who comes to England to see his old mates, and to marry Jean Kent, a girl he met during the war. But before the reunion party is over, Stevens is embroiled in fisticuffs with one of his drunken peers, then becomes the prime suspect when the man turns up murdered the next day. While dodging the police and trying to pinpoint the real killer, he succeeds in busting up a smuggling racket. Garry Marsh (right), John Bentley, Dianne Foster (centre), Bryan Coleman, John Harvey, Duncan Lamont and John Horsley also put in appearances for producers Robert S. Baker and Monty Berman and director David MacDonald. The film was made at the London Film Studios in Isleworth from a story by Robert S. Baker and Carl Nystrom and screenplay by Steve Fisher and John Gilling. RKO handled American distribution for Julian Lesser and his Royal Productions.

The law of gravity was defeated by the laws of fantasy in Walt Disney's **Peter Pan**, an animated, Technicolored version of James M. Barrie's celebrated play. Without minimizing the play's sentimental and nostalgic appeal, the Disney staff added an extra dimension of humour. Almost every scene in the fairy tale contained ample visual whimsy, from the moment Peter pilots the Darling children to Never-Never Land and throughout their adventures with pirates, Indians, mermaids, a crocodile and sundry sprites and pixies led by Tinker Bell. The most important voice behind the scenes belonged to Hans Conried, who helped make Captain Hook an even more memorable character than Peter or Tinker. Some purist critics turned up their noses because writers Ted Sears, Bill Peet, Joe Rinaldi, Erdman Penner, Winston Hibler, Milt Banta and Ralph Wright took liberties with the Barrie original, but the film did no violation to the play's ethereal spirit and was a triumph of movement, colour, visual imagination and old-fashioned fun (see illustration). Hamilton Luske, Clyde Geronimi and Wilfred Jackson were the directors of this delightful excursion into the land of make-believe, and Milt Kahl, Franklin Thomas, Wolfgang Reitherman, Ward Kimball, Eric Larson, Oliver Johnston Jr, Marc Davis, John Lounsberg, Les Clark and Norman Ferguson the directing animators. Songs included: 'Never Smile At A Crocodile' Frank Churchill, Jack Lawrence; 'Tee-Dum Tee-Dee' Oliver Wallace, Ted Sears, Erdman Penner; 'The Elegant Captain Hook', 'What Makes The Red Man Red?', 'You Can Fly, You Can Fly, You Can Fly', 'Your Mother And Mine' Sammy Cahn, Sammy Fain.

Advertised as 'The Last Word In Wild African Thrills', **Below The Sahara** was, in fact, a pretty tame sightseeing tour through big-game country (see illustration). Scenes of sea lions and pelicans along the African coast, a tusk-to-tusk elephant fight, a leopard's attack on a native guide, and a gorilla hunt by tribal warriors provided the few magnetic moments in this casual travelogue. The 65-minute picture did contain one shot that was almost worth the price of admission in itself – it showed a large conclave of penguins listening quizzically to a radio. Jerome Brondfield and Burton Benjamin earned writing credits, Jay Bonafield and Douglas Travers were the production supervisors, and producer-director Armand Denis, who headed up the expedition, also took along his young, photogenic wife Michaela. Armand Denis Productions produced for RKO Pathé, and the prints were made by Technicolor.

Angel Face was a load of heavy-breathing Freudian bunkum about a psychotic Electra figure (Jean Simmons, illustrated) and a rugged chauffeur (Robert Mitchum) whose affair with the lady sucks him into a vortex of hatred and murder. The work, however, of director Otto Preminger and his stars, was sufficiently impressive to keep the film from actually falling into the abyss. Preminger's sleek handling of Frank Nugent and Oscar Millard's script (based on a story by Chester Erskine) layered the drama with ambiguous overtones and cloaked it in a resonant, suggestive style. Other important acting jobs were delivered by Herbert Marshall, playing the father to whom Simmons is fanatically devoted, Barbara O'Neil, the stepmother whom Simmons hates with equal ferocity, and Mona Freeman, the nurse Mitchum jilts in favour of the seemingly angelic Miss Simmons. Preminger (borrowed from 20th Century-Fox) also produced, employing Leon Ames, Kenneth Tobey, Raymond Greenleaf, Griff Barnett, Robert Gist, Morgan Farley and Jim Backus to fill out the cast. Harry Stradling (on loan from Samuel Goldwyn) shot the picture in insinuating *film noir* imagery, and Dimitri Tiomkin created the suitably malignant musical score.

'In skating over thin ice,' wrote Ralph Waldo Emerson, 'our safety is in speed'. Director Don Siegel may not have read the New England philosopher, but he understood the concept, as his work on **Count The Hours** (GB: **Every Minute Counts**) demonstrated. The story (by Doane R. Hoag) and screenplay by Hoag and Karen DeWolf, was a contrived melodrama about an attorney (Macdonald Carey, right) who works frantically to extricate an itinerant ranch worker (John Craven) from the death house. Although the lawyer's motives stem from a sincere belief that his client is innocent, the people of the community believe that his interest actually is centred on Teresa Wright (centre), the wife of the convicted man. Carey almost loses his practice and the love of his wealthy fiancée (Dolores Moran) before finally bringing the real killer to bay. Siegel kept the plot flying along and reached his destination with a better picture than anyone had any right to expect. Adele Mara, Edgar Barrier, Jack Elam, Ralph Sanford and Ralph Dumke (left) also appeared for producer Benedict Bogeaus. RKO purchased the completed film from Ben-Bo Productions after its projected release through United Artists fell through.

The third and last co-production between American Pictures Corporation and RKO, **Port Sinister** was based on the dubious notion that volcanic disturbances might cause a long-submerged island filled with pirate booty to bob to the surface. James Warren and Lynne Roberts head an expedition to the peek-a-boo atoll, but are waylaid by a passel of heavies who get what's coming to them when the island decides to duck back from whence it came. Jack Rabin's special effects were not bad, especially considering the minimal budget he had at his disposal, but everything else about the film fairly begged for sarcasm. Aubrey Wisberg and Jack Pollexfen wrote and produced, Harold Daniels directed and Albert Zugsmith was the associate producer. Paul Cavanagh (centre), William Schallert (centre left), Norman Budd (centre right), Robert Bice (right), Ken Terrell (left), Marjorie Stapp, House Peters Jr, Helen Winston, Eric Colmar, Anne Kimball and Merritt Stone were also in the cast. The film was re-released by Realart Pictures in the USA in 1961 as *Beast Of Paradise Isle*.

Split Second was the only feature production photographed during the abortive Stolkin regime. Book-ended by a rousing prison break along the California-Nevada border, and a terrifying climax in which a ghost town literally comes apart at the seams, the picture generated more than enough excitement to keep viewers tingling in their chairs. Rounded up and held prisoner by escaped cons Stephen McNally, Paul Kelly and Frank de Kova in the ghost town are a strange assortment of characters: Alexis Smith, a faithless wife who offers McNally anything he wants to save her life; Jan Sterling (centre), a nightclub entertainer with all the answers; Keith Andes (left), a reporter who has been around; Arthur Hunnicutt (right), a desert rat who mixes courage with sourdough philosophy; Robert Paige, the latest boyfriend of Miss Smith; and Richard Egan, her doctor husband. Exacerbating the menace provided by the criminals is the threat of total annihilation, for the ghost town is part of an atomic testing range and a test explosion is being prepared. Dick Powell, making his debut as a director, handled the high-voltage plot in exemplary fashion. Edmund Grainger produced, and the writers were Chester Erskine and Irving Wallace (story) and William Bowers and Wallace (screenplay).

Romance, intrigue and violence were mingled in conventional fashion in **Night Without Stars**. Involving a clash between the social world and the underworld, the film starred David Farrar (right) and Nadia Gray (left), whose love affair on the French Riviera is complicated by black market profiteering and by Gray's quest for revenge against the traitor responsible for the death of her husband. Winston Graham penned the screenplay from his own novel, Anthony Pelissier directed and Hugh Stewart produced. Maurice Teynac, June Clyde, Gerald Landry, Clive Morton, Robert Ayres, Ina De La Haye and Martin Benson had supporting roles in the picture, which was produced in Britain by Europa Films. RKO managed American distribution for Thalia Productions. Song: 'If You Go' Michel Emer, English lyrics Geoffrey Parsons.

◁ There were flashes of truth and some sharply-etched moments in **Affair With A Stranger**, but they were sullied by Richard Flournoy's wordy and wearisome script. His plot was a series of reminiscences by the friends of playwright Victor Mature (left, borrowed from 20th Century-Fox) and his wife, model Jean Simmons (right), who are rumoured to be seeking a divorce. The flashbacks traced the evolution of their romantic relationship, from their first meeting to the present crisis, which has been provoked by Monica Lewis, a singer in Mature's show who is determined to deep-six his marriage. Miss Simmons was responsible, to a large extent, for the good things in the picture; she played the level-headed member of the twosome with restraint and acuity, earning a degree of sympathy and respect from the audience that none of the other players was able to evoke. Director Roy Rowland and producer Robert Sparks also gave roles to Mary Jo Tarola, Jane Darwell, Dabbs Greer, Wally Vernon, Nicholas Joy, Olive Carey, Victoria Horne, Lillian Bronson, George Cleveland and Billy Chapin. Sam Coslow penned the title song.

Winner of the Academy Award as Best Documentary Feature of 1952, **The Sea Around Us**, from Rachel Carson's non-fiction book of the same name, combined footage from various marine expeditions (see illustration) into a cinematic catalogue of undersea mysteries. The Irwin Allen production was cosmic in its approach, opening with the creation of the planet and concluding with the question of whether the Earth will eventually be submerged under rising waters resulting from the melting of the polar ice caps. It included scenes of natural phenomena (wind, rain, tidal waves, storms etc.) and some of the most interesting deep-sea footage ever shot: an octopus changing colour before the camera lens, the unusual jobs of crab herders and shark walkers, a battle between a shark and an octopus, and salmon fighting their way from the ocean to their fresh water spawning grounds to complete their life-and-death cycle. Allen also adapted Miss Carson's best-seller, writing a narration which was spoken by Don Forbes and Theodore Von Eltz. Paul Sawtell composed the music and Linwood Dunn created the imaginative photographic effects used to bridge the various sequences. ▷

◁ Raoul Walsh used only a fraction of his talent in directing **Sea Devils**. Based loosely on Victor Hugo's *Toilers Of The Sea*, the Borden Chase screenplay was set during the Napoleonic wars and chronicled the adventures of a British lady spy (Yvonne De Carlo, right) who becomes caught between the murderous ambitions of military bureaucrats and the individualism of a seaman-turned-smuggler (Rock Hudson, left). After a period of routine misunderstandings between the principals, Miss De Carlo carries out her mission and waits for rugged Rock to rescue her from the French authorities. Lavish costuming, Technicolor photography (some of it shot around the English channel islands of Jersey and Guernsey and along the French coast of Brittany) and some vigorous action scenes could not camouflage the fact that this was simply a garbled assortment of adventure film clichés, held together by a pseudohistorical plot. Also cast: Maxwell Reed, Denis O'Dea, Michael Goodliffe, Bryan Forbes, Jacques Brunius, Ivor Barnard, Arthur Wontner and Gerard Oury (as Napoleon). John R. Sloan served as associate producer and David E. Rose as producer for Coronado Productions; RKO distributed.

△

Lex Barker (right) spent much of **Tarzan And The She-Devil** as a helpless prisoner – a situation that caused considerable consternation to fans who expected all sorts of superhuman stunts from their hero. Monique Van Vooren (left) played the titular 'she-devil', an adventuress who brings her gang of ivory thieves into East Africa and has them enslave the male members of a local tribe to serve as transporters of the huge tusks. Tarzan, captured while trying to liberate the natives, must finally call upon his elephant friends – who have an obvious stake in the proceedings – to rescue him and the others, including Jane, and then trample all the baddies in sight. The foot-stomping finale notwithstanding, this was one of the dullest ever Tarzan sagas. Barker played the jungle lord for a final time, Joyce MacKenzie was Jane, and Robert Bice, Raymond Burr, Mike Ross, Henry Brandon and Michael Grainger were others in the cast. RKO's former Falcon, Tom Conway, also popped up as one of the villains. Kurt Neumann directed from a screenplay by Karl Kamb and Carroll Young. Sol Lesser produced for his own independent banner, using scenes from Frank Buck's *Wild Cargo* (1934) to pad out the movie.

Walt Disney's third film shot wholly in England, **The Sword And The Rose** contained all the *accoutrements* of first-class historical romance – opulent costumes by Valles, intricate period recreation by art director Carmen Dillon, a lusty score by Clifton Parker – and yet it lolled indolently about the screen, failing ever to vault into life. The shortcomings were rooted in Lawrence E. Watkin's enervated screenplay (based on *When Knighthood Was In Flower* by Charles Major), Ken Annakin's flaccid direction and Richard Todd's stolid performance as the male lead. Todd (left) was Charles Brandon, a commoner captain of the palace guards, enamoured of princess Mary Tudor (Glynis Johns, right), the strong-willed sister of King Henry VIII (James Robertson Justice). She defies royal edict and medieval morality to marry Brandon. Miss Johns imbued her role with a full measure of vigour and passion, but her efforts were undermined by the inherent weakness of the venture. A fine clutch of English and French actors supported. They included Michael Gough, Jane Barrett, Peter Copley, Rosalie Crutchley, John Vere, Phillip Lennard, Philip Glasier, Jean Mercure, Gerard Oury, Fernand Fabre and Robert Le Beal. Perce Pearce produced, and a title song was provided by Fred Spielman and George Brown. Marion Davies starred in a silent version of *When Knighthood Was In Flower*, produced by Hearst's Cosmopolitan Productions and released by Paramount in 1923.

An adventurer carrying a vast sum of money, a husband and wife whose marriage is on the shoals, and four criminals, slogged through the Central American jungle in **Appointment In Honduras**. Story authors Mario Silveira and Jack Cornall and screenwriter Karen DeWolf put plenty of impediments in their path – flesh-eating tiger-fish, king-sized alligators, a cloud of hornets and a jungle fire – but had some difficulty explaining why the trek was necessary in the first place. They also failed to create believable characters for Glenn Ford (left) as the adventurer, Ann Sheridan (right) and Zachary Scott as the un-loving couple, and Rodolfo Acosta, Jack Elam, Ric Roman and Rico Alaniz as the cut-throat criminals. Jacques Tourneur's no-nonsense direction was clearly superior to his material. Benedict Bogeaus produced for his Alpine Productions, and the prints were made by Technicolor. RKO distributed. Note: Ann Sheridan's participation in this film came as partial settlement of her grievances with RKO concerning *My Forbidden Past* (1951).

Howard Hughes selected **Second Chance** as RKO's first production in three-dimensions and stereophonic sound. The choice was a good one, for the Rudolph Maté-directed film represented one of the better examples of the short-lived 3-D experiment. Its boffo climax took place aboard a broken funicular cable car, suspended thousands of feet above the ground. Oscar Millard and Sydney Boehm's screenplay focused on Robert Mitchum (left) and Linda Darnell (right), each of whom is looking for a second chance in life. Prizefighter Mitchum embarks on a barnstorming tour of South America to forget an unfortunate ring experience. There, he meets and falls for Miss Darnell, the ex-girlfriend of an American mobster who has dispatched Jack Palance to make certain she will never be able to return to the States and testify against him. The three principals end up on the crippled cable car, along with two vacationers and seven natives. High above the abyss, the cat-and-mouse game between Palance and the two lovers comes to an exciting, though not unexpected, conclusion. Sam Wiesenthal produced, Edmund Grainger received his only executive producer credit, and Sandro Giglio, Rodolfo Hoyos Jr, Reginald Sheffield, Margaret Brewster, Roy Roberts, Salvador Baguez, Maurice Jara, Judy Walsh, Dan Seymour, Fortunio Bonanova, Milburn Stone and Abel Fernandez were also featured. The Technicolor film was shot in Taxco and Cuernavaca, Mexico. Note: In Britain, it was released in normal non-3-D.

The use of PatheColor and 3-D cameras failed to rescue **Louisiana Territory**, which amounted to little more than a dull 65-minute travelogue. Jerome Brondfield's half-hearted plot concerned Robert Livingston (Val Winter), the ambassador to France who engineered the $15 million bargain purchase from Napoleon in 1803. The spirit of Livingston returns to marvel at what has become of the vast wilderness he brought into the United States, and to watch over the romance of modern lovers Julian Miester and Phyliss Massicot. Though the original tract encompassed all or part of a dozen states, Livingston spends most of his time wandering around New Orleans, visiting Tulane University, the French Quarter, the city's shipping and industrial centres and, of course, the festive Mardi Gras (see illustration). Harry W. Smith directed and photographed it, with Leo Zinser and Marlene Behrens also appearing in the cast. Jay Bonafield and Douglas Travers produced for RKO Pathé. The film was never shown in Britain.

Set at the end of the nineteenth century, **Devil's** ▷
Canyon was a frenzied jail-break melodrama
without a single distinguishing feature except its
Natural Vision 3-D photography (released 'flat' in
Britain). The action involved 500 desperate men
and one female (Virginia Mayo, right, borrowed
from Warner Bros.) caged within the baking
confines of the Arizona Territorial Prison. The
men are starved for the sight and company of a
woman, but the woman, an outlaw queen –
incongruously attired in costumes with provocat-
ively plunging necklines – has eyes for only one
man (Stephen McNally). Until, that is, former US
Marshal Dale Robertson (left, borrowed from 20th
Century-Fox) arrives, and a feud between him and
McNally becomes a romantic triangle. Harry
Essex adapted a story by Bennett R. Cohen and
Norton S. Parker, and Frederick Hazlitt Brennan
penned the final screenplay, which was directed,
with a distinct lack of spark, by Alfred Werker.
Also cast: Arthur Hunnicutt, Robert Keith, Jay C.
Flippen, George J. Lewis, Whit Bissell, Morris
Ankrum, James Bell, William Phillips, Earl
Holliman and Irving Bacon. Edmund Grainger
produced in Technicolor.

Those film patrons who put the hold button on
their brains for an evening, enjoyed director-
screenwriter Frank Tashlin's **Marry Me Again**, a
screwball farce that made practically no sense at
all. Robert Cummings (left) starred as a fighter
pilot recalled to active duty in Korea just as he and
Marie Wilson (right) are about to take their
wedding vows. While he is off flying jets, she
inherits a million dollars from an eccentric aunt.
On his return from the war, Cummings can't cope
with the idea that he will be something less than
the breadwinner of the family. He decides to call
off the marriage and attempts to re-enlist, but the
◁Air Force concludes that any man who would
refuse Miss Wilson's fiscal and physical assets
must be daft. This brings Cummings into contact
with a wild group of characters, including a
psychiatrist who accuses him of not liking girls, a
pretty WAC, unscrupulous lawyers and a trio of
mobsters. Finally, the heroine gives away her
fortune to a veterans' housing project and welcomes shell-shocked Mr Cummings back to her
arms. Alex Gottlieb wrote the original story and
produced, utilizing Robert Fallon (Marie Wilson's
real-life husband) as associate producer and Ray
Walker, Mary Costa (Mrs Frank Tashlin), Jess
Barker, Lloyd Corrigan, June Vincent, Richard
Gaines, Moroni Olsen, Frank Cady, Joanne
Arnold and Bob Thomas to complete the cast.
RKO distributed for Wedding Pictures Inc. Note:
One segment of the film was a satiric gem. A brawl
breaks out in a movie theatre and, when a female
usher calls it to the house manager's attention, he
assures her that the fight is just part of the 3-D film
that is playing there.

△
Producers M. J. Frankovich and William Szekely,
associate producer Montagu Marks, treatment
author Geza Herczeg, screenwriter George
Oppenheimer and director Hugo Fregonese scrub-
bed up and watered down Boccaccio's bawdy,
saucy tales, and succeeded in turning **Decameron
Nights** into a droopy and oddly spiritless film.
The story of Boccaccio's wooing of Fiametta
provided the framework for three of his fictions:
'Paganino the Pirate', 'Wager for Virtue' and 'The
Doctor's Daughter'. In the first, a young wife
whose elderly husband prefers astrology to marital
intimacy, permits herself to be captured by a
handsome pirate in order to teach her husband a
lesson. The second concerned a merchant who
loses faith in his spouse due to circumstantial
evidence presented by a wily rogue who had
previously goaded him into a bet on the woman's
virtue. The final story dealt with a wife who finds
herself spurned by her mate who only married her
at the insistence of his king. Louis Jourdan (left)
played Boccaccio and Joan Fontaine (right) was
Fiametta; the two actors also essayed the main
parts in each of the three stories. Others cast
included: Binnie Barnes, Joan Collins, Godfrey
Tearle, Mara Lane, Melissa Stribling, Elliot
Makeham, Noel Purcell, Hugh Morton and
Marjorie Rhodes. The Technicolor picture was
shot in Spain and at the Gate Studios in Elstree,
England. RKO handled American distribution for
Amerit Film Corporation.

1954

Early in the new year, Howard Hughes devised a scheme to extricate himself from his legal problems. He offered to purchase all of the company's outstanding stock for $6 per share – a price that was slightly higher than stockholders could have obtained in the marketplace at any time following his takeover of RKO in 1948. Hughes intended to become the first individual ever to wholly own a major motion picture company. The RKO board of directors met and recommended that shareholders accept the offer and, on March 18, it was announced that the sale of the company to Hughes for $23,489,478 had been overwhelmingly approved.

President James R. Grainger continued to speak enthusiastically of his company's future, raving about production work on the 'industry's biggest picture' (**The Conqueror**, which was filmed during the year but would not be released until 1956) and an increase in colour and wide-screen presentations. In truth, however, RKO was progressing from bad to hopeless. In the fall, the studio laid off a large number of key employees, many of whom had been working at 780 Gower Street since the days of Radio Pictures. By December, a skeleton crew was handling the limited production operations.

Perhaps the only consistent thing about RKO was the quality of its 15 new releases. Nearly all of them were terrible. Walt Disney finally terminated his relationship with the blighted company and set up his own distribution arm (Buena Vista), following RKO's handling of **Rob Roy, The Highland Rogue**.

Barbara Stanwyck (right) and Ronald Reagan (left) co-starred in **Cattle Queen Of Montana**, a gun-popping action western filmed in and around Montana's Glacier National Park. Stanwyck played Sierra Nevada Jones, a tigress who fights to break the grip of avaricious land-grabbers, defies their hired killers and ultimately wins the love of undercover government agent Reagan. The above-average production values, exciting action elements and solid performances by the two principals helped overcome Robert Blees and Howard Estabrook's trite screenplay, which was based on an original story by Thomas Blackburn. Allan Dwan's skilful direction was another plus factor. Gene Evans, Lance Fuller, Anthony Caruso, Jack Elam, Yvette Dugay, Morris Ankrum, Chubby Johnson, Myron Healey and Rod Redwing led the support, and the prints were struck by Technicolor. Benedict Bogeaus produced for his Filmcrest Productions, and RKO and Filmcrest once again shared the cost of making the picture.

◁ **She Couldn't Say No** (GB: **Beautiful But Dangerous**) sank to depths hitherto unexplored by the worst of RKO's 'A'-budget comedies. The D. D. Beauchamp-William Bowers-Richard Flournoy screenplay (story by Beauchamp) had wealthy but foolish Jean Simmons (right) advancing on the small town of Progress, Arkansas, with a plan to repay the villagers who had donated money for an operation which saved her life when she was a child. The material rewards she bestows anonymously on the locals attracts all sorts of con artists, parasites and other avaricious interlopers to Progress, thus upsetting the town's delicate bucolic harmony. Practically every joke in the film landed with a deadening thud. The atrocious script was largely to blame, though director Lloyd Bacon might have salvaged something out of the fiasco by playing it as a black comedy – an alternative style that he clearly never even considered. Miss Simmons and physician-cum-fisherman Robert Mitchum (left) were completely wasted, as were all the other players except Arthur Hunnicutt, who provoked a chuckle or two as the town lush. Other unfortunates trapped in the Robert Sparks production included Edgar Buchanan, Wallace Ford, Raymond Walburn, Jimmy Hunt, Ralph Dumke, Hope Landin, Gus Schilling, Eleanor Todd and Pinky Tomlin. Note: This picture was the last of three releases made back-to-back to fulfil contractual obligations to Miss Simmons. *Angel Face* and *Affair With A Stranger* (both released in 1953) were the other two.

An instantly forgettable item from the profusion of science-fiction films made during the 1950s, **Killers From Space** featured a bunch of bug-eyed menaces from the planet Astron Delta who plan to sick an army of carnivorous insects the size of boxcars on the human race. The only thing they need to complete their mission is information concerning the next nuclear test explosion, for the isotopes and radiation from an atom bomb are necessary to the growth of their gargantuan attack force. American scientist Peter Graves (centre left) tries to warn his fellow earthlings of the threat, but they, quite reasonably, think he is far gone in the head. Taking matters into his own hands, Graves cuts off the electric power to the caves occupied by the spacemen, who are promptly blown to Astronian hell (wherever that may be). All elements of this critic-proof picture were at or slightly below the level of Saturday morning television programming. The story author was Myles Wilder, the scriptwriter Bill Raynor and the producer-director W. Lee Wilder. James Seay, Steve Pendleton, Frank Gerstle, John Merrick, Jack Daly, Ron Kennedy, Ben Welden, Robert Roark, Ruth Bennett and Mark Scott were some of the others in the cast. RKO distributed for Planet Filmplays Incorporated.
▽

Rob Roy MacGregor, the highland chief who defied a king and his armies in 1715 to save his clan from obliteration, was one of the renowned fighting men of Scottish legend. Walt Disney's **Rob Roy, The Highland Rogue** kept the hero in nearly continuous action, thundering down from crags and glens to do battle with the redcoats in order to restore the Stuart line to the British throne. Richard Todd (right) played the fearless rebel, with Glynis Johns (left) as his sweetheart, James Robertson Justice as the Minister of State for Scotland and Michael Gough as the villainous Duke of Montrose. Finlay Currie, Jean Taylor Smith, Geoffrey Keen, Archie Duncan, Russell Waters, Michael Goodliffe, Marjorie Fielding (centre), Eric Pohlmann, Ina De La Haye, Martin Boddey, Ewen Solon, James Sutherland and Malcolm Keen were also cast. Perce Pearce was the producer, Lawrence E. Watkin the screenwriter and Harold French the director. This bracing Technicolor adventure film, shot in England and Scotland, was the last of 21 Walt Disney feature productions (dating back to 1937) handled by the RKO distribution network. Song: 'The Ballad Of Rob Roy' Irving Gordon.
▽

△

'J.R. in 3D – It'll knock *both* your eyes out!'; so read one of the outrageous publicity catch phrases for **The French Line**. In reality the film was fairly tame but for the strategic placement of the 3-D and Technicolor cameras whenever a pair of mammaries (not only Jane Russell's, but those of other actresses in the cast) were in the vicinity – except in Britain where, as usual, it was released 'flat' – and one contorted, hootchy-cooch dance by Miss Russell, clad in a seven-ounce black satin costume trimmed with white, plus 10 yards of ermine wrap which she discarded early in the performance. These elements, abetted by the scandalous advertising campaign, precipitated another war between Howard Hughes and the Production Code office, though his film ultimately received a Code Seal. Tossing aside all the ballyhoo, one discovered a routine, unimaginative musical based, in part, on *The Richest Girl In The World* (1934). Texas-born Mary Carson (Russell, right) is one of the world's wealthiest women, and also one of its unhappiest. She has been engaged several times, but the bridegrooms always backed out at the last minute, unwilling to marry a corporation. On a voyage to Paris aboard the French liner *Liberté*, she pretends to be a model for a dress designer (Mary McCarty, left), hoping to land a man on the basis of her charms without her money getting in the way. A dashing French musical comedy star (Gilbert Roland) becomes the fortunate fellow and, after seen-it-all-before misunderstandings and complications, he and she are ready to live happily ever after. Mary Loos and Richard Sale wrote the screenplay, based on a story by Matty Kemp and Isabel Dawn. Edmund Grainger produced, Lloyd Bacon directed, Billy Daniel choreographed, and Arthur Hunnicutt, Joyce MacKenzie, Paula Corday, Scott Elliott, Craig Stevens, Laura Elliot, Steven Geray, John Wengraf, Michael St Angel (returning to his real name after several appearances as Steve Flagg), Barbara Darrow, Barbara Dobbins and Marilyn (later Kim) Novak also appeared. Songs included: 'Lookin' For Trouble', 'Wait 'Till You See Paris', 'With A Kiss', 'Any Girl From Texas', 'What Is This I Feel?' Josef Myrow, Ralph Blane & Robert Wells. ▷

The majestic mountain peaks of Montana's Glacier National Park seemed to look down upon Victor Mature (right, borrowed from 20th Century-Fox), Piper Laurie (left), Vincent Price and the other participants in **Dangerous Mission**, with Olympian disgust. Without question, there was plenty to be disgusted about: the muddled, episodic plot (screenplay by Horace McCoy, W. R. Burnett and Charles Bennett, from a story by McCoy and James Edmiston), the run-of-the-mill direction (by Louis King), the wretched editing (by Gene Palmer) and the complete lack of conviction and credibility displayed by the acting contingent. The story called for Mature and Price to follow Miss Laurie from New York to Glacier Park. The latter intends to kill her, while the former's job is to bring her back to Manhattan to testify about a gangland killing. A forest fire, an avalanche and a climactic battle on the glacial ice fields, plus 3-D and Technicolor, failed to make up for the film's multiplicity of shortcomings. Also cast: William Bendix, Betta St John, Steve Darrell, Marlo Dwyer, Walter Reed, Dennis Weaver and Harry Cheshire. Irwin Allen produced. The film was released 'flat' in Britain.

The Saint's Girl Friday (GB: The Saint's Return) brought back Leslie Charteris' famous sleuth after a long sabbatical from cinema screens. Louis Hayward (left), who had impersonated Simon Templar in RKO's first 'Saint' film (*The Saint In New York*, 1938), showed that he could still hypnotize the fair sex and traumatize the forces of evil in this efficient mystery thriller. Templar returns to London at the request of a former girlfriend, only to find she has been murdered. Naturally, he begins investigating right away, and discovers that mobsters running a gambling barge are responsible. He busts up the hoodlums before a similar fate comes to Naomi Chance (right, the eponymous heroine). Allan MacKinnon's serviceable screenplay also gave roles to Sydney Tafler, Charles Victor, Jane Carr, Harold Lang, Russell Enoch, Fred Johnson, Thomas Gallager and in a brief, Marilyn Monroe--like appearance, Diana Dors. Anthony Hinds produced for Hammer Films, Seymour Friedman directed, and RKO distributed for Royal Productions (Julian Lesser) in the US.

A saddle-sore western with obvious *High Noon* overtones, Silver Lode was the story of three hours in the history of a nineteenth century community and of one man's determined battle to clear himself of a murder charge. As John Payne (centre) and Lizabeth Scott (right) are being married in Silver Lode, four grim-faced strangers ride into town. Their leader, Dan Duryea, claims to be a US marshal come to arrest Payne and return him to California to stand trial for murder. Though the bridegroom is well-known and well-respected in the community, his protestations of innocence are received sceptically by many of the townspeople. He must eventually fight his way out of the set-up, without the help of the cowards and hypocrites he had formerly considered his friends. Karen DeWolf penned the derivative script and Alan Dwan contributed the mundane direction for producer Benedict Bogeaus. Also cast: Dolores Moran (Mrs Benedict Bogeaus), Emile Meyer, Robert Warwick, John Hudson, Harry Carey Jr, Alan Hale Jr, Stuart Whitman, Frank Sully, Morris Ankrum (left), Hugh Sanders, Florence Auer and Roy Gordon. The film was a co-venture between RKO and Pinecrest Productions, with prints by Technicolor.

The best things about Passion were Van Nest Polglase's art direction and the gorgeous location photography by John Alton. All other elements in this tale of vengeance, set during the early days of California, were thoroughly dispensable. Cornel Wilde starred as a young *vaquero* whose wife and grandparents are killed by terrorists, provoking a vendetta in which he dispatches the murderers one by one. The relationship between his efforts, as devised by scenarists Beatrice A. Dresher and Josef Leytes (adapted by Howard Estabrook from a story by Dresher, Leytes and Miguel Padilla), and the film's title was tenuous at best. Even the requisite love affair(s) between Wilde (right) and Yvonne De Carlo (centre), playing the wife who is murdered, as well as her younger sister were without notable impact. Allan Dwan directed, using Raymond Burr, Lon Chaney Jr, Rodolfo Acosta, John Qualen, Anthony Caruso (left) and Frank de Kova in supporting roles. Technicolor made the prints for producer Benedict Bogeaus, whose Filmcrest Productions co-sponsored the picture with RKO.

Susan Slept Here was another astonishingly dreadful major-budget comedy, produced by Harriet Parsons (her finale for RKO) and directed by Frank Tashlin. The story of a man-about-Hollywood (Dick Powell, right) and a girl of 18 (Debbie Reynolds, left, borrowed from MGM) began on Christmas eve when a policeman, knowing Powell wants to write a serious script about juvenile delinquency, deposits teenage hellion Reynolds in the bachelor's apartment as a boon to his screenwriting research. Soon enough, a triangle develops, with green-eyed Anne Francis (borrowed from 20th Century-Fox) completing the threesome, and storyteller Powell labouring to clear up all the loose ends in a plot light years beyond his comprehension. The actual author Alex Gottlieb, who developed his script from a play by Steve Fisher and himself, intended the Technicolor production to be both sexy and humorous. In the event, it was about as attractive and amusing as an afternoon in the dentist's chair. The fickle finger also points toward Leigh Harline, who composed the nearly continuous and always awful background jazz score. Glenda Farrell, Alvy Moore, Horace McMahon, Herb Vigran, Les Tremayne, Mara Lane, Rita Johnson and Maidie Norman were other members of the dispirited cast. Songs included: 'Hold My Hand' Jack Lawrence, Richard Myers; 'Susan Slept Here' Lawrence.

A brutal tale of love and lust set against the ▷ kaleidoscopic background of an American carnival company touring Bavaria, **Carnival Story** was somewhat reminiscent of the German expressionist classic, *Variety* (1925). The protagonist of Hans Jacoby and Kurt Neumann's screenplay (story Marcel Klauber and C. B. Williams) was a postwar German girl (Anne Baxter, illustrated), who drifts into carnival life as a refuge from her hard and unhappy existence. She is hungry for love and grabs it with Steve Cochran, a heel who is the spieler for the troupe. Cochran is bestial but irresistible, and the heroine finds it impossible to throw off his hold on her even after she marries Lyle Bettger, the show's high-diver, and becomes one of the stars of the outfit. Both men are eventually killed, freeing the hardened Miss Baxter to begin a new life with magazine photographer George Nader. Co-scenarist Neumann also directed, giving full vent to the animalistic drives at the core of the story and drawing carnal and powerful performances from Baxter and Cochran. Jay C. Flippen, Helene Stanley and Adi Berber were also featured for producers Maurice and Frank King. The movie was shot in Germany in Agfa Color, then distributed by RKO for King Brothers Productions with prints made by Technicolor. Song: 'Ring Down The Curtain' Willy Schmidt-Gentner, Pony Sherrell & Philip Moody. Note: A German version, entitled *Rummelplatz Der Liebe*, was shot, using a different cast – Eva Bartok, Curt Jurgens and Bernhard Wicki.

△

Sins Of Rome, a decadence and damnation epic imported from Italy, lacked colour and widescreen but had all the other ingredients of spectacle: beautiful girls at the mercy of proud tyrants, man-eating lions loose in the packed arena, hurtling chariots, sweeping battle scenes, gladiatorial contests, etc. The story by Maria Bori, and screenplay by Bori and Jean Ferry, concerned Spartacus, a Thracian slave desired by Sabina, the lustful and conscienceless daughter of a Roman noble, and loved by Amitys, daughter of a murdered Thracian leader and Sabina's personal slave. This romantic triangle becomes one of the pivots of the drama, with Spartacus' adventures in the gladiatorial arena and his leadership of a slave revolt being the two other major plot elements. Viewers eager to lose themselves in an orgy of classical posturing, and not bothered by the stilted dialogue or awkward dubbing, got some kicks out of this 72-minute panorama. Massimo Girotti played Spartacus, Gianna Maria Canale (right) was Sabina and ballerina Ludmilla Tcherina portrayed Amitys; Carlo Ninchi (left), Yves Vincent and Vittorio Sanipoli handled other important roles for director Riccardo Freda. RKO acted as American distributor for Es Establissments Sinag, a Lichtenstein corporation. The film was originally shown in Italy in 1952 as *Spartaco*, not to be confused with the more famous (and expensive) *Spartacus* (Universal, 1960), directed by Stanley Kubrick with Kirk Douglas topping an all-star cast.

Producer Hugh Brooke, director Stuart Heisler and scriptwriters Hagar Wilde and Brooke (story by Brooke) tossed frustration, deceit, murder and other supposedly standard ingredients of American home life into their sleazy cauldron and concocted **This Is My Love**. Sibling rivalry between Linda Darnell and Faith Domergue ignited the PatheColor action. Darnell (left) lives in a dream world she has constructed as an amateur writer, while her more realistic sister's marriage to Dan Duryea (right) has been dulled by an accident that confines him to a wheelchair. The situation explodes when Darnell introduces handsome stranger Rick Jason, with whom she is desperately in love, into the household, and he and Domergue immediately become involved. The filmmakers squeezed all the soapsuds possible out of the situation, giving devotees of emotional trauma a thorough dissertation on the subject. Also cast: Hal Baylor, Connie Russell, Jerry Mathers, Susie Mathers, Mary Young, William Hopper, Stuart Randall, Kam Tong, Judd Holdren and Carl 'Alfalfa' Switzer. RKO distributed for the independent Allan Dowling Pictures company. Song: 'This Is My Love' Franz Waxman, Hugh Brooke.

▽

Lacking a fresh hook on which to hang its trophies or its cinematic structure, **Africa Adventure** emerged as just another nebulous safari through the Dark Continent. Compounding the problems of familiarity was the inferior technical quality of the production, including its washed-out PatheColor footage (shot by Chester Kronfeld) and sloppy editing (no credit offered). Journalist and novelist Robert C. Ruark (centre), who wrote and narrated the picture, and ace white hunters Harry Selby (left), John Sutton (right) and Andrew Holmberg kept themselves busy bringing down a water buffalo, a rhino, a leopard and a bull elephant for the cameras, and acting out a vapid lecture on the problems of camping in the wilds. They also took armchair adventurers on visits to the Mau Mau, and to native tribes such as the Turkana and the Somalis. Jay Bonafield produced for RKO Pathé.

▽

A cast of electronically controlled puppets acted out the story of **Hansel and Gretel** to the operatic score of Engelbert Humperdinck (the original, not his pop-singer namesake). Michael Myerberg's production was charming and entertaining up to a point, but it soon became tedious, due to the static and unnatural quality of the puppetry technique and the stilted nature of the score. Irish-American poet and playwright Padraic Colum adapted Adelheid Wette's dramatized version of the Grimm fairy tale. It concerned the woodcutter's two children who go into the forest to pick strawberries and fall into the clutches of a witch who turns children into gingerbread. Amplifying the actions of the puppets (Hansel and Gretel illustrated) were the voices of Anna Russell (the cackling witch), Constance Brigham (both Hansel and Gretel), Mildred Dunnock and Frank Rogier (their mother and father). John Paul directed in Technicolor, utilizing the talents of Joseph Horstmann, Inez Anderson, Daniel Diamond, Ralph Emory, Hobart Rosen, Teddy Shepard and Nathalie Schulz who were the main animators. RKO distributed for Michael Myerberg Productions.

▽

1955

In July, Howard Hughes sold RKO for the second and final time. The buyer was General Teleradio Incorporated, a subsidiary of the huge General Tire and Rubber Company.

It was a well-known fact that the new owners controlled six television stations, and purchased RKO to gain control of its backlog of feature pictures for presentation by those stations (and possible sale or rental to other stations around the US).

To allay the many rumours about RKO's future, General Teleradio president T. F. (Tom) O'Neil announced that his regime had no intention of ending theatrical film production at the Hollywood studio. He believed there was money to be made in the movie business and intended to make RKO as active and competitive as it had been during the pre-Hughes days. Daniel T. O'Shea, a senior vice-president of the Columbia Broadcasting System who had worked for RKO as head of the legal department in the early 1930s, was named president, succeeding James R. Grainger. And William Dozier, former executive assistant to Charles Koerner during his tenure as executive producer, took over as vice-president in charge of production. The studio restructured many departments with new heads, began re-hiring a number of its old employees who had lost their jobs while Hughes held sway, and also acquired a new name. General Teleradio Inc and RKO Radio Pictures Inc merged, producing RKO Teleradio Pictures Inc, with Tom O'Neil elected chairman of the board of the new concern. RKO Radio Pictures was now a division of the corporation.

Two years after Twentieth Century-Fox set the wide screen revolution in motion with *The Robe*, RKO succumbed to it by introducing Superscope. This anamorphic process, developed by Joseph S. and Irving P. Tushinsky, provided a screen image that was approximately twice as wide as it was high. **Underwater!** became the first Superscope production.

The inevitable dispersal of the film library occurred in December. Matty Fox of C & C Corporation leased television rights in perpetuity to some 740 RKO features for a reported price of $15 million. However, in accordance with its initial intentions, the company retained video rights to the films in the six cities where RKO Teleradio owned stations (New York, Los Angeles, Boston, Memphis, Hartford and West Palm Beach).

Increased filmmaking activities at the studio would not be reflected in RKO's releases until the following year. In 1955, RKO distributed 14 new features, plus the normal run of reissues.

The best of the Benedict Bogeaus productions released by RKO, **Tennessee's Partner** recreated the roistering atmosphere of California's gold rush days. Allan Dwan's heady direction extracted plenty of guts and gusto from Bret Harte's story of the friendship between a quick-fingered gambler (John Payne, right) and a quick-on-the-draw cowboy (Ronald Reagan). The major conflict develops from Payne's attempts to prevent Reagan from marrying Coleen Gray, a gold-digger who mines her ore from men's pockets. Rhonda Fleming (left) also filled an important role as the 'Duchess', operator of a lucrative night life establishment, who is happy to give it up and marry Payne in the end. Four writers (Milton Krims, D. D. Beauchamp, Graham Baker and Teddi Sherman) worked on the screenplay, but the narrative was smooth and exciting throughout. Anthony Caruso, Morris Ankrum, Leo Gordon, Chubby Johnson, Myron Healey, Joe Devlin and John Mansfield had other significant roles in this co-venture between Filmcrest Productions and RKO. The film was in Superscope with prints made by Technicolor and had two silent antecedents: *Tennessee's Pardner*, produced by Jesse L. Lasky and released by Paramount in 1918, starring Fannie Ward; and *The Flaming Forties*, produced by Hunt Stromberg for Producers Distributing Corporation release in 1924, starring Harry Carey. Song: 'Heart Of Gold' Louis Forbes, Dave Franklin.

◁ In one of the most ludicrous publicity stunts in film history, 200 journalists and screen personalities were flown to Silver Springs, Florida, in January 1955, to attend the premiere of Howard Hughes' **Underwater!**. They donned bathing suits, aqua lungs and swim fins and viewed the film 20 feet beneath the surface of the clear spring. Those who preferred not to get wet were allowed to watch through portholes from six electrically-powered submarines. The studio should, by all rights, have left the film on the bottom after the premiere to collect the rust and slime it so patently deserved. A talky, boring treasure hunt saga, it was made primarily to give Jane Russell the opportunity to paddle around in a bikini, and other specially designed skin-diving garments. Richard Egan (left), who is 'always chasing rainbows', leads the quest for Caribbean treasure accompanied by his sceptical wife (Miss Russell, right), adventurer Gilbert Roland, priest Robert Keith and scantily-clad blonde secretary Lori Nelson (borrowed from Universal). Story authors Hugh King and Robert B. Bailey and scenarist Walter Newman plagued them with sharks, nautical bandits and a submerged ledge on which the sunken treasure ship was precariously perched. Despite the use of Technicolor and Superscope (a wide-screen process that yielded a picture whose horizontal dimensions were twice its vertical dimensions), the result was hopelessly waterlogged. Harry Tatelman produced, John Sturges directed and Joseph Calleia, Eugene Iglesias and Ric Roman also appeared. Song: 'Cherry Pink and Apple Blossom White' Louiguy, English lyrics Mack David. Note: After six weeks of shooting off the Kona Coast of Hawaii which produced very little usable footage, the picture was completed back at the studio in a giant underwater tank installed on the sound stages where Fred Astaire and Ginger Rogers had once danced their way to immortality.

In his continuing attempts to keep the Tarzan series up to date, Sol Lesser brought the jungle strong man into contact with a United Nations medical compound in **Tarzan's Hidden Jungle**. This enabled him to aid doctor Peter Van Eyck and nurse Vera Miles (right) in their efforts to cure the natives of jungle diseases and, simultaneously, to slam the door on white hunter Jack Elam whose goal is to amass 2000 barrels of animal fat, two tons of ivory and several hundred lion skins. Gordon Scott (left) played Lesser's new Tarzan; his debut was less than thunderous, thanks to a desultory script (by William Lively), perfunctory direction (by Harold Schuster) and the film's meagre production values and action ingredients. Also cast: Charles Fredericks, Richard Reeves, Don Beddoe, Ike Jones, Jester Hairston, Maidie Norman and Rex Ingram. Zippy, a regular performer on the *Howdy Doody* television series, added the monkey business in the role of Cheetah. The movie was the fourteenth Tarzan film produced by Sol Lesser's independent company, and the final one distributed by RKO.
▽

Another co-production between Benedict Bogeaus' Filmcrest Productions and RKO, **Escape To Burma** squandered the superior talents of Robert Ryan and Barbara Stanwyck on a steamy but thoroughly pedestrian jungle melodrama. Running away from a murder charge, Ryan (right) takes refuge on the teak plantation run by Miss Stanwyck (left). Romance inevitably blooms in the hothouse atmosphere until security officer David Farrar (centre) arrives to arrest Ryan for the crime. The ensuing chase, which took place largely through dense jungle, was supposed to be suspenseful and bracing, but it came off simply as a time-filler leading up to a last second *deus ex machina* – the appearance of a witness who clears Ryan of the accusations. Talbot Jennings and Hobart Donavan wrote it from a story by Kenneth Perkins, Allan Dwan directed it, and Bogeaus produced in Superscope with prints by Technicolor. Murvyn Vye, Lisa Montell, Robert Warwick, Reginald Denny, Robert Cabal, Peter Coe, Alex Montoya, Anthony Numkena, Lal Chand Mehra, John Mansfield and Gavin Muir completed the cast.
▽

The kind of experience once reserved for the illustrated lecture circuit, **Quest For The Lost City** was another foray into the deep recesses of the jungle. Dana Lamb (left) and his wife Ginger (right), seeking the last stronghold of the ancient Mayans along the Mexico-Guatemala border, completed their 2000 mile journey with no assistants, no equipment and no safari – only the gear they could carry on their backs. Using a special time exposure mechanism on their 16 mm camera, the Lambs were able to photograph themselves as well as the hardships they encountered and, thereby, added the human element to the film of their arduous trip. They lived off the land in Robinson Crusoe fashion, hacking through the undergrowth with machetes and drawing sustenance from the organic resources at hand. The colour photographic record they brought back and then blew up to 35 mm for release was unpolished by theatrical standards, but there was nothing phony about its matter-of-fact presentation of sustained heroic accomplishment. Tom Harmon, a former football star who was shot down in the jungles of the South Pacific during World War II and survived, thanks to a booklet on self-preservation written by Dana Lamb, appeared in a foreword to the film. Hal Gibney spoke the narration which was written by producer Dorothy Howell. RKO distributed for Sol Lesser Productions.
▽

◁**The Americano** combined the action of a western with the exotic atmosphere of an adventure saga set in a foreign locale. Glenn Ford (right), starred as an American cowboy, casts a shadow large enough to make Brazil's cattle kings think twice before they mark their bullets with his name. Leslie T. White's original story and Guy Trosper's screenplay dispatched Ford to deliver a cargo of prize Brahma bulls to an opulent South American ranchero. His trail leads him across angry rivers where piranhas lurk, through the jungle of the Matto Grosso, and into the domain of land-hungry murderer Frank Lovejoy. Cesar Romero as a bandit with a sense of humour, Ursula Theiss (left) as the owner of an adjoining ranch who is feuding with Lovejoy, and Abbe Lane as Lovejoy's voluptuous housekeeper, helped to make the film an exciting and unpretentious delight. Filmed partially in Brazil by director William Castle, the picture (prints by Technicolor) also featured Rodolfo Hoyos Jr, Salvador Baguez, Tom Powers, Dan White, Frank Marlowe, George Navarro and Nyra Monsour. Sam Wiesenthal was the executive producer, and Robert Stillman produced for his own company, which co-sponsored the film with RKO. Song: 'The Americano' Xavier Cugat, George Rosener & Tom Smith.

A fictional story based on the depredations of the notorious Reno Brothers gang, **Rage At Dawn** starred Randolph Scott (illustrated) as the special agent assigned by a Chicago detective company to bring the outlaws to justice. Scott pretends to be a train robber, using his criminal status to join the gang, decipher the network of judicial and political corruption that prevents prosecution of the outlaws, and then set up a train robbery to effect their capture. A forced and anti-climactic lynching scene toward the end of the picture allowed screenwriter Horace McCoy (story by Frank Gruber) to include a few sermons on the evils of mob rule. Scott sauntered through his role with tough but cavalier aplomb. Others who performed for director Tim Whelan were Forrest Tucker, Mala Powers, J. Carrol Naish, Edgar Buchanan, Myron Healey, Howard Petrie, Ray Teal, William Forrest, Denver Pyle, Trevor Bardette and Kenneth Tobey. Nat Holt produced in Technicolor; it was shot on location at the Columbia Historic State Park in northern California and was a joint venture between RKO and Holt's independent production company.
▽

Son Of Sinbad was a voyeur's delight – a ▷
seemingly inexhaustible parade of shapely females
in scanty costumes featured in various undulating
dance routines. However, filmgoers who expected
something more than a peep show for their
admission fee, were outraged by this absurd,
completely inept excuse for a movie. Aubrey
Wisberg and Jack Pollexfen's throwaway script
provided ample opportunity for Sinbad Junior
(Dale Robertson, right, borrowed from 20th
Century-Fox) to frolic in the harems of Baghdad,
which were decorated with ecdysiast Lili St Cyr
(left), Sally Forrest, Mari Blanchard (borrowed
from Universal) and more than a hundred other
eager starlets. Vincent Price played the poet Omar
the Tentmaker, ambling through the islands of
boundless epiderma and offering a few tongue-in-
cheek remarks when the spirit moved him. In the
end, Sinbad saves Baghdad from the forces of
Tamerlane, but it didn't much matter. Those
looking for a plot, and characters with some
semblance of intelligence, were long gone from the
theatre by that time, and those who remained
hadn't paid attention to anything except the
wriggling torsos anyway. Ted Tetzlaff directed
and Robert Sparks produced, though the
Technicolor and Superscope film was, in the main,
fodder for the warped fantasies of one man –
Howard Hughes. Also cast: Leon Askin, Jay
Novello, Raymond Greenleaf, Nejla Ates,
Kalantan, Ian MacDonald, Donald Randolph and
Larry Blake. **Son Of Sinbad** had major censorship problems and was condemned by the Catholic
Legion of Decency. It was also Robert Sparks' last
production for the studio.

△

Civilization and its malcontents descended on the
carefree inhabitants of an uncharted island in
Pearl Of The South Pacific. Presented in
Superscope with prints by Technicolor, the film
was congenial hokum hatched by story author
Anna Hunger and screenwriter Jesse Lasky Jr
(additional dialogue Talbot Jennings), and acted
out by Virginia Mayo (centre right, borrowed from
Warner Bros.), Dennis Morgan (right) and David
Farrar. The three westerners attempt to steal a
fortune in black pearls from the natives by passing
Miss Mayo off as a missionary. They soon learn
that the treasure is kept in an ancient burial grotto
in a deep lagoon, and guarded by a giant octopus,
but just when it appears the fortune hunters will
make off with the booty, the islanders rise up, kill
Farrar and destroy their schooner. Sorely chastened by the experience, Morgan and Mayo decide
to remain on the island, following the simple,
harmonious and non-acquisitive lifestyle of its
people. The script arranged for a jealous native girl
to burn Miss Mayo's clothes so that she could
cavort in a sarong for much of the action. This
alone made her the standout member of a cast that
also included Murvyn Vye (left), Lance Fuller,
Basil Ruysdael (centre left) and Lisa Montell.
Allan Dwan directed for producer Benedict
Bogeaus. Another RKO-Filmcrest collaboration.

Bengazi, a mildly diverting adventure yarn, began in the twisting streets of the titular North African city and ended in the grim desolation of the Sahara Desert. The Endre Bohem-Louis Vittes screenplay, based on a story by Jeff Bailey, focused on an American with a shady past (Richard Conte, left) and an Irishman without a conscience (Victor McLaglen, right) who join forces with an army deserter (Richard Erdman) in a search for gold which Arab tribesmen had hidden in a deserted mosque to keep it from falling into the hands of Rommel or Montgomery during World War II. Richard Carlson, an inspector in the British Criminal Investigation department, and McLaglen's daughter, Mala Powers, also become involved in the hunt. The gold is finally discovered, but native tribesmen take umbrage, setting the stage for a concluding battle between Arabs and plunderers. Sam Wiesenthal and Eugene Tevlin produced and John Brahm directed, shooting much of the Superscope action in the Yuma Desert in Arizona. Also cast: Gonzales Gonzales, Hillary Brooke, Maury Hill, Jay Novello, Albert Carrier and Eileen Rowe. RKO joined forces with Panamint Pictures to produce the film.

Texas Lady presented Claudette Colbert in her first role as a western heroine. The film was basically a waste of time, money and celluloid, though the fault lay with Horace McCoy's predictable screenplay and not Miss Colbert's performance. After taking revenge on gambler Chris Mooney (Barry Sullivan, right), on whom she blames her father's suicide, Prudence Webb (Colbert, centre) takes control of the newspaper in Fort Ralston, Texas, using it as an instrument of war against two lawless cattle barons (Ray Collins and Walter Sande). Mooney shows up looking for a little revenge of his own, but his attitude toward Prudence soon turns to support and then to love, as he realizes that she and her cause are worth fighting for. Any viewer who couldn't foresee the outcome of this Superscope, Technicolor-printed oater after 15 minutes or so deserved to be blackballed from every extant sagebrush fan club. Nat Holt and Lewis P. Rosen produced, Tim Whelan directed and James Bell (left), Horace McMahon, Gregory Walcott, John Litel, Douglas Fowley, Don Haggerty, Alexander Campbell, Florenz Ames, Kathleen Mulqueen and Robert Lynn completed the cast. The venture was a co-operative one between RKO and Holt-Rosen Productions. Song: 'Texas Lady' Paul Sawtell, Johnnie Mann.

Wakamba! was another mediocre African documentary with prints processed by Technicolor. Producer Edgar M. Queeny tried to pep up the usual scenes of lions (illustrated), leopards, hyenas, rhinos, hippos, gazelles and other animals, with a story about a Wakamba warrior who sets out to kill the largest elephant his tribe has ever seen in order to purchase a bride with the animal's tusks. Most of the drama inherent in his quest was defused by sloppy staging and cutting which revealed that the warrior and the prey he was supposedly stalking were nowhere near one another. The film's major advertised breakthrough entailed the use of a new directional microphone, developed by the Bell Telephone Laboratories, that brought the sounds of Africa to theatre audiences with a clarity and ambient energy never before heard in a wildlife documentary. Unfortunately, these sounds were continuously overwhelmed by a cornball narration, written by Charles L. Tedford and recited by Paul E. Prentiss. Post-production work on Wakamba! was done at the Jarville Studios in St Louis, Missouri; RKO distributed for the American Museum of Natural History (New York City).

Naked Sea was a superior 'true-life' adventure (in PatheColor), chronicling the 15,000 mile, four-month odyssey of the tuna clipper 'Star Kist' in search of its harvest from the sea (see illustration). The extras in the drama included porpoises, pelicans, squid, sharks, whales, sea turtles, poisonous sea snakes, moray eels, iguanas, an erupting volcano in the Galapagos Islands and a 'Chubasco' (a South Pacific hurricane). Producer-director-cinematographer Allen H. Miner had his 16 mm footage blown up to wide-screen 35 mm without the usual graininess or loss of definition. William Conrad did a forceful job of reciting associate producer Gerald Schnitzer's narration, and Laurindo Almeida and George Fields composed the jaunty musical score. RKO was the distributor for Theatre Productions Incorporated.

A plethora of machete-waving, machine gun-firing and dynamite-igniting action carried The Treasure Of Pancho Villa to an almost successful conclusion, in spite of its convoluted plot and risible dialogue. With the Mexican Revolution as historical background and rugged Mexican locations as scenic backdrop, Rory Calhoun (left), Shelley Winters (right) and Gilbert Roland indulged in a game of greed vs idealism. Soldier of fortune Calhoun decides he would rather steal gold for himself than for the revolution, despite the example set by dedicated Villa supporter Roland, and the nagging of Winters, who becomes a loyal supporter of the cause after her father is killed by Federal forces. In an ending reminiscent of The Treasure Of Sierra Madre, the gold is buried by an avalanche and no one gets an ounce of it. Niven Busch wrote the second-rate screenplay from a story by J. Robert Bren and Gladys Atwater, and George Sherman directed it with most of his attention given to the gunpowder-related elements. The film was produced by Edmund Grainger in Superscope and colour (prints by Technicolor) and also featured Joseph Calleia, Fanny Schiller, Carlos Mosquiz, Tony Carvajal and Pasquel Pena. RKO co-produced with Grainger's new independent company.

1956

RKO came back to life in 1956. By spring it was being called 'the busiest lot in Hollywood', and by mid-summer the RKO Teleradio regime had five completed features. Two thousand employees were working on three other movies, and six more were scheduled for production within a month. The studio also signed several new personalities, including Anita Ekberg, Diana Dors, Rod Steiger, George Gobel and Susan Strasberg, keeping the publicity office active in grinding out a storm of press copy about the actors and the forthcoming productions. In addition, the organization was making TV commercials, industrial films and short subjects. Twenty films were released in 1956, and it appeared that RKO was well on its way to full recovery.

Near the end of the year, however, the company's fortunes went into a tailspin. Insider forecasts indicated that the new pictures would be disasters, and President Daniel T. O'Shea announced that RKO was planning a substantial curtailment of production activities in 1957. He also stated that RKO was looking for 'some merger of distribution interests for purposes of economy'. Since distribution is generally the most lucrative arm of a motion picture company, O'Shea's words were more than slightly ominous. They suggested that RKO was on the verge of total collapse.

What does a smeared portrait have to do with the corpse of a beautiful model found strangled in an artist's studio? What connection does a charm from a woman's bracelet have with a mysteriously labelled bottle of chianti? What is the meaning of a sketched message on a postcard sent by a dead man? Film consumers who glued their concentration on **Postmark For Danger** (GB: **Portrait Of Alison**) were given the answers to these questions, but most paid for their efforts with outsize headaches. Ken Hughes and Guy Green's screenplay (adapted from a British TV serial by Francis Durbridge) required each viewer to work diligently just to keep the plot strands sorted out, making the picture a challenge but not a particular pleasure. Terry Moore (left) topped the cast as an actress who becomes innocently involved with diamond smugglers, and Robert Beatty (right), William Sylvester, Josephine Griffin, Geoffrey Keen, Alan Cuthbertson, Henry Oscar, William Lucas and Terence Alexander were the other featured pieces in this intricate chess game. Co-scripter and former cinematographer Green also directed for producer Frank Godwin and executive producer Tony Owen. It was made in England by Insignia Films and released in America by RKO for Tony Owen's Todon Productions.

A moody, laconic western, **Tension At Table Rock** focused on Richard Egan (left) who is reputed to be a 'black-hearted, white-livered, back-bitin' sidewinder who murdered his own best friend'. A ballad follows Egan wherever he goes, reminding him of his shooting of fellow outlaw Paul Richards, a man who was not at all the chivalric Robin Hood people believe him to have been. Egan eventually ends up in Table Rock, where he finds cowardly sheriff Cameron Mitchell (on loan from 20th Century-Fox) worried about an influx of rowdy Texas trailherders. Egan ultimately saves the sheriff and the town from destruction, then rides off alone, disregarding the fact that he and the sheriff's wife (Dorothy Malone) have fallen in love. Screenwriter Winston Miller amplified Frank Gruber's novel *Bitter Sage*, giving the picture all the *Shane* overtones he could manage to work in. Charles Marquis Warren added the plodding direction for producer Sam Wiesenthal, and Royal Dano, Billy Chapin, Edward Andrews, John Dehner, DeForest Kelley, Joe DeSantis and Angie Dickinson (right) filled out the cast. The song 'The Ballad Of Wes Tancred', by Josef Myrow and Robert Wells, was sung by Eddy Arnold. Technicolor manufactured the release prints.

◁ 'With Brains, Bullets and Women, He Fought His Way to the *Bottom!*' The fast-talking operator so identified in publicity for **Slightly Scarlet** was John Payne, whose relationships with syndicate boss Ted de Corsia, reform mayoral candidate Kent Taylor, the mayor's girl friend Rhonda Fleming (right), and Fleming's man-hungry sister Arlene Dahl (left), immerse him in a cesspool of graft and corruption. The film slipped ineluctably into the usual potboiler clichés, concluding with the not-exactly-crooked, not-exactly-straight protagonist helping to dispose of a gang of racketeers and bring back clean government to the city. Robert Blees' screenplay, based on *Love's Lovely Counterfeit*, a novel by James M. Cain, also gave roles to Lance Fuller, Buddy Baer, Frank Gerstle and Ellen Corby. Allan Dwan directed, Benedict Bogeaus produced and John Alton's photography (in Superscope with prints by Technicolor) showed the two redheads (Miss Fleming and Miss Dahl) to good advantage. **Slightly Scarlet** was a co-production between RKO and Filmcrest Productions.

△

△

The Bold And The Brave followed the lives of three American soldiers caught up in the Italian campaign of 1944. Wendell Corey (right) played an idealist who finds it hard to kill, even in battle; Mickey Rooney was an irrepressible half-pint out to win enough money in a floating crap game to open the best restaurant in New Jersey; and Don Taylor (left), a religious fanatic so afraid of committing evil that he sees hellfire in every non-conforming incident. The relationship between Taylor and prostitute Nicole Maurey (centre) represented the movie's centrepiece and also its undoing. As delineated by scriptwriter Robert Lewin, the Taylor character was so priggish, bigoted and downright unpleasant, and the love affair such a frustrating mess, that viewer involvement flew right out the window. Corey and Rooney gave their all to maintaining some excitement, but they were fighting a losing battle – with the audience, if not with the Germans. Lewis R. Foster directed in Superscope for producer Hal E. Chester, and Irving H. Levin, who received a presentation credit. Others in it were John Smith, Race Gentry, Ralph Votrian, Wright King, Stanley Adams, Bobs Watson and Tara Summers. RKO distributed for Filmakers Producing Organization (not to be confused with The Filmakers of Ida Lupino and Collier Young). Song: 'The Bold And The Brave' Mickey Rooney, Ross Bagdasarian.

Specifically aimed at the family audience, **Glory** cast the now grown-up Margaret O'Brien (left) as the owner of a racing filly. The horse constantly disappoints, until it is entered in the Kentucky Derby, and you need not be psychic to guess what happens there. Story author Gene Markey and screenwriter Peter Milne evidently decided that the saga of a perseverent girl and her beloved animal was not enough to sustain a 99-minute, Superscope, prints-by-Technicolor attraction, so they added a love triangle linking Miss O'Brien to John Lupton and Byron Palmer and also provided her with the chance to warble three M. K. Jerome-Ted Koehler tunes. The upshot was overly familiar and completely dispensable. Producer-director David Butler, whose independent company co-produced the film with RKO, employed Walter Brennan (right), Charlotte Greenwood, Lisa Davis, Gus Schilling, Hugh Sanders, Walter Baldwin, Harry Tyler, Leonid Kinskey, Paul E. Burns and Theron Jackson to complete the cast. Songs (actually sung by Norma Zimmer, dubbing for Miss O'Brien): 'Glory', 'Gettin' Nowhere Road' 'Kentucky (Means Paradise)'.

Montgomery Tully wrote and directed **The Way Out** (GB: **Dial 999**) and, therefore, was the chief target for criticism of his paltry little melodrama. Gene Nelson (left) starred as a blonde-chasing husband who kills a man in a barroom brawl. Nelson's disillusioned but loyal wife (Mona Freeman, right) agrees to help him evade the authorities; she and her brother (Michael Goodliffe) secure two trucks, shuttling Nelson from one to the other and back again, bluffing their way through roadblocks, and escaping the pursuit of Scotland Yard detective John Bentley. The finale had the wanted man run down by a bus, thus allowing Miss Freeman to become more closely acquainted with Mr Bentley. All the actors turned in sub-standard performances, including supporting troops Sydney Tafler, Charles Victor, Arthur Lovegrove, Cyril Chamberlain, Paula Byrne, Kay Callard, Michael Golden, Charles Mortimer, Margaret Harrison and Clifford Buckton. Alec Snowden produced from an original story by Bruce Graeme. The picture, a Merton Park production made in England, was distributed in the US by RKO for Todon Productions ◁ Incorporated.

△

A superb *film noir*, directed in galvanic fashion by Fritz Lang, **While The City Sleeps** was all about cold-blooded murders and back-stabbing journalism. The story had obnoxious playboy Vincent Price (right) inheriting a newspaper empire from his father, and offering a top executive job to any staff member able to discover the identity of a psychopathic killer terrorizing the women of the metropolis. Price's contest triggers vicious competition among the newspaper's personnel and eventuates in three of the men using their girlfriends as 'bait' to try to get the scoop. There was something reprehensible about nearly every character in the film, but there was nothing boring about any of them. Among the leading specimens: cynical, Pulitzer Prize-winning reporter Dana Andrews (left); tough and tricky managing editor Thomas Mitchell (centre); ruthless wire service head George Sanders; photo bureau chief James Craig, who is having an affair with Price's wife (Rhonda Fleming) and plans to use the relationship for leverage; ambitious sob sister Ida Lupino; and homicidal mama's boy John Barrymore Jr. Screenwriter Casey Robinson, working from Charles Einstein's novel *The Bloody Spur*, did a deft job of fleshing out each of the characters. Also cast: Howard Duff, Sally Forrest, Robert Warwick, Mae Marsh, Ralph Peters, Sandy White, Larry Blake, Celia Lovsky, Edward Hinton, Pitt Herbert and Vladimir Sokoloff. It is sad to report that this film, the best the studio had released in some time, was purchased from producer Bert E. Friedlob's independent company, which had originally intended to have United Artists distribute it. Thus, RKO had nothing whatsoever to do with its making. Song: 'While The City Sleeps' Herschel Burke Gilbert, Joseph Mullendore.

Somewhere deep inside a welter of empty clatter called **Cash On Delivery** (GB: **To Dorothy, A Son**), there was an amusing seed that might have germinated into a funny movie. But fertilized with a breathless succession of overstated crises, and watered with a collection of shrill, unappealing characters, the comedy yielded nothing but sour apples. Roger MacDougall (who wrote the original play) and Peter Rogers developed a plot wherein nightclub singer Shelley Winters (right) will inherit $2 million unless her ex-husband John Gregson (centre) fathers a male heir by a specified time. Gregson's new wife Peggy Cummins is, indeed, pregnant, with the arrival of the stork coming down to the wire, and international time zones, the divorce laws of Bolivia and the marriage regulations of Tonga complicating matters. Muriel Box directed in extremely broad strokes, casting Wilfrid Hyde-White (left), Mona Washbourne, Huntley Power, Martin Miller, Anthony Oliver, Joan Sims, Hal Osmond, Aubrey Mather, Ronald Adam, Charles Hawtrey, Alfie Bass, Campbell Singer, Joan Hickson, Marjorie Rhodes, Fred Berger and Joan Newell in supporting roles. Ben Schrift (Shelley Winters' father) and Peter Rogers co-produced in England for Welbeck, and RKO distributed for MacDonald Pictures in the US. Songs included: 'Give Me A Man' Paddy Roberts; 'You're The Only One' Jacques Abram; 'Juke-Box Ballet' Fred G. Moritt, George Thorn.

▽

A lady psychiatrist who knows too much for her own good became the heroine of **The Brain Machine**. When Elizabeth Allan (right) examines amnesia victim Maxwell Reed (left) with an electroencephalograph, she finds that he has the brain of a psychopathic murderer. The police exhibit no interest in her diagnosis until the patient escapes from the hospital and kidnaps Miss Allan. In their search for the missing pair, the authorities uncover a bloody trail of gang violence leading to a drug-smuggling operation. This Alec Snowden-produced film was made on a meagre budget, but its taut screenplay and direction (both by Ken Hughes) and above-average performances resulted in a satisfactory, if modest, thriller. Also among the cast: Patrick Barr, Vanda Godsell, Russell Napier, Neil Hallett, Edwin Richfield, Mark Bellamy, Bill Nagy, Anthony Valentine, John Horsley, Donald Bissett and Gwen Bacon. Another British-made import, the film was distributed in America for Berkshire Pictures Corporation.

▽

△

The Conqueror receives prominent mention in a popular book listing the 50 worst films of all time. It deserved this brand of recognition for its casting and dialogue alone. John Wayne (left) topped the acting contingent as Temujin, the Mongol leader who captures Bortai (Susan Hayward, right, borrowed from 20th Century-Fox), the tempestuous daughter of a Tartar king. 'She is a woman – much woman,' Temujin observes. She, of course, hates him until he is captured by her father and tortured. Then she loves him, as he had predicted ('I shall keep you, Bortai, in response to my passion. Your hatred will kindle into love'). Bortai helps him escape, and soon he and his warriors conquer all of the Gobi Desert tribes, at which point he becomes known as Genghis Khan. There was no denying the sweep and spectacular production values of this $6 million epic which was made in CinemaScope and stereophonic sound with prints manufactured by Technicolor. There was also no way around the astoundingly ridiculous characters, bad acting and laughable writing, or the total inaccuracy of the film's treatment of Asian history. Then again, it was just a hell-bent-for-leather western anyway, with the cowboys dressed up in some very odd costumes. Oscar Millard wrote it, Dick Powell produced and directed it, Richard Sokolove was the associate producer, Victor Young and Edward Heyman composed the title song. Also in it: Pedro Armendariz, Agnes Moorehead, Thomas Gomez, John Hoyt, William Conrad, Ted de Corsia, Leslie Bradley, Lee Van Cleef, Peter Mamakos, Leo Gordon and Richard Loo. The prime mover behind the film was Howard Hughes, who took a presentation credit and later bought the picture and all available prints from RKO so he could have **The Conqueror** completely to himself.

△

Great Day In The Morning was the odd title of a western about the machinations of Union and Confederate factions trying to seize Colorado gold for wartime financing. Set in Denver in 1861, Lesser Samuels' screenplay (based on a novel by Robert Hardy Andrews) offered Robert Stack (left, borrowed from Batjac Productions) as a cynical Southern sympathizer, Alex Nicol as a Northern secret agent, Virginia Mayo (right, borrowed from Warner Bros.) as a wild west newcomer who soon falls for Stack, and Ruth Roman as a saloon entertainer who also develops a yen for the rebel. All the proper dramatic ingredients – action, intrigue, passion, hatred, romance – were included, plus arresting Colorado scenery (in Superscope with prints by Technicolor), but the results were only a little above average. Jacques Tourneur's direction was strangely sluggish, which kept the film from ever breeding much energy or affection. Raymond Burr, Leo Gordon, Regis Toomey, Carleton Young and Donald MacDonald played secondary characters in the Edmund Grainger production. RKO co-produced with Grainger's independent company.

Followers of RKO movies through the years had had opportunities to match wits with such cinematic sleuths as Hildegarde Withers, Simon Templar and Gay Falcon. **Murder On Approval** (GB: **Barbados Quest**) introduced special investigator Duke Martin (played by former Falcon Tom Conway, left), a combination of Sherlock Holmes, The Saint and Raffles. Regrettably, the mystery he confronted, involving a valuable stamp known as the 'Barbados overplate', was unworthy of either the Duke's or the audience's attention. Dragged down by rotten dialogue, and exhibiting narrative bones picked clean long before by screenwriting buzzards, the Kenneth R. Hayles script should have been assigned to the scrap heap rather than the production stages. Brian Worth (right) played the brains behind a forgery gang, Delphi Lawrence (centre) the shapely lady who lures Conway into a killer's trap, and other significant members of a large cast were Michael Balfour, John Horsley, Ronan O'Casey, Colin Tapley, Alan Gifford, John Colicos, Mayura, John Watson, Reg Morris, Marianne Stone, Frank Pemberton, Olive Kirby and Rosamund Waring. Bernard Knowles showed absolutely no affinity for the mystery genre in his direction, and Robert S. Baker and Monty Berman produced. RKO released the British-made picture for the Barbour Corporation. Note: Conway played Duke Martin again in *Breakaway* (1956), which was released in England but not the US. See RKO British Production appendix.

Finger Of Guilt (GB: **The Intimate Stranger**) related the story of a film producer (Richard Basehart) whose career and marriage are all but ruined by a series of strange and intimate love letters from a woman he has never met. It is thought at first that the letters are part of a blackmail attempt, but when Basehart (seated right) finally catches up with the writer (Mary Murphy, left), he finds that the purpose behind her epistles is even more sinister. Also cast in this polished mystery drama: Constance Cummings, Roger Livesey, Faith Brook, Mervyn Johns, Vernon Greeves, David Lodge and Basil Dignam. The American credits for this British-made film listed Peter Howard as the screenwriter and Alec C. Snowden as the producer/director. Snowden did produce, but Howard was really blacklisted writer Howard Koch, and the film was actually directed by Joseph Losey, also on the blacklist. British credits gave Losey's pseudonym, Joseph Walton. The version distributed by RKO in the US for Todon Productions was 24 minutes shorter than the original British screening.

Death Of A Scoundrel was two hours' worth of rake's progress, complete with betrayal, thievery, multiple seduction, suicide, murder and the added fillip of watching George Sanders (right) cavort with his actual ex-wife (Zsa Zsa Gabor, left) and stab his real-life brother (Tom Conway) in the back. Writer-producer-director Charles Martin's story echoed the career of notorious financial manipulator and lothario Serge Rubenstein, but the film was the epitome of lurid trash, relieved only by several injections of comedy. Sanders portrayed the scoundrel, a penniless European who divorces himself from humanity, comes to America and begins auctioning his soul to the highest bidder. Conway was the brother he betrays; Gabor, Yvonne De Carlo, Nancy Gates and Coleen Gray were decorative stepping-stones on the road to success; and Lisa Ferraday played Conway's widow who journeys to the States to kill Sanders, but ends up committing suicide instead. Victor Jory, John Hoyt, Celia Lovsky, Werner Klemperer, Justice Watson, John Sutton, Curtis Cooksey, Gabriel Curtiz and Morris Ankrum were other cast members photographed by the ace cinematographer James Wong Howe. J. Herbert Klein worked as associate producer for Charles Martin Productions, and RKO distributed for the latter company, later purchasing full ownership in the picture to avoid certain legal complications. Note: The title was ultimately changed to **The Loves And Death Of A Scoundrel**, because it was generally felt that emphasis on the word 'Death' in a title was a detriment to box-office success.

As written for the screen by Burt Kennedy from Frank Gruber's novel *The Lock And The Key*, **Man In The Vault** told the story of locksmith William Campbell (right), a man trapped between the law and a ring of killers when he is forced to make keys for a safety deposit box containing $200,000 in cash. Anita Ekberg (left) and Karen Sharpe supplied the sex appeal, playing a two-timing gangster's moll and Campbell's high-living sweetheart respectively. Andrew V. McLaglen directed this efficient thriller on location among the streets, alleys and swank residences of Beverly Hills and Hollywood. Also cast: Berry Kroeger, Paul Fix, James Seay, Mike Mazurki, Robert Keys, Gonzales Gonzalez, Nancy Duke and Vivianne Lloyd. RKO distributed for Batjac Productions (John Wayne's company), which employed Robert E. Morrison as producer. Song: 'Let The Chips Fall Where They May' Henry Vars & By Dunham.

In 1939, John Farrow directed one of the most exciting 'B' films in company history, *Five Came Back*. Seventeen years later, producer-director Farrow came back himself, remaking his earlier triumph under the title **Back From Eternity**, but the results were only so-so. In general, the acting was better on the second trip, but a decision to pad out the basic story to 98 minutes diluted some of the compression and suspense that had fuelled the original. Crashlanding in the South American jungle, hard by the domain of head-shrinking natives, was the following, neatly shuffled deck of characters: hard-drinking pilot Robert Ryan; sultry Las Vegas superstructure Anita Ekberg (left, borrowed from Batjac Productions); criminal Rod Steiger en route to his execution; socialite Phyllis Kirk and her cowardly fiancé Gene Barry; co-pilot Keith Andes; distinguished professor Cameron Prud'homme and his wife Beulah Bondi; sadistic policeman Fred Clark, Chicago racketeer Jesse White and four-year-old Jon Provost (right). Adele Mara was also on board, but flew out a cabin door during the storm that knocked the plane out of commission. Once on the ground, abundant conflicts emerge as Ryan works feverishly to repair his craft and the survivors learn that only five of them will be able to leave once the airship is able to fly. Jonathan Latimer typed out the script, based on Richard Carroll's story, and Franz Waxman composed the effective musical score.

Beyond A Reasonable Doubt, Fritz Lang's final American film, was replete with the ambiguities and ironies that had always been a matter of fascination to him. However, the Douglas Morrow screenplay was just too contrived and far-fetched to satisfy critics or the average film patron. In it, crusading newspaper publisher Sidney Blackmer persuades his future son-in-law Dana Andrews (left) to engage in a hoax that will point up the dangers of circumstantial evidence and expose grand-standing district attorney Philip Bourneuf, who has built a career on it. Blackmer proceeds to plant clues that lead to Andrews' conviction as the murderer of a burlesque stripper. Everything is going as planned until Blackmer is killed and the documentation exonerating Andrews is destroyed. His fiancée Joan Fontaine (right), figures prominently in the attempts to secure a pardon before Andrews is executed, but the twist ending reveals that he did, in actuality, commit the murder in the first place. Arthur Franz, Edward Binns, Shepperd Strudwick, Robin Raymond, Barbara Nichols, William Leicester, Dan Seymour, Rusty Lane, Joyce Taylor, Carleton Young, Trudy Wroe, Joe Kirk, Charles Evans and Wendell Niles also appeared in the Bert Friedlob production. RKO co-sponsored the film with Friedlob's independent company. Song: 'Beyond A Reasonable Doubt' Herschel Burke Gilbert, Alfred Perry. ▷

An off-beat film of warmth and sensitivity, **The Brave One** was the love story of a boy and a bull. Gitano – or Gypsy – is the name the boy gives the bull whose life he saves during a storm. The animal follows him around like a puppy until the legal owners spirit the mature Gitano away to do battle with matador Fermin Rivera in the Plaza de Mexico bullring in Mexico City. The boy secures a 'pardon' for his pet, signed by the President of Mexico, but he arrives at the *corrida* too late. What follows is such a display of courage that the crowd finally calls for the 'undulto', a reprieve for the bull from its ritualistic death in the afternoon. Michel Ray (illustrated) played the freckled-faced lad, topping a cast of mainly unknown actors that also included Rodolfo Hoyos, Elsa Cardenas, Carlos Navarro, Joi Lansing, George Trevino and Carlos Fernandez. Jack Cardiff shot the handsome Technicolor and CinemaScope photography, Victor Young wrote the effusive musical score and Irving Rapper directed on location in Mexico. The screenplay was written by Harry Franklin and Merrill G. White, based on a story by Robert Rich which had as its inspiration a true incident that occurred in a bull ring in Barcelona, Spain in 1936. It also bore a resemblance to *The Story Of Bonito The Bull* by Robert J. Flaherty, an episode intended for Orson Welles' abortive *It's All True* project. Maurice and Frank King produced, with RKO picking up distribution rights from the independent King Bros Productions. Note: When Robert Rich was announced as winner of the 1956 Academy Award for Best Motion Picture Story, no one came forward to claim the award. In truth, Rich was an alias used by Dalton Trumbo, former RKO contract writer who had been blacklisted by Hollywood motion picture companies ever since his 1947 run-in with the House Un-American Activities Committee.

Ginger Rogers returned to her old outpost, appearing in the first film produced during the new RKO Teleradio Pictures era: **The First Traveling Saleslady**. Miss Rogers and Broadway musical performer Carol Channing (her film debut) scrambled about trying to wrench a few laughs from Stephen Longstreet and Devery Freeman's script – without demonstrable success. Ginger, the titular heroine, goes broke selling steel corset stays (the year is 1897), despite the help of her chorus girl companion (Channing). Soon enough, she is peddling barbed wire to Texas ranchers who consider the new-fangled fencing dangerous. James Arness, the biggest cattle baron in the state, vows either to stop her activities or marry her, but Ginger (left) outwits him and ends up hitched to Barry Nelson (right), a horseless carriage inventor who has followed her down south from New York. Producer-director Arthur Lubin failed to improve upon a story that lacked wit, invention and drive. Other actors giving it the old college try included Clint Eastwood (in a small role as Miss Channing's beau), David Brian, Robert Simon, Frank Wilcox, Daniel M. White, Harry Cheshire, John Eldredge, Robert Hinkle, Jack Rice, Kate Drain Lawson, Edward Cassidy and Fred Essler. RKO shared the cost of mounting the film with Arthur Lubin Productions, and prints were made by Technicolor. Songs included: 'The First Traveling Saleslady', 'A Corset Can Do A Lot For A Lady' Irving Gertz, Hal Levy.

In the remake of *Bachelor Mother* (1939), filmed under the new title of **Bundle Of Joy**, Debbie Reynolds (right, borrowed from MGM) and Eddie Fisher (left) played the parts originally created by Ginger Rogers and David Niven. Though the new version featured Technicolor photography (by William Snyder), a flock of Josef Myrow-Mack Gordon tunes, and dances choreographed by Nick Castle, it was a huge disappointment, containing only faint reverberations of *Bachelor Mother*'s delicious comic touches. Reynolds was the department store salesgirl who loses her job and finds a baby, then is saddled with it since no one will believe that the child isn't her own. Fisher, the son of the store owner, doesn't buy her story either, but he woos and wins her anyway. Director Norman Taurog played up the slapstick and the musical interludes to the detriment of the story's more subtle and witty elements. Adolphe Menjou, Tommy Noonan, Nita Talbot, Una Merkel, Melville Cooper, Bill Goodwin, Howard McNear, Robert H. Harris, Mary Treen, Edward S. Brophy, Gil Stratton, Scott Douglas and baby Donald Gray (illustrated) also took roles in the Robert Carson-Arthur Sheekman script (based on Felix Jackson's original story and Norman Krasna's 1939 screenplay). The picture was Edmund Grainger's last production for RKO. Songs included: 'Worry About Tomorrow, Tomorrow', 'All About Love', 'Some Day Soon', 'I Never Felt This Way Before', 'Bundle Of Joy', 'Lullaby In Blue' 'You're Perfect In Every Department'.

1957

In January, the shadow of doom enshrouded the RKO lot. Universal-International took over distribution of the company's important pictures, all production ground to a halt and most of the employees' contracts were terminated. A dream factory became a ghost town.

Stories circulated for months thereafter that RKO would be resurrected yet again. Chairman of the board Thomas O'Neil was said to be negotiating for enough money to reactivate production on a limited basis. RKO still had unfinished properties and outstanding commitments to stars, and an idle studio was an expensive proposition. In May, there was a report that the company contemplated putting up 100 percent of the financing for top quality European productions. But by the fall, all hope had been extinguished. O'Neil sold both the Gower Street and Culver City filmmaking plants to Desilu, the highly successful company set up by former RKO performers Lucille Ball and Desi Arnaz. The studios would be used for the production of television programs – an ironic fate, but one that was certainly better than earlier indications that they would become tire processing plants.

Ten pictures, including the long overdue **Jet Pilot**, were released during the year. All were handled by Universal-International or by States Rights companies in the United States.

Guilty? began in a British courtroom where Andrée Debar is on trial for killing a man she had every reason to hate. Debar, who had sheltered the dead man from the Nazis in France during World War II, was subsequently betrayed by him and sent to a concentration camp while pregnant with his child. Nevertheless, she insists that she had nothing to do with his knifing in a London hotel room. Her case looks hopeless until French newspaperman Frank Villard and his friend John Justin (right) take up the cause and run headlong into a gang of international counterfeiters who hold the key to the mystery. The team of Charles A. Leeds (producer), Edmond T. Greville (director), Maurice J. Wilson (screenplay) and Ernest Dudley (additional dialogue) translated Michael Gilbert's novel *Death Has Deep Roots* to the screen in well-trodden fashion. Barbara Laage (left), Donald Wolfit, Stephen Murray, Norman Wooland, Kynaston Reeves, Betty Stockfield, Hugh Morton, Leslie Perrins, Russell Napier and Sydney Tafler had other featured roles in this Gibraltar Films production, made in England and released in the US by States Rights companies.

The history of **Jet Pilot** was a perfect paradigm of the Howard Hughes era at RKO. Production began in December of 1949, was finished in May of 1951, and yet the film was not released until 1957. During the absurdly protracted post-production phase, Hughes tinkered around with it, ordering retakes, aerial shots, re-editing, a new musical score (by Bronislau Kaper) etc. A lot of top talent worked on this one, including director Josef von Sternberg, screenwriter-producer Jules Furthman, Technicolor cinematographer Winton Hoch and stars John Wayne and Janet Leigh (borrowed from MGM), but it is probably unfair to blame the horrendous results on anyone besides Mr Hughes. After all, it was his baby – the film that would supposedly rekindle the excitement of *Hell's Angels* (1930). The outlandish story was more than enough to crack up any aerial saga. Leigh (right) played a Russian spy who flees Siberia in a Mig jet, landing at an American air base in Alaska. Pretending she is a defector, the lady pilot is handed over to Colonel Wayne (left) for safekeeping. Wayne can't get much information out of her, but they have a heck of a time together, eating steaks, guzzling champagne and lounging around the pool in Palm Springs. They fall in love, marry and wing back to the Soviet Union in an American jet. Only now Wayne is the agent, gathering information for the big brains in the Pentagon. The heroine discovers what is going on just as her comrades are about to inject her man with a drug that will turn him into an idiot; naturally she opts for John Wayne (and steaks, champagne and sexy negligees) over devotion to the Communist ideology, and the young marrieds zip back to the States with Red Migs in hot pursuit. The film was filled with dizzying segues from comic to melodramatic to corny cheesecake scenes and had about as much relationship to the real military and the real cold war as Bozo the Clown has to Albert Einstein. Also cast: Jay C. Flippen, Paul Fix, Richard Rober, Roland Winters, Hans Conried, Ivan Triesault, John Bishop, Perdita Chandler, Joyce Compton and Denver Pyle. Howard Hughes received his final presentation credit on an RKO film, with Universal-International handling distribution in the US.

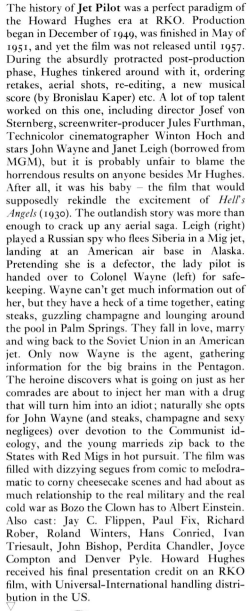

The Young Stranger introduced actor James MacArthur (right), producer Stuart Millar and director John Frankenheimer to the world of Hollywood film production. One of the better 1950s pictures dealing with the 'generation gap', it was inspired by the relationship between screenwriter Robert Dozier and his father, RKO production chief William Dozier. MacArthur played a bright, energetic teenager who is intimidated by his father, prominent film executive James Daly. The youth becomes innocently involved in a fight with a hot-tempered theatre manager, then finds that no one, his father included, believes he struck the man in self-defence. The remainder of the picture documented the boy's attempts to vindicate his honour and reclaim his self-respect; it ended happily with father and son coming to a new understanding of each one's responsibilities to the other. Kim Hunter (left), James Gregory, Whit Bissell, Jeff Silver, Jack Mullaney, Eddie Ryder, Jean Corbett, Charles Davis, Marian Seldes, Terry Kelman, Edith Evanson, Tom Pittman and Howard Price were other cast members in this searching film that touched on a number of universal concerns. The picture represented the beginning of the end for RKO, which turned it over to Universal-International for distribution throughout America. Note: The story first appeared on CBS television in 1955 as *Deal A Blow*, also written by Dozier Jr, with MacArthur in the lead and Frankenheimer directing.
▽

Public Pigeon No. 1 originated as a television comedy, starring Red Skelton, shown on CBS in September of 1955. RKO, which co-produced with Val-Richie Productions, should have left it on the small screen, for there was not enough comedic invention in this one to keep a commercial alive, let alone an RKO-Scope commercial, which this was. Skelton (right) again clowned up a storm as the eponymous sucker, a lunchroom attendant who entrusts stock swindlers with the money that he and Janet Blair have saved for their upcoming marriage. Skelton then unwittingly becomes the courier for the swindlers and winds up behind bars, precipitating a goofy jailbreak scene, and other adventures that were supposed to be wild and zany but simply broadened the definition of the word dumb. Producer Harry Tugend wrote the dreadful script, based on a story by Don Quinn and Larry Berns and a teleplay by Devery Freeman. Norman Z. McLeod directed in Technicolor, with a cast that included Vivian Blaine (left), Jay C. Flippen, Allyn Joslyn, Benny Baker, Milton Frome, John Abbott, Howard McNear, James Burke, Herb Vigran and The Seven Ashtons. Universal-International again functioned as US distributor. Songs: 'Don't Be Chicken, Chicken', 'Pardon Me, Got To Go Mambo' Matt Malneck, Eve Marley. ▷

A heart attack was the dramatic fulcrum around which **That Night!** turned. John Beal was the victim, a gray-flannel, Madison Avenue man overtaxed by the pressures of his advertising job and the upper-middle-class life style to which he and his family have become addicted. One evening as Beal is rushing to catch a commuter train from Manhattan to his Connecticut home, he feels the first stabbing symptoms of a heart seizure. The rest of the film presented, in sober, documentary fashion, the trip to the hospital, Beal's fears of death, the responses of his wife and children, a second near-fatal attack, and the slow recovery process. After the crisis atmosphere abates somewhat, the experience leads to a new understanding between Beal (right) and his wife Augusta Dabney (left), and a thorough re-examination of their values and plans for the future. Although the film was not an especially pleasurable viewing experience, it was superbly acted, honest and often compelling. Like *The Young Stranger*, the basic story (originally entitled *The Long Way Home*) had

first been dramatized on television. Robert Wallace and Burton J. Rowles wrote the screenplay, John Newland directed it, Mende Brown was the associate producer, and Shepperd Strudwick, Rosemary Murphy, Malcolm Brodrick, Denis Kohler, Beverly Lunsford, Bill Darrid and Joe Julian also appeared. Himan Brown produced in New York for his Galahad Productions outfit, and RKO turned over American distribution to Universal-International.
▽

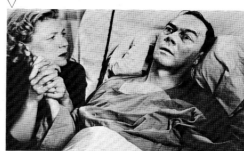

Escapade In Japan was the story of two runaway boys – one American and one Japanese – who lead the police on a merry chase through the by-ways of the island nation. Jon Provost (left) and Roger Nakagawa (right) believe the authorities are intent on putting them behind bars, while the truth, of course, is that they are simply trying to reunite the youngsters with their frightened parents. Arthur Lubin produced and directed this picaresque comedy-drama with a keen eye for such colourful settings as a Shinto temple, a theatre, the harbour of a fishing village, the busy streets of Kyoto, a geisha house, etc. In addition to providing a Cook's tour of Japan, associate producer Winston Miller's script re-emphasized the need for mutual respect and understanding between the two former enemy nations in a way that was charming and delicate rather than pompous and preachy. The two children easily stole the film from their adult colleagues, who included Teresa Wright and Cameron Mitchell as Provost's parents, Kuniko Miyake (borrowed from Daiei Motion Picture Company) and Susumu Fujita as the mother and father of the Japanese youngster, plus Philip Ober, Katsuhiko Haida, Tatsuo Saito, Ureo Egawa, Frank Tokunaga and Ayako Hidaka. William Dozier received an 'In Charge of Production' credit, and the Technicolor-Technirama film, superbly shot by William Snyder and scored by former RKO ace composer Max Steiner, was released by Universal-International in the US.
▽

△
A crazy, mixed-up western that had nothing to do with cowboys, rustlers, sheriffs or schoolmarms, **Run Of The Arrow** was worth seeing for its unbridled audacity. Writer-producer-director Samuel Fuller's movie top-cast Rod Steiger (illustrated) as the Confederate soldier who fires the last bullet in the Civil War. Steiger's hatred for the Yankees is all consuming, and he cannot accept the defeat of the South. Following a bitter argument with his mother, who suggests that 'maybe a broken neck is the best answer for what ails' him, he heads west, 'where the savages live'. There he is nearly killed by the Sioux Indians in a ritual test of strength and endurance called 'run of the arrow', marries a Sioux woman, and becomes a blood-brother of the embattled tribe. Soon enough, he is caught in the middle between his adopted people and the despised Yankees, whose soldiers are assigned to build a fort near the Indians' hunting grounds. As Captain Brian Keith suggests, Steiger is the far-West version of the 'man without a country' – neither Sioux, nor Southerner, nor American. In the end he finally accepts the American flag and leaves the Indians behind in search of a life as a whole man. One of the film's pleasures was Joseph Biroc's carefully composed Technicolor cinematography of locations around St George, Utah. Also cast: Sarita Montiel (a Spanish actress whose voice was dubbed by Angie Dickinson), Ralph Meeker, Jay C. Flippen, Olive Carey, H. M. Wynant, Neyle Morrow, Billy Miller, Frank de Kova, Frank Warner, Colonel Tim McCoy, Stuart Randall and heavily-muscled Charles Bronson (playing a Sioux chief named Blue Buffalo). RKO co-produced in this one with Fuller's Globe Enterprises company, and Universal-International took over American distribution.

A relentlessly ordinary film about 'average' people, **The Violators** featured Arthur O'Connell (right) as a parole officer, Nancy Malone as his daughter and Fred Beir as Malone's prospective husband who perpetrates a swindling scheme when O'Connell refuses to lend him the $500 needed to keep the family business going. The situation leads O'Connell to reassess his own attitudes toward teenage crime and re-evaluate his responsibilities as a father. The film came up short on nearly every count, including its verbose, prosaic script (by Ernest Pendrell, based on a story by Israel Beckhardt and Wenzell Brown), the static, claustrophobic direction (by John Newland) and indifferent performances from the principals, and from Clarice Blackburn (left), Henry Sharp, Mary Michael, Joe Julian, Bill Darrid, Sheila Copelan, Bernie Lenrow and Martin Freed in support. The sales department gave **The Violators** a full-blown exploitation treatment ('The true story of teenage law-breakers ... living recklessly, loving violently ... too young to know better, too hard to care ... caught in the remorseless web of judicial punishment...'). Only a few customers were fooled. Mende Brown was the associate producer and Himan Brown produced in New York for Galahad Productions, with Universal-International again handling American distribution.
▽

Set in 18th century France, **Cartouche** presented Richard Basehart (right) as a swordsman, adventurer and lover who is forced to flee the country after being accused of murdering a prince in a gamblers' brawl. The hero joins a troupe of strolling players, then plunges into various escapades in which he attempts to expose the real killer. Meanwhile, his enemies try to trap him with trickery and swordplay. Producer John Nasht and director Steve Sekely were in charge of this lacklustre costume romance, filmed in Italy and France, which also featured Patricia Roc (left) as

the leading lady of the itinerant performers, Akim Tamiroff as a pseudo-nobleman who has attained his title through pure rascality, and Massimo Serato as Basehart's primary enemy, plus Isa Barzizza, Nerio Bernardi, Nino Marchetti and Aldo De Franchi. The screenplay, by Louis Stevens, was based on a treatment by Tullio Pinelli. RKO was originally set to release the picture for Venturini-Nasht Productions, but it was eventually handled by different companies in different sections of the United States, a procedure commonly known as States Rights distribution. ▽

'HALF-ANGEL, HALF-DEVIL, she made him HALF-A-MAN'. So began the sleazy American advertising campaign for **The Unholy Wife**, Diana Dors' first American-made release. The amply-endowed British actress slinked her way through Jonathan Latimer's screenplay (story William Durkee) about a party girl (Miss Dors, right) who marries wealthy winery owner Rod Steiger (left), promptly falls in love with rodeo performer Tom Tryon and then decides to murder her husband. The plan backfires when she mistakenly kills Steiger's best friend. Dors escapes punishment for that homicide, but is eventually convicted of a murder she did not commit – perverse, but poetic, justice. Producer John Farrow's indolent direction deactivated the story's nasty energy and put straitjackets on the walking libidos who played it out. This, no doubt, caused plenty of unhappiness among patrons who believed the white-hot promises made by the publicity campaign. Others in the Technicolor co-production between RKO and Treasure Productions were Beulah Bondi, Marie Windsor, Arthur Franz, Luis Van Rooten, Joe DeSantis, Argentina Brunetti, Tol Avery, James Burke and Steve Pendleton. Universal-International was the US distributor. Note: The story, which bore a passing resemblance to Sidney Howard's *They Knew What They Wanted* (released by RKO in 1940), was based on a teleplay first shown on CBS in January 1956. ▽

1958-60

By 1958, RKO had drawn its last breath as a movie-making body. However, the company still had a few unreleased films of its own, contractual obligations with other organizations for productions, and several pictures acquired for outright distribution. These movies were distributed between 1958 and 1960 by various companies, including Universal-International, Warner Bros., Buena Vista, Columbia, MGM and States Rights operations.

Seven pictures were released in 1958, four in 1959 and two in 1960. All were overlooked by the Academy when Oscar time rolled around.

All Mine To Give (1958) (GB: **The Day They Gave The Babies Away**) was based on historical incidents derived from the family background of writer Dale Eunson, who penned the original story and collaborated with his wife Katherine on the screenplay. Truth may indeed be stranger than fiction, but it is not necessarily as entertaining, as this lugubrious saga demonstrated. Glynis Johns (right, borrowed from an English company called Peet Productions) and Cameron Mitchell (left, borrowed from 20th Century-Fox) played a Scottish couple who emigrate to the United States in the 1850s and raise a family of six children among the routine rigours of backwoods life. The film was an hour old before the true crisis came to the fore. Mitchell dies of diptheria and Johns of typhoid, leaving 12-year-old Rex Thompson (borrowed from Columbia) with the responsibility of finding homes for his younger brothers and sisters on Christmas day. A 'weeper' of the most old-fashioned and manipulative sort, it failed to wrest complete emotional surrender from audiences because of faulty narrative construction and weakly developed characters. Television director Allen Reisner handled his first theatrical feature for producer Sam Wiesenthal, using Patty McCormack, Ernest Truex, Hope Emerson, Alan Hale Jr, Sylvia Field, Royal Dano, Stephen Wootton, Butch Bernard, Yolanda White, Rita Johnson, Ellen Corby, Rosalyn Boulter, Francis DeSales, Jon Provost and Reta Shaw (centre) to complete the cast. Universal-International took charge of American distribution of the Technicolor film, which had had its world premiére in Britain in April, 1957 – doubtless on account of Glynis Johns' star status there.
▽

△

Herman Melville's novel *Typee* was hacked up and puréed into absolute drivel retitled **Enchanted Island** (1958). The pot was literally on the boil in this one, for Dana Andrews (right) and Don Dubbins, having escaped from a whaling ship and settled down with a tribe of South Sea islanders called the Typee, soon discover that the natives are cannibals and that they are part of a future menu. Coming to the rescue is sultry, blue-eyed princess Jane Powell (left, in one of the more 'exotic' roles of her career), whose love for Andrews evidently takes precedence over her appetite. Arthur Shields, Ted de Corsia, Friedrich Ledebur, Augustin Fernandez, Francisco Reiguera and Les Hellman also stumbled through this howling jungle farrago, which was directed in Technicolor by Allan Dwan from James Leicester and Harold Jacob Smith's screenplay. Benedict Bogeaus produced in Mexico; the film was another coproduction between RKO and Waverly Productions, distributed by Warner Bros. in the US. Song: 'Enchanted Island' Robert Allen.

The year's most unlikely casting teamed television personality George Gobel (left) and Diana Dors (right) in a numbingly unfunny comedy entitled **I Married A Woman** (1958). Goodman Ace's screenplay introduced 'Lonesome George' as the advertising hot-shot who dreamed up the 'Miss Luxemberg Beer beauty contest' and came away married to the winner (Miss Dors, borrowed from Treasure Productions). Now Gobel's frenzied boss (Adolphe Menjou) is demanding another copy-generating coup, which deflects the young man from his husbandly duties and causes his marriage to begin to crumble. How scrambling George satisfies his boss and recaptures his sensual wife made for an overdose of juvenilia that cast viewers and critics alike into a posture of frozen disbelief. Jesse Royce Landis, Nita Talbot, William Redfield, Steve Dunne, John McGiver, Steve Pendleton, Cheerio Meredith, Kay Buckley, Angie Dickinson, and John Wayne in an unbilled cameo, also performed for producer William Bloom and director Hal Kanter. RKO co-produced the film with Gomalco (Gobel's company); it was released by Universal-International in the United States. Note: **I Married A Woman** was photographed in black-and-white except for the John Wayne sequence, which was in Technicolor.

The Girl Most Likely (1958), a musicalized remake of *Tom, Dick And Harry* (1941) was the last RKO picture started and finished at the Gower Street studio. Though hardly a classic, it represented one of the better efforts of the RKO Teleradio regime. Jane Powell starred as the girl engaged to three men at the same time and having a terrible time deciding which one to marry. Her indecision is heightened by the fact that she has always dreamed of tying the knot with a rich man who would whisk her away to a life of luxury. Keith Andes almost fills the bill, but mechanic Cliff Robertson (borrowed from Columbia) and real estate salesman Tommy Noonan are also appealing prospective mates. In the end, romantic love wins out over all peripheral considerations. If anything, the story was even more sappy by 1958 standards than those of 1941, but the picture did contain several flashy musical numbers, staged by Gower Champion, (see illustration, Powell right) that transcended the plot and gave it extra pizzazz. Mitchell Leisen directed from Devery Freeman's screenplay, which also contained roles for Kaye Ballard, Una Merkel, Kelly Brown, Judy Nugent and Frank Cady. Stanley Rubin produced in Technicolor and Universal-International were the distributors. Songs included: 'The Girl Most Likely' Bob Russell, Nelson Riddle; 'All The Colors Of The Rainbow', 'I Don't Know What I Want', 'Balboa', 'We Gotta Keep Up With The Joneses', 'Crazy Horse' Hugh Martin, Ralph Blane. Note: Paul Jarrico, who had written the story and screenplay for *Tom, Dick And Harry*, was refused any sort of credit on the remake, causing more friction of *The Las Vegas Story* variety between RKO and the alliance of Jarrico and the Writers Guild. ▷

Stage Struck (1958), a remake of Zoe Akins' play *Morning Glory* which brought Katharine Hepburn her first Oscar in 1933, beautifully captured the harassed, fickle, but exciting world of the Broadway theatre. The plot, however, had become rather tarnished by years of continuous wear in similar backstage stories. Despite the polished acting of Henry Fonda (right), Susan Strasberg (left), Joan Greenwood and Christopher Plummer, it sizzled only sporadically under the direction of Sidney Lumet. Miss Strasberg was Eva Lovelace, a starry-eyed, small-town girl who arrives in New York believing she has the talent and inner fire to be a great actress. She becomes romantically involved with successful producer Lewis Easton (Fonda) and successful playwright Joe Sheridan (Plummer), but neither is responsible for her big break. Rather, it is the intransigence of temperamental star Rita Vernon (Greenwood) that shoves her into the limelight and, after her curtain calls, questions of love for Easton or Sheridan are no longer relevant. The theatre has won Eva Lovelace forever. Producer Stuart Millar recruited most of the cast members from New York, where the film was shot in its entirety. The supporting players included Herbert Marshall, Daniel Ocko, Pat Harrington, Frank Campanella, John Fiedler, Patricia Englund, Jack Weston, Sally Gracie, Nina Hansen and Harold Grau. Ruth and Augustus Goetz wrote the screenplay, and Walt Disney's Buena Vista Film Distribution Company handled bookings in the US.

Contemporary advances in the field of rocketry, and the success of Walt Disney's film based on Jules Verne's *20,000 Leagues Under The Sea* (1954), made it inevitable that someone would come up with a cinematic version of Verne's science-fantasy, **From The Earth To The Moon** (1958). The someone was producer Benedict Bogeaus, who worked out a joint arrangement between his Waverly Productions and RKO, then hired Robert Blees and James Leicester to write the screenplay, Byron Haskin to direct it and Joseph Cotten (left), George Sanders and Debra Paget to star in it. The time is shortly after the close of the Civil War when scientist Cotten announces that he has invented a source of 'infinite energy' called Power X. After some hubbub about the threat of the substance to world peace, Cotten designs a projectile to carry human beings to the moon and return them to Earth. He blasts off in the plushly appointed missile, along with his nemesis George Sanders, Sanders' stowaway daughter (Miss Paget) and crewman Don Dubbins (right). After a series of standard and rather silly adventures, including a meteor shower and a gas leak, the two lovers (Paget and Dubbins) return to Earth, leaving Cotton and Sanders behind on the cratered satellite. Warner Bros. ultimately distributed the Technicolor production, which was made in Mexico; it also featured Patric Knowles, Carl Esmond, Henry Daniell, Melville Cooper, Ludwig Stossel and Morris Ankrum.

Producer Paul Gregory, director Raoul Walsh and screenwriters Denis and Terry Sanders between them ruined Norman Mailer's powerhouse war novel **The Naked And The Dead** (1958). The production team was forced to tone down the book's language and its more brutal plot elements because of contemporary standards, but it certainly did not have to inject inappropriate slapstick interludes into a story of ugliness, horror and mania, or mutilate the drama with flashback scenes so badly staged and acted that they made a travesty of the subject matter. Nor did the filmmakers need to trot out the stereotyped old war film characters and incidents to get their points across. Aldo Ray (left) topped the cast as sadistic Sergeant Croft, killing Japanese prisoners and helpless birds with equal gusto, and telling his platoon to pry gold from the teeth of dead Japanese infantrymen. The moral centre of the picture was supposed to be Lieutenant Hearn (Cliff Robertson, right) who makes some effort to curb Croft's excesses and defies General Cummings (Raymond Massey), a believer in the theory that the more the enlisted men hate their officers, the harder they will fight. Unfortunately, Robertson played the role in so perfunctory and uncommitted a fashion that his final speech to the general about the godlike and indestructible spirit of man seemed hollow lip-service at best. The Technicolor and Warnerscope film did contain brilliant action scenes (shot, for the most part, in Panama), a scintillating score by Bernard Herrmann and fine supporting performances from William Campbell, Richard Jaeckel, James Best, Joey Bishop, Jerry Paris, Robert Gist and L. Q. Jones, but it was still a big-league disappointment. Also cast: Lili St Cyr, Barbara Nichols, Casey Adams, John Berardino, Edward McNally and Greg Roman. RKO co-produced with Gregjac Pictures, Warner Bros. handled American distribution, and Rank distributed in Britain.

Verboten! (1959) was a raw and explosive picture by the man who made *Fixed Bayonets* and *The Steel Helmet*. Producer-director-writer Samuel Fuller dealt with the early days of American military government in Germany following World War II. American Sergeant James Best (right) falls in love with German girl Susan Cummings (left) and remains behind to work with the occupation forces whose efforts are constantly being undermined by 'werewolves' – bands of youthful Germans sworn to kill every foreigner, even at the cost of their own lives. One of the gang members is Cummings' 15-year-old brother Harold Daye. He becomes the key to the destruction of the neo-Nazis after his sister takes him to the Nuremberg trials, and he is disgusted by what he sees and learns there. The trial sections enabled Fuller to include some footage of actual Nazi atrocities, reinforcing the picture's grim but weighty message. Tom Pittman, Paul Dubov, Dick Kallman, Stuart Randall, Steven Geray, Anna Hope, Robert Boon, Sasha Harden, Paul Busch, Neyle Morrow and Joseph Turkel also played roles for Fuller, whose Globe Enterprises company co-produced the film with RKO. Columbia Pictures ended up with American distribution rights. Mack David and Harry Sukman wrote the title song, an insipid love ballad totally out of synch with the sobering film it decorated.

Produced by William Gell in England for Monarch Productions, **City After Midnight** (1959) (GB: **That Woman Opposite**) related a story of blackmail and murder in the small French town of La Bandelette. When gentlemanly antique collector Wilfrid Hyde-White (right) is killed, private investigator Dan O'Herlihy must decide if Phyllis Kirk, a young divorcée whose bloodstained nightdress makes her a suspect, Jack Watling, the victim's son who had been secretly robbing his father to pay off his blackmailing mistress, a burglar, or someone else is the culprit. O'Herlihy's ratiocination was fuzzy from the start, leaving audiences slightly mystified as to how he ultimately fixed on the true murderer. Compton Bennett wrote and directed it, based on John Dickson Carr's novel *The Emperor's Snuffbox*. Also in the cast: pop singer Petula Clark (left), William Franklyn, Margaret Withers, Guido Lorraine, Andre Charisse and Robert Raikes. American distribution was handled by States Rights companies.

Though it sounded like a western, **Desert Desperadoes** (1959) was actually a sword-and-sandal epic, but one that offered *Ben-Hur* (released by MGM in the same year) no competition whatsoever. A wicked woman from Babylon, a scheming, avaricious merchant and a group of Judean refugees fleeing from King Herod's reign of terror made up a doomed caravan, winding its way through a film as flat as the desert over which it travelled. Akim Tamiroff (right) played the villainous merchant who bribes the resident Jezebel (Ruth Roman, left) to help him betray the Judeans to Herod for the reward money. His plans go awry when the woman falls in love with a soldier (Gianni Glori) whom she has seduced as part of the plot. RKO was originally to distribute this Venturini-Express-Nasht production, made on location in Italy and Egypt, but it was ultimately handled by States Rights companies in the US. Steve Sekely directed from a screenplay by Victor Stolloff and Robert Hill, and Othelo Toso, Arnoldo Foa, Alan Furlan and Nino Marchetti were also in it. John Nasht produced.

RKO acquired **The Mysterians** (1959) for US distribution from Toho Productions, then turned it over to MGM after the company's exchanges were phased out. The movie was routine Japanese sci-fi: colour, wide-screen, impressive special effects and a dizzying, paranoid plot about a race of gigantic intellects whose planet is destroyed by an atomic disaster. They naturally decide to take over Earth, mate with its women and enslave its men (see illustration). Using a giant robot beaming electronic fire-rays from its eyes, plus space stations and flying saucers against the Earth's more prosaic airships, multi-stage rockets and tanks, the invaders wreak plenty of havoc before they are finally vanquished. Takeshi Kimura wrote the screenplay, based on Shigeru Kayama's adaptation of a story by Jojiro Okami. Tomoyuki Tanaka produced it, Inoshiro Honda directed it and Kenji Sahara, Yumi Shirakawa, Momoko Kochi, Takashi Shirmura, Susumu Fujita and Hisaya Ito were among the principal players.

Julie Harris joined the Abbey Theatre Players for a rollicking romp through the Irish countryside called **The Poacher's Daughter** (1960) (GB: **Sally's Irish Rogue**). In it, Tim Seely (left) finds responsibility glowering at him in the form of a farm he is about to inherit and a lady (Miss Harris, right) he is about to marry. Rebelling against everyone who has an interest in him at all, Seely buys a motorcycle with money he has gotten by selling several of his mother's sheep and dashes away from the domestic life. But he doesn't count on Harris' strength or stamina, or the cunning nature of her father (Harry Brogan). Both are determined not to let the bridegroom go without a struggle, and they eventually snag him before a local horse-dealer (Philip O'Flynn) can force a shotgun wedding between his daughter (Finola O'Shannon) and the young man. Patrick Kirwan and Blanaid Irvine wrote the amusing screenplay, based on *The New Gossoon*, a play by George Shiels. George Pollock directed for producers Robert S. Baker and Monty Berman and executive producer Nathan Keats, with Maire Kean, Dermot Kelly, John Hoey, Geoffrey Golden, John Cowley, Brid Lynch, Eddie Golden, Noel Magee and Paul Farrell completing the cast. Emmet Dalton Productions shot the picture in Ireland, and Showcorporation of America handled US releasing.

Home Is The Hero (1960), a play by Walter Macken which opened on Broadway in 1955, was demolished by the New York critics and quickly disappeared from the boards. Substantially revised, it came to the screen a few years later with a script by Henry Keating and direction by J. Fielder Cook. Playwright Macken performed the central role, that of an Irish bully who comes home a repentant man after five years in prison. In his zealous resolve to undo old habits, Macken causes more trouble than he had before, until his crippled son (Arthur Kennedy, right) finally brings him to his senses. The 83-minute drama contained a number of flashing insights into the Irish character, and offered uniformly excellent acting from a cast that included Harry Brogan, Eileen Crowe, Joan O'Hara (left), Maire O'Donnell, Maire Kean, Philip O'Flynn, Patrick Layde, Eddie Golden, John Hoey, Michael Hennessy, Michael O'Briain, Dermot Kelly and Geoffrey Golden – most of whom were members of the Abbey Theatre Players. Robert S. Baker and Monty Berman produced and Nathan Keats was the executive producer for Emmet Dalton Productions. It was shot in Ireland and distributed in the US by Showcorporation of America.

RKO BRITISH PRODUCTION AND DISTRIBUTION

From September 1926 to June 1930, most of FBO's films, and then Radio Pictures, were distributed in Great Britain by Ideal Films Ltd. Radio Pictures Ltd was incorporated under the English Companies Act (1929) on 18 June 1930. One year later it began releasing RKO productions as well as various British films acquired by the company under the provisions of the Act. The first Radio picture distributed was **Dixiana** in 1931, and the first British film was **Sally In Our Alley**, starring Gracie Fields, in 1932.

In the early thirties, RKO entered into a co-production arrangement with Associated Talking Pictures, furnishing Basil Dean, Associated's head and producer, with technical personnel. Radio Pictures Ltd released Dean's films in England, and also distributed some (such as **Escape**, **The Perfect Alibi**) in the United States. On 30 March 1940, RKO Radio British Productions was formed, with William Sistrom and Ralph Hanbury in charge of the film-making unit at D&P Studios in Denham. World War II intervened to curtail their scheduled production activities, but **Dangerous Moonlight**, **The Saint's Vacation** and **The Saint Meets The Tiger** were among the feature films completed.

After the war, RKO entered into negotiations with J. Arthur Rank for an ambitious programme of coproductions to be made in England and on the Continent but, due to a variety of complications, only one film, **So Well Remembered**, materialised from the joint venture.

When RKO ceased production and began phasing out its world-wide network of film exchanges, it turned over British distribution of current films to J. Arthur Rank Distribution Ltd. This happened on 1 July 1958, shortly after the retirement of Robert S. Wolff, who had been managing director of RKO British operations since the early 1940's.

Over the years, a number of films in Britain were made or released by various companies under the aegis of RKO or Radio Pictures. Some of these were released in the US, but never by RKO. The brief synopses in this section deal with these films, indicating the production company and US releases. This listing is intended only as a basic reference and, as such, omits writing credits. It includes producers (except where no credit is available), and directors. The cast names embrace lead-role players and some generally well-known performers, but are not complete.

1932

Sally In Our Alley (Assoc. Talking Pictures) Gracie Fields, Ian Hunter, Florence Desmond, Ivor Barnard; Prod: Basil Dean Dir: Maurice Elvey. Musical about a café singer's love for a wounded soldier and the efforts of her jealous rival to destroy the romance.

The Face At The Window (Real Art Prods) Raymond Massey, Isla Bevan, Claude Hulbert, Eric Maturin, Henry Mollison; Prod: Julius Hagen Dir: Leslie Hiscott. Set in Paris, a crime story about a detective's efforts to expose a nobleman as a bank robber.

A Honeymoon Adventure (Assoc. Talking Pictures) Benita Hume, Harold Huth, Peter Hannen, Walter Armitage, Margery Binner; Prod: Basil Dean Dir: Maurice Elvey. Crime story in which a wife, while on honeymoon, saves her inventor husband from kidnap attempt. Released in US as **Footsteps In The Night**.

Frail Women (Real Art Prods) Mary Newcombe, Owen Nares, Edmund Gwenn, Jane Welsh, Athole Stewart, Miles Mander; Prod: Julius Hagen Dir: Maurice Elvey. Drama about an army officer who marries wartime mistress in order to give their daughter a name.

The Water Gipsies (Assoc. Talking Pictures) Ann Todd, Ian Hunter, Sari Maritza, Peter Hannen; Prod: Basil Dean Dir: Maurice Elvey. The jealous fiancée of a society artist is accidentally drowned by the gypsy girl who poses for the painter. Released in US as **The Water Gypsies**.

Nine Till Six (Assoc. Talking Pictures) Louise Hampton, Elizabeth Allan, Florence Desmond, Isla Bevan, Richard Bird, Kay Hammond; Prod/Dir: Basil Dean. Romantic drama about a dressmaker accused of stealing a dress she borrowed to wear to a dance with a peer.

The Marriage Bond (Twickenham Film Studios) Mary Newcombe, Guy Newall, Stewart Rome, Ann Casson, Florence Desmond; Prod: Julius Hagen Dir: Maurice Elvey. To protect her children, a wife leaves her drunkard husband, but returns when he is rehabilitated.

The Sign Of Four (Assoc. Talking Pictures) Arthur Wontner, Isla Bevan, Ian Hunter, Ben Soutten, Miles Malleson; Prod: Basil Dean Dir: Rowland V. Lee & Graham Cutts. Ex-convict out to get revenge on the partners-in-crime who cheated him of his booty. Released in US.

The Impassive Footman (Assoc. Talking Pictures) Owen Nares, Betty Stockfeld, Allan Jeayes, Aubrey Mather; Prod/Dir: Basil Dean. Doctor loves wife of a cruel patient; dilemma solved when latter is killed by a vengeful servant. Released in US as **Woman In Bondage**.

Love On The Spot (Assoc. Talking Pictures) Rosemary Ames, Richard Dolman, Aubrey Mather, Helen Ferrers; Prod: Basil Dean Dir: Graham Cutts. Musical in which a romance between a hotel thief and a con-man's daughter reforms both of them.

Looking On The Bright Side (Assoc. Talking Pictures) Gracie Fields, Richard Dolman, Julian Rose, Wyn Richmond; Prod: Basil Dean Dir: Dean & Graham Cutts. Musical romance about a manicurist in love with a songsmith hairdresser who, in turn, falls for a singer.

The World, The Flesh, The Devil (Real Art Prods) Harold Huth, Isla Bevan, Sara Allgood, Felix Aylmer; Prod: Julius Hagen Dir: George A. Cooper. The bastard son of a peer of the realm plans to do away with the baronet's legitimate son and heir.

1933

His Grace Gives Notice (Real Art Prods) Arthur Margetson, Viola Keats, S. Victor Stanley, Barrie Livesey; Prod: Julius Hagen Dir: George A. Cooper. A butler pays court to his employer's daughter, not letting on that he has inherited a title.

The Iron Stair (Real Arts Prods) Henry Kendall, Dorothy Boyd, Michael Hogan, Steffi Duna, Michael Sherbrooke; Prod: Julius Hagen Dir: Leslie Hiscott. Crime saga about twin sons of a wealthy man, one of whom frames his brother for forgery.

Called Back (Real Art Prods) Franklin Dyall, Dorothy Boyd, Lester Matthews, Francis L. Sullivan; Prod: Julius Hagen Dir: Reginald Denham & Jack Harris. The revolutionary efforts of a doctor in Spain are sabotaged by a blind man and an amnesiac girl.

The Medicine Man (Real Art Prods) Claud Allister, Pat Paterson, Frank Pettingell, Jeanne Stuart; Prod: Julius Hagen Dir: Redd Davis. A comedy in which a dude poses as a doctor and apprehends a bunch of crooks.

Excess Baggage (Real Art Prods) Claud Allister, Frank Pettingell, Sydney Fairbrother, Rene Ray, Gerald Rawlinson, Finlay Currie; Prod: Julius Hagen Dir: Redd Davis. Comedy about an army colonel who hunts a ghost and thinks he's killed a superior while so doing.

The Umbrella (Real Arts Prods) Kay Hammond, Harold French, S. Victor Stanley, Dick Francis, Barbara Everest; Prod: Julius Hagen Dir: Redd Davis. A comedy focusing on a man mistakenly going off with the wrong umbrella which contains a pickpocket's spoils.

The Man Outside (Real Art Prods) Henry Kendall, Gillian Lind, Joan Gardner, Michael Hogan, Louis Hayward; Prod: Julius Hagen Dir: George A. Cooper. While searching for stolen jewellery, a detective unmasks a murderer.

This Week Of Grace (Real Art Prods) Gracie Fields, Henry Kendall, John Stuart, Frank Pettingell, Minnie Rayner; Prod: Julius Hagen Dir: Maurice Elvey. Comedy in which a factory girl is sacked and her family go and manage a duchess's castle.

The Ghost Camera (Real Art Prods) Henry Kendall, Ida Lupino, John Mills, S. Victor Stanley, George Merritt, Felix Aylmer; Prod: Julius Hagen Dir: Bernard Vorhaus. A chemist fortuitously takes a photo of a murder, which saves an innocent man.

1934

Home Sweet Home (Real Art Prods)
John Stuart, Marie Ney, Richard Cooper, Sydney Fairbrother, Cyril Raymond, Eve Becke; Prod: Julius Hagen Dir: George A. Cooper. A man comes home from abroad and accidentally kills his wife's lover.

A Shot In The Dark (Real Art Prods)
Dorothy Boyd, O. B. Clarence, Jack Hawkins, Russell Thorndike; Prod: Julius Hagen Dir: George Pearson. Unusual crime twist when several people all confess to the murder of a detested recluse.

The Roof (Real Art Prods)
Leslie Perrins, Judy Gunn, Russell Thorndike, Michael Hogan, Ivor Barnard, Barbara Everest; Prod: Julius Hagen Dir: George A. Cooper. Valuable jewels left with a lawyer for safekeeping are stolen.

Mannequin (Real Art Prods)
Harold French, Diana Beaumont, Judy Kelly, Whitmore Humphries, Richard Cooper, Ben Welden, Anna Lee; Prod: Julius Hagen Dir: George A. Cooper. Romance in which a boxer deserts his true love for a society girl, but learns the error of his ways and returns.

The Pointing Finger (Real Art Prods)
John Stuart, Viola Keats, Leslie Perrins, Michael Hogan; Prod: Julius Hagen Dir: George Pearson. Familiar crime tale of a man who tries to kill his half-brother to inherit an earldom.

Say It With Flowers (Real Art Prods)
Mary Clare, Ben Field, George Carney, Mark Daly, Florrie Forde, Charles Coburn; Prod: Julius Hagen Dir: John Baxter. A musical in which a group of cockneys stage a concert to aid a sick flowerseller.

The Black Abbot (Real Art Prods)
John Stuart, Judy Kelly, Richard Cooper, Ben Welden, Drusilla Wills, Edgar Norfolk; Prod: Julius Hagen Dir: George A. Cooper. A gang of criminals hold a wealthy man to ransom in his own house.

The River Wolves (Real Art Prods)
Michael Hogan, Helga Moray, John Mills, Ben Welden, Hope Davy; Prod: Julius Hagen Dir: George Pearson. Tale of blackmail set in the Tilbury docks with a merchant-ship captain saving the day, and the landlady's daughter's sweetheart.

The Admiral's Secret (Real Art Prods)
Edmund Gwenn, Hope Davy, James Raglan, Aubrey Mather; Prod: Julius Hagen Dir: Guy Newall. A comic search by Spanish brigands for gems stolen by a retired admiral.

Tangled Evidence (Real Art Prods)
Sam Livesey, Joan Marion, Michael Hogan, Michael Shepley; Prod: Julius Hagen Dir: George A. Cooper. Police inspector proves innocence of girl accused of murdering her uncle who dabbled in the occult.

Whispering Tongues (Real Art Prods)
Reginald Tate, Jane Welsh, Russell Thorndike, Malcolm Keen, Felix Aylmer; Prod: Julius Hagen Dir: George Pearson. Aided by his butler, a man steals jewels from those responsible for his father's suicide.

The Lash (Real Art Prods)
Lyn Harding, John Mills, Joan Maude, Leslie Perrins, Mary Jerrold; Prod: Julius Hagen Dir: Henry Edwards. Drama of a self-made man's violent relationship with his selfish and dishonest son.

Music Hall (Real Art Prods)
George Carney, Ben Field, Mark Daly, Helena Pickard, Olive Sloane, Wally Patch, Derrick de Marney, Peggy Novak; Prod: Julius Hagen Dir: John Baxter. Slight story of clever showmanship saving an old music hall – just an excuse for a musical revue.

1935

Lord Edgware Dies (Real Art Prods)
Austin Trevor, Jane Carr, Richard Cooper, John Turnbull, Michael Shepley, Leslie Perrins; Prod: Julius Hagen Dir: Henry Edwards. A Hercule Poirot murder mystery from Agatha Christie's novel, with victim an elderly lord and prime suspect his young wife.

Anything Might Happen (Real Art Prods)
Judy Kelly, John Garrick, Martin Walker, Aubrey Mather; Prod: Julius Hagen Dir: George A. Cooper. A reformed criminal finds he is the double of a practising gangster.

The Silence Of Dean Maitland (Cinesound Prods) John Longden, Charlotte Francis, John Warwick, Jocelyn Howarth, Patricia Minchin, Billy Kerr; no records of other credits, nor a synopsis appear to exist.

Open All Night (Real Art Prods)
Frank Vosper, Margaret Vines, Gillian Lind, Lewis Shaw, Geraldine Fitzgerald; Prod: Julius Hagen Dir: George Pearson. Refugee Russian duke, now working in an all-night restaurant, kills himself to save a girl from a murder charge.

Flood Tide (Real Art Prods)
George Carney, Peggy Novak, Leslie Hatton, Janice Adair, Wilson Coleman; Prod: Julius Hagen Dir: John Baxter. The officer son of a Thames lock-keeper falls in love with a bargee's daughter and marries her.

The Rocks Of Valpre (Real Art Prods)
John Garrick, Winifred Shotter, Leslie Perrins, Michael Shepley, Athene Seyler; Prod: Julius Hagen Dir: Henry Edwards. In mid-19th century Belgium, an officer is freed from Devil's Island and saves his sweetheart from a blackmailer. Released in US as **High Treason** in 1937.

Lazybones (Real Art Prods)
Claire Luce, Ian Hunter, Sara Allgood, Bernard Nedell, Michael Shepley; Prod: Julius Hagen Dir: Michael Powell. A penniless baronet marries an American heiress, but their lives comically disrupted when wife is framed by her cousin for stealing official papers.

The Ace Of Spades (Real Art Prods)
Michael Hogan, Dorothy Boyd, Richard Cooper, Jane Carr, Sebastian Shaw, Geraldine Fitzgerald; Prod: Julius Hagen Dir: George Pearson. Consumed with jealousy, a girl blackmails her sister's fiancé.

Handle With Care (Embassy Pictures)
Molly Lamont, Jack Hobbs, James Finlayson, Henry Victor, Vera Bogetti; Prod: George King & Randall Faye Dir: Randall Faye. A comedy about an ex-criminal who thwarts a spy ring with the aid of a strength pill.

Street Song (Real Art Prods)
John Garrick, Rene Ray, Wally Patch, Johnny Singer; Prod: Julius Hagen Dir: Bernard Vorhaus. A musical in which a bunch of crooks reform on account of a girl, and all become radio stars.

Department Store (Real Art Prods)
Garry Marsh, Eve Gray, Sebastian Shaw, Geraldine Fitzgerald; Prod: Julius Hagen Dir: Leslie Hiscott. Crime story involving the crooked manager of the store who mistakes an ex-convict for his employer's incognito heir. Also titled **Bargain Basement**.

The Right Age To Marry (GS Enterprises)
Frank Pettingell, Joyce Bland, Tom Helmore, Ruby Miller; Prod: A. George Smith Dir: Maclean Rogers. A comedy in which a gold-digging widow sets her sights on a retired mill-owner.

Admirals All (John Stafford Prods)
Wynne Gibson, Gordon Harker, Anthony Bushell, Joan White, Wilfrid Hyde-White; Prod: John Stafford Dir: Victor Hanbury. An American star on board a battleship finds himself kidnapped by pirates. Comedy, of course.

Lend Me Your Husband (Embassy Pictures)
John Stuart, Nora Swinburne, Nancy Burne, Evan Thomas, Annie Esmond; Prod: George King & Randall Faye Dir: Frederick Hayward. Comedy in which a married man and his friend's wife spend an experimental weekend together.

Windfall (Embassy Pictures)
Edward Rigby, Marie Ault, George Carney, Marjorie Corbett, Derrick de Marney, Googie Withers; Prod: George King & Randall Faye Dir: George King. A large inheritance turns an ironmonger's son into a high-life idler.

Old Faithful (GS Enterprises)
Horace Hodges, Glennis Lorimer, Bruce Lister, Wally Patch, Isobel Scaife; Prod: A. George Smith Dir: Maclean Rogers. In his attempt to win the hand of an old cabman's daughter, a taxi-driver pretends to be a plumber.

1936

The Man Without A Face (Embassy Pictures)
Carol Coombe, Cyril Cusak, Moore Marriott, Ronald Ritchie; Prod: George King & Randall Faye Dir: George King. A wrongly convicted man escapes from jail and assumes identity of supposed dead man, who is the real culprit.

The Crouching Beast (John Stafford Prods)
Fritz Kortner, Wynne Gibson, Richard Bird, Isabel Jeans; Prod: John Stafford Dir: Victor Hanbury. A British spy is aided by an American girl reporter in stealing plans of the Dardanelles fortifications. Released in the US.

The Shadow Of Mike Emerald (GS Enterprises) Leslie Perrins, Marjorie Mars,

Martin Lewis, Vincent Holman; Prod: A. George Smith Dir: Maclean Rogers. A financier who has swindled his partners is searched for by them.

Gay Old Dog (Embassy Pictures)
Edward Rigby, Moore Marriott, Ruby Miller, Marguerite Allan, Annie Esmond, Patrick Barr; Prod: George King & Randall Faye Dir: George King. A vet is saved from the clutches of a scheming widow by his doctor brother.

Twice Branded (GS Enterprises)
Robert Rendel, Lucille Lisle, James Mason, Eve Gray; Prod: A. George Smith Dir: Maclean Rogers. A man wrongfully imprisoned for fraud is released, but forced to pose as his family's uncle.

The Vandergilt Diamond Mystery (Randall Faye Prods) Elizabeth Astell, Bruce Seton, Hillary Pritchard, Charles Paton; Prod/Dir: Randall Faye. Comedy which has some crooks and a girl searching for a pendant which has been hidden in a golf bag.

Ball At Savoy (John Stafford Prods)
Conrad Nagel, Marta Labarr, Fred Conyngham, Lu-Anne Meredith, Aubrey Mather; Prod: John Stafford Dir: Victor Hanbury. Musical set in Cannes where a baron poses as a waiter to woo an opera star, and is accused of a jewel theft.

The Beloved Imposter (John Stafford Prods)
Rene Ray, Fred Conyngham, Germaine Aussey, Penelope Parkes, Edwin Ellis; Prod: John Stafford Dir: Victor Hanbury. Musical about an egotistical writer who thinks he kills the singer who rejects his advances.

A Touch Of The Moon (GS Enterprises)
John Garrick, Dorothy Boyd, Joyce Bland, David Horne, Max Adrian; Prod: A. George Smith Dir: Maclean Rogers. Boozy bloke woos girl away from her rich American fiancé.

Pal O'Mine (Film Sales Ltd)
Charles Paton, Herbert Langley, Doris Long, Peter Cotes; Prod/Dir: Widgey E. Newman. Musical revolving round a stage doorman who takes the blame for a safe robbery, believing he is protecting his son.

This Green Hell (Randall Faye Prods)
Edward Rigby, Sybil Grove, Richard Dolman, Roxie Russell, John Singer; Prod/Dir: Randall Faye. Comedy about a daydreamer who, when in a train crash, thinks he is a famous explorer.

The Avenging Hand (John Stafford Prods)
Noah Beery, Kathleen Kelly, Louis Borell, James Harcourt, Charles Oliver; Prod: John Stafford Dir: Victor Hanbury. A group of hotel 'guests' are actually crooks looking for some hidden money.

If I Were Rich (Randall Faye Prods)
Jack Melford, Kay Walsh, Clifford Heatherley, Minnie Rayner, Henry Carlisle; Prod/Dir: Randall Faye. A Socialist barber comes into a title and changes his political tune.

Unlucky Jim (Master Productions)
Bob Stevens, Tony Jones, Agnes Lenton, Alma Aston, George Beck, Chris Hawkes; Prod: Harry Marks & Fay Davis Dir: Harry Marks. The comedy adventures that befall two lads out on a half-day holiday.

Not So Dusty (GS Enterprises)
Wally Patch, Muriel George, Gus McNaughton, Phil Ray, Ethel Griffies; Prod: A. George Smith Dir: Maclean Rogers. A rare book which has been given to two dustmen is the object of pursuit by a bunch of crooks.

To Catch A Thief (GS Enterprises)
John Garrick, Mary Lawson, H. F. Maltby, John Wood, Max Adrian; Prod: A. George Smith Dir: Maclean Rogers. A comedy about the inventor of a device to foil car thieves who catches some smash-and-grab men.

Nothing Like Publicity (GS Enterprises)
Billy Hartnell, Marjorie Taylor, Moira Lynd, Ruby Miller, Max Adrian; Prod: A. George Smith Dir: Maclean Rogers. A press agent gets a talentless actress to masquerade as an American heiress, but a crook also impersonates the same girl.

Born That Way (Randall Faye Prods)
Elliott Mason, Kathleen Gibson, Terence de Marney, Eliot Makeham, Ian Colin; Prod/Dir: Randall Faye. The tale of a Scottish spinster who takes care of her absent-minded brother-in-law's children.

Wings Over Africa (Premier-Stafford Prods)
Joan Gardner, Ian Colin, James Harcourt, James Carew, Alan Napier; Prod: John Stafford Dir: Ladislaus Vajda. An African adventure story in which the quest of rival parties for hidden jewels erupts into murder. Released in US.

Luck Of The Turf (Randall Faye Prods)
Jack Melford, Moira Lynd, Wally Patch, Moore Marriott, Sybil Grove; Prod/Dir: Randall Faye. A tipster gambles to pay for his wedding but loses on the first bet.

Busman's Holiday (GS Enterprises-Bow Bell)
Wally Patch, Gus McNaughton, Muriel George, H. F. Maltby, Isobel Scaife; Prod: A. George Smith Dir: Maclean Rogers. Some busmen are mistaken for burglars, but manage to catch the real culprits.

The Heirloom Mystery (GS Enterprises)
Edward Rigby, Marjorie Taylor, Mary Glynne, Gus McNaughton; Prod: A. George Smith, Dir: Maclean Rogers. Drama about the problems caused for the son of a cabinet maker over his father's manufacture of a fake antique.

Second Bureau (Premier-Stafford Prods)
Marta Labarr, Charles Oliver, Arthur Wontner, Meinhart Maur, Fred Groves, Joan White; Prod: John Stafford Dir: Victor Hanbury. A female German spy in France during World War I, falls in love with the French spy she has been detailed to trap. Released in the US.

All That Glitters (GS Enterprises)
Jack Hobbs, Moira Lynd, Aubrey Mallalieu, Kay Walsh, Annie Esmond, Fred Duprez, Dick Francis; Prod: A. George Smith Dir: Maclean Rogers. The part-owner of a goldmine manages to thwart swindlers.

Wake Up Famous (Premier-Stafford Prods)
Nelson Keys, Gene Gerrard, Bela Mila, Josephine Huntley Wright, Fred Conyngham; Prod: John Stafford Dir: Gene Gerrard. Complications abound in musical about hotel clerk in Cannes who is framed for theft, and then mistaken for a songwriter by a film producer.

Farewell To Cinderella (GS Enterprises)
Anne Pichon, John Robertson, Arthur Rees, Glennis Lorimer, Ivor Barnard; Prod: A. George Smith Dir: Maclean Rogers. An Australian uncle helps the drudge of a large family to find romance with an artist.

Fifty-Shilling Boxer (George Smith Prods)
Bruce Seton, Nancy O'Neil, Moore Marriott, Eve Gray, Charles Oliver, Aubrey Mallalieu; Prod: George Smith Dir: Maclean Rogers. A cockney boxer deserts the ring for show biz, but returns after failing as an actor.

Return Of A Stranger (Premier-Stafford Prods)
Griffith Jones, Ellis Jeffreys, Athole Stewart, Rosalyn Boulter; Prod: John Stafford Dir: Victor Hanbury. A disfigured man comes home from exile to discover his fiancée has married someone else. Released in the US as **The Face Behind The Scar**.

The Strange Adventures of Mr Smith (George Smith Prods) Gus McNaughton, Norma Varden, Eve Gray, Aubrey Mallalieu, Billy Shine; Prod: George Smith Dir: Maclean Rogers. A pavement artist poses as a businessman and is then accused of murdering himself.

Father Steps Out (George Smith Prods)
George Carney, Dinah Sheridan, Bruce Seton, Vivienne Chatterton, Basil Langton; Prod: George Smith Dir: Maclean Rogers. A comedy about a cheese manufacturer whose chauffeur saves him from some smooth con-artists.

Why Pick On Me? (GS Enterprises)
Wylie Watson, Jack Hobbs, Sybil Grove, Max Adrian, Isobel Scaife; Prod: A. George Smith Dir: Maclean Rogers. A henpecked bank clerk gets drunk and is taken for his lawless double.

Easy Riches (GS Enterprises)
George Carney, Gus McNaughton, Marjorie Taylor, Tom Helmore; Prod: A. George Smith Dir: Maclean Rogers. A comedy about rival cement manufacturers who bury their differences in order to get the better of some confidence tricksters.

Racing Romance (GS Enterprises)
Bruce Seton, Marjorie Taylor, Eliot Makeham, Sybil Grove, Elizabeth Kent, Ian Fleming; Prod: A. George Smith Dir: Maclean Rogers. A garage owner buys a racing filly from a girl trainer and wins the Oaks with it.

Merely Mr Hawkins (George Smith Prods)
Eliot Makeham, Sybil Grove, Dinah Sheridan, George Pembroke; Prod: George Smith Dir: Maclean Rogers. A henpecked husband finally wins his wife's admiration by outwitting con-men.

Darts Are Trumps (George Smith Prods)
Eliot Makeham, Nancy O'Neil, Ian Colin, Muriel George, H. F. Maltby; Prod: George Smith Dir: Maclean Rogers. A dart-playing clerk employs his skill to help him catch a jewel thief.

Romance A La Carte (GS Enterprises)
Leslie Perrins, Dorothy Boyd, Anthony Holles, Charles Sewell; Prod: A. George Smith Dir: Maclean Rogers. A comedy about the rivalry between a restaurant manager and a chef.

His Lordship Regrets (Canterbury Films)
Claude Hulbert, Winifred Shotter, Gina Malo, Aubrey Mallalieu; Prod: A. George Smith Dir: Maclean Rogers. An impoverished lord woos a phony heiress, only to find that his secretary, whom he really loves, is a genuine one.

1939

Weddings Are Wonderful (Canterbury Films)
June Clyde, Esmond Knight, Rene Ray, Bertha Belmore, Bruce Seton; Prod: A. George Smith Dir: Maclean Rogers. A comedy about the antics of a singer who blackmails her prospective father-in-law, as well as a socialite.

His Lordship Goes To Press (Canterbury Films)
June Clyde, Hugh Williams, Romney Brent, Louise Hampton, Leslie Perrins, H. F. Maltby; Prod: A. George Smith Dir: Maclean Williams. A Lord poses as a farmer to deceive a brash American girl newspaper reporter.

Vagabond Violinist (Twickenham-Associated Producers and Directors) John Garrick, Merle Oberon, Margot Grahame, Austin Trevor; Prod: Julius Hagen Dir: Bernard Vorhaus. A musical drama, set in France, about a composer who escapes from Devil's Island, kills his wife's lover, and writes an opera. Re-issue of 1934 film originally titled **Broken Melody**, and also released in the US under that title.

Flying Fifty-Five (Admiral Films)
Derrick de Marney, Nancy Burne, Marius Goring, John Warwick, Peter Gawthorne; Prod: Victor M. Greene Dir: Reginald Denham. A racehorse owner's son poses as a trainer and is blackmailed into losing the race.

Meet Maxwell Archer (RKO Radio Pictures)
John Loder, Leueen McGrath, Athole Stewart, Marta Labarr, George Merritt; Prod: William Sistrom Dir: John Paddy Carstairs. A private detective proves the innocence of a pilot accused of murdering a spy ring's contact man. Released in the US as **Maxwell Archer, Detective**.

Shadowed Eyes (Savoy-GS Enterprises)
Basil Sydney, Patricia Hilliard, Stewart Rome, Dorothy Boyd, Ian Fleming; Prod: Kurt Sternberg & A. George Smith Dir: Maclean Rogers. An eye surgeon, suffering from amnesia, operates on the barrister who had him convicted for the murder of his wife's lover.

Blind Folly (George Smith Prods)
Clifford Mollison, Lili Palmer, Leslie Perrins, William Kendall, Roland Culver; Prod: George Smith Dir: Reginald Denham. Comedy about a man who inherits a roadhouse where a gang of jewel thieves have hidden their loot.

The Mysterious Mr Davis (Oxford Films)
Henry Kendall, Kathleen Kelly, Morris Harvey, A. Bromley Davenport, Alastair Sim, Guy Middleton; Dir: Claude Autant-Lara. An unemployed man invents an imaginary business partner in order to foil a fraudulent financier. Originally produced in 1936 under the title **My Partner, Mr Davis**.

Honeymoon Merry-Go-Round (London Screenplays—Fanfare Films) Claude Hulbert, Monty Banks, Princess Pearl, Sally Gray; Prod: Sidney Morgan Dir: Alfred Goulding. Comedy set in Switzerland in which a honeymooner who has had a tiff with his wife is mistaken for an ice-hockey champion. Produced in 1936 under the title of **Olympic Honeymoon**.

Branded (Radius Films)
John Warwick, John Longden, Kathleen Kelly, Gabrielle Brune, Brian Buchel; Prod: Vaughn N. Dean Dir: Lawrence Huntington. A former thief intervenes to save his sister from being captured by his one-time crime boss. Reissue of film originally released in 1938 under the title of **Bad Boy**.

Law And Disorder (British Consolidated Films)
Barry K. Barnes, Diana Churchill, Alastair Sim, Edward Chapman, Ruby Miller, Leo Genn, Torin Thatcher; Prod: K. C. Alexander Dir: David MacDonald. A young solicitor uncovers a gang of saboteurs who are misdirecting bombers with the use of portable radios.

Tilly Of Bloomsbury (Hammersmith Films)
Sydney Howard, Jean Gillie, Henry Oscar, Athene Seyler, Michael Wilding, Michael Denison; Prod: Kurt Sternberg & A. Barr-Smith Dir: Leslie Hiscott. A comedy about the objections of a mother to her son's love for the daughter of a boardinghouse keeper.

1945

Journey Together (RAF Film Unit)
Richard Attenborough, Edward G. Robinson, Bessie Love, Ronald Squire, Jack Watling, David Tomlinson; Dir: John Boulting. The story of an RAF trainee who fails as a pilot but succeeds as a navigator. Released in the US in 1946.

1948

Snowbound (Gainsborough)
Robert Newton, Dennis Price, Herbert Lom, Marcel Dalio, Stanley Holloway; Prod: Aubrey Baring Dir: David MacDonald. Set in the Alps where a group looking for hidden gold become snowbound and are discovered by a scriptwriter. Released in the US in 1949.

1951

Circle Of Danger (Coronado Prods)
Ray Milland, Patricia Roc, Marius Goring, Marjorie Fielding, Dora Bryan; Prod: David E. Rose & Joan Harrison Dir: Jacques Tourneur. The dramatic quest in Wales and Scotland, of an American trying to uncover the truth about his brother's wartime death. Released in the US.

1952

Saturday Island (Coronado Prods)
Linda Darnell, Tab Hunter, Donald Gray, John Laurie, Sheila Chong; Prod: David E. Rose Dir: Stuart Heisler. A torrid romance set in the wartime tropics where a marooned pilot and a shipwrecked marine fall for the same nurse. Released in the US as **Island Of Desire**.

1956

Oklahoma (Magna Theatre Corporation)
Gordon Macrae, Shirley Jones, Gloria Grahame, Gene Nelson, Charlotte Greenwood, Eddie Albert, James Whitmore, Rod Steiger; Prod: Arthur Hornblow Jr Dir: Fred Zinnemann. Bigscreen version of the famous Rodgers and Hammerstein Broadway musical, set in the land of lusty cowhands and their gingham-aproned girls.

Breakaway (Cipa)
Tom Conway, Honor Blackman, Michael Balfour, Bruce Seton, Brian Worth, Freddie Mills; Prod: Robert S. Baker & Monty Berman Dir: Henry Cass. A girl is kidnapped by crooks who are trying to obtain a secret formula for the elimination of metal fatigue.

The High Terrace (Cipa)
Dale Robertson, Lois Maxwell, Derek Bond, Eric Pohlmann, Mary Laura Wood; Prod: Robert S. Baker & Monty Berman. Dir: Henry Cass. An American playwright admits guilt for the murder of a producer to protect the actress who actually committed the crime. Released in the US.

The Silken Affair (Dragon)
David Niven, Genevieve Page, Ronald Squire, Wilfrid Hyde-White, Richard Wattis, Irene Handl; Prod: Douglas Fairbanks Jr & Fred Feldkamp Dir: Roy Kellino. An accountant decides to break the boring bonds of respectability and starts juggling with the books of two stocking manufacturers. Released in the US in 1957.

1957

No Road Back (Gibraltar Prods)
Skip Homeier, Paul Carpenter, Patricia Dainton, Norman Wooland, Eleanor Summerfield, Alfie Bass, Sean Connery; Prod: Steven Pallos & Charles Leeds Dir: Montgomery Tully. The blind and deaf owner of a nightclub manages to save his son from being framed by jewel thieves.

Professor Tim (Emmett Dalton–Dublin Films)
Ray McAnally, Maire O'Donnell, Seamus Kavanagh, Marie Kean, Philip O'Flynn, John Hoey, Geoffrey Golden; Prod: Robert S. Baker & Monty Berman Dir: Henry Cass. Comedy about a man who returns to Ireland after 20 years of wandering, and conceals from his family the fact that he has come into an inheritance. Shown on television in the US.

1958

Rommel's Treasure (Imperial Film Prods)
Dawn Addams, Paul Christian, Bruce Cabot, Isa Miranda, Vittorio Massimo, Luigi Visconti, Andrea Checchi, Wolfgang Lukschy, John Stacy; Prod: Luigi Rovere Dir: Romolo Marcellini. Also known as **Il Tesoro Di Rommel**, this film was released in the US in 1963 under the title of **Rommel's Treasure**. There is, however, no synopsis available.

RKO NOMINATIONS AND AWARDS

1930

The only film to earn an Academy Award consideration in any category was **The Case Of Sergeant Grischa**, nominated for John Tribby's sound recording.

1931

RKO broke into the awards race thanks to **Cimarron**, which captured the Best Picture Oscar and also garnered Academy Awards for its adaptor (Howard Estabrook) and art director (Max Ree). Stars Richard Dix and Irene Dunne received nominations but lost to Lionel Barrymore (*A Free Soul*, MGM) and Marie Dressler (*Min And Bill*, MGM) respectively. Director Wesley Ruggles was also singled out, finishing behind Norman Taurog (*Skippy*, Paramount), and Edward Cronjager came in second to Floyd Crosby (*Tabu*) in the cinematography category. **Cimarron** was also named among the 'ten best' of 1931 by the National Board of Review and *Film Daily*. RKO received one additional Oscar, a special award for the development of reflex type microphone concentrators.

1932

A Bill Of Divorcement and **What Price Hollywood?** earned special accolades. Katharine Hepburn's debut production was named among the ten best pictures of the year by *Film Daily* and the National Board of Review, and **What Price Hollywood?** received an Academy nomination for its original story by Adela Rogers St John. Miss St John was bested by Frances Marion, who wrote the original on which *The Champ* (MGM) was based.

1933

It was an encouraging year for awards. Katharine Hepburn won the Best Actress Oscar for her third picture, **Morning Glory**, and **Little Women** captured a gold statuette for its adaptors, Victor Heerman and Sarah Y. Mason. The latter film was listed among the 'Top Ten' of the National Board of Review and *Film Daily*, while **Topaze** received the same honour from the National Board of Review. **Little Women** was in the running for Best Picture, and its director, George Cukor, was also nominated. They lost to Fox's *Cavalcade* and its director Frank Lloyd. Finally, Dewey Starkey won an Oscar for his work as an RKO assistant director, and **So This Is Harris**, directed by Mark Sandrich, was named the Best Comedy Short by the Academy.

1934

The Gay Divorcee was Academy-nominated for Best Picture, Best Art Direction (Van Nest Polglase and Carroll Clark), Best Scoring (RKO Music Department), Best Sound Recording (Carl Dreher) and Best Song ('The Continental' by Con Conrad and Herb Magidson). Columbia's *It Happened One Night* dominated the Awards that year and, thus, the song was the only winner, though RKO also picked up an Oscar for **La Cucaracha**, voted the Best Comedy Short Subject. Other nominees: Best Original Story (Norman Krasna for **The Richest Girl In The World**) and Best Score (Max Steiner and the RKO Music Department for **The Lost Patrol**). **The Lost Patrol** was also singled out by the National Board of Review as one of the best films of the year.

1935

The Informer dominated the Academy Awards, winning Oscars for Victor McLaglen (Best Actor), John Ford (Best Director), Dudley Nichols (Best Screenplay) and Max Steiner (Best Score), but Best Picture went to MGM's *Mutiny On The Bounty*. Other nominations: **Alice Adams** and **Top Hat** for Best Picture; Katharine Hepburn (**Alice Adams**) and Miriam Hopkins (**Becky Sharp**) for Best Actress; Van Nest Polglase and Carroll Clark for Best Art Direction (**Top Hat**); Carl Dreher for Best Sound (**I Dream Too Much**); Hermes Pan for Best Dance Direction ('The Piccolino' from **Top Hat**); George Hively for Best Editing (**The Informer**); and two designations in the Best Song category: 'Cheek To Cheek' by Irving Berlin (**Top Hat**) and 'Lovely To Look At' by Jerome Kern, Dorothy Fields and Jimmy McHugh (**Roberta**). **The Informer** was also singled out for excellence by the National Board of Review, the New York Film Critics and *Film Daily*; **Alice Adams** was honoured by the National Board of Review, and **Top Hat** by *Film Daily*.

1936

Winterset was named one of the year's best by the National Board of Review and *Film Daily*. It also attracted Oscar nominations for art director Perry Ferguson and Nathaniel Shilkret's musical score. The only Academy winner came in the Best Song category, for 'The Way You Look Tonight' by Jerome Kern and Dorothy Fields (**Swing Time**). Other nominations: Best Sound (John Aalberg for **That Girl From Paris**); Best Dance Direction (Russell Lewis for the finale from **Dancing Pirate** and Hermes Pan for the 'Bojangles' number from **Swing Time**).

1937

Though it won no major awards, **Stage Door** was the most honoured picture of 1937. Besides recognition from the National Board of Review and *Film Daily* as one of the best films of the year, it was Academy-nominated for Best Picture, Best Director (Gregory LaCava), Best Screenplay (Morrie Ryskind and Anthony Veiller) and Best Supporting Actress (Andrea Leeds). The company's only Oscar winners were Hermes Pan for Dance Direction (the 'fun house' sequence from **A Damsel In Distress**) and Walt Disney for Best Cartoon (**The Old Mill**). Other nominations: Best Art Direction (Carroll Clark for **A Damsel In Distress**), Best Score (Roy Webb and the RKO Music Department for **Quality Street**; and Frank Churchill, Leigh Harline, Paul J. Smith and the Disney Music Department for **Snow White And The Seven Dwarfs**), Best Sound Recording (John Aalberg for **Hitting A New High**) and Best Song (George and Ira Gershwin for 'They Can't Take That Away From Me' from **Shall We Dance**).

1938

The year's only Oscar was won by **Ferdinand The Bull**, a Walt Disney cartoon. There were a few nominations: Robert De Grasse for Best Cinematography (**Vivacious Lady**), Van Nest Polglase for Best Art Direction (**Carefree**), Victor Baravalle for Best Musical Scoring (**Carefree**), Victor Young for Best Original Score (**Breaking The Ice**), James Wilkinson for Best Sound (**Vivacious Lady**) and Irving Berlin for Best Song ('Change Partners' from **Carefree**). John Aalberg and the RKO sound department also received a special citation from the Academy for technical achievement.

1939

In a year dominated by MGM's *Gone With The Wind*, a Walt Disney cartoon (**The Ugly Duckling**) was once again the studio's only Oscar winner. There were, however, several nominations, particularly for **Love Affair** which garnered a notable number: Best Picture; Best Actress (Irene Dunne); Best Supporting Actress (Maria Ouspenskaya); Best Original Story (Mildred Cram and Leo McCarey); Best Art Direction (Van Nest Polglase and Al Herman); Best Song (Buddy DeSylva for 'Wishing'). Other nominations: Alfred Newman (**The Hunchback Of Notre Dame**) and Victor Young (**Way Down South**) for Best Scoring; Anthony Collins for Best Original Score (**Nurse Edith Cavell**); John Aalberg for Best Sound (**The Hunchback Of Notre Dame**) and Felix Jackson for Best Original Story (**Bachelor Mother**).

1940

Ginger Rogers walked off with the Best Actress Oscar of 1940 for her portrayal of **Kitty Foyle**. Named one of the top pictures of the year by *Film Daily*, **Kitty Foyle** also received Academy nominations for Best Picture (losing to Selznick's *Rebecca*), Best Director (Sam Wood), Best Screenplay (Dalton Trumbo) and Best Sound Recording (John Aalberg). The other RKO nominations were Best Actor (Raymond Massey, **Abe Lincoln In Illinois**), Best Supporting Actor (William Gargan, **They Knew What They Wanted**), Best Supporting Actress (Marjorie Rambeau, **Primrose Path**), Best Original Story (Leo McCarey, Bella Spewack and Samuel Spewack, **My Favorite Wife**), Best Cinematography (James Wong Howe, **Abe Lincoln In Illinois**), Best Art Direction (Van Nest Polglase and Mark-Lee Kirk, **My Favorite Wife**), Best Score (Anthony Collins, **Irene**), Best Original Score (Roy Webb, **My Favorite Wife**), Best Special Effects (Vernon L. Walker and John Aalberg, **Swiss Family Robinson**) and Best Song ('I'd Know You Anywhere' by Jimmy McHugh and Johnny Mercer from **You'll Find Out**). The Disney film **Pinocchio** produced two winners: Best Original Score by Leigh Harline, Paul J. Smith and Ned Washington and Best Song ('When You Wish Upon A Star') by Harline and Washington.

1941

Citizen Kane was the most honoured film, earning an Academy Award for its screenplay (by Orson Welles and Herman J. Mankiewicz) and further recognition from the National Board of Review, the New York Critics and *Film Daily*. The Hearst-inspired backlash prevented it from winning any other Oscars, though it was unquestionably the finest film of the year. Its other nominations were for Best Picture, Best Actor (Orson Welles), Best Director (Welles), Best Cinematography (Gregg Toland), Best Art Direction (Perry Ferguson and Van Nest Polglase), Best Editing (Robert Wise), Best Scoring for a Dramatic Picture (Bernard Herrman) and Best Sound (John Aalberg). The Best Actress Award was won for the studio for the second consecutive year when Joan Fontaine captured the statuette for **Suspicion**. That film was also nominated for Best Picture, and for Best Scoring for a Dramatic Picture (Franz Waxman). Other nominations included Goldwyn's **The Little Foxes** for Best Picture, Best Actress (Bette Davis), Best Supporting Actress (Patricia Collinge and Teresa Wright) and Best Scoring for a Dramatic Picture (Meredith Willson); **All That Money Can Buy** for Best Actor (Walter Huston) and Best Scoring for a Dramatic Picture (Bernard Herrmann won the Oscar); Goldwyn's **Ball Of Fire** for Best Actress (Barbara Stanwyck) and Best Original Story (Thomas Monroe and Billy Wilder); **The Devil And Miss Jones** for Best Supporting Actor (Charles Coburn) and Best Original Screenplay (Norman Krasna); **Tom, Dick And Harry** for Best Original Screenplay (Paul Jarrico); and **Dumbo** for Best Score for a Musical Picture (Frank Churchill and Oliver Wallace took the award). The Disney organization also won an Oscar for the Best Cartoon (**Lend A Paw**).

1942

Carroll Clark, F. Thomas Thompson and the RKO art and miniature departments received a special Academy citation for the design and construction of a moving cloud and horizon machine. Otherwise, the only Oscars were won by **Pride Of The Yankees** for Best Editing (Daniel Mandell) and the Disney organization for Best Cartoon (**Der Fuehrer's Face**). **Pride Of The Yankees** was also nominated for Best Picture, Best Actor (Gary Cooper), Best Actress (Teresa Wright), Best Original Story (Paul Gallico), Best Screenplay (Herman J. Mankiewicz and Jo Swerling), Best Cinematography (Rudolph Maté), Best Art Direction (Perry Ferguson and Howard Bristol), Best Scoring for a Dramatic Picture (Leigh Harline), Best Sound Recording (Thomas Moulton) and Best Special Effects (Jack Cosgrove, Ray Binger and Thomas T. Moulton). The **Magnificent Ambersons** picked up nominations for Best Picture, Best Supporting Actress (Agnes Moorehead), Best Cinematography (Stanley Cortez) and Best Art direction and Interior Design (Albert S. D'Agostino, Al Fields and Darrell Silvera). Other miscellaneous nominations went to **Joan Of Paris** for Best Scoring for a Dramatic Picture (Roy Webb), **The Mayor Of 44th Street** for Best Song ('There's A Breeze On Lake Louise' by Mort Greene and Harry Revel) and **Bambi** for Best Scoring for a Dramatic or Comedy Picture (Frank Churchill and Edward Plumb), Best Sound Recording (Sam Slyfield) and Best Song ('Love Is A Song' by Frank Churchill and Larry Morey).

1943

This was not a memorable year for awards. Stephen Dunn received the only Oscar – for Best Sound Recording on **This Land Is Mine**. Samuel Goldwyn's **The North Star** received nominations for Best Original Screenplay (Lillian Hellman), Best Cinematography (James Wong Howe), Best Art Direction (Perry Ferguson and Howard Bristol), Best Sound Recording (Thomas Moulton), Best Special Effects (Clarence Slifer, R. O. Binger and Thomas Moulton) and Best Scoring of a Dramatic Picture (Aaron Copland). Other nominations included **Flight For Freedom** for Best Art Direction and Interior Design (Albert S. D'Agostino, Carroll Clark, Darrell Silvera and Harley Miller); **The Fallen Sparrow** for Best Scoring of a Dramatic Picture (C. Bakaleinikoff and Roy Webb); Disney's **Saludos Amigos** for Best Sound Recording (C. O. Slyfield), Best Scoring of a Musical Picture (Edward H. Plumb, Paul J. Smith and Charles Wolcott) and Best Song ('Saludos Amigos' by Charles Wolcott and Ned Washington); and **The Sky's The Limit** for Best Song ('My Shining Hour' by Harold Arlen and Johnny Mercer). Willard H. Turner and the RKO sound department also received a special citation from the Academy for technical achievement.

1944

The awards race again generated several nominations but only one winner: Ethel Barrymore, who earned the Best Supporting Actress Oscar for her work in **None But The Lonely Heart**. A sampling of the studio's other nominations (there *were* others but very minor, and/or given to independent pictures only released by RKO): Cary Grant for Best Actor (**None But The Lonely Heart**), Albert S. D'Agostino, Carroll Clark, Darrell Silvera and Claude Carpenter for Best Art Direction and Interior Design in a Black-and-White Picture (**Step Lively**), Roland Gross for Best Editing (**None But The Lonely Heart**), Stephen Dunn for Best Sound Recording (**Music In Manhattan**) and Vernon L. Walker, James G. Stewart and Roy Granville for Best Special Effects (**Days Of Glory**). Stephen Dunn, the RKO sound department and RCA also received a special plaque for technical achievement in designing and developing the electronic compressor-limiter. This was an amplification device that gave greater smoothness, and a general increase in intelligibility, to sound reproduction, especially spoken sound.

1945

The Bells Of St Mary's dominated the Academy Awards balloting, winning an Oscar for Best Sound Recording (Stephen Dunn) and nominations for Best Picture, Best Actor (Bing Crosby), Best Actress (Ingrid Bergman), Best Editing (Harry Marker), Best Scoring of a Dramatic or Comedy Picture (Robert Emmett Dolan) and Best Song ('Aren't You Glad You're You' by Jimmy Van Heusen and Johnny Burke). The only other first-place finisher was the Goldwyn film **Wonder Man** for Best Special Effects (John Fulton and A. W. Johns). Additional nominations included George Barnes for Best Colour Cinematography (**The Spanish Main**), Roy Webb for Best Scoring of a Dramatic or Comedy Picture (**The Enchanted Cottage**), Edward Plumb, Paul J. Smith and Charles Wolcott for Best Scoring of a Musical Picture (Disney's **The Three Caballeros**) and Allie Wrubel and Herb Magidson for Best Song ('I'll Buy That Dream' from **Sing Your Way Home**).

305

1946

Samuel Goldwyn's **The Best Years Of Our Lives** took almost all the Academy Awards. In addition to recognition from the National Board of Review, the New York Critics, and *Film Daily*, the film won Oscars for Best Picture, Best Director (William Wyler), Best Actor (Fredric March), Best Supporting Actor (Harold Russell), Best Screenplay (Robert E. Sherwood), Best Editing (Daniel Mandell) and Best Scoring of a Dramatic or Comedy Picture (Hugo Friedhofer). Harold Russell also received a special award 'for bringing hope and courage to his fellow veterans' and Goldwyn picked up the Thalberg award for 'consistent high quality of motion picture production'. RKO's other nominations included James Stewart for Best Actor (**It's A Wonderful Life**), Claude Rains for Best Supporting Actor (**Notorious**), Ethel Barrymore for Best Supporting Actress (**The Spiral Staircase**), Frank Capra for Best Director (**It's A Wonderful Life**), Ben Hecht for Best Original Screenplay (**Notorious**) and John Aalberg for Best Sound Recording (**It's A Wonderful Life**).

1947

1947 was an above-average year for awards. Loretta Young won the Best Actress Oscar for **The Farmer's Daughter**; Sidney Sheldon picked up the Best Original Screenplay award for **The Bachelor And The Bobby-Soxer**; 'Zip-A-Dee-Doo-Dah' by Allie Wrubel and Ray Gilbert (from Walt Disney's **Song Of The South**) was judged the Best Song; **Design For Death** earned the statuette for Best Documentary Feature and the Goldwyn Sound Department took the top award for Sound Recording in **The Bishop's Wife**. Other nominations included: **Crossfire** for Best Picture, Best Supporting Actor (Robert Ryan), Best Supporting Actress (Gloria Grahame), Best Director (Edward Dmytryk) and Best Screenplay (John Paxton); Goldwyn's **The Bishop's Wife** for Best Picture, Best Director (Henry Koster), Best Editing (Monica Collingwood) and Best Scoring of a Dramatic or Comedy Picture (Hugo Friedhofer); **Mourning Becomes Electra** for Best Actor (Michael Redgrave) and Best Actress (Rosalind Russell); and **The Farmer's Daughter** for Best Supporting Actor (Charles Bickford).

1948

Joan Of Arc (produced by Sierra Productions for RKO release) became the first picture to win an Oscar in the newly-designated category of Colour Costume Design (Dorothy Jeakins and Karinska were responsible). The film was also honoured for Best Colour Cinematography (by Joseph Valentine, William V. Skall and Winton Hoch) and Walter Wanger received a Special Award from the Academy for 'distinguished service to the industry in adding to its moral stature in the world community by his production of **Joan Of Arc**'. The only other Oscar went to Disney's **Seal Island**, the Best Two-Reel Short Subject. **Joan Of Arc** also received nominations for Best Actress (Ingrid Bergman), Best Supporting Actor (Jose Ferrer), Best Editing (Frank Sullivan), Best Colour Art Direction-Set Decoration (Richard Day, Edwin Casey Roberts and Joseph Kish), and Best Scoring of a Dramatic or Comedy Picture (Hugo Friedhofer). **I Remember Mama** was the other company release to receive substantial recognition, garnering nominations for Best Actress (Irene Dunne), Best Supporting Actor (Oscar Homolka), Best Supporting Actress (Barbara Bel Geddes and Ellen Corby) and Best Cinematography (Nicholas Musuraca).

1949

As might be expected in what was a very undistinguished year, the RKO pictures received limited recognition during the Academy Awards ceremonies. Winton Hoch richly deserved the Oscar he won for Best Colour Cinematography (**She Wore a Yellow Ribbon**, produced by Argosy-RKO), and **Mighty Joe Young** (an Arko Production) topped its competition in the Best Special Effects category. The other nominations: Best Actress (Susan Hayward in Goldwyn's **My Foolish Heart**), Best Editing (Frederick Knudtson for **The Window**), Best Song ('Lavender Blue' by Eliot Daniel and Larry Morey from Disney's **So Dear To My Heart**; and 'My Foolish Heart' by Victor Young and Ned Washington from Goldwyn's **My Foolish Heart**), Best Cartoon (Walt Disney's **Toy Tinkers**) and Best Two-Reel Short Subject (**Boy And The Eagle**, produced by William Lasky).

1950

RKO's affiliated independents attracted the only Oscar nominations. Disney's **Beaver Valley** was named Best Two-Reel Short Subject and his **Cinderella** also received recognition for Sound Recording (the Disney sound department), Scoring of a Musical Picture (Oliver Wallace and Paul J. Smith) and song ('Bibbidi Bobbidi Boo' by Mack David, Al Hoffman and Jerry Livingston). Samuel Goldwyn's sound department was also nominated for its recording efforts on **Our Very Own**.

1951

Academy Awards were earned by **Kon-Tiki** (Best Documentary Feature), **Rashomon** (a Special Award as the Outstanding Foreign Film) and Walt Disney's **Nature's Half-Acre** (Best Two-Reel Short Subject). Predictably, RKO had nothing to do with the production of any of the victorious films. It picked up **Rashomon** for American distribution during the year, but did not release it until 1952. Other Academy nominations: Jane Wyman (Best Actress, **The Blue Veil**), Joan Blondell (Best Supporting Actress, **The Blue Veil**), Oliver Wallace (Best Scoring of a Musical Picture, Disney's **Alice in Wonderland**), Gordon Sawyer (Best Sound Recording, Goldwyn's **I Want You**), John Aalberg (Best Sound Recording, **Two Tickets To Broadway**) and Disney's **Lambert, The Sheepish Lion** (Best Cartoon).

1952

Walt Disney's **Water Birds** won the Oscar as Best Two-Reel Short Subject and **The Sea Around Us** (released in 1953) was named Best Documentary Feature. There were several nominations: Joan Crawford for Best Actress (**Sudden Fear**); Arthur Hunnicutt for Best Supporting Actor (**The Big Sky**) and Jack Palance for the same honour (**Sudden Fear**); Martin Goldsmith and Jack Leonard for Best Story (**The Narrow Margin**); Russell Harlan (**The Big Sky**) and Charles B. Lang Jr (**Sudden Fear**) for Best Black-and-White Cinematography and Harry Stradling for Best Colour Cinematography (Goldwyn's **Hans Christian Andersen**); Gordon Sawyer and the Goldwyn sound department for Best Sound Recording (**Hans Christian Andersen**); Walter Scharf for Best Scoring of a Musical Picture (**Hans Christian Andersen**); Sheila O'Brien for Best Black-and-White Costume Design (**Sudden Fear**) and Mary Wills and Madame Karinska for Best Colour Costume Design (**Hans Christian Andersen**); So Matsuyama and H. Matsumoto for Best Black-and-White Art Direction-Set Decoration (**Rashomon**); and Frank Loesser for Best Song ('Thumbelina' from **Hans Christian Andersen**).

1953

RKO films did not receive a single Academy Award nomination, though two of the Walt Disney short films did win Oscars: **Bear Country** (Best Two-Reel Short Subject) and **The Alaskan Eskimo** (Best Documentary Short Subject).

1954

The studio somehow garnered three Oscar nominations, although it had no winners. **Susan Slept Here** was recognized for Best Sound Recording (John Aalberg) and Best Song ('Hold My Hand' by Jack Lawrence and Richard Myers), while the Disney organization picked up a nomination for Best Cartoon (**Pigs Is Pigs**).

1955

The company was still handling some of the Disney cartoons at this juncture, and one of them, **No Hunting**, earned an Oscar nomination as Best Cartoon; it was the only picture with any connection to RKO that the Academy saw fit to nominate.

1956

Two of RKO's releases received recognition at Academy Awards time: **The Bold And The Brave** was nominated for Best Supporting Actor (Mickey Rooney) and Best Original Screenplay (Robert Lewin), while **The Brave One** (produced independently by the King Brothers) picked up nominations for Best Editing (Merrill G. White) and Best Sound Recording (John Myers), and won the Oscar for Best Story (Robert Rich). Years later it was formally acknowledged that Robert Rich was a pseudonym of blacklisted writer Dalton Trumbo. Shortly before his death in 1976, Trumbo received the statuette that had been denied him because of his outspoken defiance of the Communist witch-hunt in 1947.

1957-1960

RKO did not receive a single Academy Award nomination during its last four years.

Index of Film Titles

In this index the main entry for each film is denoted by the page number in bold type. If the text entry for a film indicates that it was released under a different title in Great Britain, the British title is indexed separately and, again, its main entry is denoted in bold type. Where several bold page numbers are listed against a title the inference is that more than one film was released under that title.

The index refers only to the body of the book and does not cover references in the introduction, chapter openers, year openers or appendix sections.

Index of Personnel

As in the index of film titles, this listing covers only the main body of the text. 'Personnel' is here taken to include performers, directors, producers, writers, composers, choreographers, cameramen, designers and technicians.

Where a performer is depicted in the illustration which accompanies the account of a film, the page reference is given in italics.

Spellings have been standardized and apparent anomalies and duplications should not be inferred; for example, Harry Brown (a writer) and Harry D. Brown (an actor) are, in fact, two different people, as are Fred Allen and Frederick L. Allen, and Bob and Bobby Burns. Several people, however, had a habit of using different versions of their names at different times; for example, Charles Esmond and Carl Esmond are one and the same person, as are Eddie and Edward Nugent, Larry Blake and Larry J. Blake. In these latter cases the alternative usage is indexed in parenthesis; for example, Beatty, Bob (Robert).

312

313

314

Special Photography: Robert Golden

PDO 82-0167

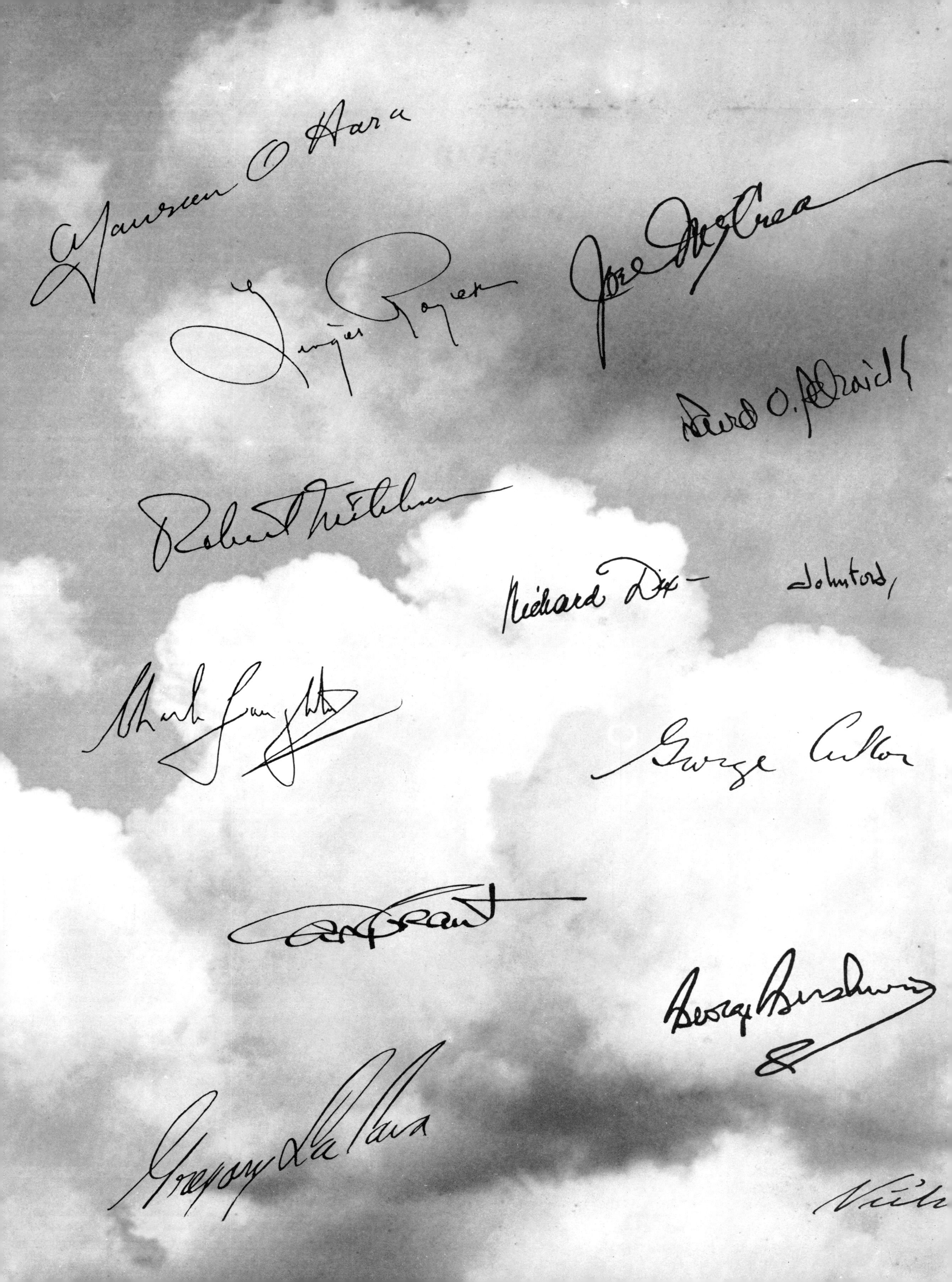